CORPUS CHRISTI

An Encyclopedia of the Eucharist

CORPUS CHRISTI

An Encyclopedia of the Eucharist

by

Michael O'Carroll, C.S.Sp.

Michael Glazier, Inc.
Wilmington, Delaware

First published in 1988 by Michael Glazier, Inc., 1935 West Fourth Street, Wilmington, Delaware 19805.

Distributed in Ireland and Britain by Dominican Publications, St. Saviour's, Dublin 1, Ireland.

Library of Congress Card Catalog number: 88-45354.

International Standard Book Number: 0-89453-687-7.

Printed in the United States of America by Edwards Brothers.

Cover design by Pat Harris.

Frontispiece by John Kelly, RHA.

Dedication

To the Sacred Alliance of the Hearts of Jesus and Mary:
An Act of Reparation
and
A Prayer for Peace in the World.

Foreword

I have been stimulated, as have others, to refresh my knowledge of Eucharistic theology and devotion by the ferment of ideas within the Church since the Second Vatican Council. The present work is the outcome of my study. In it I have tried to deal with the main themes of the Eucharist as Sacrament and Sacrifice, and to summarize the thought of those whose contribution to the subject has been noteworthy.

I have had one constant impression in the course of my reading and reflection: the voice of the centuries, right from the beginning, affirms with clarity the fundamental truths which are the commonly-held faith of our Catholic people. To know vaguely that this must be so is one thing; to meet it as one traverses age after age, to have time to identify it and the urge to identify with it, is something different, immensely rewarding. I hope that my writing may stir in the reader a similar awareness and response.

I wish to thank those who facilitated my work: three librarians, Fr. Cerckel of the Bollandistes, Fr. Brunet of Les Fontaines, Chantilly and, as ever, Fr. Dermot Fleury of Milltown Park, Dublin; Mgr. Antonio Piolanti, to whom my debt is evident throughout the work, who also generously sent me a copy of *Eucaristia*, no longer available; Dr. John Craghan, who read the manuscript and made invaluable suggestions towards its improvement.

Michael O'Carroll, C.S.Sp.

Abbreviations

AAS	*Acta Apostolicae Sedis,* 1909...
AC	*Analecta Cracoviensia.*
ACW	*Ancient Christian Writers.*
AER	*American Ecclesiastical Review,* Washington.
Ant	*Apocrypha Novi Testamenti.*
Anton	*Antonianum,* Rome.
Arch. Teol. Granad	*Achivo teologico granadino.*
Bauer	*Encyclopedia of Biblical Theology,* ed. J.B. Bauer, 3 vols. 1970.
BB	*Biblica,* Rome.
Biblz	*Biblische Zeitschrift.*
BibOr	*Bibbia e Oriente.*
BN	*Byzantion*
CBQ	*The Catholic Biblical Quarterly,* Washington.
CCCM	*Corpus Christianorum Continuatio Medievalis,* Turnhout.
CCSG	*Corpus Christianorum, Series Graeca,* Turnhout.
CCSL	*Corpus Christianorum, Series Latina,* Turnhout, 1953—.
ChQ	*Church Quarterly Review,* London, 1875.
CSCO	*Corpus Scriptorum Christianorum Orientalium,* Louvain,1903—.
CSEL	*Corpus Scriptorum Ecclesiasticorum Latinorum,* Vienna, 1866—.
CTS	*Catholic Truth Society.*
DACL	*Dictionnaire d'Archéologie Chrétienne et de Liturgie,* eds. F. Cabrol, O.S.B. and H. Leclercq, OSB., Paris, 1907—.
DBS	*Dictionnaire de la Bible,* Supplément, 1928...
DCath	La Documentation Catholique, Paris.
DHGE	*Dictionaire d'Histoire et de Géographie Ecclésiastiques,* Paris, 1912—.
DS	*Enchiridion Symbolorum,* Denziger-Bannwart, ed. 33, A. Schönmetzer, S.J.
DSp	*Dictionnaire de Spiritualité,* Paris, 1937—.
DTC	*Dictionnaire de Théologie Catholique,* Paris, 1903—.
EC	*Enciclopedia Cattolica,* 1949...
EO	*Echos d'Orient.*
EphLit	*Ephemerides Liturgicae,* Rome.
Eph Carmel	*Ephemerides Carmeliticae.*
Est Bib	*Estudios Biblicos,* Madrid.
ETL	*Ephermides Theologicae Lovanienses,* Louvain.
Eucaristia	*Eucaristia. Il mistero dell'Altare nel pensiero e nella vita della Chiesa,* ed. A. Piolanti, 1957.
Flannery, *Vatican II,* 1, 2	*Vatican Council II, Conciliar and Post-Conciliar Documents,* ed. A. Flannery, O.P.
GCS	*Die griechischen christlichen Scriftsteller der ersten drei Jahrhunderte,* Leipzig, 1897, Berlin, 1954.
Greg	*Gregorianum,* Rome.

HTR	*Harvard Theological Review.*
IDB	*The Interpreter Dictionary of the Bible.*
IER	*Irish Ecclesiastical Record,* Maynooth.
ITQ	*Irish Theological Quarterly,* Maynooth.
JBL	*Journal of Biblical Literature.*
JEH	*The Journal of Ecclesiastical History.*
JL	*Jüdisches Lexicon.*
JLW	*Jahrbuch fur Liturgiewissenschaft.*
JTS	*Journal of Theological Studies,* Oxford.
LG	*Lumen Gentium, Dogmatic Constitution on the Church (Vatican Council II).*
LTK	*Lexikon für Theologie und Kirche,* 1957.
MedSt	*Mediaeval Studies.*
Messenger, *The Reformation*	E.C. Messenger, *The Reformation, the Mass and the Priesthood,* 2 vols., London, 1936, 1937.
NCE	*New Catholic Encyclopedia,* New York, 1967.
NRT	*Nouvelle Révue Théologique,* Louvain.
NTS	*New Testament Studies,* London.
OCP	*Orientalia Christiana Periodica,* Rome.
PG	*Patrologia Graeca* (Migne).
Piolanti, A., *Il Mistero*	A. Piolanti, *Il Mistero Eucaristico,* 3rd ed., Rome, 1983.
PL	*Patrologia Latina* (Migne).
PO	*Patrologia Orientalis.*
PRE	*Realencyklopädie für protestantische Theologie und Kirche,* 1898-1913.
Prex	*Prex Eucharistica,* ed. A. Hanggi-Irmgard Pahl, Fribourg, 1968.
Quasten, *Monumenta*	J. Quasten, *Monumenta eucharistica et liturgica vetustissima,* Bonn, 1935-7.
Quasten, *Patrology*	*Patrology,* I, II, III, Washington, 1950-1960.
RAM	*Révue d'ascétique et de mystique,* Toulouse.
RB	*Révue Biblique,* Paris.
RBen	*Révue Bénédictine,* Maredsous.
REA	*Révue des Études Augustiniennes,* Paris.
REB	*Révue Études Byzantines,* Paris.
Rev. d'hist. et de phil. relig.	*Révue d'histoire et de philosophie religieuses.*
RGG	*Die religion in Geschichte und Gegenwart,* 3rd ed., Tübingen, 1957.
Riv. di Arch. Christ.	*Rivista di Archeologia Christiana,* Rome.
RHE	*Révue d'Histoire Ecclésiastique,* Louvain.
RSPT	*Révue des Sciences Philosophiques et Théologiques,* Paris.
RSR	*Recherches de Science Religieuse,* Paris.
RT	*Révue Thomiste,* Paris.
RTAM	*Recherches de Théologie Ancienne et Mediévale,* Louvain.
SC	*Sources Chrétiennes,* Lyon.
SCA	*Studies in Christian Antiquities.*
Solano, J., *Textos*	J. Solano, S.J., *Textos Eucaristicos Primitivos,* I, II, 2nd ed., Madrid, 1979.
Springtime	*Springtime of the Liturgy, Liturgical Texts of the First Four Centuries,* ed., L. Deiss, Collegeville, 1979.
ST	*Studi e Testi,* Rome.
Stone	Darwell Stone, *A History of the Doctrine of the Holy Eucharist,* 1909.
TDNT	*Theological Dictionary of the New Testament,* eds., G. Kittel and G. Friedrich, 1964-1974.
Theotokos	*Theotokos,* Michael O'Carroll, CSSp, Wilmington, DE, 1982.
ThStKr	*Theologische Studien und Kritikes.*
TQ	*Theologische Quartalschrift.*
TS	*Testi e Studi,* Rome.
TU	*Texte und Untersuchungen zur Geschichte der altchistlischen Literatur,* 1882.
ZKT	*Zeitschrift für Katholische Theologie,* Vienna.
ZNW	*Zeitschrift für die Neutestamentliche Wissenschaft.*

A

ABERCIUS, EPITAPH OF (2ND CENTURY)

The most famous of early Christian inscriptions, this was found in Phrygia in 1883 by Sir William Ramsay, and is in the Lateran Museum.[1] It is the self-composed epitaph of Abercius, who was probably bishop of Hierapolis in Asia Minor and had travelled widely in the east and to Rome; he visited the Christian churches and shared in their Eucharists. His language is mystical and symbolic which may have been dictated by the "discipline of the secret," (qv) as the inscription stood in a public place, or it may be contemporary style, evident in the writings of Tertullian (qv) and St. Clement of Alexandria (qv). The attempts of G. Ficker and A. Dieterich to show that A. was a votary, possibly a priest, of the Phrygian goddess, Cybele, have failed; as have those of A. Harnack to treat him as a syncretist. De Rossi, Duchesne, Cumont, Dolger Abel and several recent scholars concur that he was a Christian. The inscription interests Marian theologians.[2] It is the oldest monument in stone to the Eucharist. The text runs thus:

"Citizen of a famous city, I had this tomb built in my lifetime so that my body might one day rest in it. My name is Abercius. I am the disciple of a holy Shepherd who pastures his flocks of sheep on the mountains and in the plains, who has great eyes whose gaze reaches everywhere. It is he who taught me the truthful Scriptures that give life. It is he who sent me to Rome to contemplate the sovereign majesty and see a Queen clad in a golden robe and shod with sandals of gold. I saw there a people marked with a gleaming seal. I saw, too, the plain of Syria, and all the cities, Nisibis, beyond the Euphrates; everywhere I found brothers. Paul was my companion. Faith was everywhere my guide, and everywhere served me as food: a fish from a well-spring, very large and pure, caught by a holy virgin (spotless virgin) who gave it constantly to their friends to eat; she possesses a delicious wine that she serves with her bread. I, Abercius, dictated this text, and it was engraved in my presence; I was seventy-two years old. Let the brother who understands pray for Abercius. Let no one place another tomb above this under pain of a fine; two thousand gold coins for the Roman treasury and a thousand for my famous native place, Hierapolis."[3]

The "fish from a wellspring, very large and pure" is, in the symbolism, Christ, earlier spoken of as the "holy Shepherd." The "delicious wine" and the "bread" likewise refer to the Eucharist, the bread identified with the "fish from the wellspring."

[1]Text, J. B. Lightfoot, *The Apostolic Fathers*, 1889, II, 1, 492-501; Quasten, *Monumenta*, I, 21-24; id., *Patrology*, I, 171-73; H. P. N. Nunn, *Christian Inscriptions* (Texts for Students, 11), London SPCK, 1920-a photograph faces p. 24; cf. W. Ludtke-T. Nissen, *Die Grabschrift des Aberkios. Ihre Überlieferung und ihr Text*, Tübingen, 1910; A. Abel, *Etudes sur l'inscription d'Abercius*, BN 3 (1926), 321-405 bibl; A. Greiff, *Zur Verständnis der Aberkiosinschrift TheolGlaube*, 18 (1926) 78-88; A. Ferrua, S. J., *Nuove osservazioni sull'Epitaffio di Abercio, Riv. di Arch. Christ.*, 20 (1943), 279-305; H. Leclercq, DACL I, 1 (1907), 66-87; G. Bardy, *Catholicisme*, I, s.v.; [2]Cf. in my *Theotokos*, 2; S. Grill, Lexicon der Marienkunde, I, 21-23; B. Emmi, O. P., *La testimonianza mariana dell'epitaffio di Albercio, Angelicum* 46 (1969), 232-302; separate issue, Rome, 1970; [3]Tr. in L. Deiss, Springtime, 260, 61.

ABUSES IN REGARD TO THE EUCHARIST

Erros known in past or recent times are dealt with separately. (See article). Here we are dealing with the abuses or objectionable devotional practices which have been reported from different areas over the last twenty years.[1] Already in the Encyclical *Mysterium Fidei*, (qv) 1965, Paul VI (qv) drew attention to such aberrations. In the two decades following an exceptional number of Instructions dealing with the Eucharist were published by Roman authorities: in several of them the note of censure or warning is detected. In the Encyclical the Pope dealt principally with doctrinal deviations, though he did speak of those who "propose and act upon the opinion according to which in the consecrated hosts which remain after the celebration of Mass, Christ our Lord is no longer present."[2]

John Paul II (qv) has given much attention to Eucharistic devotion, in important letters and countless discourses. The Instruction, *Inaestimabile Donum*, (qv) was approved for publication by him on 17 April 1980. It contains this passage which comes after a sentence recognizing the good things achieved by the liturgical reform: "But these encouraging and positive aspects cannot suppress concern at the varied and frequent abuses being reported from different parts of the Catholic world: the confusion of roles, especially regarding the priestly ministry and the role of the laity (indiscriminate shared recitation of the Eucharistic Prayer, homilies given by lay people, lay people distributing communion while the priests refrain from doing so); an increasing loss of the sense of the sacred (abandonment of liturgical vestments, the Eucharist celebrated outside church without real need, lack of reverence and respect for the Blessed Sacrament, etc.); misunderstanding of the ecclesial character of the liturgy (the use of private texts, the proliferation of unapproved Eucharistic prayers, the manipulation of the liturgical texts for social and political ends). In these cases we are face to face with a real falsification of the Catholic liturgy: "One who offers worship to God on the Church's behalf in a way contrary to that which is laid down by the Church with God-given authority and which is customary in the Church is guilty of falsification."[3]

The generalizations in this statement have been filled in by Catholic writers. The search was carried out with special diligence in France, and the books of Michel de St. Pierre[4] may be singled out in the vast output of writing on the recent if not still contemporary crisis in the Catholic Church.[5] Even an ardent defender of the Mass of Paul VI has had to concede in regard to the formal protests that there had been instances of liturgical anarchy.[6] Against them people like Mgr. Lefebvre (qv) felt obliged to mobilize, even organize,

opinion. That assertion is a simplification of a very complex problem. The abuses are, alas, still with us.

---

[1] Besides the Roman documents mentioned cf. Michel de St. Pierre, *Les fumées de Satan*, Paris, 1978; id., *Le ver est dans le fruit*, 1978; [2] AAS 57(1965), [3] AAS 62 (1980), [4] *Op.cit., passim*, [5] For detailed inventory of the literature cf. article Lefebvre, [6] Dom Oury, cf. article Lefebvre.

ACCIDENTS, EUCHARISTIC

The unanimous, traditional teaching of the schools of Catholic theology is that, with the real presence (qv) after the wonder of transubstantiation (qv), there remain the sensible signs of bread and wine, which are now the signs of the body and blood of Christ.[1] The word 'species' is applied to these sensible signs. As to the interrelation of these species L. (Cardinal) Billot expresses the truth thus: "The accidents of bread and wine taken collectively remain miraculously in the sacrament without a subject. If, however, they are compared among themselves, we must say that the dimension of quantity alone absolutely subsists through the omnipotence of God, the others being subjected to it as to a substitute substance."[2] The same author explains another truth, the persistence of normal effects of the species, stated thus: "The accidents, as a consequence of their miraculous preservation, can do all the action which they could have done when the substance of bread and wine existed; likewise they can also decay and do decay through the change induced by a natural agent."[3] Finally, on the cessation of the real presence (qv) with the decay of the accidents L. Billot writes thus: "As often as the species decay thus so that they cease to be the accidents of bread and wine, what comes from this is in the nature of things what would happen if there had been no transubstantiation and this not by any new miracle, but by the force of the previous miracle in consecration."[4]

---

[1] Cf. F. Jansen, *Eucharistiques (accidents)*, DTC V, 1422-1452; L. Billot, S. J., *De Sacramentis*, 7th *ed.* 1932), I, 510-533; F. Filograssi, *De Eucharistia*, 6th ed., Rome, 1957, 188-207; L. Ciappi, O.P., *Le specie eucaristiche*, in *Eucaristia*, 285-299; A. Piolanti, *Il Mistero*, 324-341, *bibl.*; [2] *Op.cit.*, 511; [3] *Ibid.*, 522; [4] *Ibid.*, 525.

ACCIDIT IN DIVERSIS, 11 JUNE 1976

Decree of the Sacred Congregation for the Doctrine of the Faith on Public Celebration of Mass in a Catholic Church for other Deceased Christians.[1] Though private Masses can, and in certain cases, ought to be celebrated for such separated brethren, the discipline heretofore has been against public Masses. The Fathers of S.C.D.F. met on 9 June 1976 and decided that the discipline would remain as a general rule. Exceptions would be granted on two conditions: a) that the public Mass was requested expressly by relatives, friends or subjects of the deceased person for a genuine religious motive: b) that, in the judgement of the ordinary, there would be no scandal to the faithful. The Decree states that the conditions would be more easily verifiable in the case of the Orthodox. For other Christians present the conciliar and papal regulations in regard to *communicatio in sacris* must be faithfully observed. The Pope repealed the canons in so far as this was necessary.

---

[1] Text AAS 68 (2976), 621-622; tr. A. Flannery, O.P., II, 59-61.

ACTIO PASTORALIS ECCLESIAE, 15 MAY 1969. This is one of the many post-conciliar liturgical documents. It deals with the problems arising, and the rules to be observed, when Mass is celebrated for special groups.[1] Reference is made to the previous, substantial Instruction, *Eucharisticum Mysterium* (qv). Every aspect of the celebration dealt with comes up for advice. The whole document is an expansion of one sentence: "Everything should be disposed in such a way that, in the selection of a place, in the attitude of the persons, and in the use of things, true worship is rendered to the sacrament of the Eucharist." The church authorities to be invoked, the role of the participants at different levels, the readings, the homily, the prayer of the faithful, the time (whether Sunday or another day, the hour) are all given attention.

---

[1] Issued by the Sacred Congregation for Divine Worship; AAS, 61 (1969), 806-11; English tr., A. Flannery, *Vatican II*, 1, 142-47.

ADDAI AND MARI, THE ANAPHORA OF
Addai, according to tradition founder of the Church at Edessa, was also thought to be one of the seventy-two disciples of the Lord.[1] His role in history is part of an unusual legend about the conversion to Christianity of King Abgar V of Edessa (4 B.C. to A.D. 50). A. was allegedly sent by St. Thomas to heal the king. Identifying him with Thaddaeus, Eusebius writes in his history: "After the ascension of Jesus, Judas, who was also called Thomas, sent to him (Abgar V) Thaddaeus, an apostle, one of the seventy. When he was come he lodged with Tobias, the son of Tobias."[2] Eusebius gives an account then of the wonders which followed the arrival of this singular missionary. A prelude to the whole affair was, in the legend, the exchange of letters between Abgar and Jesus Christ.

Understandably, the Syrian liturgy was, in part, placed under the patronage of this preternatural human phenomenon; with him was associated the name of a disciple, Mari. The anaphora (qv) named for them is used by the Nestorians and by the Christians of the Chaldean and Malabar rites, who are united with Rome.

The anaphora is singular. The other Nestorian anaphoras, of Theodore of Mopsuestia and of Nestorius, are adapted from the Greek. The anaphora of Addai and Mari was probably first composed in Syriac. It has affinities in style and theology with Jewish table prayers. B. Botte dated it in the third century, broadly contemporary with that of Hippolytus (qv); L. Bouyer thought it the "oldest Christian Eucharistic composition there is." The striking omission is the institution (qv) narrative.

Did the anaphora have this element originally? Opinions divide on the answer. E. C. Ratcliff, G. Dix, W. E. Pitt, think that the institution narrative was absent from the beginning. B. Botte argued that the original text must have followed the regular pattern: thanksgiving, intercession, institution narrative, anamnesis, epiclesis. He is supported by L. Bouyer. On this view we now have a corrupted or altered text. In the sixties W. F. Macomber discovered new manuscripts, the oldest from the church of Mar Esa'ya in Mosul, from the eleventh or twelfth century, five centuries older than the manuscript thus far known. It is not necessarily the primitive text; it does rank as the oldest known. Problems still remain, about the links with the Jewish blessing and the *anamnesis*. The emphasis is on thanksgiving; the intercessory prayer most comprehensive. Some excerpts will illustrate the quality of the anaphora:

"It is right that every mouth should glorify and every tongue give thanks to the adorable and glorious name of the Father, the Son and the Holy Spirit. He created the world in accordance with his graciousness and those who dwell in it in accordance with his kindness. He saved mankind in accordance with his mercy, he has filled mortal men with great grace." There follow references to the adoration and glory given by the whole spiritual world. This is followed by the Sanctus and then comes a list of all God's saving and merciful acts—addressed to Christ the Lord. Thus this section ends: "Our Lord and God, you conquered our enemies, you gave victory to our frail, weak human nature through the abundant mercies of your grace. For all your helps and graces to us, we offer you praise, honour, gratitude and adoration, now and always and forever and ever." The prayer for "all the devout and just fathers who were pleasing to you" is made with the words "as we now commemorate the body and blood

3

of your Christ. We offer him to you upon the pure and holy altar as you taught us."[3]

After addressing God, true Father and enumerating the benefits wrought by his Son, his Beloved whom he sent, there occurs a hiatus which leaves the next part of the anaphora slightly anomalous. If the institution narrative filled the apparent vacuum, which is Dom Botte's contention, then these words following, after an introduction could be an *anamnesis*: "We rejoice and give glory, we exalt and commemorate, we praise and celebrate this great and awesome mystery of the Passion, the death and resurrection of our Lord Jesus Christ." There follows an epiclesis, archaic in form, and a distinctive doxology.

The anaphora named "of the apostles Addai and Mari" in the Syro-Malabar rite has noted characteristics different from the one described. The institution narrative is included. After it there comes this *anamnesis*: "We also, Lord, your frail and weak and wretched servants, who gathered in your name, stand before you at this moment, who have received through tradition your example, rejoicing and glorifying and recalling the memory, perform these great and awe-inspiring mysteries, holy, life-giving and divine, of the Passion, death, burial and resurrection of our Saviour Jesus Christ. And for this entire great and wonderful dispensation, which has been bestowed on us, we give you thanks and we ceaselessly glorify you openly and with confidence in your Church, (which has been) redeemed by the most precious blood of your Christ."

In the intercessions there is mention of the Pope "the Roman pontiff, head and ruler of the whole world" and of the local church ruler, as there is a mention later of the "Virgin Mary, Mother of God and of all the just and holy fathers." All these elements point to redrafting under Roman influence.

[1]*Editio princeps* of the Syriac text in *Liturgia Sanctorum Apostolorum Adaei et Maris*, Urmi, 1890-92; recently discovered text, W. F. Macomber, S.J., *The Oldest Known Text of the Anaphora of the Apostles Addai and Mari*, OCP 32 (1966), 335-71; Latin version, *Prex Eucharistica*, 375-386; Syro-Malabar anaphora, *ibid.*, 405-409; L. Ligier, 69-73; English tr., J. E. Y. Kelaita, *The Liturgy of the Church of the East*, Mossul, 1928; Brightman, 245-305; L. Deiss, *Springtime*, 159-163; cf. E. C. Ratcliff, *The Original Form of the Anaphora of Addai and Mari. A Suggestion*, JTS 30 (1928–29), 23-32; G. P. Badger, *The Nestorians and their Rituals*, II, 215-43, 1852; A. Raes, *Le récit de l'institution eucharistique dans l'anaphore chaldéenne et malabare des apôtres*, OCP 10 (1944), 216-226; *id.*, *Orientalische Liturgien, B. Einzeltypen*, LTK VI, (1961) 1089-90; G. Dix, *The Shape of the Liturgy*, 1945, 177-187; B. Botte, O.S.B., *L'Anaphore Chaldéenne des apôtres*, OCP, 15 (1949), 259-76; *id.*, *Problèmes de l'anaphore syrienne des Apôtres Addai et Mari*, *L'Orient Chrétien*, 10 (1965), 89-106; H. Engberding, *Zum anaphorischen Fürbittgebet des Apostel Addaj und Mar(j)*, OCP 41 (1957), 102-24; D. Webb, *La liturgie nestorienne des Apôtres Addai et Mari dans la tradition manuscrite*, in *Eucharisties d'Orient et d'Occident*, (Lex Orandi 47,) Paris, 1970, 25-49; E. J. Cuthrone, *The*

Anaphora of the Apostles: Implications of the Mar Esa'ya Text, ThSt, 34 (1973), 623-42; H. Rahner, S.J., LTK I, 136; J. Assfalo, VII, 24; E. Peterson, EC I, 290, 91; E. Amann, DBS I, 510, 12; [2]H. E. I, 13, 10; [3]*Prex Eucharistica*, 405-409; cf. Placid of St. Joseph, *The Present Syro-Malabar Liturgy: Menezian or Rozian?* OCP 23 (1957), 313-331; D. Webb, *Antonio de Gouvea's Version of the Nestorian Liturgy of the Apostles*, Texte und Untersuchungen zur Geschichte der altchristlichen Literatur 80, Studia Patristica 5 (Berlin 1962), 213-240; S. Congregatio Orientalis, *Revisione e ristampa del 'Messale Siro-Malabaresi,'* Rome, 1955, 26-31.

ADDUCTION THEORY OF TRANSUBSTANTIATION

An explanation of the mystery of transubstantiation (qv) which maintains that the body of Christ is brought under the species of bread and his blood under the species of wine.[1] The opinion has been attributed to Duns Scotus (qv), is expressed by St. Robert Bellarmine (qv) thus: "The body of Christ existed already, but it did not exist under the species of bread. It there exists after the words of consecration, which means that by this adduction the body of Christ which existed only in heaven exists now under the species of bread and this not by mere presence or coexistence but by a union like that which united the substance of bread to the accidents, though the accidents of bread do not inhere in the body of Christ."[2]

This theory, supported by Cardinal de Lugo (qv), among others (Vasquez, Tolet, Gregory of Valencia) was subjected to serious criticism by Lessius (qv), to criticism totally damaging by two great theologians of the present century—who differed sharply on another question about the Mass—Cardinal Louis Billot (qv) and Fr. M. de la Taille (qv). The adduction hypothesis logically implies displacement of the body of Christ and this is an untenable view, utterly so. The true corrective is the theory of St. Thomas: (qv) conversion.

[1]Cf. Louis Cardinal Billot, *De Sacramentis*, I, ed. 7, 353; M. de la Taille, *Mysterium Fidei*, 628-31; A. Piolanti, *Il Mistero*, 259-62; A. Michel, DTC, XV, 1401; [2]*Controvers. de Eucharistia*, L. I, c.XVIII; cf. De Lugo, *De Venerab. Euchar.* Sacramento, *Disp.* VII, vi, num. 89-91.

ADORATION

Jesus Christ, the eternal Son of God incarnate, fittingly receives the homage of Latria, which is due to God alone; he is God (cf. Mt 28:9, 17; Jn 5:23; 20:28; Phil 2:10; Hebr 1:6).[1] The testimony of the Fathers is clear. St. Cyril of Jerusalem (qv) says: "Bow down and, in adoration and veneration, say Amen."[2] St. Ambrose likewise: "By the footstool (Ps 98:5) is understood the earth, but by the earth the flesh of Christ which we still adore today in the mysteries."[3] St. Augustine says: "Nobody eats this flesh without previously adoring it."[4]

With the elaboration of the doctrine of Transubstantiation (qv) and the Real Presence (qv) in medieval times, the truth was so fundamental as to be utterly beyond question. The hymn *Adoro te devote, latens deitas*, attributed to St. Thomas Aquinas (qv), as well as his own hymns for the feast of *Corpus Christi*, affirm the truth explicitly or implicitly, as do so much iconography and hymnography through the centuries.

The great challenge came at the time of the sixteenth century Reformers (qv). In answer to that the Council of Trent taught as follows: "There is, therefore, no room left for doubt that all the faithful of Christ in accordance with a custom always received in the Catholic Church offer in veneration the worship of *latria* which is due to the true God, to this most Holy Scarament. For it is not less to be adored because it was instituted by Christ the Lord to be received (cf. Mt 26: 26ff). For we believe that same God to be present therein, of whom the eternal Father when introducing him into the world says: 'And let all the angels of God adore him' (Heb 1:6; Ps 96:7), whom the Magi 'falling down adored' (cf. Mt 2:11), who finally, as the Scripture testifies, (cf. Mt 28:17) was adored by the Apostles in Galilee."

To this add Canon 6: "If anyone says that in the holy Sacrament of the Eucharist the only-begotten Son of God is not to be adored even outwardly with the worship of *latria* (the act of adoration), and therefore not to be venerated with a special festive celebration, nor to be borne about in procession according to the praiseworthy and universal rite and custom of the holy Church, or is not to be set before the people publicly to be adored, and that the adorers of it are idolators: let him be anathema."[5]

The problem arose anew in the present century, even in the days of Pius XII (qv). It would take on a more serious dimension in the post-conciliar ferment of ideas. Pius XII devoted a lengthy passage of *Mediator Dei* (qv) to Adoration of the Eucharist. It is instructive and repays study:

"As everybody knows, the Eucharistic food contains 'truly, really and substantially the body and blood of our Lord Jesus Christ together with his soul and divinity.' (Trent sess. XIII, can 1). No wonder, then, that the Church has from the beginning adored the body of Christ under the appearance of bread; a fact which appears from the ritual of this august Sacrifice wherein the sacred ministers are instructed to adore the Blessed Sacrament by a genuflexion or a profound bow.

"The sacred Councils teach that it is the original tradition of the Church to pay 'one adoration to the Word Incarnate together with his flesh';[6] and as St. Augustine says: 'No one eats that flesh without having first adored it,' adding that, far from sinning by adoring it, 'we sin by not adoring it.' (cf. Enarr. in psalm, 98, 9).

"The adoration of the Eucharist, taking its origin from these doctrinal principles, developed gradually as a thing distinct from the divine sacrifice. The reservation of the sacred species for the sick and for those in danger of death gave rise to the praiseworthy custom of worshipping this heavenly food reserved in our churches. And this adoration is based upon firm and reasonable grounds. For the Eucharist is a Sacrament as well as a Sacrifice; and as a Sacrament it differs from the other Sacraments because it not only causes grace but permanently contains the Author of grace himself. When the Church, therefore, bids us adore Christ hidden under the Eucharistic veils and ask of him those spiritual and temporal blessings of which we stand in need, she is showing her lively faith in the presence of her divine Bridegroom beneath those veils, professing her gratitude to him, and rejoicing in her intimate communion with him."

The Pope then mentions the various forms this cult has taken: "devout and even daily visits to the Blessed Sacrament; Benediction of the Blessed Sacrament; solemn processions through towns and villages, especially at Eucharistic Congresses; adoration of the Blessed Sacrament exposed. Sometimes such expositions last only for a short time, sometimes for hours, even forty hours; in certain places they continue, each church taking its turn, the whole year round; and in some cases perpetual adoration is conducted day and night in religious communities, the faithful often taking part."

Pius speaks of the enrichment which the Church receives from this "perpetual worship," which "gives echo to the hymn of praise which the Church triumphant sings everlastingly to God and the Lamb 'that was slain.'" He deals with a question or difficulty sometimes raised: "Nor must it be objected that this Eucharistic worship gives rise to a false confusion between the so-called historical Christ who at one time lived on earth, the Christ who is present in the Blessed Sacrament of the altar, and the glorious Christ in heaven who now distributes to us his supernatural gifts. The answer is that by such devotions the faithful are in fact solemnly testifying to the faith of the Church, according to which the Word of God who is the Son of the Virgin Mary and suffered on the Cross, he who is present in the Eucharist, and he who reigns in heaven, are one and the same."[6]

This teaching was firm and eminently lucid, supported in subsequent lines of the Encyclical by patristic texts. Pius XII did not live to see the erratic phenomena of the post-conciliar age. With these Paul VI and John Paul II had to deal.

Paul took his stand in *Mysterium Fidei*: "The Catholic Church has always offered and still offers the cult of latria to the sacrament of the Eucharist, not only during Mass, but also outside of it, reserving consecrated hosts with the utmost care, exposing them to solemn veneration, and carrying them processionally to the joy of great crowds of the faithful."[7] The Pope supports this general statement by patristic texts and history, referring especially to the institution of the feast of *Corpus Christi* (qv).

John Paul II has been equally vigilant in regard to practice, equally explicit in doctrine: "And this adoration of ours," he writes in *Dominicae Cenae*, "contains yet another special characteristic. It is compenetrated by the greatness of that human death, in which the world, that is to say each one of us has been loved 'to the end.'[8] Thus it is also a response that tries to repay that love immolated even to death on the Cross; it is our 'Eucharist,' that is to say our giving him thanks, our praise of him for having redeemed us by his death and made us sharers in immortal life through his Resurrection.

This worship, given therefore to the Trinity of the Father, and of the Son and of the Holy Spirit, above all accompanies and permeates the celebration of the Eucharistic liturgy. But it must fill our churches also outside the timetable of Masses. Indeed, since the Eucharistic mystery was instituted out of love, and makes Christ sacramentally present, it is worthy of thanksgiving and worship. And this worship must be prominent in all our encounters with the Blessed Sacrament, both when we visit our churches and when the sacred species are taken to the sick and administered to them. Adoration of Christ in this Sacrament of love must also find expression in various forms of Eucharistic devotion: personal prayer before the Blessed Sacrament, hours of adoration, periods of exposition—short, prolonged and annual (Forty Hours)—Eucharistic benediction, Eucharistic processions, Eucharistic Congresses.[9] A particular mention should be made, at this point, of the Solemnity of the Body and Blood of Christ as an act of public worship rendered to Christ present in the Eucharist, a feast instituted by my predecessor Urban IV in memory of the institution of this great mystery. All this, therefore, corresponds to the general principles and particular norms already long in existence but newly formulated during or after the Second Vatican Council."[10]

The teaching proclaimed by the Popes is also expressed in documents emanating from Roman authorities, approved therefore by the Popes, for example *Eucharisticum Mysterium* and *Inaestimabile Donum* (qqv).

[1]Cf. L. Cattaneo, P.S.S., in *Eucaristia*, 943-956; L. Ott, *Fundamentals of Catholic Dogma*, Cork, 1954, 387; [2]*Cat. Myst.*, V,22, *Fathers of the Church* 64, 203; [3]*De Spiritu Sancto*, III, 11, 79, PL 16, 794, 95; [4]*Enarr. in Ps* 98, 9 PL 37, 1264; [5]DS 1642, 1656; [6]*CTS* tr., 53, 54; [7]*AAS*, 57 (1965), 769; [8]Jn 13:1; [9]Note to text: Cf. John Paul II, Homily in Phoenix Park, Dublin, 7, *AAS* 71 (1979), 1074ff; Sacred Congregation of Rites, Instruction *Eucharisticum Mysterium: AAS* 59 (1967), 539-573; *Rituale Romanum. De sacra communione et de cultu Mysterii eucharistici extra Missam, ed. typica*, 1973. It should be noted that the value of the worship and the sanctifying power of the forms of devotion to the Eucharist depend not so much upon the forms themselves as upon interior attitudes. [10]A. Flannery, O.P., Vatican II, 2, 67. Note to text: cf. Bull *Transiturus de hoc mundo (11 August, 1264), Aemilii Friedberg, Corpus Juris Canonici, Pars II, Decretalium Collectiones*, Leipzig, 1881, 1174-1177; *Studi eucaristici*, "VII Centenario della Bolla *Transiturus* 1264-1964," Orvieto 1966, 302-317.

AGAPE

A love feast, adopted by the early Christians, who would be mindful of the example of the Master: he shared meals during his public ministry, sometimes as at Cana (Jn 2:1-11) and in the wilderness (Mk 6:34-44) miraculously providing for the guests, sometimes honouring unlikely people by his presence at their table, or again making a meal an expression of friendship, as with the family at Bethany. Surprisingly, meals figure also in the post-Resurrection phase of his earthly existence (Lk 24:30-35, 41-43; Jn 21: 9-13; Acts 1:4—alternate reading for 'staying,' 'eating').

It would seem natural to associate such assemblies with the celebration of the Eucharist and this seems to have been done. In the human condition abuses were to occur and we have two fleeting NT references of a derogatory nature and a description of abuses. In 2 Pet 2:13 we read: "They count it pleasure to revel in the daytime. There are blots and blemishes, reveling in their dissipation (some authorities: 'love feasts'), carousing with you." Something very similar is in Jude 12: "These are blemishes on your love feasts, as they boldly carouse together, looking after themselves; waterless clouds, carried along by winds; fruitless trees in late autumn, twice dead, uprooted."

St. Paul, as a prelude to one of the great Eucharistic passages in 1 Cor, writes thus: "But in the following instructions I do not commend you, because when you come together, it is not for the better but for the worse. For, in the first place, when you assemble as a church, I hear that there are divisions among you; and I partly believe it, for there must be factions among you in order that those who are genuine among you may be recognized. When you meet together, it is not the Lord's supper that you eat. For, in eating, each one goes ahead with his own meal, and one is hungry and another is drunk. What! Do you not have houses to eat and drink in? Or do you despise the church of God and humiliate those who have nothing? What shall I say to you? Shall I commend you in this? No, I will not." (1 Cor 11:17-22).

Paul follows this with his testimony on the institution of the Eucharist and his advice on the proper behaviour of the participants (11:23-32). He concludes with some lines which serve as an epilogue to what he has said about the agape and the Eucharist: "So then, my brethren, when you come together to eat, wait for one another—if anyone is hungry, let him eat at home—lest you come together to be condemned." (11:33-34).

Paul stigmatizes certain defects in the celebration of the agape. From the tenor of the chapter it appears that in Corinth agape and Eucharist were closely associated. It is not clear, as some have contended, that Paul is aiming at the elimination of the agape. He castigates those who are exclusive, perhaps elitist, as we should say, who refuse to share, refuse to wait for others, get drunk.

The agape did not cease with the Apostles. It continued on for some generations, though the evidence is not ample or decisive. Pliny the Younger's much quoted letter (10:96) c. 112 to Trajan mentions meals taken by the Christians as "common and innocent." Chapters IX and X of the *Didache* (qv) may, it is thought, refer to an agape or Eucharist or both. They are quoted in the article on the *Didache*.

St. Ignatius in his letter to the Smyrnaeans, VIII, 2, writes thus: "Wherever the bishop appears let the congregation be present; just as wherever Jesus Christ is, there is the Catholic Church. It is not lawful either to baptize or hold an agape without the bishop; but whatever he approves, this is also pleasing to God, that everything which you do may be secure and valid."[2] Whatever may be thought of this passage, the others invoked are done so with considerable reservation. Chapter VI: 2 "But mark those who have strange opinions concerning the grace of Jesus Christ which has come to us, and see how contrary they are to the mind of God. For love they have no care, none for the widow, none for the orphan, none for the distressed, none for the afflicted, none for the distressed prisoner, or for him released from prison, none for the hungry or thirsty."[3]

If these words be taken as in some way referring to agape, it is because very quickly it was an occasion for collective charity, almsgiving. Those especially thought of were widows. Chapter VII: 1 is still more dubious as to its relevance: "They abstain from Eucharist and prayer, because they do not confess that the Eucharist is the flesh of our Saviour Jesus Christ who suffered for our sins, whom the Father raised up by his goodness. They then who deny the gift of God are perishing in their disputes; but it were better for them to have love

that they also may attain to the Resurrection."[4] The opening sentence appears to bear directly on the Eucharist; the words "to have love" may conceivably refer to agape; it is far from certain.

By the time of Tertullian (qv) the motive of relief to the needy had become dominant. He describes in a famous chapter of the *Apologeticum*, XXXIX, the meal in common, called by an expressive name signifying love (agape) in Greek. The poor benefit by it. "Since it is bound up with religion, nothing mean or improper is allowed. Before sitting at table, prayer is offered to God. We eat as hunger needs, drink as much as virtue allows. We do not go beyond good measure for we wish to be able to adore God through the night. We speak as if conscious of God's presence. After the washing of hands and lighting the lamps each one is invited to sing hymns taken from Sacred Scripture, or those he has himself composed; then one easily sees if he has drunk too much. The meal ends with another prayer."[5]

Subsequent documents tend increasingly to stress the almsgiving, especially for widows, and a later form of *agape* was the Christian funeral banquet: this is the interpretation given of the *Fractio panis* in the Capella Greca of the Catacomb of Priscilla. After the fourth century the *agape* died out. Is it being revived in the present age by religious or other groups who gather for a friendly meal after concelebrating Mass?

---

[1]Cf. R. L. Cole, *Love Feasts: A History of the Christian Agape*, London, 1916; K. Volker, *Mysterion und Agape*, Gotha, 1927; D. Tombolleo, *Le Agapi*, Rome, 1931; Esp., Bo Reicke, *Diakonie, Festfreude und Zelos in Verbindung mit altchristliche Agapefeiern*, Uppsala - Wiesbaden, 1951; C. Spicq, O.P., *Agape, Prologomènes à une étude de théologie néotestamentaire*, Studia Hellenistica 10, Louvain, 1955; H. Leclercq, O.S.B., DACL I, 775-848; L. Thomas, DBS I, 134-153; A. Romeo, EC I, 420-25; Denis-Boulet, *Catholicisme*, I, 192, 93; J. A. Jungmann, S.J. (qv) LTK, I, 180-81; E. C. Bernas, NCE I, 193, 94; [2]K. Lake, *The Apostolic Fathers*, London, 1914, I, 261; [3]*Ibid.*, 259; [4]*Ibid.*, [5]PL, 469f.

ALBERT THE GREAT, ST., DOCTOR OF THE CHURCH (C.1200-1280)

The *Doctor universalis* dealt with the Eucharist principally in works on the Sacrifice of the Mass, on the Sacrament of the Eucharist, and in his commentary on the Sentences.[1] Doubt has been cast on the authenticity of the first, but those directing the Cologne critical edition intend to publish it, as they do the second. All are in the Jammy and Borgnet editions of the works.

Dealing with the Mass A. analyzes the text of the Roman Mass phrase by phrase. In the second work he deals with problems of oblation (qv) and immolation (qv), especially enunciates his doctrine on Transubstantiation (qv), which is akin to that of his famous disciple, St. Thomas (qv): "This conversion the wise and Doctors of the Christian law have called transubstantiation, because the whole substance of bread, matter and form and union passes (*transit*) into the body of Christ without the body of Christ receiving any change or addition from this passage, if passage (*transitus*) it can be rightly called, as man was united to the Son of God, without addition or any change in the Son of God..."[2] A. insists that there is no change in the body of the Lord, the only change is in the substance of the bread and wine. In the commentary on the Sentences, Bok IV, Distinction 8 to 13, he deals mostly with the Eucharist as Sacrament, considers, in the last Distinction, the question of sacrifice with an exposition of his view on the relationship between the immolation on the Cross and the Mass. In clear advance on Peter Lombard (whose work is the basis of his commentary) (qv), he had one whole Distinction on Transubstantiation, XI.

A's theories and language in regard to the oblation and immolation are much discussed by M.de la Taille (qv).[3]

---

[1] *De sacrificio Missae* and *De Sacramento Eucharistiae* in ed., E. Borgnet, vol. 38; commentary on the Sentences, vol. 29, p. 173-399; cf. DTC. V, *Eucharistie,* 1301-1305, E. Mangenot; DTC X, *La Messe,* 1051-55, A. Gaudel; DSp, I 278-83, M. Viller; M. Lepin, *L'Idée du sacrifice,* 169-171; [2] *De Sacramento Eucharistiae,* dist. 6, tr, 3, c.1; [3] Cf. *Mysterium Fidei,* index, 18 references.

ALGER OF LIÈGE (d.c. 1132)

A., first a deacon, regent of studies and episcopal secretary in Liège, entered Cluny where he was ordained in 1121. About that time he composed his work, *De sacramentis corporis et sanguinis Domini.*[1] The treatise contains solid Eucharistic theology, especially important at the time as the effects of Berengar's teaching needed correction. It does not appear that A. saw Berengar's work, nor the tract written by Ratramnus (qv). He was effective, as much if not more so than Guitmund of Aversa (qv). A. first established the permanence of the sensible qualities after consecration (qv): "The substance of bread and wine are changed into the true body of Christ while their qualities remain."[2] Without using the word Transubstantiation (qv) he expresses the doctrine: "Though the body of Christ is in the sacrament spiritually and invisibly, it is nonetheless there substantially and truly."[3] A. had been influenced by pseudo-Eusebius of Emessa (see Faustus of Riez), as was Paschasius Radbert(qv)—he quotes the telling phrase "the author of the gift is the witness to the truth."[4]

A. insists on the need for faith in the Eucharist. And

he theorizes on the Mass: "The immolation of Christ is not spoken of on the altar in the sense that he is killed a second time, but because the immolation now represented on the altar is the same as was once effected on the cross."[5] He also shows why a visible sacrifice has to be made to the invisible God. And he made a contribution to the theology of ministry by insisting that the sacraments of Christ are not effective through the merits of the ministers—to hold such a view would, he thought, destroy the unity of the sacraments in the Church.[6]

Fr. de la Taille, (qv) who calls A. *"catholici dogmatis integerrimus assertor",*[7] refers to him twenty-four times in his monumental work. *Mysterium fidei,* attributed to A. is not genuine.

---

[1] PL 180, 737-856; cf. U. Berlière, DTC, I, 827-28; G. Hocquard, *Catholicisme,* I, 319; N. M. Haring, NCE I, 315-16; *id., A Study in the Sacramentology of Alger of Liège,* MedSt, 20 (1958), 41-78; [2] PL 180, Lib. I, c. VII, 756f; [3] *Ibid.,* c. XII, 775; [4] 777; [5] c. XVI, [6] Lib. III, c. IX; [7] *Mysterium Fidei,* 418.

ALPHONSUS DE LIGUORI, ST., DOCTOR OF THE CHURCH (1696-1787)

A., the founder, the great moral theologian and ascetical writer, in more than one of his books, treats of the Holy Eucharist.[1] He does deal with the sacrificial aspect, following here a French author, who may have been Fr. de Condren (qv), or, what is more probable, another writer dependent on the latter. A. analyses the aspects of sacrifice prefigured in OT, sees them verified in the Mass: sanctification or consecration of the victim, oblation, immolation of the victim, consumption, communion. His distinctive contribution is devotional of a very high order. His writings clearly reflect a personality richly endowed with grace; he exemplifies strikingly the Spirit's Gift of Piety. His reflections and the beautiful prayers which he composes are constantly nourished by references, short quotations, from Sacred Scripture and from sacred writers and the lives of the saints. Every page is instinct with the author's tremendous belief in the Real Presence (qv), with awe before the Blessed Sacrament. This is not the manner of our times. But is the manner of our times an absolute norm?

The Eucharist for A. is closely associated with Our Lady, whose universal mediation was for him a source of his exceptional spiritual dynamism. Remarkable, in the collection reissued lately, are the sections dealing with Preparation for Holy Communion and Thanksgiving after, Prayers for Visits to the Blessed Sacrament and Meditations for the Octave of Corpus Christi: testimony to the writer's character and a valuable treasury of true Eucharistic piety.

[1] *The Holy Eucharist*, ed. E. Grimm, New York, 1934, recently reissued, R. Tangen; cf. also in the same reissued series, *Preparation for Death*, considerations XXXIV, XXXV and *The Passion and Death of Jesus Christ*, ch. on the institution of the Holy Eucharist, 171-174.

AMALARIUS OF METZ (C. 780-850/1)

To be distinguished from Amalarius of Trier (c 809-16), A., an important figure in the history of the liturgy, deals with the Eucharist in his principal work, *De ecclesiasticis officiis*, published in PL;[1] account must be taken of corrections suggested by the great medievalist, Dom André Wilmart, O.S.B.[2] His doctrine can be taken in relation to sacrament and sacrifice. The Eucharist as sacrament may be considered in regard to a) the real presence (qv), b) the nature and effects of the sacrament of the Eucharist, and c) the taking of the Eucharist or Communion (qv). On the first he writes: "It (the Church) believes that it is the body and blood of the Lord, and by the eating of this, the souls of those taking it are filled with heavenly blessing." "In this bread Christ established his body and in the cup his blood, and he added: As often as you do this, you will do it in memory of me."[3]

A. uses the word consecration, but he deviates from doctrine in explaining it. He admits that the ordinary mode is the use of the Lord's words spoken in the Last Supper, but thinks that there are two extraordinary modes: by the recital of the Lord's prayer as he thought the Apostles did, and by contact between the wine and the consecrated host, which he thought took place on Good Friday.

A. was influenced by St. Cyprian (qv) in certain symbolist ideas. As to the effects of the Eucharist he has few things to say, but they are meaningful. It vivifies the soul; it unites us with Christ our Head and it is a pledge of our future bodily resurrection. He thought the Eucharist necessary to salvation: "And lest anyone say that the way of salvation can be in good behaviour and worship of the one omnipotent God, without sharing in the body and blood of Christ; for there is one God, he says, and one Mediator of God and men, the man Christ Jesus...."[4]

A. recommends very strongly appropriate preparation for reception of the sacrament, negative which refers to freedom from sin, positive which would be veneration for the Eucharist and love for Christ. On the question of whether to receive Holy Communion frequently or not, A. follows St. Augustine (qv) urging communion as often as one assists at Mass—which was also prescribed by a church canon which A. quotes—but without overlooking the primary motive, love of Christ.

We must not look to A. for a developed theory of sacrifice: he uses the words 'immolation,' 'oblation,' 'sacrifice' without any clear discrimination. In particular points, however, he has sure insights. He is insistent on the relationship between the sacrifice of the Mass and Calvary; the specific note of consecration in the Mass is that it is done in memory of the Passion of Christ: "the consecration of bread and wine is done in memory of the Passion of Christ, by which the author of sin was eternally laid low."[5] This is all related to A's idea of Christ as the principal offerer of the sacrifice, "through whom every sacrifice is offered to God for in him are founded all things whether in the heavens or on earth."[6] The idea is stated more emphatically in the *Eclogae de Officio Missae*, the authenticity of which is doubted.

Though A. does not mention adoration as an end of sacrifice, he does not deny it: explicitly he speaks of thanksgiving, propitiation and petition: propitiation especially: "He willed to be a victim for sinners who could not offer sacrifice to God, to have reconciliation with God through their immolation, so that they would not be frustrated but should be enabled to offer sacrifice." A. speaks of the sacrifice offered for the Church, for those who give Mass offerings, for the priest himself; and he believed in offering Masses for the dead.

One idea singular to A. aroused much opposition, some of it phrased in extreme language: his theory of the "corpus triforme Christi." He illustrated this triform theory by the three particles of the consecrated host: one put into the chalice and mingled with the Precious Blood; the second taken by the priest and the third left on the altar. The first represents the body assumed from Mary, and now risen from the dead, the second "that which walks on earth," the third "that lying in the graves." The second two parts of this symbolism are not quite clear in what he sets forth. The theory is to be related, presumably, to contemporary interpretations of the continuing presence of the Eucharist in those who received it.

A. was to some extent then instrumental in promoting an allegorical interpretation of the Eucharist. One contemporary denounced his theory as heretical; subsequent writers have been more lenient.[7]

[1] Works PL 105; critical ed. *Opera liturgica omnia*, J. M. Hannssens, S.J., Rome, ST 138-140, 1948-50; cf. R. Monchemaier, *Amalar von Metz, Kirchengeschichtliche Studien*, Bd. 1, Heft 3-4; Munster 1893; R. Sahre, *Der Liturgiker Amalarius*, Dresden, 1893; G. Morin, O.S.B., DTC, I, Paris, 1903, 933f; id., on the controversy about two writers of the name Amalarius, *RBén*, 8 (1891), 433-42; 9 (1892) 337-51; 11 (1894), 241-43: (against R. Monchemaier); E. Debroise, DACL, I, 1907, 1323-1330; with bibl; M. Besson, DGHE, II, 1912, 922f; J. Geiselmann, *Die Eucharistielehre der Vorscholastik (Forsch.*

zur christ. Literatur und Dogmengeschichte, Bd 15, Heft Paderborn, 1926 1-3; A. Cabaniss, *Amalarius of Metz,* Amsterdam, 1954; esp., S. Simonis, O.F.M., *Doctrina eucharistica Amalarii Metensis, Antonianum,* 8 (1933), 1-48; [2]*Pour une nouvelle édition du traité d'Amalaire sur les offices,* R Bén 37 (1925), 73-99; [3]*De eccl. off.,* III, 25; *ibid.,* 24; PL 105, 1042, 1141; [4]*Ibid.,* 1, 34, 1062; [5]*Ibid.,* 1, 12, 1013; [6]*Ibid.,* III, 24, 1140; [7]Cf. S. Simonis, *op.cit.,* 41-48.

AMBROSE, ST., DOCTOR OF THE CHURCH
(C. 339-397)

A. enjoyed a unique position in the Latin church in his time, which gave importance to his doctrine and liturgical practice: the first spiritual giant operating in an ecclesiastical public forum unfettered by the civil power, a Latin bishop, moreover, with knowledge of the Greek Fathers; his work on the Holy Spirit and on Our Lady gives evidence of this knowledge.[1]

A's Eucharistic doctrine is contained in the *De Sacramentis* and *De Mysteriis.* The authenticity of the former work was assumed until the sixteenth century. The assertion that it was not genuine was hardened in that age by an attack on its contents. But gradually opinion, even among Catholics, swung against its genuineness, on critical grounds: the style was different from that of A's genuine works; the contents seemed in part to reproduce other works and why should A. duplicate himself; nowhere else does A. reproach the Milanese for communicating so rarely; A. would not have taken the Roman church to task for the 'Washing of the Feet.'

Yet what seemed a solidly established structure has crumbled under persistent, expert thrust; two scholars, Fr. O. Faller and Dom R. H. Connolly, supported by Dom Botte have met all the objections and established the authenticity. Such specialized questions are not generally dealt with in a work like the present one. The present instance is important. For in the *De Sacramentis* we have probably the oldest anaphora (qv) in the west.

A. thus sets the scene of the Eucharistic celebration: "The people thus washed and wearing rich dress advance to the altars of Christ saying: 'I will approach the altar of God who gives joy to my youth.' They have left aside the remnants of the old error, their youth is renewed as that of the eagle. They hasten to approach this heavenly banquet. They come then and seeing the holy altar all adorned they cry out: 'You have prepared a table before me.' "[2]

The great doctor goes on: "Let us study this for fear that anyone seeing visible things—for what is invisible is not seen and the eyes of men cannot grasp it—would perhaps say, 'God rained manna for the Jews, he rained quails,' while for his beloved Church see he has prepared that of which it has been said, 'What eye has not seen, nor ear heard, what has not entered the heart of man God has prepared for those who love him.' So then that this should not be said, we wish very carefully to prove that the sacraments of the Church are older than the synagogue and superior to the manna."[3]

A. shows that the sacrament of the altar is superior to the manna: this belonged to heaven, whereas the Eucharist belongs to the Master of heaven; the latter is foreign to all corruption, whereas it was subject to corruption . . . the blessing changes the very nature.[4] "But," he says, "why use arguments? Let us rather use examples and establish the truth of the mystery of the Incarnation. Was it the ordinary course of nature which preceded the birth of the Lord Jesus from Mary? If we look to the order of nature, woman is accustomed to have a child after intercourse with a man. It is then clear that the Virgin had a child outside the course of nature. Well then what we produce is the body born of the Virgin. Why then look for the order of nature here in the body of Christ when the Lord Jesus himself was given birth by a Virgin outside the course of nature? It was the real flesh of Christ which was crucified, which was buried. It is then truly the sacrament of his flesh."[5]

"Christ," he affirms boldly, "is in this sacrament for it is the body of Christ. It is not then a bodily food, but spiritual."[6]

To such quotations from *De Mysteriis* one may add others from the parallel work, *De Sacramentis;* both were post-baptismal catechetical instructions. "But you perhaps say, this is my ordinary bread. But this bread is bread before the sacramental words. As soon as the consecration takes place the bread changes into the flesh of Christ. Let us then prove this. How can what is bread be the body of Christ? By what words is the consecration done and whose are these words? Of the Lord Jesus? In fact everything said before is said by the priest: praise is offered to God, prayers are said for the people, for kings, for all others. When one comes to produce the venerable sacrament, the priest no longer uses his own words, he uses the words of Christ. It is then the word of Christ which produces this sacrament. What word of Christ? Why that by which everything was made. The Lord ordered and the earth was made. The Lord ordered and all creatures came to life. You see how efficacious is the word of Christ. If then there is in the word of the Lord Jesus such great power, that what was not began to be, how much more efficacious is it to make what was to exist and be changed into something else. . . . To answer you then, before the consecration it was not the body of Christ, but after the consecration I tell you that it is henceforth the body of Christ. He spoke and it was done, he ordered and it was created."

A. then invokes other instances of divine power, notably the virgin birth, and he continues: "Does that not give you an understanding of all that the heavenly word produces? If it worked in a earthly fountain, if the word from heaven acted in the other things, does it not act in heavenly sacraments? You know then that the bread is changed into the body of Christ and that wine and water are put in the chalice, but the consecration wrought by the heavenly word makes blood of it. But you say perhaps 'I don't see the appearance of blood.' But it is the symbol of it. Just as you took the symbol of death, thus you also drink the symbol of the blood so that there should be no disgust caused by the blood, while the price of the redemption works its effect. You know then that what you receive is the body of Christ."

A. moves then into the detail of the sacrifice and sets down a passage remarkably similar to part of the Roman canon (see Eucharistic Prayers), possibly, as has been said, our first Latin anaphora: "You wish to be convinced that consecration takes place by means of the heavenly words. Here are these words: 'Grant to us,' says the priest, 'that this offering may be approved, spiritual, acceptable, because it is the figure of the body and blood of our Lord Jesus Christ, who on the eve of his Passion, took bread in his holy hands raised his eyes to heaven to you, holy Father, almighty and eternal God, blessed it giving thanks, broke it and gave it broken to his apostles and disciples saying: 'Take and eat of this, all of you, for this is my body which will be broken for you.' Pay attention. In the same way he also took the cup after supper, on the eve of his Passion, raised his eyes to you, holy Father, almighty and eternal God, blessed it giving thanks and gave it to his apostles and disciples saying, 'Take and drink of this, for this is my blood.' Observe that all the words up to 'Take the body or the blood' are of the evangelist. But from then on it is the words of Christ 'Take and drink all of this, for this is my blood.' And observe every detail. On the eve of his Passion, it says he took bread in his holy hands. Before being consecrated it is bread; but as soon as the words of Christ intervene, it is the body of Christ. Hear him say then, 'Take and eat all of this, for this is my body.' And before the words of Christ, the chalice is filled with wine and water; but as soon as the words of Christ have taken effect that becomes the blood which has ransomed the people. See then in what ways the word of Christ can transform everything. The Lord himself then assures us that we receive his body and his blood. Are we to doubt that his testimony is authoritative?"

A. enlarges his argument with other considerations. To eat this 'Bread' is to obtain remission of sins and a promise of eternal life. The communicant answering 'Amen' to the word of the priest signifies his assent to the truth enunciated by A. The sacrament was foreshadowed in figure. "Learn then," he continues, "the

greatness of this sacrament. Observe what he (Christ) says, 'Every time that you will do this, you will remember me until I return.' And the priest says: 'Recalling then his most glorious Passion, his resurrection from the dead and his ascension into heaven, we offer you this stainless victim, this spiritual victim, this unbloody victim, this sacred bread and the chalice of eternal life and we ask and beg you to accept this offering by the hands of your angels on your altar above, as you deigned to accept the gifts of your servant Abel the just, the sacrifice of our father Abraham and that which the high-priest Melchisedech offered to you."[7] A. adds the word of St. Paul 1 Cor 11:26.

A. first used the word *Mater Dei* in the west, generations after *Theotokos* was current in the east. He also probably first used the word *Missa* for the Mass (qv), in a letter to his sister.[8] There are here and there in A's writings passages which could be assembled into a theology of the Mass: such a complete synthesis was not then thought of: "We see now," he says, "good things through an image and we hold the good things of the image. We have seen the Chief Priest coming to us and we have heard him offering his blood for us; we have followed, as well as we could, the priests so that we should offer sacrifice for the people: even if weak in merit nonetheless worthy of honour by reason of the sacrifice. Because though Christ does not now seem to make the offering, he nevertheless is offered on earth when the body of Christ is offered; indeed he is shown to offer in us whose word hallows the sacrifice which is offered. And he indeed is present to the Father as our Advocate; but now we do not see him; we shall see him when the image has passed and truth (reality) has come. Then not as in a mirror but face to face those things which are perfect will be revealed."[9]

Here we have the idea of Christ's oblation (qv). A. also has the idea of the heavenly sacrifice of the Saviour: "What is more characteristic of Christ than to stand before God the Father as the advocate of peoples, offering his death for sins."[10] He had reflected on the OT figure or type: "Hear the word 'Christ our Pasch is immolated.' Recall how our forefathers acting figuratively, sectioned the lamb and ate it, thereby giving a sign of the Lord Jesus' passion, whose sacrament is our daily food."[11]

"Formerly the lamb was offered," he says, "now Christ is offered, but he is offered as a man, as one undergoing his Passion, and he offers himself as priest that he should forgive our sins, here (he is seen as it were) in image, in reality where with the Father by right he intervenes for us as our advocate."[12] Christ, A. says, was 'immolated' as our Pasch. In one powerful passage he shows us the unity of sacrament and sacrifice: "My flesh is real food and my blood is drink. You hear the word flesh, you hear the word blood and you recognize the sacraments of the Lord's death and you oppose the idea of his divinity. Hear him say, 'a spirit has not flesh and bones.' But we, as often as we take the sacraments which by the mystery of the sacred word are transformed (*transfigurantur*) into flesh and blood, announce the death of the Lord."[13] Here is an anticipation of the idea and word of transubstantiation (qv). A final word of realism: "Christ is my food, Christ is my drink, the flesh of God is my food, the blood of God is my drink. Christ ministers to me every day."[14]

Thus the theory of the man called to the episcopal office by a dramatic miracle: his exercise of the pastoral office was marked by one dramatic clash with the emperor Theodosius. A. forbade him to enter the church for the Eucharist, after a massacre committed by the imperial troops: how could he take in hands soiled with blood the 'body of Christ,' how could he who had unjustly shed so much blood, take the blood of Christ to his mouth? Doctrine and practice in noble harmony.

[1]J. Solano, *Textos,* I, 343-393; *De Sacramentis* and *De Mysteriis* critical ed. B. Botte, O.S.B., SC 25; works PL XIV-XVII and CSEL 1897ff; for authenticity of *De Sacramentis* B. Botte, *op.cit.*, 12ff: esp. P. Faller, *Ambrosius, der Verfasser von De Sacramentis Die innere Echtheitsgrunde,* 64 (1940), 81-101; R. H. Connolly, O.S.B., *The 'De Sacramentis' a Work of St. Ambrose,* Oxford, 1942; also Chr. Mohrmann, *Observations sur le 'De Sacramentis' et le 'De Mysteriis' de S. Ambroise* in *Atti del Congresso internazionale di studi ambrosiani nel XVI centenario della elezione di Santo Ambrogio alla cattedra episcopale,* Milan 2-7 Dec, 1974; ed. G. Lazzati, Milan 1976, 103-123; cf. S. Lisiecki, *Quid S. Ambrosius de SS. Eucharistia docuerit,* Wroclaw, 1910; P. Batiffol, *L'Eucharistie,* Paris, 1930, 335-349; G. Bareille, DTC V, 153; F. R. M. Hitchcock, *The Holy Communion in Ambrose of Milan,* ChQ 1941, 127-1154-58; C. Ruch, *La Messe dans l'eglise latine,* DTC X 966-997; A. Paredi, *La liturgi de S. Ambrozio,* Milan, 1940; C. Fitzgerald, *De sacrificio caelesti secundum S. Ambrosium,* Mundelein, 1944; A. Casamassa, *I grandi Padri: S. Ambrogio,* Rome, 1953 (ad usum privatum); J. Huhn, *Die Bedeutung des Wortes Sacramentum bei dem Kirchenvater Ambrosius,* Fulda, 1910; G. Segalla, *La conversione eucaristica in S. Ambrogio,* Padua, 1967; R. Johanny, *L'Eucharistie, centre de salut chez Saint Ambroise de Milan,* Paris 1968; J. H. Perez, *La ordenacion y sus 'munera' en san Ambrosio,* 347ff in *Teologia del Sacerdocio,* IX Facultad teologica del Norte de Espana, Burgos, 1977; G. Francesconi, *Storia e simbolo nella teologia di S. Ambrogio,* Brescia, 1981; A. Piolanti, *Il Mistero,* 179-84; [2]*De Myst.*, VIII, 43, SC 25, 121; [3]*Ibid.*, 44, 122; [4]*Ibid.* and IX, 50, 124; [5]IX, 53, 125/26; [6]IX, 58, 128; [7]Cf. C. Mohrmann, *op.cit.*, 103; quotations: *De Sacramentis,* SC 25, IV, 14, 15, 16, 19, 20; VI, 26-28; p. 82-86; [8]Ep. 20, 4-5, PL 16, 995; [9]In Ps 38, 25, PL 14, 1051D-52; [10]In Ps 39, 8 PL 14, 1060; [11]In Ps 43, 36, PL 14, 1107; [12]*De officiis,* I, 48, 238, PL 16, 94—cp. text quoted n. 9; [13]In Ps 98, 18, PL 15, 1461; [14]*De Fide* IV, 10, 124, PL 16, 141.

ANAMNESIS

A. is that part of the Anaphora (qv) which recalls the events in the life of Christ which gives the Eucharist meaning and efficacy.[1] The Greek word expresses a Semitic idea, that an act of divine import in being recalled comes to life in a certain way. It is not merely subjective memory but an objective memorial. There is a large OT and Jewish liturgical background to the idea as it emerged in the early liturgies and took practical shape. The form adopted in the different anaphoras is of interest. Translation of the word *anamnesis* for these reasons, presents a problem: memory, remembrance, commemoration have been suggested: each demands an added explanation.

The importance of memory is evident in OT texts: "The memory of the righteous is a blessing, but the name of the wicked will rot" (Prov 10:7); "His memory perishes from the earth, and he has no name in the street" (Job 18:17). With Ps 134:13 we have the idea of the name of God impressing his power on age after age: "Thy name, O Lord, endures for ever, thy renown, O Lord, throughout all ages." Memory should prompt obedience to God's commandments: "So you shall remember and do all my commandments, and be holy to your God" (Num 15:40); "But the steadfast love of the Lord is from everlasting to everlasting upon those who fear him, and his righteousness to children's children to those who keep his covenant and remember to do his commandments" (Ps 102:17, 18). Remembrance shall enter into the spirit of sacrifice: "And you shall put pure frankincense with each row that it may go with the bread as a memorial portion to be offered by fire to the Lord" (Lev 24:7); "On the day of your gladness also, and at your appointed feasts, and at the beginnings of your months, you shall blow the trumpets over the sacrifices of your peace offerings: they shall serve you for remembrance before the Lord: I am the Lord your God" (Num 10:10).

Remembrance seemed to bring things back: "He shall pour no oil upon it, for it is a cereal offering of jealousy, a cereal offering of remembrance, bringing iniquity to remembrance" (Num 5:15). "And she said to Elijah, 'What have you against me, O man of God? You have come to me to bring my sin to remembrance, and to cause the death of my son!'" (3 Kgs 17:18). God's covenant (qv) is the subject of remembrance (1 Chr 16:17, 18; Ex 6:5, 6). The Passover (qv) understandably is linked with this remembrance. "This day shall be for you a memorial day, and you shall keep it as a feast to the Lord; throughout your generations you shall observe it as an ordinance for ever" (Ex 12:14); "And it shall be to you as a sign on your hand and as a memorial between your eyes, that the law of the Lord may be in your mouth; for with a strong hand the Lord has brought you out of Egypt. You shall therefore keep this ordinance at its appointed time from year to year" (Ex 13:9, 10); "Observe the month of Abib, and keep the Passover of the Lord your God; for in the month of Abib the Lord your God brought you out of Egypt by night. And you shall offer the Passover sacrifice to the Lord your God, from the flock or the herd, at the place which the Lord will choose, to make his name dwell there. You shall eat no leavened bread with it; seven days you shall eat it with unleavened bread, the bread of affliction—for you came out of the land of Egypt in hurried flight—that all the days of your life you may remember the day when you came out of the land of Egypt" (Deut 16:1-3).

Recent increasing attention to the Jewish (qv) background of the Eucharist shows how strong was the idea of remembrance as objective memorial. The festive form of the third *berakah* contains this striking passage, built on the memorial theme: "Our God, and the God of our fathers, may the remembrance of ourselves and of our fathers and the remembrance of Jerusalem, thy city, and the remembrance of the Messiah, the son of David, thy servant, and the remembrance of thy people, the whole house of Israel, arise and come, come to pass, be seen and accepted and heard, be remembered and be mentioned before thee for deliverance, for good, for grace, for lovingkindness and for mercy on this such and such a day. Remember us, YHVH, our God, on it for good and visit us on it for a blessing and save us on it unto life by a word of salvation and mercy, and spare, favour and show us mercy, for thou art a gracious God and King."[2]

Fr. L. Bouyer rightly says of this passage: "What is remarkable in this text is the so abundant use made of the term memorial (in Hebrew *zikkaron*). It is impossible to imagine a better confirmation than this text for the thesis already so solidly established by Jeremias in his book on the eucharistic words of Jesus. The 'memorial' here is not merely a simple commemoration. It is a sacred sign, given by God to his people who preserve it as their pre-eminent spiritual treasure. This sign or pledge implies a continuity, a mysterious permanence of the great divine actions, the *mirabilia Dei* commemorated by the holy days. For it is for the Lord himself a permanent attestation of his fidelity to himself.... In blessing God for its meal and in acknowledging in it through the *berakah* the memorial of the mirabilia Dei of creation and redemption the community acknowledges it as the efficacious sign of the perpetual actuality within itself of these *mirabilia*, and still more precisely of their eschatological accomplishment in the future."[3] Anamnesis then had a threefold reference: to the past event, to its immediate effect in the present and to the hope it stirred for the future.

J. M. Tillard, O.P., whose advice on this point was especially welcomed by the first ARCIC (qv) meeting,

insists on the explicit precept of the *Mishnah*, 10, 5, in regard to the actualization of the Passover: "Each one is held to consider himself from generation to generation as if he had himself gone out of Egypt. For it is written: In that day when you celebrate the going out of Egypt, tell this to your Son: It is because the Lord has intervened for me when I went out of Egypt. Therefore we owe him thanks, praise, blessing, glory, homage, veneration and adoration. He does for us and for our fathers all these marvels; he led us from pain to joy, from affliction to jubilation, from darkness to great light, from servitude to redemption. Let us sing before him, Alleluia."[4] As J.M. Tillard says, the idea of *Zikkaron* is one of the richest elements in Jewish theology.

Christ was, therefore, in a supreme moment of his life attuned to a profound, living tradition of his people when he said: "Do this in remembrance of me" (Lk 22:19; 1 Cor 11:24). It should be understood as a promise as well as a precept; Jeremias suggests the translation, "Do this as my memorial." The essential point is of an objective reality which assures continuity of something before God. It is for God, is ultimately guaranteed by God's past action.

Whether the Last Supper (qv) was a Passover meal or not, this was the context and when the Lord gave his precept, he was marking a new era, the transference to himself personally of the immense meaning, mystery and power of the Passover *Zikkaron*. This is why in the Mass the anamnesis comes immediately after the institution (qv) narrative. The Lord's word to his apostles to renew the Supper was not, as with the memorial of the Passover, limited to one moment in the year, to an anniversary. The Supper, and the anamnesis so closely linked with it, were to be enacted at the choice of the apostles and their successors. Here again Christ broke the Jewish mold pointing to the universality foretold by Malachi (qv).

As to history it can be said with some degree of certainty that an anamnesis in a general sense, that is, an allusion to the Last Supper, to the Passion, death and probably resurrection and ascension of the Lord was part of the earliest liturgy, of the apostolic canon. References occur in St. Cyprian[5] and St. Justin[6] Martyr (qqv).

Examples of the anamnesis: That of St. Hippolytus (qv); "Mindful therefore of his death and resurrection, we offer you the bread and the cup, thanking you that you thought us worthy to stand before you and minister to you."[7] The Apostolic Constitutions (qv): "Mindful therefore of his Passion and death and of his resurrection from the dead and his return to heaven and his future second coming, in which he will come with glory and power to judge the living and the dead and render to each according to his works, we offer you, King and God, according to his command this bread and this cup, giving you thanks through him that you have thought us worthy to stand before you and to exercise the priesthood to you."[8] The liturgy of St. Mark: "Announcing, Ruler, Lord almighty, heavenly king, the death of your Son, Lord and God and our Saviour, Jesus Christ, and confessing his third day, happy resurrection from the dead, we also confess his ascension to the heavens, and his sitting at the right hand of you God and Father, and looking forward to his second awesome coming, when he will come to judge the living and the dead in justice and to give (to each one according to his works—spare us Lord, our God) these things, taken from what is yours, we have set before you."[9] The Euchology of Der-Balyzeh (qv): "We announce your death. We proclaim your resurrection and we pray...."[10] The Ethiopian anaphora of our fathers the apostles: "We announce your death, O Lord, and your holy resurrection: we believe in your ascension and your second coming. We praise you and confess to you; we beg and beseech you, our Lord and our God."[11] To which the priest replies: "But now, O Lord, remembering his death and resurrection, we offer you this bread (showing it) and this cup (showing it), thanking him that in him you have made us worthy of the honour of standing in your sight and exercise the priesthood for you." The Roman Canon: "Wherefore, O Lord, we thy servants as also thy holy people, calling to mind the blessed Passion of the same Christ, thy Son, our Lord, and also his glorious resurrection from the dead and his glorious ascension into heaven: do offer unto thy most excellent Majesty of thine own gifts, bestowed upon us, a pure host, a holy host, an unspotted host, the holy bread of eternal life and the chalice of everlasting salvation." Eucharistic Prayer II: "In memory of his death and resurrection, we offer you, Father, this life-giving bread, this saving cup. We thank you for counting us worthy to stand in your presence and serve you. May all of us who share in the body and blood of Christ be brought together in unity by the Holy Spirit." Eucharistic Prayer III: "Father, calling to mind the death your Son endured for our salvation, his glorious resurrection and ascension into heaven, and ready to greet him when he comes again, we offer you in thanksgiving this holy and living sacrifice." Eucharistic Prayer IV: "Father, we now celebrate this memorial of our redemption. We recall Christ's death, his descent among the dead, his resurrection, and his ascension to your right hand, and looking forward to his coming in glory, we offer you his body and blood, the acceptable sacrifice, which brings salvation to the whole world."[12]

It is for liturgical historians to trace exactly the growth of the anamnesis formulation. In the anaphora discoverable in St. Ambrose, *De Sacramentis* the institution (qv) narrative is followed by these words: "Then, know what a great 'sacramentum' it is. See what he says: 'As often as you do this, so often you will keep remembrance of me, until I come.' And the priest says: 'Therefore mindful of his most glorious Passion and his resurrection from the dead and his ascension into heaven we offer you this immaculate host, this spiritual host, this unbloody host, this holy bread and this cup of eternal life.' "[13]

In this study of evolution or development, account must be taken, as Dom F. Cabrol suggests, of curious analogies within the parts of the Mass. Thus the Secret in the pre-conciliar Roman Mass is sometimes said to be an anamnesis brought forward before the Preface. Dom Cabrol cites the example of the Secret for the feast of the Epiphany.[14]

What ultimately is the theology of the anamnesis? Not only remembrance but also oblation, a memorial which issues in oblation, an insight into the essential meaning of the Mass: "And both ideas contain an objective element as well as a subjective one. What we hold here in our hands is a memorial and an oblation. But memorial as well as oblation must be realized within ourselves, as our own remembrance and our offering. Then, and only then, can a 'worship in spirit and truth,' in the fullest sense arise to God from our hands. The *memorial* is usually referred to here in just a short phrase. This is only natural, for the whole prayer of thanksgiving is, in substance, a memorial prayer, particularly the Christological portion. In fact, even the readings of the fore-Mass, especially the Gospel, have as their aim to revive the memory of our Lord, his word and his work. The whole purpose of the yearly round of Church feasts is, in the last resort, nothing other than an enlargement of that recollection, making room for an ever-increasing store of memories. The basic theme of the Church year, too, is precisely the *Passio Domini*, the redemption accomplished by Christ's death and resurrection. In the anamnesis this theme is treated very briefly, but its contents are not analysed as a subjective memory, since it is taken for granted that the soul is already alive to everything contained therein. All that is stated here is that in the sacramental operation the divine charge to do this 'in remembrance of me' (Lk 22:19; 1 Cor 11:24ff) is being fulfilled, and that, moreover, we are thus doing what Paul had demanded in more detail, namely, to 'proclaim the death of the Lord' (1 Cor 11:26)."[15]

Fr. Jungmann traces the further phases of enrichment in western and eastern liturgies. As he points out, the remembrance should be realized by the priest and in and by the entire congregation present. To this theme of the redemption so fully recalled, rather assimilated, is added another, which affirms the sacrificial character of the Mass: Oblation. The words used, *et plebs tua sancta* (in the Roman canon), and "thy holy people" give validity to the concept of a universal priesthood of the laity (qv) implied in the words of 1 Peter 2:5, 9. All must join, each according to their degree of participation in the priesthood of Christ, in the offering of the great sacrifice.

[1]Cf. F. Cabrol, O.S.B., DACL I, 2, (1907), 1880-96; O. Casel, O.S.B., *Das Mysteriengedächtnis der Mess liturgie im Lichte der Tradition,* JLW, 6 (1926) 113-204; N. A. Dahl, *Anamnesis, Mémoire et commémoration dans le christianisme primitif, Studia Theologica* (Lund) 1 (1948), 69-95; B. Botte, O.S.B., *Problèmes de l'anamnèse, Journal Eccl. Hist.*, 5 (1954), 16-24; *id., Mysterium fidei, Bible et vie chrétienne*, 80 (1968), 29-34; B. Capelle, O.S.B., *L'evolution du 'Qui pridie' de la messe romaine,* RTAM 22 (1955), 5-16; *Travaux liturgiques*, II, 176-186; J. M. Tillard, O.P., *The Eucharist, Pasch of God's People*, New York, 1966, 212ff; L. Ligier, *Célébration divine et anamnèse dans la première partie de l'anaphore ou canon de la messe orientale, Greg* 48 (1967), 225-252; *id., Eucharisties d'Orient et d'Occident*, II 1972 (LO 47), 139-178; esp., *Prex Eucharistica*, ed. A. Hanggi and I. Pahl (contributors, L. Ligier, J. A. Jungmann, A. Raes, L. Eizenhofer, I, Pahl, J. Pinell), Fribourg, 1968 - *passim*; L. Bouyer, *Eucharist*, 1968, 83ff, 103ff; *esp.,* J. A. Jungmann, S.J., *The Mass of the Roman Rite*, II, 1955, 218-26; *id., Das Gedächtnis des Herrn in der Eucharistia, TheolQuartal*, 133 (1963), 385-99; C. Vagaggini, *The Canon of the Mass and Liturgical Reform*, 1967, 91ff, 167ff; J. Pinell, *Anamnesis y epiclesis en el antiguo rito gallicano, Didascalia*, 4 (1974), 3-130; G. Ramis, *El memorial eucaristico, concepto y formulación en los textos de las anaforas*, EL 91, 1982, 189-208; ed. A. G. Martimort, *L'Eglise en Prière*, R. Cabie, *L'Eucharistie*, Paris, 1983, 114-118, ed. S. Marsili, A. Nocen, M. Auge, A. J. Chupungco, *Anamnesis*, Rome, 1983, esp., 225-257; (see bibl. Last Supper, The); [2]Apud L. Bouyer, *op.cit.*, 84; [3]Ibid., 84, 85; [4]Op.cit., 212; [5]Cf. R. Johanny, *Cyprien de Carthage, L'Eucharistie des premiers chrétiens,* Paris 1976, 151-175; [6]Apol. 1, 66; [7]Traditio apostolica (qv), ed. B. Botte, SC 14, 32-33; [8]Prex Eucharistica, 93; [9]Ibid., 112-114; [10]Ibid., 127; L. Deiss, *Springtime*, 247, 8; [11]Prex., 148; [12]ICEL tr., 1973; [13]VI, 27, SC 25, 86; [14]Op.cit., 1890; [15]The Mass, 218, 19.

ANAPHORA

The Eucharistic Prayer, central to the Mass, the Anaphora has a history and historiography quite distinctive. The easiest way to appreciate this is by some acquaintance with a great collective work of modern scholarship.[1] This is *Prex Eucharistica*, edited by Anton Hanggi and Irmgard Pahl, the latter also one of the contributors; the others, eminent in liturgical studies, are Louis Ligier, S.J., Joseph A. Jungmann, S.J. (qv), Alphonse Raes, S.J., Leo Eizenhofer, O.S.B., and Jordi Pinell, O.S.B. Advice was forthcoming from a number of other members of the élite corps of liturgists, men like Bernard Botte, O.S.B. (qv). The language is Latin where any other language than Latin or Greek was used in the original; Latin tr. face the Greek texts, which are reproduced. Bibliographies are abundant.

The wealth of original texts critically edited reflects the research of recent years and its reward. It also points to the difficulty there is in reaching fully satisfactory solutions to some of the problems raised by the complex history of the Anaphora. From the evidence so far available it appears that the Anaphora in *The Apostolic Tradition* (qv) is the first in time known to us. Scholarly opinion oscillates on the problem of one fixed prototype of all the Anaphorae. The certainty of such a single form, once an enthroned opinion, for a while lost its status. But with some added nuances it is being viewed favourably once again.

The eastern liturgies were prolific in Anaphorae: upwards of fifty exist. They are found in different languages and are placed under the patronage of an evangelist, St. Mark, or apostle, St. John, of different Fathers of the Church, St. John Chrysostom (qv) for example. It is not generally demonstrable that those so honoured had any active part in the textual composition. With the passage of time these titles became fixed. Whereas the western Anaphorae may alter one part at different seasons, the eastern are fixed, unchangeable. As is shown in the article on the Institution Narrative, the eastern Anaphorae show slight differences from the western in the formulation, more than slight in a few cases. The eastern liturgies can also vary the Anaphora used, for example the Anaphora of Theodore of Mopsuestia (qv) is used from the first Sunday in Advent to Palm Sunday; the liturgy of Nestorius on certain feasts, five times a year. In the eastern liturgies the fore-Mass, as the part preceding the Anaphora is called, varies little, whereas, especially since Vatican II (qv), in the west, it varies very much, in the penitential rite and in the Readings, with constant change in the homily and Prayers of the Faithful.

The fore-Mass is Jewish (qv) in origin; the Anaphora, while also owing something to Jewish influence, is, in its general tenor, a Christian composition. If one is to speak of a classic pattern, there will be the following elements: 1. introductory dialogue; 2. preface or first part of the thanksgiving; 3. *Sanctus*; 4. past-*Sanctus* or second part of the thanksgiving; 5. preliminary epiclesis (alternative or additional post-Sanctus; 6. institution narrative; 7. *anamnesis*; 8. *epiclesis*; 9. diptychs or intercession, which may be divided; 10. concluding doxology.

These elements are generally found in the different Anaphorae. Exceptional are: the Euchology of Serapion of Thymuis (qv), wherein the institution narrative and the anamnesis are conflated; the Anaphora of the Holy Apostles Addai and Mari (qv), where the institution narrative is missing, but a certain number of scholars think that the original contained it; the *Apostolic Tradition* lacks the *Sanctus*, the intercessory prayers or diptychs, and a preliminary epiclesis before the institution narrative, found in the Alexandrine and Roman rites.

Each of the elements listed is dealt with separately. Here it may help to name the Anaphorae reproduced in the monumental work of Anton Hanggi and Irmgard Pahl., *Oriental Anaphorae*; I. According to the Alexandrine type: A. In the Greek Egyptian church. 1. The Anaphora of the evangelist Mark according to the Codex Rossanensis, XII century (Cod. Vatic. gr. 1970); 2. Fragmentary Anaphora of the evangelist Mark—a) Strasbourg papyrus gr. 254, IV-V century; b) Manchester John Rylands Library papyrus, 465, VI century; 3. Der-Balyzeh fragment, VI-VII century (qv); 4. The Anaphora in the Euchology of Serapion, IV century.

B. In the Coptic church. 1. The Anaphora of Cyril of Alexandria; 2. Fragment from the Louvain Coptic codex 27, VI century; 3. Fragment in the British Museum Coptic ostracon.

C. In the Ethiopian church. 1. Anaphora of our holy Fathers the Apostles; 2. Anaphora of our Lord Jesus Christ; 3. Anaphora of John, the son of thunder; 4. Anaphora of the Virgin Mary, daughter of God, composed by Abba of the city of Bahnasa; 5. Anaphora of the 318 Orthodox Fathers; 6. Anaphora of the apostolic Athanasius; 7. Anaphora of Epiphanius of Salamis; 8. Anaphora of John Chrysostom; 9. Anaphora of Cyril of Alexandria (Ia); 10. Anaphora of Dioscorus of Alexandria; 11. Anaphora of Our Lady, Mary the Mother of God, composed by Abba Georgius.

II. According to the Antiochene type. A. In commentaries of the IV-V centuries. 1. Anaphora in the Mystagogic Catecheses of Cyril of Jerusalem; 2. Anaphora in the *"Hierarchia Ecclesiastica"* (III, 3: 11, 12) of Pseudo-Dionysius the Areopagite; 3. Anaphora in Mystagogic Catechesis VI of Theodore of Mopsuestia; 4. Anaphora in the "Testament of our Lord Jesus Christ." B. In the Byzantine church: 1. Anaphora of John Chrysostom according to the codex Barber gr. 336; 2. Anaphora of Basil of Caesarea according to the codex Barber 336 gr. and the codex Grottaferr. VII; 3. Anaphora of James, brother of the Lord, according to the codex Vat gr. 2282; 4. Anaphora of Epiphanius of Salamis; C. In the Syro-Antiochene church: 1. Anaphora of the Twelve Apostles; 2. Anaphora of James the brother of the Lord; 3. Anaphora of Timothy of Alexandria; 4. Anaphora of Severus of Antioch; 5. Anaphora of Cyril of Jerusalem or of Alexandria; 6. Anaphora of Ignatius of Antioch; 7. Anaphora of John of Basorensis or Bostra; 8. Anaphora of Clement of Rome; 9. Anaphora of Julius, Pope of Rome; 10. Anaphora of Eustathius of Antioch. D. In the Maronite church: 1. Anaphora of Xystus; 2. Anaphora of the holy Roman church. E. In the Armenian church. 1.

Anaphora of Athanasius of Alexandria; 2. Anaphora of Gregory of Nazianzus; 3. Anaphora of Isaac of Sahag; 4. Anaphora of Cyril of Alexandria; 5. Anaphora of James, brother of the Lord. F. In the Egyptian church. 1. Anaphora of Basil of Caesarea; 2. Anaphora of Gregory of Nazianzus.

III. According to the Syro-eastern type.

A. In the Assyrian and Chaldean church. 1. Anaphora of the Apostles Addai and Mari. 2. Anaphora of Theodore of Mopsuestia; 3. Anaphora of Nestorius; 4. Anaphora of VI century according to the British Museum codex, Add 14669; B. In the Syro-malabar church. Anaphora of the Apostles Addai and Mari; C. In the Maronite church. Anaphora of Peter the Apostle.

Western Anaphorae (generally called Canons in the west)

I. Texts from non-liturgical books. 1. Ambrose, *De sacramentis* IV, 5, 21ff; 6, 20ff; 2. Anonymous Arian fragment from a Vatican Library codex, 5750 lat.

II. *Roman Liturgy*: Canon of the Mass with thirty-eight Prefaces added.

III. The Ambrosian Liturgy. 1. The canonical Mass; 2. Thursday in the Lord's Supper; 3. The Vigil of Easter; nineteen Prefaces.

IV. Gallican and Celtic Liturgy. 1. The Canon of Pope Gelasius followed by significant parts of twelve other Masses and three appendices: A. Thirteen *"Contestationes"* or *"Immolationes"*; B. Ten Post *Sanctus* prayers; C. Nine *Post Secreta* or *Post Mysterium*.

V. Spanish Liturgy. Significant passages from ten Masses.

In general the uniformity of the western texts is striking. There are no variations determined by different rites or by association with a varied company of Apostles, evangelists or Fathers of the Church—exceptions are the Mass of the Stowe Missal bearing the name of Pope Gelasius and three Spanish Masses with the names of St. Eugene of Toledo, St. Ildefonsus of Toledo and St. Julian of Toledo respectively. It all constitutes a rich treasury to be studied in the ages to come. For completion the three new Eucharistic Prayers given in the Novus Ordo of Paul VI (qv) must be mentioned; one is closely modelled on the Anaphora of the Apostolic Tradition. (See article Eucharistic Prayers).

---

[1]Abundant bibliographies throughout Anton Hanggi and Irmgard Pahl, *op.cit.*, cf. F. Cabrol, *Anaphore* in DACL, I, 1905, 1898-1919; *id., ibid., Canon Romain*, II, 1924, 1847-1905; B. Botte, *Le Canon de la Messe romaine. Edition critique, introduction et notes, Textes et études liturgiques*, 2, Louvain, 1935, ed. 1962; *id. Canon Missae*, RAC, 2 (1954) 842-45; W. H. Frere, *The Anaphora or Great Eucharistic Prayer. An Eirenical Study in Liturgical History*, London, 1938; A. Baumstark, *Anaphora*, RAC I (1950), 418-27; J.

Lécuyer, C.S.Sp., *La théologie de l'anaphore selon les Pères de l'école d'Antioche* in *L'Orient Syrien*, 6 (1961) 385-412; L. Ligier, *Magnae orationis eucharisticae seu anaphorae origo et significatio (Ad usum privatorum auditorum)*, Rome, 1964; id., *Textus selecti de magna oratione eucharistica addita Haggadah Paschae et nonnullis Judaeorum benedictionibus (ad usum privatum auditorum)*, Rome, 1965; id., *De la Cène de Jesus à l'anaphore de l'Eglise*, in *La Maison-Dieu* 87 (1966), 7-51; W. J. Grisbrooke, in *A Dictionary of Liturgy and Worship*, ed. J. G. Davies, London, 1972, 10-17.

ANGLICANISM

It is difficult to deal with Anglican theory and practice about the Eucharist without adverting to two events in recent history, the Papal Bull *Apostolicae Curae* (qv), which in 1896 declared Anglican Orders (qv) invalid and the Agreed Statement of the Anglican Roman Catholic International Commission (qv) in 1971 which stated that the Anglican and Roman Catholic members of the joint body had "reached agreement on essential points of Eucharistic doctrine."[1] There is much history to be explained in what preceded and followed each of these events. The approach of students, theologians or historians, has not always been free of polemical thrust.

Thomas Cranmer (qv) was a dominant figure at the outset. He cherished the idea of a council or coalition of the churches which had renounced allegiance to Rome, to offset the Council of Trent. With the death of Henry, 31 January 1547, he had a free hand to implement his policies in the matter of religious observance; henceforth his principal collaborator would be Ridley. A continuing feature of all such change was to be parliamentary action. The first parliament of the reign of Edward was asked to accept in November 1547 a "Bill for the Sacrament of the Altar" and a "Bill for the receiving of the Sacrament *sub utraque specie*"—the first to check irreverence towards the Eucharist, the second to authorize communion under both kinds.

The practical outcome was the Order of Communion which was to be within the existing Latin Mass. The terms used revealed or subtly insinuated the ideas of Thomas Cranmer, Archbishop of Canterbury and Nicholas Ridley, Bishop of Rochester (later of London): The terms *bread* and *wine* are used of the Eucharist after the consecration; the body and blood are not spoken of in administration but "*the sacrament* of the body" and "*the sacrament* of the blood." Where the Sarum rite had: "The body of our Lord Jesus Christ keep thy soul unto life everlasting," the new rite has: "The body of our Lord Jesus Christ, *which was given up for thee*, etc. The blood of our Lord Jesus Christ *which was shed for thee,* etc." There are two rubrics toward the end of the communion which are significant: the consecrated *breads* are to be broken in two pieces at least: "If the wine hallowed and consecrated doth not suffice or be enough for them that do take the Communion, the priest ... may go again to the altar, and reverently, and devoutly, prepare and consecrate another, and so the third, or more likewise, beginning at these words, 'Simili modo, postquam cenatum est,' and ending at these words, 'qui pro vobis et pro multis effundetur in remissionem peccatorum,' and without any elevation or lifting up."[2]

True, the order about the "consecrated *breads*" was followed by this sentence which seems to imply belief in the Real Presence (qv): "Men must not think less to be received in part than in the whole, but in each of them the whole body of our Saviour Jesus Christ."[3] But the content is nullified by other words used; and Cranmer at the time did not believe in the Real Presence.

The next important event was the publication of the First Prayer Book, of which the part relevant to us is "The Supper of the Lord and the Holy Communion, commonly called the Mass." The texts prescribed show a certain dilution of belief in the Real Presence, but there was not yet a clear rejection of the doctrine. Those who voted in the House of Lords debate for the Book would be deemed Protestant, whereas the Anglo-Catholics were almost entirely against it; one of the most influential, Stephen Gardiner, Bishop of Winchester, was in prison: in writing he was to hope that the Real Presence was still safe.

The year after the publication of the First Book, Cranmer published his work on Eucharistic doctrine: *A Defence of the True and Catholic Doctrine of the Sacrament of the Body and Blood of our Saviour Christ, with a Confutation of Sundry Errors concerning the Same.* Cranmer shows a knowledge of Catholic teaching in this work, giving an account of transubstantiation (qv) and the Real Presence (qv) which is fairly accurate. His own views on "How Christ is present in the Sacrament" are set forth in language such as this: "They (Catholics) teach that Christ is in the bread and wine but we say that he is *in them that worthily eat and drink the bread and wine...*" "They say that Christ is received in the mouth, and entereth in with the bread and wine. We say that he is received in the heart and entereth in by faith...."[4] Much else is in the book, showing divergence from Catholic teaching, with an occasional phrase that is less so. Gardiner answered Cranmer in a book written in prison and published in France: *An Explication and Assertion of the True Catholic Faith concerning the Most Blessed Sacrament of the Altar, with Confutation of a book written against the same.* He spoke of Christ "present truly, really, substantially, yet we say our senses be not privy to that presence, or the manner of it, but by instruction of faith...."[5] Cranmer brought out a

Rejoinder, expounding still further his idea of Christ's spiritual presence in the communicant but not in the bread and wine. Likewise he denied that there was any offering in the Eucharist—considered as a sacrifice—other than the 'sacrifice of praise and thanksgiving' and the offering of ourselves.

Cranmer's views were given freer rein in the Second Prayer Book. A typical change from the First Book shows how his decision had hardened. In the First Book the blessing of the elements was accompanied by the prayer that they might be to us "the body and blood." Bucer (qv) had objected. Cranmer now abolished the blessing of the elements and put in this prayer: "Grant that we, receiving these thy creatures of bread and wine according to thy Son our Saviour Jesus Christ's institution, in remembrance of his death and Passion, may be made partakers of his most precious body and blood." Likewise in the prayer at the consuming of the elements there is no reference to the body and blood: "Take and eat this in remembrance that Christ died for thee, and feed on him in thy heart by faith, with thanksgiving. Drink this in remembrance that Christ's blood was shed for thee, and be thankful." The Lord's Prayer follows the reception of communion and is followed by this petition: "We, thy humble servants, entirely desire thy fatherly goodness mercifully to accept this our sacrifice of praise and thanksgiving." Finally the Post-Communion prayer which in the First Book read: "We most heartily thank thee for that thou has vouchsafed to feed us in these holy mysteries, with the spiritual food of the most precious body and blood of thy Son our Saviour Jesus Christ" now becomes: "We most heartily thank thee for thou dost vouchsafe to feed us, which have duly received these holy mysteries, with the spiritual food of the most precious body and blood of thy Son our Saviour Jesus Christ."[6] The distinction is now marked between receiving of the bread and wine, and the spiritual reception by the good, of the body and blood.

The next event of importance was the appearance of the Forty-Two Articles, influenced by the Thirteen Articles already drawn up in the spirit of the Augsburg (qv) Confession. The Forty-Two were the forerunners of the later classic Thirty-Nine Articles; Cranmer was the author. Calvin wrote to encourage him and he sought advice or borrowed the views of those close to him in doctrine—the influence of articles drawn up by Bishop Hooper is patent in some of the formulas.

Article twenty-nine on the Lord's Supper reads thus: "The Lord's Supper is not only the sign of the mutual goodwill of Christians among themselves, rather it is the true sacrament of our redemption through the death of Christ. And to those taking it ritually, worthily and with faith the bread we break is a sharing in the

body of Christ (*communicatio corporis Christi*); likewise the cup of blessing is a sharing in the blood of Christ (*communicatio sanguinis Christi*). Transubstantiation of the bread and wine in the Eucharist cannot be proved from holy writ, but is opposed to the obvious words of Scripture and provides occasion for many superstitions. Since the reality of human nature requires that the body of one and the same man cannot be in many places at the same time, but must be in some one fixed place, accordingly the body of Christ cannot be present in many different places at the same time."[7]

On the Mass Cranmer wrote thus: "The offering of Christ once made is perfect redemption, propitiation and satisfaction for all sins of the whole world, original and actual; nor besides it is there any other expiation for sins. Therefore the sacrifices of the Masses in which, as was commonly said, the priest offers Christ for the remission of punishment or guilt for the living and the dead, are figments and dangerous impostures."[8]

After the Marian interlude Anglicanism was re-established under Elizabeth I. The legal measures taken were the Act of Supremacy and the Act of Uniformity. In accordance with the latter the Second Prayer Book of Edward VI with some changes was issued in 1559. A notable change was in the administration of the consecrated elements. To satisfy some belief in a kind of presence which was held by the queen, the Zwinglian significance of the Second Book was softened by adding the formula in the First Book which had been removed. The combined result read as follows: "The body of our Lord Jesus Christ which was given for thee, preserve thy body and soul into life everlasting. Take and eat this in remembrance that Christ died for thee, and feed on him in thy heart by faith with thanksgiving."[9] Some kind of Virtualism (qv) could be read into this statement.

The Thirty-Nine Articles which were approved by parliament in 1571, though the queen would have wished to impose them personally, were given the royal assent. They were influenced by previous draft summaries, and also by the lengthy *Declaration of the Returned Protestants,* 1559; these were the exiles during Mary's reign, who returned the year after her death.

This formulary was to consolidate the Anglican position. The articles relevant to Eucharistic doctrine read as follows: 28. "*Of the Lord's Supper.* The Supper of the Lord is not only a sign of the love that Christians ought to have among themselves one to another, but rather it is a sacrament of our redemption by Christ's death. Insomuch that to such as rightly, worthily and with faith receive the same, the bread which we break is a partaking of the Body of Christ, and likewise the cup of blessing is a partaking of the Blood of Christ.

Transubstantiation (or the change of the substance of bread and wine) in the Supper of the Lord cannot be proved by Holy Writ, but is repugnant to the plain words of Scripture, overthroweth the nature of a Sacrament, and hath given occasion to many superstitions.

The Body of Christ is given, taken, and eaten in the Supper only after an heavenly and spiritual manner. And the means whereby the Body of Christ is received and eaten in the Supper is faith.

The Sacrament of the Lord's Supper was not by Christ's ordinance reserved, carried about, lifted up, or worshipped." 29. "*Of the wicked which do not eat the Body of Christ in the use of the Lord's Supper.* The wicked and such as be void of a lively faith, although they do carnally and visibly press with their teeth (as St. Augustine saith) the Sacrament of the Body and Blood of Christ: yet in no wise are they partakers of Christ, but rather to their condemnation do eat and drink the sign of Sacrament of so great a thing."

30. "*Of both kinds.* The cup of the Lord is not to be denied to the lay people. For both parts of the Lord's Sacrament, by Christ's ordinance and commandment, ought to be ministered to all Christian men alike."

31. "*Of the one oblation of Christ finished upon the Cross.* The offering of Christ once made is the perfect redemption, propitiation and satisfaction for all the sins of the whole world, both original and actual, and there is none other satisfaction for sin but that alone. Wherefore the sacrifices of Masses, in which it was commonly said that the priests did offer Christ for the quick and the dead to have remission of pain or guilt, were blasphemous fables and dangerous deceits."

These are the ideas that dominated Anglican thinking on the Eucharist for centuries. They were not affected by subsequent modifications. Extensions of practices already sanctioned there might be. Thus whereas the Order of Communion of 1548 allowed for consecration of a second or third chalice, nothing similar was said of the bread. In the 1662 revision allowance was made for consecration of additional bread if it was needed. Such a practice is unknown to sound Eucharistic theology or liturgy in the east or the west.

Debate has continued about the possibility of reconciling belief in the Real Presence with the terms of these articles. By way of example two recent opinions are here cited. William Barclay writes thus: "The Risen Lord is universally present. He is not present in the sacrament any more than he is present anywhere else. As Brother Lawrence said, he felt as near to his Lord when he was washing the greasy dishes in the monastery kitchen as ever he did at the blessed sacrament. But what happens is that at the sacrament everything is done and designed *to make us aware* of that presence.

He is not specially present, but we are specially aware of his presence.... The sacrament of the Lord's Supper is not so much the place where we realize the reality of the real presence of our Lord, as the place where we realize the reality of the real presence of our Lord. The presence is not specially located in the bread and wine, nor in the Church. It is a presence which is present always, everywhere. But the sacrament is the place where memory, realization, appropriation end in encounter, because we are compelled to become aware of him There."[10] Some pages back Barclay had quoted in full the articles we are discussing.

W. G. Wilson and J. H. Templeton in *Anglican Teaching* give an exposition of the Thirty-Nine Articles; the book appeared with a preface from the Church of Ireland Archbishop of Armagh. They write thus of Article twenty-eight: "The teaching of the Article is in agreement with the sacramental principle; natural things can and do convey the divine Presence to receptive hearts and minds. Hence it rejects, on the one hand, the belief that the bread and wine in the Eucharist are mere forms, without grace, and on the other, that by consecration their own substance is replaced by that of the things they denote, and so they cease to be signs; a sign cannot signify what it is. The Real Presence of Christ in the Holy Communion is affirmed in the first section of our Article, and in the third the nature of that Presence, and how it is made available to us, is stated." On the phrase "after a heavenly and spiritual manner" and reception by faith, the authors say: "This clause is by some asserted to be a repudiation of the doctrine of the Real Presence in the Eucharist; but others declare that it is merely a denial of Christ's corporal presence in the Elements."[11]

The authors follow these words with a discussion of the objective presence and the Receptionist view, admitting the realism of the early Fathers, ending with quotations from Bishop McAdoo and the 1937 report of the Faith and Order Theological Commission favourable to the objective presence. One must note the different opinions. As to the future we have the ARCIC report and must wrestle with the question of Anglican Orders.

[1]Bibl., G. J. Cuming, *A History of Anglican Liturgy,* London, 1969, 400-430; see also bibl. to Cranmer and *Apostolicae Curae;* cf. F. A. Gasquet and E. Bishop, *Edward VI and the Book of Common Prayer,* 1891; D. Stone, *A History of the Doctrine of the Holy Eucharist,* 2 vols, 1909; esp., F. E. Brightman, *The English Rite,* 2 vols, 1915, 1921; C. W. Dugmore, *Eucharistic Doctrine in England from Hooker to Waterland,* 1942; id., *The Mass and the English Reformers,* 1958; F. Clark, *Eucharistic Sacrifice and the Reformation,* London, 1960 and other works listed to *Apostolicae Curae;*

ANGLICAN-ROMAN CATHOLIC INTERNATIONAL COMMISSION

Church of England Liturgical Commission, *Prayer Book Revision in the Church of England,* 1957; P. Dearmer, *The Parson's Handbook,* revised C. Pocknee, 1966; C. Dunlop, *Anglican Public Worship,* 1953; E. C. Messenger, *The Reformation,* 2 vols; [2]Apud E. C. Messenger, *op.cit.,* I, 362; [3]*Ibid.,* 363; [4]BkIII, ch. 2, apud E. C. Messenger, 426, 27; [5]Apud E. C. Messenger, I, 437; [6]*Ibid.,* 527; [7]*Ibid.,* 545; [8]*Ibid.,* 549; [9]E. C. Messenger, *op.cit.,* II, 219; [10]*The Lord's Supper,* 111, 112; London, 1967; [11]Dublin, 1962, 196, 197.

ANGLICAN-ROMAN CATHOLIC INTERNATIONAL COMMISSION (ARCIC)

On 24 March 1966 Pope Paul VI (qv) and Archbishop Michael Ramsey of Canterbury made a Common Declaration of mutual charity and of Christian good will and "of sincere efforts to remove the causes of conflict and to re-establish unity."[1] Looking in a Pauline spirit (Phil 3:13-14) to the future rather than the past, they made this commitment to action: "They affirm their desire that all those Christians who belong to these two communions may be animated by these same sentiments of respect, esteem and fraternal love, and in order to help these develop to the full, they intend to inaugurate between the Roman Catholic Church and the Anglican Communion a serious dialogue which, founded on the Gospels and on the ancient common traditions, may lead to that unity in truth for which Christ prayed."[2]

The immediate outcome of this decision was the Joint Preparatory Commission which held three meetings during 1967 at Gazzada in Italy, Huntercombe and Malta. Their report was optimistic and their suggestion that a Permanent Joint Commission be set up was accepted; eight members of the Preparatory Commission continued to serve on the group that succeeded it: The Anglican-Roman Catholic International Commission. The first meeting took place in 1970 and in the course of three meetings there was a conviction among members that they had reached "agreement on essential points of Eucharistic doctrine." A document stating this was ready for 7 September 1971 was then adopted. Here is the full text:[3]

Introduction:

1. In the course of the Church's history several traditions have developed in expressing Christian understanding of the Eucharist. (For example, various names have become customary as descriptions of the Eucharist: Lord's supper, liturgy, holy mysteries, synaxis, Mass, Holy Communion. The Eucharist has become the most universally accepted term.) An important stage in progress towards organic unity is a substantial consensus on the purpose and meaning of the Eucharist. Our intention has been to seek a deeper understanding of the reality of the Eucharist which is consonant with biblical teaching and with the tradition of our common inheritance, and to express in this document the consensus we have reached.

2. Through the life, death and resurrection of Jesus Christ God has reconciled men to himself, and in Christ he offers unity to all mankind. By his word God calls us into a new relationship with himself as our Father and with one another as his children—a relationship inaugurated by Baptism into Christ through the Holy Spirit, nurtured and deepened through the Eucharist, and expressed in a confession of one faith and a common life of loving service.

I The Mystery of the Eucharist

3. When his people are gathered at the Eucharist to commemorate his saving acts for our redemption, Christ makes effective among us the eternal benefits of his victory and elicits and renews our response of faith, thanksgiving and self-surrender. Christ through the Holy Spirit in the Eucharist builds up the life of the Church, strengthens its fellowship and furthers its mission. The identity of the Church as the body of Christ is both expressed and effectively proclaimed by its being centered in, and partaking of, his body and blood. In the whole action of the Eucharist, and in and by his sacramental presence given through bread and wine, the crucified and risen Lord, according to his promise, offers himself to his people.

4. In the Eucharist we proclaim the Lord's death until he comes. Receiving a foretaste of the kingdom to come, we look back with thanksgiving to what Christ has done for us, we greet him present among us, we look forward to his final appearing in the fullness of his kingdom when 'The Son also himself (shall) be subject unto him that put all things under him, that God may be all in all' (1 Cor 15:28). When we gather around the same table in this communal meal at the invitation of the same Lord and when we 'partake of the one loaf,' we are one in commitment not only to Christ and to one another, but also to the mission of the Church in the world.

II The Eucharist and the Sacrifice of Christ

5. Christ's redeeming death and resurrection took place once and for all in history. Christ's death on the cross, the culmination of his whole life of obedience, was the one, perfect and sufficient sacrifice for the sins of the world. There can be no repetition of or addition to what was then accomplished once for all by Christ. Any attempt to express a nexus between the sacrifice of Christ and the Eucharist must not obscure this fundamental fact of the Christian faith. (Footnote: The early Church in expressing the meaning of Christ's death and resurrection often used the language of sacrifice. For the Hebrew *sacrifice* was a traditional means of communication with God. The Passover, for example,

20

was a communal meal, the day of atonement was essentially expiatory; and the covenant established communion between God and man.) Yet God has given the Eucharist to his Church as a means through which the atoning work of Christ on the cross is proclaimed and made effective in the life of the Church. The notion of memorial as understood in the Passover celebration at the time of Christ—i.e., the making effective in the present of an event in the past—has opened the way to a clearer understanding of the relationship between Christ's sacrifice and the Eucharist. The Eucharistic memorial is no mere calling to mind of a past event or of its significance, but the Church's effective proclamation of God's mighty acts. Christ instituted the Eucharist as a memorial (*anamnesis*) of the totality of God's reconciling action in him. In the Eucharistic prayer the Church continues to make a perpetual memorial of Christ's death, and his members united with God and one another, give thanks for all his mercies, entreat the benefits of his passion on behalf of the whole Church, participate in these benefits and enter into the movement of his self-offering.

III The Presence of Christ

6. Communion with Christ in the Eucharist presupposes his true presence, effectually signified by the bread and wine which, in this mystery, become his body and blood. (Footnote: The word *transubstantiation* (qv) is commonly used in the Roman Catholic Church to indicate that God acting in the Eucharist effects a change in the inner reality of the elements. The term should be seen as affirming the *fact* of Christ's presence and of the mysterious and radical change which takes place. In contemporary Roman Catholic theology it is not understood as explaining *how* the change takes place.) The real presence of his body and blood can, however, only be understood within the context of the redemptive activity whereby he gives himself, and in himself reconciliation, peace and life, to his own. On the one hand, the Eucharistic gift springs out of the paschal mystery of Christ's death and resurrection, in which God's saving purpose has already been definitively realized. On the other hand, its purpose is to transmit the life of the crucified and risen Christ to his body, the Church, so that its members may be more fully united with Christ and with one another.

7. Christ is present and active, in various ways, in the entire Eucharistic celebration. It is the same Lord who through the proclaimed word invites his people to his table, who through his minister presides at that table, and who gives himself sacramentally in the body and blood of his paschal sacrifice. It is the Lord present at the right hand of the Father, and therefore transcending the sacramental order, who thus offers to his Church, in the Eucharistic signs, the special gift of himself.

8. The sacramental body and blood of the Saviour are present as an offering to the believer awaiting his welcome. When this offering is met by faith, a life-giving encounter results. Through faith Christ's presence—which does not depend on the individual's faith in order to be the Lord's real gift of himself to his Church—becomes no longer just a presence *for* the believer, but also a presence *with* him. Thus, in considering the mystery of the Eucharistic presence, we must recognize both the sacramental sign of Christ's presence and the personal relationship between Christ and the faithful which arises from that presence.

9. The Lord's words at the last supper, 'Take and eat; this is my body,' do not allow us to dissociate the gift of the presence and the act of sacramental eating. The elements are not mere signs; Christ's body and blood become really present and are really given. But they are really present and given in order that, receiving them, believers may be united in communion with Christ the Lord.

10. According to the traditional order of the liturgy the consecratory prayer (*anaphora)* (qv) leads to the communion of the faithful. Through this prayer of thanksgiving, a word of faith addressed to the Father, the bread and wine become the body and blood of Christ by the action of the Holy Spirit, so that in communion we eat the flesh of Christ and drink his blood.

11. The Lord who thus comes to his people in the power of the Holy Spirit is the Lord of glory. In the Eucharistic celebration we anticipate the joys of the age to come. By the transforming action of the Spirit of God, earthly bread and wine become the heavenly manna and the new wine, the eschatological banquet for the new man: elements of the first creation become pledges and first fruits of the new heaven and the new earth.

Conclusion

12. We believe that we have reached substantial agreement on the doctrine of the Eucharist. Although we are all conditioned by the traditional ways in which we have expressed and practised our Eucharistic faith, we are convinced that if there are any remaining points of disagreement they can be resolved on the principles here established. We acknowledge a variety of theological approaches within both our communions. But we have seen it as our task to find a way of advancing together beyond the doctrinal disagreements of the past. It is our hope that, in view of the agreement which we have reached on Eucharistic faith, this doctrine will no longer constitute an obstacle to the unity we seek."

For those instructed on the Anglican liturgy it will

not be necessary to state that this is a surprising document. (See Anglicanism.) It is not surprising that it drew comment and criticism. The Commission dealt with this response in an *Elucidation* published in 1979. They explained the terms 'substantial agreement' and considered in some detail the objections made to their use of *anamnesis* (qv). Objections were made to it from many sides: it was a veiled expression of repeated immolation; it did not sufficiently imply the reality indicated by traditional sacrificial language concerning the Eucharist; the word was not accurately or adequately interpreted. Some critics were unhappy with the realistic language, the words *become* and *change* in particular. The Commission thought that deep down there was uneasiness about the language used: Was it chosen to enable members of the two churches to see their own faith in the Agreed Statement without having in fact reached a genuine consensus?

Much of the *Elucidation* is taken up with explanation of *Anamnesis*. It runs as follows.[4]

Anamnesis and Sacrifice

5. The Commission has been criticized for its use of the term *anamnesis*. It chose the word used in the New Testament accounts of the institution of the Eucharist at the last supper. 'Do this as a memorial (*anamnesin*) of me (1 Cor 11:24-25; Lk 22:19, JB, NEB). The word is also found in Justin Martyr (qv) in the second century. Recalling the last supper he writes: 'Jesus, taking bread and having given thanks, said, 'Do this for my memorial (*anamnesin)*; This is my body;' and likewise, taking the cup, and giving thanks, he said, 'This is my blood' (*First Apology* 66; cf. *Dialogue with Trypho* 117).

From this time onwards the term is found at the very heart of the Eucharistic prayers of both East and West, not only in the institution narrative but also in the prayer which follows and elsewhere: cf., e.g., The Liturgy of St. John Chrysostom: Eucharistic Prayer I - The Roman Missal; Holy Communion, The Book of Common Prayer (1662); and Rites A and B of the Church of England Alternative Service Book (1980).

The word is also found in patristic and later theology. The Council of Trent in explaining the relation between the sacrifice of the cross and the Eucharist uses the words *commemoratio* and *memoria* (Session 22, ch 1); and in the Book of Common Prayer (1662) the Catechism states that the sacrament of the Lord's Supper was ordained 'for the continual *remembrance* of the sacrifice of the death of Christ, and of the benefits which we receive thereby.' The frequent use of the term in contemporary theology is illustrated by *One Baptism, One Eucharist and a Mutually Recognized Ministry* (Faith and Order Commission Paper No. 73),

as well as by the *General Instruction on the Roman Missal* (1970).

The Commission believes that the traditional understanding of sacramental reality, in which the once-for-all event of salvation becomes effective in the present through the action of the Holy Spirit, is well expressed by the word *anamnesis*. We accept this use of the word which seems to do full justice to the semitic background. Furthermore it enables us to affirm a strong conviction of sacramental realism and to reject mere symbolism. However the selection of this word by the Commission does not mean that our common Eucharistic faith may not be expressed in other terms.

In the exposition of the Christian doctrine of redemption the word *sacrifice* has been used in two intimately associated ways. In the New Testament, sacrificial language refers primarily to the historical event of Christ's saving work for us. The tradition of the Church, as evidenced for example in its liturgies, used similar language to designate in the Eucharistic celebration the *anamnesis* of this historical event. Therefore it is possible to say at the same time that there is only one unrepeatable sacrifice in the historical sense, but that the Eucharist is a sacrifice in the sacramental sense, provided that it is clear that this is not a repetition of the historical sacrifice.

There is therefore one historical, unrepeatable sacrifice offered once for all by Christ and accepted once for all by the Father. In the celebration of the memorial, Christ in the Holy Spirit unites his people with himself in a sacramental way so that the Church enters into the movement of his self-offering. In consequence, even though the Church is active in this celebration, this adds nothing to the efficacy of Christ's sacrifice upon the cross because the action is itself the fruit of this sacrifice. The Church in celebrating the Eucharist gives thanks for the gift of Christ's sacrifice and identifies itself with the will of Christ who has offered himself to the Father on behalf of all mankind."

The *Elucidation* also counters objections made to its doctrine of the real presence (qv), eliminating possible materialistic interpretations. There are further refinements on the reception of Christ by communicants: "Some traditions have placed a special emphasis on the association of Christ's presence with the sacramental elements; others have emphasized Christ's presence in the heart of the believer through reception by faith." The Commission thought that neither emphasis is incompatible with Eucharistic faith, provided that the complementary movement emphasized by the other position is not denied. "In the Eucharist, the sacrament of the New Covenant, Christ gives himself to his people so that they may receive him through faith."

On the question of 'reservation' (qv) and adoration

(qv) of the Eucharist, especially adoration, the Commission can scarcely hope to have given universal satisfaction. "Adoration in the celebration of the Eucharist is first and foremost offered to the Father. It is to lead us to the Father that Christ unites us to himself through our receiving of his body and blood. The Christ whom we adore in the Eucharist is Christ glorifying his Father. The movement of all our adoration is to the Father, through, with, and in Christ, in the power of the Spirit." To emphasize adoration of the Father by words such as "first and foremost" "the Christ whom we adore is Christ glorifying the Father" must not minimize the idea that Christ in the Eucharist is God.

The Commission did not deal with inter-communion, as this presupposes principles on authority and ministry; nor with the eschatological dimension, nor questions such as liberation and social justice, not divisive, not within its mandate.

The Roman Response

Consideration of the ARCIC Report cannot, however, be made without attention to the report drawn up by the Sacred Congregation for the Doctrine of the Faith, which reads as follows:[5]

"The Co-Chairmen of the Anglican Roman Catholic International Commission (ARCIC) sent to His Holiness, Pope John Paul II, the Final Report of twelve years of the Commission's work on the questions of Eucharistic doctrine, ministry and ordination, and authority in the Church. At the request of the Holy Father, the Congregation for the Doctrine of the Faith has proceeded with a doctrinal examination of this Report, and its conclusions are set forth in the following observations.

A. Overall evaluation

1) The Congregation must first of all give full recognition to the positive aspects of the work accomplished by ARCIC in the course of twelve years of an ecumenical dialogue which is exemplary on several counts. Setting aside a sterile polemical mentality, the partners have engaged in a patient and exacting dialogue in order to overcome doctrinal difficulties which were frankly acknowledged, with a view to restoring full communion between the Catholic Church and the Anglican Communion. This work achieved in common is a singular event in the history of the relations between the two Communions, and is at the same time a notable effort toward reconciliation. Worthy of particular note are:

(i) the quality of the doctrinal rapprochement achieved, in a serious attempt at a converging interpretation of the values considered fundamental by both sides;

(ii) the fact that ARCIC has been attentive to a certain number of observations which the SCDF had previously made about the Windsor, Canterbury and Venice statements, and has made an effort to respond satisfactorily in two series of elucidations on Eucharistic Doctrine—Ministry and Ordination (1979) and on Authority in the Church (1981).

2) The Congregation is obliged nevertheless to point out some negative aspects with regard to the method followed by ARCIC:

(i) The first may be considered a minor point, although it is not without relevance for the document's readers: ARCIC has thought it unnecessary to revise the original statements; rather, it has left their adjustment to two series of elucidations. The result is a lack of harmony and homogeneity which could lead to different readings and to an unwarranted use of the Commission's texts.

The following aspects are more important, for even though they pertain to the method employed, they are not without doctrinal significance:

(ii) The ambiguity of the phrase 'substantial agreement.'

The English adjective could be taken to indicate nothing other than 'real' or 'genuine.' But its translation, at least into languages of Latin origin, as 'substantiel,' 'sostanziale'—above all with the connotation of the word in Catholic theology—leads one to read into it a fundamental agreement about points which are truly essential (and one will see below that the SCDF has justified reservations in this regard).

Another source of ambiguity lies in the following fact: a comparison of three texts (Elucidations, Salisbury (1979), nos. 2 and 9; Authority in the Church I, Venice (1976), no. 26) shows that the agreement spoken of as 'substantial' while considered by ARCIC to be very extensive, is not yet complete. This does not permit one to know whether, in the eyes of the members of ARCIC, the differences which remain or the things which are missing from the document only deal with secondary points (for example the structure of liturgical rites, theological opinion, ecclesiastical discipline, spirituality), or whether these are points which truly pertain to the faith. Whatever the case, the Congregation is obliged to observe that sometimes it is the second hypothesis which is verified (for example, Eucharistic adoration, papal primacy, the Marian dogmas), and that it would not be possible here to appeal to the 'hierarchy of truths' of which no. 11 of the Decree *Unitatis Redintegratio* of Vatican II speaks (cf. the Declaration *Mysterium Ecclesiae* no. 4 par. 3).

(iii) The possibility of a twofold interpretation of the texts.

Certain formulations in the Report are not sufficiently explicit and hence can lend themselves to a twofold interpretation, in which both parties can find unchanged the expression of their own position.

This possibility of contrasting and ultimately incompatible readings of formulations which are apparently satisfactory to both sides gives rise to a question about the real consensus of the two Communions, pastors and faithful alike. In effect, if a formulation which has received the agreement of the experts can be diversely interpreted, how could it serve as a basis for reconciliation on the level of church life and practice?

Moreover, when the members of ARCIC speak about 'the consensus we have reached' (cf. Eucharistic Doctrine, Windsor (1971), no. 1) one does not always see clearly whether this means the faith really professed by the two Communions in dialogue, or a conviction which the members of the Commission have reached and to which they want to bring their respective coreligionists.

In this regard it would have been useful—in order to evaluate the exact meaning of certain points of agreement—had ARCIC indicated their position in reference to the documents which have contributed significantly to the formation of the Anglican identity (*The Thirty-Nine Articles of Religion, Book of Common Prayer, Ordinal*), in those cases where the assertions of the Final Report seem incompatible with these documents. The failure to take a stand on these texts can give rise to uncertainty about the exact meaning of the agreements reached.

The Congregation finally has to note that, from the Catholic point of view, there remain in the ARCIC Final Report a certain number of difficulties at the level of doctrinal formulations, some of which touch the very substance of the faith. These difficulties—their description and the reasons for them—will now be listed following the order of the new texts of the Final Report (Eucharistic Doctrine—Ministry and Ordination; Elucidations (Salisbury, 1979); Authority in the Church II; Authority in the Church: an Elucidation (Windsor, 1981))."

B. Doctrinal Difficulties noted by the SCDF

I - Eucharist

1) Eucharist as Sacrifice

In the Elucidations, no. 5, ARCIC has explained the reason for its use of the term *anamnesis* and has recognized as legitimate the specification of *anamnesis* as sacrifice, in reference to the Tradition of the Church and her liturgy. Nevertheless, in so far as this has been the object of controversy in the past, one cannot be satisfied with an explanation open to a reading which does not include an essential aspect of the mystery.

This text says, as does the Windsor statement (no. 5), 'the Church enters into the movement of (Christ's) self-offering' and the Eucharistic memorial, which consists in 'the making effective in the present of an event in the past,' is 'the Church's effectual proclamation of God's mighty acts.' But one still asks oneself what is really meant by the words 'the Church enters into the movement of (Christ's) self-offering' and the 'making effective in the present of an event of the past.' It would have been helpful in order to permit Catholics to see their faith fully expressed on this point, to make clear that this real presence of the sacrifice of Christ, accomplished by the sacramental words, that is to say, by the ministry of the priest saying *'in persona Christi'* the words of the Lord, includes a participation of the Church, the Body of Christ, in the sacrificial act of her Lord, so that she offers sacramentally in him and with him his sacrifice. Moreover, the propitiatory value that Catholic dogma attributes to the Eucharist, which is not mentioned by ARCIC, is precisely that of this sacramental offering (cf. Council of Trent, DS 1743, 1753; John Paul II, Letter *Dominicae Coenae,* no. 8, par. 4).

2) Real Presence

One notes with satisfaction that several formulations clearly affirm the real presence (qv) of the body and blood of Christ in the sacrament: for example, 'Before the Eucharistic Prayer, to the question: 'What is that?' the believer answers; 'It is bread.' After the Eucharistic Prayer to the same question he answers: 'It is truly the body of Christ, the Bread of Life' (Salisbury Elucidations, no. 6; cf. also Windsor Statement, nos. 6 and 10).

Certain other formulations, however, especially some of those which attempt to express the realization of this presence, do not seem to indicate adequately what the Church understands by 'transubstantiation' ('the wonderful and unique change of the whole substance of the bread into his body and of the wine into his blood, while only the species of bread and wine remain.'—Council of Trent, DS 1652; cf. Paul VI, *Mysterium Fidei,* AAS 57 (1965), 766).

It is true that the Windsor statement says in a footnote that this must be seen as 'a mysterious and radical change' effected by 'a change in the inner reality of the elements.' But the same statement speaks in another place (no. 3) of a 'sacramental presence through bread and wine,' and Elucidations (no. 6b) says 'His body and blood are given through the action of the Holy Spirit, appropriating bread and wine so that they become the food of the new creation.' One also finds the expression: 'the association of Christ's presence with the consecrated elements' (no. 7) and 'the association of Christ's sacramental presence with the consecrated bread and wine' (no. 9). These formulations can be read with the understanding that, after the Eucharistic prayer, the bread and wine remain such in their ontological substance, even while becoming the sacramental mediation of the body and blood of Christ.

(Note I) In the light of these observations, therefore, it seems necessary to say that the substantial agreement which ARCIC so carefully intended to present should receive even further clarification.

3) Reservation and Adoration of the Eucharist

Elucidations (no. 9) admits the possibility of a divergence not only in the practice of adoration (qv) of Christ in the reserved sacrament but also in the 'theological judgements' relating to it. But the adoration rendered to the Blessed Sacrament is the object of a dogmatic definition in the Catholic Church (cf. Council of Trent, DS 1643, 1656). A question could arise here about the current status in the Anglican Communion of the regulation called the 'Blank Rubric' of the *Book of Common Prayer:* ... 'the Sacramental Bread and Wine remain still in their natural substances and therefore may not be adored.' "

Note I reads as follows: One may also recall in this regard the Anglican-Lutheran statement of 1972, which reads: 'Both Communions affirm the real presence of Christ in this sacrament, but neither seeks to define precisely how this happens. In the eucharistic action (including consecration) and reception, the bread and wine, become the means whereby Christ is truly present and gives himself to the communicants.' (Report of the Anglican Lutheran International Conversations 1970-1972, authorized by the Lambeth Conference and the Lutheran World Federation, in *Lutheran World,* 19 (1972), 393).

The Observations of the SCDF then deal with the subject matter of the other ARCIC reports, Ministry and Ordination and Authority in the Church. The report suggests other subjects for consideration, apostolic succession and moral teaching and it urges the Commission members to deepen the discussion in dialogue so as to deal with the points it had raised.

---

[1]*Anglican-Roman Catholic International Commission: The Final Report,* London, CTS-SPCK, 1982; cf. also *Anglican/Roman Catholic Dialogue: The Work of the Preparatory Commission,* ed. Alan C. Clark and Colin Davey, 1974; Working Papers, *The Catholic Mind,* 64 (April 1971), 35-50; cf. J. W. Charley, *The Anglican Roman Catholic Agreement on the Eucharist,* Bramonte, 1972; H. J. Ryan, S.J., *Anglican Roman Catholic Doctrinal Agreement on the Eucharist, Worship,* 46, 1 Summer, 1972; J. M. R. Tillard, O.P., *The Deeper Implications of the Anglican Roman Catholic Dialogue, One in Christ,* 8, 3, 242-263; A. Ryder, S.C.J. and B. Byron, *The Anglican Roman Catholic Statement on the Eucharist, Comment and Discussion, Clergy Review,* 57 (1972), 163-173; *ibid.,* E. Doyle, 250-57; P. Fannon, S.M.M., 258-62; A. Ryder, *ibid., Adoration of the Eucharist,* 439-51; Letter, *The Times* 15 September 1971, Dom (later Bishop) Christopher Butler, O.S.B., a commission member); J. M. R. Tillard, O.P., *Catholiques romains et Anglicans: L'Eucharistie,* NRT, 1971 602-56—a paper by a commission member which influenced the deliberations; [2]Quotations from the *Joint Declaration on Cooperation, Vatican Council,* ed. A. Flannery, O.P., I, 479, 80; [3]Statement, *The Final Report,* 12-16; [4]*Elucidation,*

The Final Report, 18ff; [5]Text of the report, in English, AAS, 74 (1982), 1060-1074; cf. also *Response from the Bishops of England and Wales,* C.T.S., London.

APOSTOLICAE CURAE, 13 SEPTEMBER 1896

The Bull by which Leo XIII, after a historical and theological review of the question of Anglican orders, reached this firm conclusion: "Wherefore adhering entirely to the decrees of the Pontiffs, our predecessors, on this subject, and fully ratifying and renewing them by our own authority, on our own initiative and with certain knowledge, We pronounce and declare that ordinations performed according to the Anglican rite have been and are completely null and void."[1]

The decision was the final event in a series that had to end with a clear-cut statement. In the early nineties a new interest had been stirred in the question of Anglican Orders, at first in France and then inevitably in England. Books and articles were appearing in France, not only reopening the question of validity but defending an affirmative answer. The Pope was informed and expressed a wish to have reports on the matter from people whom he thought competent.

Opinion in Rome and in England had been consistently against validity, and ministers of the Anglican communion who became Catholics were, if they wished to serve as priests, obliged to seek reordination. With the influx of so many converts remarkable for learning and leadership from Anglicanism to the Catholic Church in the nineteenth century this practice was itself a kind of argument. Newman, a great theologian, and others like Manning who excelled in different ways, were in this constant stream of ministerial revaluation. This procedure went back to the sixteenth century, when, during the reign of Queen Mary (1553-1558), Cardinal Pole, with the express approval of Pope Paul IV, imposed reordination on all clerics promoted to orders according to the Edwardine Ordinal. E. C. Messenger summarizes: "As to the reason for this policy of reordination, we can only say that there is no proof whatever that it was based upon the absence of a tradition of instruments in the Anglican rite. There is, on the other hand, ample evidence to show that reordination was on the grounds of defective *form* and *intention.* This seems to have been taken for granted from the very first, in such a way that we can only say that it must have been notorious, and a fact accepted by all, that the new ministers ordained by the Anglican rite were not intended to be, never claimed to be, and were not in reality Catholic priests."[2]

From time to time, during the centuries, particular cases were referred to the Holy See for consideration and judgement. They were investigated thoroughly and always with the same result. Yet now in the late nineteenth century, which had seen acceptance of the policy by giants of the spirit, radical questioning especially from France, was heard. A link with the Frenchmen interested, Abbé Portal and the great church historian Mgr. Duchesne (though a historian of the early centuries) had been Lord Halifax. He and Abbé Portal would have a role later in the first public ecumenical initiative since the sixteenth century, the Malines Conversations, sponsored by Cardinal Mercier.

Cardinal Vaughan in England thought that a thorough examination of the question was needed. Another Roman dignitary destined to high office in the Church, Mgr. (later Cardinal) Merry del Val also thought that such an investigation should take place and that the Church should be ready to face any verdict. Those with scholarly interest were hard at work in research on the history of the Anglican ministry. A committee was set up in England by Cardinal Vaughan to gather the relevant evidence. The members' names are not known, but those of the sub-committee named to draft a historical and doctrinal essay reporting their findings are known: Mgr. Moyes, Dom F. A. Gasquet, O.S.B., a noted specialist in sixteenth-century history and Fr. David Fleming, O.F.M. Their report, entitled *Ordines Anglicani: Expositio Historica et Theologica,* was a sound piece of work.

The Pope had for a moment thought of a commission of Cardinals. He took note of the opinion forcefully expressed by Cardinal Vaughan that: "It would be impossible to exaggerate what would be the effect in England if any decision on Anglican Orders were come to in Rome reversing the practice of the Church from the very beginning of the Anglican heresy, without having, previous to such decision, fully heard the theologians and historians of the Catholic Church in England. I have no objection to French ecclesiastics identifying themselves with Lord Halifax: they do so, no doubt, with excellent intentions; and they will plead his cause more effectively than Anglicans could plead for themselves, because, among other reasons, they are less restrained and more positive than they would be had they personally adequate knowledge of English affairs. I am sure your Holiness will not allow their influence to prevail in Rome without allowing us to see their statements and their arguments, thus giving us a fair opportunity either to refute, modify, or corroborate them, as the case may be. . . . I have always advocated a thorough examination of the question of Anglican Orders."[3]

Leo XIII took heed. In March 1896 he appointed a commission of experts, representing different opinions, which simply means for or against, the validity of Anglican Orders. The commission would function more or less as a body of Consultors to the Holy Office. The results of their discussions, with the minutes of the meetings and the documents on the subject would go to the Cardinals of the Holy Office.

The members named to the Roman Commission were Mgr. Gasparri, the Abbé Duchesne, Mgr. Moyes, Dom Gasquet, Father David Fleming, O.F.M., and Fr. de Augustinis of the Gregorian University. Three members, Mgr. Moyes, Dom Gasquet and Fr. Fleming were known to oppose validity; the other three were known to take a favourable view of the Anglican claim. Duchesne's leaning in this direction has been exaggerated. The president would be Cardinal Mazella, who had taught dogmatic theology at Georgetown University, Woodstock College in Maryland and the Gregorian University. Gasparri, a future force in the Church in his special field, Canon Law—he would direct the Code of Canon Law and as Secretary of State for Pius XI negotiate the Lateran Pacts—was nevertheless uninformed on the question at issue and could not even read English.

English Catholics who favoured the Anglican claim protested that they were not represented on the Commission. With Vaughan's active support a representative of their views was sent to Rome, Fr. Scannell. To maintain numerical balance another member was then added, Fr. Jose Calasanzio de Llevanera, a Spanish Capuchin. Mgr. Merry del Val was secretary of the Commission.

Vota or statements were submitted to the Commission and Anglicans in Rome were available for their views. During meetings from 24 March to 7 May the Commission debated the matter from every possible viewpoint.

When the Cardinals met they were to consider the answers to two questions: Had the question of the validity of Anglican Orders been previously submitted properly to the Holy See, and fully determined? Had the recent inquiry shown that the previous decision was just and wise, or had it called for revision? Unanimously the Cardinals replied that the matter had been properly judged by the Holy See previously, and the recent inquiry had shown that all that had been done was just and wise and, therefore, fully justified.

All that now remained for the Pope to do was to issue a statement, which he decided to do in a special Bull, *Apostolicae Curae.* Leo XIII in the essential document reviewed the history, dealing with the rejection of Anglican Orders in the reign of Queen Mary and with the special cases of a French Calvinist in 1684 and the John Gordon case in 1704. Coming to the theological aspect the Pope had to contend with two conflicting opinions. Some Catholic theologians held that for an order to be validly received, it should be expressly mentioned in the wording of the "operative formula." This was, however, a minority opinion in the schools. Against this was the opinion of other leading theologians, including Mgr. Gasparri, that "the wording of the ordination form, even if not specifically determinate in itself, can be given the required determination from its setting, that is, from the other prayers and actions of the rite, or even from the connotation of the ceremony as a whole in the religious context of the age."

On the first and more restrictive Catholic opinion the Edwardine Ordinal was defective, for all it said was, "Receive the Holy Spirit." But the Pope took account of the other Catholic theological opinion: one more widely based. The whole Edwardine Ordinal, work of Thomas Cranmer, in its essential meaning and thrust, or as the Pope put it, "the native character and spirit of the Ordinal," rejected positively a consecrating and sacrificing priesthood: "The native character and spirit of the Ordinal, as one may call it, is thus objectively evident. Moreover, incapable as it was of conferring valid orders by reason of its original defectiveness, and remaining as it did in that condition, there was no prospect that with the passage of time it would become capable of conferring them. . . . It was in vain that from the time of Charles I some men attempted to admit some notion of sacrifice and priesthood, and then later on, certain additions were made to the Ordinal; and equally vain is the contention of a relatively small and recently formed section of Anglicans that the said Ordinal can be made to bear a sound and orthodox sense. These attempts, we say, were and are fruitless; for the reason, moreover, that even though some words in the Anglican Ordinal as it now stands may present the possibility of ambiguity, they cannot bear the same sense as they have in a Catholic rite. For, as we have seen, when once a new rite has been introduced denying or corrputing the sacrament of Order and repudiating any notion whatsoever of consecration and sacrifice, then the formula, 'Receive the Holy Ghost' (that is the Spirit who is infused into the soul with the grace of the sacrament), is deprived of its force; nor have the words, 'for the office and work of a priest' or 'bishop', etc., any longer their validity, being mere names voided of the reality which Christ instituted."

This is the principal reason for the condemnation of Anglican Orders, defect of form. It is central to the papal argument. The Pope added another, defect of intention. Here, intention is taken in the canonical sense, intending to do in a sacramental action what the Church intends that action to achieve or effect. Leo XIII elaborated the point thus: "The Church does not pass judgement on the mind or intention inasmuch as it is something directly interior; but in so far as it is

externally manifested she is bound to judge of it. Now if, in order to perform and administer a sacrament, a person has seriously and correctly used the due matter and form, he is for that very reason presumed to have intended to do what the Church does. This principle is the basis of the doctrine that a sacrament is valid even if it is conferred by a heretic or an unbaptized person, provided that the Catholic rite is used. But if, on the contrary, the rite is changed with the manifest purpose of introducing another rite which is not accepted by the Church, and of repudiating that which in fact the Church does and which by Christ's intention belongs to the nature of the sacrament, then it is evident that there is not merely an absence of necessary sacramental intention, but indeed that an intention is present which is contrary to and incompatible with the sacrament."

The principle at issue here is that of "positive contrary intention," which is basic in Catholic theology. It is not theoretical error but a deliberate act of the will directed against something which is, whether knowingly to the minister officiating or not, essential to a valid sacrament.

The personal intention of officiating Anglican ministers was not judged by *Apostolicae Curae*. The crucial case was the episcopal consecration in 1559 of Matthew Parker, first Archbishop of Canterbury in the Elizabethan hierarchy. The Roman commission of 1896 examined it carefully, for from Parker the entire Anglican clergy subsequently flowed. Bishop Barlow and his assistant bishops openly professed Protestant doctrines, and agreed to a change in the rite of consecration, abandoning the Catholic Pontifical in use during the reign of Mary, choosing rather to follow Cranmer's (qv) Ordinal. Was this an act of positive repudiation, of the kind which would nullify the sacrament? Leo XIII thought so. Hence the condemnation.

Debate has gone on among Catholic theologians as to the binding force of the papal declaration. In 1896 Leo himself wrote to the Cardinal Archbishop of Paris that his intention had been "to deliver final judgement and to settle completely that most important question of Anglican ordination." He thought that "all Catholics should receive his decision with the utmost respect, as being perpetually fixed, ratified and irrevocable."

The Pope did not use the word infallible. How then are we to interpret this passage in the ARCIC (qv) statement on Ministry: "We are fully aware of the issues raised by the judgement of the Roman Catholic Church on Anglican Orders. The development of the thinking in our two communions regarding the nature of the Church and of the ordained ministry, as represented in our Statement has, we consider, put these issues in a new context. Agreement on the nature of ministry is prior to consideration of the mutual recognition of ministries. What we have to say represents the consensus of the Commission on essential matters where it considers that doctrine admits of no divergence."

We may note that since *Apostolicae Curae* there has been much dissent from the papal findings among Anglicans, beginning from the very year of the Bull. The Old Catholic Churches and the Orthodox of the east eventually recognized Anglican Orders.

[1]Text of the Bull ASS 29 (1896-1897), 193-203; English tr. CTS Mgr. G. D. Smith, *Anglican Orders: Final Decision;* cf. F. Temple, *Answer of the Archbishops of England to the Apostolic Letter of Leo XIII on English Orders,* 1897; A. E. G. Lowndes, *Vindication of the Anglican Orders,* 2 vols, New York, 1911; G. Dix, *The Question of Anglican Orders,* London, 1944; F. Cirlot, *Apostolic Succession and Anglicanism,* El Paso, Texas, 1945; F. Clark, *Anglican Orders and Defect of Intention,* London, 1956; *id., Eucharistic Sacrifice and the Reformation,* London, 1960; *id., The Catholic Church and Anglican Orders,* CTS, 1962; *id., A Reopening of the Question of Anglican Orders, Clergy Review,* 47 (1962) 555-568; *id., Les ordres anglicans, problème oecuménique, Greg.,* 45 (1964) 60-93; E. L. Mascall, *Intention and Form in Anglican Orders, ChQuartRev.,* 158 (1957), 4-30; J. J. Hughes, *Absolutely Null and Utterly Void,* London, 1968; P. F. Bradshaw, *The Anglican Ordinal,* London, 1971; E. P. Echlin, *The Story of Anglican Ministry,* Slough, 1974; C.F. Schreiner, *The Priesthood of the Anglican Church and Apostolicae Curae,* New York, 1974; E. Yarnold, S.J., *Anglican Orders, A Way Forward,* CTS 1977; *id., Gli ordini anglicani in Il problema ecumenico oggi,* ed. C. Boyer, S.J., Brescia, 1960; E. C. Messenger, *The Reformation,* II, 508-601; E. C. Messenger, *op.cit.,* 167; Apud E. C. Messenger, *op.cit.,* 527, 28.

APOSTOLIC CONSTITUTIONS, THE
In this late fourth-century compilation of church laws, Syrian in origin but drawn from different sources, the eighth book has the Eucharistic prayer, which is preceded by a preface unique in length, with a Christian cosmology and anthropology and much on the salvation history theme; after the *Sanctus* comes a wonderful summary of the life and privileges of Jesus Christ. It ends thus: "Thus did he deliver from suffering and rescue from death those for whose sake he had come; thus did he break the bonds of the devil and free men from his deceit. He rose from the dead on the third day and remained with his disciples for forty days. He ascended to the heavens and is seated at the right hand of you, his God and Father. Remembering, therefore, the sufferings he endured for our sake, we give you thanks, O almighty God, not certainly as well as we ought, but as well as we can, and we carry out your testament."

Then comes the institution (qv) narrative: "For on the night when he was betrayed, he took bread in his holy and spotless hands, and, lifting his eyes to heaven to you, his God and Father, he broke it, gave it to his disciples, and said: 'This is the mystery of the New Testament. Take and eat this is my body which is broken for many for the forgiveness of sins.' He also filled the cup with wine and with water, he said the blessing, gave it to them, and said: 'Drink of this, all of you, this is my blood, which is poured out for many for the forgiveness of sins. Do this in memory of me. For each time that you eat this bread and drink of this cup, you will proclaim my death until I return.'"

The *anamnesis* (qv) follows: "Mindful then of his passion, of his death, of his resurrection from the dead, of his return to heaven, of his second coming in the future when he will come with glory and power to judge the living and the dead and render to each according to his works, we offer you, O King and God, according to your testament, this bread and this cup. We give you thanks through him for having judged us worthy to stand before you and exercise the priesthood for you. And we ask you to look down graciously on these offerings that we bring you, O God, who have need of nothing, and to accept them as pleasing to you, in honour of your Christ."

Then comes the *Epiclesis* (qv): "Send down upon this sacrifice your Holy Spirit, 'witness of the sufferings of the Lord Jesus' (1 Pet. 5:1), that he may make of this bread the body of your Christ and this cup the blood of your Christ.

May those who share in it be strengthened in devotion, obtain forgiveness of sins, be delivered from the devil and his errors, be filled with the Holy Spirit, become worthy of your Christ, enter into possession of eternal life, and be reconciled with you, almighty God."[2]

A litanic prayer for the bishop and one for the deacon follow. The liturgy of communion thereafter comprises a preparatory prayer, acclamation of the people, communion rites, prayer after communion and a lengthy prayer of thanksgiving. To conclude, the bishop pronounces a lengthy blessing introduced by the deacon, who is also given the very last word, 'Go in peace.'

[1]Text with Latin tr., *Prex,* 82-95 with one of the litanic prayers for the bishop and the doxology ending them; English tr. entire, *Springtime,* 227-240; ed. also PG 1, 355-1156; ed. F. X. Funk, Paderborn, 1905; bk. VIII, Brightman, LEW, 3-30; cf. F. X. Funk, *Die Apostolischen Konstitutionen,* 1891; F. Nau, DTC III (1908), 1520-1537; H. Leclercq, DACL, III (2, 1914), 2732-95; Altaner-Stuiber, 1966, 255f; Quasten, *Patrology,* I, 183-85; [2]VIII, 12, 39; tr. *Springtime.*

ARCHAEOLOGY AND THE EUCHARIST
Testimonies of early Christian monuments to the Eucharist are found in burial inscriptions, two of which are dealt with in this work (see articles Abercius, Pectorius).[1] From earliest times the symbol chosen to

represent Christ in the Eucharist was the fish. The multiplication of the loaves and fishes inspired some representations; a mosaic on the floor of a church on the shores of the Sea of Galilee is widely reproduced. (See article Art and the Eucharist.)

---

[1]Cf. G. B. De Rossi, *La Roma sotterranea cristiana*, II Rome, 1867, 328-51; *id., Inscriptiones christianae urbis Romae septimo saeculo antiquiores*, II, Rome, 1898, XII-XXVIII; G. Wilpert, *Fractio Panis*, Paris 1896; *id., Le pitture delle catacombe romane*, Rome, 1903, 260-83; *id., I sarcofagi cristiani antichi*, II, Rome, 1932, 307-10; *id., La fede delle Chiesa nascente*, Città del Vaticano, 1938, 92-114; R. S. Bour, *Eucharistie d'après les monuments de l'antiquité chrétienne*, DTC V (1913), 1183-1210; O. Marucci, *L'Eucaristia e l'Archeologia* in *Conferenze al Laterano*, March-April, 1920; A. Amore, *L'Eucaristia nell'Archeologia, Eucaristia*, 173-183; J. Quasten, "Fish, Symbolism of," NCE, V, 943-46.

ART AND THE EUCHARIST

Christian art has given us three masterpieces on the theme of the Eucharist: the Adoration of the Lamb by the brothers Van Eyck in Ghent cathedral, the Last Supper by Leonardo da Vinci on the refectory wall of the Dominican convent of Santa Maria delle Grazie in Milan, and the *Disputa del Sacramento* by Raphael in the Stanza della Segnatura in the Vatican.

Some reflection on each of these masterpieces may help the student to appreciate the relationship between aesthetics and the mysteries of the faith, exemplified in the artistic approach to the central mystery of the Eucharist.

The Adoration of the Lamb was composed for the cathedral of St. Bavon in 1432; it is, after vicissitudes caused by religious and other conflicts, now in the cathedral of Ghent. The history of the contribution made by each of the brothers, Hubert and Jan, is a matter of controversy, which can be left to historians. The style is in the rich allegorical tradition of medieval times, with the notable exception of the naturalism in the portrayal of Adam and Eve.

The genre is an altarpiece. The upper part features Christ the Pontiff centrally placed with, on his right the Blessed Virgin Mary seated beside the High Priest, and on his left the Precursor, who proclaimed the mystery of the Lamb, St. John the Baptist. Angels singing hymns and angels playing the organ fill the panels next to Our Lady and St. John. At the extreme end on the right of Christ is Adam and on the extreme left, Eve showing the apple, the forbidden fruit. Topping these extremes are minuscule OT scenes, the sacrifice of Abel and Cain over Adam, the killing of Abel by Cain over Eve.

The wide centrepiece of the lower part shows the Lamb on an altar which is situated in an open setting which fades away to elevated, attractively uneven woodland while on the horizon church towers and spires look to the sky. The hovering dove is on the summit of the visible sky.

Angels kneel adoring beside the altar of the Lamb; two in front have thuribles. Widely spaced from him but converging towards him are the hosts of prophets and saints of OT, the Apostles, Pontiffs and Doctors of the New Law, martyrs and virgins. The blood of the Lamb is taken in a chalice with sevenfold sacramental outpouring.

In two side panels to the right of the Lamb are soldiers of Christ and just judges; in two to his left are holy hermits and holy pilgrims, these led by St. Christopher. Fr. De la Taille (qv) who chose this marvellous composition as the frontispiece for his great work, *Mysterium Fidei*, supplies the moving legend: "The Lamb washed away with his blood, which gathered in the Eucharistic chalice he gave to the Church, the sin which was spread from our first parents through the whole human race; he is seated on high, a priest forever according to the order of Melchizedek." One may recall another representation of the Lamb on the altar: the remarkable group of statuary in Carrara marble executed by Professor Ferri, to depict the apparition at Knock, 21 August 1879, now standing on the site of the apparition. The shrine was honoured by a visit of John Paul II in the centenary year, to mark which event he presented the Golden Rose to Knock.

The Last Supper by Leonardo da Vinci is universally accepted as supreme in the treatment of the event. It was an innovation in taking the announcement of the betrayal as the moment to depict, not as so many others have chosen, the communion of the Apostles. Leonardo has been criticized for giving too much space to the supper room, as for placing the event in daytime. But in the strictly artistic qualities needed in such a work, purity of line, aerial perspective, grouping, character portrayal, atmosphere, this work is incomparable. "Seated in the middle of the Apostles, Christ is a picture of heavenly repose, which possesses so much the greater attraction for the spectator in view of the commotion visible among the Apostles. Amid all his sorrow the Saviour is divinely calm and serious; the Apostles, on the other hand, are amazed and indignant, each protesting with words and gestures according to the temperament which tradition has assigned to each. Each believes that he has misunderstood the words of Jesus, and turns towards his neighbour. Two groups are seen on each side of the Saviour, and these groups, notwithstanding their contrasts with one another, combine to produce an impression of perfect unity. The whole work is permeated with vitality, life and variety, but the details are so combined by the unity of the treatment that the eye of every beholder is enchanted. A deep knowledge of the human heart is shown by the figures of Peter, John and Judas whom the master combines in one group. After the head of Christ that of the Traitor is regarded as the best portion of the picture."[2]

The third masterpiece is Raphael's fresco in the Stanza della Segnatura, composed in 1509-1510. The word *La Disputa del Sacramento* should not be misunderstood. The work is to the glory of the Eucharist, and is entitled also Theology, as a response to another fresco in the same Stanza 'The School of Athens,' entitled Philosophy. Raphael would also paint the Miracle of Bolsena (see article Miracles). But *La Disputa* is his triumph on this theme. It is described as follows: "In the higher zone on the left side of Christ (as seen) are: St. Peter, Adam, St. John the Evangelist, David, St. Lawrence, the prophet Jeremiah; at the right side, St. Paul, Abraham, St. James, Moses, St. Stephen, Judas Maccabaeus. In the lower zone, the four Fathers of the (Latin) Church, Gregory, Jerome, Augustine, Ambrose in the centre (but to the right of the altar on which stands the monstrance with the Host). Among the other figures the following can be identified: to the right, St. Thomas Aquinas (qv), Pope Innocent III (qv), St. Bonaventure (qv), Pope Sixtus IV della Rovere (the uncle of Julius II), and Dante; at the left, the first of the bishops identical with the cardinal in the portrait in Madrid, Bramante, Fra Giovanni Angelico de Fiesole."[3] It is necessary to add to these details given in the Phaidon edition that the centre of the picture through all levels is the Holy Trinity: the Father with accompanying angels dominates, the Son with Our Lady on his right and St. John the Baptist on his left is enthroned above the saints and OT figures and through the cloud which separates him from those below is seen the descending dove, just over the altar and monstrance, flanked with two cherubs bearing scrolls. This indeed is a unique summary in colour and line of theology, history, Church fecundity, religious awe, unashamed piety. It is the mystery of grace, of faith, hope and love transparent through an artistic product of human genius at its summit.

What the Van Eyck brothers, Leonardo Da Vinci and Raphael expressed so powerfully has been the inspiration of succeeding generations of Christian artists and craftsmen. Art historians, such as P. D. Corbinian Wirz, O.S.B., and Maurice Vloberg, have collected the evidence for assessment of this religious impulse and its effects. Early Christian art tended to work in symbols, the fish most frequently chosen. Gradually OT and NT types and figures were depicted, the sacrifice of Abraham, the multiplication of the loaves, the miracle of Cana, the Manna, the sacrifice of Abel, the offering of Melchizedek.

Mgr. Wilpert, a famous investigator of the Catacombs, discovered the first representation of the Eucharist, the *Fractio panis* in the Capella Graeca of the Roman Catacomb of St. Priscilla. Mgr. Wilpert was convinced that it was an instance of "the breaking of the bread" in the realistic sense used in Acts: "We have here before us a liturgical picture from a time when the Apostolic expression, *fractio panis,* was still used for the Eucharistic service. The picture, however, is not exclusively realistic: the artist uses with great skill the Eucharistic prototype—the miraculous feeding of the multitude—for the clearer explanation of its antitype by painting beside the liturgical chalice two plates (one with two fishes and the other with five loaves) and to the extreme left four and to the right three baskets filled to the rim. The faithful are represented by six persons (five men and one woman) who recline as at a banquet. The woman is represented with veiled head, whereas women participating at other banquets had their heads uncovered. Finally the 'president' who breaks the bread, does not recline like the others, but sits separated from them in the foreground near the Eucharistic chalice. That the painting has a liturgical and Eucharistic import is thus proved with a certainty which excludes all doubt."[4] Not all scholars agree; some maintain that this is but a representation like others of the multiplication of the loaves and fishes, a symbol only of the Eucharist. The conclusion is valid: "However, it is certain that we have here the earliest picture dealing with the Blessed Eucharist; whether it is purely symbolical or partly symbolical and partly realistic will perhaps remain always a disputed question."[5]

The art of the Catacombs was primarily catechetical, not aesthetic and the choice of symbols or symbolic biblical episodes, such as the fish and then in places the Lamb, was also dictated by the 'discipline of the secret' (qv). With a climate of freedom, artists began to depict the essential biblical moment, the Last Supper.

Leaving aside a disputed item, we can take with certainty the origin, the first example, a mosaic in the Church of St. Apollinaris in Ravenna, city of great mosaics. With the entry of the Church into a great Eucharistic age, culminating in the thirteenth century and continuing on for some generations thereafter, artists began to turn to the subject with enthusiasm and superb skill. The very fact poses a problem not often considered: Why was genius expended with lavish generosity on this one theme? A similar question arises with regard to the Madonna, whether depicted in pigment, marble, stained glass or icon medium—which is not to fail in distinction between the underlying truths. So we are faced with a succession of great works on the Lord's Supper. Giotto and Fra Angelico lead the train and soon in the great Renaissance age they were followed by many others, Luca Signorelli, Andrea del Castagno, Dominico Ghirlandaio, Roselli, Leonardo, already mentioned, Andrea del Sarto, Titian, Tintoretto, Bonifacio Veronese. To these Italian names one must add those of the Spaniard Juan de Juanes and the Italian expatriate in Spain, Carducci. The Netherlands are represented by Dierick Bouts (Dirk van Harlem) and the great Peter Paul Rubens; France by Nicholas Poussin who painted the Last Supper three times, and his disciple Champaigne; Germany by Martin Schongauer, three woodcuts by Dürer, and two paintings by Hans Holbein, who, born in Augsburg, lived for a long time in Basel, spent his last years in England, Bartholomew Bruyn and Martin Schaffner, to end in the sixteenth century.

Whatever biblical scholars think about the meeting at Emmaus (qv) and the "breaking of the bread," the artists insinuate a Eucharistic meaning. It is a theme which has attracted Titian, Veronese, Vermeer, Rembrandt, and others. Symbolic or allegorical themes also figure in the artistic tribute to the Eucharist, such as the mystic winepress. Again, historical moments, especially in the lives of the saints, have been chosen, such as the last communion of St. Jerome. Saints noted for doctrine or devotion to the Eucharist have provided inspiration, for example, as Ruben's painting of the Champions of the Eucharist.

So the testimonies of creative art continue, though scarcely such as to rival the masterpieces of the past in scale or execution. All through history, from Byzantine times especially, there has been a multiplicity of illustrative or decorative work in material things associated with the Eucharist, altar coverings or tapestries, vestments, sacred vessels, chalices, ciboria, monstrances—even architectural work in regard to the Blessed Sacrament, chapels, part of larger church buildings. Sometimes an outstanding work of craftsmanship commemorates history and the Eucharist: witness the superb moving platform with monstrance in Valencia, gift of the women of the region to the Eucharistic Lord for the safety of their menfolk in the Spanish Civil War.

[1]Cf. J. Hoppenot, La Messe dans l'histoire et dans l'art, Paris, 1912; P. D. Corbinian Wirz, O.S.B., The Holy Eucharist in Art, Dublin, 1932; Raphael, The Phaidon Edition, London, 1941; C. (Cardinal) Costantini, Dio nascosto, Splendori di fede e d'arte nella Santa Eucaristia, Rome, 1944; esp. M. Vloberg, L'Eucharistie dans l'Art, 2 vols., Grenoble, 1946; E. Renders, Jean van Eyck et le Polyptyque, Brussels, 1950; P. B. Coremans, and others, L'Adoration de l'Agñeau, Antwerp, 1951; M. W. Brockwell, The Van Eyck Problem, London, 1954; L. van Puyvelde, L'Agneau mystique d'Hubert et de Jean van Eyck, Brussels, 1959; Eva Tea, L'Eucaristia nell'Arte, Eucaristia, 1191-1204; H. Leclercq, O.S.B., DACL VII, 2 (1927), "Ichthys," 1990-1086; J. Quasten, "Fish, symbolism of," NCE V (1967), 943-6; V. Denis, "Last Supper, Iconography of," NCE, X 399; [2]P. D. C. Wirz, op.cit., 25, 26; [3]Raphael, The Phaidon Edition, 29; [4]Apud P. D. C. Wirz, op.cit., 10; [5]Ibid., opinion of Wirz, 11.

ATHANASIUS, ST. (C. 296-373)

Eutychius of Constantinople preserves a fragment of A's sermon To the Newly-Baptized, wherein the Eucharist is dealt with: "You shall see the levites bring loaves and a chalice of wine, and place them on the table. As long as the invocation and prayers have not begun, there is only bread and wine. But after the great and wonderful prayers have been pronounced, then the bread becomes the body of our Lord Jesus Christ, and the wine becomes his blood. Let us come to the celebration of the mysteries. As long as the prayers and invocations have not taken place, this bread and this wine are simply (bread and wine). But after the great prayers and holy invocations have been pronounced, the Word descends into the bread and wine, and the body of the Word is."[1]

A passage from the Letters to Serapion[2] is sometimes quoted to justify a symbolist doctrine. The context does not justify such an interpretation. His doctrine is fully realistic as is shown in the Festal Letters, esp., "Our Saviour himself likewise passing from the figurative to the reality, promised them that henceforth they would not eat the flesh of the lamb, but his own saying: 'Take, eat and drink; this is my body and blood.'"[3]

[1]PG 26, 1325; cf. Quasten, Patrology, III, 79; cf. J. Solano, Textos, I, 215-236; P. Batiffol, L'Eucharistie, 318-325; T. Camelot, in Eucaristia, 140; [2]Ad Seraf. iv, 19, PG26, 665-668; [3]Letter V, 15, PG26, 1379c.

AUGSBURG CONFESSION, THE (1530)

In the agreed statement of Lutheran teaching drawn up at the instigation of the Emperor Charles V, article ten deals with the Eucharist.[1] The German form for which Luther was probably responsible was as follows: "The real body and blood of Christ are really present under the forms of bread and wine in the Lord's Supper, and are distributed and received." Melanchton's version in Latin was: "The body and blood of Christ are really present, and are distributed to those who eat in the Lord's Supper."[2] The difference here could be missed; it is real. In one version, "under the forms of bread and wine" make the doctrine of the presence explicit. The other version is vague, non-committal.

The Catholic theologians who replied to the Emperor on the Augsburg Confession pointed out the deficiency of this statement. A later version in 1540 was still vaguer: "Together with the bread and wine, the body and blood of Christ are really exhibited to those who eat in the Lord's Supper." This formula reduces the idea of presence still more.

In regard to the Mass, the Confession made against Catholics an accusation that has died hard: "There was added an opinion which infinitely increased the number of private Masses, namely that Christ by his Passion made satisfaction for original sin, and instituted the Mass, in which oblation should be made for daily sins, mortal and venial; hence arose a public opinion that the Mass was a work washing away the sins of the living and the dead *ex opere operato*; here it began to be disputed whether one Mass said for many availed as much as if each Mass were said for each: this dispute brought forth an infinite number of Masses."[3] The authors of the Confession say that they retain the Mass and celebrate it with greatest reverence; private Masses they had abolished because of the erroneous opinion they held about Catholics.

Catholic theologians at the time repudiated the opinion as characteristic of their doctrine; no name was mentioned in support of the allegation. Bellarmine (qv) summed up accurately: "No Catholic ever taught such a thing."[4]

[1]Bibl. K. Schottenloher, *Bibliographie zur Deutschen Geschichte im Zeitalter der Glaubensspaltung,* 1517-1585, IV 1938, 35-45; on the *Confutation* 45f; W. Gussmann, *Quellen und Forschungen zur Geschichte des Augsburgischen Glaubenbekentnisses,* 2 vols, 1911; J. Ficker, *Die Konfutation des Augsburgischen Bekentnisses,* 1891; W. E. Nagel, *Luthers Anteil an der Confessio Augustana, (Beiträge zur Forderung christlicher Theologie,* 34, Hft. 1, 1930); T. Kolde, PRE, ed. 3., II, 1897, 242-250; H. Bornkamm, EKL, I, 1956, 254-8; *id.,* RGG 3 ed, I, 1957, 733-36; E. C. Messenger, *The Reformation,* 121-35; M. Lackmann, *The Augsburg Confession and Catholic Unity,* New York, 1932; DTC Tables, XVI, 1, 1089-91; [2]*Corpus Reformatorum,* XXVI, 559; [3]Le Plat, *Monumenta,* II, 391; [4]*Judicium de libro,* 88.

AUGUSTINE, ST., DOCTOR OF THE CHURCH (354-430)

A. calls the Eucharist "the sacrament of piety, the sign of unity, the bond of charity."[1] Protestant writers, notably Frederich Loofs, have maintained that A. is the forerunner of Berengar (qv), that he gives a purely symbolist doctrine of Christ's presence in the Eucharist, not believing in a real presence. The main point here is A's use of the word sign: he must then, Loofs and others contend, imply mere symbolism (qv). Apart from and in spite of a certain plausibility, this view is untenable.

That A. had at times a symbolist approach is manifest. His doctrine, which is clear on the central point of the real presence must be seen in the context of African thinking, that of St. Cyprian (qv) and Tertullian (qv). We must not overlook his problem with the 'discipline of the secret.' Generally he formulates a

distinction which is a clue to his thought: *aliud est sacramentum, aliud virtus sacramenti.*[2] Consecration or sanctification in the Eucharist, is guaranteed as he applies this principle: "The Lord did not hesitate to say: 'This is my body' since he was giving a sign of his body."[3] There is then a sign, a *res sacra,* a *sacramentum.* But consecration does more: to the sign it adds a gift, none other than the body and blood of Christ himself:" "The bread which we see on the altar, sanctified by God's word, is the body of Christ. The chalice, that is what the chalice contains, sanctified by the word of God, is the blood of Christ."[4] Such texts could be multiplied: "not all bread, but that which receives the blessing of Christ, becomes the body of Christ."[5] Speaking of the sacrament which we take for our spiritual nourishment, he adds, "though it is brought to its visible appearance (i.e., of bread and wine) by mens' hands, it is not sanctified to become such a mighty sacrament save by the Spirit of God acting invisibly."[6] Within the sign is a gift, a reality, food for the soul, but a gift accessible only to faith, though it is not created by faith, since children can receive it: it is due to the action of the Spirit of God.

Further texts from A. are invoked to show how he believed in the real presence (qv): "That which you see is the bread and the chalice and see that your eyes assure you of this. But what your faith wishes to know is that the bread is the body of Christ and the chalice the blood of Christ."[7] "The same who gave to his disciples the bread and the chalice, is the one who today consecrates these things. It is not a man who consecrated the body and blood of Christ here before him, but the same Christ, crucified for you. The words are spoken by the mouth of the priest but the body and blood are consecrated by the power and grace of God." "This true Mediator ... preferred, as a man, to be the sacrifice than to receive it so as not to give anyone the pretext of believing that this honour could be given to a creature. Thus he is the priest who offers and the victim offered..."[8] For A., in a word, the Eucharistic bread and the body of Christ are identified.

A. speaks of Christ "being borne in his hands when giving his own body; he said, 'This is my body.' For he bore that body in his hands."[9] It is, moreover, impossible to understand his teaching on the adoration (qv) due to the sacrament, apart from belief in the real presence. Pondering a verse in the psalms, 'Adore the footstool of his feet,' he reaches this explanation: "Divided in mind, I fear to adore the earth lest I be condemned by him who made heaven and earth, while on the other hand I fear not to adore the footstool of my Lord. In doubt I turn to Christ and find how the earth can be adored without impiety.... Flesh is from the earth and he received flesh from the flesh of Mary;

he walked here in the very flesh and gave that flesh to us to eat for our salvation; but no one eats that flesh without first adoring it. Thus we have found how such a footstool of our Lord's may be adored. Not only do we not sin by adoring, but we sin by not adoring."[10]

A's teaching on unworthy communion is likewise unintelligible unless he is taken to believe in the real presence. He says that the sinner "eats the body of Christ and drinks his blood"[11] without receiving the grace of the sacrament. He warns against sins of the flesh in these words: "You already know your dignity, you already know where you are approaching, what you are eating, what you are drinking—even more, whom you are eating, whom you are drinking. Restrain yourself, therefore, from fornication."[12]

There is the question of A's use of signs and figures. "He entrusted and handed over to his disciples the figure of his body and blood."[13] In Letter 98 he expounds a general theory. The sacramental signs, because they resemble the realities which they represent, are given the names of these realities. Christ was really immolated only once, but he is said to be immolated daily. As "in one way the sacrament of the body of Christ is the body of Christ so the sacrament of faith is the faith."[14]

Commentators thus explain these texts: the Eucharist besides producing a special grace is composed of a double element: one invisible, the body of Christ; the other, the only visible one, the accidents (qv) of bread which remain. The accidents or species, what is seen as bread, are a sign of the body, which only our faith perceives. A., moreover, uses the word *sacrament* for the visible palpable element, not as we do for the body of Christ.

A. likewise speaks of a figurative eating, understandable on his terms, ruling out carnal eating in the Capharnaite sense, urging a spiritual eating, that is, true interior dispositions. His rich doctrine on the Eucharist as the symbol of the Church, continues a strand of thought from long before him, one that continues to the present time; it is ultimately Pauline in origin.[15]

A's writing on the Eucharist merits patient study. His total orthodoxy is certain from the fact that never for a moment did he think himself in any disagreement whatsoever from his predecessors, especially from St. Ambrose to whom he was so close in mind and heart; and it is notable that his opponents ever on the look out for grounds of criticism, did not dare question his Eucharistic doctrine.

[1]J. Solano, *Textos*, II, 105-284; Cf. K. Adam, *Die Eucharistielehre des hl. Augustinus*, Paderborn, 1908; *id.,* same title, *TheolQuartal*, 1931, 490-553; P. Batiffol, *L'Eucharistie*, 422-453; G. Lecordier, *La doctrine de l'Eucharistie chez S. Augustin*, Paris, G. Bracci, *Victima sancta. Pensiero, dottrina, e insegnamento del S. Dottore Agostino sull'Eucaristia*, Turin, 1930; J. Rivière, *L'Eucharistie et S. Augustin, Rev. Apolog.*, 1930, 513-531; H. Lang, *S. Augustini Textus eucharistici selecti, Florilegium Patristicum*, Fasc. 25, Bonn 1933; B. Busch, *De initiatione christiana sec. doctrinam S. Augustini*, Rome, 1939; Th. Camelot, *Réalisme et symbolisme dans la doctrine eucharistique de S. Augustin*, RSPT 31 (1947), 394-410; H. de Lubac, S.J., *Corpus Mysticum* 2nd ed., Paris, 1949, 200-225 and *passim*; F. Krueger, *Synthesis of Sacrifice according to St. Augustine*, Mundelein, 1950; F. Filograssi, *De Eucharistia*, Rome, 1953, 140-150; L. J. Van der Lof, *Eucharistie et présence réelle selon Saint-Augustin*, REA 10 (1964) 289-294; J. Pintard, *Expérience et enseignement de l'Eucharistie chez S. Augustin, Esprit et Vie*, March, 1978, 177-87; M. Fr. Berrouard, *L'être sacramentel de l'Eucharistie selon S. Augustin*, NRT 109 (1977), 702-721; A. Garrido Sanz, *Realismo y simbolismo eucaristico agustiniano, Estudio Agustiniano* 14 (1979), 521-540; W. Gessel, *Eucharistiche Gemeinschaft bei Augustin*, Würzburg, 1966, A. Sage, *L'Eucharistie dans la pensée de Saint Augustin*, REA 15 (1969) 209-240; E. Portalié, DTC I, 2418-2426, English tr. *A Guide to the Thought of St. Augustine*, London, 1960, 247-260; G. Bareille, DTC V, 1173-79; C. Boyer, *Eucaristia*, 165-71; A. Piolanti, *Il Mistero*, 193-98; [2]*In Joa.* tr XXVI, 11, PL 35, 1611; [3]*Contra Adminat*, Xii, 3, PL 42, 144; [4]*Serm* 227, PL 38, 1099; [5]*Serm* 234, *ibid.*, 1116; [6]*De Trin.* III, iv, 10 PL 42, 874; [7]*Serm* 272 PL 38, 1246; [8]*Serm* 143 ed Card. Mai, apud A. Piolanti, op.cit., 195; *De Civ. Dei*, Lib X, c. 20, PL 41, 298; [9]*In ps* 38, *enar.* 1, 10, PL 36, 306; [10]*In ps* 98, IX, PL 37, 1265; [11]*Serm* 71, XI, 17, PL 38, 453; *De bapt. contra Don.*, V, 8, 9, PL 43, 181; [12]*Serm* IX, 4, PL 38, 85; [13]*In ps.* 9, X, 14, PL 36, 73; [14]Ep. 98, 9, PL 364; [15]Cf. E. Portalié, *op.cit.*, 257f; P. Bertiocchi, *Il Simbolismo ecclesiologico dell'Eucaristia in S. Agostino*, Bergamo, 1937; H. de Lubac, *op.cit.*

AZYMES

Unleavened bread used for the Eucharist in the Latin Church, opposed by the Orthodox, the occasion of controversy since the eleventh century. The problem had existed even before Photius, who did not become personally involved. But the really sharp debate begins in the eleventh century with the Patriarch Michael Cerularius. A document of heated polemic associated with him, the *Panoplia*, the authenticity of which is debated, gives the argumentation used by Michael Cerularius, supported soon by others whom he called on, the Metropolitan Leo, a Bulgarian and a monk, Niceta Stethatos, author of four treatises of a polemical nature. The latter's general conclusion, "All Scripture prohibits the use of azymes," sums up the arguments then used: they concentrated on Scripture, especially seeking to show that the Lord himself had broken with Jewish tradition and had not used unleavened bread at the Last Supper. One way of proving this was to argue that he had first celebrated the Passover and then his own Eucharistic meal using leavened bread for this; another to maintain that he celebrated the Last Supper on 13 Nisan, when he would have been obliged to use it.

The Reunion Council at Florence (qv) settled the question. But controversy went on, "The discussion of the azymes, which started in the eleventh century, was generally entangled in arguments of purely symbolic nature (the Greeks maintained, for example, that the Eucharistic bread had to be leavened in order to symbolize the *animated* humanity of Christ, while the Latin use of azymes implied Apollinarianism, i.e., the denial that Jesus had a human soul), but the controversy also recognized that the Byzantines understood the Eucharistic bread to be necessarily consubstantial with humanity, while Latin medieval piety emphasized its supersubstantiality, its other worldliness." Yet, Fr. Jugie comments that, with the exception of Cerularius, who closed down Latin churches in Constantinople and had his sacristan profane the consecrated hosts (for, they said, the divinity could not dwell in unleavened bread), no great Orthodox theologian contends that

consecration of unleavened bread is invalid. We have to hope for a triumph of the spirit of Florence. (See article Orthodox, The)

Cf. M. Jugie, A.A., *Theologia dogmatica Christianorum orientalium ab Ecclesia catholica dissidentium,* III, Paris, 1930, 232-256; Th. Spacil, *Doctrina theologiae Orientis separati de SS. Eucharistia,* 2, *Orientalia Christiana* 14 (1929), n. 50, 118-150; S. Runciman, *The Eastern Schism. A Study of the Papacy and the Eastern Churches during the XIth and XIIth Centuries,* Oxford, 1955, 40ff; esp., D. Stiernon, A.A., *Incrinature dottrinali delle Cristianità separate dell'Oriente, Eucaristia,* 511-531 bibl, esp. on the authenticity of the Panoplia, 520, n. 53; 2J. Meyerndorff, *Byzantine Theology,* New York, 1974, 204.

B

BASIL, ST. (C. 330-379)

One letter of B. is highly informative on belief and practice in regard to the Eucharist in the fourth century:[1] "It is good and beneficial to communicate every day, and to partake of the holy body and blood of Christ. For he distinctly says 'He that eats my flesh and drinks my blood has eternal life.' And who doubts that to share frequently in life, is the same thing as to have manifold life? I, indeed, communicate four times a week, on the Lord's day, on Wednesday, on Friday, and on the Sabbath, and on the other days if there is a commemoration of any saint. It is needless to point out that for anyone in times of persecution to be compelled to take the communion in his own hand without the presence of a priest or minister is not a serious offence, as long as custom sanctions this practice from the facts themselves. All the solitaries in the desert, where there is no priest, take the communion themselves, keeping communion at home. And at Alexandria and in Egypt, each one of the laity, for the most part, keeps the communion at his own house, and participates in it when he likes. For when once the priest has completed the offering and given it, the recipient, participating in it each time as entire, is bound to believe that he properly takes and receives it from the giver. And even in the church, when the priest gives the portion, the recipient takes it with complete power over it, and so lifts it to his lips: with his own hand. It has the same validity whether one portion or several portions are received from the priest at the same time."[2]

The passage shows belief in the real presence (qv), in the custom of reservation in private homes and in daily communion (qv). His words here must be borne in mind when interpreting what he says elsewhere on communion: "'He that eats me,' he says, 'he also shall live because of me;' for we eat his flesh and drink his blood, through his Incarnation and his visible life being made partakers of his Word and his Wisdom. For all his mystic sojourn among us he called flesh and blood, and set forth the teaching consisting of pratical science, of physics and of theology, whereby our soul is nourished and is meanwhile trained for the contemplation of actual realities. This is perhaps the intended meaning of what he says."[3]

In the *Moralia*, which G. Bardy thought authentic, B., in Rule XXI, gives important directives, to each of which is attached a scripture quotation or quotations: "That participation in the body and blood of Christ is necessary to eternal life" (Jn 6:33, 34); "That he who approaches communion without consideration of the method whereby participation in the body and blood of Christ is given, takes no benefit from it, and he who receives unworthily should be condemned" (Jn 6:53; 1 Cor 11:27-29); "By what method the body of Christ should be eaten and his blood drunk, in remembrance of the obedience of the Lord to death, that those who live should no longer live to themselves, but to him who died and rose for them" (Lk 22:19, 20; 1 Cor 11:23-26; 2 Cor 5:14, 15; 1 Cor 10:16, 17); "That God should be praised in a hymn by him who has participated in the sacred things" (Mt 26:26, 30); "And when they had sung a hymn, they went out to the Mount of Olives."[4]

[1]J. Solano, *Textos*, 399-410; Cf. G. Bardy, DTC, V, 1147-48; *id.*, DGHE, VI, 1111-1126; J. Maier, *Die Eucharistielehre der drei grossen Kappadozier*, Freiburg i. B., 1915; P. Batiffol, *L'Eucharistie*, 392-96; [2]Letter 93 to the Patrician Caesaria, LNPF, VIII, 179; [3]Letter 8 to the Caesareans, *ibid.*, 118; [4]PG 31, 738-42.

BASIL, LITURGY OF ST.

The Byzantine Liturgy which replaces that regularly used, of St. John Chrysostom (qv), on ten days of the year, the Sundays in Lent, except Palm Sunday, Holy Thursday, the Eves of Easter, Christmas and the Epiphany, and on the feast of St. Basil, 1 January.[1] It is accepted that the origin of this Liturgy has some connection with St. Basil (qv), but since there have been alterations since the first known MSS, dated in or about the ninth century, there may also have been changes adopted before that from the usage in Cappadocia.

[1]Text, Brightman, *Liturgies, Eastern and Western,* I, 309-344; 400-11; PG 31, 1629-56; Anaphora, *Prex* 230-243; (Cod Barber. gr. 336, Grottaferr, Tb VII); cf. M. Jugie, A.A., *L'Epiclèse et le mot antitype de la messe de saint Basile, Echos d'Orient,* 9 (1906) 193-98; M. Orlov, *Liturgia S. Basilii Magni,* St. Petersburg, 1909, 164-255, Greek text, Slav tr.; E. Peterson, *Die Bedeutung von 'anadeichnumi' in den griechischen Liturgien* in *Festgabe Adolf Deissmann,* Tubingen, 1927, 320-26; H. Engberding, *Das eucharistische Hochgebet der Basileosliturgie,* Munster, 1931; *id., Das anaphorischische Fürbittgebet der Basiliusliturgie, Oriens Christianus* 47 (1963) 16-52; S. Euringer, *Die äthiopische Anaphora des hl. Basilius,* Rome, 1934; M. J. Lubatschiwskyj, *Des heiligen Basilius liturgischer Kampf gegen den Arianismus. Ein Beitrag zur Texgeschichte der Basiliusliturgie,* ZKT, 66 (1942) 20-38; S. Salaville, A.A., *Liturgies orientales,* II, *La messe—Bibliothèque Catholique des Sciences Religieuses,* 91, Paris, 1942; M. G. H. Gelsinger, *The Epiclesis in the Liturgy of Saint Basil, Eastern Churches Quarterly,* 10 (1953-54), 243-48; A. Raes, *L'authenticité de la liturgie byzantine de saint Basile,* REB 16 (1958) 158-161; id., *Un nouveau document de la liturgie de saint Basile,* OCP 26 (1960), 401-11; J. Döresse-E. Lanne, *Un témoin archaique de la liturgie cope de saint Basile;* appendix by B. Capelle, O.S.B., *Les Liturgies basiliennes et saint Basile,* (Bibliothèque du Museon, 47) 1960; W. E. Pitt, *The Origins of the Anaphora of the Liturgy of St. Basil, Journal of Eccl. Hist.,* 12 (1961), 1-13; P. de Meester, O.S.B., DACL VI, 2 (1925), 1596-1604, *Grecques (liturgies), Authenticité des liturgies de Saint Basile et de Saint Jean Chrysostome.*

BELLARMINE, ROBERT, ST., DOCTOR OF THE CHURCH (1542-1621)

The great Counter-Reformation controversialist B. could not avoid clashing with the Reformers in their ideas about the Mass.[1] Faced with the idea of the Reformers that sacrifice implied essentially destruction, he sought to show that the Mass embodied this reality. His definition of sacrifice was: "An external oblation made to God alone, by which for the acknowledgement of human weakness and recognition of the divine majesty something physical and lasting is by a lawful minister in a mystical rite consecrated and transformed."

Remarking that every sacrifice is an oblation but not every oblation a sacrifice, B. goes on to say: "For sacrifice, besides oblation, requires the change and consumption of what has been offered, which simple oblation does not require." He held that for true sacrifice it is necessary that what is offered to God cease to be what it was before. It must be entirely destroyed, changed, to achieve this end.

How is this realized in the Mass? Certain elements of the Eucharistic rite B. thinks necessary to its integrity, the oblation of bread and wine preceding the consecration, the oblation following it, the breaking of the host; but these elements are not of the essence of sacrifice. What will make this is the true, real destruction, the death, for example, of the victim. He rejects too the opinion of those who see in the consecration, wherein the species *seems* to divide the body and soul, the virtual representation of Christ's death and, therefore, the essence of the sacrifice of the Mass. This mystic immolation cannot be the true meaning of sacrifice. Those holding it are obliged to add that the death of Christ which the sacrifice of the Mass must signify is prevented by his glorious presence in heaven. This, in B's opinion, means that the glorious presence of Christ prevents the sacrifice being real: not only the use but the very substance must be destroyed. There must be real destruction if there is to be real sacrifice; this mystic immolation by separation affects the *materia ex qua,* not the real victim. If, under the old law, the priest, in the Temple, had struck the animal being sacrificed a blow meant to be mortal but void of this effect, there would not have been sacrifice, but the will to offer sacrifice.

B. is guided by the overriding idea that sacrifice is the highest proclamation of our dependence on God, the supreme act of external worship. He finds it fulfilled in the consecration in a singular way: 1. a profane thing becomes sacred, when the bread is changed into the body of Christ; 2. this object, sacred from having been profane, is offered to God on the altar; 3. by the consecration the sacred object is "ordered to a change, a true, real, external destruction" which is required, according to B., in sacrifice.

The host, by consecration, takes the form of food: the consecration is directed towards the consumption, by eating, of the host. Christ does not lose his existence by this form of destruction, but he does lose his sacramental existence, ceasing to be on the altar, losing his quality of natural food.

For B. then, the priest's communion is intrinsic to the sacrifice of the Mass. No other real destruction of the victim takes place and without the priest's communion there would be no destruction at all. B. does not mention the theory of Casal, an immediate predecessor, who concentrated on the diminished condition of Christ after the consecration, deprived of the use of his senses.

Though not triumphant at once in the schools of theology, B.'s thesis began to gain ground and well into the next generation it was being widely espoused, occasionally with some alteration. Among those who rallied to it entirely, dropping his previous opinion, was St. Alphonsus Liguori. (See article Adduction)

[1]Principal work as source, *Controversia de Missa*, 1, V. *Opera*, Paris, 1870, vol I, 296ff; cf. J. de la Servière, *La théologie de Bellarmin*, Paris, 1908, 435ff; M. Lepin, *La Messe*, 383-87; A. Michel, DTC, X, 1176-79.

BERENGAR OF TOURS (C. 1010-1088)

Tours was B's family background, though he was at Chartres studying under St. Fulbert, and at Angers in service to the Count of Anjou; he was for a while archdeacon and treasurer of the cathedral. He fell out of favour and returned to Tours as Scholasticus, Master of the schools, until c. 1080, when he became a hermit on an island near Tours.[1]

B. is significant for the Eucharistic writings he provoked, for the stimulus he gave to theological reflection on the subject; this would eventually lead to the development of the doctrine of transubstantiation (qv). His letter to Lanfranc[2] was reported to Rome and from then on the Popes were directly involved in the controversy: Leo IX in 1050 and again at a legatine synod in Tours, 1054; Victor II in the Synod of Florence, 1055; Nicholas II in the Synod of Rome; Gregory VII in two councils in Rome, 1078, 1079: the second was a landmark in Eucharistic doctrine.

The champions of the faith who opposed B. were John of Fecamp, Hugh of Langres, Durand of Troarn, Lanfranc of Bec and Guitmond of Aversa (qqv); Alger of Liège (qv) also contributed.

B. adopted a rationalist approach to the interpretation of Scripture; he would not accept authority. On such a principle he refused to accept that the substance of bread and wine ceased, the *conversio sensualis*, in his own terms, of the elements into the body and blood of Christ. Since the elements remain what they were, they cannot be the body and blood of Christ. He frequently, however, used current realist phraseology, so that his denial of the real presence (qv) is ambiguous and has given rise to much controversy. During his lifetime denial of the real presence was attacked as his specific error.[3]

B. held that the bread and wine, while remaining what they were, become spiritually—*quantum ad spiritualitatem*—for faith and understanding, the true body and blood of Christ. Hence it is sometimes said that, whatever about his ideas on transubstantiation, he did have an idea of the real presence.[4] He thought that the body of Christ in itself is only in heaven and not *actually* present in the sacrament. He had studied the Fathers and he especially invoked St. Augustine (qv) on his side. The elements, while remaining what they are, by consecration undergo a mystical change, take on the sacramental function of *symbols* and thus become, for faith and understanding, the body and blood of Christ. They can then arouse devotion and nourish the soul with spiritual life. The doctrine has been called "Dynamic Symbolism." Its influence in later times is a matter of interest.

The final important doctrinal event in the Berengarian controversy was the oath taken by Berengar at the Roman Council in 1079. The preliminaries are noteworthy. B. was summoned to Rome in the autumn of 1078 to answer for his doctrine; though he had submitted outwardly twenty years previously in 1059, the debate had continued. Gregory VII presided over the Council which met on 1 November 1078. B. was required to accept this profession of faith: "I profess that the bread of the altar, after consecration, is the true body of Christ born of the Virgin, which suffered on the Cross, which is seated at the right hand of the Father, and that the wine of the altar, after it is consecrated is the true blood of Christ which flowed from the side. And as I orally proclaim I confirm that I interiorly hold."[5]

This is the doctrine of Paschasius Radbert (qv), on the identity of the Eucharist with the historical body of Christ. B. disliked it and how he meant his acceptance is a matter for conjecture. His critics suspected his sincerity and asked that a final solution be delayed until the Lenten Council of the following year. It took place in the Lateran on 11 February and Berengar was required to subscribe to a new formula, more tightly composed than the previous one and containing two very important words by way of addition (here italicized): "I in my heart believe and with my lips confess that through the mystery of the sacred prayer and the words of our Redeemer, the bread and wine which are placed on the altar are *substantially changed* into the true and proper and life-giving flesh and blood of our Lord Jesus Christ, and that after the consecration it is the true body of Christ which was born of the Virgin and which, offered for the salvation of the world, hung on the Cross, and is seated at the right hand of the Father, and the true blood of Christ, which was poured out from his side, not only through the sign and power of the sacrament, but in its property of nature and in truth of substance, as here briefly in a few words is contained, and I have read and you understand. Thus I believe, nor will I teach contrary to this belief. So help me God and these holy Gospels of God."[6]

B. knew well what he was saying and afterwards expressed his dissatisfaction.[7] With the Council statement dogmatic progress was assured.

---

[1]Sources: Berengar's *De Sacra Coena*, ed. A. F. and F. T. Vischer, Berlin, 1934; critical ed., W. H. Beekenkamp, *Kerkhistorische Studiën*, II, The Hague, 1941; for the Council of 1079, Berengar's *Acta Concilii Romani*, Martène et Durand, IV, 103-109; Bernold of Constance, *De Berengarii heresiarchae damnatione multiplici*, PL 148, 1456; id., *Chronica*, PL 148, 1377; letters, ed. C. Erdmann, N. Fickermann, *Briefsammlung der Zeit Heinrichs IV*, MGH, *Die deutschen Geschichtsquellen des Mittelalters 500-1500*, V, 1950, 132-172; Lanfranc, *De corpore et sanguine Domini*, PL 150, 411 a later insertion; M. Matronola, O.S.B., *Un testo inedito di Berengario di Tours il Concilio Romano del 1079*, Orbis Romanus, VI, 1936; H. Sudendorf, *Berengarius Turonensis, oder eine Sammlung ihn Betreffender Briefe*, Hamburg, 1850; for discussion cf. J. Gieselmann, *Die Eucharistielehre der Vorscholastik*, Paderborn, 1926, 290-299, 331-365; C. Erdmann, *Gregor VII und Berengar von Tours, Quellen und Forschungen aus italienischen Archiven und Bibliotheken*, XXVIII, 1937-38, 48-74; A. J. Macdonald, *Berengar and the Reform of Sacramental Doctrine*, London, 1930; *The Real Presence in the Early Middle Ages*, Clergy Review 8 (1934), 420-460; R. W. Southern, *Lanfranc of Bec and Berengar of Tours*, in *Studies in Medieval History Presented to Frederick Maruice Powicke*, ed. R. W. Hunt, W. A. Pantin, R. W. Southern, Oxford, 1948, 27-48; C. E. Sheedy, *The Eucharistic Controversy of the 11th Century*, Washington, 1947; O. Capitani, *Studi su Berengario di Tours*, Lecce, 1966; J. de Montclos, *Lanfranc et Berengar, La controverse eucharistique du XIe siècle*, Spicilegium S. Lovaniense, 38, 1971, 3-245; M. Cappuyns, DGHE, VIII, 1935, 385-407, bibl., Stone, 244-59 esp. F. Vernet, DTC, II, 1910, 722-742; id., DTC V, *Eucharistie du IXe a la fin du XIe siècle*, 1218-24; [2]PL 150, 63; [3]Cf. Hugh of Langres, PL 142, 1327; Durand of Troarn, PL 149, 1377; Lanfranc PL 150, 415A; Adelmann, *Epist. ad Berengarium*, PL 143, 129OB; Deoduin of Liège, *Epist. ad Henricum I*, 146, 1439B; Wolpelm of Brauweiler, *De sacramento Eucharistiae*, PL 154, 413AB; Gozechin of Mainz, *Epist. ad Walcherum*, PL 143, 900D; [4]Cf. F. Vernet, op. cit., V, 1218; [5]*Acta Concilii Romani*, 103a; [6]DS 700; [7]*Acta Concilii Romani*, 107e.

BIBLIOGRAPHY

Il Mistero[1] by Mgr. A. Piolanti (qv) provides excellent bibliographies on every aspect of the Eucharist; these reading lists are distributed throughout the volume, run to over 35 pp. The collective work edited by Mgr. Piolanti, *Eucaristia*, with the collaboration of 50 contributors—some responsible for more than one article—covers every aspect of the subject, is the most comprehensive of its kind, over 1230 pp. Bibliographies accompany the separate contributions.

The large collections are likewise equipped: esp. DTC V (the Eucharist), C. Ruch, G. Bareille, R. Bour, F. Vernet, J. de Ghellinck, E. Mangenot, F. Jansen, 989-1430; DTC X (The Mass), C. Ruch, L. Ruch, A. Gaudel, A. Michel, 795-1316; DSp IV, 2 (1960), A. Hamman, E. Longpré, E. Bertaud, G. Vassali-E. G.

Nunez-R. Fortin, A. Rayez-A. de Bonhomme, 1553-1653; DACL V, H. Leclercq, F. Cabrol, 681-692.

Large works used frequently here are notable for highly select bibliographies, esp. *Prex*. J. Solano, *Textos*, has bibliographies to the first edition, 1952. Substantial studies like M. de la Taille, *Mysterium Fidei* and M. Lepin, *L'idée*, provide much bibliographical material with the text.

Note also R. Laurentin, *Jésus Christ Présent*, Paris, 1980 bibl. 161-168; *L'Eucharistie, le sens des sacraments*, ed. R. Didier, Lyons, 1971, bibl., 315-318; *L'Eucharistie des premiers chrétiens*, articles published in *Parole et Pain*, Paris, 1976.

The Theological Faculty of Northern Spain brought out between 1969 and 1982 fourteen volumes under the general title, *Teología del Sacerdozio*; from the Instituto 'Juan de Avila,' Ediciones Aldecoe, Burgos. Every aspect of the subject is dealt with and the bibliographies are exhaustive. The work is one of collective authorship, mostly, but not only Spanish. Production is of a high order and the scope of the bibliographies may be seen by examples of some interest: vol I, Methodological Guidelines, 280-337; vol. II, Ministerial and Lay Priesthood, 373-441; vol. III, The Priest, Minister of the Church, 245-319; vol. IV, Theology of the Priesthood in the First Centuries, 455-526; vol V, The Permanent Charism of the Ministerial Priesthood, 453-527; vol. VI, The Priestly Character, 287-356; vol VII, Priests: Ten Years after *Presbyterorum ordinis*, 587-664; vol. VIII, The Power of Orders, 213-232.

The fourteen volumes constitute the most comprehensive study of the priesthood in modern times; they provide the fullest documentation available anywhere. Logically many of the articles are in part relevant to Eucharistic theology. As an example cf. M. Guerra, *El sacerdocio y el ministro de la eucaristia en las primeras comunidades cristianas*, Vol IX (1977) 43-118. The detailed study of the Fathers (qv) must prove beneficial to all future research and reflection. The most important bibliographical work, however, is R.I.C. Supplement, *The Eucharist*, 96-98 covering the years 1975-1984, Cerdic Publications, Strasbourg, 1985. In *Cena*, Fribourg, 1984, Irmgard Pahl, joint editor of *Prex*, has with several collaborators, provided an invaluable source book for the liturgies of the Reformation, over 600 pp. of explanatory material with original texts fully reproduced. Those interested in the additional Eucharistic Prayers approved recently have an illustrative collection in *Preghiere Eucaristiche della Chiesa Italiana*, five Eucharistic Prayers, two for reconciliation, three for children, two Ambrosian, Centro Catechistico Salesiano, Turin, 1984. Source material is found in R. Raczynski; *Enchiridion Documentorum Instaurationis Liturgicae*, 1963-1973, Turin, 1975 and ICEL, *Docu-*

ments on the Liturgy, Conciliar, Papal, Curial, 1963-1979, Collegeville, 1982.

---

[1]For full titles cf. Abbreviations.

BIEL, GABRIEL (C. 1420-1495)

Sometimes called the last of the scholastic theologians, B. treated of the Eucharist in two works, in the *Collectorium* or Commentary on the Sentences of Peter Lombard (qv) and the *Expositio Canonis Missae.*[1] It is possible to extract from these works a body of Eucharistic doctrine. The author was a follower, though not in a slavish sense, of Scotus (qv) and William of Ockham, having especially adopted the nominalist principles of the latter. St. Thomas (qv) had little influence on him, though he is not averse to quoting the Angelic Doctor. He was rigidly attached to Sacred Scripture, the Fathers and the Church, though on some points he missed church teaching.

B. covers most of the aspects of the Eucharistic mystery, showing a clear grasp of sacramental theology. He has much to say on the Real Presence, especially on the central question of Transubstantiation (qv), splendidly settled by St. Thomas. He has been wrongly accused of proposing the opinion of annihilation in this matter.[2] "B's Eucharistic doctrine is sound, confirmed by profound philosophical studies; the different questions are clearly and wisely set forth, exhaustively treated, the nominalist philosophical ideas are harmonised with church teachings in masterly fashion, (ecclesiastical) canons and decrees never called in doubt, so that nothing is taught contrary to Catholic doctrine, except the opinion that wheaten bread is not necessary matter for consecration, which does not conform to the decrees of the Council of Florence. But B. defends it, because he did not know this decree, stating many times that there was no decision from the Church in this respect. In disputed questions, wherein philosophy has to give its help, he naturally behaves and pronounces according to the principles derived from Scotus and Ockham. Various opinions of his are still defended by Catholic doctors while others are generally rejected, such as that the body of Christ is in the Sacrament without its quantity. From reading the *Expositio Canonis* and the *Collectorium,* one can touch the truth of the eulogies given to our Gabriel, which we read in dictionaries and in the books dealing with him; in him wonderfully merge vast culture and sharpness of reasoning power, an intelligence uncommon and exalted together with love of the truth and a humble regard for his own judgement."[3]

---

[1]Ed. of *Canonis Missae Expositio,* H. A. Oberman and W. J. Courtenay, *Veroffentlichungen des Instituts für europäische*

Geschichte, Mainz, 31-34; 1963-67; of *Collectorium;* Cf. H. A. Oberman, *The Harvest of Medieval Theology; Gabriel Biel and Late Medieval Nominalism,* Cambridge, Mass, 1963; P. Anatriello, *La dottrina di G. Biel sull'Eucaristia,* Milan, 1957; M. Cappuyns, O.S.B., DHGE, VIII (1935), 1429-35; V. Heynck, NCE, II (1967), 552; [2]Cf. P. Anatriello, op.cit., 103-106; [3]*Ibid.,* 175.

BILLOT, LOUIS (1846-1931)

B. was a great speculative theologian, Professor for many years at the Gregorian University, named Cardinal for his services to Catholic theology.[1] He was a Thomist and his great treatises are commentaries on the relevant parts of the *Summa Theologica* of the Angelic Doctor (see article Thomas Aquinas, St.). B. composed a treatise on the sacrament and sacrifice of the Eucharist, which was well structured and philosophically consistent. Two sections therein are distinctive: on transubstantiation (qv) and on the Mass as a mystic immolation (see articles Oblation and Immolation).

B. was radically opposed to De la Taille's (qv) thesis on the unicity of the Last Supper and Calvary as sacrifice: "According to Trent not only is the offering of the (Lord's) Supper not to be considered as an essential or integral part of the sacrifice of the Cross, but it is to be considered on the contrary as fully distinct from it; it is opposed to it, as that which represents to the thing represented, as a memorial to the reality which is to be remembered forever, as what was ordered to be repeated until the end (of time) and to be assisted at continuously, to that which was only once to be effected, nowhere to be repeated."[2]

B. maintained that this was the only interpretation of the words of Trent: "He, therefore, our God and Lord, *though* he was about to offer himself once to God the Father upon the altar of the Cross by the mediation of death, so that he might accomplish an eternal redemption there, *nevertheless,* that his sacerdotal office might not come to an end with his death (Heb 7:24, 27) at the Last Supper, on the night he was betrayed, so that he might leave to his beloved Spouse, the Church, a visible sacrifice (as the nature of man demands) whereby that bloody sacrifice once to be completed on the Cross might be represented, and the memory of it remain even to the end of the world (1 Cor 11:23ff) ... he offered to God the Father his own body and blood under the species of bread and wine...."[3] For B. the contrast between *though* and *nevertheless* clearly indicates two separate realities—he urges the example "though he was going to build a house, nevertheless, he laid the foundations" to show how absurd would be the usage in Trent if it was speaking of one and the same sacrifice: no one would use the phrase he quotes about a building.

B's main contribution to modern Eucharistic theology was in the long section (p. 332-449) on Transubstantiation. His aim was to restore the authentic doctrine of St. Thomas. He held that for the Angelic Doctor the notion of transubstantiation was so closely linked with that of the real presence (qv) that if the first were to be denied, denial of the second would logically follow: this he thought stemmed from the general theory of the Scholastics.

The pages in which this position is developed and argued are among the most powerful to emerge from the Catholic universities in modern times, utterly free of the defects occasionally found in manualistic theology. B. shows the reasons why ideas of annihilation, of production and adduction (qqv) should be discarded and transubstantiation pinned to conversion: always he insisted that no change in the heavenly body of Christ can be thought of.

In B's treatise on the Eucharist there are many other striking sections, on the manner in which Christ is in the Sacrament, on remaining accidents after consecration, on the form of the Sacrament, especially on the effects of the Sacrament of the Eucharist: "The specific *res Eucharistiae* is the spiritual transformation of man into Christ through charity, and this is not given to the communicant only as a quality, but is also stirred to action; this sacrament achieves in the spiritual life every effect that material food and drink work in the bodily life, sustaining, increasing, restoring, delighting."[4] B. also deals with the questions of communion and adoration (qqv).

It would be unfair to so great a theologian to present his theology of the Mass so sketchily as to make a caricature of it. He enunciates it thus: "The Mass, as to its essence, consists in the sole consecration of each species, though from the nature of the reality the communion of the celebrant must be added, which, consequently, is prescribed by a law which does not permit dispensation. But the consecration has in itself the true meaning of sacrifice, formally and precisely in so far as it is an unbloody immolation of Christ, representative of the bloody immolation of the Cross, through a sacramental or mystical separation of the body from the blood, under the distinct species of bread and wine."[5]

The author, having given special consideration to concomitance (qv), did not need to be reminded that the whole Christ, body and blood, is present under each species. B. was convinced that immolation or destruction was essential to sacrifice. Physical destruction as on Calvary was not to be suggested. Other forms of mystical immolation, such as that implied in communion by the priest, or in a so-called state of deprivation, wherein the body of Christ would be seen

to exist on the altar." He argued brilliantly his own theory, which gained a number of important adherents in the seminaries in the decades following his teaching years at the Gregorian.[6]

Billot in footnotes to his text frequently quotes large extracts, in the original French, from the writings of Bossuet.

[1]Cf. H. le Floch, C.S.Sp., *Le Cardinal Billot*, Paris, 1947; M. Lepin, *L'idée du sacrifice*, 606-10; J. Lebreton, S.J., *Catholicisme*, II, 61-63; J. Galot, S.J., NCE, II, 557-58; DTC Tables, XVI, 1, 443-46; [2]*De Sacramentis*, 7th ed., Rome, 1932, 605—on the Eucharist as sacrament and on the sacrifice of the Mass, 313-661; [3]DS 1739; [4]549ff; [5]624ff; [6]L. Labauche, *Leçons de théologie dogmatique. Dogmatique spéciale*, IV, *Les Sacrements*, Paris, 1918, 269ff; A. Tanquerey, *Synopsis theologiae dogmaticae*, ed. 16, Tours, 1919, III, 484ff; N. Gihr, *Die heiligen Sacramente der Kirche*, Freiburg i. Br., 1897, 657ff.

BONAVENTURE, ST. (C.1217-1274)

B., thinking in the noontide of scholasticism, accepted all the theological gains acquired thus far.[1] His Eucharistic theology is of interest in the domain of the existential, of experience. He deals with the effects of the Eucharist and the Mass in *De sanctissimo corpore Christi*, which was composed for the feast of *Corpus Christi* (qv). In *Liber Sententiarum IV*, he speaks of the Eucharist as assimilated directly to the love which unites to God, and gives a certain experience of God, an experimental knowledge influenced by the gift of wisdom. With the help of figures taken from the OT, B. elaborates different aspects of the soul's union with God in the moment of Eucharistic communion, an outstanding combination of theology and spiritual experience.

[1]Text of *De sanctissimo corpore Christi, Opera*, ed. Quaracchi, V, 553-566; cf. F. X. Kattum, *Die Eucharistielehre des hl. Bonaventura*, Munich-Freising 1920; E. Longpré, O.F.M., *L'Eucharistie et l'union mystique selon la spiritualité franciscaine*, RAM 25 (1949), 306-333; id. DSp, IV, 2 (1960), 1598-1599.

BOSSUET, JACQUES BENIGNE (1627-1704)

The great orator dealt with the Eucharist, especially the sacrifice of the Mass in his meditations, sermons and apologetic works.[1] In the eloquent pages which he has left us, he developed an idea of the Mass which is broadly one with that of the French school, notably Fr. de Condren and Fr. Jean-Jacques Olier (qqv): links then with the Oratory and St. Sulpice. The ideas which show the relationship are: the sacrifice of Christ begins from the first moment of his existence; the Eucharistic offering is united with Christ's offering in heaven; the Church is closely associated with the oblation of its

Head. Fr. M. Lepin (qv) in his account of B's theory assembles texts which he interprets in the sense of his own doctrine, on the Mass as essentially an oblation. Cardinal Billot (qv) among the extracts from B. which he adds as footnotes to his text—unusual in a Latin treatise—can choose one which expresses his own theory of the mystic immolation signified by the separate consecration of the bread and wine: "There is his body; there is his blood; they are separated, yes, separated: the body on one side, the blood on the other: the word has been the sword, the cutting edge which made this mystical separation.... To impress on this Jesus who does not die any more the character of the death he really suffered, the word comes, which puts the body on one side, the blood on the other, and each under different signs. Here he is then clothed with the character of death, this Jesus formerly our victim through the shedding of his blood, and again today our victim in a new manner, by the mystical separation of this blood from this body."[2]

"In the consecration," he says elsewhere, "the body and blood are mystically separated, because Jesus Christ said separately: 'This is my body, this is my blood': which contains a vivid and effective representation of the violent death he suffered. Thus the Son of God is placed on the holy table, by virtue of these words, clothed with the signs which represent his death. That is what the consecration effects; and this religious action bears with it recognition of the sovereignty of God, in so far as Jesus Christ present renews and perpetuates, in a certain way, the memory of his obedience unto the death on the Cross; so that nothing is wanting in it for a real sacrifice."[3]

The great orator deals with equal compelling power with many of the great Eucharistic truths, as Cardinal Billot was happy to show by quotation: the Real Presence, the form of the sacrament, Holy Communion, the liturgical presentation of the sacrifice. B. exemplifies, as does Newman, that rhetoric, accurate and disciplined, may by the perfection of its adherence to truth, help to develop the content of the truth proclaimed.

[1]M. Lepin, *L'idée du sacrifice*, 505-13; L. Billot, S.J., *De Sacramentis*, ed. 7, 1932, 313-661, *passim*; [2]*Méditations sur l'Evangile, 57e jour*, apud Billot, op. cit., 636, n. 2; [3]*Exposition de la doctrine de l'Eglise catholique*, 1671, Oeuvres, 18, 128-29, apud M. Lepin, op.cit., 507.

BUCER, MARTIN (1491-1551)

B. had been a follower of Luther (qv), having been a Dominican and dispensed by the Pope from his monastic vows.[1] He tried vainly to mediate between Luther and Zwingli (qv), became the leader of the Reformed Churches in Switzerland and South Ger-

many after the death of Zwingli. He was a participant in unsuccessful meetings arranged to reconcile Catholics and Protestants. Having in vain resisted the Augsburg Interim of Charles V in 1548, he came to England the following year. Named Regius Professor of divinity in Cambridge by the king, he was an advisor to Cranmer (qv), and certainly influenced the Anglican Ordinal of 1550.

B's views are affirmed in nine propositions which he published in 1530; the latter are relevant to the Eucharist: 1. We deny transubstantiation. 2. We deny that the body of Christ is locally in the bread. 3. We affirm that the body of Christ is really in the Supper, and that Christ actually present feeds us with his real body and his real blood, using for this purpose his own words which the ministers recite, and the holy signs of bread and wine. 4. As by baptism there is the power of regeneration so the very body and blood of Christ are "exhibited" (*exhiberi*) by the symbols of the Eucharist.... 6. He is really and actually present in the Supper ... through symbols that are received by faith."[2] This is realism and symbolism inextricably entwined, which means that realism loses.

Three years later B. still used the word "exhibited" and in a statement made shortly before his death he expressed himself thus: "Scripture must agree with itself, and therefore the texts which say that Christ dwells in us and that we eat him must agree with those which say that he is in heaven, and hath a body and is therefore limited and bound in one place. And may not be placed in all or many places at one time. Hence Christ's presence whether in the word or in the sacraments is no presence of place, neither of senses nor of reason, nor yet no earthly presence, but a spiritual presence, a presence of faith, and a heavenly presence, forasmuch as we are conveyed into heaven by faith.

"The antichrists make the simple people to believe by these words that we receive and have Christ here present after some worldly fashion, that is to say, either enclosed with the bread and wine, or else that he is present under their accidents, so that there he ought to be honoured and worshipped.

"Let them be taught that there is no presence of Christ in the supper, *but only in the lawful use thereof*, and such as is obtained and gotten *by faith* alone.

"He offereth himself, *being in heaven*, to be received by us. Christ is present *realiter* and *substantialiter* if one would understand by the presence of the Lord really and substantially, that he is received verily indeed by faith, and his substance is given in the sacrament, but if he would interlace any worldly presence with these words I will deny it, because the Lord is departed this world.

"The bread and wine be *signs exhibitive*, that is to

say, such signs as do give the things signified . . . after the same manner as he gave his disciples the Holy Ghost by the sign of breathing of his mouth.

"This is my body' means 'The thing which by this sign I give unto you is my body.'

"Three things are given and received in the Lord's supper of them that rightly communicate. . . . First, bread and wine, *nothing in themselves changed*, but that they are, by the words and ordinance of the Lord, made all only the signs. Secondly, the selfbody and blood of the Lord. . . . Thirdly, the establishing of the New Testament of the forgiveness of sins."[3] With such words B. expressed his notion known as 'receptionism,' presence 'with,' not 'in' or 'under' the bread and wine.

B. rejected the idea of the Mass as a sacrifice, taking destructive action against what was associated with it. He composed a new Communion service to replace it. The ministry he conceived as directed not to a sacrificial action, but to administration of the Word and the sacraments. He designed a new ordination rite embody-ing his ideas and this he would bring to England where it would directly influence Cranmer. For B. arrived in England in April 1549. He was Cranmer's guest for some months that summer and took up his post in Cambridge in November. It was at this time that Cranmer was engaged on the composition of the new Ordinal. Hence the presence in the liturgical work of Bucer's ideas, at times of his phrasing, done into English.

[1]Works ed. F. Wendel, F. Staehelin, R. Stupperich, and others, Paris-Gutersloh, 1954f; cf. H. Eells, *Martin Bucer*, Yale, 1931; R. Stupperich, *Bibliografia Bucerana*; G. Klingenburg, *Das Verhältnis Calvins zu Butzer*, Bonn, 1912; C. Hopf, *Martin Bucer and the English Reformation*, Oxford, 1946; H. Bornkamm, *Martin Bucers Bedeutung für die europäische Reformationsgechichte*, 1952; B. Thompson, *Bucer Study since 1918, Church History*, 25 (1956), 63-82; P. Polman, DHGE, X (1938), 1015-91, *bibl.*; H. Bornkamm, RGG, I, 1453-57; P. Iserloh, LTK, II, 845-46; E. C. Messenger, *The Reformation*, I, 162-69; [2]*Scripta anglicana*, 611; [3]*Life of Cranmer*, J. Strype, London, 1694, app 46.

C

CABASILAS, NICHOLAS (14th century)

The Byzantine theologian quoted on the Eucharist with probably the greatest respect by western theologians, C. is not well known biographically. Probably born c. 1320 and dying before 1390, he became involved in the Hesychast controversy.[1] His relevant works to our theme are *The Exposition of Divine Liturgy*,[2] and *On Life in Christ*.[3] In the first he gives a commentary, enriched with profound theological insights, of the Byzantine Eucharistic rite. The work was used in the preparatory phase of the Council of Trent, which had the sacrifice of the Mass high on its programme, as a witness to tradition. It drew from Bossuet (qv) the eulogy of its author, "one of the soundest theologians of the Greek church." It is treated with great respect by modern Catholic authors, such as F. S. Renz and J. Kramp and, above all, most strikingly by M. de la Taille (qv). *On Life in Christ* is a powerful exposition of Christocentrism, in which the author deals with Baptism, Confirmation and the Eucharist as sources of union with Christ. Part IV deals with the Eucharist in detail.[4]

In the *Exposition of the Divine Liturgy*, C. proceeds somewhat like Innocent III, who studied the Roman rite of his day. But he is led to greater consideration of theological issues. De la Taille, whose many quotations from C. would make an anthology on its own, seizes on the Greek author's notion of the bread and wine as first-fruits of human life, *Quod haec dona Deo offeruntur tanquam vitae humanae primitiae* and quotes him thus: "We consecrate these gifts to God as the first-fruits of human life, as they are the human nutriment, on which bodily life rests; and life does not rest only on nutriment, but it is also signified by it. . . . We call human nutriment that which pertains to man alone; to need making bread that he may eat and wine that he may drink is a strictly human characteristic."[5]

Christ, says C., is the priest, the altar and the victim. He is the eternal intercessor, which here means mediator: "For Christ is the intercessor through whom we have attained all good things given us by God, all that are ever given. He did not withdraw after being once an intercessor and having given us all for which he interceded, but he is ever interceding, not by certain words or prayers, as legates are accustomed to do, but in reality. What is that reality? To join us with him and through himself to bestow appropriate graces on us."[6] Likewise, in regard to the notion of Christ's immolation continuing in the Eucharist, C. expresses ideas acceptable to the Latins.

In the great Oriental tradition, C. insists on the role of the Spirit. As so many others in that tradition, he sees an analogy between the Incarnation and the Eucharist: "The Holy Spirit 'formed' the body and blood of the Infant in the womb of the Blessed Virgin and so, also, in the Eucharist the Gifts are overshadowed by the same Holy Spirit so as to be 'made' the body and blood of Christ."[7]

Thus he describes the great moment of the consecration: "When the priest has made mention of that awesome Supper and how the Lord delivered it to his holy disciples before his Passion and that he received the cup and took bread and hallowed the Eucharist, and that he spoke the words by which he manifested the mystery, and when he in turn has uttered the same words, he bows down and prays and implores God, applying those divine words of his only-begotten Son, our Saviour, to the gifts offered on the altar, that they, receiving this all-holy and almighty Spirit may be changed, the bread into his precious and holy body itself, and the wine into his stainless and holy blood itself. And when this has been said, the whole of the priestly rite has been accomplished and completed, and the gifts have been consecrated, and the sacrifice has been perfected, and the great sacrifice and victim which was slain for the sake of the whole world is seen to lie on the Holy Table; for the bread is no longer a figure of the Lord's body, nor an offering which bears an image of the real gift, nor an offering which gives us a pictorial memorial of the sufferings which save us, as a picture might do, but it is the real gift itself, the body itself of the all-holy Master, which really experienced all the insults, violence and stripes, which was crucified, which was slain, which witnessed before Pontius Pilate the good confession, which was flogged, which was tormented and spat upon, which tasted the gall. In like manner also the wine is the blood itself which leapt out of the slain body, this body, this blood which was conceived by the Holy Spirit, which was born of the holy Virgin, which was buried, which rose on the third day, which ascended into heaven, which sits at the right hand of the Father."[8]

Unfortunately in two chapters of his splendid work C. treats the epiclesis polemically. To deal dispassionately with him, we should recall his view on Pentecost and the Eucharistic ministry: "He said: '*This is my body. This is my blood.*' He also commanded the Apostles and through them the whole Church to do it: '*Do this*' he said '*in memory of me.*' But he would not have ordered them to do it, if he were not about to give them the power, by which they could do so. And what was the power? The Holy Spirit, the power which descending from on high equipped the Apostles, in accordance with the word spoken to them by the Lord: '*Remain in the city of Jerusalem . . . you shall receive power.*'[9]

The opening lines of ch XXIX declare that "certain Latins" reproach the easterns with attaching undue importance to the prayer of invocation, with making an unnecessary addition to the already effective words of the Lord in the institution (qv) narrative. "That is why," they continue, "those who, after repeating the words of Christ, again name the bread and wine and beseech consecration on them, as if they were not already consecrated, apart from the fact that their faith is sickly, do something needless and superfluous. Blessed Chrysostom," they say, "certifies that it is this word (of the Saviour) which consecrates the offerings, when he

declares that, as the creative word of God, 'Increase and multiply,' was once spoken by God but is continuously operative, likewise the word of the Supper, once pronounced by the Saviour continues to produce its effect."[10] The Latins, C. thinks, go further: they accuse the easterns of esteeming their own prayer more highly than the word of the Lord. This means that they reckon this word as powerless, count more on themselves than on the Lord, and render the sacrament dependent on something uncertain, that is, human prayer.

C. tries to turn the tables on the adversary he has evoked. By pressing the analogy—surely, despite the authority of St. John Chrysostom, not one to be too rigidly interpreted—with 'Increase and multiply' he argues that just as these words will not have their effect without marriage and all that goes with it, so the words of the Master, at the Last Supper, though assuring the possibility, need the special prayer to become operative in each instance. He summarizes his thought thus: "That is why we entrust the consecration in this sacrament to the priest's prayer, relying not on human power but on that of God (we are certain of the result) not because of the man who prays, but because of God who hears him; not because man has requested, but because God, Truth itself, has promised to give."[11]

C. butresses his argument by appealing to the practice in other sacraments, where prayer is necessary for the effect. B. Bornert, editor of SC ed., points out the difference between the Eucharist and these sacraments, quoting St. Thomas (III, q. 78, art 1) thus: "The sacrament of the Eucharist differs in two ways from the other sacraments. First, it is accomplished in the consecration of the matter, while the others are operative through the usage of matter already consecrated. Again in Baptism, Confirmation, Orders, etc., consecration consists in a blessing from which the consecrated matter receives instrumentally spiritual power which can be attached to an inanimate instrument by the animated instrument, which is the minister; but in the Eucharist the consecration implies the miraculous change, which God alone can operate, of the substance of bread and wine."[12]

In the next chapter C. advances into the Latin camp. He tries with all the ingenuity he can muster to prove that the Latins do, in fact, use a prayer similar to the epiclesis, the *Supplices te rogamus*: "This prayer can signify nothing other for the offerings than their transformation into the body and blood of the Lord." He concludes on a conciliatory note: "It is then evident that to despise the prayer said for the offerings after the words of the Saviour is not at all the policy of the Latin Church in general, but only of a few rare innovators, who had done it harm in other matters too: these are people whose only pastime is to 'say or listen to something new.' (Acts 17:21)."

C. has written some of the most eloquent lines on the effects of the Eucharist on the soul of the communicant. The Eucharist is the crowning of the great movement of God towards man begun in the Incarnation. It is union, a marriage celebrated with many hymns, a light for those already purified, purification for those still awaiting purification. This is a food which assimilates those who take it, contrary to what happens ordinarily.

We are divinised by the Eucharist and C., singularly, links our adoptive sonship especially with the Eucharist. Then comes the passage of which F. de la Taile wrote: "Nothing has been said more beautifully and more truly of the Eucharist: Moreover, after being author of our life and education, he did not withdraw (as do our parents); he is ever present and united with us; by the very fact of his presence giving us life and education. Nothing prevents those separated from their parents from survival; death is the only survival to those separated from Christ. Why should I not say more? To stand on their own is not possible to children, save apart from their parents; indeed this separation means that they can be parents to others, other children; sonship, which is based on the mysteries, consists in union and communion, and it is the same thing to have it dissolved and non-existing ... (he contrasts natural generation with spiritual sonship). But by so much does the second birth surpass the first that of this neither trace or name remains. And thus the sacred bread, ushering in the new man, banishes utterly the old. For that is the work of the sacred table. Those who have received him, he said, are not born of blood. But when have we *received* (*taken*) him? We know the word, we know on the occasion of what mystery it was spoken, the word I say *Take*. It is clear that by that word we are called to the supper, in which we truly receive Christ with our hands, and take him with our mouth, and mingle with his soul and unite with his body and abide with his blood."[13]

In so much, C. joins the greatest, most intense thinking on Eucharistic grace through the ages. In another way he is of the same great tradition: his profound theology of Our Lady. In the three great Marian homilies published in this century by Fr. Martin Jugie, A.A., on the Nativity of Mary, on the Annunciation and the Dormition (Assumption), this doctrine is seen to be in the noble Byzantine tradition. C. could write: "The incarnation of the Word was not only the work of the Father, of his power and of his Spirit, but also was the work of the will and faith of the Virgin; without the consent of the Immaculate one, without the contribution of her faith, this plan was as unrealisable as without the intervention of the three divine persons themselves."[14]

[1]Works, PL 150, 367-772, including his life of St. Theodore; cf. S. Salaville, A.A., *Le christocentrisme de Nicholas Cabasilas, Echos d'Orient*, 1936; id., *Les principes de la dévotion au Sacré Coeur dans l'Eglise orientale: la doctrine de Nicholas Cabasilas, Regnabit* (review), March 1923, 298-308; id., *De cultu SS Eucharistiae in Oriente* in *Acta primi conventus pro studiis orientalibus*, Ljublana, 1925; id., DSp, II (1953), 1-9; id., Catholicisme, I, 341; id. *Vues sotériologiques chez Nicolas Cabasilas, Etudes Byzantines*, 1 (1943), 19-47; M. Jugie, A.A., *Theologia dogmatica Christianorum Orientalium ab Ecclesia Catholica Dissidentium*, III, 1930, 284ff; G. Horn, *La vie dans le Christ de Nicolas Cabasilas, RAM*, 3 (1922) 20-45; M. Lot-Borodine, *Nicolas Cabasilas. Un maître de la spiritualité byzantine au XIVe siècle*, Paris, 1958; N. S. Craig, *Nicolas Cabasilas: An Exposition of the Divine Liturgy, Studia Patristica* 2, TU 64, Berlin, 1957, 21-28; J. H. McKenna, *Eucharist and Holy Spirit. The Eucharistic Epiclesis in 20th Century Theology*, London, 1976, 75-77; W. Volker, *Die Sakramentsmystik des Nikolaus Kabasilas*, Wiesbaden, 1977; C. N. Tsirpanlis, *The Liturgical and Mystical Theology of Nicholas Cabasilas*, New York, 1979, 2nd ed., 52-59; F. Vernet, DTC, II, 1202-1205; J. Gouillard, DHGE, XI (1949), 14-21; [2]PG 150, 367-491; French tr. SC 4 (1943) S. Salaville; revised R. Bornet, O.S.B., J. Gouillard, 1967 SC 4 bis, 1947 - with Greek text; English tr. J. M. Hussey and P. A. McNulty, intro. R. M. French, 1960; [3]PG 150, 49; French tr. S. Broussaleux, *Nicolas Cabasilas, La Vie en Jésus Christ*, Amay, 1931; [4]Part IV, PG 150, 581-625; F. S. Renz, *Die Geschichte des Messopfer-Begriffs*, Freising, 1902, I, 651-656; J. Kramp, *Die Opferanschauungen der römischen Mess Liturgie*, 2nd ed. Regensburg, 1926, 112-167; J. Rivière, *La dogme de la Rédemption, Etudes critiques et documents*, Louvain, 1931, 281-303; id., *Le dogme de la Rédemption au début du moyen âge*, 1934, 286, 445; M. de la Taille, *Mysterium Fidei*, 3rd ed., 1931; viii, 23, 36, 108, 153, 164, 167, 229; 242, 276, 300, 332, 333, 337, 436, 450, 482, 496, 514, 571, 576, 600, 615; [5]PG 150, 377; [6]PG 150, 464; [7]PG 150, 425, 452; [8]PG 150, 425ff; [9]PG 150, 425, 8; [10]SC 4bis, 180; [11]*Ibid.*, 184; [12]*Ibid.*, 188, n. 1; [13]PG 150, 597-601; [14]*In Annunt* 4, *Patrologia Orientalis* 19, 488; on C's Marian doctrine cf. M. O'Carroll, C.S.Sp., *Theotokos*, Wilmington, 1983, 92, 93.

CALVIN, JOHN (1509-1564)

Before taking up permanent residence in Geneva, C. spent some years by way of interlude in Stasbourg, where he met Bucer (qv); there too he signed the Augsburg Confession (qv) "in the sense of its author" (Melanchton).[1] C. rejected all but two Sacraments, Baptism and the Lord's Supper. He sought a middle way between Luther and Zwingli in his Eucharistic doctrine. He did not accept the real and substantial presence of the body and blood of Christ under the appearances of bread and wine, but taught a spiritual presence, which acts on the faithful by the Holy Spirit. The faithful soul is lifted up on the wings of faith to heaven, where it spiritually communes with its Saviour. The presence is not attached to the bread and wine. Christ gives us from heaven, through the sacrament, the grace he wishes us to have.

Though C. borrows language from others, he gives the words his own meaning. He favours use of the word 'exhibited.' "They are greatly deceived who suppose that there is no presence of Christ in the Supper unless it is placed in the bread. For by such an idea they leave nothing to the secret operation of the Spirit who unites

Christ himself to us. Christ does not seem to them to be present unless he descends to us, as if we did not equally possess his presence if he draws us up to himself." C. thinks that "Christ is to be adored spiritually in the glory of heaven rather than this so dangerous way of adoration devised, full of a carnal and gross idea of God." "What," he asks, "is idolatry if it be not to worship the gifts instead of the Giver? In which there is doubly a sin, for the honour is taken away from God and bestowed on a creature, and God himself is dishonoured in his polluted and profaned gift, when from his holy Sacrament a dreadful idol is made."

In regard to the Eucharist, Calvin rejected the notion of sacrifice in the Catholic sense: "He has given us a table at which to feast, not an altar on which to offer a sacrifice. He has not consecrated priests to sacrifice, but ministers to distribute the sacred banquet." A sacrifice of expiation has for its object to appease the wrath of God. "The real sacrifice of this kind," says C., "was offered by Christ alone, by him alone because it could not be offered by any other. And it was offered once for all, because the efficacy and power of that one sacrifice which was offered by Christ is eternal." Nothing was lacking, he thought, which would leave room for another sacrifice. Sacrifice, for him then, could only be "prayers, praises, thanksgiving and whatever is done by us for the worship of God." This kind of sacrifice, he thought, had nothing to do with appeasing the wrath of God, or obtaining remission of sins. "This kind of sacrifice the Lord's Supper cannot be without, in which, while we announce his death and return thanks, we offer nothing else than a sacrifice of praise. From this duty of sacrifice we Christians are all called a royal priesthood."

It is inherent in C's position that there is no Christian priesthood in the Catholic sense. "All those do an injury to Christ who say that they are priests who offer a sacrifice of reconciliation. It is he who was ordained by the Father, and consecrated with an oath as priest according to the order of Melchisedek.... We are indeed all priests in him, but merely for the offering of praise and thanksgiving to God, and chiefly to offer ourselves and all that is ours." "The priesthood of the Catholics is therefore a 'damnable sacrilege' and it is impudent to call it a sacrament." "In the matter of the ceremonies of ordination, we must reject all that does not correspond to the reality, as for instance the words 'Receive the Holy Spirit,' which Christ could say, but no one after him, and again unction."

The doctrine of the founder was expressed in Confessions of Faith as the *Catechism of Geneva*, 1537 and 1545, the *Consensus Tigurinus,* 'Consent of Zurich,' 1549, wherein agreement was reached between Zwinglians and Calvinists on sacramental doctrine; this document influenced developments in England in the reign of Edward VI. Noteworthy also are the *Gallican Confession* of 1559, the *Belgian Confession* of 1561, the *Heidelberg Catechism* of 1563 and the *Second Helvetic Confession,* work of Bullinger and adopted in Germany and Switzerland in 1566. The last two documents are authoritative statements of Calvinist doctrine. Recent writers like Max Thurian credit Calvin with a belief in the Real Presence.

Such interpreters would appeal to a passage like the following to show C's belief in the real presence: "For otherwise what would it mean that we eat the bread and drink the wine as a sign that his flesh is our food and his blood our drink if he gave only bread and wine and left the spiritual reality behind? Would it not be under false colours that he instituted the mystery—the mutual substance is joined with the visible signs and as the bread is distributed by hand so the body of Christ is communicated to us, so that we are made partakers of it. If there were nothing more we have good reason to be satisfied when we realize that Jesus Christ gives us in the supper the real substance of his body and his blood so that we may possess him fully and possessing him take part in his blessing."[6]

[1]Cf. R. S. Wallace, *Calvin's Doctrine of the Word and Sacrament,* Edinburgh, 1953; H. Scholl, *Der Dienst des Gebetes nach Johannes Calvin*, Zurich, Stuttgart, 1968; L. Cristiani, *Calvin tel qu'il fut* (texts), Paris, 1955; id., *Réforme,* DTC XIII, 2077-81; id., *Sacramentaire (controverse),* XIV, 441-46; *id., Eucaristia,* 547-551; K. McDonnell, O.S.B., *John Calvin, the Church and the Eucharist,* Princeton, 1967; id., *Concilium* 42 (1969), 75-84; J. Cadier, in *Eucharisties d'Orient et d'Occident,* Paris, 1970, *La Prière eucharistique de Calvin,* 171-180; *La présence réelle dans le Calvinisme, Etudes théologiques et religieuses* 13 (1938), 293-309; *La doctrine calviniste de la Sainte Cène, ibid.,* 26 (1951), 3-158; B. Burki, *Calvin avait-il le sens liturgique* in *Communio Sanctorum,* Mélanges J. J. von Allmen, Geneva, 1982, 157-172; E. C. Messenger, *The Reformation,* I 173-78; M. Thurian, *L'Eucharistie,* Paris, 1963, 262ff; DTC Tables, XVI, 1, 1095-97; [2]*Institutes,* IV, 17, 35-36; [3]*Ibid.,* IV, 12, 18; [4]IV, 19, 28; [5]*Ibid.,* 29,31; [6] *Short Treatise on the Lord's Supper,*1541, *The Library of Christian Classics,* Westminster Press, Philadelphia, Vol XXII, 148.

CASEL, ODO (1886-1948)

A Benedictine at Maria Laach, C., one of the greatest of liturgical theologians in church history, was chaplain to the nuns at Herstelle.[1] His death, suddenly on Easter night after he had intoned the *Lumen Christi* of the Easter Vigil, has been seen as symbolic of his lifework, which was centered on the Paschal Mystery. His written work comprising over 100 papers mostly in the *Jahrbuch für Liturgiewissenschaft,* is summarized in *The Mystery of Christian Worship,* 1962.

C. thought of relating Christian worship to the pagan mystery cults, a controversial opinion. His permanent contribution, which he spent time in refining, was in the domain of mystery as embodied in liturgy. Mystery is first in God, then it is incarnate in Jesus Christ. With his resurrection and ascension into heaven, the Mystery, an action, not a truth beyond our understanding as we generally mean by the word, is divine reality given to men and expressed in the appropriate, though inevitably inadequate doctrinal language. Christ, triumphant in his human existence on earth, preserves the mysteries by which he lived for us and saved us in one entity, which has manifold effect for us. What he accomplished is the heart of the mystery, but it is reflected in the different events of his life which culminated in the Paschal Mystery.

Efforts have been made to root the theory in the Pauline concept of mystery, which is not a mere rite, as in the pagan mysteries, but God's plan for salvation, centered, triumphant in the Cross of Christ. Much reflection is still needed to extract *fully* and integrate with the Christian synthesis, the precious essence, abiding and creative, of C's thought. He welcomed the statement of Pius XII (qv) in *Mediator Dei*: ("Our Lord) does (in the Mass) what he did on the Cross."

C., who searched the Fathers closely, enlarges on the presence of Christ. "Unless Christ's death is made present we can make no sense of Romans VI. In the Eucharist the passion of Christ is present, as even the opponents of the mystery are beginning to admit; but the passion can in no way be taken out of the context of the whole saving action, for the pain as such did not redeem us. In ancient Christian language the *passio* was conceived as *pascha*, and contained his glorification as a normal concomitant."[2]

"The making present of the saving act in mystery," C. continues, "takes place in a sacramental manner; the saving work then receives, in addition to its natural mode of being, a new sacramental mode of being. This does not imply any change in the work; it remains what it was, yet in this new manner it is made present to us, so that we enter into it and can make it our own."[3] C. rejects any superficial interpretation of his theory, such as that the Child Jesus comes on the altar at Christmas. "What we meant is that the whole *oikonomia*, the whole design of salvation from the incarnation to the *parousia* which has not yet appeared in point of time, does take on a sacramental presence and therefore can be the subject of our co-participation in the most vivid way."[4]

C. does not hesitate to draw daring, though in a sense inevitable, conclusions. As the saving presence of the act is considered a communion with Christ, it implies that we are his "contemporaries"—we "have already entered into God's eternal now." "When we go with Christ in his way he becomes contemporary with us. He is neither past nor to come but present to us; he is

always with us. And not only his person but also his saving act belongs to this present. There can be no deeper communion of living than that we should share the essential life and action of another."[5] "Above all," C. continues, "it is the death and resurrection of Christ in which we have this immediate share: Later he can develop his thought like this: "What Christ did by dying and rising was not an historical event like any other, it was saving action, saving history. As such it burst the bonds of time and history. Christ dies to leave the world of sin and open the new age of divine order.... The death and resurrection of Christ are, then, the turning point in the history of the world."[6]

Such intuitions are the essential contribution of C. to the theology of the liturgy; he was ready to dismiss the speculation on the relation of Christian mystery to the pagan mysteries; as indeed most commentators on his theory have dismissed them. His abiding doctrine of mystery remains untouched by the fortunes of what is in fact not even an ancillary theory; rather is it a prolegomenon, but in this case somewhat unnecessary, if not irrelevant.

[1]Works of C.: *Das gadächtniss des Herrn in der altchristlichen Liturgie*, Freiburg i. B., 1918; *Die Liturgie als Mysterienfeier*, Freiburg 1922; *The Mystery of Christian Worship*, Westminster, Maryland, 1962; *La Fête de Pâques dans l'Eglise des Pères*, Paris, 1963; *Das Mysterium des Kommenden*, Paderborn 1952; *Das Mysterium des Kreuzes*, Paderborn, 1954; *Mysterium der Ekklesia*, Mainz, 1961; his articles from 1921-1941; Cf. T. Filthaut, *Die Kontroverse über die Mysterienlehre*, Warendorf, 1947; *Maison-Dieu*, 14 (1948), 1-106; *Liturgie und Monchtum* 3 (1949), 1949; *Das Paschamysterium P. Odo Casel zum Gedächtniss*; A. Mayer et als. ed., *Vom christlichen Mysterium*, Düsseldorf, 1951, *Gesammelte Arbeiten zum Gedächtniss von Odo Casel, O.S.B.*, bibl. his works, 363-75; T. Kampmann, *Gelebter Glaube*, Warendorf, 1957, 105-115; L. Bouyer, *Life and Liturgy*, London, 1956, 86-98; C. Davis, *Liturgy and Doctrine*, London, 1960, 66ff; B. Poschmann, *Mysteriengegenwart im Lichte des hl. Thomas, Theologische Quartalschrift*, 125, 1935, 53-116; O. D. Antiagada, *Dom O. Casel, Contributo monografico per una bibliografia generale delle sue opere degli studi sulla, sua dottrina e sulla sua influenza sulla teologia contemporanea, Archiv für Liturgiewissenschaft*, 1976, 7-77; A. Triacca, *Dom B. Neunheuser, interprete di O. Casel, Rassegna bibliografica, Salesianum* 40 (1978), 625-32; B. Neunheuser, *La théologie des mystères de Dom Casel dans la tradition catholique, EphLit* 94 (1980), 297-311; Id., LTK II: 966; Id., NCE III, 176-77; G. Penco, *La prima penetrazione in Italia del pensiero di P. Casel, Benedictina* 29 (1982), 365-380; A. Schilson, *Theologie also Sakramenttheologie Die Mysterientheologie Odo Casels, Tübinger theologische Studien*, 18, Mainz, 1982; A. Piolanti, Il Mistero, 455-66; DTC Tables, XVI, 1, 542; [2]*The Mystery of Christian Worship*; [3]*Op.cit.*, 154; [4]*Ibid.*; [5]*Ibid.*; [6]*Op.cit.*, 155.

CIENFUEGOS, ALVAREZ (1657-1739)

The Spanish Jesuit, who taught Philosophy at Compostela and Theology at Salamanca, was prominent as a bishop in relations with the Austrian power, was in Rome member of several Congregations. His Eucharistic doctrine is contained in the *Vita abscondita*, Rome, 1728.[1] He defended views of startling originality, without departing from orthodoxy, and without gaining any support from theologians. His principal ingenious idea was that by the consecration at Mass Jesus Christ in the Eucharist had the full use of his senses, but that he voluntarily suspended this use immediately and thus on the altar fulfilled the definition of sacrifice which he gives: "the offering made to God by the change of something sensible, from lawful institution, as a sign of his supreme dominion over all things, of life and death." However, the Saviour takes back his sensory powers again at the moment of the mingling of the fragment of the consecrated host with the Precious Blood: this moment symbolizes the resurrection. "This life Christ the Lord himself, as high priest, immolates alone, offers at the same time, in so far as he suspends or removes by the command of his human will, vital acts miraculously produced...."[2] Cardinal Franzelin (qv) thought that this opinion would frighten a careful theologian; Hurter found it "singular;" Cardinal Billot (qv) was of the opinion that "the opinion of Cardinal Cienfuegos, more than singular, is rightly and deservedly shattered by all."[3]

---

[1]M. Lepin, *L'idée*, 523-25; [2]Apud M. Lepin, ibid., 524; [3]*De Sacramentis*, 1932 ed., I, p. 625, n. l.

CLEMENT OF ALEXANDRIA, ST. (c. 150 - c. 215)
C. saw the Eucharist as instrumental in the accomplishment of the task undertaken by the Logos of God to bestow on men immortality.[1] His writing on sacrifices, which he appears to reject, must be read in the context of his thinking on pagan and Jewish sacrifices. He knows the requirements of Eucharistic celebration for he condemns those who "celebrate the Eucharist with mere water;" he invokes a canon of the Church which prescribes bread and wine and he speaks of "Melchizedek, king of Salem, priest of the most high God, who gave bread and wine, furnishing consecrated food for a type of the Eucharist."[2]

The Eucharist is a sacrifice. It is also the food for believers: "'Eat ye of my flesh,' he says, 'and drink my blood' (Jn 5:53). Such is the suitable food which the Lord ministers, and he offers his flesh and pours forth his blood, and nothing is wanting for the childrens' growth. O amazing mystery! We are enjoined to cast off the old and carnal corruption, as also the old nutriment, receiving in exchange another regimen, that of Christ, receiving him if possible, to hide him within; and that, enshrining the Saviour in our souls, we may correct the affections of our flesh." C. goes on then to speak allegorically: "But you are not inclined to

understand it thus, but perchance more generally. Hear it also in the following way. The flesh figuratively represents to us the Holy Spirit; for the flesh was created by him. The blood points out to us the Word, for as rich blood the Word has been infused into life; and the union of both is the Lord, the food of babes— the Lord who is Spirit and Word."[3]

C. distinguishes between the human and Eucharistic blood of Christ: "The blood of the Lord is twofold. For there is the blood of his flesh, by which we are redeemed from corruption; and the spiritual, by which we are anointed. And to drink the blood of Jesus, is to become partaker of the Lord's immortality; the Spirit being the energetic principle of the Word, as the blood is of the flesh. Accordingly, as wine is blended with water, so is the Spirit with man. And the one, the mixture of wine and water, nourishes to faith; while the other, the Spirit, conducts to immortality. And the mixture of both—of the drink and of the Word — is called Eucharist, renowned and glorious grace; and they who by faith partake of it are sanctified both in body and soul."[4]

---

[1]Works PG 8, 9; GCS 1-3, O. Stählin; J. Solano, *Textos*, I, 105-109; cf. J. Brinktine, *Der Messopferbegriff in den ersten zwei Jahrhunderten*, Freiburg l. B., 1918, 105-110; P. Batiffol, *L'Eucharistie*, 248-261; F. R. M. Hitchcock, *Holy Communion and Creed in Clement of Alexandria*, ChQ 129 (1939), 57-70; [2]*Strom.* 4:25; [3]*Paed.*, I, 6, 42, 3-43, 2; [4]*Ibid.*, II, 2, 19, 4-20, 1.

COMMUNION, HOLY
The principal aspects of this question are treated in this order: effects of Communion; first Communion; frequent Communion; spiritual communion.[1]

Effects of Communion
The effects of receiving the Eucharist in communion are listed as follows: a) Sacramental union with Jesus Christ, with all that this entails, eventually leading to union with the Holy Trinity (qv). This union is modelled, with respect for the essential differences, on the mystery of the Incarnation. b) Increase in sanctifying grace; this truth is of faith from the Council of Trent.[2] The Decree for the Armenians promulgated by the Council of Florence was already quite explicit on the subject: "The effect of this sacrament which he operates in the soul of him who takes it worthily is the union of man with Christ. And since through grace man is incorporated with Christ and is united with his members, it follows that through this sacrament grace is increased among those who receive it worthily; and every effect that material food and drink accomplish as they carry on corporal life, by sustaining, increasing,

restoring and delighting, this the sacrament does as it carries on spiritual life, in which, as Pope Urban says, we renew the happy memory of our Saviour, are withdrawn from evil, are greatly strengthened in good, and proceed to an increase of the virtues and the graces."[3]

So much is implied in the Eucharistic promise Jn 6:27ff, in particular 50-58: "This is the bread which comes down from heaven, that a man may eat of it and not die. I am the living bread which came down from heaven; if any one eats of this bread he will live forever; and the bread which I shall give for the life of the world is my flesh.... Truly, truly I say to you, unless you eat the flesh of the Son of man and drink his blood, you have no life in you; he who eats my flesh and drinks my blood has eternal life, and I will raise him up at the last day. For my flesh is food indeed, and my blood is drink indeed. He who eats my flesh and drinks my blood abides in me and I in him. As the living Father sent me, and I live because of the Father, so he who eats me will live because of me." To which promise add the words: "I came that they may have life and have it abundantly" (Jn 10:10). Note in particular the present tense "eats" and "has eternal life." c) Sacramental grace: The grace proper to the sacrament is help in assimilation to Jesus Christ. It is the pledge on Jesus' side to further the whole programme of life which is distinctively his. The communicant gives himself to Christ and Christ is committed to moulding him to his own likeness.

Indirect effects: a) Whether the Eucharist absolves sin, that is venial sin, directly or by stirring up such a degree of charity that they disappear is debated. But such sins, with fervent reception of Communion, are removed from the soul. b) In like manner the Eucharist relieves the soul of the debt of punishment due because of sin. c) It also preserves the soul from collapse through mortal sin; as d) it more and more eliminates venial sin from the life of the communicant. e) It protects the soul from the assaults of the demon, nourishes the soul, stirs it to fervour and brings to it a certain sweetness, a true Christian joy and peace. Lastly it facilitates prayer.

The moment, the intensity, the degree of these effects varies according to the dispositions of the communicant. St. Catherine of Siena summarized a wealth of theology by the simple advice given to a disciple: Desire him. This is what matches the very nature of the sacrament, hunger of the soul, the deep sentiment of utter want, dependence, emptiness.

First Communion

For reasons which appear in the next section the time of receiving first communion had been, in the eighteenth and nineteenth centuries, very much retarded. St. Pius X (qv) had already considerably altered, in the direction of frequent and daily Communion, a baneful custom of restriction and rigorism. By the Decree 'Quem singulari' issued through the Congregation on the Sacraments, 8 August 1910, he effected an equivalent revolution in the matter of first communion. The principal criteria were as follows:

I. The age of discretion both for confession and for Holy Communion is that at which the child begins to reason, that is, at about the seventh year, more or less. The obligation of satisfying both precepts of confession and communion begins from that time.

II. For first confession and for first communion a full and perfect knowledge of Christian doctrine is not necessary. But the child will be obliged afterwards to learn gradually the whole catechism in accord with his intelligence.

III. The knowledge of religion which is required in a child, that he may prepare himself fittingly for his first communion, is that by which in accord with his capacity he perceives the mysteries of faith necessary by a necessity of means, and by which he distinguishes Eucharistic bread from the common and corporeal, in order that he may approach the most blessed Eucharist with that devotion which his age carries."

Five other provisions in the Decree deal with the duties of parents and confessors in regard to the moment of the first communion, of pastors who must arrange general communions for children once or several times a year, of the need to inculcate habits of frequent, even daily, communion in the young. There are severe strictures on those who do not confess or absolve children past the use of reason—there is mention of "the remedy of the law" as of severe treatment to those who do not administer Viaticum and extreme unction in similar cases.[4]

Frequent Communion

The Lord himself in recalling the manna of the Old Testament implied frequency in reception of Holy Communion. He directly invites communion in the words of Institution (qv) "take and eat" . . . "Drink, all of you." St. Paul insists on this truth: "The cup of blessing which we bless, is it not a participation in the blood of Christ? The bread which we break, is it not a participation in the body of Christ?" (1 Cor 10:16). But the apostle insists on the requisite purity: "Let a man examine himself, and so eat of the bread and drink of the cup" (1 Cor 11:28); he excludes those unworthy: "Whoever, therefore, eats the bread or drinks the cup of the Lord in an unworthy manner will be guilty of profaning the body and blood of the Lord. For anyone who eats and drinks without discerning the body eats and drinks judgement upon himself" (1 Cor 11:27, 29).

Practice in obedience to these injunctions, frequency in receiving Holy Communion, has varied through the centuries. At first, if we follow the evidence of Acts, of the Didache (qv) and of St. Justin (qv), it was weekly. By the third century on the testimony of St. Cyprian (qv) and Tertullian (qv), the faithful communicate daily if the sacrifice is offered, as it generally is. Quite young children are allowed to receive Communion and the faithful are allowed to take consecrated bread to their homes and communicate freely at their own choice.

Thus things continued until, with the end of the era of persecution and the advent of masses of neophytes to the Church, a decline set in. Curiously this change was affected too by a change in attitude to the Eucharist, where one would not expect it, in the monasteries: respect for the Sacrament and fear of losing this through familiarity.

The Fourth Lateran Council, 1215, intervened to establish a clear obligation and the fact and tenor of the statement imply much: "Let everyone of the faithful of both sexes, after he has arrived at the years of discretion, alone faithfully confess all his sins at least once a year to his own priest, and let him strive to fulfill with all his power the penance enjoined upon him, receiving reverently the sacrament of the Eucharist at least in Paschal time, unless by chance on the advice of his own priest for some reasonable cause it shall be decided that he must abstain from the precept temporarily; otherwise both while living let him be barred from entrance to the church, and when dying let him be deprived of Christian burial. Therefore, let this salutary law be published frequently in the churches, lest anyone assume a pretext of excuse in the blindness of ignorance."[5]

The lives of the saints in that and the subsequent century afford evidence of the restrictive spirit prevailing. In the twelfth century St. Elizabeth of Schönau (d. 1165) received communion only on feast days; St. Hildegarde (d. 1179), once a month or thereabouts. In the thirteenth century St. Mechtilde (d.c. 1298) and St. Gertrude (d.c. 1302) were given communion on Sundays and feast days. St. Lucardie at Oberweimar, St. Liutgarde (d. 1246) lived under the same regime. It was with a special authorization from Rome that Venerable Ida of Louvain (d. 1300) approached the altar daily.

Though St. Francis encouraged devotion to the Eucharist this did not lead to frequent communion. St. Clare's rule, approved by Pope Innocent IV in 1253, allowed Communion only seven times a year: Christmas, Holy Thursday, Easter, Pentecost, the Assumption, All Saints and the feast of St. Francis. St. Elizabeth of Hungary (d. 1231) and her namesake of Portugal (d. 1336) were allowed to communicate three times a year; St. Louis of France (d. 1270), six times. St.

Margaret of Cortona (d. 1297), once a month. Blessed Robert Malatesta (d. 1482) despite a very special devotion to the Eucharist received Communion only once a week. Blessed Emilia Brichieri, a Dominican, was allowed to receive three times a week. St. Gilbert of Sempringham (d. 1189) drew up a rule for his institute granting Communion eight times a year; the Teutonic Order, in the rule of 1442, foresaw seven times a year. The Carthusians, who were not priests, were allowed to receive Communion on the first Sunday of each month and on the following feasts: Christmas, Holy Thursday, Easter, Pentecost, Corpus Christi and on the feast of St. Bruno.

Slowly but surely a movement favouring more frequent Communion gathered strength in different parts of Europe; the institution of the feast of Corpus Christi (qv) due to the inspiration of Blessed Juliana of Liège was an influential factor, as was the appearance in different countries of spiritual leaders convinced of the importance of frequent Communion, John Tauler (d. 1361), John Gerson (d. 1429), Gabriel Biel (d. 1493) (qv), the author of the *Imitation of Christ*. The final clarification was given by the Council of Trent (qv) with such words as these... "that they may believe and venerate these sacred mysteries of his body and blood with that constancy and formness of faith, with that devotion of soul, that piety and worship, as to be able to receive frequently that 'supersubstantial bread' (Mt 6:11), and that it may be to them truly the life of the soul and the perpetual health of mind...."[6] ..."The holy Synod would wish indeed that at every Mass the faithful present receive Communion not only by spiritual desire, but also by the sacramental reception of the Eucharist, so that a more abundant fruit of this most holy Sacrifice may be brought forth in them...."[7] In that age a great spiritual force in Italy, St. Charles Borromeo (d. 1584), worked arduously to win the faithful to the practice of frequent Communion.

Different trends were, nevertheless, apparent in the centuries following Trent; a certain laxist idea was offset by what may be called partial rigorism—favouring Communion once a week. Then came the extreme rigorism of the Jansenists (qv), a baneful period in Eucharistic history. The freedom proclaimed by the Council of Trent was not to be lost, but the exaggerated demands of Saint-Cyran and Antoine Arnauld inhibited many from approaching the Sacrament. So great was the personal purity which they thought necessary in the communicant that, as the wise St. Vincent de Paul exclaimed, "St. Paul would have dreaded receiving Communion." The order of things had been inverted: souls were being denied the essential means of gaining and preserving purity, on the grounds that they must possess such purity as a condition of using such means.

There would be another return to doctrinal sanity. It was preceded by hopeful signs, the liturgical revival—or reawakening if that be too strong a word—associated with Dom Prosper Gueranger, increasing help given by the Popes to those seeking an end to the Jansenist influence. Religious works centered on the Eucharist arose and flourished in the nineteenth century: the movement of Nocturnal Adoration, founded in Rome in 1810 extended to France in 1851 and widely adopted—by 1896 seventy-five French dioceses had taken it up; the movement of Adoration in reparation and of Communion in reparation, a basic practice of the Apostleship of Prayer; the foundation of the Congregation of Priests of the Blessed Sacrament in 1856 by St. Pierre Julien Eymard (qv), the International Eucharistic Congresses (qv) initiated in 1881. The change did not come without a clash of ideas; this was evident up to the year when St. Pius X (qv) officially supported those who defended the practice of frequent, daily Communion.

The decisive papal act came on 20 December 1905, *Sacra Tridentina Synodus*. The Pope had already given indications of his thinking: by a Brief to Mgr. Ricard, Bishop of Angoulême on 11 May of that year, on the occasion of a Eucharistic congress, by an indulgence granted for the recitation of a prayer to obtain the extension of frequent communion, 30 May, and by the address he gave to the Rome Eucharistic congress in June.

The Decree of the Congregation of the Holy Council, approved by the Pope read as follows: "The desire (indeed) of Jesus Christ and of the Church, that all the faithful of Christ approach the sacred banquet daily, is especially important to this, that the faithful of Christ being joined with God through the Sacrament may receive strength from it to restrain wantonness, to wash away the little faults that occur daily, and to guard against more grievous sins to which human frailty is subject; but not principally that consideration be given to the honour and veneration of God, nor that this be for those who partake of it a reward or recompense for their virtues. Therefore, the Sacred Council of Trent calls the Eucharist "an antidote, by which we are freed from daily faults and preserved from mortal sins."

"Because of the plague of Jansenism, which raged on all sides, disputes began to arise regarding the dispositions with which frequent and daily Communion should be approached, and some more than others demanded greater and more difficult dispositions as necessary. Such discussions brought it about that very few were held worthy to partake daily of the most blessed Eucharist, and to draw the fuller effects from so saving a Sacrament, the rest being content to be renewed either once a year or every month, or at most once a week. Such a point of severity was reached that entire groups were excluded from frequenting the heavenly table, for example, merchants, or those who had been joined in matrimony.

"In these matters the Holy See was not remiss in its proper duty.... Nevertheless the poison of Jansenism which had infected even the souls of the good, under the appearance of honour and veneration due to the Eucharist, has by no means entirely disappeared. The question about the dispositions for frequenting Communion rightly and lawfully has survived the declarations of the Holy See, as a result of which it has happened that some theologians even of good name, rarely, and after laying down many conditions, have decided that daily Communion can be permitted to the faithful.

"...But his Holiness, since it is especially dear to him that the Christian people be invited to the sacred banquet very frequently and even daily, and so gain possession of its most ample fruits, has committed the aforesaid question to this sacred Order to be examined and defined. (Hence the Congregation of the Holy Council on 16 December 1905, made the following decisions and declarations).

1. Let frequent and daily Communion ... be available to all Christians of every order or condition, so that no one, who is in the state of grace and approaches the sacred table with a right and pious mind, may be prevented from this.

2. Moreover, right mind is in this, that he who approaches the sacred table, indulges not through habit, or vanity, or human reasonings, but wishes to give pleasure to God, to be joined with him more closely in charity and to oppose his infirmities and defects with that divine remedy.

3. Although it is especially expedient that those who practise frequent and daily Communion be free from venial sins, at least those completely deliberate, and of their effect, it is enough, nevertheless, that they be free from mortal sins, with the resolution that they will never sin in the future....

4. ...Care must be taken that careful preparation for holy Communion precede, and that actions befitting the graces follow thereafter according to the strength, condition, and duties of each one.

5. ...Let the counsel of the confessor intervene. Yet let confessors beware lest they turn anyone away from frequent or daily Communion, who is in the state of grace and approaches (it) with a right disposition....

6. ...Finally, after the promulgation of this decree, let all ecclesiastical writers abstain from any contentious disputation about dispositions for frequent and daily Communion."[8]

That was the liberating charter which inaugurated a

CONCELEBRATION

new era in the Catholic Church. The evil was denounced; the terms of the reformed discipline, a return to older things as is clear from history, were firm and clear.

Spiritual Communion

Spiritual communion is union of the soul with Jesus in the Eucharist, not through sacramental reception, but through desire for this reception. The phrase "spiritual eating" and "spiritual use of the sacrament" are found in medieval times, though not always with the same meaning. From those times there is evidence of the practice of spiritual Communion. St. Thomas Aquinas (qv) taught that one who received the Sacrament *in voto* could receive the same benefit as by receiving it *in re*.

The Council of Trent (qv) supported the idea: "As to its use (the Eucharist) our Fathers have rightly and wisely distinguished three ways of receiving this holy Sacrament. For they have taught that some receive it sacramentally only, as sinners; others only spiritually, namely those who eating with desire the heavenly bread set before them, by a living faith 'which worketh by charity' (Gal 5:6), perceive its fruit and usefulness; while the third receive it both sacramentally and spiritually."[9]

Understandably then the practice spread. It was encouraged by great authorities in the spiritual life, such as St. Teresa of Avila and St. Francis de Sales. Theologically the basis was sound: spiritual communion is the expression of desire, desire directed towards the Eucharist, preferably explicit. The source of this desire is faith in the real presence (qv) of Jesus in the Eucharist. This desire supplies for the act.

The effects can be the same, even greater than from sacramental Communion. But these effects depend on the disposition of the communicant, for the effects follow not *ex opere operato,* but *ex opere operantis.* The practice is a matter of personal decision, with the advice, if need be, of a spiritual director.

[1]. Cf. E. de Gibergues, *Holy Communion,* New York, 1913; E. Demoutet, *Le désir de voir l'hostie et les origines de la dévotion au Saint Sacrement,* Paris, 1926; id., *Le Christ selon la chair et la vie liturgique au moyen age,* Paris, 1932; P. Browe, *De frequenti Communione in Ecclesia Occidentali usque ad annum c. 1000, Textus et Documenta,* series theologica 5, Rome, 1932; id., *Die Verehrung der Eucharistie im Mittelalter,* Munich, 1933; id., *Die häufige Kommunion im Mittelalter,* Münster, 1938; C. Clinton, *The Paschal Precept,* Catholic University of America, Canon Law Studies, Washington, 1932; J. McCarthy, *Sacramental and Spiritual Communion, Irish Eccl. Record.,* 63 (1944), 194-98; M. M. Crotty, *The Recipient of First Holy Communion,* Catholic University of America, Canon Law Studies, Washington, 1947; P. F. Palmer, *Sacraments and Worship,* (Sources of Christian Theology), Westminster, Md. 1955; J. Cavagna, *Dispositions required for Communion, Emmanuel* 63 (1957), 315-18; F. Costa, *Nature and Effects of Spiritual Communion,* Proceedings of the Catholic Theological Society 13, 1958, 139-48; J. A. Jungmann, S.J., *The Early Liturgy to the Time of Gregory the Great,* tr. F. A. Brunner, 1959; J. B. Collins, ed, *Catechetical Documents of Pope Pius X,* Paterson 1964; E. Dublanchy, Communion (fréquente), DTC III, 515-552; H. Leclercq, O.S.B., Communion, DACL, III, 2457ff; esp. J. Duhr, DSp, II, 2, 1234-1291; N. Mitchell, *Cult and Controversy: The Worship of the Eucharist outside Mass,* New York, 1982; [2]DS 1639; [3]DS 1322; [4]DS 3530-3533; cf. Code of Canon Law, 1983, cc. 913, 914; cf. *Commentary of the Canon Law Society of America,* New York, London, 1985, ed. J. A. Coriden, T. J. Green, D. E. Heintschel, 652, 653; [5]DS 812; [6]DS 1649; [7]DS 1747; [8]DS 3375-3383; [9]DS 1648.

CONCELEBRATION

One of the features of Catholic liturgy since the changes introduced after Vatican II is the widespread use of concelebration, especially in religious communities. The essence of the practice as thus instituted is the recital of parts of the Eucharistic prayer, especially the institution (qv) narrative together. The capital text in regard to this recent practice is in the Constitution on the Liturgy, *Sacrosanctum Concilium,* 4 December 1963. It runs as follows:

(1) "Concelebration whereby the unity of the priesthood is appropriately manifested has remained in use to this day in the Church both in the East and the West. For this reason it has seemed good to the Council to extend permission for celebration to the following cases:

1. a) On the Thursday of the Lord's Supper, not only at the Mass of the Chrism, but also at the evening Mass.

b) At Masses during Councils, Bishops' Conferences and Synods.

c) At the Mass for the Blessing of an abbot.

2. Also, with permission of the Ordinary, to whom it belongs to decide whether concelebration is opportune:

a) At conventual Mass, and at the principal Mass in churches when needs of the faithful do not require that all priests available should celebrate individually;

b) At Mass celebrated at any kind of priests' meetings whether the priests be secular or religious.

(2) 1. The regulation, however, of the discipline of concelebration in the diocese pertains to the bishop.

2. Each priest shall always retain his right to celebrate Mass individually, though not at the same time in the same church as a concelebrated Mass nor on the Thursday of the Lord's Supper.

58. A new rite for concelebration is to be drawn up and inserted into the Pontifical and into the Roman Missal."[2]

The practice of concelebration was taken up widely in the years after the Council. The subject has been dealt with in a number of Roman documents since then. In *Inter Oecumenici* (qv) in the section dealing with the 'Liturgical formation of the spiritual life of the Clergy,' the paragraph on Sundays and greater feasts states: "Priests who are not needed for individual

Masses for the faithful may concelebrate, especially on the more solemn feasts, after the new rite shall have been published."[3]

In 1965 the Sacred Congregation for Rites issued *Ecclesiae Semper* dealing with Concelebration and Communion under both species. Three distinctive properties are singled out in the Mass: the unity of the sacrifice of the Cross, the priesthood, and the action of the People of God. "These three characteristics," we are told, "are found in every Mass, but they are vividly apparent in the rite by which several priests concelebrate the same Mass."

There follow some theoretical and practical considerations: "In this manner of celebrating Mass, several priests act together with one will and one voice, by the power of the same priesthood and in the place of the high priest, together they consecrate and offer the one sacrifice, in one sacramental act, and together they participate in it.

"Consequently, when the sarifice is thus celebrated, the faithful are taking an active part, aware of what they are doing, and as befits a community, the principal manifestation of the Church is realized—especially if the bishop is presiding—in unity of sacrifice and priesthood, in one sole act of thanksgiving around one sole altar, with ministers and holy people.

"Thus it is that the rite of concelebration expresses and inculcates vividly truths of great moment for the spiritual and pastoral lives of priests and the Christian formation of the faithful.

"For these reasons, much more than for merely practical considerations, concelebration of the mystery of the Eucharist has existed in the Church from antiquity, in different forms, and has survived to our own day, evolving differently, in both East and West.

"It was for these same reasons that liturgical experts had been pursuring researches into the matter, submitting requests that permission for concelebration be extended and that the rite be reformed.

"Finally the Second Vatican Council, having considered the matter carefully, had extended the faculty of concelebrating to a number of cases and had ordered the preparation of a new rite of concelebration, to be inserted into the Pontifical and the Roman Missal. Consequently, after he had solemnly approved and proclaimed the Constitution on the Sacred Liturgy, His Holiness Pope Paul VI commissioned the Concilium charged with the implementation of the constitution to prepare a rite of concelebration as soon as possible. While the rite was being prepared, it was several times examined by the members and consultors of the Concilium and was considerably revised. Finally, the Concilium unanimously ratified it on 19 June 1964, ordaining that, if the Holy Father approved, it should be experimented with in different parts of the world and in varying circumstances before being definitely approved.

"The Concilium for the Implementation of the Constitution on Sacred Liturgy, in accordance with the wishes of the council, also prepared a rite for the administration of Communion (qv) under both species, all over the world. When the secretary had received reports and comments on these experiments, both rites were submitted to a final revision in the light of the experience gained and were submitted to the Holy Father by Cardinal Giacomo Lercaro, President of the Concilium.

"The Holy Father considered the two rites very carefully, with the assistance both of the Concilium and of the Sacred Congregation of Rites, and he approved and confirmed them, *speciali modo,* in their entirety and in all parts, in virtue of his authority, in an audience with Cardinal Arcadio Maria Larraona, Prefect of the Sacred Congregation of Rites. He ordered it to be published and to be observed by everybody from Holy Thursday, 16 April 1965, and to be accurately transcribed into the Pontifical and Roman Missal."[4]

In 1967 the Sacred Congregation for Rites published *Eucharisticum Mysterium* (qv) on the worship of the Eucharistic Mystery. This document also deals with concelebration as follows:

"Concelebration of the Eucharist aptly demonstrates unity of the sacrifice and of the priesthood. Moreover, whenever the faithful take an active part the unity of the People of God is strikingly manifested, particularly if the bishop presides.

"Concelebration both symbolizes and strengthens the brotherly bond of the priesthood, because 'by virtue of the ordination to the priesthood which they have in common, all are bound together in an intimate brotherhood.'

"Therefore, unless it conflicts with the needs of the faithful, which must always be consulted with the deepest pastoral concern, and although every priest retains the right to celebrate alone, it is desirable that priests should celebrate the Eucharist in this eminent manner. This applies both to communities of priests and to groups which gather on particular occasions, as also to all similar circumstances. Those who live in community or serve the same church should welcome visiting priests into their concelebration.

"The competent superiors should, therefore, facilitate, and indeed positively encourage concelebration, whenever pastoral needs or other reasonable motives do not prevent it.

"The faculty to concelebrate also applies to the principal Masses in churches and public and semipublic oratories of seminaries, colleges and ecclesiastical

CONCELEBRATION

institutes, and also of religious orders and societies of clergy living in community without vows. However, where there is a great number of priests, the competent superior may give permission for concelebration to take place even several times on the same day, though at different times or in different places."

The Bread for Concelebration
If a large host is used for concelebration, as permitted in the *Ritus servandus in concelebratione Missae,* n. 17, care must be taken that, in keeping with traditional usage, it should be of such a shape and appearance as befits so great a sacrament."[5]

The General Instruction on the Roman Missal appeared in 1970. A section deals with concelebration, laying down the rules for observance. Questions were raised about two numbers (76 and 158) and to deal with them the Sacred Congregation for Divine Worship, shortly after 7 August 1972, issued *In Celebratione Missae.* It reads as follows: "Everyone has the right and duty, when sharing in the celebration of Mass 'to play his proper role in accordance with the diversity of orders and functions ... in such wise that the very ordering of the celebration will manifest the Church in its various ranks and ministries.' Priests ordained by the special Sacrament of Orders, perform the function that is properly theirs in the celebration of Mass whenever, individually or with other priests, they effect and offer the sacrifice of Christ sacramentally and receive Holy Communion.

"It is fitting that at Mass priests should celebrate or concelebrate, so as to play their part more fully and in the manner proper to themselves, and that they should not communicate merely, as do the laity."

The problems arising about a priest concelebrating after he had celebrated Mass for pastoral reasons are then settled. There is a reminder that Mass celebrated without the participation of the faithful "remains at the same time the center of the entire Church and the heart of priestly existence." The following paragraph ends the document: "For this reason, every priest ought to be allowed the right to celebrate Mass alone. To ensure priests' liberty, everything should be made available to facilitate such celebrations: time should be set aside, there should be a place where single celebration is possible and an altar server should be at hand, and whatever else is needed should be made available."[6]

Such are the official church decisions and directives instituting and ordering one of the great changes in liturgy since the Council. The ecclesiastical documents appeal to history and to current practice in the East and the West. Such facts as the following are mentioned: Pope Anicetus invited St. Polycarp to join him in the Eucharist—Rome, second century; regional councils

like Arles, 314, decreed that visiting bishops could be invited to concelebrate—this is evident too in the fifth century *Statuta Ecclesiae Antiqua.* There is evidence that priests concelebrated with the Pope in Rome until the sixth century and until the twelfth on great feasts. An eighth century Ordinal decrees that the Canon should be recited together.

In the East there is similar evidence, facts from time to time, nothing at the outset, anymore than in the West, like a universal practice. Thus a third-century Syrian version of the *Didascalia Apostolorum* provides for two bishops who concelebrate, one the bread and the other the wine. Between the fourth and sixth centuries the practice is found in Asia Minor, Syria and Egypt. Evidence is forthcoming from the Councils of Ephesus and Chalcedon. In the ninth century Pope John VIII (d. 882) authorized his delegates to concelebrate with the Patriarch Photius. Action in favour of concelebration is reported of Peter Moghila, Metropolitan of Kiev (1597-1646), and Pope Benedict XIV (d. 1758) in 1743. Silent concelebration is practised in the Greek, Coptic and Ethiopian Orthodox rites; in many other rites the words of consecration (qv) are spoken aloud.

Fr. A. Piolanti publishes in his book *Il Mistero Eucaristico* an essay on concelebration by Fr. R. Michael Schmitz, devoted to the question whether in concelebration one Mass is said or as many as the celebrants. The answer which he supports with arguments from the magisterium and from theologians of stature is one Mass. He then puts the question to individual priests whether they have the right to deny the Church the benefits accruing from Masses celebrated individually. He knows that priests concelebrating are allowed to accept stipends as if they were saying individual Masses, but explains this on the general grounds of the infinite fruits of the Mass.[7] The 1983 Code of Canon Law gives legal form to the teaching of the Council and Roman authorities.[8]

[1]For bibliography S. Madeja, *Bibliografia sulla concelebrazione eucaristica, EphLit* 97 (1983) 262-73; cf. J. M. Hanssens, S.J., *De concelebratione eucharistica,* in *Periodica de re morali, canonica, liturgica* 16 (1927), 143-154, 18 (1928), 93-127, 21 (1932), 133-213; Lambert Beauduin, O.S.B., *La concélébration, La Maison Dieu, 7* (1946), 7-26; P. Dalmais, O.P., *Concélébration,* Catholicisme, IV, 1949, 1435-38; B. Botte, O.S.B., *Note historique sur la concélébration dans l'église ancienne, La Maison Dieu, 35* (1953, 3) 13; A. Raes, S.J., *La concélébration eucharistique dans les rites orientaux, La Maison Dieu, 1953, 3),* 24-47; B. Schultze, *Das theologische Problem der Konzelebration, Greg* 36 (1955), 212-271; P. le Guillou, O.P., *La concélébration: manifestation du Mystère,* in *Parole et Pain,* 1 (1964) 18-25; P. Tihon, S.J., *De la concélébration eucharistique, NRT,* 86 (1964), 579-607; id., English tr., *Yearbook of the Liturgical Society,* VI, 1965; J. C. McGowan, *Concelebration, Sign of the Unity of the Church,* New York, 1964; J. Kleiner, *Théologie de la concélébration,* in *Esprit et Vie* 89 (1979), 671-680; Joseph de Sainte Marie, O.C.D.,

L'eucharistie, salut du monde, sa célébration, sa concélébration. Etudes sur le Saint Sacrifice de la Messe, Paris 1982; these articles by the same author in *La Pensée catholique: Réflexions et questions au sujet de la concélébration*, 180 (May-June) 1979, 21-36; *Note sur une théologie de la concélébration*, 180 (January-February) 1980, 13-41; *L'Eglise demande la multiplication des Messes* 185 (March-April) 1980, 42-58; *La concélébration; histoire d'une histoire*, 186-87 (May-August) 1980, 62-69 - bibl.; R. M. Schmitz, *Zur Theologie der Konzelebration, Theologisches* 139 (November 1981), 4323-4334; P. de Puniet, DACL III, 2, 2470-88; J. A. Jungmann, S.J., and K. Rahner, S.J., LTK², VI, 524-25; A. Cornides, NCE, IV, 103-105; ²Art. 57, 58, *Vatican II*, 1, 19; ³*Ibid.*, art. 15, 49; ⁴*Ibid.*, 58ff; ⁵*Ibid.*, 128; ⁶*Ibid.*, 222ff; ⁷*Op.cit.*, 501-520; ⁸Cf. with commentary by the American Canon Law Society, cc. 276, 835, 844, 846, 884, 902, 908; ed. J. A. Coriden, T. J. Green, D. E. Heintschel, New York, London, 1985.

CONCOMITANCE

The necessary bond between things united so that where one exists the other must also be. As St. Thomas says, it is only by a process of mental abstraction that things united are considered separately.[1] Since the body, blood and soul are physically one, it follows that wherever the body of Christ is there is the blood and the soul, and wherever the blood of Christ is there too is the body and soul. This is so because Christ's body is risen and in itself unchangeable. This total presence of the man Christ follows the law of natural concomitance. But since by the hypostatic union, the divinity of the Word is united really to the body and soul of Christ, by supernatural concomitance wherever the body and soul are, there is the divinity. This is not to be confused with "ubiquismus," a theory of some Lutherans that wherever the Word is there too is Christ. The Word is where Christ is, but Christ is not everywhere that the Word is. This would be so if two realities were so united that each adequately contained the other, but the sacred humanity of Christ cannot exhaustively contain the Word, who by his infinite power contains all things and surpasses them immeasurably.

The doctrine of concomitance is taught by the Council of Trent: " ... And this belief has always been in the Church of God, that immediately after the consecration the true body of our Lord and his true blood together with his soul and divinity exist under the species of bread and wine; but the body indeed under the species of bread and the blood under the species of wine by the force of the words, but the body itself under both by force of the natural connection and concomitance by which the parts of Christ the Lord, 'who has now risen from the dead to die no more' (Rom 6:9) are mutually united, the divinity also because of that admirable hypostatic union (can. 1 and 3) with his body and soul. Therefore, it is very true that as much is contained under either species as under both. For Christ whole and entire exists under the species of bread and under any part whatsoever of that species, likewise the whole (Christ) is present under the species of wine and under its parts (can. 3)."[2]

[1]Cf. Bibl to articles Presence, real, and Transubstantiation; St. Thomas (qv) III, q. 76, a. 1; L. Billot, *De Sacramentis*, 7 ed., 476-487; A. Piolanti, *Il Mistero*, 299-301; ²DS 1641; cp 3231.

CONDREN, CHARLES DE (1588-1641)

A great spiritual writer of the French school, C. deals with the Eucharist in his great work, accepted as faithful to his thought though it was composed by disciples and appeared after his death, *L'idée du sacerdoce et du sacrifice de Jesus Christ*, 1677.[1] He lays down the principal characteristics of sacrifice and applies them to the Mass: sanctification of the victim, oblation, slaying or immolation, consumption or burning, communion. The immolation he sees in the mystic separation of the species in the consecration.

De C's ideas are understandably imbued with the outlook of the French school of spirituality, identification with the mysteries of the Incarnate Word, theocentrism which in life thus means Christocentrism. This carries into the existence of the Saviour in glory, and an important idea in de C's synthesis on the Mass is the heavenly sacrifice of Christ.

[1]New ed., 1858; cf. M. Lepin, *L'idée*, 476ff.

CONFERENTIARUM EPISCOPALIUM,
28 October 1974

A Note on the Obligation to use the new Roman Missal; it was issued by the Sacred Congregation for Divine Worship.[1] It is the nearest there is in Roman documents to an outright prohibition to use the Tridentine Mass. It has to be read carefully. It recalls a previous note, published with the approval of Paul VI, on the role of episcopal conferences in regard to translations of liturgical books. The remainder of the note does not carry this papal approval. It states that once such vernacular versions have been made, Mass may not be celebrated save according to the rite of the Roman Missal promulgated by order of Paul VI, 7 April 1969. Ordinaries, as was previously permitted, may allow priests for reasons of age or ill-health, to celebrate Mass according to the 1962 edition of the Roman Missal, with the changes introduced in 1965 and 1967: but never for Mass with a congregation. Ordinaries, religious and local, are urged to secure the acceptance of the new Roman Missal by clergy and laity, seeing that priests "by dint of greater effort and greater reverence comprehend the treasures of divine wisdom and liturgical and pastoral teaching which it contains."

---

[1]Text *Notitiae*, November, 1974, 353, tr. A. Flannery, O.P., 1281-82.

CONGRESSES, INTERNATIONAL EUCHARISTIC

A manifestation of faith and devotion centred in the Eucharist, organised around liturgical assemblies, open-air with international participation, each day filled with related activities, sectional or general meetings to discuss aspects of Eucharistic doctrine or practice.[1] Latterly each congress is given a theme around which lectures can be selected. At Lourdes, 1981, it was "Bread broken for a new world," at Nairobi, 1985, "The Eucharist in Family Life." To benefit by the event those in the host diocese should fulfill a lengthy pastoral program beforehand. Proceedings, diary of events, texts of lectures, official documents are customarily published.

The origins are in the life work of a Frenchwoman, Marie Marthe Emilia Tamisier (1834-1910) who first exercised her particular apostolate by directing people to places where Eucharistic miracles had occurred. The first attempt to organise a congress failed. In 1881 thanks to the initiative and generosity of Philibert Vrau, a Catholic Lille industrialist, the first international congress took place at Lille with the blessing of Leo XIII; attendance has been put at 800.

Including the most recent at Nairobi, forty-three congresses have been held. Landmarks were Jerusalem in 1893, the first attended by a papal legate and Montreal, 1910, first in the western hemisphere. Pius XI presided at the Rome congress in 1922; he decided that henceforth one should take place every two years. He broadcast for the first time to Dublin in 1932. Cardinal Pacelli, the future Pope Pius XII, was legate to Buenos Aires in 1934 and to Budapest in 1938. Manila, 1937, was the first city in the Far East to host a Congress; it was recalled in a National Eucharistic Year followed by a National Congress in 1987.

Europe was dominant for a long time, having hosted 30 altogether—France led with 11. Recently the choice has gone generally outside Europe, North and South America, Australia, Asia and Africa. The congress at Bombay in 1964, third year of the Second Vatican Council was the first outside Rome to which a Pope travelled. The reception given to Paul VI on his arrival by the government and especially by the people was unexampled. John Paul II was similarly acclaimed in Nairobi. He had been prevented from attending the

Lourdes congress in 1981, as had been his intention, by the attempt on his life in St. Peter's Square, 13 May, that year.

---

[1]Cf. J. Vaudon, *L'oeuvre des congrès eucharistiques: ses origines*, Paris, 1911; F. Vrau, *Les triomphes eucharistiques dans les 25 premiers congrès eucharistiques internationaux*, Paris, 1920; G. Jacquemet, M. E. Point, *Cath.* III, 30-32; B. Spini EC IV, 350-52

CONSECRATION

In Eucharistic theology the word that denotes the essential moment in the Mass when bread and wine are changed into the body and blood of Christ. A Mass wherein the words of consecration are omitted is not valid. When Mass is concelebrated the concelebrants join in the words of consecration with the principal celebrant. The words of consecration are within the Institution Narrative (qv): "This is my body, which will be offered up for you"; "This is the cup of my blood, the blood of the new and everlasting covenant; it will be shed for you and for all for the forgiveness of sins."

CORPUS CHRISTI: THE FEAST

The feast of Corpus Christi, not always called by that name, dates from the thirteenth century.[1] It originated in a great centre of Eucharistic and liturgical piety, Liège, which had already given the Church the feast of the Most Holy Trinity. From 1208 St. Juliana (1192-1258), first abbess of the nearby Augustinian convent of Mont Cornillon, had symbolic visions which she interpreted as God's call to her to work for a special feast in honour of the Blessed Sacrament. In 1230 she shared her secret with two friends, the recluse Eve of Liège and Isabelle, a Béguine at Huy, later a nun in Mont Cornillon. Isabelle secured the good offices of Jean de Lausanne, of the chapter of Saint Martin in Liège. Theologians consulted were favourable. Juliana composed an office. But chapter members and some of the clergy disagreed.

Jean d'Eppes (d. 1238), bishop of Liège, lacked interest. So did his successor, Robert de Torote, until he met Juliana. He established the feast of the Blessed Sacrament probably in June 1246 (*Inter alia mira*) and decreed its celebration on the Thursday after the Octave of Pentecost. He died in October of that year; he had the Mass celebrated in his presence before death. In 1247 the canons of Saint Martin celebrated the Mass. But opposition hardened; Juliana left Mont Cornillon for good.

Yet in the autumn of 1251 the Dominican Cardinal Hugh de St. Cher, legate of Innocent IV to Germany visited Liège. He celebrated the feast himself in St. Martin's and by decree, *Dum humani generis*, 29 December 1252, he extended the feast to the territory to which he was delegate. The decision was confirmed by his successor, Cardinal Peter Capocci, 30 November 1254. Archdeacon Jacques de Troyes, who had known Juliana, was elected Pope in 1261, taking the name Urban IV. On 11 August 1264, by the Bull *Transiturus de hoc mundo*, he extended the feast of the Blessed Sacrament to the universal Church. On 8 September he informed Eve of the fact: "*Laetare . . . quia omnipotens Deus tribuit tibi desiderium cordis*"; Urban said that the feast had been celebrated in his presence.

The Pope died on 2 October and the Bull ramained a dead letter for fifty years. The decree of Bishop Robert was included in the statutes of the diocese of Liège in 1288, but not many dioceses adopted the feast—Apt 1277, Venice 1295, Würzburg 1298, Amiens before 1306; the Carmelites took up the feast in 1306.

It was Clement V (d. 1314) who saved the day. Within the Council of Vienne he promulgated the Bull of Urban IV anew; John XXII included it in the Clementines in 1317; setting up an octave and ordering a procession. It was welcomed by the dioceses and religious orders in the fourteenth century.

The text of the office of Corpus Christi has been the subject of considerable research in recent times. When the *Festum Eucharistiae* was instituted, John of Mont Cornillon, a young Augustinian, composed an office on the advice of Juliana, *Animarum cibus*. He had borrowed from the work of Alger of Liège (qv)*De sacramento altaris*. The sequence of the Mass was *Laureata plebs fidelis*. This office had been approved by Urban IV. But when he instituted the feast he may have called on St. Thomas Aquinas (qv). The saint's biographer, Tolomeo de Lucca, says that he composed the office using one already in existence—some of the lessons in this had come from John of Cornillon.

In recent years detailed research has been conducted on the available documents to determine exactly what is due to St. Thomas and to others.

---

[1]Cf. G. Morin, *L'office cistercien pour la Fête-Dieu comparé avec celui de St. Thomas d'Aquin*, *RBen* 27 (1910), 236-246; E. Dumoutet, *Les origines de la fête et de la procession du Saint Sacrement*, in *La vie et les arts liturgiques*, 11 (1925), 345ff; id., *Corpus Domini, Aux sources de la piété eucharistique mediévale*, 1942; P. Browe, *Die Ausbreitung des Fronleichnamfestes* in *JLW* 8 (1928), 107-44; id., *Die Verehrung der Eucharistie im Mittelalter*, Munich, 1933; id., *Textus antiqui de Festo Corporis Christi*, Münster i. W., 1934; G. Simenon, *La Fête-Dieu et sa signification* in *La Vie eucharistique de l'Eglise*, Collection Cours et Conferences des semaines liturgiques (Liège 1934, vol 12, Louvain, 1935; id. *Juliana de Mont Cornillon*, Brussels, 1946; E. Denis, *La vraie vie de Ste. Julienne de Liège*, Tournai, 1935; esp. C. Lambot, O.S.B., *L'office de la Fête-Dieu; Aperçus nouveaux sur les origines*, *RBen* 54 (1942), 61-123, id. with l.

Fransen, O.S.B., *L'Office de la Fête-Dieu primitive, Textes et mélodies retrouvés,* Maredsous, 1946; id., with F. Baix, *La dévotion à l'Eucharistie et le VIIe centenaire de la Fête-Dieu,* Gembloux-Namur, 1946, bibl. 151-160; id., *La Bulle d'Urbain IV à Eve de Saint-Martin sur l'institution de la Fête-Dieu*, Scriptorium, 2 (1948), 69-77; id., *L'ufficio del SS.mo Sacramento*, in *Eucaristia*, 827-835; *Studia Eucharistia, DCC Anni de Condito Festo Sanctissimi Corporis Christi 1246-1946,* Antwerp, 1946, bibl. R. M. Gallet, 415-450; A. Renard, *Un opuscule théologique sur l'Institution de la Fête-Dieu*, in *Revue du moyen age latin*, 2 (1946), 269-276—a work dated 1270-1272; C. Hontoir, *Sainte Julienne et les cisterciens*, *Collectanea ordinis cisterciensium reformatorum*, vol. 8, 1946, 109-111; S. Roisin, *L'hagiographie cistercienne dans le diocèse de Liège au 13e siècle*, Louvain-Brussels, 1947; G. Simenon, *Juliana de Mont Cornillon*, Brussels, 1947; L. M. J. Delaisse, *A la recherche des origines de l'office du Corpus Christi dans les manuscrits liturgiques*, Scriptorium 4 (1950), 220-239; P. Rai, *La Fête-Dieu chez les Melchites*, in *Bolletino di Grottaferrata*, 6 (1952), 32-39; A. Kern, *Aus alten Handschriften. Die ursprungliche Fassung des Fronleichnams Offiziums vom hl'Thomas in der Universitätsbibliothek Graz gefunden*, Gratz, 1952; id., *Das Offizium De Corpore Christi in Oesterreichischen Bibliotheken*, *RBen* 64 (1954), 46-67; F. Callaey, *Origine e sviluppo della festa del Corpus Domini*, in *Eucaristia*, 907-933; F. Oppenheim, EC II (1950), 611-13; Righetti II, 142-44; R. Naz DDC V, 1, 832-33; J. Gaillard, Catholicisme, IV, 1215-19; W. Duling - J. A. Jungmann, LTK, IV 405-407.

COVENANT, THE

The agreement between God and his people, described on the model of human agreements, especially solemn because the initiative was divine and the people, though beneficiaries of God's favour and liberality, were bound by divine law.[1] Much recent research into newly discovered materials relevant to the peoples of the ancient Near East has shown the historical complexities of the subject, the allowance that must be made for alliances of an economic-political kind which, though secular and profane in character, were nonetheless bound up with the unfolding of salvation history. The transference to the purely religious domain of the idea expressed in the common word for all these alliances, *b'erit*, afforded a thought pattern of immense significance; it was not a contractual agreement but a divine warrant for future largesse. There was no question of equal partners. God was dominant, for he was sole source of salvation.

The covenant idea became, with the passage of time and its different manifestations all suited to the need of a particular moment, and the mode of enrichment designed by the supreme Author, fundamental to the entire revelation of the OT, an indispensable key to understanding of this phase of salvation history. How much remains to be clarified is stated by an expert: "There can be no doubt that the covenant was connected with cult. The importance of sacrifice and the theophany in covenant-making as exemplified for instance in Sinai show this. Moreover, there is the striking fact that the apparent sequence of cultic ceremonies reflects in large part the actual sequence of covenant treaty documents. This, of course, raises the question, the vexed question, of the covenant feast.... The relationship between the prophets and the covenant needs further study. The studies of the curses and condemnations of the prophets show that they use imagery analogous to the imagery of the covenant curses. However, these curses were part of the common Near Eastern patrimony and they occur in other types of documents such as boundary stones and the law codes and building inscriptions of the ancient Near East. The *rib* pattern that we have discussed is more convincing at present. Still the troubling question remains, why do the prophets avoid the word 'covenant'? Finally the relationship between the Davidic and the Mosaic covenants remains to be clarified. Was there really a tension, an opposition or even, as some extreme proponents of this idea hold, a basic incompatibility? And yet the kingship is a basic element in the theology of the OT and of supreme importance because it is the source of messianism. We have seen that the attempt to make the Davidic covenant formally identical with the Mosaic has not succeeded. The Davidids have a special relation to Yahweh because they are patrons of the temple worship. Moreover, it is a promissory, an absolute covenant; they will be favoured and especially united to Yahweh, and through them the people will receive grace in spite of their failing. This is not in form or in content the treaty-type covenant. How did the man of ancient Israel integrate this with the Mosaic covenant?"[2] The same author summarizes the overall significance: "With the added realization of its responsibilities and of the moral character of union with Yahweh, Israel always knew itself to be not a mere vassal or hired minion but the very family of God, the harbinger of the people of the new dispensation who 'born again of water and the Holy Spirit' would be called and be the sons of God."[3] A cultic act was essential to the Sinai covenant. Hosea uses the word twice.

Covenant was then the framework of religious thought, motivation, prayer, self-judgement: sin was a failure in due observance; in moments of crisis the ultimate resource and pledge of recovery, as the deep well of divine compassion and forgiveness, were to be found in the covenant.

This vast treasure would be surpassed in the NT. The Septuagint used the word *diatheke*, a word related to a last will and a statement of provisions to be effected, to translate *b'erit*. The emphasis is on divine transcendence, initiative, condescension: all most appropriate to the new creation.

The word is found 26 times in the NT, 7 quotations from the OT, 16 allusions thereto. The one capital use of the word for the biblical theology of the Eucharist is in the words of the Last Supper (qv). This, outside Zechariah's *Benedictus*, is the only occasion when the idea occurs in the gospels. This, still more significantly, is the only occasion on which Jesus used the word. The uniqueness is eloquent, as is the echo of Ex 24 in the mention of blood. But here the author of the new covenant makes his own blood the pledge of its efficacy and endurance, takes wholly unprecedented means to guarantee perpetuity in its working. Nowhere in the OT evolution of the covenant idea is there question of blood miraculously provided, of blood the priceless sign of the covenant, its very source, blood poured out with effects intrinsic to the very inmost spiritual being of every beneficiary of this totally new, totally unmerited divine dispensation.

The OT covenants looked to Christ, made a people of God, fashioned Israel as his chosen one. The new covenant is inaugurated by Christ, is moment by moment building up the heavenly Jerusalem as its citizens make up the "great cloud of witnesses," has enlarged the concept of a chosen people to embrace all mankind.

The Dombes Group (qv) have written beautifully about the new covenant: "Jesus Christ, *Mediator of the New Covenant.*

58. The New Covenant is, in regard to the Old, in a line of continuity and discontinuity. On the one hand it means to take on its meaning, to prolong and accomplish it; on the other, it brings with it a complete innovation in the person of Jesus Christ, the only Mediator between God and men, he on whom the Spirit of God rests in fullness and who, when his reconciling Pasch was concluded, sends the promised Spirit in a manner definitive and irreversible.

A certain number of analogies appear then between the two Covenants, each of which gives structure to an existence in history, the growth of a people in its relations with God.

59. The founding event of the New Covenant is the Pasch of Jesus, accomplished once for all by him who was true man and true God. In Jesus Christ, the new Adam, whose filial response was perfect and whose fraternal love was brought to its extreme, God succeeds in giving himself to us, he frees us from sin and makes us a people who are saved.

60. Henceforth the law is not lapsed for it is at last fully received as a Law of liberty and of love; thanks to the gift of the Holy Spirit, it becomes the New Law of the New Covenant. The Spirit acts at the heart of our freedom as a source of faith, of hope and of love; he assures the cohesion of the believing community.

61. To allow his people to live until the end of time by the definitive gift of the New Covenant and by the Law

of the Spirit, the Lord Jesus gave his disciples the twofold commandment to baptize (Mt 28:19), and to celebrate the Supper of the new Pasch (Lk 22:19). The community of the New Covenant has always recognised that it was founded by these two acts, wherein it perceives, according to two different and complementary modalities, the memorial of the founding event.

62. Such are the Christian Sacraments where the Spirit introduces us and renews us in the New Covenant with God. They ensure our encounter, in his absence, with the crucified one risen, ever present. They enable us to live the filial and fraternal relations which the Spirit arouses in the living memory of Christ Jesus.

63. By reason of the call of God and his promise, the New Covenant is directed to a precise future: the kingdom of God, the fullness of which will arrive in the world through the Lord's return. The disciples of Jesus have received, with the gift of the Spirit, the mission of announcing the Kingdom and opening the world to its coming, by struggling against all forms of evil, for just, brotherly and liberating relations between all men.

64. The diverse traditions of the NT express, each in its own way, the fundamental conviction that the New Covenant, sealed in the event of Jesus Christ, constitutes the definitive gift of the Spirit to men. It is the same Spirit who passes from Jesus to the community called together in his name and to which the pagans are summoned. It is the gift of this same Spirit that the pilgrim community is invited to receive, to celebrate and to live in the Sacraments of Baptism and the Eucharist."[4]

[1]Cf. L. G. da Fonseca, *Diatheke—foedus and testamentum*, BB 8 (1927), 31-50, 161-181, 290-319, 418-441; H. Cazelles, *Etudes sur le Code de l'Alliance*, Paris, 1946; G.E. Mendenhall, *Covenant Forms in Israelite Tradition*, BiblArchaeol 17 (1954), 50-76; *id., Law and Covenant in Israel and the Ancient Near East*, Pittsburgh, 1954; E. F. Siegman, *The Blood of the Covenant*, AER 136 (1957), 167-174; J. L'Hour, *L'Alliance de Sichem*, RB 69 (1962), 5-36, 161-184, 350-368; N. Lohfink, *Die Bundesurkunde des Konigs Josias*, BB 44 (1963), 261-288, 461-498; J. Lecuyer, C.S.Sp., *Le Sacrifice de la nouvelle Alliance*, Le Puy, Lyon, 1962; J. Coppens, *La Nouvelle Alliance en Jer 31:31-34*, CBQ 25 (1963), 12-21; N. Lohfink, Das Siegeslied am Schiffmier, Frankfurt, 1964, 129-50; L. Krinetzki, *Der Bund Gottes mit den Menschen nach dem AT und NT*, Dusseldorf, 1963; esp. D. J. McCarthy, S.J., *Treaty and Covenant*, AB, Rome 1963; *id., Three Covenants in Genesis*, CBQ 26 (1964), 179-189; *Covenant in the Old Testament: The Present State of Inquiry*, CBQ 27 (1965), 217-240; *id., Notes on the Love of God in Deuteronomy and the Father Son Relationship between Yahweh and Israel*, ibid., 144-147; *id., Der Gottesbund im Alten Testament* (Stuttgarter Bibelstudien 13; S. Katholisches Bibelwerk), 1966; V. M. de La Taille, *Mysterium Fidei*, ed. 1931, 53-65; V. Hamp and J. Schmid, LTK 2:770-778; J. Hempel and L. Goppelt, RGG 1:1512-18; Bauer, I, 140146; A. Vonick, NCE, 4:401-405; [2]D. J. McCarthy, op.cit., 240; [3]D. J. McCarthy, *Treaty and Covenant*, 177; [4] *L'Esprit Saint, l'Eglise et les Sacraments*,—agreed statement, Presses de Taizé, 1979.

CRANMER, THOMAS (1489-1556)

A key figure in the establishment of Anglicanism, principal architect of its early liturgy, C. has been the center of polemical writing. It is better in his case, in regard to the Mass, to let facts and texts, that is his own words, speak.[1] C. was well informed on theology in the centuries before the Reformation. In his writings he refers to theologians such as Peter Lombard (qv), Hugh of St. Victor, St. Thomas Aquinas (qv), Durandus, Duns Scotus (qv), John Gerson (qv), Biel (qv). An attempt to reconstruct his personal library has shown that it contained, among other works, those of St. Albert the Great, (qv) Alexander of Hales, Richard of St. Victor, William of Ockham, St. Antoninus, Richard of Middletown, Denis the Carthusian.

C. had invited a number of continental Reformers to England, where they were well received, mostly given lucrative posts, "come over to us and labour in the harvest of the Lord." It is well known that Henry VIII had given no support to the Lutheran theologians who had entered into agreements with some English divines of his time. C. cast a wide net and got Peter Martyr of Vermigil, Martin Bucer from Strasburg, Bernardino Ochino from Siena, Paul Fagius from Switzerland, John Lasco (Laski), nephew of a Polish cardinal. All were opposed to the Catholic idea of the Mass as sacrifice, some were ex-priests.

C. was restrained in his liturgical and doctrinal ambition by Henry VIII. The king died in January 1547 and was succeeded by Edward VI, a minor. In the autumn of that year, in the name of the new Supreme Head of the English Church, a questionnaire was addressed to the English bishops as follows: 1. Whether the sacrifice of the altar was instituted to be received of one man for another, or to be received of every man for himself? 2. Whether the receiving of the said sacrament of one man doth avail another? 3. What is the oblation and sacrifice of Christ in the mass? 4. Wherein consisteth the Mass by Christ's institution? 5. What time the accustomed order began first in the Church, that the priest alone should receive the sacrament? 6. Whether it be convenient that the same custom continue still in this realm? 7. Whether it be convenient that masses satisfactory should continue, that is, priests hired to sing for souls departed? 8. Whether the gospel ought to be taught at the time of the mass, to the understanding of the people being present? 9. Whether in the mass it were convenient to use such speech as the people may understand?

C's answers to these questions reveal his mentality: 1. The sacrament of the altar was not ... instituted to be received of one man for another, but to be received of every man for himself. 2. The receiving of the said sacrament by one man doth avail and profit only him

CRANMER

that receiveth the same. 3. The oblation and sacrifice of Christ in the mass is so called not because Christ indeed is there offered and sacrificed by the priest and the people (for that was done but once by himself on the cross) but it is so called, because it is a memory and representation of that very true sacrifice and immolation which before was made upon the cross. 4. The mass by Christ's institution consisteth in those things which be set forth in the Evangelists Mk XIV, Lk XXII; 1 Cor X and XI. 5. I think the use that the priest alone did receive the sacrament without the people began not within six or hundred years after Christ. 6. I think it more agreeable to the scripture and primitive Church, that the first usage should be restored again, and that the people should receive the sacrament with the priests. 7. I think it not convenient that satisfactory masses should continue. 8. I think it very convenient, that the gospel concerning the death of Christ and our redemption should be taught to the people in the mass. 9. I think it convenient to use the vulgar tongue in the mass, except in certain secret mysteries, whereof I doubt."[2]

To appreciate fully C's ideas, the degree of his personal variation from what was, at the time, accepted doctrine, one should read the views of six of the bishops consulted: these views are set in parallel by Gregory Dix. They are set forth under the name of Bishop Boner. The replies to questions 3 and 7 are particularly informative: 3. "I think it is the presentation of the very Body and Blood of Christ being really present in the sacrament; which presentation the priest maketh at the mass in the name of the church unto God the Father, in memory of Christ's passion and death upon the cross, with thanksgiving therefore and devout prayer that all christian people, and namely they which spiritually join with the priest in the said oblation and of whom he maketh special remembrance, may attain the benefit of the said passion." 7. "I think that such of the schoolmen as do write of masses satisfactory, do define them otherwise than is declared in this question; nevertheless, I think it is not against the word of God but that priests praying in the mass for the living and the dead, and doing other things in the church about the ministration of the sacraments, may take a living for the same."[3]

C. was, moreover, quite explicit on the meaning the Mass had for him, on the 'presence' of Christ therein. "The eating of Christ's flesh and drinking of his blood is not to be understand(ed) simply and plainly, as the words do properly signify, that we do eat and drink him with our mouths; but it is a figurative speech spiritually to be understand(ed), that we must deeply print and fruitfully believe in our hearts that his flesh was crucified and his blood shed for our redemption. And this, our belief in him, is to eat his flesh and drink his

blood, although they be not present here with us, but be ascended into heaven. As our forefathers, before Christ's time, did likewise eat his flesh and drink his blood, which was so far from them that he was not yet born."[4] Or again: "But as the devil is the food of the wicked, which he nourisheth in all iniquity and bringeth up into everlasting damnation, so is Christ the very food of all them that be lively members of his body, and them he nourisheth, bringeth up and cherisheth unto everlasting life. And every good and faithful Christian man feeleth in himself how he feedeth of Christ, eating of his flesh and drinking of his blood. For he putteth the whole hope and trust of his redemption and salvation in that only sacrifice which Christ made upon the cross, having his body there broken and his blood there shed for the remission of his sins. And this great benefit of Christ the faithful man earnestly considereth in his mind, cheweth and digesteth it with the stomach of his heart, spiritually receiving Christ wholly into him and giving again himself wholly unto Christ. And this is the eating of Christ's flesh and drinking of his blood."[5]

On the contrast between his ideas and those of Catholics, C. has this to say: "The papists say that every man, good and evil, eateth the Body of Christ: We say, that both do eat the sacramental bread and drink the wine, but none do eat the very Body of Christ and drink his Blood, but only they that be lively members of his Body. They say that good men eat the Body of Christ and drink his Blood only at that time when they receive the sacrament. We say that they eat, drink and feed of Christ continually, so long as they be members of his Body. . . . They say that the fathers and prophets of the Old Testament did not eat the Body and drink the Blood of Christ. We say that they did eat his Body and drink his Blood although he was not yet born nor incarnated."[6]

Eating the Body of Christ and drinking his Blood for C. was "an inward, spiritual and pure eating with heart and mind, which is to believe in our hearts that his flesh was rent and torn for us upon the cross and his Blood shed for our redemption, and that the same Flesh and Blood now sitteth at the right hand of the Father, making continual intercession for us. . . ."[7]

C. saw the purpose of the Lord's Supper in the same terms it was to prompt an exercise of faith and comfort at the "remembrance of Christ's benefits." In regard to Consecration (qv) he thinks only of "the separation of any thing from a profane and worldly use into a spiritual and godly use" and he asserts that the bread and wine cannot be "partakers of any holiness or godliness or can be the Body and Blood of Christ; but they represent the very Body and Blood of Christ."

C. wrote reverently of the "holy supper of the Lord" which puts us in remembrance of his death and he thought that reception of the sacrament "with a true faith" would ensure forgiveness of sins, that "to eat Christ's flesh and to drink his blood" was to have everlasting life by him.[8] But the fundamental position was what he had stated clearly; it would affect his idea of ministry, for he thought that the ministers of the Eucharist were acting as such, simply as officials of the secular government of the christian state. From such principles came his liturgies.[9]

---

[1]Works: *Writings on the Lord's Supper: Miscellaneous Writings and Letters*, 2 vols., Cambridge, 1844, 1846; *The Remains of Thomas Cranmer*, ed. H. Jenkins, 4 vols., Oxford, 1833; *Cranmer's Writings and Disputations Relative to the Sacrament of the Lord's Supper*, ed. E. Cox, London, The Parker Society, cf. C. H. H. Wright, *Cranmer's Defence of the True and Catholic Doctrine of the Last Supper*, London, 1907; G. W. Bromley, *Thomas Cranmer, Theologian*, 1956; E. C. Ratclif, *The Liturgical Work of Archbishop Cranmer*, JEH, 7 (1956), 189-203; C. W. Dugmore, *The Mass and the English Reformers*, 1958; P. Brooks, *Thomas Cranmer's Doctrine of the Eucharist*, 1965; esp., G. Dix, *The Shape of the Liturgy*, London, 1945, 640-650; esp. F. Clark, *Eucharistic Sacrifice and the Reformation*, 150-162; E. K. Burbridge, *Remains of the Library of Thomas Cranmer*, London, 1892; [2]*Apud* G. Dix, 640-42; [3]*Ibid.*, [4]*Ibid.*, 648, *Defence*, III, 10, 381; [5]*Defence IV*, 2, 426f; Jenkins, II; [6]Jenkins, 357; [7]404; [8]307; [9]cf. Messenger, *The Reformation* I, 286.

CUM HAC NOSTRA AETATE, 14 February 1966

Decree of the Sacred Congregation of Rites on the administration of holy Communion in hospitals.[1] The rules are simplified to allow holy Communion to be given with respect for the difficulties in hospital administration.

---

[1]Text *AAS* 58 (1966) 525-26; English tr., A. Flannery, O.P., I, 61.

CYPRIAN OF CARTHAGE, ST. (d. 258)

C. deals with the Eucharist in his classic treatise on the Lord's Prayer; in his great pastoral document, on the problem of those who had lapsed during persecution and were seeking a return to the Church, *De Lapsis*, but especially in Letter 63, which has been called a little treatise on the Holy Sacrament.[1]

In the *De dominica oratione* he links the prayer 'Give us this day our daily bread' with the Eucharist, recalling the words of the Master, that he is the bread of life, promising eternal life, his warning, too, that those who do not eat his flesh and drink his blood will not have life in them, to end thus: "and therefore we beg that our bread, that is Christ, be given to us daily, so that as we remain and live in Christ, we should not depart from his sanctification and body."[2]

In the *De Lapsis* C. speaks of those still reeking with their defilement by pagan worship doing violence to the body of the Lord; by thus doing violence to his body and blood—since their ill deed has not been purged "they sin even more with their hands and mouth against the Lord than when they denied the Lord."[3]

Yet C. would allow the *lapsi* to communicate if threatened by a new persecution, that they should be "strengthened by the blood and body of Christ." "For how shall we teach or urge them to shed their blood in confessing the name, if we deny them the blood of Christ in the moment of combat?"[4]

With this realism C. is also a great exponent of symbolism (qv), as would be St. Augustine (qv) in the Latin church and as had been St. Clement and Origen (qqv) in the Greek church. Passages in which he insists on the duty of using wine and not water only in the Eucharist, expounding the symbolism of the water and the wine, taken out of context and apart from his other writings, have been used to support the contention that he viewed the Eucharist symbolically only: this is to misrepresent him totally.

On the Mass as a sacrifice C. is more explicit and satisfying than any of his predecessors: "For if Jesus Christ our Lord and God is himself the chief priest of God the Father, and has offered himself a sacrifice to the Father, and has commanded this to be done in commemoration of himself, certainly that priest truly discharges the office of Christ who imitates that which Christ did; he then offers a true and full sacrifice in the Church of God the Father, when he proceeds to offer it according to what he sees Christ himself to have offered."[5]

C. thought that both the Last Supper and the Eucharistic sacrifice of the Church are the representation of Christ's sacrifice on the Cross. "We make mention of his passion in all sacrifices because the Lord's passion is the sacrifice which we offer. Therefore we ought to do nothing else than what he did." Our oblation and sacrifice must respond to his passion. The sacrifice is offered for the departed—as for the martyrs. It is in such a clear doctrinal setting that his teaching on symbolism is acceptable: "In this very sacrament our people are shown to be made one, so that in like manner as many grains, collected and ground and mixed together into one mass, make one bread, so in Christ, who is the heavenly bread; we may know, that there is one body, with which our number is joined and united." Again on the water and wine: "When the water is mingled in the cup with wine, the people are made one with Christ, and the assembly of the believers is associated and conjoined with him on whom it believes."[6]

This symbolism of the species as a sign cannot be a denial of the real presence, not with one who said: "Who was more a priest of the most high God than Our

Lord Jesus Christ, who offered a sacrifice to God the Father, offering the same that Melchizedek offered, that is bread and wine, namely his body and blood."[7]

---

[1]Texts: *S. Cypriani opera*, ed Hartel; Vienna 1868-71; CSEL III, 1-3: J. Solano, *Textos*, I, 140-183; Quasten, *Monumenta*, 356-58; cf. Peters, *Cyprians Lehre über die Eucharistie*, *Der Katholik*, 53 (1873) I, 609-687, II, 25-39; A. Schweiler, *Die Elemente der Eucharistie in den ersten drei Jahrhunderten* (FLD), Mainz, 1903, 10-119; A. Struckmann, *Die Gegenwart Christi in der hl. Eucharistie nach den schriftlichen Quellen der vornizanischen Zeit*, Vienna, 1905, 306-321; G. Rauschen, *Eucharistie und Bussakrament in den ersten sechs Jahrhunderten der Kirche*, Freiburg i.B., 1910; W. C. Bishop, *The African Rite*, *JTS* 13 (1911-12); 263ff; F. Cabrol, O.S.B., *Afrique*, II, 1, DCAL I, 1591-619; G. Bareille, DTC V, 1132-1135; Quasten, *Patrology*, II, 381-83; M. Lepin, *L'idée du sacrifice*, 70ff; A. D'Ales, *La théologie de Saint Cyprien*, Paris, 1922, 249-271; P. Batiffol, *L'Eucharistie*, 227-247; [2]CSEL, III, 1, 280-81; [3]*Ibid.*, 248; [4]*Epist* 57, CSEL III, 2, 652; [5]*Epist* 63, 14, CSEL III, 3, 713; [6]*Epist*. 63, 13; [7]*Epist* 63, 4, 703.

CYRIL OF ALEXANDRIA, ST., DOCTOR OF THE CHURCH (d. 444)

The great doctor of Ephesus adverts to the mystery of the Eucharist in many of his writings, his biblical commentaries, in the latter case especially dealing with the institution (qv) narratives and at length with the Johannine Eucharistic passages.[1] He can take up Eucharistic themes also in his controversial writings. In fact the Christological problem which occupied him so much is never far from his reflection on the Eucharist. He excels in his account of the effects of the Sacrament. His key word here is 'vivifying,' 'life-giving.'

Some extracts from Fr. D. J. Sheerin's excellent work, *The Eucharist* in *The Message of the Fathers of the Church* series:

"But he said quite plainly, 'This is my Body,' and 'This is my Blood,' so that you may not suppose that the things you see are a type; rather, in some ineffable way they are changed by God, who is able to do all things, into the Body and Blood of Christ truly offered. Partaking of them, we take into us the life-giving and sanctifying power of Christ. For it was needful that he, through the Holy Spirit in us, in a manner proper to God, be mixed, as it were, with our bodies by means of his holy flesh and precious blood. These are ours for a life-giving blessing in the bread and wine, so that we may not be appalled seeing flesh and blood offered on the holy tables of the churches. For God puts the power of life into the offerings, bringing himself down to our weakness, and he changes them into the energy of his own life."[2]

"Then let those who, because of their folly have never accepted faith in Christ listen to this: 'Unless you eat the flesh of the Son of Man, and drink his blood, you do not have eternal life in you.' For completely, without a

share, indeed without a taste in the life in holiness and blessedness do they remain who have not received Jesus through the mystic blessing. For he is life by nature, according as he was begotten by the Living Father (Jn 6:57). Moreover, his holy Body is not less life-giving, for it was, in a way, gathered to, and, in an indescribable manner, united to the Word who engenders life in all things."[3]

"For he (Luke) tells us that he took a cup and gave thanks, and said: 'Take this, and divide it with one another.' Now by his giving thanks, by which is meant his speaking to God the Father in the manner of a prayer, he signified to us that he, so to speak, shares and takes part in his good pleasure in granting to us the life-giving blessing which was bestowed upon us, for every grace, and every perfect gift (cf. Ja 1:17) comes to us from the Father by the Son in the Holy Spirit."[4]

"And not as common flesh do we receive it, not at all, nor as a man sanctified and associated with the Word according to the unity of dignity, or as having had a divine indwelling, but as truly the life-giving and very flesh of the Word himself."[5]

"We celebrate in the churches the holy, life-giving, and unbloody sacrifice. The Body and also the Precious Blood, which is offered we believe not to be that of a common man and of anyone like us, but we receive it, rather, as having become the very Body and Blood of the Word who gives life to all."[6]

---

[1]J. Solano, *Textos*, II, 335-445; D. J. Sheerin, *The Eucharist, Message of the Fathers of the Church* series, Wilmington, 1986, 224, 226, 229, 275; cf. J. Mahé, *L'Eucharistie d'après Saint Cyrille d'Alexandrie*, RHE 8 (1907), 677-696; id., DTC III, 2520ff; P. Batiffol, *L'Eucharistie*, 466-477; H. du Manoir, S.J., *Dogme et Spiritualité chez Saint Cyrille d'Alexandrie*, Paris, 1944, 181f; 185-218; 435f; H. Chadwick, *Eucharist and Christology in the Nestorian Controversy*, JTS, NS, 2 (1951) 145-164; E. Gebremedhin, *Life-Giving Blessing: An Inquiry into the Eucharistic Doctrine of St. Cyril of Alexandria*, Uppsala, 1977; [2]*Commentary on Matthew*, fragments, TU 61, 255-56; Sheerin, 225; [3]*Comment on the Gospel of John*, IV, 2, ed. P. E. Pusey, Oxford, 1872, 1, 518, Sheerin, 227; [4]*Homily on the Gospel of Luke*, No. 142; ed. R. Payne Smith, 664, Sheerin, 230; [5]*Third Letter to Nestorius*, ACO, 1, 1, 1, 37-38, Sheerin, 277; [6]*Explanation of Eleventh Anathema*, ACO, 1, 1, 5, 24-25, Sheerin, 278.

CYRIL OF JERUSALEM, ST., DOCTOR OF THE CHURCH (c. 315-386)

With his contemporaries Ambrose and John Chrysostom (qqv), C. ranks as a great Doctor of the Eucharist. His doctrine is contained in the Fourth and Fifth Mystagogical Lectures.[1] At once there arises a question of authenticity. The Greek manuscript tradition names Cyril as author. But one codex gives as author John II, Cyril's successor in the see of Jerusalem;

four codices attribute them to both Cyril and John. There are differences of style in the Lectures, when they are compared with the Lenten Lectures, which are of undoubted authenticity. One hypothesis is that the text of the Mystagogical Lectures was taken down by a scribe, used subsequently and finally revised by John II of Jerusalem. They are associated with C. and do represent teaching in his church.[2]

In the Fifth Mystagogical Lecture, C. gives an account of the Eucharistic Liturgy: The Hand-washing; The Kiss; The Dialogue; The Memorial of Creation and Sanctus; The Epiclesis and Consecration; The Intercession; The Lord's Prayer; The Communion.

The Institution Narrative (qv) is not included, either because it was too well known or too sacred—reserved from the uninitiated—or possibly, a remote possibility, because it was not used. The Epiclesis reads thus: "Next after sanctifying ourselves by these spiritual songs, we implore the merciful God to send forth his Holy Spirit upon the offering to make the bread the body of Christ and the wine the blood of Christ. For whatever the Holy Spirit touches is hallowed and changed."[3] The opening sentence in the next section is significant: "Next, when the spiritual sacrifice, the bloodless worship, has been completed, over that sacrifice of propitiation we beseech God for the public peace of the Churches, for the good estate of the world, for the Emperors, for the armed forces and our allies, for those in sickness, for the distressed: for all, in a word, who need help, we all pray and offer this sacrifice."[4]

One may contend that the Institution Narrative would easily fit between these two sections of the liturgical account.

In the Fourth Lecture, C. expresses his doctrine of the real Presence unequivocally—though attempts have been made to interpret his clear words in a virtual (qv) or dynamic sense (see article Berengar of Tours). His words are: "The teaching of the blessed Paul is of itself sufficient to give you full assurance about the divine mysteries by admission to which you have become one body and blood with Christ. For Paul just now proclaimed that 'on the night in which he was betrayed our Lord Jesus Christ took bread and, also giving thanks, broke it and gave it to his disciples saying, 'Take, eat: this is my body'; then, taking the cup, he gave thanks and said, 'Take, drink: this is my blood.' When the Master himself has explicitly said of the bread, 'This is my body,' will anyone still dare to doubt? When he is himself our warranty, saying, 'This is my blood' who will ever waver and say it is not his blood?"[5]

C. recalls the miracle in Cana in Galilee: "Once at Cana in Galilee he changed water into wine by his sovereign will; is it not credible, then, that he changed wine into his blood? If as a guest at a physical marriage he performed this stupendous miracle, shall he not far more readily be confessed to have bestowed on 'the friends of the bridegroom' the fruition of his own body and blood?

"With perfect confidence, then, we partake as of the body and blood of Christ. For in the figure (typos) of bread his body is given to you, and in the figure of wine his blood, that by partaking of the body and blood of Christ you may become of one body and blood with him. For when his body and blood become the tissue of our members, we become Christ-bearers and as the blessed Peter said, 'partakers of the divine nature.'"

C. recalls the error of the Jews who took Jesus' words for physical eating of his flesh and he makes the contrast with the loaves of proposition of the Old Testament. He repeats his doctrine: "Do not think then of the elements as bare bread and wine; they are, according to the Lord's declaration, the body and blood of Christ. Though sense suggests the contrary, let faith be your stay. Instead of judging the matter by taste, let faith give you an unwavering confidence that you have been privileged to receive the body and blood of Christ."[6]

C. then looks for foreshadowing of the Eucharist in OT texts. He returns to his main thesis: "In this knowledge, and in the firm conviction that the bread which is seen is not bread, though it is bread to the taste, but the body of Christ, and that the visible wine is not wine, though taste will have it so, but the blood of Christ, and that it was of this that David sang of old: 'oil to make his face shine, and bread to strengthen man's heart,' strengthen your heart, partaking of this bread as spiritual, and make cheerful the face of your soul."[7]

This is very clearly the doctrine of the Real Presence, though C. does not advance an explanation of how it comes about, or its mode. He uses the word *metaballestai*, for the change, but it seems forcing the texts to see in them the theory of transubstantiation (qv). He considers the invocation of the Holy Spirit by the epiclesis as that which effects the change of the bread and wine into the body and blood of Christ. He is the first to give the form of the epiclesis which will become general for the Oriental Liturgies.

C., as is clear from the passage quoted from the Intercession, thought of the Eucharist as a sacrifice, spiritual, bloodless, propitiatory. In the passage on the Intercession he expresses two other important points: the sacrifice is "most dread" (awe-inspiring), an idea which would continue through the other sources of the Antiochene liturgy, St. John Chrysostom, Theodore of Mopsuestia and Narses (qqv); and he justifies prayers for the dead at Mass: "Next we pray also for the holy Fathers and Bishops who have fallen asleep, and generally for all who have gone before us, believing that this will be of the greatest benefit to the souls of those on whose behalf our supplication is offered in the presence of the holy, the most dread sacrifice." To those who ask how can this supplication avail, he replies: "Well, suppose a king banished persons who had offended him, and then their relatives wove a garland and presented it to him on behalf of those undergoing punishment, would he not mitigate their sentence? In the same way, offering our supplications to him for those who have fallen asleep, even though they be sinners, we, though we weave no garland, offer Christ slain for our sins, propitiating the merciful God on both their and our own behalf."[8]

[1]Text: W. K. Reischl and J. Rupp, Munich 1848, 1860; J. Quasten, *Monumenta eucharistica*, 69-111; F. L. Cross, *St. Cyril of Jerusalem's Lectures on the Christian Sacraments*, S.P.C.K., London, 1951—text and English tr.; French tr., A. Piedagnel, *Cyrille de Jerusalem, Catéchèses mystagogiques*, text with tr., SC 126, 1966; English, E. H. Gifford, LNPF, VII, 1894; L. P. McCauley, S.J. and A. A. Stephenson, The Fathers of the Church, 64, 1970—used here; German, P. Hauser, *Des heiligen Cyrillus . . . Katechesen* (Bibliothek der Kirchenväter), Munich, 1922; J. Solano, *Textos*, I, 322-337; J. Bouvet, *Cyrillus Hierosolymitanus, Catéchèses baptismales et mystagogiques*, Namur, 1962; Cf. Becker, *Der hl. Cyrillus von Jerusalem uber die reale Gegenwart Christi in der heiligen Eucharistie, Der Katholik* 1 (1872), 422-449; 539-554, 641-661; V. Schmitt, *Die Verheissung der Eucharistie (Joh 6) bei den Antiochern Cyrillus von Jerusalem und Johannes Chrysostomus und Johannes Chrysostomus*, Würzburg, 1903; R. Rios, *St. Cyril of Jerusalem on the Holy Eucharist: Pax* 25 (1935), 77-81; J. Quasten, *Mysterium tremendum. Eucharistische Frömmigkeits-auffassungen des vierten Jahrhunderts: Vom christlichen Mysterium (Festschrift O. Casel)*, Düsseldorf, 1951, 66-75; K. Baus, *Die eucharistische Glaubensverkundigung (Festschrift J. A. Jungmann)*, ed. F. X. Arnold and B. Fischer, Freiburg i. B. 1953, 55-70; P. Batiffol, *L'Eucharistie*, 371-381; X. le Bachelet, DTC, III, 1908, 2527-2577; G. Bareille, *ibid.*, V, 1143-44; J. Quasten, *Patrology*, III, 362-377; L. Deiss, *Springtime*, 269-289; G. Bardy, DSp II, 2, 2683--2687; [2]For the authenticity cf. *The Fathers of the Church*, vol II, 143ff; [3]*Ibid.*, 196; [4]*Ibid.*, 197; [5]*Ibid.*, 181; for commentary cf. Appended Note C, 186-190; [6]*Ibid.*, 182, 183; [7]185, 186; [8]*Ibid.*, 198; cf. E. Yarnold, *The Authorship of the Mystagogical Catecheses attributed to Cyril of Jerusalem, Heythrop Journal, 19* (1978) 143-61; Clairs Patrum Graecorum, II, 297. D. Sheerin, *The Eucharist*, 64-73.

D

DE LA TAILLE, MAURICE (1872-1933)

The publication of *Mysterium Fidei*, 1921, was the outstanding theological event since the appearance of M. J. Scheeben's *The Mysteries of Christianity*.[1] No other theological work between the two world wars rivalled the intellectual impact of De la Taille's monumental treatise. The author was French, had been educated in England, had held academic posts in the Catholic University of Angers and the Gregorian in Rome; as a military chaplain he had wartime pastoral experience. Though completed in 1915 his work was not published until 1921.

De la T's starting point in study had been the *Epistle to the Hebrews*; with time he accumulated massive erudition, in every relevant domain, biblical, patristic, liturgical, magisterial, historical development. When he later appealed to "the teaching of the whole of patristic antiquity as well as of Holy Writ," to the "doctrine of the liturgies ... the doctrine preferred at the Council of Trent by the most eminent among the Fathers"[2] he was speaking at first hand, which did not automatically imply acceptance by other scholars. It is possible that many who were captivated by his theory were principally influenced by his exceptional learning—so erudite a scholar could not have gone astray! To which add another important factor: Catholic theologians had not yet recovered from the constricting, at times unjust, procedures adopted against Modernism; most of them chose safe, conventional options. Here was a startlingly original thinker, unafraid of the effect which his bold conception would produce. A fighter, too, as he proved in a whole series of articles in

different theological reviews replying to his critics—his command of English was here an advantage.[3] The third ed. of his work, carried over 100 pp. of *Vindiciae* (justifications), added to the 650 p. volume in large format; pages packed with scholarship.

For De la T. the essence of sacrifice is oblation (qv), but he links immolation with it: "The word 'to sacrifice' then refers to the act of a priest sacrificing, that is making or bearing a gift to God, and as such it signifies oblation *in recto*, and only *in obliquo* immolation of slaying. For true sacrifice then it suffices that something be offered either as about to be immolated or as immolated."[4] The victim may be offered as to be immolated, or it is offered by immolation, or it is offered as having been immolated.

Applying this general principle to Christ's sacrifice De la T. put forth a theory of amazing originality: At the Last Supper Christ made the ritual, liturgical oblation necessary for the sacrifice of the cross, in such wise that the two were one. When most people think of De la T., it is this idea which occurs to them: "I hold," he wrote in one of the apologetic essays called forth by the controversy, "that Christ our Lord on the night of the Last Supper by consecrating the bread into his body delivered up to death for us and the wine into his blood shed for many unto the remission of sins, visibly, ritually, liturgically offered up to God and his death and Passion, whereby he was to be immolated at the hands of the Jews, a Victim for the ransom of the world. Thus in that sacred mystery of our faith which is the redemption of mankind by the sacrifice of the Body and Blood of our Saviour, I distinguish a twofold immolation. One perfectly real, even bloody, another previous to that in the Supper, not real, but representative, symbolical, sacramental (all these words in the present case express but one thought) not bloody but unbloody. I hold that the unbloody immolation which represented the bloody one to come, was the act by which Christ pledged himself in the sight of the Father and of men; thus making over to God the Lamb to be slain, and by the very fact offering, in the ritual sense of the word, not internally, but outwardly, not by a mere purpose or promise to give but by the actual giving and delivering up of the gift, not in mere figure but most really and formally, the Victim that was henceforth sacred to God and as such due to its ultimate fate. I consider then that Christ offered as High Priest according to the order and likeness of Melchizedek and yet in that very same capacity offered nothing but the sacrifice of redemption, the sacrifice of his Passion and Death; but he offered it in the Eucharist of the supper night."

De la T. maintained his central thesis: "I do not therefore admit that there were two distinct and complete sacrifices, offered by Christ, one in the Cenacle, the other on Calvary. There was a sacrifice at the Last Supper but it was the sacrifice of redemption; and there was a sacrifice on the Cross, but it was the self-same sacrifice continued and completed; he offered it to be immolated; he offered it as immolated of old."[4]

"Thus," he says elsewhere, "the Supper and the Passion answer each other. They complete and compenetrate each other. The one presents to our eyes the sacerdotal, sensible, ritual oblation, wherein consists the mystic immolation; the other adds to it the real, bloody, all-sufficient immolation, of which the first was the figure. In the Supper Room, amid a scene of splendour which he has designedly procured, Christ is chiefly the priest; on Calvary, in his silence and nakedness, he is chiefly the victim. On the one hand we have the Body and Blood symbolically separated, and under cover of this appearance, doomed to the death whose image they bear. On the other hand we have the Blood that flows till it is drained, in order to substantiate the prediction made at the Supper, realize the sacramental figure and carry out the oblation. The whole Passion is sacrifice, because the whole Passion is bloody immolation offered by the Priest; and the Supper is the same Sacrifice, one and indivisible, because it is the gesture of the Priest, offering, in an unbloody rite, the same bloody immolation. The Passion is *immolatio hostiae oblatae*; the Supper is *oblatio hostiae immolandae*: OBLATION WHICH PERSEVERES, AND THAT VISIBLY, THROUGH THE TORMENTS OF THE SAVIOUR, INASMUCH AS IT IS NOWHERE REVOKED, INASMUCH AS IT IS EVERY-

WHERE COUNTERSIGNED BY THE BLOOD THAT FLOWS TO RATIFY IT. (Author's capitals). And thus, there are not two sacrifices of our Redeemer, an unbloody sacrifice, followed by a bloody sacrifice; but there is one only Sacrifice, complete and perfect, both on the part of the Priest who celebrates with bread and wine, and on the part of the Victim put to death.[5]

But Christ is now in glory and Mass is celebrated on our altars. In a general way De la T. offered this idea: "But it is permissible to argue back to the Supper from Mass. For if Christ is offered in the Mass as (having been) immolated on the cross, he must have been offered in the Supper as about to be immolated on the cross. If we offer the death of Christ as having taken place, Christ (as we contend) must have offered his death which was imminent. One cannot be affirmed of the Mass unless the other is concluded as to the Supper. Unless you agree with us as to the Supper, you will appear to give little consent to the Council (of Trent, qv)."[6]

More positively the author laid down such theses as these: "Offered in the Supper and delivered in the passion Christ's sacrifice received a certain consummation in the resurrection and ascension, and it continues eternally as is clear from Scripture, the Fathers and theological argument."[7] "Christ instituted a Eucharistic rite to be celebrated by us."[8]

A crucial point for De la T. was Christ's role in each Mass. How is the identity between the sacrifice of Christ and the Mass ensured? De la T. laid down this thesis: "Although Christ is the priest of all our sacrifices, nevertheless he does not in each particular case himself make a new oblation."[9] In heaven Christ is in the state of a victim formerly immolated and in this sense a 'passive sacrifice.' The active, new oblation repeated each time, from which the Mass has its quality of proper, genuine sacrifice, this oblation is made solely by the Church, or the priest, its representative.... Eucharistic oblation is then an act not of Christ but of the Church. The immolation is on one side and the other purely representative, the oblation on the contrary is absolutely real, oblation by Christ at the Supper, at Mass by the Church.

Christ has given his Church the power and the order to offer him; he remains the principal and universal cause of the sacrifical action: really the unique priest. The priest, minister of the Church acts as a particular, subordinate cause. He offers in virtue of the unique oblation once for all made by Christ. There are differences: Christ offered himself to suffer death, whereas we offer him as put to death long ago; he offered himself prefiguring his future immolation, but we offer him recalling in tangible form his past immolation.

Is the identity between the Mass and the sacrifice of Christ preserved in this aspect of De la T.'s theory? Is the identity guaranteed only—as for Scotus—by the institution by Christ? Other questions have been raised: Who, before De la T., held that the Supper and Calvary were one sacrifice? He appealed to St. Gregory of Nyssa (qv) and Procopius as indirectly supporting the view, and as direct supporters to St. Ambrose (qv), Hesychius, Cassiodorus, as to many ancient liturgies. He defended himself too against those who cited Trent against him.[10]

How does De la T. stand in the history of theology? We are not here concerned with some other work which he published, on the nature of contemplative prayer, on grace and the divine indwelling. Foreseeing a sale for his huge book of some thirty copies, he passed 3,000 before too long: itself an achievement. He could count names like Bishop MacDonald, Dom Lambert Beadouin, O.S.B. and Fr. Ramirez, O.P., with other enthusiastic admirers, as he had caustic critics like Fr. V. McNabb, O.P., and the inflexible opposition of his fellow professor at the Gregorian, Louis Billot (qv). More powerful perhaps was the criticism of another learned theologian of the Mass, Marius Lepin (qv), because he agreed with De la T. on the idea of oblation.[11] Will some elements of his synthesis, notably the identity of sacrifice in Supper and Calvary survive and find their place in the ultimate solution to the problem?

---

[1] Principal relevant works, besides definitive ed. *Mysterium Fidei*, 1931, *Esquisse du mystère de la foi*, ed. 2, Paris 1924; English tr. *Outline of the Mystery of Faith*, London, 1930; in *Eucharistia, Encyclopédie populaire sur l'Eucharistie*, 1934, 153-181; articles from many reviews, with *Outline* ed. J.B. Schimpf, S.J., *The Mystery of Faith and Human Opinion contrasted and defined*, London, 1930; as well as many review articles and notices, cf. as favourable: A. d'Alès, S.J., *De Eucharistia*, Paris, 1929, 109-124; J. Connell, *De sacramentis Ecclesiae*, Bruges, 1933, 271-73; Girolamo da Fallette, *Stato attuale degli studi riguardo al sacrifício della S. Messa, Palestra del Clero*, 1933, 124-140; also approximating to De la T.F. de Laversin, *Esquisse d'une synthèse du sacrifice, RSR* (1927), 193-209; G. Albarelli, *Il santo sacrifizio della Messa*, Pesaro, 1937; among critics of De la T. cf. Anonymous, *L'Ami du Clergé*, 1923, 72ff; J. Brodie Brosnan, *The Sacrifice of the New Law*, London, 1926; J. Clesse, *Etude critique de certaines propositions du'Mysterium Fidei*, Dolbin, 1927; *id., Le sacrifice de la Messe, Etudes Religieuses*, n. 433-434; Liège 1938, 5-19; V. Cremers, *Quelques réflexions sur le 'Mysterium Fidei', Studia Catholica*, 1925/1926, 57-70, 179-202; V. McNabb, O.P., *A New Theory of the Sacrifice of the Mass, IER*, 1924, 561-573; V. Héris, O.P., *Le Mystère du Christ*, Paris, 1928, 362; J. Puig de la Bellacasa, *La esencia del sacrificio de la Misa, EstEccl*, 1929, 265-380 (On the Billot [qv] De la T. controversy); *id., ibid.*, 1931, 65-96, 385-406, 538-553; *ibid.*, 1932, 95-103; A. Verhamme, *De distinctione sacrificium Crucis inter et sacrificium Missae, Collationes Brugenses* 1936, 230-36; further details in *The Mystery of Faith and Human Opinion, passim*; summary I. Jimenez, *En el cinquantenario del 'Mysterium Fidei' de Maurice de la Taille*, Santiago de Chile,1971 pp. 305; A. Michel, DTC X, 1245, 46; M. Lepin (qv), *L'Idée du sacrifice de la Messe*, etc., 658-720; J. Lebreton, S.J., *RSR 24*

(1934), 5-11; B. Leeming, S.J., *The Month*, 163 (1934), 31-40; M. J. O'Connell, S.J., NCE IV 726-27, DTC Tables, XVI, 2, 2896; [2] *The Mystery of Faith . . .* 13, 14; [3] *Mysterium Fidei*, I, 12; [4] *The Mystery of Faith*, 231; [5] *Outline, ibid.*, 13; [6] *Mysterium Fidei*, Elucidatio XII, 130; [7] *Elucidatio*, XII, 130; [8] *Elucidatio*, XVI, 182; [9] *Elucidatio* XXIII, 394; [10] *Vindiciae*, 724; [11] *Op.cit.*

DE LUGO, JOHN CARDINAL (1583-1660)

The Spanish Jesuit, who had been a lawyer before entering the Society, was educated in Salamanca and taught for some years in Spain before coming to Rome where he quickly acquired a considerable reputation as a theologian: he was rewarded with the Cardinal's hat. In the domain of Eucharistic theology his theory centred on the idea of sacrifice as destruction. "We say that it is of the essence of sacrifice to be the affirmation of the divine excellence as such that our life may fittingly be destroyed in its worship, whether this be real destruction of our own life or of some other thing through which our disposition is expressed, our own destruction not being allowed or appropriate."[1] To establish this position De L. seeks to eliminate the other opinions which had been proposed on the subject.

Thus De L. dismisses the theory of a vocal oblation, made either before (the Offertory) or after (Anamnesis) (qv), the Consecration,—sacrifice must comprise real action, distinct from words; likewise he is not happy with the theory of Cano, which puts the essence of the sacrifice in the breaking of the bread, for this rite is not universally used—Cano's theory was generally abandoned: nor will De L. agree that the essence of the sacrifice is in the Communion, though he considers this integral to the Mass.

The final option is for the Consecration as the essence of the Mass, and the next step is to show how the idea of destruction, dear to the author, is realized therein. Not by the destruction of the substance of bread and wine, to God's honour, for this is insufficient in relation to the sacrifice of the body and blood of Christ; nor, as Suarez would have it, by the disappearance of the bread and wine to allow for the production (qv) of the body and blood, what is principally offered to God—an opinion not acceptable to most theologians; nor again, as Vasquez maintained, by eliminating the idea of destruction in a relative or memorial sacrifice, as the Mass is—but this would reduce it to a mere memorial, not a true sacrifice. Lessius, with whom Vasquez had already disagreed, thought that there was a virtual immolation in the double consecration, for this is an image of immolation, not the real thing.

To his own opinion then: though the Communion is essential to the sacrifice, this substantially has taken place in the Consecration. To justify his idea of destruction in the Consecration he resorts to a piece of subtle word play: "To explain how consecration is substantially sacrificial action, note that when we claim that destruction is of the essence of sacrifice the word destruction is not always to be understood in the sense of substantial physical or metaphysical corruption of the host, so that the host, by the force of sacrificial action, in so far as it is at the end of that action, may be in a state of diminution, at least ceasing to be in a human manner. With this assumption, it will be easy to explain how by the consecration the body of Christ is sacrificed. For, though it is not substantially destroyed by the consecration, it is so in a human manner, in so far as it is placed in a state of diminution, such that it is rendered useless for ordinary needs of the human body, adapted to other different uses in the way of food. From the human point of view it is as if it had become bread and were made ready as food. But such a change is sufficient to have sacrifice."[2] To become eatable and serve no other use is greater change than any other in this context.

Though the sacrifice begins and is essentially in existence at the Consecration, the Communion completes the 'destruction' of the host. The sacrifice lasts then until the Communion and is completed and ended by it: "I add that each action pertains to the substance of sacrifice in this way, that the Consecration having taken place, already substantial sacrificial action has taken place, but as the communion takes place another part of the same substance is present."[3] De L. is firm in the view that the double Consecration must be made. "The answer to arguments of the contrary opinion is in the will of Christ, who instituted such a sacrificial rite, by which his death is clearly represented."[4] Not even the Pope can dispense from this obligation.

---

[1]Works, *Opera omnia*, Lyons 1636ff, esp. *Tractatus de venerabili Eucharistiae sacramento*, Migne, *Theologiae cursus completus*, 1841, vol 23; cf. P. Bernard, DTC, IX (1926), 1071ff; A. Michel, DTC X 1185-87; M. Lepin, *L'Idée du sacrifice de la Messe*, 426-430; D. Stone, *A History of the Doctrine of the Holy Eucharist*, II (1909), 373-7; quotation, *Op.cit.*, disp. 19, sect. i, number 1; Migne, 703; [2]*Ibid.*, number 67, 730; [3]*Ibid.*, number 64, 729; [4]*Ibid.*, number 112, 749.

DER BALYZEH, THE EUCHOLOGY OF

In the ruins of the monastery of Balyzeh near Assiout in Upper Egypt, a number of Greek papyrus fragments were discovered in 1907; the monastery had been destroyed more than a thousand years before. With such small items intelligent guesswork was necessary. Most scholars accepted the suggestion that they were from the prayers of the Mass. The conjecture was confirmed when, some forty years later, further fragments were discovered. The original text was a euchology; what interests us is the anaphora, (qv) that of the ancient Mass. Restoration has been attempted by experts—italics show their additions to what is in the fragments. The papyrus is of the sixth century; part of the text is clearly much earlier. That of the Liturgy of the Mass is here given:

Prayer of Intercession: *May* your bless*ing come upon your* people *who do your will.* Raise up the fallen, bring back those who have strayed, console the faint-hearted. For you are above every principality, power, force, and dominion, above everything that can be named in this world and *in the world to come.*
Preface: *Near to you* stand *the thousands of holy angels and the* numberless *hosts of archangels. Near to you* stand the Cherubim with many eyes. Around you stand the Seraphim, each with six wings; two to hide the face, two to hide the feet, and two to fly. Unceasingly they all proclaim your holiness. With all their acclamations of your holiness receive also our acclamation who sing to you:
Sanctus: Holy, holy, holy is the Lord, the God Sabaoth! Heaven and earth are filled with your glory (Is 6:2-3).
Epiclesis: Fill us with your glory! And deign to send your Holy Spirit on these offerings that you have created, and make this bread to become the body of our Lord and Saviour Jesus Christ, and this chalice to become the blood of the New *Testament* of our Lord, God, and Saviour, Jesus Christ.
Prayer for the Church: *And* as this bread was scattered *on the mountains,* the hills, and in the valleys, and was gathered to become a single body . . . and as this wine, sprung from the *holy* vine of *David,* and this water, sprung from the spotless Lamb, were mixed and became a single mystery, so too gather the catholic Church of Jesus Christ.
Institution Narrative; For our Lord *Jesus Christ,* on the night when he *was betrayed, took bread in his holy hands, gave* thanks and *blessed it, sanctified and broke it, gave* it to his *disciples* and apostles, saying: '*Take and eat* of it, all of you. This *is* my body which is given for you in forgiveness of sins.'

Likewise after the supper, he took the chalice and blessed it, drank of it and gave it to them, saying: 'Take, drink of it, all of you. This is my blood which is poured out for you for the forgiveness of sins. *Do this in memory of me.*' Each time that you eat this bread and that you drink this chalice, you announce my death, you proclaim my resurrection, *you make mem*ory *of me.' Anamnesis*: We announce your death, *we procl*aim your resurrection, and we pray. . . .
Communion prayer: Give *your servants* the power of

the Holy Spirit, the confirmation and increase of faith, the hope of eternal life to come, through our Lord Jesus Christ. Through him, glory to you, Father, with the Holy Spirit for ever. Amen."

The lines "Raise up the fallen ... fainthearted" are borrowed from the 'Great Prayer' of St. Clement of Rome. There is a borrowing from the *Didache* in the Prayer for the Church—the "bread scattered on the mountains. . . . " The place of the Epiclesis before the consecration was thought for a long time to be unique. In 1940 Lefort found an ancient anaphora with the same peculiarity. Opinions vary on the date of the Der-Balyzeh Papyrus: T. Schermann and P. Drews, c. 225; F.E. Brightman, c. 350; B. Capelle, c. 575.

---

[1]Ed. P. de Puniet, *Report of the 19th Eucharistic Congress held in Westminster* 9-13 September 1908, London, 1909; id., *Le nouveau papyrus liturgique d'Oxford, RBen* 26 (1909), 34-51; T. Schermann, TU XXXVI, 1b, 1910; C. Wessely, PO XVII, 1924; C.H. Roberts (text) and B. Capelle, O.S.B., (commentary), *An early Euchologium. The Der-Balyzeh Papyrus enlarged and reedited, Bibliothèque du Muséon*, 23, Louvain, 1949; cf. S. Salaville, A.A., *Le nouveau fragment d'anaphore égyptien de Deir Balyzeh, Echos d'Orient* 12 (1909), 329-335; id., *La double épiclèse des anaphores égyptiennes, ibid.*, 13 (1910), 133f; A. Bugnini, C.M., *L'eucologio di Der-Balyzeh, EphLit*, 65 (1951), 157-170, Latin tr. A. di Clemente, 160-170; P.E. Kahle, *Bala'izah*, Coptic texts from Deir Bala'izah in Upper Egypt, 2 vols, 1954; K. Gamber, *Das Eucharistiegebet im Papyrus von Der-Balyzeh und die Samstagabend-Agapen in Ägypten*, in *Ostkirchliche Studien*, 7 (1958), 48-65; J. Van Haelst, *Une Nouvelle Reconstruction du Papyrus Liturgique der Der-Balizeh, ETL*, 14 (1969), 444-55; J. Quasten, *Monumenta*, 37-45, bibl. 37; F. Cabrol, O.S.B., DACL II, 1910, 1881-95; H. Leclercq, O.S.B., XI, 1933, 624-66; *Prex*, 124-27.

DESCARTES, RENÉ (1596-1650)

With his special cosmology D. was led to deny transubstantiation and veered more in the direction of impanation (qv). He did not use the word and his idea must be seen in the context of his idea of bodily substance, which for him is constituted by local extension—his cosmological principle; and in that of his psychological principle: according to this the union between the joint principles of the human essence is not substantial, but consists in the hegemonic action of the soul on the body. In virtue of the first principle, since quantity remains in the species, the substance of bread remains, which rules out transubstantiation— on his terms. But since the soul exercises a hegemonic action on the body, so the soul of Christ informing the substance (for him the extension) of bread exercises action, power, on it through which there is a presence to it. To avoid ecclesiastical censure D. allowed his views to circulate solely among friends and disciples.

Responsiones quattuor objectionibus Antonii Arnauld, R. Descartes, *Oeuvres*, ed Ch Adam et P. Tannery, Paris, 1913, vol VII,

Appendix; *Lettres au Père Mesland*, S.J., *Ibid.*, vol IV, 162ff, 216ff, 345ff, 374ff; cf. P. Lemeire, *Dom Robert Desgabets*, Paris, 1902; S. Zardoni, *Cartesio e Cartesiani di fronte al Mistero Eucaristico*, 2 vols, Rome, Diss. Universita Urbaniana, 1952—second vol. with unpublished matter; A. Chollet, DTC *Descartes*, IV, 555-560; B. Jansen, (Accidents) Eucharistiques, DTC V, 1422-30.

DIDACHE, THE

Since the discovery in 1875 of this MS and its publication in 1883 by P. Bryennios, much ink has flowed on its origin, date, contents.[1] The dust of controversy has largely settled with this general result: this document is of first-century origin, probably from Syria, contemporary with the four canonical gospels. Therefrom arises the interest of theologians in the Eucharistic prayer contained in chapters IX and X and in the injunction on Sunday observance contained in chapter XIV. As to the first passage controversy still persists on the question whether the celebration described is an agape or a Eucharist strictly called: various intermediate positions have been adopted—it is an adaptation of Eucharistic prayers to a fraternal agape, it is an agape followed by a Eucharist.[2]

With these provisos, here are the prayers, which, therefore, may be the first of their kind:

"As for the Eucharist give thanks like this: First, for the cup: We give thee thanks, our Father, for the holy vine of David, thy servant, that thou hast revealed to us through Jesus, thy Child. Glory to thee for ever! Next, for the broken bread: We give thee thanks, our Father, for the life and knowledge that thou hast revealed to us through Jesus, thy Child. Glory to thee for ever! Just as this bread which we break, once scattered over the hills, has been gathered and made one, so may thy Church too be assembled from the ends of the earth into thy kingdom! For glory and power are thine for ever. No one is to eat or drink your Eucharist except those who have been baptized in the name of the Lord; for in this regard the Lord said: 'Do not give holy things to the dogs.' After you have eaten your fill, give thanks like this: We give thee thanks, O holy Father, for thy holy name which thou has made to dwell in our hearts, for the knowledge, faith and immortality that thou hast revealed to us through Jesus, thy Child. Glory to thee for ever! It is thou almighty Master, who hast created the world, that thy name may be praised; for their enjoyment thou hast given food and drink to the children of men; but us thou hast graciously favoured with a spiritual food and with a drink that gives eternal life, through Jesus thy Child. Above all, we give thee thanks for thine own great power, Glory to thee for ever! Amen. Remember, Lord, thy Church, to deliver her from evil, to make her perfect in thy love. Gather her from the four winds, this Church thou hast sanctified, into the kingdom thou hast prepared for her. For power and glory are thine for ever. Amen. May the Lord come and may this world pass away! Amen. Hosanna to the house of David! He who is holy, let him approach. He who is not, let him do penance. Marana tha! Amen."[3]

It will be noted that the institution (qv) narrative is not given and that the thanks offered for the cup precedes that offered for the "bread which we break."

The text of ch XIV refers to the Sunday celebration of the Eucharist: "On the Lord's Day of the Lord come together, break bread and give thanks (hold Eucharist) after confessing your transgressions that your sacrifice be not defiled. But let none who has a quarrel with his companion join in your meeting until they be reconciled, that your sacrifice be not defiled. For this is that which was spoken by the Lord, 'In every place and time offer me a pure sacrifice, for I am a great king' says the Lord, 'and my name is wonderful among the heathen.'"[4]

D. in this passage recalls the word of the Acts of the Apostles: "On the first day of the week, when we were gathered together to break bread, Paul talked with them, intending to depart on the morrow" (20:7). Pliny the Younger in his famous letter to the emperor Trajan (c. 112), says that the Christians assemble on Sunday evening to "take their food, which, despite what is said, is ordinary and innocent." It does not appear from D. that the agape and the Eucharist were yet held separately: this separation would come about the time of St. Justin Martyr (qv).

D. has relevance to the Jewish (qv) origin or influence in Christian liturgy. "It does not appear improbable that D. X is, or is meant to seem, a careful adaptation of the *Birkat ha-mazon* to the requirements of the Lord's Supper (qv), which has become *zebah-todah*: the Eucharistic sacrifice."[5]

[1]Text: K. Lake, *The Apostolic Fathers*, I, London, 1914, 305-333; J. Kleist, *The Didache*, Westminster, Md., 1948: each with English tr.; L. Deiss, English tr. *Springtime*, 74-77; J.P. Audet, O.P., *La Didache, Instruction des apôtres*, Paris, 1958; W. Rordorf and A. Tuilier, *La doctrine des douze apotres (Didache)*, SC 248, Paris, 1978: each with French tr.; J. Quasten, *Monumenta*, 8-17, Latin tr.; cf. F.E. Vokes, *The Riddle of the Didache*, London, 1938; S. Giet, *L'Enigme de la Didache*, Paris, 1970; W. Rordorf, *The Didache*, in *The Eucharist of the Early Christians*, ed. R. Johanny, tr. M.J. O'Connell, New York, 1978, 1-23; J.A. Jungmann, *The Mass*, 11-13; J. Quasten, *Patrology*, I, 29-39, bibl.; on possible links with Jewish prayers, cf. T.-J. Talley, *De la Berakah à l'Eucharistie: Une question à réexaminer*, La Maison-Dieu 125, (1976), 28ff; *Prex*, 66-69.

DISCIPLINE OF THE SECRET, THE

The origin of the practice is controverted: it meant broadly a restriction in public on diffusion of knowledge about the essential Christian truths and practices, esp. the liturgical practice of the Eucharist, which the Christians maintained during the early centuries.[1] It has been suggested, argued, that the Christians took it from the pagan mystery religions. A view widely defended by Catholic scholars is that its origin goes back to the Master and the Apostles. He was deliberately reserved in certain moments, about certain truths. Some secrecy was forced on Christians during the long persecutions by the Roman powers; whence arose a problem as to the duty of publicly professing the faith. Disguise of one kind or another has been used during phases of persecution, from the first century to the twentieth. The "Discipline of the secret" has been occasionally, for the purposes of fiction or drama, presented colourfully, or again enigmatically. It was at times due to sensitive regard for the sacred, at times a protective device, always a matter of skill in judgement and behaviour. A particular application of the practice was the exclusion of catechumens from the most sacred part of the Eucharist. This is mentioned by a number of the Fathers.

[1]Cf. P. Batiffol, *Etudes d'histoire et de théologie positive*, Paris, 1902, 3-41; id., DTC, I (1903), 1738-58; F.X. Funk, *Das Alter der Arkandisziplin*, in *Kirchengeschichtliche Abhandlungen und Untersuchungen*, III (1907), 42-57; E. Vacandard, DHGE III (1924), 1497-1513; F. Oppenheim, O.S.B., EC (1949), 1793-97; O. Perler, *RAC*, I (1950), 667-76.

DOMBES GROUP, THE

The nucleus of this important study group was created by the remarkable French ecumenist, Fr. Paul Couturier. He died in 1953, did not live to see how the original number would be increased and their work encouraged by Vatican II (qv). Following a lead given by Faith and Order, the Dombes group, with representatives of Catholic and different Protestant communions, undertook the preparation of an agreed statement on the Eucharist, which they had achieved in September 1972. This text is as follows:[1]

"1. Today, when Christians celebrate the Eucharist and announce the gospel, they feel themselves more and more brothers among men, with the mission and urgency to bear witness together to the same Christ by word and action and by the celebration of the Eucharist. That is why, for some years the Dombes group has studied the meaning and conditions of mutual Eucharistic openness and of celebration together.

2. A particularly important condition of this sharing of the Lord's table is substantial agreement on what it is, despite theological differences.

3. The Dombes Group makes its own the agreed text of Faith and Order (1968), seeking to clarify it, to adapt it and to complete it with a view to the interconfessional situation today in France.

I. The Eucharist, the Lord's meal

4. The Eucharist is the sacramental meal, the new paschal meal of the People of God, which Christ, having loved his disciples to the end, gave them before his death, that they should celebrate it in the light of the Resurrection until he comes.

5. This meal is the efficacious sign of the gift which Christ makes of himself as the bread of life through the sacrifice of his life and of his death, and through his Resurrection.

6. In the Eucharist Christ accomplishes in a privileged manner his promise to make himself present to those who gather in his name.

II. The Eucharist, thanksgiving to the Father

7. The Eucharist is the great thanksgiving to the Father for all that he has accomplished in creation and redemption, for all that he is accomplishing now in the Church and in the world despite the sins of men, for all that he wishes to accomplish through the coming of the kingdom. Thus the Eucharist is the blessing (berakah) through which the Church expresses her gratitude to God for all his benefits.

8. The Eucharist is the great sacrifice of praise in which the Church speaks in the name of all creation. For the world which God has reconciled to himself in Christ is present at the moment of every Eucharist: in the bread and wine, in the person of the faithful and in the prayers which they offer for all men. Thus the Eucharist opens to the world the way to its transfiguration.

III. The Eucharist, memorial of Christ

9. Christ instituted the Eucharist as the memorial (anamnesis) of his whole life, especially of his Cross and of his Resurrection. Christ, with all that he accomplished for us and for all creation is himself present in this memorial, which is also a foretaste of his kingdom. The memorial, in which Christ acts through the joyful celebration of his Church, implies this re-presentation and this anticipation. It is not therefore merely a question of recalling a past event or even its meaning. The memorial is the effective proclamation by the Church of God's great work. The Church, by its communion with Christ, shares in the reality from which it draws life.

10. The memorial, as re-presentation and anticipation, is lived in thanksgiving and intercession. Accomplishing the memorial of the Passion, Resurrection and Ascension of Christ, our high priest and intercessor, the Church presents to the Father the unique and perfect sacrifice of his Son and asks him to bestow on each man the benefit of the great work of the redemption which she proclaims.

11. Thus, united with our Lord who offers himself to his Father and in communion with the universal Church in heaven and on earth, we are renewed in the covenant sealed by the blood of Christ, and we offer ourselves in a living and holy sacrifice which should find expression in all our daily life.

12. The memorial of Christ is the essential content of the word proclaimed as of the Eucharist. The Eucharist is not celebrated without announcing the word, for the ministry of the word is directed towards the Eucharist and reciprocally the latter presupposes and accomplishes the word.

IV. The Eucharist, gift of the Spirit

13. The memorial, in the large meaning which we have given it, assumes the invocation of the Spirit (epiclesis). Christ, in his heavenly intercession, asks the Father to send his Spirit on his children. For this reason the Church, living in the new covenant, prays with confidence to obtain the Spirit, that it may be renewed and sanctified by the bread of life, led into all truth and strengthened to fulfil its mission in the world.

14. It is the Spirit who, invoked on the assembly, on the bread and wine, makes Christ really present to us, gives him to us and makes us discern him. The memorial and the invocation of the Spirit (anamnesis and epiclesis), which are directed to our union with Christ, cannot be accomplished independently of communion.

15. The gift of the Spirit in the Eucharist is a foretaste of the kingdom of God; the Church receives the life of the new creation and the assurance of the Lord's return.

16. We recognise that the whole Eucharistic prayer has the character of an epiclesis.

V. Sacramental presence of Christ

17. The Eucharistic action is gift of the person of Christ. In fact, the Lord said: 'Take and eat, this is my body given up for you.' 'Drink you all of it, for this is my blood, the blood of the covenant poured out for the multitude for the remission of sins.' We confess then unanimously the real, living, acting presence of Christ in this Sacrament.

18. Discernment of the body and blood of Christ requires faith. Nevertheless, the presence of Christ to his Church in the Eucharist does not depend on the faith of each one, for it is Christ himself who binds himself, by his words and in the Spirit, to the sacramental event, sign of his presence which is given.

19. The act of Christ being gift of his body and of his blood, that is of himself, the reality given under the signs of bread and wine is his body and his blood. It is in virtue of the creative word of Christ and by the power of the Holy Spirit that the bread and wine are made sacrament and therefore 'communion in the body and blood' of Christ (1 Cor 10:16). They are thereafter in final truth, beneath the external sign, the given reality, and remain so to be consumed. What is given as body and blood of Christ remains given as body and blood of Christ, and requires to be treated as such.

20. Taking note of the diversity of practice among the Churches, but drawing the consequences of the preceding agreement, in view of the ecclesial conversion (metanoia) recognised as necessary (cf. thesis no. II of 1969 and theses of 1970) we ask:

—that, on the Catholic side, it be recalled, especially in catechesis and preaching, that the primary intention of Eucharistic reservation is distribution to the sick and absent;

—that, on the Protestant side, steps should be taken to ensure the best way of showing the respect that is due to the elements which have served in the Eucharistic celebration, that is, their eventual consumption, without excluding their use for the communion of the sick.

VI. The Eucharist, communion in the body of Christ

21. In giving himself to communicants, Christ gathers them into the unity of his Body. It is in this sense that it can be said: if the Church makes the Eucharist, the Eucharist makes the Church. Sharing in the same bread and in the same cup in a given place creates the unity of communicants with the whole Christ, among themselves and with all other communicants at every time and in every place. In sharing the same bread they make clear that they belong to the Church in its catholicity, their eyes are opened to the mystery of the redemption and the whole Body grows in grace. Communion is thus the source and the strength of all community life among Christians.

22. By his Cross Christ has overthrown all the walls which separated men. We cannot then communicate truly in him, without working to ensure that, in the conflicts wherein we are caught, the walls within the Church between races, nationalities, languages, classes, confessions ... should disappear.

23. According to the promise of Christ, every believer who is a member of his Body obtains in the Eucharist remission of his sins and eternal life, and he is nourished in faith, hope and love.

24. The solidarity in Eucharistic communion in the body of Christ (agape) and the care which Christians have for one another and for the world should find expression in the Liturgy: by mutual forgiveness of sins, the kiss of peace, offering of gifts meant for community meals, and distribution among brethren in need, by a fraternal welcome to all in a pluralism comprising political, social and cultural positions.

VII. The Eucharist, mission in the world

25. Mission is no simple consequence of the Eucharist. Every time that the Church is truly the Church, mission is part of its life. In the Eucharist the Church is fully itself and is united to Christ in his mission.

26. The world is already present in thanksgiving to the Father, wherein the Church speaks in the name of the whole creation; in the memorial, wherein, united to Christ the redeemer and intercessor, she speaks for the world; in the invocation of the Spirit, wherein she hopes for sanctification and the new creation.

27. Reconciled in the Eucharist, the members of Christ's Body become servants of reconciliation among men and witnesses of the joy of the Resurrection. Their presence in the world implies solidarity in suffering and hope with all those on whose behalf they are called to a commitment to represent the love of Christ in service and in striving. Celebration of the Eucharist, breaking the bread necessary to life, is a motive to refuse acceptance of conditions in which men are deprived of bread, justice and peace.

28. The Eucharist is also the feast of continuous apostolic harvest where the Church rejoices at the gifts received in the world.

VIII. The Eucharist, banquet of the kingdom

29. It was for the time between his Ascension and his return that the Lord instituted the Eucharist. This is the time of hope, this is why the celebration of the Eucharist orients us towards the coming of the Lord and brings him near to us. It is a joyous anticipation of the heavenly banquet, when the redemption will be fully accomplished and all creation will be delivered from all enslavement.

30. Thus the Lord, in giving the Church the Eucharist allows her, as she lives in weakness until the end, in the midst of sufferings and struggles, to renew her courage and to persevere.

31. This Church which Christ nourishes all along its way, sees clearly that the eschatological rendezvous is an ecumenical rendezvous, where Israel and all the nations will be gathered in one people.

IX. Presiding over the Eucharist

32. Christ, in the Eucharist, gathers and nourishes his Church inviting her to the meal over which he presides.

33. His action of presiding has a sign in that of a minister whom he has called and sent. The mission of ministers has its origin and norm in that of the Apostles; it is passed on in the Church by the imposition of hands with the invocation of the Holy Spirit. This passing on implies continuity of the ministerial office, fidelity to the apostolic teaching and conformity to the life of the Gospel.

34. It is made clear by the minister that the assembly is not proprietor of the action which it performs, it is not in control of the Eucharist; it receives this from another, Christ living in his Church. The minister, though he remains a member of the assembly is also the one sent to signify the initiative of God and the link between the local community and the other communities in the universal Church.

35. By their mutual relations the Eucharistic assembly and the president live their dependence on the unique Lord and Great Priest. In its relation to the minister, the assembly exercises its royal priesthood as a gift of Christ, the priest. In his relation to the assembly, the minister lives his presiding function as a service to Christ the Pastor.

X. Conclusion

36. At this stage of our research, we give thanks that the fundamental difficulties about Eucharistic faith have been lifted.

37. We recognize nevertheless that clarification is necessary of the permanence of the sacramental presence and of the precise form of apostolic succession in the ministry. It seems to us that all Eucharistic participation in common calls for a real effort to overcome these difficulties, and, eventually, on one side and the other, abandonment of everything of a polemical nature within confessional positions.

38. The pursuit of our research must enrich us still further with spiritual values, complementary, which make our life. We shall never exhaust understanding of a mystery which surpasses all comprehension and invites us ceaselessly to move out of ourselves to live in thanksgiving and wonder before this supreme gift of Christ to his Church.

XI. Recommendations

39. People often ask today what degree of agreement in the faith is needed to allow welcome of a Christian by another Church at its Eucharistic table. Without claiming to resolve here the other questions raised by different cases of Eucharistic openness, we think that access to Communion should not be refused, on the grounds of Eucharistic faith, to Christians from another communion who are ready to make their own the faith here professed.

40. That is why we ask the authorities of our

Churches to consider attentively the new situation created by this Eucharistic agreement in their evaluation of the requests for hospitality which will be addressed to them."

In a further statement the Group made suggestions on the ministry.[2]

---

[1] *Vers une meme foi eucharistique*, Presses de Taizé, 1972; cf. special number of *Unité des Chrétiens*, 67, July 1987, *Le Groupe des Dombes a 50 ans*; several contributors, esp. D. Alger, *Le document sur l'Eucharistie et son impact sur nos Eglises*, 9-12; [2] *Pour une réconciliation des ministeres*, Presses de Taizé, 1973.

DOMINICAE CENAE, 24 February 1980
Second letter for Holy Thursday sent by John Paul II (qv) to bishops.[1] Like Paul VI (qv) he also felt the need to emphasize the essentials of Eucharistic theology and discipline—within little over five weeks he was to publish *Inaestimabile Donum* (qv). The Pope's stated purpose in *Dominicae Cenae* was "to devote it to the Eucharist, and in particular to certain aspects of the Eucharistic mystery and its impact on the lives of those who are ministers of it." Together with the Bishops the letter was addressed to priests, and, in their own rank, to the deacons too. The basic principle is thus enunciated: "The Eucharist is the principal and central *raison d'être* of the Sacrament of the priesthood (qv), which effectively came into being at the moment of the institution of the Eucharist, and together with it." In the first chapter, *The Eucharistic Mystery in the life of the Church and of the Priest*, as well as practical advice on forms of worship, the Pope deals with the "close relationship between the Church's spiritual and apostolic vitality and the Eucharist, understood in its profound significance and from all points of view." In the second chapter John Paul concentrates on the idea of sacrifice, which, as he well knew, had been devalued by some recent writers. He ends with a plea that the Liturgy be not a cause for disunity, especially the Eucharist. Before that he penned these words: "As I bring these considerations to an end, I would like to ask forgiveness—in my own name and in the name of all of you, venerable and dear Brothers in the episcopate—for everything which, for whatever reason, through whatever human weakness, impatience or negligence, and also through the at times partial, one-sided and erroneous application of the directives of the Second Vatican Council, may have caused scandal and disturbance concerning the interpretation of the doctrine and the veneration due to this great Sacrament. And I pray the Lord Jesus that in the future we may avoid in our manner of dealing with this sacred mystery anything which could weaken or disorient in

any way the sense of reverence and love that exists in our faithful people."

The annotation contains references to many recent conciliar and Roman documents, as to the Fathers, the ancient liturgies and recent writers, the Byzantine scholar, M. Jugie, A.A., the theologian, H. (Cardinal) de Lubac, S.J.

---

[1]Text, *Notitiae*, 1980, 125-154; A. Flannery, Vatican II, II, 64-92, repr. tr. Vatican Press Office.

DURANDUS OF TROARN (c. 1010-1088)

Abbot of Troarn D. was an opponent of Berengar (qv), author of the first treatise against him, *De Corpore et Sanguine Domini*.[1] He has a significant place in the development of the doctrine of the Eucharist in so far as he adds to the volume of opinion stressing the importance of substantive change, thereby preparing the way for the doctrine of transubstantiation (qv). D. thought that Berengar's basic error was to believe in the permanence of the bread and wine after consecration: "The gifts of bread and wine borne to the altar remain after consecration what they were, and thus are in some way the body and blood of Christ not naturally but figuratively." There could thus be no real presence (qv). D. puts it thus: "For although something else is perceived by human powers, although it is not denied that this may reasonably, usefully signify something else, nonetheless what is established as being altogether substantially here (*substantialiter esse*) is nothing but the true body and true blood of Christ." This may be the first use of the word *substantialiter*. D. opposes *substantiva veritas* to *figura*. This excludes all merely virtual or dynamic presence—*non solum per virtutis efficaciam*—and is explicitly opposed to figure or shadow. *Substantialiter* denotes the reality of a thing. D. does not consider the metaphysical nature of the species, though he distinguishes in the sacrament the appearances of bread and the true flesh. He argues from the words of institution like Hugh of Langres, without being exhaustive. The change he takes as one of nature, but the process he leaves a mystery.

---

[1]PL 149, 1375-1424; R.F.N. Sauvage, *L'Abbaye de Saint Martin de Troarn au diocèse de Bayeux*, Caen, 1911; R. Heurtevent, *Durand de Troarn et les origines de l'hérésie berengarienne*, Paris, 1912; C. Poras, DHGE, XIV, 1159-60.

E

ECCLESIAE SEMPER, 7 March 1965

Decree of the Sacred Congregation of Rites on Concelebration (qv), and Communion under both species.[1] The special advantages of concelebration are given: it manifests the unity of the sacrifice of the Cross, the unity of the priesthood and action by the entire people of God. An officially prepared rite is announced. Likewise for Communion under both species.

---

[1]Text *AAS* 57 (1965), 410-412, English tr. A. Flannery, O.P., I, 57-60.

ECOLOGY

The relevance of the Eucharist to ecology is akin to the social effects of the sacrament and sacrifice. A recent writer says: "Much of what was said above in relation to Baptism also applies today in any serious discussion of the Eucharist. St. John in chapter 6 of his Gospel, and the Church through the centuries, presented the Eucharist as the Bread of Life. If the Eucharist symbolizes food and drink and sharing a meal in the memory of Jesus, who lived, died and rose from the dead, the most important challenge facing any celebration of the Eucharist today is not the legitimacy of the priest's orders or the appropriateness of the liturgical text, but the fact that the Eucharist is today celebrated in a world where over one thousand million people are regularly hungry."[1] The author lists the ugly features of this global situation—hunger, malnutrition, lack of opportunities to grow and harvest food, exploitation of varying kinds, and goes on: "One cannot celebrate the Eucharist today without being challenged to do something about this appalling reality." He quotes the former Superior General of the Jesuits, Pedro Arrupe, speaking at the International Eucharistic Congress in Philadelphia, 1974: "If there is hunger anywhere in the world then our celebration of the Eucharist is somehow everywhere incomplete in the world. He comes to us not alone but with the poor, the oppressed, the starving of the earth. Through him they are looking for help, for justice, for love expressed in action. Therefore we cannot properly receive the Bread of Life unless at the same time we give bread for life to those in need, wherever, whoever they may be." Prophetic words calling for a vast programme of reform, renewal, relief on the part of the disciples of the Eucharistic Lord. He is the motive, the source, the guarantee of this urgently needed change.

---

[1]S. McDonagh, *To Care for the Earth*, London, 1986, 171; quotation from Fr. Arrupe, *ibid.*, 172.

ECUMENISM

The Decree on Ecumenism from Vatican II has this to say about the Eucharist and the separated churches. In regard to the Orthodox: "It is well known with what love eastern Christians celebrate the sacred liturgy, especially the Eucharist, source of life for the Church and pledge of heavenly glory. In this way the faithful united with the bishop can approach God the Father through the Son, the Word incarnate, dead and glorified in the outpouring of the Holy Spirit. Thus they enter into communion with the most Holy Trinity and become sharers in the divine nature (2 Pet 1:4). In this way even through the celebration of the Lord's Eucharist in each particular church, the Church of God is built up and grows (cf. St. John Chrysostom, *Hom in Jo.* 46, PG 59, 260-262), the communion between them is shown in concelebration. . . . Since these Churches, though separated, have true Sacraments, especially in virtue of the apostolic succession, priesthood and the Eucharist, which unite them intimately with us, some *'communicatio in sacris,'* in favourable circumstances, with the approval of ecclesiastical authority, is not only possible but advisable."[1]

On the separated brethren of the West the Council's words were: "Certainly the ecclesial communities separated from us have not the full unity which derives from Baptism, and we believe, especially as a result of the absence of the Sacrament of Orders, that they have not kept the full proper reality of the Eucharistic mystery. Nevertheless, in celebrating in the Holy Supper the memorial of the death and resurrection of the Lord, they profess their belief that life consists in communion with Christ and they await his glorious return. Doctrine on the Lord's Supper, on the other Sacraments, on the worship and ministries of the Church must then be the object of dialogue."[2]

The Eucharist is the cause, exemplar, prime factor and both essential and existential bond of unity among Christ's followers. It is therefore of pre-eminent importance that in the Eucharist itself there should be the greatest degree of agreement and harmony possible, and this at the deepest level, in the celebration and the sacramental use. The tragedy is that Christian unity has at times been broken because of different theological opinions of the Eucharist, different interpretations of the Lord's words. All the more imperative, in the improved ecclesial climate of the present age, with improved resources for research into the sources of divine revelation, biblical, traditional, especially patristic, is the call to endeavour in this field. History can also be studied in a more scientific and serene light, can throw its light on past differences, show where distortion has been caused by mistaken loyalty and the irruption into doctrine and worship of political, social and economic factors. Nor must we overlook the recurring phenomenon of history: the disciples, at two or more generations removed from the pioneers or founding fathers, tend to harden and narrow the theses of their spiritual forebears, as they easily forget historical contexts necessary to full understanding.

Much of the present work is taken up with the laudable efforts of many ecumenists to elucidate

differences and seek genuine agreement in regard to Eucharistic doctrine and worship. (See articles on ARCIC; Lutheran, Roman Catholic Dialogue on Eucharist and Ministry; Dombes, Group of; Lima agreement, Orthodox). Interest should also be given to agreements reached between ecclesial communities of the West conducting dialogue between themselves without reference to the Roman Catholic Church; likewise to the past internal history of one Orthodox Church, the Russian, in regard to the form of the Eucharist. The subject of Inter-communion is dealt with separately. Since 1980 the Joint International Commission for Theological Dialogue between the Roman Catholic Church and Orthodox Churches has been active. Its first report, available from the Secretariat for Christian Unity was issued in 1981 on *"The Mystery of the Church and the Eucharist in the Light of the Mystery of the Holy Trinity."*

---

[1] Texts of agreement issued by the Commission on Faith and Order: *'The Eucharist in Ecumenical Thought,'* Faith and Order, Louvain, 1971; *Study Reports and Documents,* Faith and Order Paper No. 59, Geneva 1971, 71-77; 'Beyond Inter-communion,' *ibid.*, 54-70; 'The Eucharist,' *One Baptism, One Eucharist and a Mutually Recognized Ministry: Three Agreed Statements,* Faith and Order Paper No. 73, Geneva, 1975, 18-28; Texts of agreement issued by the Group of Les Dombes, France, consisting of French-speaking Roman Catholic, Lutheran and Reformed Theologians: 'Towards a Common Eucharistic Faith?', *Modern Eucharistic Agreement,* London, 1973, 51-64; 'Pastoral Agreement: The Meaning of the Eucharist,' *ibid.*, 65-78; Documents of the bilateral conversations (of Lutherans) with the Anglican Church: 'Report of the Anglican-Lutheran International Conversations 1970-1972. Authorized by the Lambeth Conference and the Lutheran World Federation,' *Lutheran World,* XIX (1972), 387-399; Reports of the official dialogue of Roman Catholics and Lutherans in the U.S.: 'The Eucharist as Sacrifice,' *Lutherans and Catholics in Dialogue,* ed. P. C. Empie and T. Austin Murphy, Washington, D.C. and New York, 1967, vol III, 187-200; 'Eucharist and ministry,' *Lutherans and Catholics in Dialogue,* Washington, New York, 1970, vol. IV, 7-33, *Luthériens et Réformés de France; Déclaration,* 22 March, 1981, DCath 1981, 512, 13; J. Desseaux, *Dialogues théologiques et accords oecuméniques,* Paris, 1982; L. Swindler, ed., *The Eucharist in Ecumenical Dialogue,* New York, 1976; M. Thurian, ed., *Ecumenical Perspectives on Baptism, the Eucharist and Ministry;* esp. M. Thurian, *The Eucharist, Memorial Sacrifice of Praise and Supplication,* 90-103, and J.M. Tillard, O.P., *The Eucharist, Gift of God,* 104-118; K. Osborne, O.F.M., *Ecumenical Eucharist, Journal of Ecumenical Studies,* 6 (1969) 598-619; id., *The Christian Sacraments of Initiation, Baptism, Confirmation, Eucharist,* New York, 1987; I.T. Ramsey, *Thinking about the Eucharist,* London, 1972; R.C.D. Jasper and C.J. Cumming, *Prayers of the Early and Reformed Liturgy,* London, 1975; L. Swidler, ed., *The Eucharist in Ecumenical Dialogue,* New York, 1976; T. Klauser, *A Short History of the Western Liturgy,* Oxford, 1981; Le Groupe Agape, *L'Eucharistie de Jésus aux Chrétiens d'aujourhui,* 1981, esp. B. Rollin, *Textes patristiques,* 45-173; J. Desseaux, *L'Eucharistie dans le dialogue oecuménique,* 369-544—21 declarations in 13 years; R. A. Keifer, *Blessed and Broken,* Wilmington, 1982; J. Reumann, *The Supper of the Lord,* New York, 1980; E. J. Kilmartin, *Towards Reunion,* 1979; id., *Church, Eucharist and Priesthood,* 1981.

ELEVATION AT MASS, THE

There is a little elevation of the Host and Chalice at the words *Per ipsum et cum ipso et in ipso est tibi Deo Patri omnipotenti in unitate Spiritus Sancti omnis honor et gloria per omnia saecula saeculorum. Amen.* But the important elevation in Eucharistic history is that which takes place after the Consecration at Mass.[1] We first have certain evidence of the practice in the *Praecepta synodalia* of the Bishop of Paris, Eudes (Odo) of Sully (d. 1208): "Let the priests be instructed that when holding the host in the canon of the Mass they have begun, *Qui pridie*, they are not to raise it too high immediately to be seen by all the people, but they should hold it breast-high until they have said; *Hoc est corpus meum*, and then they should raise it so that it may be seen by all."[2]

This evidence is firm though the practice may have been in vogue elsewhere earlier. The purpose was to prevent adoration of the bread before the moment of consecration and to satisfy a popular desire to see the host. The custom spread rapidly and within fifty years was adopted throughout the West. Mistaken views sometimes arose. People thought that to look on the host was the equivalent of communion and some left the church after the moment of elevation. Merely to look on the host was thought to be a protection on the individual who did so.

The highly symbolic action was in keeping with so much else in the thirteenth century which expressed profound faith in the real presence (qv) and was manifest in most sensitive attitudes towards the Eucharist. In the present century St. Pius X (qv) characteristically indulgenced the action of looking reverently, with an accompanying prayer, on the Host and the Chalice. But the elevation of the Chalice was not in use until later than that of the Host. One difficulty was that the contents of the Chalice were not visible. It was St. Pius V (qv) who prescribed the twofold elevation with the reform of the Missal in 1570. The Carthusians have not adopted the practice of elevation.

[1]E. Dumoutet, *Le désir de voir l'hostie et les origines de la dévotion au Saint-Sacrament*, Paris 1926; Cf. V.L. Kennedy, *The Moment of Consecration and the Elevation of the Host*, Medieval Studies, 6 (1944), 121-150; id., *The Date of the Parisian Decree on the Elevation of the Host*, Medieval Studies, 8 (1946), 87-96; Righetti, III, 236, 37; F. Cabrol, O.S.B., DACL IV, 2, 2662-70; E. Mangenot, DTC IV, 2, 2320-28; I. Cecchetti, EC V, 226-28; Emile Bertaud, DSp IV, 2, 1626, 27; Paul Viar, DSp, IV, 2, 1678-80; A. Guny, *Eudes de Sully*, in *Catholicisme* IV, 665, 66; W. J. O'Shea, NCE V, 265, 66; [2]Mansi XXII, 628.

EMMAUS, APPARITION OF THE RISEN JESUS AT, Lk 24:13-35

Lk's resurrection narratives deal with the encounter between the women and the angels at the empty tomb, the meeting between two disciples and Jesus on the road to Emmaus, and the apparition to the "eleven" and those who were with them, prior to his ascension.[1] The Emmaus incident is told lengthily and with suggestive detail. It is considered a narrative gem, an artistic triumph on Lk's part.

The relevance to the Eucharist is strongly suggested, and remains, in final analysis, tantalizing, mysterious rather.

The paschal mystery (qv) is evoked by Jesus: "Was it not necessary that the Christ should suffer these things and enter into his glory?" (24:30). This is the mystery that will continue in the Eucharist as we have been so strongly reminded in our time, not least by Vatican II. The words of Jesus open a theological reflection which Mk in his brief reference to the event did not think of raising: "After this he appeared in another form to two of them, as they were walking in the country. And they went back and told the rest, but they did not believe them" (16:12-13).

To lead up to his incisive summary and to the further explanation of the Scriptures, "he interpreted to them in all the Scriptures the things concerning himself," there is an illuminating example of catechetical pedagogy. Jesus stirs his companions to express their faith in him: "Concerning Jesus of Nazareth, who was a prophet mighty in deed and word before God and all the people." Then they cannot conceal their disappointment, "and how our chief priests and rulers delivered him up to be condemned to death, and crucified him. But we had hoped that he was the one to redeem Israel" (24:20-21).

The dialogue continues as they relate the episode of the women and the empty tomb and the "vision of angels, who said that he was alive." Thereon Jesus rebukes them: "O foolish men, and slow of heart to believe all that the prophets have spoken" (24:25). Then Jesus unfolds his privileged knowledge to them; his words are revelatory.

This was the prelude to the final scene, when he would eat with them. Before this, however, he appeared to be going further and it was they who constrained him to stay. They offered him hospitality. Since as yet they had not recognized him, it was not a case of "Where two or more are gathered in my name." Then comes the first story of a meal by the Risen Jesus. The last, three days previously, had been the Eucharistic banquet; inevitably this one has been compared with it. Rightly so since it is related by the one evangelist who has the anamnesis (qv) theme in the words of

Jesus, 'Do this in remembrance of me' (Lk 22:19).

The phrasing in Lk's account of the two meals is almost identical. "And he took bread, and when he had given thanks, he broke it and gave it to them . . . (Lk 22:19); "When he was at table with them, he took the bread and blessed, and broke it and gave it to them" (Lk 24:30). It is noteworthy and not often noted, that the unknown guest—as he still was until this moment—presided at the table, as he had done at the Last Supper taking the place of the father of the family.

"The lesson," says J. Fitzmyer, "in the story is that henceforth the risen Christ will be present to his assembled disciples not visibly (after the ascension) but in the breaking of bread."[2] The same author thinks that the question: Did Jesus celebrate a Eucharist at Emmaus is an impossible one to answer; he does deal with the Eucharistic aspect of the episode. Yet one must bear in mind the fact that it was in "the breaking of the bread" that he was known to them. Was it merely the physical act that enlightened them? How and why should this be? Was it a mere memory of the Last Supper? Or was it a fulfilment of the *anamnesis* he had himself commanded? There is a further complication: the two were not of the "eleven"; how then did they know what the "breaking of the bread" could signify, unless there was some supernatural effect of his action on them? Why did he "vanish out of their sight?" Why did they then recall and appraise the effect of his words earlier? "Did not our hearts burn within us, while he talked to us on the road, while he opened to us the Scriptures?" (Lk 24:32).

If it was a Eucharist it was already in a pattern which would eventually become normal, unfolding of the Scriptures as the suitable setting, the word of God in the Scripture to accompany the coming of the Word of God in the Eucharist. And it was followed by what will also be the practice: proclamation. "Then they told what had happened on the road and how he was known to them in the breaking of the bread" (Lk 24:35). What do those words "made known" enclose as meaning? It is pertinent to remark that the same author in his second book, Acts, uses the phrase "breaking of the bread" for the Eucharist. He only relates it after the descent of the Spirit (see article Spirit, the Holy). But in the Emmaus episode we are dealing with the one who would send the Spirit.

There is a further point. Apparently the two disciples were believed at once: not treated skeptically as the women had been. Why should "the breaking of the bread" as their motive of credibility, evoke the response of faith? What did the words signify to their listeners? Something apparently which was now full of Christlike meaning, sacred, therefore, and not to be used save

with the greatest seriousness. It was in a way a password in this instance, the hallmark of credibility so profound was the memory of the Lord's action at the Last Supper.

There are other aspects of the wonderful incident which call for reflection and comment. Already the kerygma, the summary of faith of the Christian community is adumbrated in the words spoken during the dialogue. And, most significantly, if we may accept the breaking of bread in its Eucharistic sense, we have linked two mysteries which must henceforth be actively associated, the Eucharist and the Resurrection (qv). "The Scriptures bear witness to the risen Christ, but it is the Eucharist which gives the risen Christ, living and present, to the faithful. So it is that for Christians the Eucharist is the great sign of the Lord's Resurrection, the sign by which they recognize the Lord living and present."[3]

The site of the ancient village of Emmaus is disputed: It is sometimes said to be Amwas on the Jerusalem Jaffa road, 20 miles from Jerusalem, whereas Lk speaks of 60 stadia, about 7 miles. From the thirteenth century El-Qubeiheh, 8 miles northwest of Jerusalem has gained support.

---

[1]Cf. commentaries on Lk 24:13-35, esp. J. Fitzmyer, S.J., *The Gospel according to Luke*, Anchor Bible, II, (1985), 1553-1572; bibl 1570-72; J. Dupont, O.S.B., *The Meal at Emmaus* in *The Eucharist in the New Testament*, London, 1964, 105-123; [2]Fitzmyer, 1569; [3]J. Dupont, *op.cit.*, 121. J.A. Grassi, *Emmaus revisited*, CBQ 26 (1964), 463-67; L. Dussaut, *Le triptyque des Apparitions en Luc 24 (Analyse structurelle)*, RB (1987), 161-213.

EPHRAEM, ST., DOCTOR OF THE CHURCH (c. 306-373)

A teacher in his native town, Nisibis, where he was also in charge of liturgy, E. there and in Edessa, whither he withdrew after the Persian entry to Nisibis, carried on constant literary activity.[1] Some of his writing is lost; what remains, now fortunately available in critical editions, justifies his title, greatest of the Syrian Fathers. Unavoidably caught in controversy, his thinking is rooted in the Bible, which he saw as one entity, OT and NT interpreted one by the other and each in regard to the other; the mould of his expression is often liturgical, his horizons clearly ecclesial.

Dom Edmund Beck draws mostly for his summary of E's Eucharistic doctrine on the Hymns *De Fide (Contra scrutatores)*, *Contra Haereses*, *De Nativitate*, *De Azymis*, *De Virginitate* and *Carmina Nisibena*; Fr. Pierre Yousif uses some more of the surviving E. texts.

E. saw Christ's priesthood, ultimate source of the Eucharist, in a biblical context. "The priests of the former people slaughtered the High Priest. Then our

Priest became the offering. Through his offering he abolished theirs. At that time the priests were from the earth, whereas the Lamb descended from heaven. He himself alone became the offering and the offerer ... the stainless lamb was the Victim for peace and freed those high and low with his all-freeing blood.... He broke the bread with his hands, the prototype of the offering of his body, mixed the chalice with his hands, the prototype of the offering of his blood. He offered, as Priest brought himself our expiation. He clothed himself in the priestly office of Melchizedek, his type, who brought no offering but gave bread and wine."[2]

E. links the Eucharist with the Adam Christ typology: "While Adam without praising God, gathered (as animals), our Saviour praised God and broke (the bread), for as he absolved (Adam's) faults, on the bread he accomplished thanksgiving."[3] The Eucharist made reparation for the sin of Adam, "the Eucharistic bread entered into them, making atonement for the greed by which Adam rejected God."[4] The contrast is between the Supper and Eden. The bread earned by the sweat of (Adam's) brow becomes the source of joy and blessing: one food was the cause of the curse on man, another, the Eucharist, has become the height of divine favours, communion in which abolishes the curse.

What we lost through Eve by the serpent's effort, we have gained through the Eucharist. E. has Mary speak thus: "Eve became for us a hole and a tomb. For the accursed serpent who entered her and dwelt in her she became his bread (Gen 3:14), she who turned into dust. It is You (Christ) who are our bread; it is you who are our nuptial chamber, the robe of our glory."[5] The forbidden fruit caused death to mankind; the Eucharist gives back life. "You, whom a fruit in Eden killed (Gen 3:6), have regained freely life thanks to a fruit. Adam stretched out his hand (Gen 3:6), and took the fruit which had death hidden in it. Stretch out your hands and receive the bread which holds life."[6]

Ardent devotee of Our Lady that E. was, it is not surprising that he intertwines his thinking on the Eucharist with striking poetic images related to Mary. But he goes deep into the mystery of the Incarnation to announce: "His (Christ's) body has become bread to vivify our immortal being." The Eucharist is the culmination, in the present order of things, of the Incarnation. Again and again E. comes back to Mary in this context: "Happy your dwelling (he is addressing the Cenacle) in which was broken the Bread (come) from the sheaf. In you was pressed the grape bunch (born) of Mary, Chalice of salvation."[7]

"Mary gave us the comforting bread in place of the bread of weariness which Eve had given us."[8]

Beck illustrates very fully a distinctive idea in E's Eucharistic doctrine, the presence of the Spirit in the Eucharist with Christ.[9] A recently discovered Armenian antiphon, 48, reveals the Trinitarian element in the Syrian doctor's thought on the subject: to the Trinity is due the mystery of Christ's coming into the Eucharist, the Father operating through the Spirit 'his right hand.' The presence of the Spirit is important for E's theory of spiritualisation through the Spirit and Christ. "Spirit in your Bread, Fire in your Wine, a sublime wonder, which our lips receive."[10] "Here is the power hidden in the veil of your Holy Spirit, power which no thought has ever grasped. His love was lowered, descended and hovered over the veil of the altar of reconciliation."[11] "Fire and Spirit in the womb of your Mother; Fire and Spirit in the river wherein you were baptised; Fire and Spirit in our baptism (Lk 3:16); in the Bread and in the Cup, Fire and Holy Spirit."[12]

There was place in E's synthesis for symbolism: "He took and broke the Bread which is other and unique, mystery (symbol) of his unique body which came from Mary."[13] This must be seen along with his whole-hearted belief in the real presence (qv). "O happy place (the Cenacle), none has seen or will see what you have seen, namely the Lord become the true altar, the priest, the bread and chalice of salvation. He of himself is sufficient for all and none can suffice for him, he the altar and the lamb, the victim and minister, priest and food."[14]

This certainty and other important Eucharistic truths are affirmed in the remarkable Hymn XVI De Nativitate, wherein E. shows Mary addressing Jesus in the Eucharist: "He who hates your bread is truly like the one who hates your body, and the distant one who loves your Bread is as the one near to you who cherishes your image (Eph 2:13). The first and the last have seen you in the Bread and in the Body."[15]

A Eucharistic theology nourished on Sacred Scripture, enlightened by highly personal insights, set in a solid frame of genuine mysticism, coloured by a unique poetic gift.

[1]For editions and editors, CSCO, Louvain, 1955 ... chiefly E. Beck, O.S.B., H. Leloir, O.S.B.; PO; Le Muséon; cf. P. Yousif, in *Etudes Mariales* (BSFEM), 1979-80, 73; for texts (but not from recent critical editions), J. Solano, *Textos*, 1, 259-299; J. Hobeika, *Saint-Ephream et la sainte Eucharistie*, Beyrouth, (1926); monographs, E. Beck, O.S.B., *Die Eucharistie bei Ephräm, Oriens Christianus*, 38 (1954), 41-67; F. Graffin, *L'Eucharistie chez Saint Ephrem, Parole d'Orient*, 4 (1973), 112-114; S.P. Brock, *Mary and the Eucharist, Sobornost, inc. Eastern Churches Review*, 1 (1979), 50-59; P. Yousif, *Etudes Mariales*, (BSFEM), 1979-80, *La Vierge Marie et l'Eucharistie chez Saint Ephrem de Nisibe et dans la pastristique syriaque antérieure*, 49-80; id., *L'Eucharistie et la Sainte Ecriture d'après St. Ephrem de Nisibe*, R.H. Fischer ed., *A Tribute*

to *Arthur Voobus*, Chicago, 1977, 235-46; id., *Les controverses de St. Ephrem et l'Eucharistie*, Euntes Docete, 33 (1980), 405-426; id., esp. *L'Eucharistie chez Saint Ephrem de Nisibe, Orientalia Christiana Analecta*, Rome, 1984; [2] *De Azymis*, 3, C, II, 3-8; Solano, 268, 69; Beck, 41-42; [3] *Mere de Mensa*, Yousif, 56; [4] *Diatesseron*, XIX, 4; Yousif, 56; [5] *De Nativitate, XVII*, 6, Yousif, 57; [6] *Sequence* I, Yousif, 57; [7] Hymn *De Crucifixione*, III, 9, Yousif, 65; Solano, 277; [8] *De Azymis*, VI, 7; Yousif, 66; Solano, 269; Beck 48; [9] *Op.cit.*, 51ff; [10] *De Fide*, X, 8, Beck, 53; [11] *Ibid.*, X, 16, Yousif, 63; [12] *Ibid.*, X, 17, Yousif, 64; [13] *Carmen Nisibenum*, XLVI, 120, Beck, 47; [14] Hymn *De Crucifixione*, III, 10, Solano, 277; [15] *De Nativitate*, XVI, 5, 6, Beck, 64, Yousif, 78, 79.

EUCHARISTIAE PARTICIPATIONEM, 27 April 1973

A Circular Letter on the Eucharistic Prayers from the Sacred Congregation for Divine Worship.[1] Once the rigid framework of the Roman Missal was loosened, it was inevitable, given the tendencies of human nature, that individuals would seek still more liberty in liturgical composition. The Congregation notes in this letter that requests are received for approval of new texts of presidential and Eucharistic prayers "or that others be permitted to grant them approval, texts more in keeping with modern modes of thought and speech." But several authors, it is stated, had, for scientific purposes, composed and published Eucharistic Prayers. "Furthermore priests frequently use these privately-composed texts in liturgical celebrations, in spite of the prohibitions of Vatican II and of bishops." (The reference is to art. 22 of the Liturgical Constitution—so often quoted in post-conciliar documents.)

Paul VI (qv) requested the Congregation to take the matter in hand. The members studied the matter and sought the advice of experts from different parts of the world. Result: It is not advisable to cede to the episcopal conferences "a general permission for the composition or approval of Eucharistic prayers." Catechetical instruction on the Eucharistic prayer is needed. The Holy See will consider requests from episcopal conferences sympathetically; it will state the norms to be observed. Some considerations are offered to facilitate understanding and application of the decision; the final conclusion is that not novelties are required but deeper understanding "of the character, the structure and the elements of the celebration and especially of the Eucharistic prayer—to enable the faithful to take part more fully and with greater awareness in the celebration.

[1] Text *AAS* 65 (1973), 340-347; tr. A. Flannery, O.P., I, 233-240.

EUCHARISTIAE SACRAMENTUM, 21 June 1973

Issued by the Sacred Congregation for Divine Worship, it deals with Holy Communion and the Worship of the Eucharistic Mystery outside Mass:[1] reservation of the Blessed Sacrament; the times at which Holy Communion may be distributed outside Mass "priests should readily accede to the request"; the minister of Holy Communion; the place; the disposition required in those receiving Holy Communion. Directives are given in regard to worship of the Blessed Sacrament; special consideration is had for exposition of the Blessed Sacrament.

[1] A. Flannery, O.P. I, 242-253; tr. Dom Matthew Dillon, O.S.B.

EUCHARISTICUM MYSTERIUM, 25 May 1967

Instruction of the Sacred Congregation of Rites on the Worship of the Eucharistic Mystery.[1] It was given wide distribution, as it met a need. The very increased participation in Eucharistic celebration along with the theological upheaval which followed the Council (see article Paul VI) prompted undue liberty in certain quarters, both as to doctrine and practice. Some felt the need for reassurance. It was given on the basis of the conciliar and papal documents. The document contains the essentials of Eucharistic theology, set in the context of instruction of the faithful.

[1] Text *AAS* 59 (1967), 539-573; English tr. issued by the Congregation, A. Flannery, O.P., I, 100-136 and CTS.

EYMARD, SAINT PIERRE JULIEN (1811-1868)

Religious founder and apostle whose life and work were centred on the Eucharist (see Hagiography), P. J. was born in La Mure d'Isère, had been a secular priest and member of the Marist Congregation before undertaking, with the approval of Mgr. A. D. Auguste Sibour, the foundation of his congregation in 1856; it would later be called the Congregation of the Blessed Sacrament.[1] With the cooperation of Marguerite Guillot and this time the approval of Mgr. Guillaume Angebault of Angers, he founded the female institute, the Servants of the Blessed Sacrament. Approved by the Church both institutes spread to other countries. The founder was canonised in 1962. P.J.'s work coincided with a stirring of Eucharistic piety manifest in the Forty Hours and Perpetual Adoration (qqv).

He was especially influential through his religious communities and his sermons. His writings are slight, the Constitutions and a Directory; but these are augmented by diverse material, letters and notes of his lectures. From these A. Terniere edited with P.J's name a number of works: *La divine Eucharistie, Première serie; La présence réelle*, 1870; *La Sainte Communion et la vie de communion à Jesus Hostie*, 1871; *Retraite aux pieds de Jésus—Eucharistie*, 1873. On these and other works from the same editor and still more from E. Couet a critical problem arises: Are these the founder's authentic words? Certainly his spirit is captured and, with verbatim quotations from letters, his words.

---

[1]For further detail, bibl. and statement of the critical position cf. André Guitton, DSp XII, 1679-1691.

F

FAST, THE EUCHARISTIC

For the first three centuries there was no apparent practice of abstinence from food for a fixed time before reception of Holy Communion (qv); the practice of Agape (qv) evidently did not permit this.[1] By the fourth century, abstinence from food before Communion was widespread; it was universal in the Middle Ages. Down to the present century the fast was from midnight: so the 1917 Code of Canon Law confirmed the practice (808, 858). During the Second World War relaxations were given. After the war Pius XII in the Apostolic Constitution *Christus Dominus*, 16 January 1953,[2] laid down that water did not break the fast, nor medicine. By the *Motu proprio, Christus Dominus*,[3] 19 March 1957, he prescribed a three-hour fast from solid food and alcoholic drink and a one-hour fast from non-alcoholic drink; a priest celebrating Mass was to calculate the time from the beginning of Mass. Paul VI by *Pastorale Munus*,[4] 6 November 1963, allowed the ordinary to permit priests to take liquid between Masses even if one hour did not elapse. On 21 November 1964, he fixed the Eucharistic fast at one hour before the reception of Holy Communion; priests would now calculate from the time of Communion, not the beginning of Mass. All these changes are embodied in the new Code of Canon Law, 919: "1. One who is to receive the Most Holy Eucharist is to abstain from any food or drink, with the exception only of water and medicine for at least the period of one hour before Holy Communion; 2. A priest who celebrates the Most Holy Eucharist two or three times on the same day may take something before the second or third celebration even if the period of one hour does not intervene. 3. Those who are advanced in age or who suffer from any infirmity, as well as those who take care of them can receive the Most Holy Eucharist even if they have taken something during the previous hour."

The Code goes further than the previous decisions in some particulars. Whereas formerly the dispensation from the fast to priests celebrating two or three Masses depended on the Ordinary, now it is given to all by the law; they can take solids as well as liquids. There is no mention of the quarter of an hour fast for the infirm or those taking care of them. In the general prescription, the words "at least" imply an encouragement to fast for longer.

Among the Orthodox the practice prevails of strict Eucharistic practice from the time of rising. Practice has changed from time to time among Protestants. Anglicans often have the same practice as the Catholic Church.

[1] J.M. Frochisse, S.J., *A propos des origines du jeûne eucharistique, RHE* 28 (1932), 594-609; W. Conway, *The New Law on the Eucharistic Fast*, Dublin, 1954; T.F. Anglim, *The Eucharistic Fast*, Washington, 1964; *The Code of Canon Law, A Text and Commentary*, ed. J.A. Condren, T.J. Green, D.E. Heintschel, 1985, 655; A. Bride, *Dictionnaire de Droit Canonique*, VI (1957), 142-181; A.M. Carr, NCE V (1967), 847; F.L. Cross, 477-78; [2] *AAS* 45 (1953), 15-24; [3] *AAS* 49 (1957), 177 [4] *AAS* 56 (1964), 5-12; [5] *AAS* 57 (1965), 186.

FATHERS OF THE CHURCH, THE

The patristic revival in recent times has proved beneficial to study of the Eucharist.[1] The scientific approach which aims at clarifying and appraising the ideas of the Fathers, not merely using them as a quarry for support to theses framed independently of them, is assured of more lasting results. In research into Eucharistic doctrine certain distinctive features are quickly discerned. There were no prolonged theological battles as happened with other Christian mysteries, Christological and Trinitrian especially. Controversy was not frequent. This was partially due to another special characteristic of the doctrine. It was from the outset seen vitally, not merely theoretically: it was the very center of the Church's life. Belief in the reality was the very test of the following of Christ: not only belief but commitment, worship, participation. Many of our early testimonies are either directly liturgical, like the *Didache* and the *Apostolic Tradition* (qqv) or issued from the liturgy like the account given by St. Justin Martyr (qv), or again *Catecheses* prompted by liturgical events, as in the case of St. Cyril of Jerusalem (qv). With the passage of time we get elaborate reflection, yet, as with St. Ambrose, reproduction of a liturgical text, his special anaphora (qv).

Such reflection in patristic times, even with the great St. Augustine, never reaches the systematically developed theories of medieval times. The real presence of Jesus Christ was quite clearly affirmed, at times as with St. John Chrysostom (qv) very realistically, but no doctrine like that of transubstantiation (qv) was formulated.

One important service rendered to Christian thought by the Fathers was to relate their ideas to Sacred Scripture. It is an assumption that we make nowadays in regard to method. The tracks were firmly laid down by the early Christian writers. Sometimes they turned their attention to the Eucharist in the course of discussions on other subjects, incidentally as it were. They had not at their disposal, for the reason already mentioned, accurately chiselled terms, could, accordingly, speak in a way that may strike us as inaccurate. And we must not forget the *'disciplina arcani'* (qv), the discipline of the secret, which dictated a policy of silence about the sacred mysteries in the early centuries, possibly down to the fifth century in places.

The Fathers are dealt with individually and it is clear from the text which of them wrote or preached significantly on the Eucharist. It is not always evident from the quantity of passages reproduced in anthologies what value in the development of doctrine their content may have. The rules of scientific interpretation have to be applied.

---

[1]In addition to sources used in the present work—Quasten, *Monumenta*, and Solano, *Textos*, cf. D. Sheerin, *The Eucharist*, in

Message of the Fathers, Wilmington, Delaware, and *L'Eucharistie des premiers chrétiens*, Paris, 1976, ed. R. Johanny, English tr., M.J. O'Connell, *The Eucharist of the Early Christians*, New York, 1978 (contributors: W. Rordorf, G. Blond, R. Johanny, M. Jourjon, A. Hamman, A. Mehat, V. Saxer); A. Hamman, *Prière des premiers chrétiens*, 1952; id., *Prières eucharistiques des premiers chrétiens*, 1957; E.J. Kilmartin, *The Eucharist in the Primitive Church*, 1965.

FAUSTUS OF RIEZ, ST. (c. 408-490)

A homily found among the dubious works of St. Jerome (qv) is now restored by scholars to F.[1] There is, however, a question of textual criticism: the homily may have been retouched in the century after the author's death—it is well known that a collection of sermons bearing for centuries the name of Eusebius of Emesa come from F. The present homily has been ascribed to many different authors. It is much quoted in subsequent ages, by, e.g., Paschasius Radbert, Guitmund of Aversa, Haymon of Halberstadt, Peter Lombard (qqv).

Terminology, which would prove capital centuries later, is found or hinted at in his reflections on the Eucharist—*fide non specie* and above all this which has been called—with some hyperbole, doubtless—transubstantiation without the word (DTC, lc.): *"Sicut autem quicumque ad fidem Christi veniens ante verba baptismi adhuc in vinculo est veteris debiti, his vero memoratis, mox exuitur omni faece peccati; ita quando benedicendae verbis caelestibus creaturae sacris altaribus imponuntur, antequam invocatione sui nominis consecrantur, substantia illic est panis et vini, post verba autem corpus et sanguis est Christi."*[2] It is striking in Latin, even if it was one of the passages retouched in the century after F. "What wonder," he continues, "is it if by a word he could convert (*convertere*—another key word) created things, which by a word he was able to create. Indeed it already seems a smaller miracle to change what it is agreed that he created from nothing, from its created condition to something better. Think what could be difficult to him who easily fashioned man from the matter of clay; to endow him also with the image of his divinity, and then again easily to recall him from the depths, to rescue him from perdition, lift him up from the dust, raise him from earth to heaven, make him an angel from a man, give him a human body conformed to his own body of brightness, exalt his form to share in his kingdom; so that he who assumed the body of our frailty should assume us into the body of his immortality; may he who lives and reigns for ever and ever deign to prepare us by pious works for that glorious resurrection. Amen."[2]

Here the mystery of the Eucharist is set in the entire

Christian anthropology and salvation: a perspective of man's origin, fall and redemption. In the same sermon restored to F. from Eusebius of Emesa, we read: "His (Christ's) food are the heavenly sacraments of the altar, of which it is said, 'He gave them bread from heaven, man ate the bread of angels.' (The Church) saw his holocausts, the mysteries of prayers doubtless and of supplications; and it wondered seeing the inestimable riches of its Lord."[3]

[1]Text PL 30, 271D-276A; J. Solano, *Textos*, II, 511-521; cf. G. Morin, O.S.B., *La collection gallicane dite d'Eusèbe d'Emèse et les problèmes qui s'y rattachent, ZNW*, 34 (1935), 107; G. Bareille, DTC V; [2]Sermo 57, PL 39, 2172; [3]*Ibid.*

FIRMA IN TRADITIONE, 15 June 1974

An Apostolic Letter from Paul VI (qv) on Mass stipends,[1] which referring to previous papal texts on the subject states the present discipline in regard to fulfillment, and alteration, of conditions accepted in regard to time and place, identifying also the authorities competent henceforth in these matters.

[1]Text *L'Osservatore Romano*, 11 July 1974, tr. A. Flannery, O.P., I, 277-280.

FRANZELIN, JOHN BAPTIST, CARDINAL (1816-1886)

The Austrian Jesuit, who taught for many years in the Roman College, was a man of vast erudition, a linguist, sensitive to every advance in the history of theology.[1] His prestige was enhanced when Pius IX chose him as papal theologian at the First Vatican Council. By his many theological treatises he gave importance to positive theology, may be said to have revived it. His work on the Eucharist abounds in reference to the Fathers and to previous theologians; he was also attentive to the writings of his time, dealt with Pusey's (qv) work.

F. revived the theory of de Lugo on destruction as the essence of sacrifice. He thought that sacrifice was "the offering to God of something perceptible to the senses for its real or equivalent destruction, by virtue of a lawful institution, with the intention of either recognising the supreme dominion of God, or since the existence of sin, of proclaiming his justice and the expiation which the fault deserves."[2]

It was clear that there would be a substitution of victims for men themselves "who profess themselves entirely subject to God, the origin and end of all creation, and acknowledge that they are guilty of death because of sin." He elaborates thus: "The meaning and purpose of sacrifice are made clear by this substitution of the thing sacrificed for the very life of man. In relation to God, (which may be called its theological meaning), it is the objective expression by the thing's destruction, of his supreme dominion over all things, as to whether they should or should not exist, and for man in a fallen state the recognition of divine justice to be appeased; in relation to man, which may be called the moral meaning of sacrifice, it is the external expression of the interior acknowledgement of and submission to this dominion of God, with the disposition to sacrifice one's life and one's whole being to God, and the interior acknowledgement of guilt, which deserves death."[3] "Destruction of some kind," he thinks, "is in all (sacrifices) the form of the oblation to be made."[4]

How to apply this general idea of sacrifice to the Mass? It is not, as Vasquez and Lessius would have it, that the body and blood of Christ appear to be put to death by the double consecration. The separate presence under the appearance of bread and wine is in appearance only. Christ, living and glorious, is whole and entire under each of the species. True, the double consecration is needed that the Mass be a memorial of the cross, so much so that to take away this sensible relationship with the bloody immolation would be to nullify the Eucharistic sacrifice itself; but it is not this necessary relationship with the cross which constitutes the essential form of the sacrifice of the altar. "If the mystical pouring of blood," he says, "shows us that the Mass is a relative sacrifice, it does not sufficiently explain, of itself, how the Mass is a true, proper sacrifice."[5] F. likewise rejects the opinion of Suarez, though without any detailed analysis.

He opts for De Lugo's (qv) opinion: "We think, therefore, with Cardinal de Lugo and several theologians after him, that the intrinsic form of sacrifice consists in this that Christ, the high priest, through the ministry of priests offering in his name, puts his body and blood under the appearances of bread and wine, in a certain deprivation as to functions and principles of being normal to his most sacred humanity, (so as to be) in the condition of food and drink."[6]

This is broadly the position of De Lugo, though F. differs from his predecessor in holding that the essence of the Mass as a sacrifice is in the consecration alone. He is too generous in his estimate of "several" theologians who have followed De Lugo. He certainly gives his thesis some sweep: "The first born of all creatures, head of the Church, holding the primacy in all things, he gives himself to the Church, through the priests who are his ministers, to be set by his body and blood in such a mode of existence under the species of bread and wine, that he is really in the condition of food and drink; so that (formally in so far as he is under these species) every normal act of his corporeal life depending on his senses ceases; so that he cannot at all act in terms of his body; so that the body and blood, in so far as his presence is bound to the species, is subject in a certain manner to the choice of creatures, not otherwise than if he were inanimate; he has placed himself in such a condition that he the high priest for the whole Church, of which he is the Head, and the Church, through him, should express in his most sacred body and blood God's sovereignty and the absolute dependence of every creature, of which he the man Jesus Christ is the first-born, and should also express and manifest the satisfaction formerly accomplished on the cross for sins by the surrender of this body and the outpouring of this blood."[7]

F. was certain that this restriction of existence *(exinanitio)* contains all that is needed to fulfill the ends of true sacrifice. "More than that, with the exception of the bloody sacrifice of the cross, it is impossible to conceive a more sublime real and more profound form of true sacrifice. There is, therefore, no doubt that, in this sacramental mode of existence of the body and blood of Christ, the suitability and, assuming the insitution, the actual sacrificial meaning, and consequently the intrinsic principle of true and proper sacrifice are contained not only sufficiently, but magnificently."[8]

---

[1]Principal work, *Tractatus de SS Eucharistiae Sacramento et Sacrificio,* ed. 3, 1878; later ed. by J. Filograssi, S.J., 1932; cf. *Commentarius de Vita Eminentissimi Auctoris,* preface to author's *Theses de Ecclesia Christi,* 1867, v-xxxi; N. Walsh, *John Baptist Franzelin, S.J., A Sketch and a Study,* Dublin, 1895; P. Bernard, DTC VI (1920), 765-767; M. Lepin, *L'Idée du sacrifice,* 587-91; A. Michel, DTC, X, 1190-92; [2]p. 318; [3]p. 315; [4]313; [5]388; [6]*Ibid.;* [7]403; [8]*Ibid.*

FRUITS OF THE MASS, THE

Considerable attention was given in the relevant literature formerly to the question of the fruits of the Mass.[1] If this was in some places excessively rigid and positive, the cause may have been insistence on the institutional character of the Church, legalism unchecked. We are faced with a mighty mystery, and this sense of mystery has to inform all reflection on its effects. With this proviso consideration should be given to the important distinction between the Mass as a sacrifice of praise and thanksgiving infinite in value because of the essential offerer, Christ, and the Father to whom in the Spirit his offering is made, and the Mass as propitiation or atonement, and impetration or entreaty. Atonement is intrinsic to the Mass, as the continuation of the sacrifice of the Cross. To benefit by the atonement obtained by the Mass, individuals or whole congregations must have the requisite dispositions, previous sacramental absolution from grave sin, inner conversion from all sin with firm resolve to adhere to God's will. On the subjective disposition here, on submission to divine Providence, as in all sacramental grace, in the final analysis, much depends. The object of all prayer must be related to salvation. The whole Church benefits by the general fruit of the Mass, independently of the celebrant's motivation; those for whom the Mass is specifically offered benefit, in a special way, and the decision to offer specially for named persons, living or dead, is supported by a tradition going back to Tertullian,[2] St. Cyprian,[3] St. Augustine.[4] Pius VI condemned an opposing view held by the Synod of Pistoia (qv)[5], Finally there is a personal fruit accruing to the priest who offers (again depending on his disposition) and to those who offer with him (likewise).

---

[1]Cf. M. de la Taille (qv), *Mysterium Fidei,* Paris, 1931, 319-393; L. Billot (qv), *De Sacramentis,* Rome, 1932, 640-658; L. Ott, *Fundamentals of Catholic Dogma,* Cork, 1954, 412-415; L. Godefroy, DTC, VI, 933-944; [2]*De monogomia,* 10; [3]Ep., 1, 2; [4]*Confessions,* IX, 12ff; [5]DS, 1630.

G

GAUDENTIUS OF BRESCIA (4th-5th century)
A friend of St. Ambrose G, a reluctant Bishop of Brescia, was involved in the attempt to save St. John Chrysostom from ill-treatment at the emperor's hands, but to no avail. A number of his sermons survive. In one we read this wonderful passage on the Eucharist: "The heavenly sacrifice which Christ instituted is truly the bequest of his new testament, a bequest which he left us as the pledge of his presence on the night he was handed over to be crucified. This is the food which sustains and nourishes us on our journey through life, until we depart from this world and are united with Christ. This is why the Lord said: 'Unless you eat my flesh and drink my blood, you will have no life in you.' It was his will that his gifts should remain among us; it was his will that the souls which he redeemed should continue to be sanctified by sharing the pattern of his own passion. For this reason he appointed his faithful disciples the first priests of his Church and enjoined them never to cease to perform the mysteries of eternal life. These mysteries must be celebrated by every priest in every church in the world until Christ comes again from heaven, so that we priests, together with the congregation of the faithful, may have the example of Christ's passion daily before our eyes, hold it in our hands, and even receive it in our mouths and in our hearts and so keep undimmed the memory of our redemption. . . .

"Besides, since bread is made from many grains of wheat ground into flour, mixed with water and baked by fire, it is appropriate that we should receive the sacrament of Christ's body in the form of bread. For we know that Christ has become one body made up of the many members of the human race and brought to completion by the fire of the Holy Spirit. He was born of the Holy Spirit and since it was fitting for him to fulfill all righteousness, he entered the waters of baptism in order to consecrate them. Then, full of the Holy Spirit, who had come down on him in the likeness of a dove, he returned from the Jordan, as St. Luke tells us: 'And Jesus, full of the Holy Spirit, returned from the Jordan.' So too the wine of his blood is made from many grapes, the fruit of the vineyard he planted himself, which are gathered and pressed in the wine press of the cross; by its own energy the wine ferments in those who, with faithful hearts, receive him like capacious jars. Escape, all of you, from the domination of Egypt and Pharaoh, I mean the devil, and join us in receiving this sacrifice of the saving Pasch, with all th eagerness of a religious heart, so that the Lord Jesus Christ himself, whom we believe to be present in his sacraments, may sanctify our inmost hearts. For the power of this sacrifice is beyond worth, and endures forever."[1]

---

[1]Works PL 20, 827-1002; J. Solano, *Textos,* II, 17-24; here quoted, Tractate 2 on Exodus, 31ff, p. 22, 23; cf. E. Peterson, EC, V, 1950, esp. P. Viard, DSp VI, 139-143, ample bibl.

GERMANUS OF CONSTANTINOPLE (c. 634-733)
The Patriarch of Constantinople, famous for his defence of sacred images and for his elaborate teaching on Our Lady, whose universal mediation of grace he

defended eloquently, is probably the author of the *Historia Mystica Ecclesiae Catholicae*, an interpretation of the Byzantine liturgy, best known until the advent of the work by Nicholas Cabasilas (qv).[1] The textual history appears to be confused and there may have been interpolations. Through the text, as we have it, there are characteristic Byzantine points, especially the emphasis on the Holy Spirit and a plenary confession of the Trinitarian mystery, as in this excerpt: "Whence also the Holy Spirit, by the good pleasure of the Father and the will of the Son invisibly present, shows forth divine power and bears witness to the hand of the priest, and seals and accomplishes the change of the proferred holy gifts into the body and blood of Christ our Lord who said, 'For them I make myself holy' (Jn 17:19) so that 'He who eats my flesh and drinks my blood abides in me and I in him.'"

---

[1]ed. N. Borgia, *Il Commentario liturgico di S. Germano*, 2nd ed., Grottaferrata, 1912, revised by D. Sheerin, *Historia Ecclesiastica: The Contemplation of the Divine Liturgy by ... Germanus*, Fairfax, Virginia, 1984; cf. F. Cayre, DTC, VI, 1914, 1300-1309; J. Darrouzes, DSp, VI, 309-311; H.-G. Beck, *Kirche und theologische Literatur im byzantinischen Reich*, Munich, 1959, 473-476; esp. M. Geerard, *Clavis Patrum Graecorum*, III, 1979, 508-509; D. Sheerin, *The Eucharist*, Wilmington, 1986, 116-127; [2]Apud Sheerin, *op. cit.*, 124-25.

GREGORY OF NYSSA, ST. (c. 330-c. 395)

G. deals with the Eucharist in the *Oratio catechetica*, the Great Catechism.[1] "What," he asks, "is this remedy?" (for the poison that dissolved our nature). "Nothing else than the body which proved itself superior to death and became the source of our life. For, as the apostle observes, a little yeast makes a whole lump of dough like itself. In the same way, when the body which God made immortal enters ours, it entirely transforms it into itself. When a poison is combined with something wholesome, the whole admixture is rendered as useless as the poison. Conversely, the immortal body, by entering the one who receives it, transforms his entire being into its own nature. Now nothing can enter the body unless it is assimilated in the system by eating and drinking. Hence the body must receive the life-giving power in the natural way. Now only that body in which God dwelt acquired such life-giving grace; and we have already shown that our body cannot become immortal unless it shares in immortality by its association with what is immortal. We must, therefore, inquire how that one body can be perpetually distributed to so many thousands of the faithful throughout the world, and yet be received in its entirety in the portion each gets, and still remain whole in itself."

After some considerations on human nutrition and a parallel with divine things, G. expounds his faith explicitly: "We have good reason, then, to believe that now too the bread which is consecrated by God's word is changed into the body of God the Word. For that body as well was once virtually bread, though it was sanctified by the indwelling of the Word in the flesh. Therefore the means whereby the bread was changed in that body, and was converted into divine power, are identical with those which produce a similar result now. For, in the former case, the grace of the Word sanctified the body which derived its subsistence from bread, and which, in a way, was itself bread. In the latter case, similarly, the bread (as the apostle says) is consecrated by the Word of God and prayer. It is not, however, by being eaten that it gradually becomes the body of the Word. Rather is it immediately changed by the Word into the body, as the Word himself declares: 'This is my body.'

But all flesh is nourished by the element of moisture as well; for the earthly part in us could not continue to live unless it were combined with this. Just as we sustain the solid mass of the body by firm and solid food, so we supplement its moisture from what is akin to us. By entering us it is changed into blood by assimilation; and this is especially the case if it derives from wine the capacity of being changed into heat. Now the flesh in which God dwelt used this element too to maintain its existence. The reason, moreover, that God, when he revealed himself, united himself with our mortal nature was to deify humanity by this close relation with Deity. In consequence, by means of his flesh, which is constituted by bread and wine, he implants himself in all believers, following out the plan of grace. He unites himself with their bodies so that mankind too, by its union with what is immortal, may share in incorruptibility. And this he confers on us by the power of the blessing, through which he changes ('transelements,' *metastoicheiusas*) the nature of the visible elements into that immortal body."[2]

---

[1]J. Solano, *Textos*, I, 424-437; cf. M. Canevet, DSp VI, (1967), 971-1011; J. Maier, *Die Eucharistielehre der drei grossen Kappadozier*, Freiburg i.B., 1913; [2]*Or. Catech.*, 37, PG 45, 93A-97B.

GUITMUND OF AVERSA (d. 1090/1095)

A Norman monk, Abbot of Le Bec, who later became Archbishop of Aversa, in Italy, 1088, G. published an important treatise against Berengar (qv), *De corporis et sanguinis Domini veritate libri tres*.[1] It was in the form of dialogue with one Roger. Berengar's opinion is thus described: Berengar and those following him assert that the Eucharist of the Lord is not truly and substantially *(vere substantialiterque)* the body and blood of the Lord, but is only called thus by name, in so far as by shadow and figure it signifies the body and blood of the Lord."

Besides these followers of Berengar who speak of shadows and figures there are the *impanatores*: "But others say that the body and blood of the Lord are truly contained but in a hidden way and are subject in a kind of manner to impanation, as I have said, that they may be taken." Both the *umbratici*, those who believe in shadows, and the *impanatores*, those who think of some kind of union allowing the body and the bread to co-exist, are subjected to searching criticism by G. In the course of his exposition, in which he draws on the Fathers, Augustine, Ambrose (qqv), Leo the Great, Gregory the Great and Hilary, he notably advanced systematic thinking on the Eucharist by applying the distinction of substance and accidents and by his use of the word substantially, especially with the verb to change: the way was open for the full doctrine of transubstantiation. He did think that the real presence survived corruption of the accidents. Berengar himself had spoken of the distinction of substance and accidents, but incorrectly. Its first orthodox application was by G. He also worked heavily from the words of institution.

[1]PL 149, 1427-1490; cf. J. Leclercq, *Passage authentique inédit de Guitmund d'Aversa, RBen* 57, (1947), 213-14; P. Shaugnessy, *The Eucharistic Doctrine of Guitmund of Aversa*, Rome, 1939; A. Piolanti, EC VI 1302-03; F. Vernet, DTC VI, 2, 1989-92; *Geiselmann*, LTK, IV, 1272; F. Dellray, *Catholicisme*, V, 422-23; B. Gregoire, NCE, VI, 858-59.

H

HAGIOGRAPHY

More than the other Sacraments, the Eucharist is a recurring theme in Christian hagiography.[1] Progress in holiness, of necessity, means growth in devotion to the Eucharist, the centre of Christian life. There is a large field for research in regard to the Eucharistic devotion of saints, such as St. Catherine of Siena who lived miraculously without food, deriving sustenance from the Eucharist, or again of those in very different walks of life, the contemplatives, as John of the Cross, Teresa of Avila and others, as well as those engaged in secular pursuits, those living the consecrated life and those in the married state. Some of the saints are thought of more immediately in this context: St. Paschal Baylon, patron of Eucharistic Congresses (qv), St. Pierre Julien Eymard (qv), founder of religious institutes especially dedicated to Eucharistic devotion; St. Margaret Mary, who received her glowing revelations before the Blessed Sacrament; the great preachers on the Eucharist like the Curé of Ars, the builders of churches like St. John Bosco: the list is happily interminable.

---

[1]Cf. Ephrem Longpré, O.F.M., *Expérience eucharistique dans l'hagiographie*, DSp IV, 2, 1615-1619.

HEART, THE EUCHARISTIC

Since devotion to the Sacred Heart of Jesus has been brought into the public worship of the Church, the cult of his Eucharistic Heart has come as a logical sequel. Much of what is said in Sacred Scripture on the love which Jesus Christ has for men, much of the theology of the Fathers and medieval writers on the same theme, is equally applicable to devotion to the Sacred Heart and to the Eucharisic heart of Jesus. In our cult of the Sacred Heart we honour, serve and love this Heart as the immediate source and inspiration of his entire redemptive and sanctifying mission and achievement. In our devotion to the Eucharistic Heart we look to the sublime gift wherein all that is embodied, himself in the Eucharist, not only his gift, but his presence, his sacrificial immolation, his union with us in our sacramental communion.

Already in the seventeenth century St. John Eudes (d. 1680) spoke of the Heart of Jesus as a furnace of love for us in the most holy Sacrament. In that age too, according to present knowledge, *Cor eucharisticum* and *Cor Jesu eucharistici* were used for the first time. They are found in the work of a German parish priest, Anthony Ginther (1655-c.1740): *Speculum amoris et doloris in sacratissimo ac divinissimo Corde Jesu incarnati, eucharistici et crucifixi orbi christiano propositum*, Augsburg, 1706, ed. 4,1743. A French Maurist, about the same time, Jean-Paul du Sault (1650-1724) wrote of "the divine Heart of Jesus in the Most Holy Sacrament of the Altar," 5 vol., Toulouse, 1701-1703, in his *Entretiens avec Jésus Christ dans le Très-Saint Sacrement de l'autel.*

The private revelation of a devout French lady, Sophie Prouvier, had an effect in spreading devotion to the Eucharistic Heart; a prayer composed by her in 1854 was, in that year, indulged by Mgr. Mabile, Bishop of Saint-Claude. Sermons—the first by St.

Pierre-Julien Eymard (qv)—articles, papers at national and international Eucharistic congresses, took up the idea and expounded or defended it. Official action was not lacking. Pius IX in 1868 indulgenced an invocation to the Eucharistic Heart of Jesus. Important figures in the Catholic life, especially of France, wholeheartedly espoused the cause. Many confraternities were established under the exalted patronage. In 1872 Francois Blot, S.J., published two volumes entitled *Le Coeur Eucharistique ou le Coeur de Jésus dans le Saint Sacrament* (Paris). A review of the Archconfraternity of the Eucharistic Heart was launched in Rome in 1903 and in 1914 in Paris, *Le Prêtre du Coeur Eucharistique de Jésus.*

Warnings came from Rome against excesses, in the domain of iconograpy. Despite many requests from bishops, despite the fact that St. Pius X, in 1911, enrolled himself as a member of the association of Priests of the Eucharistic Heart of Jesus which he approved, it was a restrictive decision which emanated in 1914 from the Congregation of Rites. There seemed to be contradiction in its directives with the position officially taken in the Raccolta and especially in the Papal Brief by which Leo XIII, 16 February 1903, had approved the Archconfraternity of the Eucharistic Heart of Jesus. Further clarification was given, making it clear that the devotion was approved, but as yet no liturgical ceremony was sanctioned.

The change came on 9 November 1921 when the Congregation of Rites approved a Mass and Office in honour of the Eucharistic Heart of Jesus, to be celebrated the Thursday after the octave of Corpus Christi (qv). What then is the official teaching of the Church on the meaning of the devotion and its place in the liturgy? The answer is principally in the following illuminating texts—which naturally permit of explanation and development.

The Brief of Leo XIII: "This archconfraternity bears this name because it expresses the twofold object of the devotion, the cause and the effect, that is the loving Heart of Our Lord Jesus Christ, and the Holy Eucharist, which is its work par excellence."[2] A note in the *Raccolta*, composed by Cardinal Gotti and attached to a prayer to the Eucharistic Heart, which had been enriched with indulgences by Leo XIII, 17 June 1902, stated that "worship of the Eucharistic Heart of Jesus takes as a special object of veneration, love, gratitude and mutual appeal the act of supreme love by which the Heart of Jesus instituted the Eucharist and remains with us until the end of time."[3]

Pius XII, in one of the great Christological documents in church history, *Haurietis Aquas* on the Sacred Heart of Jesus, 15 May 1956: "It is also our dearest wish that all those who glory in the name of Christian, and who labour to establish the Reign of Christ in the world, should regard the practice of devotion to the Heart of Jesus as a standard and source of unity, salvation and peace. At the same time no one must think that this devotion entails any belittlement of the other forms of religious piety whereby the Christian people, under the Church's guidance, honour the divine Redeemer. Far from it. Without any doubt a burning devotion to the Heart of Jesus will cherish and advance our reverence for the august Sacrament of the Altar. For we dare assert—and this is wonderfully borne out by the revelations vouchsafed by Jesus Christ to St. Gertrude and St. Margaret Mary—that only those have a proper understanding of Jesus Christ crucified who have penetrated the mystic secrets of his Heart. Nor is it easy to fathom the might of that love, constrained by which Christ has given himself to us as the food of our souls, unless we go out of our way to foster the cult of the Eucharistic Heart of Jesus; the which cult, if we may borrow the words of our Predecessor of happy memory, Leo XIII, recalls that 'act of supreme love by which our Redeemer, pouring out all the riches of his Heart in his desire to be with us all days even to the end of the world, instituted the adorable Sacrament of the Eucharist.' (The Pope then quotes St. Albert the Great) 'For not the least gift of his Heart is the Eucharist, which he bestowed upon us out of the immense charity of his Heart.'"[4]

The prayer of the Mass approved in 1921: "Lord Jesus Christ, who in pouring out the riches of your love for men, have instituted the Eucharist, grant, we beseech you, that we may be empowered to love your most loving Heart and always receive this so great Sacrament worthily."

The Decree of approval: "This new feast has the purpose of commemorating very specially the love of which our Lord Jesus Christ gives us proof in the mystery of the holy Eucharist. Another purpose is to stir the faithful to approach with ever greater confidence the holy Eucharist, to set their souls aflame with the divine love, the source of which our Lord Jesus Christ has in his heart burning with an infinite love, which instituted the holy Eucharist, which loves his disciples and keeps them in his Sacred Heart, since he lives and dwells in them as they dwell in him, he who, through the Eucharist, offers and gives himself to each one of us, in his quality of victim, companion in exile, food, viaticum and finally, pledge of heaven."[5]

---

[1]Cf. A. Lepidi, *De cultu Cordis Jesu Eucharistici explicatio dogmatica* Rome, 1905; French tr. with history of the devotion by E. Hugon, Paris, 1926; F. Bouchage, *Rayons du Coeur Eucharistique*, Saint-Etienne, 1922; F. Jansen, *Le Coeur Eucharistique,*

N RT 54 (1927), 112-122; D. Castelain, *De cultu eucharistici Cordis Jesu. Historia, doctrina, documenta*, Paris, (1928); R. Garrigou-Lagrange, O.P., *Le Coeur eucharistique et le don parfait de lui-même, Vie Spirituelle*, 29 (1931), 225-237; L. Garriguet, *Eucharistie et Sacré Coeur. Etude comparative de théologie et d'histoire sur les deux dévotions*, Paris ,1925; id., *Les deux grandes dévotions de l'heure présente. Devotion à l'Eucharistie et dévotion au Sacré Coeur*, Paris, 1926; A. Vermeersch, S.J., 7th ed., *Pratique et doctrine de la dévotion au Sacré Coeur*, 136-140, Tournai-Paris, 1930; Auguste Hamon, *Histoire de la dévotion au Sacré Coeur*, vol 5, Paris, 1940, 247-254; [2]*A A S* 35, 1902-1903, 582; [3]*Raccolta*, no. 121, 194; [4]*A A S* 48 (1956), 351; reference to St. Albert, *De Eucharistia*, works e du Burgnet, vol. 38, 358; [5]*A A S* 13 (1921), 545.

HILARY OF POITIERS, ST., DOCTOR OF THE CHURCH (c. 315-67)

H's doctrine on the Eucharist is found in his great work on the Trinity (qv). Replying to those who maintain that there is not a unity of nature between the Father and the Son but of will only, he appeals to the analogy of the Eucharist through which Christ is in us. The whole passage deserves quotation:

"Now our Lord has not left the minds of his faithful followers in doubt, but has explained the manner in which his nature operates, saying, 'That they may be one, as we are one; I in them and Thou in me, that they may be perfect in one.' Now I ask those who bring forward a unity of will between Father and Son, whether Christ is in us today through verity of nature or through agreement of will. For if in truth the Word has been made flesh and we in very truth receive the Word made flesh as food from the Lord, are we not bound to believe that he abides in us naturally, who, born as a man, has assumed the nature of our flesh now inseparable from himself, and has conjoined the nature of his own flesh to the nature of the eternal Godhead in the sacrament by which his flesh is communicated to us? For so are we all one, because the Father is in Christ and Christ in us. Whoever then shall deny that the Father is in Christ naturally must first deny that either he is himself in Christ naturally, or Christ in him, because the Father in Christ and Christ in us make us one in them. Hence, if indeed Christ has taken to himself the flesh of our body, and that man who was born from Mary was indeed Christ, and we indeed receive in a mystery the flesh of his body (and for this cause we shall be one, because the Father is in him and he in us) how can a unity of will be maintained, seeing that the special property of nature received through the sacrament is the sacrament of perfect unity?

"For as to what we say concerning the reality of Christ's nature within us, unless we have been taught by him our words are foolish and impious. For he says himself: 'For my flesh is food indeed and my blood is drink indeed. He who eats my flesh and drinks my blood abides in me, and I in him' (Jn 6:55, 56). As to the verity of the flesh and blood there is no room left for doubt. For now both from the declaration of the Lord himself and our own faith, it is verily flesh and verily blood. And these when eaten and drunk, bring it to pass that both we are in Christ and Christ in us. Is not this true? Yet they who affirm that Christ Jesus is not truly God are welcome to find it false. He therefore himself is in us through the flesh and we in him, whilst together with him our own very selves are in God.

"Now how it is that we are in him through the sacrament of the flesh and blood bestowed upon us, he himself testifies saying, 'Yet a little while and the world will see me no more, but you will see me; because I live, you will live also. In that day you will know that I am in my Father, and you in me and I in you' (Jn 14:19, 20). If he wished to indicate a mere unity of will, why did he set forth a kind of gradation and sequence in the completion of the unity, unless it were that, since he was in the Father through the nature of the Deity, and we on the contrary in him through his birth in the body, he would have us believe that he is in us through the mystery of the sacraments? And thus there might be taught a perfect unity through a Mediator, whilst we abiding in him, he abode in the Father, and as abiding in the Father abode also in us; and so we might arrive at unity with the Father, since in him who dwells naturally in the Father by birth, we also dwell naturally, while he himself abides naturally in us also.

"Again, how natural this unity is in us he has himself testified in this wise, 'He who eats my flesh and drinks my blood abides in me, and I in him' (Jn 6:56). For no man shall dwell in him, save him in whom he dwells himself, for the only flesh which he has taken to himself is the flesh of those who have taken his. Now he had already taught before the sacrament of this perfect unity, saying, 'As the living Father sent me, and I live because of the Father, so he who eats me will live because of me' (ibid. 57). So he lives through the Father and as he lives through the Father in like manner we live through his flesh."[2]

H. takes the divine unity as *exemplar* and Eucharistic unity as *exemplatum*. His aim is to establish from the analogy of Christ's unity with us, which is physical, the natural bond in nature between the Father and the Son. But despite the advantage of seeing the Eucharist in a Trinitarian setting, the distinction must be preserved between unity in the Godhead and unity between the communicant and Christ.

[1] *Textos*, I, 309-320; PL 10, 285f; cf. C. Kannengeisser, S.J. DSp., VII, 466-99; [2] *De Trinitate*, Bk VIII, 13-16, *Textos*, 313-16.

HIPPOLYTUS OF ROME, ST (c. 170-c. 236)

One of the great triumphs of recent patristic scholarship has been the successful attribution to H. of *The Apostolic Tradition*, a unique source for the structure of the Roman Church and its liturgical practice, at the beginning of the third century.[1] Scholars of international repute, E. Schwartz, R.H. Connolly, G. Dix, and B. Botte have established the identity of the work and given reliable editions. We are concerned here with the anaphora (qv) found in H's work. The thanksgiving contains these words: "You sent him from heaven into the womb of the Virgin. He was conceived and became flesh, he manifested himself as your Son, born of the Spirit and the Virgin. He did your will, and, to win for you a holy people, he stretched out his hands in suffering to rescue from suffering those who believe in you." Then comes the institution narrative: "When he was about to surrender himself to voluntary offering in order to destroy death, to break the devil's chains, to tread hell underfoot, to pour out his light upon the just, to establish the covenant and manifest his resurrection, he took bread, he gave you thanks and said: 'Take, eat, this is my Body which is broken for you.' In like manner for the cup, he said: 'This is my Blood which is poured out for you. When you do this, do (it) in memory of me.'"

Thereon comes the anamnesis (qv): "Remembering therefore your death and your resurrection, we offer you the bread and the wine, we thank you for having judged us worthy to stand before you and serve you." Next is the epiclesis (qv): "And we pray you to send the Holy Spirit on the offering of your holy Church, to bring together in unity all those who receive it. May they be filled with the Holy Spirit who strengthens their faith in the truth. May we be able to thus praise and glorify you through your child Jesus Christ." The Doxology follows: "Through him glory to you and honour, to the Father and the Son, with the Holy Spirit, in your holy Church now and for ever and ever. Amen."[2]

[1] For H. cf. esp., M. Richard s.v. DSp, VII, 1, 531-571—he leaves the *Apostolic Tradition* to a separate article to appear; for recent history and bibl. L. Deiss, *Springtime*, 123-127; text follows; *Prex*, with bibl. 80, 81; [2] *Springtime*, 130, 131.

HOLY HOUR, THE

Since the seventeenth century, due to the influence of St. Margaret Mary, the custom prevails in the Catholic Church of spending one whole hour in adoration before the Blessed Sacrament. On certain occasions the Blessed Sacrament is exposed and large or small groups are organised. The hour chosen may be from 11 o'clock to midnight on Thursday, or some one hour from the afternoon to midnight on Friday or at any other time. The words of Our Lord spoken to the saint sometime in June 1674 were: "Every week between Thursday and Friday I will grant you a share in that mortal sadness which I chose to feel in the Garden of Olives. You shall keep me company in the prayer I then offered to my Father."

In 1829 a French Jesuit, Fr. Robert Debrosse, founded an association which eventually became the Archconfraternity of the Holy Hour, spreading the devotion into different countries; the centre is at Paray le Monial.

The Holy Hour as a practice is based on the identity which Christ wishes to establish between him and the Christian, a truth admirably expounded and developed by the French school of spirituality, with its cardinal principle the assimilation of the faithful soul to the mysteries of Christ's life. The practice is supported by the further truth that the historic mysteries of Christ's life—in this case as the Saviour explained to St. Margaret Mary, the Agony in the Garden—are made present to his faithful in a mysterious communion which transcends the limitations of time and space. Hence the conviction of the great mystics of living with Christ what he endured.

Three further important truths are implied in the devotion: the infinite love of Christ for us symbolised in his adorable Heart, the Eucharist seen as the supreme, sublime gift of this love and the urgent call on all those truly faithful to him to reparation for the sins and offences offered to him by others. The basis of this reparation, which ultimately implies participation in the redemptive Passion of the Saviour, is the vital bond which unites all in the Communion of Saints, its concrete manifestation, the Mystical Body of Christ.

The practice of the Holy Hour has been much supported in the Church by the many religious institutes founded in the nineteenth and twentieth centuries with an explicit orientation towards Eucharistic devotion, perpetual adoration notably. Perpetual adoration, vigils before the Blessed Sacrament are frequently organised at the great Marian shrines. Great apostles maintain the practice daily. In a busy life Bishop Fulton Sheen never missed a single day in his fidelity to the practice.

The Holy Hour is distinctive of the Catholic ethos and way of devotional life. Some Catholic ecumenists, thinking that to achieve Christian unity it would be helpful to shed such distinctive elements, discouraged the Holy Hour. On the occasion of his visit to Paray le Monial, John Paul II (qv) handed a letter to the Superior General of the Jesuits, recalling them to their historic vocation to spread devotion to the Sacred Heart: he referred explicitly to the Nine Fridays and the Holy Hour.[2]

The Basilica of the Sacred Heart in Montmartre has perpetual exposition of the Blessed Sacrament to attract devotees of the Holy Hour; all-night vigils are organised for groups.

[1]F.M. Catherinet, *Ce qu'il faut savoir pour bien comprendre et bien faire l'Heure Sainte*, Paray le Monial, 1932; K. Rahner, S.J., *Heilige Stunde und Passionsandacht*, Freiburg i. B., 1960; [2]*L'Osservatore Romano*, weekly ed., November 3, 1986.

HOMILY

The homily in its classical sense was spoken during the celebration of the liturgy to explain some biblical text that had been read and to enforce its claim on intellectual assent or moral commitment. There have been great moments in the history of the genre: the age of the Cappadocians and those who gave them their model, notably Origen in the east with St. John Chrysostom as a crowning light; Ambrose and Augustine, high luminaries in the West, but not overshadowing others who happen to be less well known, or not directly associated with the homily—St. Leo the Great, thought of as a great ruler and official teacher, Maximus of Turin, Zeno of Verona, much earlier, Hippolytus.

With time and the evolution of the Liturgy, biblical texts were chosen to fit the feasts newly created and this called for explanation of the feast itself. Hence the many homilies on the Annunciation, and, in the East especially, on the *Hypapante* or the Presentation of Jesus, as on the Presentation of Mary in the Temple; or again the many homilies preached in the West on Christmas.

With the rise and expansion of monasticism a new kind of homily was called for, one spoken to a special audience. St. Jerome, St. Gregory the Great, Venerable Bede exemplify the type. St. Bernard was conspicuous in such a product. But practice changed, deteriorated even, and one of the reforms put forward by the Council of Trent was in these terms: "The holy Synod commands pastors and everyone who has the care of souls to explain frequently during the celebration of the Masses, either themselves or through others, some of the things which are read in the Mass, and among other things to expound some mystery of this most

holy Sacrifice, especially on Sundays and feast days." Exhortation by the Code of Canon Law and a papal encyclical, *Humani Generis Redemptionem*, 5 June 1917, did not have major effect. The real change came with the liturgical movement, with the realization that there was a vitally close link between the Liturgy of the Word and the Liturgy of the Eucharist, and that the homily must make this link explicit and meaningful. This is not to belittle the great pulpit orators of the seventeenth century.

It was then logical that in the liturgical reform directed and outlined by Vatican II, the homily would have a place. Thus we read in the Constitution on the Liturgy:

"That the intimate connection between the rite and words may be apparent in the liturgy: 1. In sacred celebrations a more ample, more varied and more suitable reading from Sacred Scripture should be restored; 2. The most suitable place for a sermon ought to be indicated in the rubrics, for a sermon is part of the liturgical action whenever a rite involves one. The ministry of preaching is to be fulfilled most faithfully and carefully. The sermon, moreover, should draw its content mainly from scriptural and liturgical sources, for it is the proclamation of God's wonderful works in the history of salvation, which is the mystery of Christ ever made present and active in us, especially in the celebration of the liturgy."[2]

This general idea is applied to the Mass as follows: "By means of the homily the mysteries of the faith and the guiding principles of the Christian life are expounded from the sacred text during the course of the liturgical year. The homily, therefore, is to be highly esteemed as part of the liturgy itself. In fact at those Masses which are celebrated on Sundays and holy days of obligation, with the people assisting, it should not be omitted except for a serious reason."[3]

[1]Cf. C.H. Dodd, *The Apostolic Preaching and its Developments*, 10th print., R.H. Fuller, *What is Liturgical Preaching*, London, 1957; *Initiation à la pratique de la théologie*, ed. J.B. Refoulé, Paris, 1982, V, *La prédication*, bibl. 150-153; R. Spiazzi, *Verbum Salutis, Storia e Teologia della predicazione*, Rome, 1963; O. Semmelroth, *Parole éfficace, Pour une théologie de la prédication*, Paris, 1963; J. Murphy-O'Connor, O.P., *La prédication selon St. Paul*, Paris, 1966; E. Haensli, *La prédication d'aujourdhui, fruit d'une théologie vivante*, in *Questions théologiques aujourdhui*, Paris, 1966, III, 61-89; D. Grasso, *L'Annonce du salut, Théologie de la parole*, Paris, 1969; J.-B. Schneyer, *Geschichte der katholischen Predigt*, Freiburg, 1969; R. Bohren, *Predigtlehre*, Munich, 1971; J.J. von Allmen, *Le Prédicateur, témoin de l'Evangile*, Irenikon, 49 (1976), 333ff; 453ff; G. Ebeling, *Fundamentaltheologische Erwagungen zur Predigt, Wort und Glaube*, Tubingen, III, 1975, 554-573; A. Dumas, *La prédication de Jésus Christ*, RSR 65 (1977), 227-238; G. Garrone, *Parole et Eucharistie, Réflexions sur l'homélie*, Paris, 1978; D.T. Holland, *The Preaching Tradition, A Brief History*, Nashville, Abingdon, 1980; D. Grasso, *L'annuncio della salvezza: Teologia*

della predicazione, Naples, 1960; Z. Alszeghy, *Il problema teologica della predicazione,* Greg. 40 (1959) 671-744; S. Maggiolini, *La predicazione nella vita della Chiesa,* Brescia, 1961; E. Robben, *Il problema teologico de la predicazione,* Rome, 1962; esp. C. Vagaggini, O.S.B. (qv), *Theological Dimensions of the Liturgy,* Collegeville, 1976, 859-887; [2]*Constitution on the Liturgy,* 35; [3]*Ibid.,* 52.

HUGH OF LANGRES (11th Century)

Author of the first work against Berengar, a letter, probably written before 1049, shorter than the treatises of Durandus, Lanfranc or Guitmund of Aversa (qqv), but well argued.[1] H. could not use the word transubstantiation (qv), which did not yet exist, but he had the essentials of the doctrine. He pointed out to Berengar that his error was that the "nature and essence of bread and wine are not changed." On this change depends the real presence. Berengar speaks of the body but really makes it incorporeal—"that the body should exist without the nature and essence of the bread and wine changing: and you make the body which you had said was crucified intellectual (i.e., spiritual)." "For if the essence and nature of bread and wine continue really present after the consecration , no change-over can be thought of, and if what is added is by the sole power of the intellect, it does not really take place." He presses the point forcibly appealing to the words of the institution, "This is my body." "You agree that he said this, but you cease not to deny it. For you say that it is a body and not a body, his and not his."

Briefly H. teaches that the elements of the bread and wine—apart from the species—become flesh and blood, though he does not develop his thinking on the species. As to manner, H. must accept it as a mystery like the Incarnation or the regeneration of a soul. He uses the miracle of Cana by way of illustration.

[1]PL 142, 1325-1334;

HYMNOGRAPHY

Hymns to the Blessed Sacrament are not found so frequently in early times. L. Deiss reproduces two, one from the third century, the other from the fourth.[1] The Eithiopian liturgy has a collection of Eucharistic hymns to be sung at the end of Mass. They are attributed to a sixth-century saint Yared, but critical scholarship assigns a later date.[2] The Antiphonary of Bangor (end of seventh century) reproduces a Eucharistic hymn, *Sancti, venite, Christi corpus sumite.* From the twelth century on, more and more prayers to the Eucharist are found and in the next century we get the great hymns. Authorship of the best known was at one time taken for St. Thomas; the *Adoro te* is now controverted, its beauty and power are not in doubt.[3] *Lauda Sion* probably is authentic—it has the sobriety and accuracy of the *Summa Theologiae.* The other hymns attributed to St. Thomas are the *Pange lingua, Sacris sollemniis, Verbum supernum.* The stimulus was the feast of *Corpus Christi* (qv). The *Orationale Augiense* (Reichenau, 14th-15th century) contains the largest collection of Eucharistic hymns of those times, twenty-six items, including the *Ave verum,* even more popular than the *Adoro te.* The *Ave verum* was first a prayer said at the Elevation (qv). It is found, in its own right, in a 14th-century Cluny Missal and a 15th-century Angers Missal.

Translations have been made of the classic Eucharistic hymns, the *Lauda Sion* and others—a difficult task.

[1]*Springtime,* 255, 257; cf. E. Bertaud, DSp, IV, 2, 1629, 30; J.S. Phillimore, *The Hundred Best Latin Hymns,* London, 1926—8 Eucharistic hymns, *Ave vivens, hostia* by John Peckham in addition to those mentioned; [2]Cf. B. Velat, *Hymnes eucharistiques éthiopiennes, Rythmes du monde, nouv.* série, 1 (1953), 26-36. art. Ethiopio, DSp IV, 1473; [3]A. Wilmart, O.S.B., *Auteurs spirituels et Textes dévots du Moyen Age,* Paris, 1932.

I

IGNATIUS OF ANTIOCH (d. c. 110)

The testimony of this most important pastor in the post-apostolic age is of prime importance for an understanding of the place the Eucharist had from the beginning of the Church.[1] The texts are well-known and, fittingly, often quoted. In Ephesians I. writes: "Let no one deceive himself: unless a man is within the sanctuary, he has to go without the *Bread of God.* Assuredly, if the prayer of one or two has such efficacy, how much more that of the bishop and the entire Church. It follows then: He who absents himself from the common meeting, by that very fact shows pride and becomes a sectarian; for the Scripture says: *God resists the proud.*"[2]

In the same letter he writes: "Make an effort, then, to meet more frequently to celebrate God's Eucharist (K. Lake tr. 'to give thanks') and to offer praise. For when you meet frequently in the same place, the forces of Satan are overthrown, and his baneful influence is neutralized by the unanimity of your faith. Peace is a precious thing: it puts an end to every war waged by heavenly or earthly enemies."[3] And again: "I will do so (i.e., send further teaching) especially if the Lord should reveal to me that you—the entire community of you!—are in the habit, through grace derived from the name, of meeting in common, animated by one faith and in union with Jesus Christ—who *in the flesh was of the line of David* (Rom 1:3), the Son of Man and the Son of God—of meeting, I say, to show obedience with undivided mind to the bishop and the presbytery, and to break the same Bread, which is the medicine of immortality, the antidote against death, and everlasting life in Jesus Christ."[4]

Here we have a theology of the Eucharist as the central ecclesial act, as the source of power against Satan, and as the pledge of immortality. On it unity in the Church rests. I. can accomodate, with his manifest realism, a suggestive symbolism, as he shows in his epistle to the Trallians: "Take up the practice, then, of kind forbearance and renew yourselves in faith, which is the Flesh of the Lord and in love which is the Blood of Jesus Christ."[5]

The Eucharist as the very centre of Christian living and well-spring of hope is evident in these lines to the Romans: "I have no taste for corruptible food or for the delights of this life. *Bread of God* is what I desire, that is, flesh of Jesus Christ, who was of the seed of David, and for my drink I desire his Blood, that is, incorruptible love."[6] Has there ever been a more sublime, more authentic Eucharistic piety?

That the Eucharist links us directly with the Redemption, bringing hope of future resurrection, I. conveys to the Smyrnaeans, "From Eucharist they (those in error) hold aloof, because they do not confess that the Eucharist is the Flesh of our Saviour Jesus Christ, which suffered for our sins, and which the Father in his loving kindness raised from the dead. And so those who question the gift of God perish in their contentiousness. It would be better for them to have love, so as to share in the resurrection."[7]

The Eucharist is the essential test of orthodoxy as I. tells the Philadelphians: "Take care, then, to partake of one Eucharist; for, one is the flesh of our Lord Jesus Christ, and one the cup to unite us with his

Blood, and one altar, just as there is one bishop assisted by the presbytery and the deacons, my fellow servants. Thus you will conform in all your actions to the will of God."[8]

---

[1]Text F.X. Funk, revised by K. Bihlmeyer, *Die Apostolischen Väter*, I. Teil, Tubingen, 1924; English tr., K. Lake, *The Apostolic Fathers*, I, (Loeb Classical Library), London, 1917; J.A. Kleist, S.J., ACW, 1,1946, used here; Solano, *Textos*, I, 43-51; D.J. Sheerin, *The Message of the Fathers, The Eucharist*, Wilmington, 1986, 241-44; bibl., P.S. Zanetti, *Bibliografia eucaristica ignaziana recente, Studi G. Lercaro*, Rome, 1966, 341-389; cf. P. Batiffol, *L'Eucharistie*, Paris, 1930, 39-50; J. Moffat, *An Approach to Ignatius, Harvard Theol. Review*, 29 (1936), 1-38; W. Scherer, *Zur Eucharistielehre des heiligen Ignatius von Antiochien, Theolpraktische Quartalschrift*, 76 (1923), 628ff; P.T. Camelot, O.P., *Ignace d'Antioche, Lettres*, SC 10, 1944, 38ff; O. Perler, *Eucharistie et Unité de l'Eglise d'après St. Ignace d'Antioche*, 35th International Eucharistic Congress, Barcelona, 1954, 424-29; S.M. Gibbard, *The Eucharist in the Ignatian Epistles, Studia Patristica*, VIII, 2 TU 92,1966, 214-218; M. Jourgon, *La présidence de l'Eucharistie chez Ignace d'Antioche, Lumière et Vie* 84 (1967) 26-32; W. Bieder, *Das Abendmahl im christlichen Lebenszussamenhang bei Ignatius von Antiochien, Evangelishce Theol*, 16 (1956), 75-77; DTC V, 1126-27, G. Bardy; DSp VII, 2, 1250-66, esp., 1260-61; P.T. Camelot, DSp IV, 2, 1568-69; [2]V, 2, 62; [3]XIII, 65; [4]XX, 2, 67, 8; [5]VIII, 1, 77; [6]VII, 3, 83; [7]VII, 1, 92; [8]IV, 86.

IMMENSAE CARITATIS, 25 January 1973

Instruction of the Sacred Congregation for Divine Worship on facilitating Sacramental Eucharistic Communion in Particular Circumstances.[1] It deals with a) extraordinary ministers for the distribution of Holy Communion; b) a more extensive faculty for receiving Holy Communion twice in the same day; c) mitigation of the Eucharistic fast for the sick and the elderly; d) the piety and reverence owing to the Blessed Sacrament whenever the Eucharist is placed in the hand of the communicant. The norms are specific, compassionate.

---

[1]Text *AAS* 65 (1973), 264-271; English tr. Vatican Press Office, A. Flannery, O.P., I, 225-232.

IMPANATION

A theory of the real presence which maintains, on a false analogy with the hypostatic union, that the body and blood of Christ are united with the substance of the bread and wine, which remains.[1] The word is first found with Guitmund of Aversa (qv), who said that some think that the body and blood of the Lord "are truly present, but hidden, in such a way that they can, in a certain manner, be received, that is to say that they are impanated" (*revera sed latenter contineri, et ut sumi possint, quodammodo, ut ita dixerim,*

impanari).[2] Alger of Liege (qv) makes the point about the false analogy with the incarnation. Certain heretics, he said, "assert that Christ is, in person, impanated in the bread just as God was in person incarnate in human flesh" (*ita personaliter impanatum Christum sicut in carne humana personaliter incarnatum Deum*).[3]

Rupert of Deutz (qv) has been accused of the heresy, though he has his valiant defenders. John of Paris (d. 1306) held or proposed tentatively a similar view: the bread remains with its accidents, but not with its suppositum, which through the mediation of the flesh is drawn to the suppositum of the Word.[4]

A curious, ingenious theory was put forward in the pages of the American review, *The Catholic World*, (1873-75) purely as a hypothesis, by Fr. Joseph Bayma, S.J. It was thus summarised and condemned in a Decree of the holy Office, 7 July 1875:

"Reply to a question: Whether the explanation of transubstantiation in the sacrament of the most holy Eucharist can be tolerated, which is comprehended by the following propositions:

1. Just as the formal reason for hypostasis is 'to be through itself,' or, 'to subsist through itself,' so the formal reason for substance is 'to be in itself' and 'actually not to be sustained in another as the first subject'; for, rightly are those two to be distinguished: 'to be through itself' (which is the formal reason for hypostasis), and 'to be in itself' (which is the formal reason for substance).

2. Therefore, just as the human nature in Christ is not hypostasis, because it does not subsist through itself but is assumed from a superior divine hypostasis, so finite substance, for example the substance of bread, ceases to be substance by this alone and without any change of itself, because it is sustained supernaturally in another, so that it is not already in itself, but in another as in a first subject.

3. Thus, transubstantiation, or the conversion of the entire substance of bread into the substance of the body of Christ our Lord, can be explained in this way, that the body of Christ, while it becomes substantially present in the Eucharist, sustains the nature of bread, which by this very fact and without any change in itself, but in another sustaining; and, indeed, the nature of bread remains, but in it the formal reason for substance ceases; and so there are not two substances, but one only, that, of course, of the body of Christ.

4. Therefore, in the Eucharist the matter and form of the elements of bread remain; but now, existing supernaturally in another, they do not have the nature of substance, but they have the nature of supernatural accident, not as if in the manner of natural accidents they affected the body of Christ, but on this account,

INAESTIMABILE DONUM—INNOCENT III

insofar as they are sustained by the body of Christ in the manner in which it has been said."

The reply is that "the doctrine of transubstantiation, as it is set forth here, cannot be tolerated."[5] In other words, the parallel invoked by Bayma, between the hypostatic union and transubstantiation, is not valid as he expounds it; he confuses the order of essence and of existence.

---

[1]A. Piolanti, *Il Mistero*, 237, 38; *Oxford Dictionary of the Christian Church*, 694, s.v.; [2]PL 149, 143OD; [3]PL 170, 754B; [4]*Determinatio de modo existendi corporis Christi in sacramento altaris alio quam sit ille quem tenet Ecclesia*, London, 1686, 86-87; cf. Mangenot, DTC V, 1309-10; H. Weisweller, *Die Impanationslehre des Joannes Quidort, Scholastik*, 1931, 161-195; [5]DS 3121-3124; cf. J.B. Franzelin, *De Eucharistia*, 291-98; A. Piolanti, *Bayma, Giuseppe*, EC II, 1086-87.

INAESTIMABILE DONUM, 3 April 1980

This is an Instruction issued by the Sacred Congregation for the Sacraments and Divine Worship, following the letter of Pope John Paul II, *Dominicae Cenae* (qv), giving particulars of abuses (qv) in the Eucharistic Liturgy.[1] The fundamental principle is that "the faithful have a right to a true Liturgy." "Undue experimentation, changes and creativity bewilder the faithful." The Council admonition is recalled: "No person, even if he be a priest, may add, remove or change anything in the Liturgy on his own authority." Pope Paul's words in the same sense were: "Anyone who takes advantage of the reform to indulge in arbitrary experiments is wasting energy and offending the ecclesial sense." The Instruction, in twenty-seven points, indicates where aberrations have taken place, where correction is required: in regard to readings, to the parts of the Mass where the priest alone may function, to the manner of concelebration, the reverence due to the consecrated hosts, Eucharistic worship outside Mass. It reads like an indictment, which is what it is. The program of reform is clear and detailed.

---

[1]Text, *Notitiae*, 1980, 287-296; tr. A. Flannery, Vatican II, II, 93-102, from Vatican Press Office.

IN CELEBRATIONE MISSAE, 7 August 1972

A Declaration of the Sacred Congregation for Divine Worship on concelebration (qv). Questions had arisen on the interpretation of two articles in the *Institutio Generalis* (qv). The principal point was about the right of those who celebrate Mass for the faithful to join in concelebration to which they would, otherwise, be entitled—as members of chapters or communities of institutes of perfection, those concelebrating at the principal Mass on the occasion of a pastoral visitation, or a special gathering of priests—for example, during a pastoral gathering, a congress or a pilgrimage. The answer is yes in each case. But they may not take a stipend for the concelebrated Mass. Some points of interest are added: those with authority must ensure dignity and true piety; concelebrants must be free; though concelebration is excellent, Mass without the participation of the faithful is also "the centre of the entire Church and the heart of priestly existence." Every priest ought to be allowed the right to celebrate Mass alone; everything needed for such celebration should be made available.

Why the difference in tone and directives between this Instruction and *Ecclesiae Semper*? The Episcopal Synod had met in the meantime—its text *De Sacerotio Ministeriali* is quoted. It was trying to deal with the crisis in the Catholic priesthood: identity crisis; flight from the ministry; decline in recruitment. Had the mode of adopting concelebration devalued the personal fulfilment inherent in the priestly office?

---

[1]Text *AAS* 60 (1972), 561-563; English tr. A. Flannery, O.P., I, 222-224.

INNOCENT III (1160-1216, Pope 1198)

Before his election to the Papacy, I. composed a work on the Mass, *De sacro altaris mysterio*.[1] It is largely a study of the ceremonies and rites of the papal Mass, following the sequence of prayers and actions prescribed. It is a capital witness to the Roman Mass in the twelfth century. Occasionally, in the course of the six books, despite a declared intention not to become involved in theological speculation, he enunciates a truth of doctrinal import. Thus on the offering prayer to the Holy Trinity: *Quod sacrificium altaris aequaliter offertur toti Trinitati. Totius igitur individuae Trinitatis indivisa est adoratio quae principaliter exhibetur in sacrificio*.[2] This is his justification of the prayer *Suscipe sancta Trinitas;* to deny its validity would be to risk moving towards subordinationism. Some present-day liturgical publicists who advocate prayer only to the Father through the Son in the Spirit have to beware of this danger. Pius XII (qv) in *Mystici Corporis Christi* pointed out that to say that "our prayers should not be directed to the person of Jesus Christ but rather to God, or to the eternal Father through Christ, since our Saviour, as Head of the Mystical body, is only 'mediator of God and men' is not only opposed to the mind of the Church and to Christian usage, but false."[1]

I. bore in mind the controversies of the previous

century, had a chapter dealing with the "confession of Berengar" (qv), dealt at length with the "truth of the body and blood of Christ under the appearance of bread and wine,"[3] devoted four chapters of the fourth book to Transubstantiation (qv). He also clarified the effects of the Eucharist, its *virtus unitatis*, the causal action of the real body on the Mystical Body, the spiritual nourishment given by the sacrament.

I. as Pope saw the great Lateran Council (qv) IV assemble and publish its doctrine; one important item was on transubstantiation (qv). The Eucharist is also dealt with in a number of his letters as Pope. In '*Cum Marthae circa*' to a certain John, Archbishop of Lyons, 29 November 1202, he sought to allay anxiety about the addition of '*Mysterium Fidei*' to the words of the Lord as recorded in the gospels: "You have asked (indeed) who has added to the form of the words which Christ himself expressed when he changed the bread and wine into the body and blood, that in the Canon of the Mass which the general Church uses, which none of the evangelists is read to have expressed.... In the Canon of the Mass that expression, '*Mysterium fidei*' is found interposed among his words.... Surely we find many such things omitted from the words as well as from the deeds of the Lord by the evangelists, which the Apostles are read to have supplied by word or to have expressed by deed.... From the expression, moreover, concerning which your brotherhood raised the question, namely '*Mysterium fidei*', certain people have thought to draw a protection against error, that which says that in the sacrament of the altar the truth of the body and blood of Christ does not exist, but only the image and species and figure, inasmuch as Scripture sometimes mentions that what is received at the altar is sacrament and mystery and example. But such run into a snare of error, by reason of the fact that they neither properly understand the authority of Scripture, nor do they reverently receive the sacraments of God equally 'ignorant of the Scriptures and the power of God' (Mt 22:29).... Yet '*Mysterium fidei*' is mentioned, since something is believed there other than what is perceived. For the species of bread and wine is perceived there, and the truth of the body and blood of Christ is believed, and the power of unity and love...."[4]

I. then goes on to some general principles of Eucharistic theology: "We must, however, distinguish accurately between three things which are different in this sacrament, namely the visible form, the truth of the body, and the spiritual power. The form is of the bread and wine; the truth, of the flesh and blood; the power, of unity and of charity. The first is the 'sacrament and not reality.' The second is the 'sacra-

ment and reality.' The third is 'the reality and not the sacrament.' But the first is the sacrament of a twofold reality. The second, however, is a sacrament of one and the reality (is) of the other. But the third is the reality of a twofold sacrament. Therefore, we believe that the form of the words, as found in the Canon, the Apostles received from Christ, and their successors from them...."[5]

In the same letter the great Pope dealt with various opinions about the change effected in the water mixed with wine in the Mass. He concludes: "But among the opinions mentioned that is judged the more probable which asserts that the water with the wine is changed into blood."[6] In another letter, to Hugo, Bishop of Ferrara, 5 March 1209, he reassures his friend that it was water that flowed from the side of Christ.[7] Yet again, writing this time to the rectors of the Roman brotherhood, he censures a celebrant of Mass, who being in a state of sin, chooses to feign the ceremony. It is bad to celebrate in a state of sin; still worse to feign celebration: such a one not only mocks God but deceives the people.[8]

---

[1]PL 217, 773-916; cf. G. Barbero, S.S.B., *La dottrina eucaristica negli scritti di Papa Innocenzo III*, Rome, 1953; M. Maccarrone, DSp VII, 2, 1767-1773; id., *Innocenzo III come teologo dell'Eucaristia, Divinitas* 10 (1966), 352-412; W. Imkamp, *Das Kirchenbild Innocenz III* (Päpste und Papstum 22), Stuttgart, 1963; [2]Lib III, c. 8; [3]Lib IV, c. 7; [4]Ibid., cc 17-20, 868-71; [5]DS 782, 83; [6]DS 784; [7]DS 788; [8]DS 789.

INSTITUTIO GENERALIS, Roman Missal, 1970
General Instruction on the Roman Missal, found in all printed versions of this liturgical book.[1] With a preface which in fifteen points summarizes the Eucharistic outlook of those who composed it, overseen carefully by Paul VI (qv), the Instruction sets forth in detail an explanation of the different parts of the Mass and a justification of the changes, not an explanation covering every change, every addition.

---

[1]Text in Roman Missal; English tr. Clifford Howell, S.J., CTS, A. Flannery I, 154-205.

INSTITUTION NARRATIVE, THE
The Institution Narrative, inset in the Eucharistic Prayers is found substantially the same in four NT accounts:[1] in Mt and Mk, as the texts here laid out make clear, there is so much resemblance that they seem to derive from the same tradition; one is led to a similar conclusion about the texts of Lk and Paul. Mt 26:26-29: "Now as they were eating, Jesus took bread,

and blessed, and broke it, and gave it to the disciples and said, 'Take, eat; this is my body.' And he took a cup, and when he had given thanks he gave it to them, saying, 'Drink of it all of you; for this is my blood of the covenant, which is poured out for many for the forgiveness of sins. I tell you I shall not drink again of this fruit of the vine until that day when I drink it new with you in my Father's kingdom.'"

Mk 14:22-25: "And as they were eating, he took bread, and blessed, and broke it, and gave it to them, and said, 'Take; this is my body.' And he took a cup, and when he had given thanks he gave it to them, and they all drank of it. And he said to them, 'This is my blood of the covenant, which is poured out for many. Truly, I say to you, I shall not drink again of the fruit of the vine until that day when I drink it new in the kingdom of God.'"

Lk 22:15-20: "And he said to them: 'I have earnestly desired to eat this passover with you before I suffer; for I tell you I shall not eat it until it is fulfilled in the kingdom of God.' And he took a cup, and when he had given thanks he said, 'Take this and divide it among yourselves; for I tell you that from now on I shall not drink of the fruit of the vine until the kingdom of God comes.' And he took bread, and when he had given thanks he broke it and gave it to them, saying, 'This is my body which is given for you. Do this in remembrance of me.' And likewise the cup after supper, saying, 'This cup which is poured out for you is the new covenant in my blood.'"

Paul, 1 Cor 11:23-26: "For I received from the Lord what I also delivered to you, that the Lord Jesus on the night when he was betrayed took bread, and when he had given thanks, he broke it and said, 'This is my body which is for you. Do this in remembrance of me.' In the same way also the cup, after supper, saying, 'This cup is the new covenant in my blood. Do this, as often as you drink it, in remembrance of me.' For as often as you eat this bread and drink the cup, you proclaim the Lord's death until he comes."

The kernel of this institution narrative is found in all the anaphorae, with the exception—in its present state, at least—of that of Addai and Mari (qv), but, in the versions used by the four Eucharistic Prayers, sanctioned by the *Novus Ordo* (qv), there are variations. Prayers I, II, III, use the same words from "Take this all of you and eat it" and "When supper was ended" ... but introduce them differently as follows: I: "The day before he suffered he took bread in his sacred hands and looking up to heaven, to you, his almighty Father, he gave you thanks and praise. He broke the bread, gave it to this disciples, and said..." II: "Before he was given up to death, a death he freely accepted, he took bread and gave you

thanks. He broke the bread, gave it to his disciples, and said..." III: "On the night he was betrayed, he took bread and gave you thanks and praise. He broke the bread, gave it to his disciples, and said...." Prayer IV differs even after "Take this, all of you, and eat...." "While they were at supper, he took bread, said the blessing, broke the bread, and gave it to his disciples, saying: 'Take this all of you, and eat it: this is my body which will be given up for you.' In the same way, he took the cup, filled with wine. He gave you thanks, and giving the cup to his disciples, said: 'Take this all of you, and drink from it: this is the cup of my blood, the blood of the new and everlasting covenant. It will be shed for you and for all men so that sins may be forgiven. Do this in memory of me.'"

There are points of interest in the gospel texts. Scholars think them derived from liturgical usage. There are two evident traditions, Mk and Mt from a Palestinian setting, Lk and Paul from a Hellenistic background. Only Lk and Paul have the Lord's appeal for an *anamnesis* (qv). Only Lk and Paul speak of the covenant as "new." Paul has not the "vow of abstinence" reported, with slight variations, by all three Synoptics: "I tell you I shall not drink again of this fruit of the vine until that day when I drink it new with you in my Father's kingdom"—thus Mt whereas Mk who retains the word "new" speaks of the "kingdom of God," and Lk says "until the kingdom of God comes" without the word "new." Mk's "for many" becomes "for many unto the forgiveness of sins" with Mt. Lk and Paul add "which is given for you" or "which is for you" to "This is my body"; but they do not have "Take" as have Mk and Mt. All four texts have the announcement of a new covenant. Jesus identifies himself with the covenant, recalling Isaiah 42:6: "I have given you as a covenant to the people, a light to the nations." Likewise such phrases as "poured out" and "for many unto the forgiveness of sins" evoke the Suffering Servant of Isaiah 53: "because he poured out his soul to death, and was numbered with the transgressors; yet he bore the sin of many, and made intercession for the transgressors (v. 12)."

---

[1]Commentaries on the relevant passages in exegetical and theological works; cf. J. Delorme, et al., *The Eucharist in the New Testament*, London, 1964; G. Ruffino, *L'Eucaristia nel Nuovo Testamento*, in *Eucaristia*, 31-110 with bibl 110-114.

INTER-COMMUNION

Vatican II (qv) in the Decree on Ecumenism laid down rules for common worship by Catholics and those of other Christian churches and communities.[1] "Yet," it says in the essential passage, "sharing in liturgical worship *(communicatio in sacris)* is not to be considered as a means to be used indiscriminately for the restoration of unity among Christians. There are two main principles upon which the practice of such common worship depends: first, that of the unity of the Church which ought to be expressed; and second, that of the sharing in the means of grace. The expression of unity very generally forbids common worship. Grace to be obtained sometimes commends it."[2]

The Ecumenical Directory, part one, issued 14 May 1967, outlined the application of these principles and laid down rules. There is a clear distinction between what is permitted between Catholics and the Orthodox Eastern Churches and Catholics and the other separated brethren. Through "the close communion in matters of faith" and the fact that these Churches (i.e., the Orthodox) possess true sacraments, above all—by apostolic succession—the priesthood and the Eucharist the Directory declares: "This offers ecclesiological and sacramental grounds for allowing and even encouraging some sharing in liturgical worship—even Eucharistic—with these Churches 'given suitable circumstances and the approval of church authorities.'" The faithful should be instructed and before any decision in regard to the sacraments of penance, the holy Eucharist and anointing of the sick there should be "satisfactory consultations with the competent authorites (at least local ones) of the separated Oriental Church."

In regard to the separated brethren of the other communities, the following directives were given: "Celebration of the sacraments is an action of the celebrating community, carried out within the community, signifying the oneness in faith, worship and life of the community. Where this unity of sacramental faith is deficient, the participation of the separated brethren with Catholics, especially in the sacraments of the Eucharist, penance and anointing of the sick, is forbidden. Nevertheless, since the sacraments are both signs of unity and sources of grace (cf. Decree on Ecumenism, n. 8), the Church can, for adequate reasons, allow access to those sacraments to a separated brother. This may be permitted in danger of death or in urgent need (during persecution, in prisons) if the separated brother has no access to a minister of his own communion, and spontaneously asks a Catholic priest for the sacraments—so long as he declares a faith in these sacraments in harmony with that of the Church, and is rightly disposed. In other cases the judge of this urgent necessity must be the diocesan bishop or the episcopal conference. A Catholic in similar circumstances may not ask for these sacraments except from a minister who has been validly ordained."[4]

[1]For background cf. articles, Anglicanism, Luther, Calvin, Cranmer, Bucer, Zwingli, ARCIC, Lutheran-Roman Catholic Dialogue, Lima Agreement; Eucharistic Sharing, NCE, 17, 214-17, bibl., M.A. Fahey.; [2]Art. 8, A. Flannery, Vatican II, 1, 461; [3]nn. 40, 42, *ibid.*, 496, 7; [4]n. 55, *ibid.*, 499.

INTER OECUMENICI, 26 September 1964
An instruction from the Sacred Congregation of Rites giving directives for the implementation of the Constitution on the Liturgy.[1] It deals with the training necessary to those who will be responsible for liturgical services, with the proper authority, the commissions, regional and diocesan, to be established so that proper programs should be drawn up and carried out, matters of general principle, such as the equality of all the faithful, and particular questions, such as Bible services and sacramentals.

[1]*AAS* 56 (1964), 877-900; tr. with certain articles omitted; A. Flannery, O.P., I, 45-56;

IRENAEUS, ST. (c. 130-200)
I. has left us a precious testimony on the belief of the Church in his time and, in one passage, a problem which has agitated many commentators.[1] On the Eucharist he writes thus: "To his disciples too he gave this advice, to offer to God the first fruits of his creatures, not that he had need of them, but that they should be neither sterile nor thankless. He took the bread, which comes from creation, and he gave thanks, saying: 'This is my body.' And likewise the cup, which comes from the creation to which we belong, he declared it his blood and he taught that it was the new oblation of the new covenant. It is this oblation which the Church has received from the apostles, which she offers to God in the whole world, to him who gives us food, first fruits of his gifts in the new covenant."

Of this, among the twelve prophets, Malachi spoke beforehand in these terms: "I have no pleasure in you says the Lord of hosts, and I will not accept an offering from your hand. For from the rising of the sun to its setting my name is great among the nations, and in every place incense is offered to my name and a pure offering: for my name is great among the nations, says the Lord of hosts. He signified thus that the first people would cease to make offerings to God, while in every place a sacrifice would be offered to him, a pure one."[2]

Again on the theme of the Church's oblation he

writes thus: "Since then the Church makes its offering with simplicity, her gift is rightly deemed a sacrifice to God, according to Paul's word to the Philippians: 'I have received full payment, and more; I am filled, having received from Epaphroditus the gifts you sent, a fragrant offering, a sacrifice, acceptable and pleasing to God' (4:18). For we must make an oblation to God and in all things be found grateful to God the Creator, in a pure disposition and faith without hypocrisy, in firm hope, in ardent charity, offering the first fruits of his own creatures. The Church alone offers this oblation pure to the Creator, offering him with thanksgiving what comes from his creation."[3]

I. goes on to mention those who like the Jews or heretics cannot make an offering to God: "Besides, how will they have the certainty that the Eucharistic bread is the body of their Lord and the cup his blood, if they do not say that he is the Son of the Creator of the world, that is his Word, through whom the wood fructifies, springs flow, the earth gives first grass and then the ear full of corn."[4]

With that passage linking the Eucharist with the divinity of Christ, compare this which recalls the promise of Christ in Jn 6:39: "How can they still say that the flesh departs to corruption, having no share in life, when it is nourished by the body of the Lord and his blood? Let them then change their way of thinking, or let them desist from offering what we have mentioned. As for us, our way of thinking is in harmony with the Eucharist and the Eucharist in turn confirms our way of thinking. For we offer him what is his, proclaiming in harmonious fashion the communion and union of the flesh and the Spirit, for as the bread, which comes from the earth, is no longer ordinary bread, but the Eucharist, comprising two things, one earthly, the other heavenly, thus our bodies which share in the Eucharist, are no longer meant for corruption, since they have the hope of the resurrection."[5]

The two elements, earthly and heavenly have been the subject of differing interpretations.[6] Luther, Calvin, Baur and Steitz interpret the earthly element as the bread, varying on the second: Luther, the body of Christ; Calvin the power of the holy Spirit; Baur the Word of God; Steitz the words of consecration. Massuet and Batiffol think the two elements respectively, the body of Christ and the Word of God, whereas Perpetuité de la Foy think they represent the sensible appearances and the body of Christ. On the last theory I. was close to the very doctrine of transubstantiation (qv). A subject awaiting final solution.

Thus far, I. in the fourth book of *Adv. Haer.* He returns to the subject in the fifth book: "Futile, in every way, are those who reject the whole 'economy' of God, deny the salvation of the flesh, despise its regeneration, declaring that it is incapable of taking on incorruptibility. If there is no salvation for the flesh, then the Lord has not redeemed us by his blood, the cup of the Eucharist is not communion in his blood, and the bread which we break is not a communion in his body. For blood cannot flow but from veins, from flesh and from the rest of the human substance, and it was to become all that that the Word of God redeemed us by his blood, as the Apostle says: 'in whom we have redemption by his blood, the forgiveness of sins' (Col 1:14). And because we are his members and are nourished by means of his creation—creation which he himself gives us, making the sun rise and the rain fall according to his will, the cup drawn from creation he has declared to be his own blood, by which our blood is strengthened, and the bread, taken from creation, he declares to be his own body, by which our bodies are strengthened."

"If then the cup which has been mingled and the bread which has been made receive the word of God and become the Eucharist, that is to say the blood and body of Christ, from which the substance of our flesh is increased and strengthened, how can these people say the flesh is incapable of receiving the gift of God which is eternal life, when it is nourished by the blood and body of Christ and is his member, as the blessed Apostle says in the letter to the Ephesians: 'We are members of his body, formed of his flesh and of his bones' (5:30). It is not of any spiritual or invisible man that he says that 'for a spirit has neither bones nor flesh' (Lk 24:39), but he speaks of a genuinely human organism, composed of flesh, nerves and bones, which is nourished from the chalice which is his blood and strengthened from the bread which is his body. As the wood of the vine, after it has lain in the earth, bears fruit in its time, as 'the grain of wheat after falling into the ground and being there dissolved, rises in multiple form through the Spirit of God who supports all things, later, as a result of skill, they come to be used by men, and then receiving the word of God, they become the Eucharist, that is, the body and blood of Christ—likewise our bodies, which have been fed by this Eucharist, after having lain in the ground and there dissolved, will rise in their time 'for the glory of God the Father' (Phil 2:11)."[7]

For I. then places the Eucharist at the centre of the new creation: Christ assumed human nature in its totality and the bread and wine are offered by the Church as elements of the sacrifice of the new covenant, Christ, first-born in creation, is also first-born from the dead, first-fruits of the new covenant. Redemption corresponds to creation in I's synthesis,

Christ through whom the world was made, gives by his flesh incorruptibility to man. It is the Eucharist integrated into I's grand design of recapitulation in Christ. The firm reality of essential change, from bread and wine into the body and blood, is explicit.

It is more difficult to say what I. thinks of the Eucharistic minister: is he necessarily the bishop? This seems to be implied in a letter preserved by Eusebius.[8] "For neither could Anicetus (i.e., the Pope) persuade Polycarp," he is quoted as writing, "not to observe what he had always observed with John the disciple of the Lord, and the other apostles with whom he had associated; neither could Polycarp persuade Anicetus to observe it, as he said that he ought to follow the customs of the presbyters that had preceded him. But though matters were in this shape, they communed together, and Anicetus conceded the administration of the Eucharist in the church to Polycarp, manifestly as a mark of respect."[9]

---

[1]Works relevant PG 7, Harvey, vol II, sp., SC 100, 152, 211; J. Solano, *Textos*, I, 67-79; cf. A. d'Alès, *La doctrine eucharistique de S. Irénée, RSR* 13 (1923) 24-46; P. Batiffol, *L'Eucharistie*, ed. 9, 1930, 167-183; V. Couckle, *Doctrina eucharistica apud S. Irenaeum, Collationes Brugenses*, (1929), 163-70; H.D. Simonin, A propos d'un texte eucharistique de S. Irénée, *RSPT*, 23 (1934), 281-92; Quasten, *Monumenta*, 346-348; Bareille, DTC V, 1128-30; A.W. Ziegler, *Das Brot von unseren Feldern. Ein Beitrag zur Eucharistielehre des hl Irenaus, Pro Mundi Vita Festschrift zur eucharistischen Weltkongress*, Munich, 1960, 21-43; A. Hamman, DSp 1569-70; id., *Irénée de Lyons, L'Eucharistia des premiers chrétiens*, Paris, 1976, 89-99; D. Unger, *The Holy Eucharist according to St. Irenaeus, Laurentianum* 20 (1979), 103-64; A. Piolanti, *Il Mistero*, 158-166; D. van den Ende, *Eucharistia*, 126ff; G. Celada, O.P., *Ministerio y Tradición en S. Ireneo*, in *Teología del Sacerdocio, Faculdad del Norte de España*, IX 148ff; [2]*Adv. Haer.* IV, 17, 5, SC 100, 590-92; [3]*Ibid.* 18, 4, 606; [4]*Ibid.*; [5]*Ibid.*, 18, 5, 608; [6]Cf. A. d'Ales, *op. cit.*, esp., 42; [7]*Adv. Haer.*, V, 2, 2-3, SC 30-36; [8]Cf. A. d'Alès, *op. cit.*; G. Celada, op, cit.; [9]H.E., IV, 24, 16-17.

ISIDORE OF SEVILLE (c. 560-636), ST., DOCTOR OF THE CHURCH

The great Christian encyclopaedist, in some passages of his works, speaks of the Eucharist.[1] In the *Etymologiae* he has this to say about the Mass: "The Mass, in the time of sacrifice is when the catechumens are put outside, as the levite cries out, 'If there is still any catechumen, let him leave.' Then the Mass takes place, for those not born to a new life cannot take part in the sacraments of the altar. It is called sacrifice, doing of a sacred thing, because it is consecrated for us in memory of the Lord's passion; therefore at his command we call it the Body and Blood of Christ. For though it is from the fruits of the earth, it is sanctified and becomes a Sacrament, with the Spirit of God operating invisibly; this Sacrament of the bread and chalice the Greeks call Eucharist, which in Latin means kind thanks. And what is better than the Blood and Body of Christ?"[2]

In the *De officiis ecclesiasticis* I. provides a source book for the Mozarabic Rite. His treatment of the Eucharist occurs in Book I. He deals with the prayers and behavioural rules related to the Mass. On sacrifice he writes: "Now the sacrifice which is offered to God by Christians was first instituted by Christ, our Lord and Teacher, when he revealed his Body and Blood to the Apostles before he was handed over, as we read in the gospel: 'Jesus took bread and the cup and blessed and gave it to them' (Mt 26:26). Melchizedek, the King of Salem, was the first to offer this Sacrament figuratively as a type of the Body and Blood of Christ, and was the first to present, by way of an image, the mystery of such a great sacrifice.... These (bread and wine, of which he suggested the symbolism) are visible things, but consecrated by the Holy Spirit, they change into the Sacrament of the divine Body."[3] Later he adds an interesting point on the frequency of Holy Communion: "Some say that unless sin stand in the way, the Eucharist should be received daily, for we ask that this Bread be given to us daily, as the Lord commands, when we say 'Give us this day our daily bread.' They are right about this, if they receive with religion and devotion and humility, and do not do it relying on their own righteousness with the presumption of pride."[4]

When I., in his work *De fide catholica ex Veteri et Novo Testamento contra Judaeos*, deals with the Eucharist, he develops the Melchizedek (qv) theme at length.[5]

---

[1]Texts PL 82, 83; Solano, *Textos*, II, 695-708; cf. J.H. Geiselmann, *Die Abendmahlslehre an der Wende de cristlichen Spätantike zum Frühmittelalter Isidor von Sevilla und das Sakrament der Eucharistie*, Munich 1933; J. Havet, *Les Sacraments et le rôle de l'Esprit Saint d'après Isidore de Seville*, ETL, 16 (1939), 32-93; G. Bareille, DTC, VIII, 1, 1924, 98-111; J. Fontaine, *Isidore de Seville et la culture classique dans l'Espagne wisigothique*, 2 vols., 1959; id., *Catholicisme*, VI, 154-166; id., DSp VII, 2, 1971, 2104-21116; J. Madoz, EC VII, 254-58; [2]PL 82, 255B-256B; [3]ch. 18, PL 82, 754B; [4]Pl 82, *ibid.*; [5]Bk. II, ch. 27, PL 83, 535B.

J

JANSENISM

The rigorist views of this movement were made to bear on the Eucharist, on holy Communion, as one of the well-known books in the history of the age vividly testifies. In August 1643, the year of Saint Cyran's death, his destined successor as leader of the Jansenist movement, Antoine "the Great" Arnauld published a work which was to have an immense impact on French spirituality. A clash of personal practice between two noble ladies was the occasion of the ensuing debate. The Princess de Guemène directed by Abbé de Saint Cyran was shocked to see her friend the Marquise de Sable, directed by P. de Sesmaisons, S.J., communicate frequently despite a rather worldly lifestyle. The Jesuit composed a booklet to reassure his dirigée: *Question: s'il est meilleur de communier souvent que rarement.*

Antoine Arnauld's reply was a volume in several hundreds of pages: *De la Fréquente Communion où les sentiments des Pères, des Papes et des Conciles touchant l'usage des sacrements de Pénitence et d'Eucharistie sont fidèlement exposés pour servir d'adresse aux personnes qui pensent sérieusement à se convertir à Dieu et aux Pasteurs et confesseurs zélés pour le bien des âmes.*[1]

The work went into five editions before 1773 and had a very great effect. It was a call to the mentality, as the author saw things, of the early Church, was stringent on conditions needed to approach the Communion table, spelled out the qualities required in a spiritual director, whose role was maximised, was based on one essential falsehood: Holy Communion was the reward of *merit*, not the indispensable food of the soul without which there can be no merit. The merit, in the view adopted, was acquired not only by absence of mortal sin and venial sin, but by a resolve to purify the soul of inclinations which would lead to the latter.

Plausibly and lengthily argued, widely disseminated, matching perhaps a certain mood in French Catholicism, the Jansenist ideas of Arnauld went deep and they hardened. Their effects remained down to the reforms of St. Pius X (qv) and led to practices which now seem barely credible, such as the regulation by confessors of the number of times the pentitent could communicate weekly—rarely was daily communion allowed—even denying Holy Communion for a period of time as a penance in confession! One predictable result was that the daily communicant passed for a paragon of virtue, and, in the human condition, probably himself agreed with the judgement. It was historically inevitable that the magnificent missionary movement from France from the seventeenth to the twentieth century, and the French contribution to seminary training over the same period should widely implant Jansenist ideas about the Eucharist.

[1] *Oeuvres*, Paris, 1773-1783, vol XXVII, 71-693; bibl., J. Willaert, *Bibliotheca janseniana belgica*, 3 vols, Brussels, 1950; cf. A. de Meyer, *Les premières controverses jansenistes en France (1640-49)*, Louvain, 1947; H. Bremond, *Histoire du sentiment religieux en France*, IV, 1920, *La conquête mystique*, L'Ecole de Port Royal, 281-317; L. Cognet, *Le Jansenisme*, Paris, 1961; J. Carreyre, DSp, I 881-87, S.V. Arnauld; *id.*, DTC VIII, 1, 1924, 460-66; 471-74; *id.*,

DHGE, IV, (1930), 447-85; J. Brucker, DTC I (1903), 1978-83; L.J. Cognet, NCE VII (1967), 820-24;

JEROME, ST., DOCTOR OF THE CHURCH
(c. 342-420)

The great biblical scholar was content to believe the words of Scripture in regard to the Eucharist and like many, if not all of the Fathers, he did not seek to elaborate a philosophical system based on the biblical data.[1] He was realistic and forthright: "Let us hear that the bread which the Lord broke and gave to his disciples is the body of the Lord and Saviour as he said to them,' 'Take and eat, this is my body' and the chalice that of which again he said, 'Drink of this, all of you. This is my blood of the New Testament, which will be poured out for many for the forgiveness of sins'; that is the chalice of which we read in the prophet, 'I will take the chalice of salvation and invoke the name of the Lord'; and in another place 'My chalice is intoxicating, how excellent it is.' For if the bread which came down from heaven is the body of the Lord and the wine, which he gave his disciples is his blood of the New Testament, which was poured out for the forgiveness of all sins, let us reject Jewish fables and let us go up with the Lord to the great cenacle, adorned and cleaned and let us receive from him again the chalice of the New Testament, and celebrating there with him the pasch let us become drunk with the wine of sobriety, 'For the kingdom of God does not consist in eating and drinking, but in righteousness and pace and joy in the Holy Spirit' (Rom 14:17). Nor did Moses give us the true bread—it was the Lord Jesus who did so, he the guest and the banquet, he who eats and is eaten; we drink his blood and without him we cannot drink."[2] "Far be it from me to say anything sinister about those who have succeeded to the apostolic hierarchy and who, by their sacred mouth, make the body of Christ."[3]

In another passage J's knowledge of Scripture prompts him to a generalization not original but so well phrased: "There is as great a difference between the loaves of proposition and the body of Christ as between the shadow and bodies, between the image and the truth, between the models of future things and those which were prefigured by the models. How then should the bishop, to a degree above all the laity, especially have meekness, patience, sobriety, modration, detachment from profit, hospitality and kindness?"[4] To which J. adds further counsels on priestly holiness.

J. in his OT commentaries returns to Eucharistic themes: he comments on Melchizedek (qv)[5] as a figure of Christ, reflects on the ancient Passover, passes to the NT to admire the new and lasting one: "And it happened that when Jesus had completed all these discourses he said to his disciples: You know that after two days it will be the Passover and the Son of man will be delivered to be crucified. Let those blush who think that the Saviour feared death, that through panic over the Passion he said, 'Father if it be possible, let this chalice pass from me.' As he would celebrate the Pasch after two days, he knew that he would be delivered to be crucified, yet he does not avoid snares, does not take flight in terror; so much so that when the others do not wish to go, he advances fearlessly, as Thomas said, 'Let us also go and die with him.' Wishing to end the feast of flesh, and as the shadow passed, to perform the true Pasch, he said, 'With desire I have desired to eat this Pasch with you before I suffer.' For Christ, our Pasch, has been immolated, provided that we eat it in the unleavened bread of sincerity and truth. (Here J reproduces the words of Institution.) ... After the Pasch, which was the type, had been fulfilled, and he had eaten the flesh of the lamb with the apostles, he takes bread, which strengthens the heart of man, and changes over to the true sacramental Pasch, that as Melchizedek, the priest of the most high God, prefiguring him had offered bread and wine, he also would make present in truth his body and blood."[6] For 'to make present' he uses a word of Tertullian, *representare*.

The Saviour made the Last Supper (qv) a type of his Passion.[7] While pointing to the two ways in which flesh and blood may be understood, he shows the true identity.[8] He can speak of the Bishop Exuperius reduced, through his largesse to the poor in imitation of Christ having nothing but "a wicker basket to hold the body of the Lord and a glass container his blood."[9] Always realistic in his interpretation of the Lord's word.

---

[1] Texts, J. Solano, *Textos*, II, 38-75; cf., G. Bareille, DTC, V, 1152-54; M.S. Weglewicz, *Doctrina Sancti Hieronymi de ss. Eucharistia*, Rome, 1931; [2] *Epist.* 120, PL 22, 985; [3] *Epist.* 14, CSEL 54, 54; PL 22, 352; cp. Epist 44, 611; Epist 146, 1193; [4] *In Epist. ad Titum*, I, 5, 8, PL 26, 569A; [5] Cf. *In Gen 14;* 15, PL 23, 961 AB; infra n. 6; *Epist.* 73, 3, PL22, 678. [6] *In Mt.*, I,26, PL26, 190-195; [7] *Adv. Jovin.*, II, 17, PL 23, 311; [8] *In Epist. ad Eph.*, I, 1, 7, PL26, 451; [9] *Epist.* 125, PL22, 1085.

JEWISH BACKGROUND TO THE EUCHARIST

Some facts of the history of theology will illustrate the immense increase of interest in this subject in very recent times.[1] Treatises on the Eucharist circulating among Catholics, many of them designed for academic use, manuals, had no space for description of Jewish rites or analysis of Jewish liturgical formulas which would shed light on their subject. The great classical works mentioned in the present compilation, the treatise of Cardinal Billot (qv) or the nomumental opus of Fr. de la Taille (qv), the latter enriched with vast, varied erudition, comprising patristic, medieval and modern authors and liturgical texts of varied provenance, did not set out Jewish prayers or blessings as having relevance. Down to recent times Catholic literature did not have this dimension.

Not so long ago Dom Odo Casel turned to the mystery religions to help understanding of the Eucharistic mystery: not to Jewish sources. When Jesus Solanos, S.J., published his two volume *Textos eucaristicos primitivos* in 1952 he did not think of including any formulas from the treasury of Jewish liturgy. A well-known scripture scholar could write of the "alleged influence" of Jewish practice on the origins of the Eucharist.

A notable change in approach was to come and, as in such matters, to accelerate, after some initial hesitancy. Gregory Dix gave attention to the subject in *The Shape of the Liturgy*, 1949. Articles by R. le Déaut, C.S.Sp.,[2] and J.P. Audet, O.P.,[3] opened new perspectives and showed that this was a matter for serious scholarship. Then came Vatican II and its varied impact on Catholic thinking and Catholic life. In the middle sixties Louis Bouyer's work on the Eucharist showed a completely new appreciation of the Jewish origins—the proportion of his book given to it was an indication.[4] Simultaneously Louis Ligier, S.J., issued studies which confirmed independently the value of this insight.

Scholars work within the intellectual climate of their time, and they may be influenced by currents of thought which will not find direct expression in their writings; it is a question of a direction which they follow, a stimulus to research, new horizons and perspectives which challenge them. The new attitude towards the Jewish people which found expression in the teaching of Vatican II was surely such a stimulus: "There is first that people to which the covenants and promises were made, and from which Christ was born according to the flesh (cf. Rom 9:4-5); in view of the divine choice, they are a people most dear for the sake of the fathers, for the gifts of God are without repentance (cf. Rom 11:28-29)." The longer passage in the *Declaration on the Non-Christian Religions* enlarges on this insight and contains this directive: "Since Christians and Jews have such a common spiritual heritage, this sacred Council wishes to encourage and further mutual understanding and appreciation. This can be obtained, especially, by way of biblical and theological enquiry and through friendly discussion."[5]

Certain other factors helped to concentrate interest in the Jewish background to the Eucharist. There has been a change from the essentialist approach to divine revelation to a personalist analysis, with recognition of the historical dimension. Abstract debates on the Mass—which retain their validity—have given way to reflection on the Paschal Mystery (qv), result of Dom Casel's insight, stimulus to study of the biblical background, of the circumstances and existential elements composing crucial events in Christ's life.

Simultaneously a Jewish scholar, Louis Finkelstein, in a paper which was to become seminal, reconstructed an important Jewish prayer.[6] It was then too that Joachim Jeremias achieved his great monograph on the Last Supper and established the fact that we have the *ipsissima verba* of the Lord.[7] From now on it would be impossible to overlook such prime, determinant facts as that Jesus was a devout Jew, steeped in the traditions of his people, surrounded by fellow Jews, that everything he did embodied the very best elements of Jewish thought and practice, that this very fact enhanced and clarified his singular, his highly powerful and utterly original action in the Last Supper. It was unique, but it has been torn from the framework within which its uniqueness was realized.

The great liturgist and hymnographer, Lucien Deiss, C.S.Sp., who has accepted the idea of Jewish influence, issues some advice: "An unbridled apologetic approach to these marvellous texts could well reduce them to a state of enslavement. Such an approach might assert, on the one hand, that 'there is nothing new, since the Christian liturgy was born of the Jewish liturgy.' On the other hand, it might claim that 'everything is new, since the Christian liturgy broke away from the Jewish liturgy.'"[8] As an indication of the change in Catholic literature, one may take L. Deiss' own book, *Springtime* . . . which devotes Ch I, 3-19, to *The Sources of Jewish Prayer*, or more striking still, *Prex,* ed. A. Hanggi, I. Pahl, where *Pars Prima*, by L. Ligier is devoted, 5-57, to *Textus Liturgiae Judaeorum*, about one-tenth of the work; J. Quasten's valuable collection has no such entry.

The first obvious theme to take is the Last Supper as a Passover meal. It is well-known that the synoptics support the view, while St. John seems to reject it, or make it impossible to hold. Joachim Jeremias took up the challenge and argued powerfully that the Supper was a Passover meal. Briefly his arguments are in ten points: Jesus came to Jerusalem to eat the Passover; the Last Supper took place at night—community meals took place usually before nightfall; at the Passover meal there should be, at least, ten—there were at least twelve; the Passover meal was taken reclining; hors d'oeuvres, green herbs and bitter herbs were taken before the Passover meal—Mk says, "While they were eating, he took bread..." (14:22); wine is drunk at the Passover meal, not necessarily at others; it was customary to give the poor something to eat—cf. Jn 13:29 "that he should give something to the poor"; hymns were customarily sing—cf Mk 14:26; Jesus did not leave the city during the Passover night—he went to the Garden of Olives; Jesus interprets the meaning of the bread and wine—corresponding to the explanation given by the head of the family, according to the "seder."

There are objections to the thesis of Jeremias; the difficulty arising out of Jn's account; Mk tells us the chief priests did not wish to arrest Jesus "during the feast"—according to this text the Supper had taken place before the feast of 14/15 Nissan; the Sanhedrin did not generally meet for judgement at this time; nor did the buying of a shroud take place; chiefly there is no mention of eating the lamb. Jeremias has an answer to these objections and persists in his opinion.

Louis Bouyer thinks the matter of no major importance: "In the first place, the Passover setting is no less relevant to the Last Supper whether it preceded Passover (the immolation of the lambs coinciding in time with the death of the Saviour in this case), or was actually the Passover meal. But—and this is of special importance—the paschal references were present not only in the prayers of this one night but in all the meal prayers. And in fact, whether the Supper was this special meal or another, there is no doubt that Jesus did not connect the Eucharistic instutition of the new covenant to any of the details that are proper to the Passover meal alone. The connection is solely with what the Passover meal had in common with every meal, that is, the breaking of bread in the beginning and the rite of thanksgiving over the cup of wine mixed with water at the end. And, we may add, this is what made it possible for the Christian Eucharist to be celebrated without any problem, as often as one might wish, and not only once a year."[9]

Out of the rich treasury, by way of illustration, let us take some passages, ending with judgements by experts. From the *Kiddush* for the Sabbath and Feast Days (*Kiddush* means 'sanctification'): "You are blessed, Lord our God, King of the universe, you who created the fruit of the vine." The words are spoken by the master of the house, as the lamp has been lit and as he holds a cup of wine in his hand, and has recited Gen 1:31b-2:1-3 on the institution of the Sabbath. Then follows the blessing to sanctify the day of the Sabbath or the feast: "You are blessed, Lord our God, King of the universe. You have sanctified us by your commandments, you have given us as an inheritance the Sabbath of your holiness, out of love and good

will, as a memorial of the works of your creation (Lev 23:3). This day is the first of your holy convocations. It is the memorial of the exodus from Egypt. You have chosen us among all peoples, you have sanctified us, you have given us as an inheritance the Sabbath of your holiness, out of love and good will. You are blessed, O Lord, who sanctify the Sabbath."[10] Those present take some wine into their cups and drink it after the father of the family has drunk. The father then takes the bread and raises it saying: "You are blessed, Lord our God, King of the universe, you who have brought bread forth from the earth." The reader will recognise in this *Kiddush* the origin of the prayers now said in the Roman Missal for the presentation of the offerings.

From the *Birkat ha-mazon,* thought to have been the model of the Christian anaphoras (qv): "You are blessed, Lord our God, King of the universe, you who nourish the entire world with goodness, tender love, and mercy. You are blessed, O Lord, you who nourish the universe. We will give you thanks, Lord our God, for you have given us a desirable land for our inheritance (that we may eat of its fruits and be filled with its goodness). You are blessed, Lord our God, for the land and the food. Lord our God, take pity on Israel, your people, and Jerusalem, your city, on Zion, the place where your glory dwells, on your altar and your sanctuary. You are blessed, O Lord, who build Jerusalem. You are blessed, Lord our God, King of the universe (you who are) good and filled with kindness"!

Extracts from the liturgical text according to the Siddur Rav Saadja: "We will give you thanks, Lord our God, for you have given us for our inheritance: a desirable land, good and widespread, the covenant and the law, life and food. For all these (blessings) we give you thanks and we bless your name eternally and for ever. You are blessed, O Lord, for the land and the food.... You are blessed, Lord our God, King of the universe, God our Father, our King, our Creator, our Redeemer, good and beneficent King. Day after day you are solicitous to do good to us in many ways. It is you who give us increase for ever through grace, tender love, spirit, mercy, and every good."[11]

To these typical passages one could add others as from *Shemone Esre* (Eighteen Blessings) or the *Birkat Yotser,* of the *Shema Israel,* this latter certainly resembling a Christian anaphora, even to the Sanctus. All raise the question so often put *From Barakah (blessing) to the Eucharist.* J. Coppens gave this judgement: "By the simplicity of the rite and by the depth and meaning, by the mystic-sacramental and sacrificial aspects, by the mysterious and wonderful union of all the elements which make it up, the

Eucharist is a unique rite which defies comparison with the Old Testament data, and the institutions of Palestinian and Hellenistic Judaism."[12]

Louis Ligier, writing to conclude his study *De la Cène à l'Anaphore*, with the centrality of the memorial of Christ in mind says: "Such unity and thrust have their ultimate foundation in the Trinitarian structure which, beyond the 'economic' structure, makes the theological unity of the Christian Eucharistic prayer. The anaphora has not borrowed it from Jewish prayer. It is its own proper and primary reality. Its primary source is the example of Christ at the Supper: as the Gospel of John relates, he addressed the Father to celebrate, for the last time, his name, and he also invited the Apostles to pray 'in his name.' In his time Paul recalls also this direction of Christian thanksgiving, to the Father through the Son. That is why every anaphora is addressed to the Father in memory—*unde et memores*—of the Son and of his paschal mystery, in the fellowship of the Spirit. This Trinitarian schema is inherent not only in the words, but also in the movement of the anaphora. The direction towards the Father, particularly marked at the beginning, explains the style of the Eucharistic prayer. Christ's mediation is fixed particularly in the anamnesis and in the entirety of the memorial. Fellowship with the Holy Spirit comes at the epiclesis. And finally the three themes corresponding to the three Persons, meet and are joined in the final unity of the doxology of the 'name.'"[13]

In a thoughtful, well argued article, Thomas-Julian Talley comes to this conclusion: "From the beginning, it appears, the similarity between the Christian liturgy and the Jewish liturgy is accompanied by differences which claim our attention. Yes, as Gregory Dix says, Jesus was a Jew and our search for origins may never forget it. Nevertheless the relationship between Christianity and Judaism is more complex than that between the New Testament and the Old. Jewish liturgy and Christian liturgy were both the object of swift development in the first two centuries of the common era; to evaluate the influence of one on the other demands a kind of precision, of which, I fear, these remarks have only, once again, established the need. As Fr. Ligier has shown, theological and thematic similarities alone would not suffice. To reach firm conclusions attention must be given to the form of the *berakoth* and to the entire structure surrounding them. Having at least attempted that, I must conclude: no, the *berakah* is not a synonym for *Eucharist*, we can hope that further studies will help us to understand the meaning and consequences of this fact which is, after all, rather strange."[14]

Studies then must continue. One theme, which has certainly been very fully explored and with enlightening consequences, is the meaning of memorial in Jewish tradition and liturgy.

[1]W.O.E. Oesterley, *The Jewish Background of the Christian Liturgy*, Oxford, 1925; J. Coppens, *Les soi-disant analogies juives de l'Eucharistie*, ETL 8 (1931), 238-248; id., *Eucharistie*, DBS II, *Eucharistie et les prétendues analogies juives*, 1192-1193; G. Dix, *The Shape of the Liturgy*, 5th ed., London, 1952; J.P. Audet, *Esquisse historique du genre littéraire de la "bénédiction" et de l'Eucharistie chrétienne*, RB 65 (1958), 371-399; L. Ligier, *Autour du sacrifice eucharistique. Anaphores orientales et anamnèse juive du Kippur*, NRT 82 (1960), 40-55; id., *Anaphores orientales et prières juives*, Proche Orient Chrétien, 13 (1963), 4-21, 99-113; id., *Textus selecti de magna oratione eucharistica addita Haggadah Paschae et nonnullis Judaeorum benedictionibus*, 2nd ed., Rome, 1965; id., *De la Cène de Jesus à l'anaphore de l'Eglise*, LMD, 97 (1966), 7-51; id., *La benedizione e il culto nell'Antico Testamento* in *Il canone*, Padua, Centro di Azione liturgica, 1968 (*Liturgica nuova serie*, 5); id., *La "Benedizione" e la Cena pasquale di Gesu, ibid.*, 23-37; id., *Della Cena di Gesu all'anafora della Chiesa, ibid.*, 39-54; J. Godart, *Aux origines de la célébration eucharistique*, QL 46 (1965), 8-25; 104-121; C.P. Price, *Jewish Morning Prayers and Early Christian Anaphoras, Anglican Theological Review*, 43 (1961), 153ff; L. Bouyer, *Eucharist: Theology and Spirituality of the Eucharistic Prayer*, London, 1968, 70-115; H. Cazelles, *L'Anaphore et l'Ancien Testament*, in *Eucharisties d'Orient et d'Occident* 1, Paris, 1970, 11-22; K. Hruby, *L'action de grâce dans la liturgie juive, ibid.*, 23-31; id., *La Birkat ha-Mazon*, in *Mélanges ... Dom Bernard Botte*, Louvain, 1972, 205-222; J. Vellian, *The Anaphoral Structure of Addai and Mari Compared to the Berakoth preceding the Shema in the Synagogue Morning Service, Le Muséon* 85 (1972), 201-223; T.J. Talley, *De la "berakah" à l'Eucharistie, une question à réexaminer*, LMD 125 (1976), 11-39; G. Rouwhorst, *Bénédiction, action de grâce, supplication. Les oraisons de la table dans le Judaisme et les célébrations eucharistiques des chrétiens* QL 61 (1980), 211-240; H. Wegman, *Généalogie hypothétique de la prière eucharistique, ibid.*, 263-278; L. Deiss, *It is the Lord's Supper*, New York, 1977; id., *Springtime*, 3-19; G. Giraudo, *La struttura letteraria della preghiera eucaristica. Saggio sulla genesi di una forma*, Rome, 1981, (Analecta Biblica 92); A. Schenker, *L'Eucaristia nell'Antico Testamento*, Milan, 1982; I.M. Sanchez Caro, *Benedicion y Eucaristia* in *Salamantencis*, 30 (1983), 123-147; A. Piolanti, *Il Mistero*, 52-91; *Prex*, (L. Ligier), 5-60; H.H. Guthrie, Jr., *Theology as Thanksgiving: From Israel's Psalms to the Church's Eucharist*, New York, 1981; C. de Sante, *La prière d'Israel. Aux sources de la liturgie chrétienne*, Paris, 1986.; [2]*Le titre de 'Summus Sacerdos'donné à Melchisedech est-il d'origine juive*, RSR 50 (1962) 222-29; [3]*Esquisse historique du genre littéraire de la "benediction" et de l'Eucharistie chrétienne*, RB 65 (1958), 371-99; [4]*Eucharist: Theology and Spirituality of the Eucharistic Prayer*, London, 1968 (French ed. 1966), 70-115; [5]*Constitution on the Church*, 16, A. Flannery ed., 1, 367; *ibid., Declaration*, 4, 741; [6]*The birkat ha-mazon*, in *The Jewish Quarterly Review* 19 (1928, 29) 211-262; [7]Cf. *La dernière Cène; Les Paroles de Jésus*, French ed., 1972, 238-240; [8]*Springtime*, 4; [9]*Op. cit.*, 99; [10]Apud L. Deiss, *op. cit.*, 6; [11]*Ibid.*, 8, 9; [12]*Op. cit.*, 1193; [13]*Op. cit.*, 50; LMD, 1966; [14]*Op. cit.*, LMD, 1976, 39.

JOHN CHRYSOSTOM, ST., DOCTOR OF THE CHURCH (c. 347-407)

Called the "Doctor of the Eucharist," C. merited the title by his idea so often expressed of the important place which the Eucharist has in Christian life, and by his teaching on the Real Presence (qv).[1] On the latter point he was realistic to the point of using language which should not be taken too literally. He certainly taught the reality of Transubstantiation (qv), but he lacked the philosophical equipment to make all the necessary distinctions.

In a classic passage C. says: "Let us then have faith in God, with no denial, even when what he testifies appears contrary to our reason and our sense. Let us behave thus in regard to the Eucharist, not considering what lies before our eyes, but believing in his words. His word is infallible, while our judgement is easily mistaken; his word never fails, our senses can be wanting in so many things. When he then says: 'This is my Body,' let us adhere closely to what he says and believe, contemplating it with the eyes of the spirit. How many are they who say: I would like to see his external appearance, his bearing, his clothes, his shoes. But, behold, you see him, you touch him, you eat him. You wish merely to see his clothes, but he gives himself to you, not only to see but to touch, to eat, to be taken within you."[2]

C's realism is very explicit: "Parents often get strangers to feed their children. It is not thus with me. I feed mine with my own flesh, I give myself to you as food. I wished to become your brother, to have, on your behalf, the same flesh and the same blood as you; well then, I give you this flesh and this blood by which I have become your race."[3] Commenting on 1 Cor 10:16, 'The cup of blessing which we bless, is it not a participation in the blood of Christ?,' C. writes: "Here are words full of faith and awe-inspiring. This is what the Apostle says: What is in the chalice is the same thing which flowed from the side of Christ and we participate in it."[4] Or again: "It is no longer in the crib that the body of Christ appears to you, but on the altar. He is no longer in the hands of a mere woman. See the priest holds him; and you not only see him, but you touch him; you not only touch him, but you eat him and take him to your homes."[5]

The note of awe as proper in the presence of the Eucharist is stressed by C.J. Quasten lists with exact references several texts of C. which express this idea of awe, reverence required, a sentiment of dread.[6] The same patristic scholar quotes the passages where C's realism seems to go beyond the limits. "Reflect, O man, what sacrificial flesh you take in your hand! To what table you will approach. Remember that you, though dust and ashes, do receive the blood and the body of Christ."[7] That is highly acceptable, but the following seems over-realistic: "Not only ought we to see the Lord, but we ought to take him in our hands, eat him, set our teeth upon his flesh and most

intimately unite ourselves with him."[8] "What the Lord did not tolerate on the Cross (i.e. the breaking of his legs) he tolerates now in the sacrifice through the love of you; he permits himself to be broken in pieces that all may be filled to satiety."[9] As J. Quasten rightly remarks, C. "here transfers to the substance of the body and blood of Christ what is strictly true of the accidents of bread and wine, in order to make the truth of the real presence and the identity of the Eucharistic sacrifice with the sacrifice of the Cross as clear as possible."[10]

It is the same Christ who is offered everywhere: "There is one Christ everywhere, complete both in this world and in the other; one body. As then, though offered in many places, he is but one body, so there is but one sacrifice. We offer that now which was offered then; which is indeed inconsumable.... We do not then offer a different sacrifice from what the high priest formerly did, but always the same; or rather, we celebrate a memorial of a sacrifice."[11]

Christ is the sacrificing priest and the consecration takes place the moment that the words of institution are pronounced. "It is not man who causes what is present to become the body and blood of Christ, but Christ himself who was crucified for us. The priest is the representative when he pronounces these words, but the power and grace are those of the Lord, 'This is my body,' he says. This word changes the things that lie before us and as that sentence 'increase and multiply,' once spoken extends through all time and gives to our nature the power to reproduce itself; even so, that saying, 'This is my body,' once uttered, does at every table in the churches from that time to the present day, and even till Christ's coming, make the sacrifice complete."[12]

---

[1]J. Solano, *Textos*, I, 441-664; cf. F. Probst, *Die antiochenische Messe nach den Schriften des heiligen Johannes Chrysostomus dargestellt: ZKT* 7 (1883), 250-303; J. Sorg, *Die Lehre des hl. Chrysostomus über die reale Gegenwart Christi in der Eucharistie und die Transubstatiation: TQ* 79 (1897) 259-297; A. Nagele; *Die Eucharistielehre des hl. Johannes Chrysostomus, des Doctor Eucharistiae*, Freiburg i. B., 1900; E. Michaud, *St. Jean Chrysostome et l'Eucharistie; Rev. Internat. de Théol.*, 11 (1903) 3-111; E. S. Salaville, *L'épiclèse d'après St. Jean Chrysostome et la tradition occidentale*, EO 11 (1908) 101-112; A. D'Alès, *Un texte eucharistique de St. Jean Chrysostome, RSR* 24 (1933) 451-462; W. Lampen, *Doctrina S. Joannis Chrysostomi de Christo se offerente in Missa*, Ant. 18 (1943) 3-16; G. Fittkau, *Der Begriff des Mysteriums bei Johannes Chrysostomus*, Bonn, 1953; G. Stocker, *Eucharistiche Gemeinschaft bei Chrysostomus* ST II (TU) 64, Berlin, 1957, 309-316; [2]*In Matth. Homil.* 82, PG 58, 743; [3]*In Joannem Hom* 46, PG 59, 261; [4]*In 1 Cor Hom* 24, 1, PG 61, 199; [5]*Ibid.*, 5; [6]*Op. cit.*, 480; [7]*Hom. in nat. Dom.*, 7, PG 49, 361; [8]*Hom* 46 *in Johannem*, 3, PG 59, 260; [9]*Hom.* 24 *in 1 Cor*, 2, PG 61, 200; [10]*Op. cit.*, 480; [11]*Hom.* 17 *in Hebr. 3*; [12]Hom 1 de prod. Judae, 6, PG 49, 380; 389.

JOHN CHRYSOSTOM, LITURGY OF ST.

This is the Liturgy generally used in the Byzantine rite.[1] It bears the name of the saint because of the importance of Constantinople, where he was patriarch, capital of the eastern empire, in the Church second only to Rome after the Council of 381; his own fame as a preacher doubtless, possibly also his Eucharistic doctrine, contributed to the attribution. Grounds to justify it are very weak. In time it displaced the other eastern liturgies, eclipsing that of St. James and St. Mark (qv); these had gradually shed most of their differences from it. It is used in many different languages in the Orthodox churches.

[1]Text Brightman, *Liturgies Eastern and Western*, I (1896), 309-344; modern text, 353-399; anaphora in *Prex* (Cod. Barber gr. 336, 223-229); cf. P. de Meester, *Les origines et les développements du texte grec de la liturgie de saint Jean Chrysostome*, in *Chrysostomika*, papers for XVth centenary of his death, 407-1907, Rome, 1908; S. Salaville, *L'Epiclèse d'après saint Jean Chrysostome et la tradition occidentale*, *Echos d'Orient*, 11 (1908) 101-112; A. Strittmatter, 'Missa Graecorum'—'Missa Sancti Joannis Chrysostomi'. *The oldest Latin version known of the Byzantine Liturgies of St. Basil and St. John Chrysostom*, *EphLit* 55 (1941), 2-73; A. Raes, *L'Authenticité de la Liturgie byzantine de saint Jean Chrysostome*, OCP 24 (1958) 5-16; J. Matéos, *L'Action du Saint Esprit dans la liturgie dite de saint Jean Chrysostome*, in *Proche-Orient Chrétien*, 9 (1959), 193-208; H. Engberding, *Das anaphorische Fürbittgebet der Byzantinischen Chrysostomusliturgie*, *Oriens Christianus* 45 (1961) 20-29; id., *Die Angleichung der byzantinischen Chrysostomusliturgie an die Basiliusliturgie*, in *Ostkirchliche Studien*, 13 (1964) 105-122; G. Khouri-Sarkis, *L'origine syrienne de l'anaphore byzantine de saint Jean Chrysostome*, *L'Orient Syrien*, 7 (1962), 3-68; C. Kucharek, *The Byzantine-Slav Liturgy of St. John Chrysostom; Its Origin and Evolution*, Allendale, New York, 1971; G. Wagner, *Der Ursprung der Chrysostomus-liturgie (Liturgie wissenschaftliche Quellen und Forschungen*, 49) 1973.

JOHN OF DAMASCUS, ST., DOCTOR OF THE CHURCH (c. 675-c. 749)

In ch 13 of bk IV of his great work *De Fide Orthodoxa*, J., the 'last of the Fathers,' brought together into an orderly and harmonious synthesis the teaching of his predecessors on the Eucharist. The statement marks a completed stage, as it were, in theological reflection, is admirable in its own right, not aiming at originality but fidelity to tradition.

Central to the exposition is the magnificent parallel between the Incarnation and the Eucharist: "God said 'This is my body' and 'This is my Blood,' and 'Do this,' and it is done at his omnipotent command until he comes. For it was in this sense that he said '...until he comes.' And the overshadowing power of the Holy Spirit becomes, through the epiclesis, the rain to the new cultivation. For just as God made all that he made by the energy of the Holy Spirit, so also now the energy of the Spirit performs those things which are above nature, which it is not possible to comprehend except by faith alone. 'How shall this be,' said the Virgin, 'since I know not man?' And the Archangel Gabriel answered her: 'The Holy Spirit shall come upon you, and the power of the Most High shall overshadow you' (Lk 1:34, 35). And now you ask how the bread becomes Christ's Body and the wine and water Christ's Blood, and I say to you: The Holy Spirit comes and does these things which surpass description and understanding.... The Body from the Holy Virgin is in truth Body united to divinity, not because the very Body which was taken up (Mk 16:19) descends from heaven, but because the bread and wine are changed into God's Body and Blood. But if you ask how this happens, it is enough for you to hear that it is through the Holy Spirit, just as also from the holy Theotokos through the Holy Spirit, the Lord made flesh to subsist for himself and in himself."[1]

[1]Bk IV, ch 13 PG 94, 1136-1153; Solano, *Textos*, 760-772; here quoted 765-66; tr. D.J. Sheerin, *Message of the Fathers, The Eucharist*, 169f; cf. P. Benoit, *The Eucharistic Teaching of St. John Damascene*, diss., Washington, D.C., 1946.

JOHN PAUL II (1920, Pope 1978...)

No one in history has celebrated the Eucharist before such vast crowds in so many different parts of the world as John Paul II.[1] From this continuous, worldwide celebration has come a flow of homiletic teaching which is at once a testimony of high quality, powerful exhortation and, indirectly, a record of popular faith and practice at the level of the local church. From the beginning of his pontificate John Paul II chose to turn attention to the priesthood (qv) and the Eucharist.

Like Paul VI (qv), the Pope had requests for laicisation piling up on his desk—it is reported that 500 awaited his immediate attention on his election. He emphasized the link between the priestly office and the Eucharist in face of this disarray: "A priest is worth what his Eucharistic life is worth."[2] The Pope marked his concern in the first year of his pontificate. For Holy Thursday 1979, he sent letters to the Bishops and to the Priests of the Church. There is a notable difference in the dimensions of the two documents: that to the Bishops takes six pages of the Catholic Truth Society ed., that to the Priests, thirty-three. The following year for Holy Thursday John Paul sent a letter to Bishops on the mystery and worship of the Eucharist, in which he begins with considerations on the priesthood. Thereafter when he issues a document for Holy Thursday, it is written primarily for priests: 1982, 1983, 1985, 1986. In addition the Pope has taken every possible opportunity to speak to priests or future priests, even the laity on the sacred office. No Pope in history has, within an equivalent period of time, published so much pastoral and spiritual teaching on the Catholic priesthood. This the Pope has continued to do to groups or assemblies organised on the theme of the priesthood; in special encounters with priests and seminarians in Italy or in the course of his many travels; when he also often ordains priests in special ceremonies timed for his visit; on the days set aside to pray for vocations throughout the world.

The Pope has also powerfully countered the wave of timidity in faith, if not doubt concerning the Eucharist itself. The very letter mentioned, the Apostolic Exhortation *Dominicae Cenas*, (qv), 24 February 1980, elaborates a doctrine on the Eucharist as sacrament and sacrifice, notable for the strong insistence on the great traditional truths. The Instruction issued by the Congregation for the Doctrine of the Faith, concerning the worship of the Eucharist, *Inaestimabile Donum,* 3 April 1980, coming so soon after the other document just mentioned, indicated a sense of urgency, if not of crisis, in this most important of all areas of Christian living.

In practice the Pope has wished to lead by example and by positive practical exhortation. He has given a very elaborate character to the Holy Thursday celebration, as the feast of the priesthood and the Eucharist, presiding at Mass with very large numbers of concelebrants. He has encouraged public honour to the Eucharist, processions and vigils and especially congresses. His fixed policy is to attend every International Eucharistic Congress, from which he is not physically barred; he was so through the effects of an assassination attempt from Lourdes in 1981.

In John Paul II the two trends, pastoral, so strongly accentuated by St. Pius X (qv), and liturgical, growing through the pontificate of Pius XII (qv), Vatican II (qv) and Paul VI (qv) meet and enrich the spiritual patrimony of the Church and the world.

In published work John Paul II is, with due regard for the time scale, the most prolific Pope in history. His varied pronouncements, with the exception of the year 1980, when his output was diminished by a criminal attack on his person, run to over one million, two hundred thousand words, the equivalent of twelve substantial books, annually; he uses at least eight languages: Latin, Polish, Italian, French, German, English, Spanish, Portuguese. Within this vast corpus what he has said on the Eucharist and the priesthood constitutes a substantial part, as does his teaching on the Blessed Virgin Mary. If John Paul II is a Eucharistic and a Marian personality, then he himself merits examination by experts interested in the possible

enlargement of natural power and talent by the supernatural, channeled through exceptional mystical forces, in the present instance those flowing from the Eucharist and through the Blessed Virgin Mary. St. Thomas Aquinas presents a similar problem.

Faced with such an 'embarras de richesses' one can but make a selection, hoping it will be representative. In the first letter on the priesthood the Pope writes in the line of Vatican II, the *presbyterium*: "From the very beginning I wish to express my faith in the vocation that unites you to your Bishops, in a special communion of sacrament and ministry, through which the Church, the Mystical Body of Christ, is built up. Today, in fact, there is a special circumstance that impels me to confide to you some thoughts that I enclose in this Letter; it is the nearness of Holy Thursday. It is this, the annual feast of our priesthood, that unites the whole Presbyterium of each diocese about its Bishop in the shared celebration of the Eucharist.... The Second Vatican Council, which so explicitly highlighted the collegiality of the Episcopate in the Church, also gave a new form to the life of the priestly communities, joined together by a special bond of brotherhood, and united to the Bishop of the respective local Church .... (A reference follows to Priests' Councils, which, in conformity with the Council and *Ecclesiae Sanctae* of Paul VI, should be universal.) All this is meant to ensure that each Bishop, in union with his Presbyterium, can serve ever more effectively the great cause of evangelization. Through this service the Church realizes her mission, indeed her very nature."[2]

In the following year the Pope writing to the Bishops of the Church on the Eucharist, dealt with the Eucharist and the priesthood as follows: "In reality, the ministerial and hierarchical priesthood, the priesthood of the Bishops and the priests, and, at their side, the ministry of the deacons—ministries which normally begin with the proclamation of the Gospel—are in the closest relationship with the Eucharist. The Eucharist is the principal and central *raison d'être* of the priesthood, which effectively came into being at the moment of the institution of the Eucharist, and together with it. Not without reason the words 'Do this in memory of me' are said immediately after the words of Eucharistic consecration, and we repeat them every time we celebrate the Holy Sacrifice."[3]

Here the idea of the presbyterium is muted, certainly not denied. A similar comment may be made on the words spoken by the Pope at the Holy Thursday Mass: "We are therefore priests of his priesthood. We are priests of this sacrifice, which he offered in his body and in his blood on the Cross and under the species of bread and wine at the Last Supper. We are also 'priests for men,' in order that all, by means of the sacrifice we carry out by virtue of his power, may become 'a kingdom of priests' and offer spiritual sacrifices in union with his sacrifice of the Cross and of the Upper Room."[4]

Later in the month the Pope spoke thus to the priests of Turin: "I remind myself and you that there are some fundamental properties, which unite all those who share in the ministerial priesthood in the Church, though exercising different tasks. The first one is a participation with the one Priest, sovereign and eternal, who is Jesus Christ; all of us, in fact, 'have been sanctified through the offering of the body of Jesus Christ once for all' (Heb 10:10), even if we always bear within us a sense of unworthiness for this extraordinary call which makes us 'unworthy servants' (Lk 17:10). The second one consists in the peculiar pastoral responsibility, which distinguishes priests from the faithful on whom the ordinary baptismal priesthood has been bestowed, and reserves for them a specific task in the preaching of the word, the celebration of the sacraments and safe guidance of the community.... The third characteristic, closely connected with the preceding ones, concerns our special conformation to Christ, so that his sacrifice and his love become also our norm of life. Each member of the faithful should be able to say of each of us what every Christian, with St. Paul, confesses with regard to Jesus: he 'loved me and gave himself for me' (Gal 2:20), as the Holy Shroud, preserved here, opportunely reminds us."

It is in his final remark that the Pope speaks of the ecclesial aspect "and urges his priest listeners to "cultivate close communion with their bishops"; he adds a well-known passage from St. Ignatius of Antioch on the presbyterium.

In the following month John Paul spoke to priests in Kinshasa on their sacred office. He said not a word about the presbyterium, took as his central point this truth: "To be a priest means a mediator between God and men, in the Mediator par excellence who is Christ." "Christ," he said a little later, "exercised his office as mediator mainly by offering up his life in the sacrifice of the Cross, accepted out of obedience to the Father. The Cross remains the necessary way for the meeting with God. It is a way on which the priest first and foremost must embark courageously. As I recalled in my recent letter on the Eucharist, is he not called to renew 'in persona Christi', in the Eucharistic celebration, the sacrifice of the Cross? According to the fine expression of the African Augustine of Hippo, Christ on Calvary was 'priest and sacrifice, and therefore priest because he was sacrifice' (Confessions, X, 43, 69)."[6]

"Beloved brothers," the Pope ends, "have faith in your priesthood. It is the priesthood of always, because it is a participation in the eternal priesthood of Christ, who 'is the same yesterday and today and forever' (Heb 13:8; cf. Rev 1:17 ff). Yes, if the demands of the priesthood are very great, and if I have not hesitated, however, to speak to you about them, it is because they are simply the consequence of the closeness of the Lord, of the confidence he shows in his priests. 'No longer do I call you servants ... but I have called you friends' (Jn 15:15). May this song of the day of your ordination remain for each of you, as for me, a permanent source of joy and trust. It is this joy that I call upon you to renew today. May the Virgin Mary always sustain you on the way, and may she introduce you more and more every day to intimacy with the Lord!"[7]

In the same month the Pope spoke to French priests with as his central thesis, "We have been taken from among men, and we ourselves remain poor servants, our mission as priests of the New Testament is sublime and indispensable. It is that of Christ, the one Mediator and Sanctifier, to such an extent that it calls for the total consecration of our life and being."[8]

In July of that year the Pope performed an ordination ceremony in Rio de Janeiro and spoke on the priesthood. Talking of the identity which Christ willed with his priests "in the exercise of the powers which he has conferred on us, that our personality disappears, in a way before his, since it is he who acts through us," the Pope continued a little later: "As you can see, we are here at the peak of Christ's priesthood, in which we particpate and which made the author of the letter to the Hebrews exclaim; 'grandis sermo et ininterpretabilis ad dicendum'—'about this we have much to say which is hard to explain' (Heb 5:11). The expression 'sacerdos alter Christus,' 'the priest is another Christ', created by the intuition of the Christian people, is not just a way of speaking, a metaphor, but a marvellous, surprising and consoling reality."[9]

The manifold mystery of the Eucharist is a theme proclaimed unceasingly by John Paul II. In his first Encyclical, *Redemptor hominis*, we get his outlook: "The Eucharist is the sacrament in which our new being is most completely expressed and in which Christ himself unceasingly and in an ever new manner 'bears witness' to the Holy Spirit in our spirit (cf. 1 Jn 5:5-11), that each of us, as a sharer in the mystery of the Redemption, has access to the fruits of the filial reconciliation with God that he himself actuated and continually actuates among us by means of the Church's ministry. It is an essential truth not only of doctrine but also of life, that the Eucharist builds the

Church, building it as the authentic community of the people of God, as the assembly of the faithful, bearing the same mark of unity that was shared by the Apostles and first disciples of the Lord. The Eucharist builds ever anew this community and unity, ever building and regenerating it on the basis of the sacrifice of Christ, since it commemorates his death on the Cross, the price by which he redeemed us. . . . The Church lives by the Eucharist, by the fullness of this sacrament, the stupendous content and meaning of which have often been expressed in the Church's magisterium from the most distant times down to our own days." With all the greater reason, then, it is not permissible for us, in thought, life or action, to take away from this truly most holy sacrament its full magnitude and its essential meaning. It is at one and the same time a sacrifice-sacrament. And, although it is true that the Eucharist always was and must continue to be the most profound revelation of the human brotherhood of Christ's disciples and confessors, it cannot be treated merely as an 'occasion' for manifesting this brotherhood."[10] From this truth, as the Pope insists, flows the obligation to "carry out rigorously the rules of worship offered to God himself." More than a hint on irregularities!

The Eucharist is linked by the Pope to the Incarnation: "The Eucharist brings us closer to God in a stupendous way. And it is the sacrament of his closeness to man. God in the Eucharist is precisely the God who wished to enter the history of man. He wished to accept humanity itself. He wished to become a man. The sacrament of the body and blood reminds us continually of his divine humanity. We sing, 'Ave verum corpus, natum de Maria Virgine.' And living with the Eucharist we find again all the simplicity and depth of the mystery of the Incarnation."[11]

The Pope points to the Trinitarian dimension of Eucharistic worship: "This worship, given therefore to the Trinity of the Father and of the Son and of the Holy Spirit, above all accompanies and permeates the celebration of the Eucharistic liturgy."[12]

Hence too John Paul is led to consider the Eucharist at some length in his Encyclical, *Dominum et vivificantem*, on the Holy Spirit: "The most complete sacramental expression of the 'departure' of Christ through the mystery of the Cross and resurrection is the Eucharist. In every celebration of the Eucharist his coming, his salvific presence, is sacramentally realized: in the sacrifice and in communion. It is accomplished by the power of the Holy Spirit as part of his own mission. Through the Eucharist the Holy Spirit accomplishes that 'strengthening of the inner man' spoken of in the Letter to the Ephesians. Through the Eucharist, individuals and communities, by the action

of the Paraclete-Counsellor, learn to discover the divine sense of human life, as spoken by the Council: that sense whereby Jesus Christ 'fully reveals man to man himself,' suggesting a certain likeness between the union of the divine persons, and the union of God's children in truth and charity.' This union is expressed and made real especially through the Eucharist, in which man shares in the sacrifice of Christ which this celebration actualizes, and he also learns to 'find himself ... through a ... gift of himself, through communion with God and with others, his brothers and sisters."[13]

For John Paul, "The Eucharist is above all else a sacrifice (qv). It is the sacrifice of the Redemption and also the sacrifice of the New Covenant, as we believe and as the Eastern Churches clearly profess: 'Today's sacrifice,' the Greek Church stated centuries ago, 'is like that offered once by the Only-begotten Incarnate Word; it is offered by him (now as then) since it is one and the same sacrifice.' Accordingly, precisely by making this single sacrifice of our salvation present, man and the world are restored to God through the paschal newness of Redemption. This restoration cannot cease to be; it is the foundation of the 'new and eternal covenant' of God with man and of man with God. If it were missing, one would have to question both the excellence of the sacrifice of the Redemption, which in fact was perfect and definitive, and also the sacrificial value of the Mass. In fact, the Eucharist, being a true sacrifice, brings about this restoration to God."[14]

The Pope continues to preach regularly on the Eucharist, for example, several times during his visit to Poland in 1987, at the time of the national Eucharistic Congress.

---

[1]All the Pope's pronouncements in *Insegnamenti*, Vatican City, or *AAS*; cf also *L'Osservatore Romano*, weekly ed.; English tr. Catholic Truth Society, A. Flannery, *Vatican II, 2;* on the Priesthood cf. *A Priest Forever*, Papal texts ed. Seamus O'Byrne, Athlone, down to July 1981; texts from 1978-1986, *Jean Paul II. Avec vous je suis prêtre, Homélies et Exhortations de Jean Paul II.* Présentation P. Raffin, O.P., Paris, 1986; on the Eucharist, S. O'Byrne, *The Bread of Life*, texts to July 1982, Athlone, 1982; [2]A. Flannery, O.P., Vatican II, 2, 346, 47; [3]*Ibid.*, 65; [4]*A Priest Forever*, 97; [5]*Ibid.*, 97, 98; [6]*Ibid.*, 100; [7]*Ibid.*, 105, 106; [8]*A Priest Forever*, 110; [9]*Ibid.*, 119; [10]*The Bread of Life*, 22, 23; [11]*Ibid.*, 34; [12]*Dominicae Cenae*, A. Flannery, O.P., Vatican II, 2, 67; [13]Catholic Truth Society ed., 124, 25; [14]*Dominicae Cenae*, A. Flannery, O.P., 75.

JUNGMANN, JOSEPH ANDREW (1889-1975)

The appearance in Vienna in 1948 of *Missarum Sollemnia* was a landmark in Catholic publishing.[1] The work, known in English as *The Mass of the Roman Rite* (2 vols, 1951, 1955), is accurately described as "the most authoritative and complete work on the history of the growth of the Liturgy of the Roman Mass that has ever appeared." The story of its composition has to be read in the author's own words:[2] the narrative of his immense research carried out during the vicissitudes of persecution and war, when sources, libraries, collections were dispersed or unavailable; the success, nevertheless, of resilience supported by much generosity. A few sentences often summarize yards and yards of collated columns, with dozens, even hundreds of smaller strips. Checking the citations took more than six months of strenuous work.

J., ordained a secular priest, joined the Society of Jesus after some years. He has taught at Innsbruck University and during the war did some ministry in a country parish—writing all the time. Editor of the *Zeitschrift für Katholische Theologie*, contributor to reviews and collections, esp. *LTK*: his other major work is *Die Stellung Christi im liturgische Gebet, The Place of Christ in Liturgical Prayer*. His message: Christian joy in the centrality of Christ. J. had been offered a *Festschrift* on his 50th birthday, *Die Messe in der Glaubenverkündigung* (Freiburg i. Brisgau) and for his 60th, *Paschalia Sollemnia* (Freiburg i. B.).

---

[1] W. Croce, S.J., in *Catholicisme*, VI, 1261; DTC Tables, XVI, 2, 2750-51; [2] Author's Foreword to vol I.

JUSTIN MARTYR, ST (c. 100-c. 165)

The testimony of J., the highly literate Palestinian, greatest of the Apologists, is precious because of his cultural background, and his conversion in adult years and his wide acquaintance with the world of his time from Palestine and Ephesus—where he probably became a Christian c. 130—to Rome where he died, after openly defending his Christian faith to the emperor, Antoninus Pius and the senate.[1] In these two defences, the *Apologies*, and in his *Dialogue with Trypho*, J. communicates much that is valuable on the subject of the Eucharist. He first describes the Eucharist which follows Baptism: "After we have cleansed the person who believes and has joined our ranks, we lead him in to where those we call 'brothers' are assembled. We offer prayers in common for ourselves, for him who has just been enlightened, and for all men everywhere. It is our desire, now that we have come to know the truth, to be found worthy of doing good deeds and obeying the commandments, and thus to obtain eternal salvation. When we finish praying, we greet one another with a kiss. Then bread and a cup of wine mixed with water are brought to him who presides over the brethren. He takes them and offers prayers, glorifying the Father of the universe through the name of the Son and of the Holy Spirit, and he utters a lengthy eucharist because the Father has judged us worthy of these gifts. When the prayers and eucharist are finished, all the people present give their assent with the 'Amen!' 'Amen' in Hebrew means 'So be it!' When the president has finished his eucharist, and the people have all signified their assent, those whom we call 'deacons' distribute the bread and the wine and water, over which the eucharist has been spoken, to each of those present; they also carry them to those who are absent.

"This food we call 'eucharist,' and no one may share it unless he believes that our teaching is true, and has been cleansed in the bath of forgiveness for sin and of rebirth, and lives as Christ taught. For we do not receive these things as if they were ordinary food and drink. But just as Jesus Christ our Saviour was made flesh through the word of God and took on flesh and blood for our salvation, so too (we have been taught) through the word of prayer that comes from him, the food over which the eucharist has been spoken becomes the flesh and blood of the incarnate Jesus, in order to nourish and transform our flesh and blood. For, in the memoirs which the apostles composed and which we call 'gospels,' they have told us that they were commissioned thus: Jesus took bread and, having given thanks, said: 'Do this in memory of me; this is my body.' And in a like manner he took the cup and, having given thanks, said: 'This is my blood.' And he gave these to the apostles alone."[2]

On the liturgy of the Lord's Day J. writes as follows: "Those of us who have any resources come to the aid of all who are in need, and we are always assisting one another. For all that we eat we thank the Maker of the universe through his Son, Jesus Christ, and the Holy Spirit. On the day named after the sun, all who live in city or countryside assemble. The memoirs of the Apostles or the writings of the prophets are read for as long as time allows. When the lector has finished, the president addresses us and exhorts us to imitate the splendid things we have heard. Then we all stand and pray. As we said earlier, when we have finished praying, bread, wine, and water are brought up. The president then prays and gives thanks according to his ability, and the people give their assent with an 'Amen'! Next, the gifts over which the thanksgiving has been spoken are distributed, and everyone shares in them, while they are also sent via the deacons to the absent brethren. The wealthy, who are willing, make contributions, each as he pleases, and the collection is deposited with the president, who aids orphans and widows, those who are in want because of sickness or some other reason, those in prison, and visiting strangers—in short, he takes care of all in need. It is on Sunday that we all assemble, because Sunday is the first day; the day on which God transformed darkness and matter and created the world, and the day on which Jesus Christ our Saviour rose from the dead. He was crucified on the eve of Saturn's day, and on the day after, that is, on the day of the sun, he appeared to his Apostles and disciples and taught them what we have now offered for your examination."[3]

The word 'eucharist' means thanksgiving in these passages, save in the phrase: "This food we call eucharist"; this is the first time that the word is used not merely for the prayer of thanksgiving, but to denote the bread and wine over which the prayer (i.e. the consecration) has been said. There is considerable discussion as to whether there is an allusion in Apol 66, 2 to the words of institution.[4] The Mass here described contains elements to be fixed in the Christian celebration: reading of the word of God, homily of the celebrant, common prayer, Eucharist. The reference to a reading "from the memoirs of the Apostles or the writings of the prophets" echoes Acts 2:42: "And they devoted themselves to the Apostles' teaching and fellowship, to the breaking of bread and the prayers."[5]

J. has a passage in *The Dialogue* which has stirred controversy: Does he consider the Eucharist a sacrifice? "God therefore has long since borne witness that all sacrifices offered by his name, which Jesus the Christ enjoined, namely at the thanksgiving of the bread and the cup, which are offered in every place on earth by Christians, are well pleasing to him. But those that are made by you, and by means of those priests of yours, he utterly rejects, saying: 'And your sacrifices will I not accept from your hands; because from the rising of the sun unto its setting my name has been glorified,' he says, 'among the Gentiles, but ye do profane it.' And until now do you say in your love of controversy, that God did not accept the sacrifices in Jerusalem in the case of those who were called Israelites and dwelt there then, but that he has said that the prayers of that race who in truth were then in the Dispersion did please him, and that he calls their prayers sacrifices. Now that both prayers and thanksgivings, when made by worthy people, are the only perfect and acceptable sacrifices to God, I also must affirm. For these alone were Christians taught to make, even at the remembrance of their food, both dry and liquid, in which also the suffering which the Son of God has suffered for their sake is brought to mind."[6]

Earlier in *The Dialogue* J. had evoked OT events and passages as foreshadowing the Eucharist: "The offering of fine flour, Gentlemen, I said, which was ordered to be offered on behalf of those who were being cleansed from leprosy, was a type of the bread of the Eucharist. For Jesus Christ our Lord ordered us to *do this in remembrance* (see *Anamnesis*) of the suffering which he suffered on behalf of those who are being purged in soul from all iniquity, in order that we should at the same time give thanks to God for having created the world with all that is in it for man's sake, and also for having set us free from the evil in which we had (hitherto) been, and for having destroyed the powers and the authorities with a complete destruction by means of him who became liable to suffering according to his will. Wherefore God says thus concerning the sacrifices that were offered up by you at that time, speaking, as I said before, by Malachi, one of the Twelve: 'I have no pleasure in you, says the Lord, and your hosts, and I will not accept an offering from your hands. For from the rising of the sun to its setting my name is great among the nations, and in every place incense is offered to my name, and a pure offering; for my name is great among the nations, says the Lord of hosts, But you profane it ... (Mal 1:10, 11).' He speaks at that time, so long beforehand, concerning the sacrifices that are being offered to him in every place by us Gentiles, that is to say, the bread of the Eucharist and likewise the cup of the Eucharist, saying also that we glorify his name, but you profane it."[7]

Again quoting a passage from Isaiah (33:13-19) he adds: "It is plain therefore that in this prophecy he speaks of the bread which our Christ taught us to do in remembrance of his incarnation for those who believe in him, for whom he became even liable unto suffering; and also of the cup which he taught us as we give thanks to do in remembrance of his blood. And this prophecy declares that we shall see this very King (surrounded) with glory."[8]

In summary, allowing for divergent interpretations of particular texts, the Eucharistic doctrine of J. is remarkably enlightened. The Eucharistic mystery is directly related to the Incarnation. Food of the soul, it is brought into being by the words of Christ. The object of the Incarnation is the flesh and blood of Christ, the efficient cause is God's creative word, the final cause is man's salvation. The parallel with the Eucharist is striking: Christ's word is the efficient cause; his flesh and blood, the reality; and the final cause is the spiritual nourishment of the Christian. J. also lays down the conditions for receiving the body and blood of the Lord: faith and Baptism.

The praise of J's Eucharistic doctrine by patrologists is impressive. "The Eucharist," says P. Batiffol, "is not considered by J. apart from the Incarnation, of which it is an application, a sequel and a fulfillment; the healing and the immortal destiny of our nature has been won for us by the Incarnation and they are communicated by the Eucharist."[9] "The wealth of J's Eucharistic doctrine is apparent," says G. Bardy. "Later centuries will bring greater precision in formulation; they will add nothing, apparently, to the statement of the old Apologist."[10]

[1]Texts, PG 6; Quasten, *Monumenta* 16-21; 337-39; J. Solano, *Textos*, I, 57-67; E.J. Goodspeed, *Die Ältesten Apologeten*, Göttingen, 1914, 74-76, 138, 234f; *Prex Eucharistica*, 68-75; English tr., L. Deiss, *Springtime*, 89-94; bibl., Quasten, *Monumenta*, 16, 337; id., *Patrology*, I, 219; cf. M. Goguel, *L'Eucharistie des origines à Justin Martyr*, Paris, 1909; M.J. Lagrange, O.P., *St. Justin*, Paris, 1914; O. Casel, O.S.B., *Die Eucharistielehre des hl. Justinus Martyr, Der Katholik*, 94 (1914), 153-76; 243-63; 331-55; 414-36; J. Brinktine, *Der Messopferbegriff in den ersten zwei Jahrhunderten, Freiburger Theologische Studien* 21 (Freiburg i. Br. 1918), 85-105; G. Bardy, *Melchisedech dans la tradition biblique partristique, RB* 35 (1926), 496-509; 36 (1927) 25-45; P. Batiffol, *L'Eucharistie*, 6-32; O. Perler, *Logos und Eucharistie nach Justinus I Apol. 66, Divus Thomas* (Frib.) 18 (1940), 296-316; Otilio del Niño Jesús, *Doctrina eucaristica de san Justino, filósofo y martir, Rev. Española de teol.*, 4 (1944), 3-58; M. Jourjon, *Justin*, in *L'Eucharistie des premiers chretiens*, Paris, 1976, 75-88; A. Piolanti, *Il Mistero*, 152-156; [2]*Apologia*, I 65-66, PG 6, 428; [3]*Ibid.*, 67, PG 6, 429; [4]Cf. O. Perler, *op. cit.*, [5]Cf. L. Deiss, *God's Word and God's People*, tr. M.J. O'Connell, Collegeville, 1976, 253-72; [6]*Dialogue* 117, tr. A.L. Wiliams, London, 1930, 240-42; [7]*Ibid.*, 41, p. 81, 82; [8]*Ibid.*, 70, 150; [9]*Op. cit.*, 30; cf. G. Bareille, DTC, V, 1128; [10]*Histoire du dogme eucharistique, Eucharistia*, Paris, 41.

K/L

KNOWLEDGE OF CHRIST, THE

The object here is not to take up all the aspects of the problem of Christ's knowledge and consciousness, to seek to integrate in one satisfying synthesis official teaching, the findings of biblical scholars and the reflection of theologians. Vatican II, taking up an idea from Pius XI's *Mit brennender Sorge*, proclaimed that Christ is "the Mediator and the fullness of divine revelation."[1] The ITC has issued the first part of its report on the problems recently agitated which has some relevance to what is here suggested: all such analyses should include a special application to the moment of Eucharistic institution. It may appear unwarranted to formulate the question thus: What knowledge was in the mind of Christ on the night of the Last Supper?

Preliminaries must be assumed. It is known that until recently the scholastic distinction of threefold knowledge in Christ, acquired, infused, beatific, was not challenged by Catholic theologians: some now reject the idea of beatific science in the Saviour. Again, no one who believes in his divine sonship, consubstantial with the Father, can hold an opinion about him which implicitly or explicitly denies his transcendence. Account must be taken of the *kenosis*, which he accepted in the Incarnation. These are parameters. Within them biblical scholars operate with their skills: one, R.E. Brown reverently, sensitively, gives an evaluation of the gospel evidence taking care to insist that the evaluation "*does not predetermine the theological interpretation to be drawn from it.*"[2] He has no means of contending which of two schools of theology, which he briefly mentions, may be right, though as a biblicist he would be happier with one.

The great biblical scholar sees a difficulty: "Those prone to reject authority may object that if Jesus' knowledge was limited his views were those of his day and can be rejected by the much more learned twentieth century." He answers: "On the other hand, we have indicated an area where his views were not at all those of his time, namely the area of belief and behaviour called for by the coming of the kingdom. And in this area, in my personal opinion, his authority is supreme for every century, because in this area he spoke for God."[3] This is an edifying act of faith, but it remains, in point of scientific value at the empirical level.

A higher stage must be entered, that of theology. Drawing on important disciplines as it has always done, it must provide explanation above the empirical level: the disciplines here are psychology, logic and epistemology. Psychologically, how was Christ's knowledge acquired? Logically, how was it given rational coherence? Epistemologically, what gave it validity and certainty for Christ himself? Why did he speak as one with authority, and how was he equipped to judge a degree of acceptance in his own milieu, of full response from so many in the ages since he lived on earth?

Until these questions are satisfactorily answered many may agree with Jean Galot, S.J., who has written much on this problem that "faced with the witness of Scripture, the scholastic doctrine of a threefold human knowledge, beatific, infused and acquired in Christ does not appear as arbitrary as it might appear at first sight. We have shown that it has a solid foundation."[3] He nuances the idea of beatific knowledge and pleads for an understanding of growth in Christ's consciousness of divine truth: "Every kind of knowledge possessed by Christ, even that of higher origin, is intertwined with the progressive development of his psychology."[4] Later, writing coincidentally with the appearance of the ITC report, in the same review, Fr. Galot grapples anew with the problem of Christ's vision: "When Jesus asserts that he has seen the Father, the assertion relates to the eternal pre-existence of the Son, and corresponds to what the Johannine prologue declares about the Word who from the beginning was with God. The vision is therefore a divine vision. One is not justified in concluding that since there is divine vision there is human vision. Jesus does not now say that he sees the Father, but that he knows him, that he recognises him or knows who he is."[5]

But Jesus said that he and the Father "are one," that he can only do the works which he *sees* the Father doing, that he is in the Father and the Father in him, that he will send the Spirit from the Father—all Johannine reports (10:30; 5:19; 14:10; 15:26) to be taken with Jean Galot's opinion, based also on Jn, to weaken it. It labours, moreover, from an intrinsic weakness. If Jesus had a divine vision, was this before he became man? How did he, as a man, know of this vision, without experiencing it? What relevance at all has it to his knowledge as a man? Why should he mention it, if it were not logically coherent with other layers of his knowledge—this problem of the inner cohesion of his knowledge, its logically interdependent organisation, is central. Jean Galot seems to give him vision for a while! K. Rahner is quite positive on the point.

Theologians must apply their theses to the crucial case of the Eucharist. St. Thomas Aquinas thought it a greater miracle than the act of creation. How did Jesus Christ know that what he was doing was compatible with the laws of nature? It is a mighty thing for a human being to say of bread that it is his body, and wine that it is his blood. Rightly the comment has been made that only God could think of such a thing and only God made man could do it. This was adding a dimension to cosmic reality utterly undreamt of, apart from that supremely solemn moment. Moreover, Jesus knew that he was setting off a chain of similar sensational departures from previously known cosmic laws; acts identical with his own then and there, throughout the universe. There is here a field for the student of Christ's knowledge. A similar

problem has been stated, in the present author's work, *Trinitas*, in regard to Christ's knowledge of the Trinity.[6]

[1]*Constitution on Divine Revelation*, 2; for report of ITC cf. *Greg.* 67, 3 (1986), 413–442—*La conscience que Jesus avait de lui-même et de sa mission*; for reading: A. Durand, *La science du Christ*, NRT 71 (1949), 497–503; J. Galot, S.J., *Science et conscience de Jésus*, NRT 82 (1960) 113-131; id., *Esprit et Vie*, 92 (82), 145-152; id., *Le Christ terrestre et la vision Greg.*, 67, 3, 442-450; T.E. Clarke, *Some Aspects of Current Christology*, in *Thought* 36 (1961), 325-343; K. Rahner, *Dogmatic Considerations on Knowledge and Consciousness in Christ* in *Dogmatic vs. Biblical Theology*, Baltimore, 1964, 241-267; ed H. Vorgrimler; id., *Dogmatic Reflections on the Knowledge and Self-consciousness of Christ*, in *Theological Investigations* V (1966), 193-215; Philippe de la Trinité, O.D.C., *A propos de la connaissance du Christ. Un faux problème théologique*, *Ephemerides Carmeliticae*, 11 (1960), 1-52; B. Lonergan, S.J., *De Verbo Incarnato*, 3rd ed., Rome, 1964, 332-416; J. Mouroux, *La connaissance du Christ et le temps*, RSR 47 (1959), 321-44; R.E. Brown, *How Much Did Jesus Know? A Survey of the Biblical Evidence*, CBQ 29 (1967), 315-345; *Jesus, God and Man*, London, 1968, 39-102; the following articles in *Doctor Communis*, special issue, 36 (1983), 123-411; B. de Margerie, S.J., *De la science du Christ, Science, prescience, conscience, même prepascales du Christ Rédempteur*, 123-157; A. Feuillet, P.S.S., *La science de vision de Jésus et les Evangiles*, 158-179; J.-M. Salgado, O.M.I., *La Science du Fils de Dieu fait homme: Prises de position de Pères et de la Pré-scolastique (IIe-XIIe siècle)*, 180-286; L. Iammmarrone, O.F.M. Cap., *La visione beatifica di Cristo Viatore nel pensiero di San Tommaso*, 287-320; L. Bogliolo, S.D.B., *Strutture antropologiche evisione beatifica dell'anima di Cristo*, 321-346; R.M. Schmitz, *Christus Comprehensor. Die 'Visio beatifica Christi Viatoris' bei*, M.J. Scheeben, 347-359; M.-J. Nicolas, *Voir Dieu dans la'condition charnelle'* 384-394; P. Toinet, *Un progrès hors du commun; de la clairvoyance à la cecité*, 360-383; D. Ols, O.P., *A propos de la vision beatifique du Christ Viateur: Notes de lecture*, 395-405; M. Corvez, O.P., *Le Christ voyait-il l'essence de Dieu pendant sa vie mortelle?* 406-411; abundant references throughout to bibl.; [2]*Op. cit.*, 99; [3]*Ibid.*, 101; [4]*Op. cit.*, 131, 130; [5]Op. cit., 449. [6]See article Faith of Jesus in *Trinitas*, Wilmington, 1986.

LAMB OF GOD, THE

This is a rich biblical title of the Saviour given prominence in the liturgy of the Mass.[1] In the *Gloria* we recite: "Lord Jesus Christ, only Son of the Father; Lord God, Lamb of God, you take away the sin of the world." Before the Communion we say three times: "Lamb of God, who takes away the sins of the world." And immediately before receiving Holy Communion we hear the priest say: "This is the Lamb of God, who takes away the sins of the world. Happy are those who are called to his supper." The Preface for Easter sees Christ, our Pasch, as the true Lamb.

NT designation of Christ as Lamb of God is frequent. John the Baptist so names him: Jn 1:29, 36, as does 1 P 1:19; in Rev the title occurs twenty-eight times. St. Paul in 1 Cor 5:7 speaks of Christ "our paschal lamb" who has been sacrificed. Scholars trace different meanings of the title.

There is the Servant of Yahweh theme in Is 53.

John the Baptist seemingly echoes Is 53:12: "he bore the sin of man"; John says: "he takes away the sin of the world." The Servant is "like a lamb that is led to the slaughter, and like a sheep that before his shearers is dumb" (53:7). J. Jeremias suggests a linguistic explanation: the original Aramaic word 'talya' means both lamb and slave and there has been a mistranslation in Jn 1:29, 36.

The other OT theme is one rooted in the mighty saving act of God for his people. When Israel was delivered from bondage to Egypt, the saving sign for the Jews from the avenging angel was the blood of a lamb on the lintels over the door. With the passage of time Jewish tradition gave a redemptive power to the blood of the lamb: the blood marked a moment of destiny for the Jews, the beginning of their identity as a consecrated people, chosen by God, subject to the Torah. That was a figure of the new Israel, the Church of God: "You know," says 1 Pet 1:19, "that you were ransomed from the futile ways inherited from your fathers, not with perishable things like silver and gold but with the precious blood of Christ like that of a lamb without blemish or spot" (cp Ex 12:5).

R.E. Brown agrees, after careful analysis of the arguments, "that the evangelist intended the Lamb of God to refer to the Suffering Servant and to the paschal lamb," sees "no serious difficulty in maintaining that John intended both references. Both fit into John's Christology and are well attested in 1st-century Christianity. Indeed, a similar twofold reference can probably be found in 1 Pet where, although the paschal theme is prominent, the Suffering Servant theme also appears (2:22-25=Is 53:5-12). Brown points out that the two themes are woven together in the late 2nd-century homily of Melito of Sardis "for while Melito says that Jesus came in place of the paschal lamb, he describes Jesus' death in terms of Is 53:7 . . . "led forth as a lamb, sacrificed as a sheep, buried as a man."[2] And the biblical scholar also suggests that John the Baptist hailed Jesus as the lamb of Jewish apocalyptic expectation. Three levels may be distinguished: for John, the fiery eschatological lamb, for Jesus, the Suffering Servant, for the Christians, the paschal lamb.[3]

The title Lamb of God encapsulates the entire saving role and destiny of Jesus Christ. It does so in the texture of biblical symbolism of the most valid kind. It satisfies a desire for imaginative presentation of divine truth, that can prevent it being lodged only in the upper sector of the mind where concepts are isolated, devoid of vital influence.

The mention of the Lamb in the Gloria of the Mass goes back to the fourth century; this hymn was introduced at Rome for episcopal Masses by Pope Symmachus (498-514). According to the *Liber Pontificalis* the Syrian Pope Sergius I (687-701) decreed *"ut tempora confractionis dominici corporis 'Agnus Dei qui tollis peccata mundi miserere nobis' a clero et populo decantetur."* Older Roman *ordines* laid it down that when the archdeacon had distributed the consecrated hosts so that the fraction could begin, he should intimate to the singers to begin the *Agnus Dei*; it was then a *confractorium*. The response and the repetition varied somewhat down to the present form. Of interest to note is that usage was earlier in the East where the word 'Lamb' was used to refer to sacrificial gifts. Before the sixth century the West Syrians were using the invocation to the Lamb of God who takes away the sins of the world.[4]

On 21 August 1879 in the evening, an apparition took place at the end wall of the parish church in the village of Knock, Co. Mayo, Ireland. Diocesan inquiries over a lengthy period of time have yielded satisfactory results. The shrine, a statuary group in Carrara marble, work of the Italian sculptor, Professor Fersi, now represents the figures seen that evening. This is a national centre of piety associated with the Blessed Virgin Mary. The group has one unique feature. Besides the Virgin crowned, St. Joseph and St. John the Evangelist, a lamb standing on an altar was clearly seen: angels were hovering in the background.

When John Paul II went on pilgrimage to Knock on 30 September 1979 he presented the Golden Rose to the shrine and raised the large new church to the rank of Basilica.[5]

---

[1]Cf. J. Jeremias, *Lamb of God—Servant of God* (original Greek), *ZNW* 34 (1935), 115-123; *id., TDNT* I, 338-41; V, 702; E.E. May, *"Ecce Agnus Dei." A Philological and Exegetical Approach to Jn 1:29-36*, Washington, 1947; C.K. Barrett, *The Lamb of God*, NTS 1 (1954, 55), 210-218; J. Leal, *Exegesis catholica de Agno Dei in ultimis 25 annis, Verbum Domini, 28 (1950),* 98-109; M.E. Boismard, O.P., *Du baptême à Cana*, Paris, 1956, 43-60; I. de la Potterie, S.J., *Ecco l'Agnello di Dio, BibOr,* 1 (1959), 161-69; S. Virgulin, *Recent Discussions of the Title, Lamb of God, Scripture,* 13 (1961), 74-80; R.E. Brown, *The Gospel According to John*, Anchor Bible, 1966, I, 58-63; for the Liturgy, J.A. Jungmann, *The Mass of the Roman Rite*, II, 1955, 332-340. [2]R.E. Brown, *op. cit.,* 63; [3]Communication from Dr. Craghan to the author; [4]J.A. Jungmann, *op. cit.;* [5]For bibl. on Knock cf. *Theotokos*, 212, s.v.

LATERAN COUNCIL IV, 1215.
Called by Innocent III (qv) at the summit of his mighty career, the Council dealt briefly with the Eucharist. The passage is, however, noteworthy as marking the first official use of the word transubstantiation (qv): "One indeed is the universal Church of the faithful, outside which no one at all is saved, in

which the priest himself is the sacrifice, Jesus Christ, whose body and blood are truly contained in the sacrament of the altar under the species of bread and wine; the bread (changed) into his body by the divine power of transubstantiation, and the wine into the blood, so that to accomplish the mystery of unity we ourselves receive from his (nature) what he himself received from ours. And surely no one can accomplish this sacrament except a priest who has been rightly ordained according to the keys of the Church which Jesus Christ himself conceded to the Apostles and to their successors."[1]

---

[1]DS 802.

LÉCUYER, JOSEPH, C.S.Sp. (1912-1973)

A theologian of the Mass and the priesthood, L. won a doctorate in the Gregorian University, 1945, for his thesis: *Le sacerdoce céleste du Christ selon les premiers commentateurs de l'epître aux Hébreux*.[1] He was spiritual director in the French Seminary, Rome, lecturer in Regina Mundi and the Lateran University, consultor of Roman Congregations, esp. for the Doctrine of the Faith. He was an expert to Vatican II, secretary of the commission on the Ministry and Life of Priests, his hand evident in certain passages, as in the section on collegiality in LG—he has specialized in the subject. Principal task in Council history, expanding the skeleton set of propositions rejected at the third session to the more ample text submitted at the fourth and seeing this through the hundreds of lengthy written submissions and over ten thousand *Modi* (amendments).[2]

Besides a large number of important articles dealing with the priesthood and worship, L. published *Abraham, Notre Père*, 1955; *Le Sacerdoce dans le mystère du Christ, Le sacrement de l'ordre*, 1957; *Prêtres Christ*, 1957; *Le sacrifice de la nouvelle Alliance*, his most important work, 1962; *Etudes sur la collégialité épiscopale*, 1964; *Eucharistie et vivante tradition*, 1981; *Le sacrement de l'ordination*, 1983; for six years, 1968-'74, Superior General of his congregation he also published work on its history, such as *(Bienheureux) Jacques Laval, Extraits de sa correspondance*, 1978. L's theological work was characterised by thorough knowledge of the Fathers, especially the Greek Fathers, particularly the school of Antioch and by an informed approach to the relevant biblical texts: a "return to the sources," fully informed, balanced in judgement.

---

[1]*Catholicisme*, (Bulletin of the French Seminary, Rome) esp. *Echos*

de Santa Chiara, May, 1984, many authors, 45-81; his bibliography, 71-81; DTC Tables, XVI, 2, 2932-33; [2]*Acta Synodalia*.

LEFEBVRE, MARCEL (1905-)

L's service to the Church before Vatican II was quite remarkable: thirty years' missionary service in Africa, in the 'bush,' as seminary director, finally, first Archbishop of Dakar and simultaneously Delegate Apostolic for all French-speaking Africa; Bishop of Tulle; Superior General of the congregation of the Holy Ghost and the Immaculate Heart of Mary.[1] He was a member of the Central Preparatory Commission for the Council—as Superior General he had transferred the mother house of his congregation from France to Rome and directed admirably the preparation of the renewal chapter following the Council.

Since the early seventies L. is at the head of the Society of St. Pius X, a movement viewed with distrust by Rome. When he ordained the first priests of the Society, 29 June 1976, Paul VI (qv) suspended him: the Pope, noting the quantity and quality of support for L. received him, with no preconditions, on 11 September of that year. John Paul II (qv) also received him and took no action against him or his Society, which, at this writing, has four major seminaries, 70 houses and over 250 priests.

L. contends that the church has been influenced by Protestant, liberalising, modernist forces, even in the composition of conciliar documents—he refused to sign the Pastoral Constitution on the Church in the Modern World and the Declaration on Religious Liberty.

By retention of the 'Tridentine' Mass (qv) in the priories and churches served by members of his society L. has sharply separated himself and his followers from the main body of the Catholic Church. He objects strongly to phrases like 'the Lord's meal,' 'the Eucharistic meal.' L. sees in the Mass "codified by Pius V and not invented by him, as we are often given to understand, clearly expresses these three realities: sacrifice, real presence and priesthood of the priests."[2] Or again: "At Mass it is always the same Priest, the same victim, the same mystical Body united with the Priest who is Christ. The ministers offer the sacrifice only *'in persona Christi.'*

"The more deeply we enter into these considerations the more we must realise how close and how real is the bond between the Cross and Mass—that the bond between the eternal Priest and his ministers is necessary.

"Here we put our finger on the three realities which are essential in the Mass for it to be the continuation of the sacrifice of the Cross—the reality of Sacrifice, that is the oblation of the Victim brought about in the consecration, the real and substantial presence of the Victim which must be offered and thus the necessity of transubstantiation, the need of a priest who is the minister of the principal Priest who is Our Lord, and consecrated by his priesthood.

"The Church, to which Our Lord bequeathed his ministerial priesthood to accomplish it till the end of time, has carried out the sacrifice of the Mass with love and devotion, it has ordained its prayers, ceremonies and rites to signify these realities and to preserve our faith in these realities willed and determined by God himself."[3]

L. contends that "to weaken and blur" faith in these essential realities "would lead to the most disastrous consequences, for the Sacrifice of the Mass is the heart, the soul and the mystical wellspring of the Church."

L. considers the 'Novus Ordo Missae,' product of the liturgical reform, which he rightly characterizes as "most singular, unique in the history of the Church." His judgement, after recalling the three fundamental truths already quoted: "the whole reform attacks these three truths essential to the Catholic faith." He finds everything in the new order nearer "the Protestant conception than the Catholic."

The liturgical changes embodied in Vatican II's *Constitution on the Sacred Liturgy* were unacceptable to L. This, together with his divergence from other decrees of the Council, his disavowal of freedom of conscience, his disapproval of ecumenism, and his determination to have his own views accepted in his prolonged disagreements with Paul VI and John Paul II and Vatican authorities, made negotiations for reconciliation extremely difficult. After final Vatican efforts at accommodation faltered, L. rejected the personal entreaties of Pope John Paul II, and in June 1988 ordained four of his followers bishops. Thus a schism was created; and L. and the four newly ordained bishops were excommunicated.

[1]Extensive literature on Mgr. Lefebvre and the movement deriving from him. His own works: *Un évêque parle*, Paris, 1975; English tr. *A Bishop Speaks*, Edinburgh, 1976, additional matter; *Letters to Friends and Benefactors*, published occasionally from Ecône, first seminary; *Le coup de maître de Satan, Econe face à la persécution*, Martigny, 1977; *J'accuse le Concile; Eté chaud, 1976; Ecône, portes ouvertes*; cf. bibl., R. Guelly, *La crise de l'Eglise de France dans livres francais de 1976-1979*, Rev. Theol. Louvain, 11 (1980), 201-244; cf. R. Gaucher, *Monseigneur Lefebvre, Combat pour l'Eglise*, Paris, 1976; *NON, Entretiens de Jose Hanu avec Mgr. Lefebvre*, 1977; Y. Congar, O.P., *La crise dans l'Eglise*, Paris, 1976; esp. M. Davies, *Apologia for Archbishop Lefebvre*, 2 vols; Lettre ouverte aux catholiques perplexes, Paris, 1985; [2]*Lettre ouverte*, 43; [3]*A Bishop Speaks*, 91; [4]*Ibid.*, 92; for the references to quotations from Protestants, cf. L. Salleron, *La nouvelle Messe*, Paris, 1976, 9f; 237ff; Guy Oury, O.S.B., *La Messe de S. Pie V a Paul VI*, Solesmes, 1976, 123.

LEGISLATION

Canons 897 to 958 of the new Code of Canon Law give the laws to be followed in regard to "the most venerable of the Sacraments." These canons are in Book Four, The Sanctifying of the Church, Part One, The Sacraments, Title Three, The Eucharist. Separate consideration is given to the celebration—the minister, participation, rites and ceremonies, time and place—the reservation and veneration, and the offering to be made for Mass. The canons codify the essential discipline imposed by the magnitude of the mystery and the alteration in the particulars of this discipline where change was possible, since the Second Vatican Council.

LEO I, 'THE GREAT' (d. 461)

The great Pope of Chalcedon was happy to accept the words of Scripture and did not follow a line of speculation either from St. Ambrose or St. Augustine (qqv):[1] "Manifesting this belief, with all your hearts, dearly beloved, reject the impious fictions of heretics so that your fasting and alms may not be soiled by contact with any error; the offering of sacrifice is pure and the outpouring of mercy holy when those who perform these things understand what they do. For as the Lord said: 'Unless you eat the flesh of the Son of man and drink his blood, you will not have life in you,' You must communicate at the sacred table in such wise that you have no doubt whatever about the truth of the body and blood of Christ. Here what is believed in faith is received in the mouth and in vain is *Amen* answered by those who argue against what is received."[2]

L. had the wide perspective of Christ's priesthood and sacrifice in his thinking: "It is not then, truly beloved, rashly but faithfully that we confess the Lord Jesus Christ present among believers, and though he sits at the right hand of God the Father, until he makes his enemies a footstool for his feet, he is nonetheless not absent from the congregation of his bishops, and rightly the whole Church and all the priests sing to him: 'The Lord has sworn and will not change, You are a priest forever according to the order of Melchizedek.' For he is the true and eternal Pontiff, whose rule cannot change or end. He is the one whom Melchizedek foreshadowed in figure, not offering Jewish victims to God, but immolating the sacrifice of the sacrament which the redeemer consecrated in his body and blood. He is the one whose priesthood the Father established with an unbreakable oath, not according to the order of Aaron, which would pass with the time of the law, but according to the order of Melchizedek, which would be celebrated forever."[3]

On sacrifice he is likewise clear: "But Jesus, sure in his design and intrepid in the work the Father had planned, fulfilled the Old Testament and instituted the new Pasch. Seated with his disciples to eat the mystical supper, as in the hall of Caiphas the plot to kill Christ was being hatched, he, establishing the sacrament of his body and blood, taught what victim should be offered to God, not excluding from this mystery the traitor himself."[4]

L. linked his thought on the Eucharist with his resistance to Monophysitism: if the Saviour was not really a human being, then any belief in his presence in the Eucharist would be an illusion. He also taught the special effect of the Eucharist uniting us with Christ, "what is given, what is received in that mystical sharing of spiritual nourishment is that those of us who receive the power of the heavenly food should pass into the flesh of him who became our flesh."[5] Hence L's concern that no one should be denied the Eucharist without grave reason—it should not be done at the whim of the priest and not without serious fault: to deprive the communicant of the Eucharist would leave him open to the assaults of the demon.[6]

---

[1]Texts, J. Solano, *Textos*, II, 501-506; cf. DTC V, G. Bareille, 1179-80; [2]*Sermo* 91, 3, PL 54, 452A-B; [3]*Sermo* 5, 3, PL 54, 154 B-C; [4]*Sermo* 58, 3, PL 54, 333C, 334A; [5]*Epist.* 50, 2 to the citizens of Constantinople, PL 54, 868B; C. Silva-Tarouca, S.J., *S. Leonis Magni, epistolae contra Eutychis haeresim, Textus et Documenta, ser. theol. fasc 15*, Rome, 1934, 41; E. Schwartz, *Acta Conciliorum oecumenicorum*, II, iv, 34; [6]*Epist.* 10, 8, PL 54, 635AB.

LEO XIII (1810-1903, Pope, 1878)

The reform of Eucharistic custom and regulations within the Church is generally associated with St. Pius X (qv). Sufficient attention has scarcely been given to the very considerable changes which took place during the pontificate of Leo XIII (see article on Communion). Important Roman rulings and decrees were issued. In 1885 the Archbishop of Cambrai asked the Congregation of Rites what was to be thought of religious who were receiving Communion every day, with ecclesiastical approval, but against their religious rule and the opinion of numerous theologians. The reply was that the custom was praiseworthy; frequent Communion should be promoted according to the directives of the Council of Trent. On 23 December 1886, the Sacred Penitentiary ruled that daily Communion by religious was praiseworthy, but should have the confessor's permission in each individual case, in agreement with the rules laid down by approved authors, especially St. Alphonsus Liguori. On 4 April 1888, the Congregation for Bishops and Religious ruled that clauses in the rules of religious orders and congregations limiting the number of communions were to be taken as directives, not prescriptive. The Holy Office made a similar reply to a chaplain of the Sisters of Charity. Leo XIII by the decree *Quemadmodum,* 17 December 1890, confirmed this decision. On 17 August 1891, the Congregation for Bishops and Religious abrogated those sections of the rules and constitutions of religious orders and congregations which forbade communion outside certain days. Finally on 28 May 1902, Leo, then in his ninety-third year, published one of the great Encyclicals on the Eucharist, *Mirae caritatis* (qv), the most important doctrinal statement on the subject until *Mediator Dei* (qv) issued by Pius XII (qv) in 1947. For though St. Pius X accomplished so much in this domain, he did not publish an Encyclical.

---

[1]J. Duhr, DSp., II, 2, 1283, 84; A. Bride, *La communion du XVIIe siècle à nos jours*, in *Eucharistia*, Paris, 1934, 280-300.

LEPIN, MARIUS (1870-1953)

A Sulpician who entered the anti-modernist fray with a series of publications, extending his interest to Christian apologetics and Sacred Scripture, L. made an important contribution to the theology of the Mass evolving in his time under the impact of M. de la Taille's (qv) monumental work; his interest in the subject went back much further, to his doctorate thesis, presented at the Catholic Institute of Toulouse, *L'idée du sacrifice dans la religion chrétienne principalement d'après le P. de Condren et M. Olier,* 1897.[1] He then saw that offering (*oblation* in French) was the essential element in sacrifice. Almost thirty years later appeared *L'idée du sacrifice de la Messe d'après les théologiens depuis l'origine jusqu'à nos jours,* 1926. *Jesus souverain Prêtre* appeared in 1937, with the special Mass of the priesthood sanctioned by Pius XI—L. had founded an association so inspired. In that year also appeared *La Messe et nous*—in 1927 L. had published *Pour la Messe et la communion.* Apart from his many works in Christology, apologetics and Scripture, one other work has some relevance, *Marie servante du Christ Jésus et de l'Eglise,* 1949.

L'idée du sacrifice is a survey of the work of every theologian who has treated of the Mass through the ages, with, all in all, space proportionate to the importance of the author. L. understandably gives much attention to the French school. His attention turns around the two ideas, oblation and immolation. He saw a deviation after the Reformation in Catholic thinking and traced the different theories of destruction for three centuries, real destruction and mystical. He concluded that the two main currents of thought, physical destruction and mystical destruction, could not be justified, the first because it was strictly impossible, the second because it was not destruction in the real sense.[2] The opposition he thought futile, as both, in his opinion, were astray.

So he clung to the idea of oblation as guaranteed by tradition, as he saw things. How does he generally see it? "According to the most constant tradition and in harmony with all we have set forth, the Eucharistic oblation is first and essentially the oblation of Christ by himself under the sense-perceptible species which recall his past immolation."[3] The Mass itself he was prepared to define thus: "The oblation which Christ makes of himself and which the church makes of Christ under the representative signs of his past immolation."[4]

There can be no question of the value of L's contribution to the theology of the Eucharist in the historical context. He made an invaluable survey of Christian thought on the subject through the ages. One point of importance in the theory of oblation was to puzzle him. In his first book he had been captured by the idea of Christ's offering to his Father, from the first moment of his existence, a particular reading of a text in Hebrews: "Consequently when Christ came into the world, he said, 'Sacrifices and offerings thou hast not desired, but a body thou hast prepared for me; in burnt offerings and sin offerings thou hast taken no pleasure. Then I said, Lo I have come to do thy will, O God, as it is written of me in the roll of the book' (10:5-7)." In this L. was following the ideas of the two masters of the French school, De Condren and Olier, whom he admired: "Such is the solemn oblation which Jesus Christ makes of himself to his Father in the Temple. It is the manifestation of the first oblation which he made in the womb of Mary. It is also the preparation for the bloody oblation which he must one day make on the Cross."[5] M. Olier sees the oblation also as made "in the quality of victim in the womb of the most Blessed Virgin, as on an altar, to be one day immolated and consumed to the glory of his divine majesty."[6]

This idea was severely criticised by M. de la Taille in the *Vindiciae* added to the final edition of *Mysterium Fidei*.[7] Over several pages he sought to demonstrate, with lengthy quotations, that the authorities adduced by L. in support of his thesis, the most important of them certainly, did not hold the opinion, certainly not Salmeron, Cornelius a Lapide, Bossuet or Berulle. "Was it not an oblation of this kind of which the author of the Epistle to the Hebrews speaks, when he shows us Christ, from his entry into the world offering himself in place of the ancient victims" said L. De la T. sums up: "Let one Father (of the Church) be quoted

who says that Christ fulfilled his priestly office, performed his sacrifice, was actually victim and offering in the moment of the Incarnation."[8]

---

[1]Cf. A. Michel, DTC X, 1246ff; J. Noye, DSp, IX, 681; J. Trinquet, *Catholicisme*, VI, 55; A. Loisy, *Mémoires pour servir à l'histoire de notre temps*, Paris, 422, 23; A. Piolanti, *Il Mistero*, 431-434; [2]*Op. cit.*; [3]*Op. cit.*, 753; [4]*Op. cit.*, 754; [5]*L'idée du sacrifice dans la religion.*, 122; [6]*Ibid.*; [7]*Op. cit.*, 699ff; Lepin, *L'idée du sacrifice*, 742, 43; [8]*Op. cit.*, 703.

LIMA TEXT, FAITH AND ORDER PAPER, NO. 111

In January 1982, over one hundred theologians from different communions met in Lima and accepted a statement on Baptism, Eucharist and Ministry which had been drawn up, discussed, refined by the Faith and Order Commission of the World Council of Churches at Accra (1974), Bangalore (1978), and Lima itself.[1] Between the Plenary Commission meetings, a steering group on Baptism, Eucharist and Ministry worked on textual drafting, after 1979 under the presidency of Frère Max Thurian of the Taizé Community. The Commission had sought to bring the local churches into the doctrinal process. The Fifth Assembly of the World Council (Nairobi, 1975), authorized the distribution of an earlier draft (Faith and Order Paper No. 73) to encourage study by the local churches. Over a hundred churches, widely representative geographically and in church tradition, sent detailed comments. These were assessed at a consultation in Crêt-Bérard (Faith and Order Paper No. 84). While this work was in progress, research and dialogue continued in other contexts and situations. Representatives of Orthodox Churches considered the draft text at Chambésy, 1979. Finally the Faith and Order Commission was authorized by the World Council's Central Committee, Dresden (1981) to distribute the document finally revised (Lima, 1982) to the churches, asking for a response.

William H. Lazareth, Director of the Secretariat on Faith and Order, and Nikos Nissiotis, Moderator of the Commission, comment on the changes taking place in the life of the churches; they note spontaneous interfaith growth of biblical and patristic studies, with the liturgical movement and the need for common witness. They make this claim in regard to the text: "The Lima text represents the significant theological convergence which Faith and Order has discerned and formulated. Those who know how widely the churches have differed in doctrine and practice on baptism, Eucharist and ministry, will appreciate the importance of the large measure of agreement registered here. Virtually all the confessional traditions are included in the Commission's membership. That theologians of such widely different traditions should be able to speak so harmoniously about baptism, Eucharist and ministry is unprecedented in the modern ecumenical movement. Particularly noteworthy is the fact that the Commission also includes among its full members theologians of the Roman Catholic and other churches which do not belong to the World Council of Churches."[1]

The writers do not confuse agreement with "consensus," by which they mean "that experience of life and articulation of faith necessary to realize and maintain the Church's visible unity." They also make it clear that the statement does not aim to give "a complete theological treatment" of the subjects; it "purposely concentrates on those aspects of the theme that have been directly or indirectly related to the problems of mutual recognition leading to unity." Two texts are offered: the main one "demonstrates the major areas of theological convergence"; added commentaries "either indicate historical differences that have been overcome or identify disputed issues still in need of further research and reconciliation." The section of the whole text dealing with the Eucharist reads as follows:

I. *The Institution of the Eucharist.*

1. The Church receives the Eucharist as a gift from the Lord. St. Paul wrote: "I have received from the Lord what I also delivered to you, that the Lord Jesus on the night when he was betrayed took bread, and when he had given thanks, he broke it, and said: 'This is my body, which is for you. Do this in remembrance of me' (*anamnesis* qv). In the same way also the cup, after supper, saying: 'This cup is the new covenant in my blood. Do this, as often as you drink it, in remembrance of me'" (1 Cor 11:23-25; cf. Mt 26:26-29; Mk 14:22-25; Lk 22:14-20).

The meals which Jesus is recorded as sharing during his earthly ministry proclaim and enact the nearness of the Kingdom, of which the feeding of the multitudes is a sign. In his last meal the fellowship of the Kingdom was connected with the imminence of Jesus' suffering. After his resurrection, the Lord made his presence known to his disciples in the breaking of the bread. Thus the Eucharist continues these meals of Jesus during his earthly life and after his resurrection, always as a sign of the Kingdom. Christians see the Eucharist prefigured in the Passover memorial of Israel's deliverance from the land of bondage and in the meal of the Covenant on Mount Sinai (Ex 24). It is the new paschal meal of the Church, the meal of the New Covenant, which Christ gave to his disciples as the *anamnesis* of his death and resurrection, as the anticipation of the Supper of the Lamb (Rev 19:9).

Christ commanded his disciples thus to remember and encounter him in this sacramental meal, as the continuing people of God, until his return. The last meal celebrated by Jesus was a liturgical meal employing symbolic words and actions. Consequently the Eucharist is a sacramental meal which by visible signs communicates to us God's love in Jesus Christ, the love by which Jesus loved his own 'to the end' (Jn 13:1). It has acquired many names: for example, the Lord's Supper, the breaking of bread, the holy communion, the divine liturgy, the Mass. Its celebration continues as the central act of the Church's worship.

II *The Meaning of the Eucharist*

2. The Eucharist is essentially the sacrament of the gift which God makes to us in Christ through the power of the Holy Spirit. Every Christian receives this gift of salvation through communion in the body and blood of Christ. In the Eucharistic meal, in the eating and drinking of the bread and wine, Christ grants communion with himself. God himself acts, giving life to the body of Christ and renewing each member. In accordance with Christ's promise, each baptized member of the body of Christ receives in the Eucharist the assurance of the forgiveness of sins (Mt 26:28), and the pledge of eternal life (Jn 6:51-58). Although the Eucharist is essentially one complete act, it will be considered here under the following aspects: thanksgiving to the Father, memorial of Christ, invocation of the Spirit, communion of the faithful, meal of the Kingdom.

A. *The Eucharist as Thanksgiving to the Father.*

3. The Eucharist, which always includes both word and sacrament, is a proclamation and a celebration of the work of God. It is the great thanksgiving to the Father for everything accomplished in creation, redemption and sanctification, for everything accomplished by God now in the Church and in the world in spite of the sins of human beings, for everything that God will accomplish in bringing the Kingdom to fulfillment. Thus the Eucharist is the benediction (*berakah*) by which the church expresses its thankfulness for all God's benefits.

4. The Eucharist is the great sacrifice of praise by which the Church speaks on behalf of the whole creation. For the world which God has reconciled is present at every Eucharist in the bread and wine, in the persons of the faithful, and in the prayers they offer for themselves and for all people. Christ unites the faithful with himself and includes their prayers within his own intercession so that the faithful are transfigured and their prayers accepted. This sacrifice of praise is possible only through Christ, with him and in him. The bread and wine, fruits of the earth and of human labour, are presented to the Father in faith and

thanksgiving. The Eucharist thus signifies what the world is to become: an offering and hymn of praise to the Creator, a universal communion in the body of Christ, a kingdom of justice, love and peace in the Holy Spirit.

B. *The Eucharist as Anamnesis or Memorial of Christ.*

5. The Eucharist is the memorial of the crucified and risen Christ, i.e. the living and effective sign of his sacrifice, accomplished once and for all on the cross and still operative on behalf of all humankind. The biblical idea of memorial as applied to the Eucharist refers to this present efficacy of God's work when it is celebrated by God's people in a liturgy.

6. Christ himself with all that he has accomplished for us and for all creation (in his incarnation, servanthood, ministry, teaching, suffering, sacrifice, resurrection, ascension and sending of the Spirit) is present in this anamnsesis, granting us communion with himself. The Eucharist is also the foretaste of his *parousia* and of the final kingdom.

7. The anamnesis in which Christ acts through the joyful celebration of his Church is thus both representation and anticipation. It is not only a calling to mind of what is past and of its significance. It is the Church's effective proclamation of God's mighty acts and promises.

8. Representation and anticipation are expressed in thanksgiving and intercession. The Church, gratefully recalling God's mighty acts of redemption, beseeches God to give the benefits of these acts to every human being. In thanksgiving and intercession, the Church is united with the Son, its great high Priest and intercessor (Rom 8:34; Heb 7:25). The Eucharist is the sacrament of the unique sacrifice of Christ, who ever lives to make intercession for us. It is the memorial of all that God has done for the salvation of the world. What it was God's will to accomplish in the incarnation, life, death, resurrection and ascension of Christ, God does not repeat. These events are unique and can neither be repeated nor prolonged. In the memorial of the Eucharist, however, the Church offers its intercession in communion with Christ, our great High Priest.

9. The *anamnesis* of Christ is the basis and source of all Christian prayer. So our prayer relies upon and is united with the continual intercession of the risen Lord. In the Eucharist, Christ empowers us to live with him, to suffer with him and to pray through him as justified sinners, joyfully and freely fulfilling his will.

10. In Christ we offer ourselves as a living and holy sacrifice in our daily lives (Rom 12:1; 1 Pet 2:5); this spiritual worship, acceptable to God, is nourished in the Eucharist, in which we are sanctified and reconciled in love, in order to be servants of reconciliation in the world.

11. United to our Lord and in communion with all the saints and martyrs, we are renewed in the covenant sealed by the blood of Christ.

12. Since the *anamnesis* of Christ is the very content of the preached Word as it is of the Eucharistic meal, each reinforces the other. The celebration of the Eucharist properly includes the proclamation of the Word.

13. The words and acts of Christ at the institution (qv) of the Eucharist stand at the heart of the celebration; the Eucharistic meal is the sacrament of the body and blood of Christ, the sacrament of his real presence. Christ fulfills in a variety of ways his promise to be always with his own even to the end of the world. But Christ's mode of presence in the Eucharist is unique. Jesus said over the bread and wine of the Eucharist: 'This is my body ... this is my blood....' What Christ declared is true, and the truth is fulfilled every time the Eucharist is celebrated. The Church confesses Christ's real, living and active presence in the Eucharist. While Christ's real presence in the Eucharist does not depend on the faith of the individual, all agree that to discern the body and blood of Christ, faith is required.

C. *The Eucharist as Invocation of the Spirit.*

14. The Spirit makes the crucified and risen Christ really present to us in the Eucharistic meal, fulfilling the promise contained in the words of institution. The presence of Christ is clearly the centre of the Eucharist, and the promise contained in the words of institution is therefore fundamental to the celebration. Yet it is the Father who is the primary origin and final fulfillment of the Eucharistic event. The incarnate Son of God by and in whom it is accomplished is its living centre. The Holy Spirit is the immeasurable strength of love which makes it possible and continues to make it effective. The bond between the Eucharistic celebration and the mystery of the Triune God reveals the role of the Holy Spirit as that of the One who makes the historical words of Jesus present and alive. Being assured by Jesus' promise in the words of institution that it will be answered, the Church prays to the Father for the gift of the Holy Spirit in order that the Eucharistic event may be a reality; the real presence of the crucified and risen Christ giving his life for all humanity.

15. It is in virtue of the living word of Christ and by the power of the Holy Spirit that the bread and wine become the sacramental signs of Christ's body and blood. They remain so for the purpose of communion.

16. The whole action of the Eucharist has an

"epikletic" character because it depends upon the work of the Holy Spirit. In the words of the liturgy, this aspect of the Eucharist finds varied expression.

17. The Church, as the community of the new covenant (qv), confidently invokes the Spirit, in order that it may be sanctified and renewed, led into all justice, truth and unity, and empowered to fulfill its mission in the world.

18. The Holy Spirit through the Eucharist gives a foretaste of the Kingdom of God; the Church receives the life of the new creation and the assurance of the Lord's return.

D. *The Eucharist as Communion of the Faithful.*

19. The Eucharistic communion with Christ who nourishes the life of the Church is at the same time communion within the body of Christ which is the Church. The sharing in one bread and the common cup in a given place demonstrates and effects the oneness of the sharers with Christ and with their fellow-sharers in all times and places. It is in the Eucharist that the community of God's people is fully manifested. Eucharistic celebrations always have to do with the whole Church, and the whole Church is involved in each local Eucharistic celebration. In so far as a church claims to be a manifestation of the whole Church, it will take care to order its own life in ways which take seriously the interests and concerns of the other churches.

20. The Eucharist embraces all aspects of life. It is a representative act of thanksgiving and offering on behalf of the whole world. The Eucharistic celebration demands reconciliation and sharing among all those regarded as brothers and sisters in the one family of God and is a constant challenge in the search for appropriate relationships in social, economic and political life (Mt 5:23f; 1 Cor 10:16f; 1 Cor 11:20-22; Gal 3:28). All kinds of injustice, racism, separation and lack of freedom are radically challenged when we share in the body and blood of Christ. Through the Eucharist the all-renewing grace of God penetrates and restores human personality and dignity. The Eucharist involves the believer in the central event of the world's history. As participants in the Eucharist, therefore, we prove inconsistent if we are not actively participating in this ongoing restoration of the world's situation and the human condition. The Eucharist shows us that our behaviour is inconsistent in face of the reconciling presence of God in human history; we are placed under continual judgement by the persistence of unjust relationships of all kinds in our society, the manifold divisions on account of human pride, material interest and power politics and, above all, the obstinacy of unjustifiable confessional oppositions within the body of Christ.

21. Solidarity in the Eucharistic communion of the body of Christ and responsible care of Christians for one another and the world find specific expression in the liturgies: in the mutual forgiveness of sins; the sign of peace; intercession for all; the eating and drinking together; the taking of the elements to the sick and those in prison or the celebration of the Eucharist with them. All these manifestations of love in the Eucharist are directly related to Christ's own testimony as a servant, in whose servanthood Christians themselves participate. As God in Christ has entered into the human situation, so Eucharistic liturgy is near to the concrete and particular situations of men and women. In the early Church the ministry of deacons and deaconesses gave expression in a special way to this aspect of the Eucharist. The place of such ministry between the table and the needy properly testifies to the redeeming presence of Christ in the world."

The section which follows on *The Eucharist as Meal of the Kingdom* develops the idea of a cosmic effect from the Eucharist. It also calls for "solidarity with the outcast," for Christians "to become signs of the love of Christ who lived and sacrificed himself for all and now gives himself in the Eucharist."

A final part of the document, *The Celebration of the Eucharist,* lists in order the elements of the liturgy, urges renewal, allows for diversity, encourages celebration on Sunday "as the Eucharist celebrates the resurrection (qv) of Christ, frequent communion and reverent reservation.

---

[1] *Baptism, Eucharist and Ministry,* World Council of Churches, 5th printing, 1983.

LITURGIAE INSTAURATIONES, 5 September 1970

Third Instruction on the correct Implementation of the Constitution on the Sacred Liturgy.[1] Stating that "the reforms which have so far been put into effect in implementing the Liturgical Constitution have been concerned above all with the celebration of the Eucharistic mystery" the Instruction maintains that "the gradual introduction of the new liturgical forms has taken into consideration both the overall renewal programme and the great variety of local conditions throughout the world." The wide choice of readings and the flexibility of the rubrics facilitated adaptation. And the result, after six years? Despite a good reception by the majority, there was here and there some resistance and impatience. No proof is given for this generalization, beyond a reference to an address by Paul VI. Why then did "many bishops, priests and laymen ask the Holy See to intervene?" Because two sets of abuses were noticed: those attached to ancient customs would not accept the reforms; the impatient who "made changes, additions or simplifications which at times went against the basic principles of the liturgy. This only troubled the faithful and impeded or made more difficult the progress of genuine renewal." The bishops were told to exercise their own authority. "It is they whom the Holy Spirit has made rulers of the Church of God" (Acts 20:28). They are to be informed and to work with their commissions. The Instruction was designed to aid them "to restore the orderly and disciplined celebration of the Eucharist." Rules and guidelines were supplied: dignity should be preserved, not sacrificed to undue simplicity; liturgical reform is not desacralization, not the occasion for the secularization of the world; deeper insight, not the constant search for novelty, is needed; priests should refrain from individualism and idiosyncrasy which "offends the rights of the faithful"; "he should not add any rite which is not contained and authorized in the liturgical books"; readings should be from the Bible, not from past or present, sacred or profane authors. The homily is the task of the priest; the faithful should refrain from dialogue, comments, etc. The Liturgy of the Word and the Liturgy of the Eucharist should not be celebrated at different times or places.

Again the precept of the Council against arbitrary change is recalled. Where alternatives are provided (the Penitential Rite, the Eucharistic Prayer, the acclamation of the people, the final blessing), choice is free; invention is not. Music should be encouraged; innovation needs approval by the episcopal conference. Places where the priest may say a few words to the people are indicated (at the beginning, before the readings, before the preface and before the dismissal); not during the Eucharistic Prayer. Ministers of lower rank than the priest may not read any part of the Eucharistic Prayer. Unleavened wheat bread is to be used. Rules are given for the distribution of Holy Communion. What women may and may not do are stated. The material things used for worship are dealt with; so are the places of worship. A realistic document, revealing on the actual situation inside the Catholic Church, six years after the inception of the liturgical reform.

---

[1] Text *AAS* 62 (1970), 692-704; English tr. issued by the Congregation, A. Flannery, O.P., I, 209-221.

LORD'S SUPPER, THE

The last encounter between the Saviour and his disciples was a shared meal, the final one of a number recorded in the gospels (Mk 6:32; 14:3; Lk 7:36; Jn 2:1ff).[1] "In reality," says J. Jeremias, "the 'founding meal' is only one link in a long chain of meals which Jesus shared with his followers and which they continued after Easter."[2] There are, in regard to this final meal (before his death), some sharp points of debate, if not controversy. Our information about it derives from the gospels (see Institution Narrative; John the Evangelist; Passover, The; Covenant) and St. Paul. The account in the Synoptics includes, as well as the institution of the Eucharist, the preparation and the foretelling of the betrayal by Judas: (a) the preparation, "And on the first day of Unleavened Bread, when they sacrificed the passover lamb, his disciples said to him, 'Will you have us go and prepare for you to eat the Passover?' And he sent two of his disciples, and said to them, 'Go into the city, and a man carrying a jar of water will meet you; follow him and wherever he enters, say to the householder, The teacher says, "Where is my guest room, where I am to eat the Passover with my disciples?" And he will show you a large upper room, furnished and ready; there prepare for us.' And the disciples set out and went to the city, and found it as he had told them; and they prepared the Passover" (Mk 14:12-16). "You know that after two days the Passover is coming, and the Son of man will be delivered up to be crucified.... Now on the first day of Unleavened Bread the disciples came to Jesus, saying, 'Where will you have us prepare for you to eat the Passover?' He said, 'Go into the city to a certain one, and say to him, The Teacher says, my time is at hand; I will keep the Passover at your house with my disciples.' And the disciples did as Jesus had directed them, and they prepared the Passover" (Mt 26:2, 17-19). "Now the feast of Unleavened Bread drew near, which is called the Passover.... Then came the day of Unleavened Bread, on which the passover lamb had to be sacrificed. So Jesus sent Peter and John, saying, 'Go and prepare the Passover for us, that we may eat it.' They said to him, 'Where will you have us prepare it?' He said to them, 'Behold, when you have entered the city, a man carrying a jar of water will meet you; follow him into the house which he enters, and tell the householder, The Teacher says to you, "Where is the guest room where I am to eat the Passover with my disciples?" And he will show you a large upper room furnished; there make ready.' And they went, and found it as he had told them; and they prepared the Passover." (Lk 22:1, 7-13).

(b) the foretelling of the betrayal: "And when it was evening he came with the twelve. And as they were at table eating, Jesus said, 'Truly, I say to you, one of you will betray me, one who is eating with me.' They began to be sorrowful, and to say to him one after another, 'Is it I?' He said to them, 'It is one of the twelve, one who is dipping bread into the dish with me. For the Son of man goes, as it is written of him, but woe to that man by whom the Son of man is betrayed! It would have been better for that man if he had not been born'" (Mk 14:17-21). "When it was evening, he sat at table with the twelve disciples; and as they were eating, he said, 'Truly I say to you, one of you will betray me.' And they were very sorrowful, and began to say to him one after another, 'Is it I, Lord?' He answered, 'He who has dipped his hand in the dish with me, will betray me. The Son of man goes, as it is written of him, but woe to that man by whom the Son of man is betrayed! It would have been better for that man if he had not been born.' Judas, who betrayed him, said, 'Is it I, Master?' He said to him, 'You have said so'" (Mt 26:20-25). (After the Institution) "'But behold the hand of him who betrays me is with me on the table. For the Son of man goes as it has been determined; but woe to that man by whom he is betrayed!' And they began to question one another, which of them it was that would do this" (Lk 22:21-23).

St. John (qv) presents a divergent treatment of the theme. What has to be interpreted is contained in these texts: "Now before the feast of the Passover, when Jesus knew that his hour had come to depart out of this world to the Father, having loved his own who were in the world, he loved them to the end" (13:1). "'Truly, truly, I say to you, one of you will betray me.' The disciples looked at one another, uncertain of whom he spoke. One of his disciples, whom Jesus loved, was lying close to the breast of Jesus; so Simon Peter beckoned to him and said, 'Tell us who it is of whom he speaks.' So lying close to the breast of Jesus, he said to him, 'Lord, who is it?' Jesus answered, 'It is he to whom I shall give this morsel.' He gave it to Judas, the son of Simon Iscariot. Then after the morsel, Satan entered into him. Jesus said to him, 'What you are going to do, do quickly.' Now no one at the table knew why he said this to him. Some thought that, because Judas had the money box, Jesus was telling him, 'Buy what we need for the feast'; or that he should give something to the poor. So, after receiving the morsel, he immediately went out; and it was night" (13:21-30). "Then they led Jesus from the house of Caiaphas to the praetorium. It was early. They themselves did not enter the praetorium, so that they might not be defiled, but might eat the Passover" (18:28). "When Pilate heard these words, he brought Jesus out and sat down on the judgement seat at a place called the Pavement, and in Hebrew, Gabbatha. Now it was the day of Preparation of the Passover; it was about the sixth hour" (19:13, 14).

Though there is, in the Synoptics, no mention of

eating the lamb, and though the words recorded by Lk only, "Do this in remembrance of me," seem to imply more than merely annual celebration, an essential characteristic of the Passover, it is generally thought that the Last Supper as reported by these gospels was a Passover meal; it must at least have been a meal in a Passover context. There are internal problems in regard to the Institution Narrative, in particular the mention of two cups by Lk, which need elucidation; the big difficulty, as yet not satisfactorily resolved, is the apparent impossibility of interpreting Jn's narrative as that of a Passover meal. There are other matters, such as the silence of Jn on the Institution Narrative, with some phrases of which he has parallels in the discourse of promise in ch six; and the factor which has been much investigated in recent times, the influence of the whole body of Jewish custom and ritual on the Lord's behaviour on that important night. Meals were given a religious significance by formal introductory blessings and ceremonial acts like the 'breaking of bread.'

A remarkable monograph published in 1957 by Annie Jaubert claimed to solve the problem of Johannine chronology. The prescription of Lev on the time of the Passover was: "In the first month, on the fourteenth day of the month in the evening is the Lord's Passover" (23:5). According to the official calendar in use in Jesus' time, 14 Nisan could fall on any day of the week. But Mlle. Jaubert used a sectarian, priestly calendar from the book of Jubilees—which she thought earlier—to show that since 14 Nisan always fell in this calendar on Tuesday, Jesus could have used it to celebrate the Passover. There are echoes of the calendar in early Christian literature; and there were links with Qumran, certain from their use of the calendar, nebulous if one seeks to bind them to Jesus personally. The great exegete, Pierre Benoit, O.P., raised serious objections to Mlle. Jaubert's thesis: "In the present case, the chronology given to the Passion after the event by a certain particular Jewish-Christian current of thought is interestingly explained by the calendar of certain Jewish circles, but by no means proves that Jesus really followed the calendar. In order to assert this last point two things must be established; that an Essene Passover was not surprising from Jesus, but was his habitual custom; and that the Synoptics had forgotten about it.... To state that in an action as important as the celebration of the Passover, Jesus departed from official Judaism, and attached himself to the calendar of archaic-sounding conventicles, one needs strong arguments, based on the whole gospel. I do not think that Mlle. Jaubert has provided them."[4] The problem which she set out to solve, the contradiction between Jn and the

Synoptics as to the day on which 15 Nisan fell, Friday or Saturday, is, P. Benoit thinks, one on which exegetes have spent themselves in vain.

The story of Judas is part of the Last Supper; it is not often dealt with at length. Lk places an abbreviated version after the Institution. But Jn who does not reproduce the Institution Narrative adds detail and dialogue, bringing in Simon Peter and the 'beloved disciple' to the dialogue. Jn had given the account of the washing of the feet with the Master's explanation. What is his explanation of the lengthy Judas story? Is it given in the naming of one whom, in this episode, the Synoptics do not mention, Satan? "Then after the morsel, Satan entered into him." The whole Judas event, the choice of that solemn moment by Jesus to disclose his imminent treachery, his presence, despite Jesus' knowledge of his evil intention, all serves to draw within the confines of the Upper Room the very essence of salvation in Christ, the whole drama of our redemption, the Eucharist as the indispensable focus of Christian recovery and renewal. There is another valid comment: the very unusual nature of the happening, where a man intent on lethal opposition is allowed to witness the most sacred, secret innovation designed to give enduring reality to a vast creative scheme of universal import, carries proof of its own historicity. This is one instance of what could not have been thought of had it not happened. In another of the many contexts to which the Lord's Supper has relevance, Judas is a reminder of the abuse and rejection which Jesus Christ will, through the ages, meet in the supreme gift of his love. The sublime Gift is at risk from the first moment until the end of time.

[1]Cf. G. Dalman, *Jesus-Jeshua*, 1921, English tr. 1929, 86-184; Rittans, *Eucharistic Origins*, 1927; C.H. McGregor, *Eucharistic Origins, A Survey of the Evidence*, London, 1929; M.J. Lagrange, O.P., *Evangile selon St. Marc*, ed. 5, 1935, 354-363; O. Casel, O.S.B., (qv), *Art und Sinn der ältesten christlichen Osterfeier, JL*, 14 (1938), 1-78; A. Arnold, *Der Ursprung des christlichen Abendmahls*, ed. 2, Freiburg, 1939; Y. de Montcheuil, *Mélanges théologiques*, Paris, 1949, 23-48; F.J. Leenhardt, *Le Sacrement de la sainte Cène*, Neuchâtel, 1948; id., *Ceci est mon corps*, Neuchâtel, 1955; H. Schürmann, *Die Anfänge christlicher Osterfeier, TQ* 131 (1951) 414-25; id., *Der Paschamahlbericht Lk 22* (7-14, 15-18) I *Teil einer quellenkritischen Untersuchung des lukanischen Abendmahlsberichtes Lk 22, 7-38, (Neutestamentliche Abhandlugen, XIX Bd., 5 Heft, Münster-Westph.*, 1953; id., *Der Einsetzungsbericht Lk 22, 19-20; II Teileiner quellenkritischen Untersuchung des lukanischen Abendmahlsberichtes Lk 22, 7-38 (NT Abhdl XX, 4)* Münster Westph. 1955; id., *Die Gestalt der urchristlichen Eucharistiefeier, Münchener Theol Zeitschrift 6 (1955)*, 107-131; C. Mohrmann, *Pascha, Passio, Transitus, EphLit* 66 (1952), 37-52; A.J.B. Higgins, *The Lord's Supper*, London, 1952; O. Cullmann, *Early Christian Worship*, London, 1953; R.H. Fuller, *The Mission and Achievement of Jesus*, London, 1954, 64-77; V. Taylor, *Jesus and his Sacrifice*, London, 1955; N. Moccia, *L'istituzione della S. Eucaristia secondo il metodo della Storia delle Forme*, Naples, 1955; J. Jeremias, *The Eucharistic Words of Jesus*, London, 1955;

D. Daube, *The New Testament and Rabbinic Judaism*, London 1958, 186-95; J.P. Audet, *Esquisse historique du genre litteraire de la bénédiction juive et de l'eucharistie chrétienne, RB* 65 (1958), 371-399; J. Dupont, *"Ceci est mon corps," "Ceci est mon sang,", NRT*, 18 (1958), 1025-41; H. Lietzmann, *Messe und Herrenmahl*, ed. 3, Berlin, 1958; P.W. Skehan, *Date of the Last Supper, CBQ* 20 (1958), 192-99; B. Cooke, *Presentation of the Eucharist as Covenant Sacrifice, TS*, 21 (1960), 1-44; C. Vollert, S.J., *The Eucharist: Quests for Insights from Scripture, TS* 21 (1960) 404-443; G. Sloyan, *Primitive and Pauline Concepts of the Eucharist, CBQ* 23 (1961), 1-13; G. Zeiner, *Die Brotwunder im Markusevangelium, BiblZ* 4 (1960) 282-85; P. Neuenzeit, *Das Herrenmahl: Studien zur paulinischen Eucharistieauffassung*, Munich, 1960; P. Benoit, O.P., articles in *Exégèse et Théologie*, 1, Paris, 1961; *Le récit de la Cène, Luc, XXII, 15-20; Les études de H. Schürmann; Les récits de l'institution de l'Eucharistie et leur portée; Note sur une étude de J. Jeremias; Notes sur deux études de F.J. Leenhardt; La date de la Cène*, 163-261; E.J. Kilmartin, *The Eucharistic Cup in the Primitive Liturgy, CBQ* 24 (1962), 32-43; E. Käsemann, *The Pauline Doctrine of the Lord's Supper, Essays on New Testament Themes*, Naperville, Ill., 1964, 108-35; J. Delorme, P. Benoit, O.P., M.E. Boismard, O.P., D. Mollat, S.J., *The Eucharist in the New Testament*, London, 1964; L. Bouyer, C. Orat., *Eucharistie*, Tournai, 1966; J. Jungmann, *The Mass of the Roman Rite*, 1955 II, 194-201; C. V (1912), 990-1121; id., ibid., Mgr. Ruch, DTC, X, (1928), 795-863; J. Coppens, DBS II, 1146-1215; H. Haag, DBS VI, 1144-1149; X. Léon-Dufour, ibid., 1454-58; H. Schürmann, *Abendmahl*, LTK I, (1957), 26-31; J. Betz, LTK, III, 1142-57; C. Bernas, NCE V, 594-599; id., NCE VIII, 397-99; E. Schweizer, RGG, ed. 3, I, 10-21; TDNT, *Diatheke*, (G. Quell, J. Behm), II, 106-124, 124-134; ibid., *Pascha* (J. Jeremias), V, 896-904; [2]*Op. cit.*, 21, 67; [3]*Op. cit.*; [4]*Exégèse et Théologie*, 261.

LUTHER, MARTIN (1483-1546)

Three years after the initial incident of the 95 theses, L. issued his three Reformation treatises: "Manifesto to the German Nation"; the "Babylonian Captivity"; the "Address to the German Nobility."[1] In the second he expounds his doctrine on the mode of Christ's presence in the Eucharist, and he rejects the idea of the Mass as a sacrifice. On the first point he defends a theory which has become known as Consubstantation: "The Lord Cardinal of Cambrai (Pierre d'Ailly) once gave me food for reflection, at a time when I was drinking in scholastic theology, by that passage in the fourth book of his 'Propositions,' where he argues most acutely that it would be much more plausible and would entail fewer redundant miracles if it were asserted that not only the accidents but also the reality of bread and wine remained in the sacrament of the altar—had not the Church determined otherwise! Afterwards when I realized what the church was, which so determined, namely the Thomist, i.e. the Aristotelian, Church, I grew more bold. I have been hesitating between the devil and the deep sea, but now at last I brought my conscience to rest in my former opinion; which was, that the bread and wine are really bread and wine and the true flesh and blood of Christ is in them in the same fashion and the same degree as they hold them to be beneath their accidents. I took this step because I saw that the Thomist opinions whether they be approved by pope or by council, remain opinions and do not become articles of faith, even if an angel from heaven should decide otherwise. For that which is asserted without the authority of Scripture or of proven revelation may be held as an opinion, but there is no obligation to believe it."[2] L. thought that transubstantiation (qv) was to be "considered as an invention of human reason, since it is based neither on Scripture nor sound reasoning."[3]

"Why," asks L., "could not Christ confine his body within the substance of bread, just as in the accidents? Fire and iron are two substances; yet they are so mingled in red-hot iron that any part is at once iron and fire. What prevents the glorious body of Christ from being in every part of the substance of bread?"[4] L. is here using the terminology of Aristotelian philosophy and refusing to reckon with its content.

On the Mass as a sacrifice he has this to say: "The third captivity of this sacrament is that most sacrilegious abuse by which it has come about that at this day there is nothing in the Church more generally received or more widely held than that the Mass is a good work and a sacrifice. This abuse has brought an endless flood of other abuses, until faith in the sacrament has been utterly extinguished and a divine sacrament has been turned into an article of trade, the subject of bargaining and business deals. Hence arise fellowships, fraternities, intercessions, merits, anniversaries, memorials; and such like pieces of business are bought and sold, and contracts and bargains are made about them. The entire maintenance of priests and monks depends on such things. . . . Another scandal must be removed . . . namely, the general belief that the Mass is a sacrifice which is offered to God. This opinion seems to be in harmony with the words of the Canon: 'These gifts, these offerings, these holy sacrifices'; and later 'This oblation.' And then there is the unambiguous prayer that 'this sacrifice may be accepted just as the sacrifice of Abel, etc.' Hence Christ is called the victim of the altar. And besides these the sayings of the Holy Fathers are adduced, and many precedents and the universal and uninterrupted observance of this way of speaking."[5]

"Because they take their stand so obstinately on these grounds we must with equal steadfastness set against them the words of Christ. . . . For in them there is no mention of a 'work' or a 'sacrifice'. . . . The offering of a sacrifice is incompatible with the distribution of a testament or the reception of a promise; the former are received, the latter we give. The same thing cannot be at once received and offered, nor be given and accepted by the same person at the same time. . . ."[6] L. was convinced that the gospel did not allow the Mass to be a sacrifice.

Logically he was led to deny the Catholic doctrine of the priesthood: "The Sacrament (of Order) is not known to the Church of Christ, it has been invented by the Pope's Church. Not only is there no promise of grace attached to it, but in the whole of the New Testament there is no mention of it. It is ridiculous to affirm the existence of a sacrament when the divine institution of it cannot in any way be proved."[7]

To implement his ideas about the Mass, L. drew up a new Latin Mass in 1523 and three years later a German version. He excluded whatever, in his view, implied the notion of sacrifice. Hence the Offertory and Canon were eliminated; the priest was, however, to pronounce aloud over the bread and wine the words of consecration from 1 Cor 11:23-25.

Luther disagreed with Zwingli (qv) on the Eucharist. The conference arranged between the two at Marburg, with a view to solidarity among the Reformers, failed on this one point. Efforts by "moderates," such as Melanchton (qv) and Bucer (qv) to heal the breach were unavailing.

The historian will welcome the agreements recently reached by different representative Lutheran bodies with members of other communions. Some will see in this the abiding faith in the Eucharist which derived from Luther, which was not essentially affected by his preference for the word "consubstantiation" to "transubstantiation."

---

[1] Cf. V. Vajta, *Die Theologie des Gottesdientes bei Luther*, Gottingen, 1959; D. Reed, *The Lutheran Liturgy*, Philadelphia, 1959; H.C. Schmidt Lauber, *Die Eucharistie als Enfaltung der Verba Testamenti. Eine formgeschichtlich-systematische Einführung in die Probleme des lutherischen Gottesdienstes und seiner Liturgie*, Kassel, 1957; E.C. Messenger, *The Reformation*, 115-120; DTC Tables, X, 1086-89; [2] *The Babylonian Captivity*, B.J. Kidd, *Documents Illustrative of the Continental Reformation*, No. 36; [3] *Ibid.*; [4] *Ibid.*; [5] *Ibid.*; [6] *Ibid.*; [7] Weimar ed., VI, 572.

LUTHERAN-ROMAN CATHOLIC DIALOGUE: EUCHARIST

In 1980 the Lutheran World Federation published *The Eucharist*, a document presented for discussion, the work of the Lutheran-Roman Catholic Joint Commission established by the Secretariat for Promoting Christian Unity and the Lutheran World Federation.[1] The chairpersons, Bishop Hans L. Martensen of Copenhagen and Professor George A. Lindbeck of Yale University, announced in their preface that the document had been passed unanimously by the commission members. "Agreement has been reached on significant points. In large measure it has been possible to make a common witness. Thus we are confident that those questions which remain open will be clarified mutually."

The text, which comes in the wake of a number of other texts drawn up by mixed Lutheran-Roman Catholic groups in Europe and elsewhere, one of which in the U.S. dealt with the subject of the Eucharist as sacrifice and reached an optimistic conclusion, is distinctively comprehensive and very thoroughly documented. It falls into the following parts: I, Joint Witness; II, Common Tasks; III, The Liturgical Celebration of the Eucharist; IV, Supplementary Studies.

Part I, Joint Witness, deals with these matters: 1. The legacy of Christ according to the Scripture; 2. Mystery of Faith; 3. Through, with and in Christ; 4. In the unity of the Holy Spirit; 5. Glorification of the Father; 6. For the life of the world; 7. With a view to the future glory. There are some admirable things in this section. For example: "Finally, the mystery of the Eucharist unites us to the ultimate mystery from, through, and towards which all things exist: the mystery of the triune God. Our heavenly Father is the first source and final goal of the Eucharistic event. The incarnate Son of God is the living centre of the Eucharistic event: the One in, with and through whom it unfolds. The Holy Spirit is the immeasurable power of love which gives the Eucharist life and lasting effect."

In I, 3, occur these remarkable words: "In the sacrament of the Lord's Supper, Jesus Christ, true God and true man, is present wholly and entirely, in his body and blood, under the signs of bread and wine. Through the centuries Christians have attempted various formulations to describe this presence. Our confessional documents have in common affirmed that Jesus Christ is 'really,' 'truly' and 'substantially' present in this sacrament. This manner of presence 'we can scarcely express in words,' but we affirm his presence because we believe in the power of God and the promise of Jesus Christ, 'This is my body.... This is my blood'.... Our traditions have spoken of this presence as 'sacramental,' 'supernatural' and 'spiritual.' These terms have different connotations in the two traditions, but they have in common a rejection of a spatial or natural mode of presence and a rejection of an understanding of the sacrament as only commemorative or figurative."

I, 4, treats amply of the Spirit with a key passage thus: "It is also through the Holy Spirit that Christ is at work in the Eucharist. All that the Lord gives us and all that enables us to make it our own is given to us through the Holy Spirit. In the liturgy this becomes particularly clear in the invocation of the Holy Spirit (*epiklesis*). In remembrance of the intercession of Christ its High Priest, the Church asks with confidence for his Spirit in order to be renewed and sanctified through the Eucharistic gifts and so strengthened to accomplish its mission in the world. In the power of the Holy Spirit the bread and wine become the body and blood of Christ through the creative word. The Spirit of love causes the sacrament of love to become real in that the divine love seeks us in our earthly reality in order to bring us home again. Only in the Holy Spirit does the congregation come to the faith without which it cannot celebrate the Eucharist. Thus the *epiklesis* is also the prayer for a living faith which prepares us to celebrate the remembrance of the suffering and Resurrection of Christ. The Eucharist is not an automatic means for the salvation of the world; it presupposes the presence of the Holy Spirit within the believers."

I, 5, on glorification of the Father begins thus: "The union with Christ into which we are drawn in the Eucharist through the power of the Holy Spirit ultimately leads to the eternal Father. This occurs at different levels and in varying, yet internally related ways." The document then considers proclamation, thanksgiving, intercession, praise and self-giving. This section concludes with a passage borrowed from the U.S. documents: "Our two traditions agree in understanding the Eucharist as a *sacrifice of praise*. This is neither simple verbal praise of God, nor is it a supplement or a complement which people from their own power add to the offering of praise and thanksgiving which Christ has made to the Father. The Eucharistic sacrifice of praise has only become possible through the sacrifice of Christ on the Cross; therefore this remains the main content of the Church's sacrifice of praise. Only 'by him, with him, and in him, who is our great High Priest and intercessor we offer to the Father, in the power of the Holy Spirit, our praise, thanksgiving and intercession."

I, 6, has telling points to make on the "Eucharist's relation to the world" and on "the responsibility of Christians to the world." So has I, 7, on the eschatological dimension: "In the Eucharist we proclaim 'the Lord's death until he comes' (1 Cor 11:26). In it the future glory is promised, as well as, in an initial way, revealed and mediated."

Part II, Common Tasks, has three sections: overcoming controverted positions; liturgical form; reception. The problems are identified clearly, impartially: the explanation of Eucharistic presence and Eucharistic sacrifice given on either side, the practice of Communion, especially under both species, ministry and fellowship. It is urged that in regard to liturgical form which should correspond to the faith held, "without impairing diversity" compatible with this faith "greater *agreement in certain basic patterns* needs to be sought." By 'reception' is meant the "response and co-responsibility" from fellow Christians which is thought desirable.

The document reproduces verbatim Roman Catholic and Lutheran texts used, for the celebration of the Eucharist in the first place, for the order of Holy Communion in the second: the common prayers of the Mass and four Eucharistic prayers for Catholics, six Lutheran texts used respectively by those in the Federal Republic of Germany, the U.S., France, Czechslovakia, Netherlands, Sweden.

A Lutheran and a Catholic member of the commission prepared papers on the controverted issues in the light of historical research and ecclesiastical developments. These the commission accepted and submits as attached appendices. They add to what is already a very valuable contribution, by way of statement, analysis and honest appraisal, to Ecumenical dialogue on the central act of Christian worship.

---

[1]The report is published by Lutheran World Federation, printed by Imprimerie La Concorde, Lausanne; parallel issue in German *Das Herrenmahl*, Frankfurt am Main, 1978; cf. bibliography to Ecumenism; quotations here indicated by sections of the official text.

LUTHERAN-ROMAN CATHOLIC DIALOGUE: MINISTRY

The nationally constituted mixed group, with scholarly representatives on both sides issued their statement on Eucharist and ministry in St. Louis, Missouri, in 1970.[1] Part one contains common observations; part two, reflections of the Lutheran participants; and part three, reflections of the Roman Catholic participants. It is the concluding or culminating paragraph in each of the latter two parts which is of primary interest. Part two ends thus: "As Lutherans we joyfully witness that in theological dialogue with our Roman Catholic partners we have again seen clearly a fidelity to the proclamation of the gospel and the administration of the sacraments which confirms our historic conviction that the Roman Catholic Church is an authentic church of our Lord Jesus Christ. For this reason we recommend to those who have appointed us that through appropriate channels the participating Lutheran churches be urged to declare formally their judgement that the ordained Ministers of the Roman Catholic Church are engaged in a valid Ministry of the gospel, announcing the gospel of Christ and administering the sacraments of faith as their chief responsibilities, and that the body and blood of our Lord Jesus Christ are truly present in their celebrations of the sacrament of the altar."[2]

Part three had this passage, which was by way of conclusion, though "clarifications" were added: "As Roman Catholic theologians, we acknowledge in the spirit of Vatican II that the Lutheran communities with which we have been in dialogue are truly Christian churches, possessing the elements of holiness and truth that mark them as organs of grace and salvation. Furthermore, in our study we have found serious defects in the arguments customarily used against the validity of the Eucharistic ministry of the Lutheran churches. In fact, we see no persuasive reason to deny the possibility of the Roman Catholic Church recognizing the validity of this Ministry. Accordingly we ask the authorities of the Roman Catholic Church whether the ecumenical urgency flowing from Christ's will for unity may not dictate that the Roman Catholic Church recognize the validity of the Lutheran Ministry and, correspondingly, the presence of the body and blood of Christ in the Eucharistic celebrations of the Lutheran churches."[3]

The theologians on each side take cognisance of their historical antecedents, the Lutherans referring to the *Book of Concord* and the Catholics wrestling with the teaching of the Council of Trent (qv). The "clarifications" added to the declaration just quoted make such points as that the Catholic theologians are dealing with the present situation, do not assert that recognition would either constitute or confirm validity, reject private intitiatives, are not questioning the "age-old insistence on ordination within our own Church or covertly suggesting that it be changed," and are not dealing with other churches, communities or movements that have the practice of ordination by priests": each would demand separate study. They have not discussed, they add, the implications their suggestion would have for inter-communion or Eucharistic sharing.[4]

---

[1]Text in *Modern Ecumenical Documents on the Ministry*, London, SPCK, 1975; [2]p. 66; [3]p. 74; [4]p. 75f.

M

MALACHI, 1:10-11

"Oh, that there were among you who would shut the doors, that you might not kindle fire upon my altar in vain; I have no pleasure in you, says the Lord of hosts, and I will not accept an offering from your hand. For from the rising of the sun to its setting my name is great among the nations, and in every place incense is offered to my name, and a pure offering; for my name is great among the nations, says the Lord of hosts."[1]

Of this passage traditionally applied to the Mass the Council of Trent spoke as follows: "And this, indeed is that 'pure offering,' which cannot be defiled by any unworthiness or malice on the part of those who offer it; which the Lord foretold through Malachi must be offered in every place as a pure offering (Mal 1:11) to his name which would be great among the nations. . . ."[2]

The preceding verses of this first chapter of Mal express the divine displeasure at the unworthy victims offered by the priests to Jahweh, "polluted food upon my altar" (1:7). In contrast the Lord singles out an offering that is pure and, more singular still in view of his preference for Israel, recalled in the opening verses, world-wide, universal. Here the last of the prophets records the decision of Jahweh to break the exclusive Israelite mould; a feature, as is made clear elsewhere, of messianic times. Guided by Trent, in the messianic context, Catholic exegetes interpret the passage in the light of NT and see it as a prophecy about the Mass. The interpretation is reached by stages in which form it may be partially acceptable to others. One stage is thus expressed by a Catholic exegete: "We hold that the text looks forward to a ritual sacrifice of the messianic age, a fulfillment and perfection of the Mosaic rite, which will be offered by all men and accepted by God."[3]

Explanations offered of the text vary—even on the question whether it may refer to the future or only to the present. Those who think in terms of the present suggest that the prophet had in mind Jews of the Diaspora, or Gentile proselytes of the Jewish faith, or pagans genuinely devoted to their own gods. Each suggestion is open to serious criticism: Mal seems clearly to imply that the offering will be not merely on Gentile soil, but by Gentiles; the number of Gentile proselytes were too few to justify the sweeping optimism of the passage; the pagans as such would scarcely be praised so highly by a prophet who affirms his belief in the election of Israel.

The question remains what contemporary religious practice may have caught Mal's attention, become the starting point of his insight—always under divine inspiration? Was he influenced by the cult offered by the Persians to Ahura-Mazda, the 'god of heaven,' and did he think of a future development more sublime? Such attempts to analyse the working of his mind do not invalidate a Christian view of the final import of what he says.

The Christian view intimated in the *Didache* is found among the Fathers, beginning with St. Justin (qv), *Dialogue*, 116.

---

[1]Cf. Commentaries and dictionaries s.v. and A. Rembold, *Die eucharistische Weissagung des Propheten Malachias, Theol. und*

Glaube 16 (1924), 58-70; B. Mariani, *De sacrificio a Malachia praedicto, Anton.* 1934, 193-242; 361-282; 451-474; G. Rinaldi, *La profezia di Malachia, 1:11 e la Messa, Eucaristia,* 23-30; M. Rehn, *Das Opfer der Volker nach Malachias, 1:11,* in *Lex Tua Veritas,* ed. E.H. Junker, Trier, 1961, 193, 94; C. Stuhlmueller, *Sacrifice Among the Nations, The Bible Today,* 22 (1984), 223-25; J. Swetnam, *Malaci 1:11: An Interpretation,* CBQ 31 (1969); P.A. Verhoef NGTT 21 (1980), 21-30; J. Scharbert, *'Erwahlung im Alten Testament im Licht von Gen 12:1-3; Dynamik im Wort, Festschrift ... des Katholischen Bibelwerks in Deutschland,* Stuttgart, Katholisches Bibelwerk, 1983, 13-33; P. Sacchi, *Ordine cosmico e prospettiva ultraterrena nel postesilio. Il problema del male e l'origine dell'apocallitica RivB* 30 (1982), 11-33; ²DS 1739; ³C. Stuhlmueller, JBC, 400.

MARK, LITURGY OF ST.,

The Greek Eucharistic Liturgy of the Church of Alexandria, given the name of the evangelist whom tradition claims as the founder of its Christian community—Alexandria, be it recalled, was politically second only to Rome and was for centuries the chief ecclesiastical centre, the cultural fountain-head, of the eastern Mediterranean, with its immense library, its catechetical school and its mighty Fathers and Doctors, Clement, Origen, Athanasius and Cyril.[1] The Liturgy is preserved in three MSS, the Cod. Rossanensis (Vat gr. 1970, dated thirteenth century), the Rotulus Vaticanus (Vat gr. 2281, thirteenth century) and the Rotulus Messanensis (Cod. Messin. gr. 177, twelfth century). The text was reproduced by the seventeenth-century French liturgist, E. Renaudot,[2] by Brightman[3] and by Quasten, *Monumenta;*[4] the text of the anaphora from Cod. Rossanensis is in *Prex.*[5] Peculiarities of the anaphora (qv) are the placing of the Intercessions before the Sanctus, and Epiclesis said twice, before the Institution Narrative (qv) and again after the anamnesis which follows the latter; the anamnesis is in the past tense. Changes have been made with the passage of time, it is thought.

Part of the original anaphora was identified in a Strasbourg Papyrus, dated fourth or fifth century, in 1928; another in John Rylands Library Papyrus 465. Coptic Monophysites and Abyssinians use an altered version of the Liturgy in their respective languages, Ethiopian in the latter case.

---

[1]Cf. *Prex* 101-123; C.A. Swainson, *The Greek Liturgies,* 1884, 2-73; H. Engberding, *Neues Licht über die Geschichte des Textes der agyptischen Markusliturgie, Oriens Christianus,* 40 (1956), 40-68; id., *Zum Papyrus 465 der John Rylands Library zu Manchester, ibid.,* 42 (1958), 68-76; id., *Das anaphorische Fürbittgebet der griechischen Markusliturgie,* OCP 30 (1964), 398-446; M. Andrieu-P. Collomp, *Fragments sur papyrus de l'anaphore de Saint Marc,* RSR 8 (1928), 489-515; S.G. Mercati, *L'anafora di san Marco riconosciuta in un frammento membranaceo del Museo Britannico, Aegyptus* 30 (1950), 1-7; K. Gamber, *Das Papyrusfragment zur Markusliturgie und das Eucharistiegebet im Clementsbrief,* in *Ostkirchliche Studien* 8 (1959), 31-45; C.H. Roberts, *Catalogue of the Greek and Latin Papyri in the John Rylands Library, Manchester,* III, Manchester, 1938, Papyrus 465, pp. 25-28; A. Gastoué-H. Leclercq, DACL I (1907), 1182-1204, s.v. Alexandrie (liturgie), bibl. A. Fortescue, *Catholic Encyclopaedia,* I (1907), 303-6, s.v. Alexandrine Liturgy; A. Raes, S.J., EC (1949), I, 769-73, s.v. Alexandria d'Egitto, 5, Il rito alessandrino; ²*Liturgiarum Orientalium Collectio,* I, Paris, 1716, 131-65; ³*Liturgies, Eastern and Western,* I, 1896, 115-88; ⁴I, 1935, 44-48; ⁵101-115; Strasbourg Papyrus, *ibid.,* 116-119; Manchester Papyrus, *ibid.,* 120-23.

MARTIMORT, AIMÉ, GEORGE (1911-   )

One of the best-known Catholic liturgists of recent times, M. had a broad-based training, French religious history—in the Gallican phase—and archaeology.[1] Involved in rescue work during the war, especially with Jews, he helped in Paris to launch in 1943 the *Centre de Pastorale Liturgique,* which he helped to direct between 1946 and 1964; he also occupied the chair of Liturgy in the Catholic University of Toulouse. His writings, widely read and translated, helped prepare the climate for Vatican II (qv). Chief of his books: *La Prière de l'Eglise,* 1954; *Les signes de la nouvelle alliance,* 1960; *L'Eglise en Prière, Introduction à la Liturgie,* 1961, 199 thousand, 1970; new ed. 1983, vol. III, *L'Eucharistie,* by R. Cabie, his successor in the professorship in Toulouse. Numerous articles bring his bibl. to 140 items.

M. had an important role in Vatican II as a consultor to the Preparatory Liturgical Commission and expert during the sessions, much appreciated by Cardinal Lercaro. He was named a member of the Consilium set up by Paul VI in 1964 to implement conciliar teaching and directives. He has been one of the principal figures turning theological thinking on the Mass away from purely dogmatic speculation—always valid—to pastoral issues.

---

[1]Indispensable the *Festschrift, Mens concordet voci,* 1983 offered by his colleagues in Toulouse to commemorate 40 years of the CPL and 20 since Vatican II; bibl 15-22; cf. esp. C.A.M. Roguet, *Le Centre de Pastorale Liturgique,* 371-380; C. Braga, *La Preparazione della Constituzione Sacrosanctum Consilium,* 381-403; C.J.C. Inard, *Le Consilium,* 404-418.

MARY AND THE EUCHARIST

In 1980 the French Society for Marian Studies, decided to deal, in the annual session, with the theme, *Marie et l'Eucharistie.* The contributors were scholars of stature, some of them unrivalled in their respective specialized areas.[1] Twenty-eight years previously a similar collective work had been published by the Spanish review, *Ephemerides Mariologicae, La Virgen y la Eucaristia.*[2] The subject is then not restricted to hagiography, nor to publications of a kind which have less than strictly scientific theological scope. It challenges theological science directly.

The scriptural basis will be sought in the sacramental significance seen in the sign of Cana and in the participation possible to Mary in the Paschal Mystery (qv). Did she take part in the Last Supper? Since it was Passover time and we know—if we accept the historicity of Jn 19:25-27—that she was in Jerusalem at the time, we have to seek an answer to the question: Where did she celebrate the festival? Lk 2:41 tells us that when Jesus was a child his parents went annually to Jerusalem for the Passover. If she was in the city, with whom rather than her Son would she have celebrated the Passover? The solemn blessing of the lamp was an important rite of the evening meal of sabbath or festivals. It was the privilege of the mother of the family to light the sabbath lamps; then the head of the family, in this case Jesus, would speak the blessing, "Blessed are you, Lord our God, eternal Kingdom, O you who created the lamps of fire."[3] Of course this is problematic—as is much that is written enthusiastically about the Jewish background (qv) to the Last Supper. We need to reconstitute the whole picture. If Mary was present would she have received Communion? Did she see the Risen Lord? An ancient eastern patristic tradition answers affirmatively. Can we do likewise to the other question? We must remember that her name does not figure in the accounts of the preparation for the last Passover in the life of Jesus (Mt 26:17-19; Mk 14:12-17; Lk 22:7-13).

The text of the inscription of Abercius (qv) well known and discussed, is a first pointer in early Christian, patristic times. Two extremes are to be avoided in this search for evidence: dismissal of material as irrelevant; exaggeration of its significance. With this provision we can look for some symbolic thrust in the words of Ignatius of Antioch: "I have no pleasure in the food of corruption or in the delights of this life. I desire the 'bread of God,' which is the flesh of Jesus Christ, who was of the 'seed of David,' and for drink I desire his blood, which is incorruptible love."[4] Experts look elsewhere for results.[5] One of the strongest texts is in St. Ambrose (qv). Comparing the Eucharist with the virgin conception he writes: "The body which we make (by the accomplishment of the sacramental rite) has a Virgin as its origin. Why do you seek the laws of nature in the body of Christ, since it was by an exemption of the natural order that the Lord Jesus himself was given birth by the Virgin! Assuredly then this flesh is the true flesh of Christ which was crucified and buried."[6]

This association of the Virgin Mother and the Eucharist is re-echoed in the literature of Carolingian times. After some discretion it occurs in the Oath of Berengarius: "after consecration it is the true body of Christ which was born of the Virgin and which, offered for the salvation of the world, was suspended on the Cross, and which sitteth at the right hand of the Father."[7]

A further step was to proclaim the parallel between Mary and the priest who consecrates, an intuition from which certain abuses predictably flowed. Such thinking, to be corrected in the writings of the great, came logically in the twelfth and thirteenth centuries, when Eucharistic and Marian doctrine and Christian living touched a summit of perfection. St. Bonaventure could speak of Mary giving example to the priest: "Priest, you offer the blood of Christ. You must offer it with purity and piety. Who taught you this? The glorious Virgin. You offered her Son in the hands of the Church, as he did in the hands of the just Simeon."[8] The Franciscan doctor went further: "One does not reach the benefit of the Sacrament without the patronage of the Virgin. And for this reason the holy Body which has been given to us must also be offered by her hands; and by her hands to be received under the Sacrament which was obtained for us and born of her womb."[9] A similar idea was discovered by the great Byzantine scholar, Martin Jugie, A.A., in the writings of Isidore Glabas (d.c. 1397).[10] Gerson, in the West, was expansive calling Mary 'Mother of the Eucharist.'

If we move forward to the seventeenth century we meet massive compositions on the subject, unequal in value, sometimes advancing the strangest ideas. With the increase in Marian literature in the present century, in the years between the movement for a definition of Mary's universal mediation, launched by Cardinal Mercier, and the death of Pius XII, 1921-1958, publications of the kind mentioned earlier began to appear.[11]

The reflection of the ages, when purified of its excesses, leaves us with a perspective in which the subject can be studied. There is a link between the Eucharist and the Incarnation in which mystery Mary had a vital role; she participated in the Passion of her divine Son: "Thus the Blessed Virgin advanced in her pilgrimage of faith, and faithfully persevered in her union with her Son unto the cross, where she stood, in keeping with the divine plan enduring with her only-begotten Son the intensity of his suffering, associated herself with his sacrifice in her mother's heart, and lovingly consenting to the immolation of this victim which was born of her."[12] It is this sacrificial act of Christ which is renewed in the Mass.

Finally Mary's communion with the first Christians after Pentecost in the breaking of bread affords a basis for meditation on the profound, mysterious relationship between her and the Eucharistic Christ become the food of our souls. This is example in the most powerful, most creative sense. The vast question of Mary and the priesthood is dealt with in *Theotokos*.[13]

[1]*Etudes Mariales, Bulletin de la Societe Francaise d'Etudes Mariales,* Paris, 1980; contributors, R. Laurentin, H. Crouzel, S.J., P. Yousif, M.L. Therel, B. de Margerie, S.J., A. Gouhier, J.H. Nicolas, O.P., Jos. de Ste Marie, O.C.D., M.J. Nicolas, O.P., H. Cazelles; for extensive bibl. cf. article *Eucharist, The* in *Theotokos*, M. O'Carroll, Wilmington, 1985, 138; further bibl, R. Laurentin in *Eucaristia*, 629-649; [2]Madrid, 1952; [3]Cf. L. Bouyer, *La première eucharistie dans la dernière Cène*, Paris, 1951, Appendice 3, 302; [4]Rom VII, 3, ed., H. Lake, 235; [5]Cf. R. Laurentin, op. cit., 20ff; article Ephraem, St., in present work; [6]Apud R. Laurentin, 31; [7]DS 700; [8]Opera I, 160; [9]Sermo 3 De corpore Christi, Quarrachi, V, 559B; [10]Ed. M. Jugie, A.A., *La Vierge Marie et l'Eucharistie*, in *Eucharistie* 2 (1911), 33; for Gerson, Commentary on the Magnificat, Opera, ed. P. Glorieux, VIII, 413 and *passim*; [11]Cf. R. Laurentin, op. cit., 27; [12]*Constitution on the Church*, 58; [13]293-96, s.v.

MEDIATOR DEI, 20 November 1947

With the address to the International Liturgical Congress at Assisi in 1956, *Mediator Dei* constitutes a principal contribution of Pius XII (qv) to the liturgical movement which culminated in the Council.[1] It is the most important single text on the subject to emanate directly from the papacy. Part two deals explicitly with Eucharistic Worship, though part one on the nature, origin and development of the Liturgy, and part four on pastoral instruction, have some relevance too.

There are four chapters in part two: nature of the Eucharistic Sacrifice; the part taken by the faithful in the Eucharistic Sacrifice; Holy Communion; Adoration of the Eucharist.

Pius XII, recalling the teaching of the Council of Trent (qv), affirms the identity of the Mass and Calvary; he recalls the four ends of sacrifice: praise, thanksgiving, propitiation, impetration. He shows the harmony there exists between the all-sufficiency of the sacrifice on Calvary and the need for the Mass: "Therefore if individual sinners are to be purified in the blood of the Lamb, Christians themselves must co-operate. Although Christ, universally speaking, has reconciled the whole human race to the Father by his death, yet he has willed that all men should come and be brought to his Cross, especially by means of the Sacraments and the Mass, and so take possession of the fruits which through the Cross he has won for them." "Among the instruments for distributing to believers the merits that flow from the Cross of the divine Redeemer, the august Sacrifice of the altar is pre-eminent: 'As often as the commemoration of this victim is celebrated, the work of our Redemption is performed.'"[2]

In chapter II the Pope touches on the priesthood of the laity: "By reason of their baptism Christians are in the Mystical Body and become by a common title members of Christ the Priest; by the 'character' that is graven upon their souls they are appointed to the worship of God, and therefore, according to their condition, they share in the priesthood of Christ himself."[3] There follows an analysis of the offering which the faithful are empowered to make, with practical advice on the mode of participation then allowed. Pius expounds the church outlook on Communion (qv) (see Pius X, St.), mentioning in passing the desirability of Communion by the faithful from particles consecrated at the actual Mass; he sets forth succinctly the theological justification for adoration (qv) of the Eucharist.

The Encyclical had an immense impact not only in liturgical circles, but also within the whole Church. It was for long the charter of the liturgical movement. The conciliar Constitution on the Liturgy borrows textually from it, but without the acknowledgement made to borrowing from the Popes, including Pius XII, in all the other documents.

[1]Text *AAS*, 39 (1947); [2]English tr., Mgr. G.D. Smith, CTS, London; CTS, 36; [3]*Ibid.*, 39; see article Faithful, Priesthood of.

MELCHIZEDEK

"And Melchizedek, king of Salem, brought out bread and wine; he was priest of God Most High. And he blessed him and said, 'Blessed be Abram by God Most High, maker of heaven and earth; and blessed be God Most High, who has delivered your enemies into your hand!' And Abram gave him a tenth of everything" (Gen 14:18-20). "The Lord has sworn and will not change his mind, 'You are a priest for ever after the order of Melchizedek'" (Ps 110:4). "So also Christ did not exalt himself to be made a high priest, but was appointed by him who said to him, 'Thou art my Son, today I have begotten thee'; as he says also in another place, 'Thou art a priest for ever, after the order of Melchizedek.' In the days of his flesh, Jesus offered up prayers and supplications, with loud cries and tears, to him who was able to save him from death, and he was heard for his godly fear. Although he was a Son, he learned obedience through what he suffered; and being made perfect he became the source of eternal salvation to all who obey him, being designated by God a high priest after the order of Melchizedek. . . . For this Melchizedek, king of Salem, priest of the Most High God, met Abraham returning from the slaughter of the kings and blessed him; and to him Abraham apportioned a tenth part of everything. He is first, by translation of his name, king of righteousness, and then he is also king of Salem, that is, king of peace. He is without father or mother or genealogy, and has neither beginning of days nor end of life, but resembling the Son of God he continues a priest for ever.... But this man who has not their genealogy (that of the descendants of Levi) received tithes from Abraham and blessed him who had the promises. It is beyond dispute that the inferior is blessed by the superior.... One might even say that Levi himself, who receives tithes, paid tithes through Abraham, for he was still in the loins of his ancestor when Melchizedek met him. Now if perfection had been attainable through the Levitical priesthood (for under it the people received the law), what further need would there be for another priest to arise after the order of Melchizedek, rather than one named after the order of Aaron? For when there is a change in the priesthood, there is necessarily a change in the law as well. For the one of whom these things are spoken belonged to another tribe, from which no one has ever served at the altar. For it is evident that our Lord was descended from Judah and in connection with that tribe Moses said nothing about priests. This becomes even more evident when another priest arises in the likeness of Melchizedek, who has become a priest, not according to a legal requirement concerning bodily descent but by the power of an indestructible life. For it is witnessed of him, 'Thou art a priest for ever after the order of Melchizedek'" (Heb 5:5-10; 7:1-3, 6-16).

Catholics have been accustomed to hear the name of Melchizedek in the canon of the Mass (now the first Eucharistic Prayer), "the gifts of thy just servant Abel, the sacrifice of our patriarch Abraham, and that which your high priest Melchizedek offered to you, a holy sacrifice, an unspotted victim." Behind this liturgical mention there is much biblical and patristic history. The Council of Trent considered the question clarified sufficiently to pronounce thus: "Since under the former Testament (as the apostle Paul bears witness) there was no consummation because of the weakness of the Levitical priesthood, it was necessary (God the Father of mercies ordaining it thus) that another priest according to the order of Melchizedek (Gen 14:18; Ps 110: 4; Heb 7:11) arise, our Lord Jesus Christ who could perfect (Heb 10:14) all who were to be sanctified, and lead them to perfection."[3] Trent keeps to the priestly typology, whereas the Roman Canon mentions sacrifice.

The noted biblical scholar, J. Fitzmyer, S.J., has brought into focus the precise question of sacrifice in the Gen phrase, "brought out bread and wine." As he says, the author of Heb illustrated the superiority of Jesus' priesthood over that of Aaron by three elements: the lack of genealogy, the reception of tithes, and the

blessing bestowed. The author of Heb is apparently unaware of a sacrificial implication in the words "brought out bread and wine." The exegete continues: "In a composition that is otherwise so closely bound up with the notion of sacrifice, it is difficult to understand how he would have omitted it, if it were so understood in his day.... But it is well known that some of the Fathers understood these words in Gen in terms of the sacrifice of Melchizedek. Their exegesis of the text, however, manifests the same midrashic, haggadic development as that of the author of Heb; it lacks only the charism of inspiration. However, it should be admitted with V. Hamp that even if the verb *hosi* (brought forth) can in no wise be forced into a sacrificial expression, nevertheless the bringing out of "bread and wine" by the priest Melchizedek does prefigure the loving care of the high priest Christ who provides food to still the spiritual hunger of his chosen warriors in their earthly campaign. In this sense Gen 14:18 can be said to prefigure the Eucharist."[4] The author gives an exhaustive set of references to the Fathers, who did not and who did see the element of sacrifice in the text.[5] He maintained and enlarged his position in face of a criticism made by J.F.X. Sheehan, S.J., in *Sciences Ecclésiastiques*.[6]

Meanwhile Qumran finds have added to the literature on Melchizedek—besides Gen and Ps 110, his legend is already found in the *Genesis Apocryphon*, Philo, Josephus and the Targums. On Qumran, J.P.M. van der Ploeg makes this communication: "The greater part of the fragments held by the Academy of Amsterdam have been matched, according to their script in 1963 by J.P.M. van der Ploeg. Save for very small fragments containing only a few letters, the work was relatively easy; it was even exciting, for the individual character of the script evoked the writer. It was like making contact with a world disappeared for two millennia."

"*Fragments of the Midrash of Melchizedek.* The remains of a text which deals with the role of Melchizedek in the kingdom of God were gathered and placed under glass by J.P.M. van der Ploeg in 1963. The photograph of it taken with infra-red rays, which bears the number PAM 43.979 of the Palestinian Museum (PAM) has been studied and published by A.S. van der Woude, author of a doctorate thesis *Die messianischen Vorstellungen der Gemeinde von Qumran* (Assen, 1957). The text and the provisional *editio princeps* bear the title, *Melchisedech als himmlische Erlösergestalt in den neugefundenen midraschim aus Hohle XI, Oudtestamentische Studien*, XIV, 1965, pp. 354-373 + 2 pl. With M. de Jonge, A.S. van der Woude published an improved edition of the text in *New Testament Studies*, XII, 1965-66, pp. 301-326.

Later in 1972, J.T. Milik published a new transcription with translation and commentary; he had been able to use our PAM photograph, lent in a 'friendly spirit' by ... John Strugnell."

In 1972, J.T. Milik had published three fragments, from 4Q, of a work in Aramaic which he had called *Q Visions d'Amram* (RB, 79, 1972, pp. 77-97), a work the contents of which seemed to him related to the one of which *11Q Melch* had preserved remains. See *Milki-sedeq et Milki-resa dans les anciens écrits juifs et chrétiens*, in *Journal of Jewish Studies*, XXIII, 1972, pp. 95-144. In this article the master decoder of Qumran has advanced our knowledge of this important text by locating fragments 11 and 13 and proposing convincing new readings. According to J.T. Milik the fragments would date from the middle of the first century before our era, 'perhaps even from the years 75-50.'[7]

J. Fitzmyer has translated the fragments published by A. van der Woude, with explanatory comments. "What is to be noted above all, therefore, in this text are the associations which are made with Melchizedek. He is associated with the deliverance of divine judgement, with a day of atonement, with a year of jubilee, and with a role that exalts him high above the assembly of heavenly beings. Such associations make the comparison in Hebrews between Jesus, the high priest, and Melchizedek all the more intelligible. The tradition is not the same; but what we have in 11Q Melch at least furnishes new light on the comparison. It reveals an almost contemporary Jewish understanding of Melchizedek, which is not without its pertinence to the midrash on him which is incorporated into Heb 7."[8] Later he says, "Even though it is not possible to say that the presentation of Melchizedek, which is found in it, directly influenced the midrash on him in Heb 7 (because the latter is developed almost exclusively in terms of the classic OT loci, Gen 14 and Ps 110), nevertheless its exaltation of Melchizedek and its view of him as a heavenly redemption-figure make it understandable how the author of the epistle to the Hebrews could argue for the superiority of Christ the high priest over the levitical priesthood by appeal to such a figure. The exalted status of Melchizedek which is presented in this text gives another aspect to the Christology of the epistle in which Jesus is depicted as a priest *kata ten pazin Melchizedek.*"[9]

---

[1]Cf. commentaries of the relevant passages of Gen and Heb, and biblical dictionaries s.v.; F.J. Jerome, *Das geschichtliche Melchisedech-Bild und sein Bedeutung im Hebraerbriefe*, Strasbourg, 1917; W.F. Albright, *The Historical Background of Genesis XIV, Journal of the Society of Oriental Research*, 10 (1926), 231-269; id., *Abram the Hebrew, Bull. American School of Oriental Research*, 163 (1961), 36-54; Landsdorfer, *Das Priesterkönigtum von Salem,*

Journal of Society Or. Research, 9 (1925); G. Wuttke, *Melchisedech der Priesterkönig von Salem. Ein Studie zur Geschichte der Exegese*, Giessen, 1927; G. Bardy, *Melchisedeq dans la tradition patristique* RB 35 (1926) 496-509; 36 (1927) 25-45; P.F. Cremin, *According to the Order of Melchisedech; the Patristic Interpretation and its Value*, IER 51 (1938) 469-87; 52 (1938) 37-45; 53 (1939) 487-500; R. Galdos, *Melquisedec en la patristica*, EstEc, 19 (1945), 221-46; P. Samain, *Melchisedech a-t-il offert un sacrifice, figure de l'Eucharistie?, RevDiocTournai*, 1 (1946), 38-41; I. Hunt, *Recent Melchizedek Studies*, in *The Bible in Current Catholic Thought*, ed. J.L. McKenzie, New York, 1962, 21-33; R. le Déaut, C.S.Sp., *Le titre de 'Summus Sacerdos' donné à Melchisedech est-il d'origine juive?*, RSR 50 (1962) 222-29; J.A. Fitzmyer, S.J., *"Now this Melchizedek...."* CBQ 23 (1963), 305-321; id., *Further Light on Melchizedek from Qumran Cave XI*, JBL 1967, 25-41; F. Moriarty, *Abel, Melchizedek, Abraham*, The Way 5 (1965), 95-104; J.F.X. Sheehan, *Melchisedech in Christian Consciousness, ScEccl*, 18 (1966), 127-38; J.P.M. van der Ploeg, *Les Manuscrits de la Grotte XI de Qumran, Revue de Qumran*, June 1985, 4-5, XII, 1; A.S. van der Woude, besides op. cit. in text, IDB Supplementary Vol, s.v., 585, 586; G.R. Castellino, in *Eucaristia*, 11-22; J.F. Mattingly, NCE IX, 626-27; E. Spadafora, E. Jost, EC VIII, 635-37; M. de Jonge and A.S. van der Woude, *Melchizedek and the NT*, NTS, 12 (1966), 301-332; M.P. Miller, *The function of Isa 61:1-2 in 11Q Melchizedek*, JBL 88 (1969), 457-69; M. Delcor, *Melchizedek from Genesis to the Qumran Texts and the Epistle to the Hebrews*, JSJ 2 (1971), 115-35; J. Carmingnac, *Le document de Qumran sur Melkisedeq, Revue de Qumran* 7 (1970), 343-78; F. Laubacher, *God's angel of truth and Melchizedek; A Note on 11Q Melch 13b*, JSJ 3 (1972), 46-51; K. Berger, *Der Streit des guten und des bösen Engels um die Seele: Beobachtungen zu 4QAmr und Judas 9*, JSJ 4 (1971), 1-18; J.A. Sanders, *The OT in 11Q Melchizedek*, JANES 5 (1973), 373-82; C. Gianotto, Melchisedek et la sua tipologia, Brescia, 1984; [2]Roman Missal; [3]DS 1739; [4]*op. cit.,* 321; [5]CBQ 1963, 320, n. 61; [6]*op. cit.;* [7]*op. cit.,* 9; [8]*op. cit.,* 31; [9]*Ibid.,* 41.

MEMORIALE DOMINI, 29 May 1969

Instruction of the Sacred Congregation for Divine Worship on the Manner of Distributing Holy Communion.[1] The question at issue was placing the Host in the hand of the communicant. The Instruction explains that since requests for this practice had been received from "a small number of episcopal conferences" it was decided to consult the Church's bishops. Results of a questionnaire: Do you think that attention should be paid to the desire that over and above the traditional manner, the rite of receiving Holy Communion on the hand should be admitted? Yes: 597; No: 1,233; Invalid votes: 20. Is it your wish that this new rite be first tried in small communities, with the consent of the bishop? Yes: 751; No: 1,215; Invalid votes: 70. Do you think that the faithful will receive this new rite gladly, after a proper catechetical preparation? Yes: 835; No: 1,185; Invalid votes: 128. The Instruction concluded that "from these returns it is clear that the vast majority of bishops believe that the present discipline should not be changed, and that, if it were, the change would be offensive to the sentiments and the spiritual culture of these bishops and of many of the faithful." The Pope, influenced by the findings, decided to make no change. All were urged to "obey carefully" the law which is still valid. However, episcopal conferences could separately apply for permission to make the change: the mode of application and the conditions were prescribed.

---

[1]Text, AAS 61 (1969), 541-547; English tr. A. Flannery, I, 148-153.

MIRAE CARITATIS, 28 May 1902
The great Encyclical on the Eucharist publishd by Leo XIII, toward the end of his mighty career, one marked by special excellence in the Encyclical genre, *Rerum Novarum*, 1891, his best known example; the Pope died on 20 July 1903, four months past his ninety-third birthday.[1]

The Encyclical was the climax to a liberalising programme which had been accelerated in the last decade of the pontificate; several restrictions on the reception of Communion had been lifted. The document also reflected the Pope's preoccupation with doctrinal questions in his last years: it is shown in *Divinum illud munus*, 1897, on the Holy Spirit, *Annum sacrum*, 1899, on the Sacred Heart of Jesus, *Tametsi*, 1900, on Jesus Christ, our Redeemer, and finally in the present substantial text.

The Pope begins on a personal note: "It was toward the close of his mortal life that Christ our Lord left this memorial of his measureless love for men, this powerful means of support for the life of the world. And precisely for this reason we, being so soon to depart from this life, can wish for nothing better than that it be granted to us to stir up and foster in the hearts of all men the dispositions of mindful gratitude and due devotion towards this wonderful Sacrament, wherein most especially lie, as we hold, the hope and the efficient cause of salvation and of that peace which all men so anxiously seek."[2]

Though conscious of the tension between outmoded rules and the sentiment of the faithful at the time he was writing, Leo expounded a profound theology of the Eucharist. It is "a most divine gift proceeding from the very Heart of the Redeemer, who 'with desire desireth' this singular mode of union with men, a gift most admirably suited to be the means whereby the salutary fruits of his Redemption may be distributed." "To know with an entire faith what is the excellence of the most Holy Eucharist is in truth to know what that work is which, in the might of his mercy, God-made-man carried out on behalf of the human race. For as a right faith teaches us to acknowledge and to worship Christ as the sovereign cause of our salvation, since he by his wisdom, his laws, his ordinances, his example, and by the shedding of his blood, made all things new;

so the same faith likewise teaches us to acknowledge him and to worship him as really present in the Eucharist, as truly abiding through all time in the midst of men, in order that as their Master, their Good Shepherd, their most acceptable Advocate with the Father, he may impart to them of his own inexhaustible abundance the benefits of that Redemption which he has accomplished."[3] The Pope recalls the immediate effects of the Incarnation in human affairs: "there at once burst forth a certain creative force which issued in a new order of things and pulsed through all the veins of society, civil and domestic. Hence arose new relations between man and man; new rights and new duties, public and private; henceforth a new direction was given to government, education, to the arts; and most important of all, man's thoughts and energies were turned towards religious truth and the pursuit of holiness."[4]

Leo relates the Eucharist most closely to the Incarnation: "The Eucharist, according to the testimony of the holy Fathers, should be regarded as in a manner a continuation and extension of the Incarnation. For in it and by it the substance of the Incarnate Word is united with individual men, and the supreme Sacrifice offered on Calvary is in a wondrous manner renewed, as was signified beforehand by Malachi in the words: 'In every place incense is offered to my name and a pure offering' (Mal 1:11)."[5]

The Eucharist is the very centre of the Christian life: "But no one has ever fittingly expressed praise for or worshipped with veneration this Sacrament, which is so great, manifesting all power. The Sacrament, whether one reflects devoutly on it, or duly adores it, or, what is more important, receives it with purity and sanctity, is to be considered the centre of the Christian life in every dimension. The other means of piety, whatever they may be, eventually lead to it and cease with it. And Christ's kindly invitation and still more kindly promise, 'Come to me all who labour and are heavy laden, and I will give you rest' (Mt 11:28), have effect especially in this mystery and are fulfilled daily. It is, so to speak, the soul of the Church, towards which the very fullness of sacerdotal grace through the different degrees of orders is directed. From thence too the Church draws and holds all in its power and its glory, the ornaments of all charisms, all good things; wherefore it is particularly vigilant that it should instruct and lead the minds of the faithful to intimate union with Christ through the Sacrament of his body and blood."[6]

The Pope was especially full and explicit on the effects of the Sacrament: "Now if anyone will seriously consider the benefits which flow from the Eucharist he will understand that conspicuous and chief among them all is that in which the rest, without exception, are included; in a word, it is for men the source of life, of that life which best deserves the name. 'The bread which I will give is my flesh, for the life of the world (Jn 67:52).'[7] "Now the venerable Sacrament of the Eucharist is both the source and the pledge of blessedness and glory, and this not for the soul alone, but for the body also. For it enriches the soul with an abundance of heavenly blessings, and fills it with a sweet joy which far surpasses man's hope and expectations; it sustains him in adversity, strengthens him in the spiritual combat, preserves him for life everlasting, and as a special provision for the journey, accompanies him thither. And in the frail and perishable body that divine Host, which is the immortal body of Christ, implants a principle of resurrection, a seed of immortality which one day must germinate."[8]

Christ, says the Pope, binds us to himself in this Sacrament. With it we are especially bound to the divine nature and given an increase in all the supernatural virtues, especially in faith—the Pope recalls the words *Mysterium fidei* applied to the Eucharist. Here too is the remedy for human pride and for everything that threatens to deprave human life. With his sense of history he notes: "History bears witness that Christian civilization flourished in times when communion was frequently received. On the other hand it has been found that when men neglected the Bread of heaven and seemed to weary of it, the vigour of Christian commitment declined." The Pope noted with joy the Eucharistic renewal taking place in his lifetime and was happy to record the approval he had officially given to various forms of this renewal, confraternities, congresses and the like." "Away then" he exclaimed, "with the widespread but mischievous error of those who give it as their opinion that the reception of the Eucharist is in a manner reserved for those narrow-minded persons (as they are deemed) who rid themselves of the cares of the world in order to find rest in some kind of professedly religious life. For this gift, than which nothing can be more excellent or conducive to salvation, is offered to all those, whatever their office or dignity may be, who wish—as every one ought to wish—to foster in themselves that life of divine grace whose goal is the attainment of the life of blessedness with God...."[9] The Pope, quoting the Council of Trent (qv) and Pope Innocent III (qv) at length, urges frequent Communion on all. He adds some enlightening passages on the Eucharist as sacrifice, meeting the essential religious needs of man. The reader will probably agree that his Encyclical has scarcely received due recognition.

Leo, when there is question of the Eucharist, is most frequently thought of in regard to Anglican Orders, on which subject he delivered an official judgement, after hearing from the commission which he established to report to him thereon (see article *Apostolicae Curae*). Others think of him as preoccupied with the social, and indeed political question. His teaching was finely balanced between radical diagnosis of the world's ills and exhortation to piety of the most informed kind— witness his nine Encyclicals on Our Lady, and his insistence on the Rosary, the prayer of Blaise Pascal and his housekeeper, of the two intellectual giants of recent times, Newman and Lonergan (qqv). Leo's teaching on the Eucharist is the pinnacle of this mighty edifice.

[1]Text, ASS 34 (1902), 641-655; *Acta Leonis* XIII, VIII, 109-122; cf. Anne Freemantle, *The Papal Encyclicals in their Historical Context*, New York, 1956, 161-166; John Wynne, S.J., *The Great Encyclicals of Leo XIII*, New York, 1903, 516-529; [2]*Acta* quoted, 110; [3]111; [4]*Ibid.;* [5]114; [6]118-119; [7]111; [8]115; [9]112.

MIRACLES OF THE EUCHARIST

The Eucharist itself is the wonder of wonders surpassing in idea and realization all that could possibly be thought of by a human being.[1] Only God could think of it and only God-made-man could accomplish it. But miracles in the sense traditionally defined and with one required element, that is that they should be perceptible to the senses, have been reported through the ages; scientific evidence is not always available. One which took place at Bolsena, 1264, was depicted in a famous painting by Raphael (see article Art and the Eucharist). Such miraculous happenings have been classified as follows: sacred hosts which showed signs of apparent bleeding, Lanciano (8th century), Ferrara (1171), Alatri (1228), Florence (1230), Bolsena (1264), Offida (1273), Berlin (1510), etc.; sacred hosts miraculously preserved, Santarrem (13th century), Morovalle (1562), Favernay (1618), Siena (1730), etc; luminous appearance of sacred hosts, Turin (1453), Paterno near Naples (1772), etc; apparition of Jesus in the sacred host, Braine (1153), Ulmes in the diocese of Angers (1668), esp. in the life of St. Catherine Labouré, etc; punishment of those who profaned the Eucharist, Louvain-Brussels (1369), Volterra (1471), Boston (1834), etc.; prodigious cures, Paris (1725), Lourdes, Loreto, Fatima and many other Marian shrines at the blessing of the Blessed Sacrament. Thus was fulfilled the word of St. Pius X, the 'Pope of the Eucharist,' when he was told that Lourdes would detract from personal devotion to Christ: "No, the Son will be seen to work miracles at the intercession of the Mother."

[1]List by A. Piolanti, EC VIII, 1067, cf. B. Pesci, O.F.M., *Il Miracolo di Bolsena, Eucaristia*, 1025-1033.

MISSALE ROMANUM, 3 April 1969

The Apostolic Constitution whereby Paul VI (qv) presented the new Order of the Mass (qv) to the Catholic Church.[1] He explained the origin of the Missal in conciliar decisions, and mentioned the principal differences between it and the Roman Missal, the addition of three new Canons, the addition of many new Prefaces, the wide variety of readings and the responsorial psalm. The rites have been simplified, care being taken to preserve their substance. "Elements," says the Pope, "which, with the passage of time, came to be duplicated or were added with but little advantage have now been discarded, especially in the rites concerned with the preparation of bread and wine, the Breaking of bread and the Communion" (part of this sentence is a quotation from The Constitution on the Liturgy, art 50). Elements which had been lost were brought back: the Homily, the Prayer of the Faithful and the Penitential Rite.

---

[1]Text in Roman Missal, English tr. by Clifford Howell, S.J., CTS, A. Flannery, O.P., I, 137-141.

MUSICAM SACRAM, 5 March 1967

Instruction on Music in the liturgy, prepared by the Consilium set up by Paul VI (qv) and issued by the Sacred Congregation of Rites.[1] It identifies sacred music, proceeds from the principle: "Liturgical worship is given a more noble form when it is celebrated in song, with the ministers of each degree fulfilling their ministry and the people participating in it." "Indeed," the Instruction continues, "through this form prayer is expressed in a more attractive way, the mystery of the liturgy, with its hierarchical and community nature, is more openly shown, the unity of hearts is more profoundly achieved by the union of voices, minds are more easily raised to heavenly things by the beauty of the sacred rites, and the whole celebration more clearly prefigures that heavenly liturgy which is enacted in the holy city of Jerusalem."

There is a reminder of the interior spirit which is needed in all prayer. As to the sung Mass, specific distinction is made between three degrees of participation: "These degrees are so arranged that the first may be used even by itself, but the second and third, wholly or partially, may never be used without the first. In this way the faithful will be continually led towards an ever greater participation in the singing. The following belong to the first degree: a) In the entrance rites: the greeting of the priest together with the reply of the people; the prayer. b) In the Liturgy of the Word: the acclamation of the Gospel. c) In the

Eucharistic Liturgy: the prayer over the offerings; the preface with its dialogue and the *Sanctus*: the final doxology of the Canon; the Lord's prayer with its introduction and embolism; the *Pax Domini*; the prayer after the Communion, the formulas of dismissal. The following belong to the second degree: a) the *Kyrie, Gloria* and *Agnus Dei*; b) the Creed; c) the prayer of the faithful. The following belong to the third degree: a) the songs at the Entrance and Communion processions; b) the songs after the Lesson or Epistle; c) the *Alleluia* before the gospel; d) the song at the Offertory; e) the readings of Sacred Scripture, unless it seems more suitable to proclaim them without singing. Further directives are given.

---

[1]Text *AAS* 59 (1967) 300-320; English tr. by the Congregation, reproduced A. Flannery, O.P., I, 80-97.

MYSTERIUM FIDEI, 3 September 1965

The Encyclical Letter issued by Paul VI (qv) to correct abuses noted in the Church in the immediate wake of Vatican II (qv), to deal with those acting as if "everyone were permitted to consign to oblivion doctrine already defined by the Church or else to interpret it in such a way as to weaken the genuine meaning of the words or the recognized force of the concepts involved."[1] Examples given by the Pope of such errors: "to exaggerate and emphasize what is called 'communal' Mass to the disparagement of Masses celebrated in private; or to exaggerate the element of sacramental sign as if the symbolism, which all certainly admit in the Eucharist, expresses fully and exhausts completely the mode of Christ's presence in this Sacrament ... to discuss the mystery of transubstantiation without mentioning what the Council of Trent stated about the marvellous conversion of the whole substance of the bread into the body and of the whole substance of the wine into the blood of Christ, speaking rather of what is called 'transignification' and 'transfiguration'; or finally to propose and act upon the opinion according to which, in the consecrated hosts which remain after the celebration of the Sacrifice of the Mass, Christ our Lord is no longer present."

To counter such pernicious error the Encyclical deals with the Eucharist as a mystery of faith, as verified in the sacrifice of the Mass; subsequent sections deal with the sacramental presence of Christ, transubstantiation, the latreutic worship of the Eucharist; there is finally an exhortation to promote the cult of the Eucharist.

The teaching of the Encyclical is supported throughout by solid erudition, particularly in the domain of patrology and of conciliar and papal teaching.

[1]*AAS* 57 (1965), 753-774; translations available.

MYSTICISM

The direct, essential response to communion in the Eucharist is faith. Yet the very nature of the encounter provides a setting in which mystical experience may be possible to those called by God to this privilege. There is consequently a considerable history of the phenomenon. Fortunately much of it has been documented by the saints and servants of God so favoured.[1] Much wisdom is needed to discriminate what is genuine mystical experience from what may be, if not necessarily spurious, at least tinged with the artificial.

[1]Cf. Ephrem Longpré, DSp IV, 2, 1586-1621.

N

NEW ORDER OF MASS, THE

The Mass of the Second Vatican Council, composed in the years that followed it by the liturgical experts named by Pope Paul VI (qv);[1] it was proposed to the Catholic Church by the Apostolic Constitution, *Missale Romanum*, 3 April 1969 (qv); it has as an introductory recommendation and explanation, the *Institutio Generalis* (qv), and translated around the world was ready for use in 1970. As the so-called Tridentine Mass (qv) was the result of the Council of Trent (qv), this Mass is the fruit of Vatican II. There were Protestant observers present at the drafting committee; what influence they may have had has been a matter of conjecture.

As the Mass is universally celebrated its distinctive features are well known. Three Eucharistic Prayers (qv) were added. The Roman Canon was slightly altered but still remains Eucharistic Prayer one: the name of St. Joseph had been added by John XXIII during the first session of the Council; to "This is my body" is added "which will be given up for you"; instead of "Whenever you do this," there is "Do this in memory of me"; "Mysterium fidei," which was not in Christ's words is now used after them in a formula inspired by St. Paul, "(We proclaim) that Christ has died."

Outside the Eucharistic Prayers the changes are: a penitential rite to begin the Mass; the responsorial psalm which follows the first reading, the addition of a second reading on Sundays and solemnities, with variations and a wide choice of biblical texts; the suppression of the prayers said over the bread and wine—*Suscipe sancte Pater* . . .; *Offerimus tibi, Domine* . . .; *Veni Sanctificator omnipotens*, of the psalm said at the washing of the hands, psalm 26:6-12; of the prayer of oblation to the Holy Trinity, *Suscipe Sancta Trinitas*.

The *Institutio generalis* does not mention these omissions at all; it speaks of the preparation of the altar, the antiphon which may be sung during the offertory procession, the washing of the hands. *Missale Romanum* has this passage: "As regards the Order of the Mass 'the rites have been simplified, due care having been taken to preserve their substance. Elements which with the passage of time, came to be duplicated or were added with but little advantage have now been discarded' (Liturgical Const., art. 50) especially in the rites concerned with the preparation of the bread and wine, the Breaking of the Bread, and the Communion."

At the height of the controversy over the Mass, along with other matters, in France in 1976 centering on Mgr. Lefebvre (qv), a principal liturgist of Vatican II, Mgr. A.G. Martimort (qv) wrote a defence of the New Order for *La Croix*; it was widely distributed, taken up by *L'Osservatore Romano*. He thus justified what had been done: "It is of course the Offertory, which has given rise, in the Commission of the Roman *Consilium*, to the liveliest controversies. Theologians and liturgists had been discussing it for three centuries. It is this that has undergone the most decisive change. Most of the prayers which the priest used to say in a low voice repeated one another, and regretfully encroached upon the formulas of the Eucharistic Prayer.

Then too, in popular pastoral work in the years 1935-1950, allegorical interpretations of the Offertory had proliferated, which threatened dangerously to make people forget the essential: simplification was therefore necessary."

Two questions remain unanswered in these statements: Why was the oblation to the Holy Trinity omitted after eleven hundred years—what did it "repeat" that would not be missed? What is the origin of the prayers substituted, 'Blessed are you, Lord God of all creation...' (twice), 'Lord God we ask you to receive us and be pleased....?' The first question has a deep theological import: for eleven hundred years the Mass was offered to the Trinity, applying thereto the teaching of the two great Fathers who saved the west from the danger of subordinationism, Hilary and Augustine, each author of a prayer directly to the Trinity. This prayer should not prevent or be prevented by prayer to the Father, through the Son in the Spirit. The indirect danger of exclusive use of the second from of address is obvious.

The new prayers whose origin is unexplained bear a striking resemblance to Jewish table prayers. It would have been preferable to admit this publicly if the borrowing was made (see Jewish background).

Mgr. Martimort contends that "from the *Pater* to the end of the Mass the changes are very slight." The *Libera*, said after the *Pater* (which itself has been given three new introductory formulas) is now "Deliver us, Lord, from every evil and grant us peace in our day. In your mercy keep us free from all anxiety as we await the coming of our Saviour, Jesus Christ. For thine is the kingdom, the power and the glory." Formerly it read: "Deliver us, we beseech thee, O Lord, from all evils, past, present, and to come; and by the intercession of the blessed and glorious ever Virgin Mary, Mother of God, and of the holy Apostles, Peter and Paul, and of Andrew, and of all the saints, mercifully grant peace in our days, that through the assistance of thy mercy we may be always free from sin, and secure from all disturbance. Through the same Jesus Christ, thy Son, our Lord, who with thee in the unity of the Holy Spirit lives and reigns, God, world without end. Amen."

The prayer for peace formerly came after the *Agnus Dei*; now it precedes it, with an invitation to the congregation to share the peace. It was one of three prayers said consecutively before Communion. One of these is now entirely dropped in so far as a choice is allowed between the remaining two: only one is to be said. Before the Communion, now the priest says: "This is the Lamb of God, who takes away the sin of the world; happy are those who are called to his supper." The reply is, "Lord, I am not worthy...."

Formerly the priest said, "I will take the Bread of heaven, and I will call upon the name of the Lord." Then he said three times: "Lord I am not worthy...." He said then as he says now, "The body of our Lord Jesus Christ preserve my soul unto life everlasting." But before the Cup he said, "What return shall I make the Lord for all he has given to me? I will take the chalice of salvation, and call upon the name of the Lord. Praising I will call upon the Lord, and I shall be saved from my enemies." He makes a similar invocation to what he said over the host.

Formerly the priest pronounced the twofold formula of forgiveness, "May almighty God have mercy on you.... May the almighty and merciful Lord grant you pardon...." He held aloft the host to the faithful and announced, "Behold the Lamb of God...." Then he said three times, "Lord, I am not worthy...."

While engaged on the ablution, the priest said: "May thy body, O Lord, which I have received, and thy Blood which I have drunk cling to my inmost being; and grant that no stain of sin may remain in me, who have been fed with this pure and holy Sacrament; who live and reign for ever and ever. Amen." This is now omitted. So is the prayer said before the final blessing: "May the performance of my homage be pleasing to thee, O holy Trinity; and grant that the sacrifice which I, though unworthy, have offered up in the sight of thy majesty, may be acceptable to thee, and through thy mercy, be a propitation for me, and for all those for whom I have offered it. Through Christ our Lord. Amen."

One may discuss whether the changes were beneficial; one can scarcely say they were very slight ("minimes" is Mgr. Martimort's word).

In 1969 a booklet appeared in Rome entitled *Breve esame critico del 'Novus Ordo Missae'* by two Italian priests, one an official in the Curia, another a seminary, or university, professor. The booklet was addressed to Paul VI by Cardinals Ottaviani and Bacci; they complained that the New Order, in its new elements, did not conform to the Catholic theology of the Mass and asked that access should be permitted to the "complete and fruitful Roman Missal of St. Pius V." The press exploited this letter which was also published in France. The publicity annoyed Cardinal Ottaviani, who eventually said he was satisfied with the doctrinal clarifications given by Paul VI in two addresses in November 1969. The Congregation for the Doctrine of the Faith examined the entire dossier. No valid criticism was made of the Order of the Mass, it was thought.

---

[1]Bibl. to articles mentioned. 'Articles by Mgr. Martimort, *La Croix*, 26 August 1976; repr. *D Cath* 1976, 1062-64.

NEWMAN, JOHN HENRY (1801-1890)

N. presents the interesting case of a man of genius, with immense spiritual potential, expressing his thought on the Eucharist from within two different Christian communions, in the successive phases of his religious pilgrimage. His attitude to Anglican Orders (see article *Apostolicae Curae*) is not without interest.[1] All is of importance in view of the intellectual role he is destined to play in the Catholic Church. Relevant to study of this Newman question are two sermons and a controversial letter from his Anglican days and some passages in the correspondence after he had become a Catholic; to which must be added some devotional papers always, with N., nourished on doctrine.

As an Anglican, N. believed in the real presence, without accepting the doctrine of transubstantiation (qv); he would also see the Eucharist as a sacrifice, without any elaborate theological theory—this he did not achieve as a Catholic either. He had an opportunity to express his considered opinion in a lengthy letter written to the Margaret Professor of Divinity, Rev. Godfrey Fausset, in defence of his friend Hurrell Froude, who had died young, whose *Remains*, mostly spiritual diaries, had been edited by N.: Froude had, among other things, expressed himself strongly on priesthood and sacrifice.

Dealing with the Eucharist, N. proceeds thus: "As regards then this most sacred subject, three questions offer themselves for consideration: first, whether there is a Real Presence of Christ in this Holy Sacrament, next what it is, and thirdly where. 1. On the Real Presence I shall not use many words of my own, because on the one hand it is expressly recognized by the Catechism and Homilies (not to mention the language of the Service itself), and on the other because you do not absolutely condemn such language, only you think it 'highly objectionable and dangerous' when 'systematically and studiously adopted.' I shall not, therefore, debate a point which the formularies of our Church decide, when they declare that 'the Body and Blood of Christ' are *verily and indeed* taken and received by the faithful in the Lord's Supper; that 'the Body of Christ is *given, taken and eaten* in the Supper'; and that 'thus much we must be sure to hold, that in the Supper of the Lord there is no vain ceremony, no bare sign, *no untrue figure of* a thing absent, but as the Scripture saith, . . . the communion of the Body and Blood of the Lord, in a marvellous incorporation, which by the operation of the Holy Ghost, the very bond of our conjunction with Christ, is through faith wrought in the souls of the faithful, whereby not only their souls live to eternal life, but they surely trust to win to their bodies a resurrection to immortality.'[2] These passages seem to determine

that the Body and Blood of Christ are not absent but present in the Lord's Supper; and if really, and in fact Christ's Body be there, His Soul is there and His Divinity; for, as the article says, the two natures are 'never to be divided'; therefore he is there, 'One Christ', whole and entire." In support of this contention N. quotes a long passage from Hooker's *Treatise on the Laws of Ecclesiastical Polity*.

"So much," he continues, "on the testimony of our Church and of her celebrated divine to the doctrine of the Real Presence. But here it is objected that such a Presence is *impossible*; and this brings us to the question *how* Christ is present, which stands next for consideration. The objection takes this form—if He is *really* here, he is *locally* here, but he is locally in heaven not here, therefore he cannot be here, but is only said to be here."

N. refers to Bellarmine's (qv) opinion. He goes on to expound the Anglican view as he understood it: "Our Church, however, incidentally argues that a body cannot be in two places at once; and that the Body of Christ is not locally present, in the sense in which we speak of the Bread as being locally present. On the other hand she determines, as I have already said, that the Body of Christ is in some unknown way, though not locally, yet really present, so that we after some ineffable manner, partake of it. Whereas then the objection stands, Christ is not really here, because he is not locally here, she answers, he is really here, yet not locally."[3]

N. comes to his second point, "what is the meaning of saying that Christ is really present, yet not locally?" "Presence then," he says, "is a relative word, depending on the channels of communication existing between the object and the person to whom it is present. It is almost a correlative of the senses. A fly may be as near an edifice as a man; yet we do not call it present to the fly, because he cannot see it, and we do call it present to the man, because he can." "As sight for certain purposes annihilates space, so other unknown conditions of our being, bodily or spiritual, may practically annihilate it for other purposes. Such may be the Sacramental Presence. We kneel before the Heavenly Throne, and distance vanishes; it is as if that Throne were the altar close to us." "This is my first suggestion; my second is as follows: Our Lord not only 'did rise again from death', as the Article says, 'and took again his Body with flesh, bones and all things appertaining to the perfection of man's nature', but he rose with what St. Paul terms 'a spiritual body'; so that now he is in heaven, he is not subject to the laws of matter, and has no necessary relations to place, no dependence on its conditions; and for what we know, his mode of making himself present òn earth, of coming and going, is as different from the mode natural to bodies by locomotion, nearness being determined by intervals and absence being synonymous with distance as spirit is different from matter. He may be literally present in the Holy Eucharist, yet, not having become present by a movement and a transit, he may still be continuously on God's right hand: so that, though he be present with us in deed and in truth, it may be impossible, it may be untrue, to determine that he is in or about the elements, or in the soul of the communicant. These may be serviceable modes of speech, according to the occasion; but the true result of all such inquiries is no more than the assertion with which we began, that he is present in the Holy Eucharist but not locally present. We to whom the idea of space is a necessity, and who have no experience of spirits, are of course unequal to the conception of such an idea, and can only call a mystery what is as transporting and elevating to the religious sense, as it is difficult to the intellect."[4]

When N. comes to the third point, the relation of the consecrated elements to "those Realities of which they are the outward signs," he writes thus: "The Roman Church, we know, considers that the elements of Bread and Wine depart or are taken away on Consecration, and that the Body and Blood of Christ take their place. This is the doctrine of Transubstantiation; and in consequence they hold that what is seen, felt and tasted, is not Bread and Wine but Christ's Flesh and Blood, though the former look, feel and taste remains." N. agreed later that this is not an exact statement of transubstantiation (qv). He also rejects the Lutheran idea of consubstantiation.

For fuller insight into the mind of N. on our subject two sermons must be read. The first on *The Resurrection of the Body* was preached in 1832, and is of interest to N's idea of 'life,' the 'unity' of the human person and especially the eschatological aspect of the Eucharist.[5] As so often happens with N. much of what he says here is in harmony with Catholic teaching. This would also be true of his remarkable sermon on *The Eucharistic Presence*, for which his text was Jn 6:50. We do well to recall that presence for N. meant during the Eucharistic celebration.

Singling out Holy Communion in what he calls the Sacramental Season (from Ash Wednesday to Trinity Sunday), "Christ, who died and rose again for us, is in it spiritually present, in the fullness of his death and resurrection. We call his presence in this Holy Sacrament a spiritual presence, not as if 'spiritual' were but a name or mode of speech, and he were really absent, but by way of expressing that he who is present there can neither be seen or heard; that he cannot be approached or ascertained by any of the senses; that he is not present in place, that he is not present carnally, though he is really present. And how this is, of course, is a mystery. All that we know or need know is that he is given to us, and that in the Sacrament of Holy Communion."[6] N. has interesting remarks on the contrast between the Johannine Eucharistic text, which he is expounding, and the synoptic narratives. Again he refers to the Catholic doctrine of Transubstantiation, disagreeing (as he understood it) but citing it as a sign of the importance attached to the Eucharist. N. considers other questions arising out of the Johannine text, the typology of the manna and the implied pedagogy of the miracle of the loaves and fishes.

N. before and for some time after his ordination as a Catholic priest believed in the validity of Anglican Orders; within a year he abandoned this belief—he would always allow for the reception of grace through the spiritual disposition of the ordinand. This had surely been true in his own case. There is a wealth of evidence to show his intense Eucharistic piety as a Catholic, especially his devotion to the Blessed Sacrament; he loved visiting churches where the Sacrament was reserved.[7] Editing the works of his Anglican days after his conversion he added notes to state the true Catholic doctrine; they are admirable for lucidity.[8] So are his Eucharistic prayers or meditations: "In the Holy Mass the One Sacrifice on the Cross once offered is renewed, continued, applied to our benefit."[9]

---

[1]Cf. Dom Placid Murray, O.S.B., *Newman the Oratorian*, Dublin, 1969, ch. III, *The Eucharistic Ministry*, 43-58; [2]*The Via Media*, II, ed., 1877, 220, 21; [3]*Ibid.*, 223, 25; [4]*Ibid.*, 227, 29; [5]*Parochial and Plain Sermons*, I, Sermon 21; text *Sermons on Subjects of the* Day, ed. 1871, 411ff; [6]*Parochial and Plain Sermons*, vol. VI, 136, 37; [7]For texts in support cf. P. Murray, *op. cit.*, 48, n. 13; for meditations and prayers cf. Meditations and Devotions, London, 1894, 291, 351, 391 (a visit), 560-570 (The Holy Sacrifice—The Mass, Holy Communion, The Food of the Soul); [8]Cf. *Via Media, op. cit.*, 220, n.6; 223, 24, n.1; [9]*Meditations and Devotions*, 291.

O

OBLATION

What is the primary constituent of sacrifice: offering of a gift, or destruction, i.e., immolation of a victim? The question was brought into focus in theological debate by the work of Fr. M. de la Taille, *Mysterium Fidei* (qv). His contemporary, M. Lepin (qv), made a survey of writing on the Eucharist from the earliest times to seek support for his own theory, that offering, oblation, was generally seen as the essential element in sacrifice, *L'Idée du sacrifice*. He would not, nor would others who hold this view, exclude the idea of immolation altogether. But they would consider it an adjunct imposed by the fact of sin.

OT evidence needs careful interpretation (cf. Melchisedek, Malachi), and experts in the history of religions are also to be heard. A theology of optimism based on the first design of God in creation, a design in part thwarted by sin but essentially primordial, will emphasize oblation as intrinsic to sacrifice.

[1]Cf. M. Schmidt, *Notions générales sur le sacrifice dans les cycles culturels, Semaine d'ethnologie religieuse tenue à Tilbourg*, 1922, Enghien, 1923, 229-244; M. de la Taille, S.J., *op. cit.,; id., Distinctio oblationis et immolationis in traditione dogmatica, ETL,*, 4 (1927) 384-404; G. Graneris, *La religione nella storia delle religioni*, Turin, 1935, 263-68; M. Lepin, *op. cit.*; A. Gaudel, DTC, XIV, 1, (1939) 662-692.

OECOLAMPADIUS, JOHN (1482-1531)

Not an original theologian of the Reformation, a communicator rather, an expert linguist, resolute also in applying decisions taken, O. takes his place with Ulrich Zwingli, whom he accompanied with Bucer, at the crucial, epoch-making Colloquy of Marburg, 1529, where they discussed possible points of agreement with Martin Luther (qv) and Melanchton, failing to succeed only on the Eucharist. O. (real name Hussgen or Heussgen or Hauschein), born in Weinsberg, (Palatinate) studied law at Bologna, theology at Heidelberg, was for a while cathedral preacher in Basle. He withdrew from the scene of active life to a Brigittine monastery in Austria but left after two years. Back in Basle he was vicar of St. Martin's and a reader at the University. Busied himself with lecturing and disputation on behalf of the Reform. Due to his efforts with those of Zwingli in 1528, Berne adopted the new faith and in the following year the Mass was abandoned in Basle. Like Zwingli he refused to accept Luther's idea of Consubstantiation. He rejected also Luther's idea of ubiquity, preferring to think of the universal presence of the Holy Spirit. The Eucharist was explainable metaphorically, he thought, yet he thought of it as a means of grace. He quickly shrugged off the early Lutheran influence while he was in Augsburg; it issued in his work *Canonici indocti*.

[1]Cf. E. Staehelin, *Das theologische Lebenswerk Johannes Oekolampads (Quellen und Forschungen zur Reformationsgeschichte, 21)* 1939; id., *Oekalampads-Bibliographie*, ed. 2, Nieuwkoop, 1963; L. Cristiani, DTC XI, 1, 947-951.

OFFICIUM MIHI, 13 December 1980

A communication from the Sacred Congregation for

the Sacraments and Divine Worship stating that the permission to use the Eucharistic Prayers for Children and for Reconciliation which had expired at the end of 1980 had been, in an audience granted to Cardinal Knox by Pope John Paul II, extended indenfinitely.[1]

---

[1]A. Flannery, O.P., II, 118.

OLIER, JEAN-JACQUES (1608-1657)

The founder of the Society of Saint-Sulpice treated of the Eucharist in his writings centered on the priesthood, and on the spiritual life. His teaching embodies the ideas and ideals of the French school of spirituality. It will be found principally in: *La Journée chrétienne*, 1655, the *Catéchisme chrétien pour la vie intérieure*, 1656; *L'Introduction à la vie et aux vertus chrétiennes*, 1657; *L'Explication des cérémonies de la grand'messe en paroisse, 1657*; two posthumous works, *Lettres Spirituelles* and *Traité des saints ordres*, published by M. Tronson in 1672 and 1675.

Deep devotion to the Eucharist was a cardinal principle in O's spirituality—he would have wished to name his society the Fathers of the Blessed Sacrament and he exhorted his followers to this practice. In *L'Explication des cérémonies de la grand'messe en paroisse* we get his theology of the Mass, which strongly resembles that of De Condren (qv). He deals with four parts of the sacrifice of Christ, oblation, immolation, consummation and communion. Oblation is the key word and for O. this began with the Incarnation: "Our Lord coming into the world offered himself once as victim to God his Father in the womb of the Most Blessed Virgin, as on an altar, to be one day immolated and consumed to the glory of his divine majesty. And this offering was the offering and the sanctification of the whole Church, which he wished to sacrifice with him." "It was then in the secrecy of the Most Blessed Virgin that the holy religion of Jesus Christ had its beginning."[2]

O. has another interesting idea more fully developed with him than it is found elsewhere, the sacrifice of Christ in heaven: "It is a strange idea for most people to say that there is sacrifice in heaven; I am speaking about people in general, for the others who know what constitutes religion and its first duty which is sacrifice, have no doubt that there should be sacrifice in heaven, for even on earth those who believe in God offer sacrifice: *Sacrificat qui putat esse Deum*."[3] O. taught that the Mass was the sacrifice of heaven, but distinct, special to the Church militant: "There is a sacrifice in paradise, which at the same time is offered on earth since the victim which is there presented is borne on the altar of heaven; it differs only in this that

here it is presented under veils and symbols and there it is offered openly, without any veil."[4] O. supports all this theory with pertinent remarks on the priesthood of Christ according to the order of Melchizedek.

The great Sulpician develops a theory of the union of Christ with his Church in the sacrifice, and of the union of the Church with Christ: "Jesus Christ and all his saints, comprised in the *Communicantes*, all his mysteries and all his gifts are but one Victim offered and presented to God, one that is pure, holy and spotless in heaven." "The Church is on the altar in spirit, well represented as a victim by the bread and wine composed of several grains, pointing to the unity of the faithful assembled in spirit with the Victim, to offer, consecrate and immolate themselves to God."[5]

---

[1]*Oeuvres*, ed. J.P. Migne, Paris, 1856; cf. H. Bremond, *Histoire littéraire du sentiment religieux en France depuis la fin des guerres de religion jusqu'à nos jours*, Paris, 1916 ... II (1921), 419-507; R. Levesque, DTC XI, 1, (1931), 419-507; esp., M. Lepin, *L'Idée*, 486-496; I. Noye and M. Dupuy, DSp, XI, 737-751; [2]Apud M. Lepin, 489; [3]*Ibid.*, 490; [4]*Ibid.*, 491; [5]*Ibid.*, 495.

OPPORTUNUM ESSE, 1 November 1974

Instruction on the Eucharistic Prayers for Masses for Reconciliation, issued by the Sacred Congregation for Divine Worship. Approval for texts specially designed to match the Holy Father's purpose in regard to the forthcoming Holy Year, on the theme of reconciliation.[1] Directives on their use.

---

[1]Text *Notitiae*, 11 (1975), 6; tr. A. Flannery, O.P.,II, 58.

ORIGEN (c. 185-c. 254)

The astonishing genius of Alexandria expounded his ideas of the Eucharist on two levels: he stated the faith of the Church, held by all, ordinary people especially and he developed a doctrine for the more intellectually advanced. But the final judgement on his teaching has to leave some unresolved questions, allow that there are passages difficult of explanation. In the *Contra Celsum* he writes thus: "We give thanks to the Creator of all and, along with thanksgiving and prayer for the blessing we have received, we also eat the bread presented to us; and this bread becomes by prayer a sacred body, which sanctifies those who sincerely partake of it."[2] He is more explicit in the following passage: "You who are wont to assist at the divine Mysteries, know how, when you receive the body of the Lord, you take reverent care, lest any particle of it should fall to the ground and a portion of the consecrated gift (*consecrati muneris*) escape you. You consider it a crime, and rightly so, if any particle thereof fell down through negligence."[3]

O. in the commentary on St. John writes thus of the Last Supper: "As he who unworthily eats the bread of the Lord or drinks his chalice, eats and drinks to his judgement, as the greater force, which is in the bread and the chalice, effects good things in a good soul and evil things in a bad, the morsel given (to Judas) by Jesus was of the same kind; that which he gave to the other Apostles saying 'Take and eat' was salvation for them, but judgement for Judas, so that after the morsel Satan entered into him. The bread and chalice are understood by the more simple people in the ordinary meaning of Eucharist, but by those who have acquired a higher knowledge in the more divine meaning of the nourishing truth of the Word."[4]

Here we enter the realm of allegory, well-known to students of O. He develops the idea elsewhere: "That bread which God the Word (*deus verbum*) owns to be his body, is the Word which nourishes the soul, the Word which proceeds from God the Word (*verbum de deo verbo procedens*), and that bread from heavenly bread which is placed upon the table, of which it is written: 'Thou hast prepared a table before me, against them that afflict me' (Ps 22:5). And that drink, which God the Word owns to be his blood, is the Word which saturates and inebriates the hearts of those that drink it, they drink in that cup of which it is said: How goodly is thy inebriating chalice (Ps 22 *ibid.*). . . . Not that visible bread, which he held in his hands, did the divine Logos call his body, but the word, in the mystery of which the bread was to be broken. Not that visible drink did he call his blood, but the word, in the mystery of which this drink was to be poured out. For the body of the divine Logos or his blood, what else can they be than the word which nourishes and the word which gladdens the heart?"[5]

About this passage G. Bareille thinks that it shows that O. had not sought to make a synthesis of his ideas in this whole theological domain, while P. Batiffol thinks that his doctrine is here incomplete. Passages as the following must be noted: "If you go up with him to celebrate the pasch, he gives you the chalice of the new testament, he gives you the bread of the blessing, he dispenses his body and his blood."[6] "Formerly in figure baptism was in the cloud and the sea, but now regeneration is in water and the Holy Spirit. Then in figure the manna was food, but now is disclosed the flesh of the Word of God is true food, as he himself said, 'For my flesh is food indeed and my blood is drink indeed.'"[7] What it means to approach such great and such wondrous sacraments."[8]

That O. knew and adhered to the faith of the Church cannot be questioned; that he succeeded in applying his allegorical method satisfactorily can.

[1]Works Quasten Monumenta, 349-352; J. Solano, *Textos*, I, 127-140; cf. A. Scheiwiler, *Die Elemente der Eucharistie in den ersten drei Jahrhunderten*, Mainz, 1903, 66-85; A. Struckmann, *Die Gegenwart Christi in der hl. Eucharistie nach den schriftlichen Quellen der vornizanischen Zeit*, Vienna, 1909, 143-194; G. Rauschen, *Eucharistie und Bussakrament in den ersten sechs Jahrhunderten der Kirche*, Freiburg i. B., 1910, 6-10; P. Batiffol, *L'Eucharistie*, 262-284; E. Klostermann, *Eine Stelle des Origenes* (In Mt ser. 85), ThStKr 103 (1931), 195-198; F.R.M. Hitchcock, *Holy Communion and Creed in Origen*, ChQ, 1941, 216-329; O. Casel, O.S.B. (qv), *Glaube, Gnosis und Mysterium*, JL 15 (1941), 164-195; L. Grimmelt, *Die Eucharistiefeier nach den Werken des Origenes. Eine liturgiegeschtliche Untersuchung*. Dissertation, Münster, 1942; G. Bareille, DTC, V, 1137-39; Quasten, *Patrology*, II, 85-87; [2]CGS Orig. 2, 249; PG 11, 1566 C; [3]In Exodum Hom. 13, 3, CGS 6, 274; [4]In Johannem 32, 24 CGS 4, 468, Preuschen; [5]In Matthaeum comment. ser 85, CGS Orig. 11, 196, 19-197, 6 Klostermann; [6]In Jeremiam Hom. 19, 13, CGS Orig. 3, 169, Klostermann; [7]In Numeros Hom 7, é2, CGS 7, 39, Baehrens; [8]In Ps 37 Hom. 2, 6, PG 12, 1386D, D. Sheerin, *The Message*.

ORTHODOX, THE

The table of contents of the great work of Panagiotis N. Trembelas, *Dogmatique de l'Eglise Orthodoxe Catholique* (French tr., Archimandrite Peter Dumont, O.S.B.),[1] in the section dealing with the divine Eucharist, gives an indication of the similarity that exists between Orthodox and Catholic teaching on the subject. The divine Eucharist is treated as the third sacrament. The treatment falls into four parts entitled respectively: I, Definition, importance, designations, types (figures), divine institution; II, Sensible aspect of the Sacrament; conditions for celebration and participation; III, Invisible aspect of the Sacrament of the Eucharist. Sub-sections of the first part include: Food of supernatural transformation and sacrifice celebrated by the Saviour; and Excellence of the Sacrament in comparison with the others. The second part deals with the questions of the kind of bread and of wine, the words of consecration, the ministers and the participants in the Sacrament. There are two main sub-divisions in the third part: the first deals with the real presence of Christ and its consequences; the second with the divine Eucharist as sacrifice and its fruits.

The opening summary of Eucharistic doctrine shows also the similarity with so much Latin thinking: "The divine Eucharist is the Sacrament where Christ is really and substantially present under the appearances of bread and wine, offered in a sacrifice unbloody and a representation of that which was offered only once and forever on the cross, then given to the faithful as life-giving food and communion. The Eucharist thus has a double aspect, it is sacrament and sacrifice. The very many names used for it by Scripture and Tradition in the Church express these two aspects which are equally serious. By them it is exalted either as a sacrament which nourishes the souls of the faithful, uniting them to Christ and among themselves in one bread and one body, or again as a sacrifice which represents, in a manner which is unbloody and mysterious, but nevertheless really, the sacrifice which the High Priest offered in his blood on the Cross. Since the body and blood of the Lord are given as food and drink to the faithful through this sacrament, its exceptional excellence and importance are clearly evident, making it the centre towards which the other sacraments and the whole Christian life lead."[2]

Compare with this authoritative statement the following words of the 'Decree on the Ministry and Life of Priests' from Vatican II: "But the other sacraments and indeed all ecclesiastical ministries and works of the apostolate are bound up with the Eucharist and are directed towards it. For in the most blessed Eucharist is contained the whole spiritual good of the Church, namely Christ himself our Pasch and the living bread which gives life to men through his flesh—that flesh which is given life and gives life through the Holy Spirit."[3]

Words in the statement also recall the well-known definition of Trent (qv): "And since in this divine sacrifice, which is celebrated in the Mass, that same Christ is contained and immolated in an unbloody manner, who on the altar of the Cross 'once offered himself' the holy Synod teaches that this is truly propitiatory and has this effect, that if contrite and penitent we approach God with a sincere heart and right faith, with fear and reverence, 'we obtain mercy and find grace in seasonable aid' (Heb 4:16)."[4]

To show the textual resemblance with Trent, we should have to quote a passage further on in the same Orthodox work: "(The Eucharist) is also a propitiatory sacrifice and a sacrifice of intercession, wherein offering the victim, offered on the Cross for our salvation, we ask for remission of our sins, having been assured that God is propitious in their regard."[5]

To revert to our author's sequence of ideas, we note that he prescribes as species of the sacrament "leavened bread and wine with which a little water is mixed." Here we have the controversy on the point of difference between the Orthodox and the West: the azymes (qv).

The eastern churches used leavened bread from the outset. The argument is put forward that they continue thus the practice of the first centuries. St. Irenaeus (qv) and St. Justin Martyr (qv) are cited in support of the view, from the words that, "after the thanksgiving pronounced on (the bread)" it is no longer "common bread," "ordinary bread"; it was therefore, so runs the inference, common or ordinary before; it was not unleavened. Again the example of Melchizedek (qv) is invoked; he certainly did not use unleavened bread.

Nor can the Last Supper be used as an argument—to show that the Lord used unleavened bread: according to the reading of Jn's account, the last meal took place before the Passover and the Lord was crucified on the eve of the Passover. The problem is discussed in the relevant article. The frequent "breaking of the bread" mentioned by Acts was outside the pattern of the Jewish Passover; so it cannot be argued that the Passover prescription about unleavened bread was binding.

Unfortunately with the eleventh century break between east and west, the difference of opinion and liturgical practice added to the other differences. "The discussion on the azymes, which started in the eleventh century, was generally entangled in arguments of purely symbolic nature (the Greeks maintained, for example, that the Eucharistic bread had to be leavened in order to symbolize the *animated* humanity of Christ, while the Latin use of the azymes implied Apollinarianism, i.e., the denial that Jesus had a human soul), but the controversy also recognized that the Byzantines understood the Eucharistic bread to be necessarily consubstantial with humanity, while Latin medieval piety emphasized its 'supersubstantiality,' its otherworldliness."[6] This is the view of a determined Orthodox!

Panagiotis M. Trembelas takes the view that it is the epiclesis which achieves the consecration: "(The sensible species) are consecrated by the epiclesis of the Holy Spirit pronounced over them, added immediately after the ecphonesis of the words of institution and the precept of the anamnesis."[7]

The change which takes place is thus described: "An ineffable transformation and conversion which transcends human understanding take place in the consecrated species of bread and wine, in such wise that under their external appearances, Our Lord himself is present, truly, really and substantially, not typically, not symbolically or by impanation, and that he is given to the faithful."[8]

The difficulty arising from the use of symbolic language by certain of the Fathers is splendidly met: the reference to symbols or equivalent terms like type and anti-type is sometimes on the basis of the elements before consecration, sometimes it is based on consideration of the species only, or again it is a symbolism, such as St. Paul (qv) used between the Eucharist and the Church; or, as with St. Augustine, who is much quoted in these pages, if the language of signs and symbols is used, nowhere is it said that there is question of mere signs and symbols, empty of reality. Throughout the exposition, the eastern Fathers are abundantly quoted.

Panagiotis M. Trembelas deals with the adoption at

a certain time of the western, Latin, idea of transubstantiation. He first lists various words used from the fourth century on, in the east, to express the wondrous change: *metaballein*, to change, to transform (Cyril of Jerusalem, Theodore of Mopsuestia), *metapoiein* and *metapoiesthai*, to convert (Gregory of Nyssa, Cyril of Alexandria, John of Damascus), *metastiecheioun*, to change the nature (Gregory of Nyssa), *metaskeuazein*, *metarruthmizein*, to transform. After the approval given by the Fourth Lateran Council, 'transubstantiation' begins to appear in Greek, noun and adjective, *metousiosis, metousiousthai*. In 1282 Michael Paleologus used it in a letter to Pope Gregory; so did George Scholarius in his homily on the sacramental body of our Lord Jesus Christ. "The word was more widely used among us in the seventeenth century, on the occasion of discussions provoked by the confession of faith attributed to Cyril Lucaris and by other Calvinistic influences. It was taken up ... in the Confessions of Mogila and Dositheus, and utilised as a synonym for the words 'change' and 'conversion,' without admitting acceptance of the theory by which the Roman Catholic Church sought to explain the dogma and justify it philosophically."[9] J. Meyerndorff makes the reservation sharper.[10] Fr. Jugie is also to be read on the subject.[11]

Our Orthodox authority also stresses the notion of sacrifice in consideration of the Eucharist. "The sacrificial character of the Eucharist, prefigured already in the Old Testament, is also made evident by the separate consecration of the Eucharistic species, at the time of the institution of the sacrament, and by the Saviour's words which declare the shedding of blood and its character as blood of the New Covenant."[12]

The particulars of this theory thus summarily presented are worked out by the author, in a way that Latin readers will find congenial. In fact the broad agreement between east and west in Eucharistic theology is most impressive and, in its essential lines, is not touched by the controversies about the azymes (qv) or the epiclesis (see article, Cabasilas, Nicholas). On Nestorians and Monophysites the reader is referred to Fr. Jugie's work.[13]

---

[1]Chevetogne, 1966; cf. also M. Jugie, A.A., *Theologia dogmatica Christianorum Orientalium ab Ecclesia catholica dissidentium*, 1933, vol III, 177-330; J. Meyerndorff, *Byzantine Theology*, New York, 1974, 200-215; Th. Spacil, *Doctrina theologiae Orientis separati de SS. Eucharistia*, Rome Orientalia Christiana, 14 (1929); A. Schmemann, *L'Eucharistie, Sacrament du Royaume*, esp. 235-251, *Le Sacrament de l'Esprit Saint*; M. Jugie, A.A.A., *La Messe du rite byzantin*, DTC, X, 2, 1331-1346; [2]*Op. cit*, III, 157; [3]Art. 5; [4]DS 1742; [5]*Op. cit.*, 232; [6]J. Meyerndorff, *op. cit.*, 204; [7]*Op. cit.*, 168; [8]189; [9]209; [10]*Op. cit.*, 204; [11]*Op. cit.*, 193-227 [12]232. [13]M. Jugie, *op. cit.*, V, 664-719; cf. also D. Stiernon, A.A., in *Eucaristia*, 512-518.

P

PASCHAL MYSTERY, THE

One of the valuable insights, in part a recovery, of recent times, is the unity of the passion, death and resurrection of Jesus Christ as the saving mystery of mankind, the core of the Liturgy, especially of the central act of the Liturgy, the Eucharist.[1] Many trends converged to reach this satisfying, creative concept. Reflection on the ideas of Dom Odo Casel (qv) was a preparation, as was the seminal study of F.-X. Durrwell, C.SS.R., on the Resurrection, *Mystery of Salvation*; L. Bouyer, C. Orat., published a pioneering work, *Le Mystère pascal,* in 1945; R. le Déaut, C.S.Sp., had clarified the Jewish background in a penetrating study, *La nuit pascale. Essai sur la signification de la Pâque juive à partir du Targum d'Exode XII*, 1963. Significantly the treatment of the Redemption in the great dogmatic collective work of the post-Vatican II era, *Mysterium Salutis*, by renowned theologians, Hans Urs von Balthasar and Aloysius Grillmeier, S.J., was under the title *The Paschal Mystery* (German ed. vol II, 2, Einsiedeln, 1969, 133-392—many translations). Research shows that though *Pascha-Passio* for a while was proposed as an interpretation, *Pascha-transitus* was seen as a valid, profound insight favoured by St. Augustine: the 'passage' of Christ through death to victory and glorification at the right hand of the Father makes possible our passage through grace from bondage to freedom, from darkness to illumination. We 'rise' from sin through rebirth in water and the Spirit made possible in the Easter vigil; we are destined to a second resurrection, a return to life of our bodies, already accomplished in Christ, promised to those saved in him.

Vatican II (qv) fully accepted the doctrinal finding, valid through patristic times: "The wonderful works of God among the people of the Old Testament were but a prelude to the work of Christ Our Lord in redeeming mankind and giving perfect glory to God. He achieved his task principally by the paschal mystery of his blessed passion, resurrection from the dead and glorious ascension, whereby 'dying he destroyed our death, and rising, restored our life.' For it was from the side of Christ as he slept the sleep of death upon the cross that there came forth 'the wondrous sacrament of the whole Church.'"[2]

The Sunday observance is enriched by the thought: "By a tradition handed down from the apostles, which took its origin from the very day of Christ's resurrection, the Church celebrates the paschal mystery every seventh day, which day is appropriately called the Lord's Day or Sunday. For on this day Christ's faithful are bound to come together into one place. They should listen to the word of God and take part in the Eucharist, thus calling to mind the passion, resurrection and glory of the Lord Jesus, and giving thanks to God who 'has begotten them again, through the resurrection of Christ from the dead into a living hope'" (1 Pet 1:3).[3]

Originally the 'Fifty Days' from Easter to Pentecost was celebrated as one feast, a "great Sunday." But with development of Trinitarian theology, especially at the hands of the great Cappadocians in the fourth century, the fortieth and fiftieth days were detached,

Ascension and Pentecost. There is some echo of the ancient idea in recent liturgical prayers. Vatican II does not include Pentecost in the Paschal Mystery; to do so rigidly might smack of subordinationism—all of which will be dealt with in a work prepared by the present author, *Veni Creator Spiritus*.

"Mystery" is used in the sense expounded by Dom Odo Casel.

---

[1]Besides the works mentioned, cf. esp. R. Cantalamessa, *La Pascua nella Chiesa antica*, Turin, 1978, French tr. *La Pâque dans l'Eglise ancienne*, Berne, 1980; ample bibl.; Odo Casel, O.S.B., *Art und Sinn der ältesten christlichen Osterfeier, Jahrbuch für Liturgiewissenschaft*, 14 (1934), 1-78; French tr. *La fête de Pâques dans l'Eglise des Pères*, Paris, 1963; H. Haag, *Pâque,* DBS, VI, 1960, 1120-49; *id.*, *Vom alten zum neuen Pascha. Geschichte und Theologie des Osterfestes*, Stuttgart, 1971; W. Huber, *Passa und Ostern. Untersuchungen zur Osterfeier der alten Kirche*, Berlin, 1969; A.J. Chupungco, *The Cosmic Elements of Christian Passover*, Rome, 1977; Cl. Richard, *Il est notre Pâque. La gratuité du salut en Jésus Christ*, Paris, 1980; esp. I.H. Dalmais, *Pâques. Résonances spirituelles du mystère pascal*, DSp, XII, 171-182; *id.*, *Introduction to the Liturgy*, Baltimore, 1961; [2]*Constitution on the Liturgy*, 5; [3]*Ibid.*, 106.

PASCHASIUS, RADBERT St. (c. 790-c. 865)

A Benedictine monk, abbot of the monastery of Corbie, P. was the author of the first treatise devoted explicitly to the Eucharist, *De corpore et sanguine Domini*; he composed it between the years 831 and 833.[1] Controversy arose about this work, which by the realism expounded by its author offended those clinging to a symbolism which they attributed to St. Augustine (qv). Opponents of P. included Rabanus Maurus, Ratramnus and Gottschalk.

His basic belief, repeated many times, was the identity between the body of the historical Jesus and his body in the Eucharist. This is the work of the entire Trinity. It is a mystery surpassing all the miracles ever known; these miracles occurred so that it should be believed; the other miracles of Christ were worked so that we should have his body and blood. None must be ignorant of this. But it demands faith.

"To this end the 'Word became flesh and dwelt among us,' that through God the Word made flesh, the flesh could advance to God the Word. This flesh of the Word in this mystery becomes edible and the food of the faithful, while it is believed to be flesh for the life of the world, nothing other than the flesh of Christ's body, by which Christ remains in us that we through it should be transformed into him, who became nothing else than God-flesh in his condescension that he should dwell in us. If therefore he dwells in us it is right that we should remain in him, for we are in him that we should live from him. And therefore we eat the flesh of the Word and drink his blood."[2]

P. relates the wonder of the real presence (qv) to the omnipotence of God: "For the invisible priest with his secret power by his word converts visible creatures into the *substance* (italics added) of his body and blood, speaking thus: 'Take and eat, for this is my body'; and having repeated the blessing, 'Take and drink, this is my blood.' Therefore, he says, as at the behest of the Lord giving order suddenly from nothing exist the heights of the heavens, the depths of the seas, the expanse of lands; with like power in spiritual sacraments the very power of the word gives order and the real effect follows.... Behold the sacred body of your God, look on his blood, wonder with honour, approach it with your mind, take it with the scope of your heart, especially grasp it interiorly to the full."[3]

P. compares the Eucharistic conversion with the mystery of the virginal conception: "Whence it is not to be wondered at that the Holy Spirit, who created, without (male) seed, the man Christ in the womb of the Virgin, should also effect by his invisible power through the sacred action of his sacrament, that the *substance* (italics added) of the bread and wine become the body and blood of Christ, though it is not perceived by the sight externally or by taste, since in reality spiritual things are grasped with fullest certainty by faith and the mind, as Truth foretold."[4] Or again: "He it is who, through the Holy Spirit, makes this his flesh and pours out *(transfundit)* his blood. For who else could by a creative act have caused the Word to become flesh. In the same way in this mystery it is to be believed that by the same power of the Holy Spirit through the word of Christ, by invisible action, the flesh and blood of Christ are wrought."[5]

P. was conscious of the soteriological aspect of the Eucharist: "A sacrament is whatever in any divine celebration is given to us as a pledge of salvation, when the visible action invisibly works interiorly something invisible vastly different which must be received in a holy manner. Wherefore the sacraments are said to be secret, because the divinity achieves through the corporeal appearance, something within most secretly, or from the consecration of sanctification, because the Holy Spirit remaining hidden in the body of Christ, the great divine power invisibly works all these sacramental mysteries, beneath a covering of visible things, for the salvation of the faithful."[6]

Salvation means eternal life: "Therefore since he willed it thus that his flesh and blood should be this mystery, have no doubt, if you believe in God, but hold it in your mind, with true faith, that this is that flesh which was offered for the life of the world, and he who eats it will not see death forever."[7]

P. was conscious of the sacrificial aspect of the

Eucharist with reference to both oblation (qv) and immolation (qv). "This oblation is repeated daily, though Christ suffered once in his flesh through one and the same endurance of death, once saved the world.... And therefore since we fall daily, Christ is immolated mystically for us daily and the passion of Christ is given to us in mystery."[8]

P. explains the immolation in a passage in the commentary on Mt: "Immolation is not used rightly according to the proper meaning of the name and word unless the slaughter of the victim ensues. Nevertheless in the bread and wine the priest is rightly said to immolate, since in it Christ, as I believe, in this oblation to God the Father is made victim, as victim for our sins, or in the food of salvation."[9]

Christ is the altar: "Do you think that there is any other altar where Christ assists as *pontifex* than his own body, through which and in which the prayers of the faithful and the faith of believers are offered to God. And if the body of Christ is truly believed to be that heavenly altar, think not that you take flesh and blood from anywhere else than the body of Christ"[10]

P. distinguishes the reality and the figure in the offering of the Eucharist: "But it seems to be a figure while it is being broken, while under the visible appearance something else is understood than is perceived by the sight of bread and the taste, while in the chalice the blood is mixed with water. Nonetheless, that sacrament of faith is rightly called reality. Reality therefore it is while the body and blood of Christ is wrought from the *substance* (italics added) of bread and wine at his own word, by the power of the Spirit, but a figure while by the priest as if performing something externally, because of the memorial of the sacred Passion, ... the Lamb is immolated daily." "But if we look into things truly," he goes on, "it can rightly be spoken of as reality and figure at the same time, so that it may be a figure or image of the reality that is externally perceived, the reality itself being whatever is rightly or interiorly grasped or believed of the mystery. Not every figure is shadow or falsehood."[11]

P. Batiffol thought that P. came closer to the doctrine of transubstantiation (qv) than anyone before him. "Think then if anything corporeal more sublime can exist than that the substance of bread and wine is effectively changed interiorly into Christ's body and blood"—this is a fairly accurate statement of the meaning of transubstantiation.

P. was indebted to the Fathers, Cyprian, Ambrose, Hilary, Augustine, John Chrysostom, Jerome, Gregory, Isidore, Hesychius, Bede. In one aspect of his thinking his debt was to Faustus of Riez (qv), author of the homily attributed to Eusebius of Emessa by P. To Faustus perhaps Batiffol's compliment should be

addressed. Christ the high priest, Christ the victim, bread and wine substantially changed, salvation daily available the direct effect, the Eucharist sacrament and sacrifice—such are the great themes opened up by P. whose synthesis ushers in the Middle Ages, a great Eucharistic epoch.

[1]Works PL 120, critical ed. *De corpore et sanguine Domini*, B. Paul, O.S.B, CCCM 16 (1969), here used. Cf. H. Peltier, *Pascase Radbert*, Amiens, 1938; Id., DTC, XIII, 2 (1937) 1627-39; J. de Ghellinck, DTC V (1913) 1213ff; A. Gaudel DTC X (1929), 1009-1022; D. Stone, *A History of the Doctrine of the Holy Eucharist*, London, 1909, 216-22; J. Geiselmann, *Die Eucharistielehre der Vorscholastik, (Forschungen zur christlichen Literatur und Dogmengeschichte*, XV, Hftt. 3-4, Paderborn, 1926); C. Gliozzo, *La dottrina della conversione eucaristica in Pascasio Radberto e Ratramno*, Palermo, 1945; J. Brinktine, *Zur Lehre der mittelalterlichen Theologen über die Konsekrationsform der Eucharistie. Von Pascasius Radbertus bis zu Hugo von St. Cher, Theol. und Glaube* 45 (1955), 188-207; [2]CCCM 16, I, 19; [3]*Epistle to Fredugardus, ibid.* 149, 50; [4]III, 27; [5]XXI, 77; [6]III, 23; [7]I, 17; [8]IX, 52; [9]In Mt 26, PL 120, 894D; [10]VIII, 43; [11]IV, 28, 29.

PAUL, ST.

It is significant that the first written testimony to the Eucharist is from one who had not known Jesus Christ prior to his death and resurrection, who was a convert from the persecutors of Christ's followers, who, because of his life work and mission, is known as the Apostle of the Gentiles.[1] The testimony is rich in factual content and spiritual import. It is contained in 1 Cor, which Paul wrote during his two-year stay in Ephesus, at the beginning, towards 55, or at the end, towards Easter 57. This is some years before the first gospel, St. Mark's. The first account of the institution is from one who was not present at the Last Supper (qv).

Paul's words are: "I want you to know, brethren, that our fathers were all under the cloud, and all passed through the sea, and all were baptized into Moses in the cloud and in the sea, and all ate the same supernatural food and all drank the same supernatural drink. For they drank from the supernatural Rock which followed them, and the Rock was Christ. Nevertheless, with most of them God was not pleased; for they were overthrown in the wilderness" (1 Cor 10:1-5).

"Therefore, my beloved, shun the worship of idols. I speak as to sensible men; judge for yourselves what I say. The cup of blessing which we bless, is it not a participation in the blood of Christ? The bread which we break, is it not a participation in the body of Christ? Because there is one bread, we who are many are one body, for we all partake of the one bread. Consider the people of Israel; are not those who eat the sacrifices partners in the altar? What do I imply then? That food offered to idols is anything, or that an idol is anything? No, I imply that what pagans sacrifice they offer to demons and not to God. I do not want you to be partners with demons. You cannot drink the cup of the Lord and the cup of demons; you cannot partake of the table of the Lord and the table of demons" (1 Cor 10:14-21).

"For I received from the Lord what I also delivered to you, that the Lord Jesus on the night when he was betrayed took bread and when he had given thanks, he broke it, and said, 'This is my body which is for you. Do this in remembrance of me.' In the same way also the cup after supper, saying, 'This cup is the new covenant in my blood. Do this, as often as you drink it, in remembrance of me.' For as often as you eat this bread and drink the cup, you proclaim the Lord's death until he comes. Whoever, therefore, eats the bread or drinks the cup of the Lord in an unworthy manner will be guilty of profaning the body and blood of the Lord. Let a man examine himself, and so eat of the bread and drink of the cup. For any one who eats and drinks without discerning the body eats and drinks judgement upon himself. That is why many of you are weak and ill, and some have died. But if we judged ourselves truly, we should not be judged. But when we are judged by the Lord, we are chastened so that we may not be condemned along with the world" (1 Cor 11:23-32).

Paul first links the Eucharist with baptism and recalls the Exodus which prefigured the great mystery. He evokes sacrificial meals to emphasize the sacrificial quality of the Eucharistic meal. "Because there is one bread, we who are many are one body, for we all partake of the one bread." Here in Paul's first explicit statement of the doctrine of the Mystical Body, of which he had an intimation in the word of Christ, "Saul, Saul, why persecutest thou me?" (Acts 9:4) is the link between the Eucharist and the Body: Paul sees in the Eucharist that we form one body living the life of Christ, which comes to all from it.

It is clear that for Paul the Eucharist is attached to the Last Supper and to Christ's will that it be repeated constantly. His account of the institution (qv) agrees broadly with that of Mk and Mt; but there are distinctive differences. Mk says: "And as they were eating, he took bread, and blessed, and broke it, and gave it to them, and said, 'Take, this is my body'" (14:22). Paul does not say "he gave" but it is implied. He adds to the word 'body' "which is for you" probably implying "being given": possibly a theological addition. "Do this in remembrance of me" is peculiarly Pauline; it is repeated for the cup, whereas Lk reproduces the formula once only, after the consecration of the bread (22:19).

Though nothing suggests that Paul is giving something new, hitherto unknown to his readers, it is, nonetheless, a fact that this is, in writing, the first teaching on the *anamnesis* (qv) with all that this implies.

Paul says of the cup that Christ spoke the words over it "after supper." If it was during a paschal meal that the Last Supper took place, this would have been the fourth, the last and most solemn cup taken after the completion of the meal.

"This cup is the new covenant in my blood." Mk has "This is my blood of the covenant, which is poured out for many" (14:24). Scripture scholars point out that though the order of the words "covenant" and "blood" is reversed, the memory of the ancient covenant (Lev 1:5) and Semitic usage explain the apparent difference: "In Mk the formula 'my blood of the covenant' signifies 'my blood which ratifies the Alliance' (covenant); in Paul, the expression 'the new covenant in my blood' signifies 'the new Alliance (covenant) ratified, concluded by my blood,' as so often in the New Testament, under the influence of the Semitic languages, the proposition 'in' has a causal sense: 'by means of.' Paul, then, repeats substantially the form of consecration as Mk has handed it down to us; but he alters the literary form by substituting the effect for its cause. In short, then, it must be understood in this way: 'The wine contained in this cup is my blood which establishes and ratifies the new Alliance.'"[2]

What is the intrinsic meaning of the words "This is my body" for Paul? Is it a metaphor as when Christ says "I am the vine, you are the branches"? Or does it signify reality? The Apostle leaves us in no doubt whatever on this question: "Whoever," he says, adding the word "therefore" for emphasis, "eats the bread or drinks the cup of the Lord in an unworthy manner will be guilty of profaning the body and blood of the Lord"—he does not say "will show disrespect to the memory of the Lord," or "will profane words made sacred by usage at the Lord's supper." Consequently before eating or drinking in this case there must be an examination of conscience. To eat and drink here "without discerning the body" is to invite the wrath of God. Paul mentions the kind of punishment, illness and death. What is at issue is sacrilege: desecration not only of the sacred, but also of the Author of all that is sacred. The entire scale of moral values, of the theocentric ethical code of God's chosen people, takes on a new, substantial element which gives it indefinable enrichment.

Later centuries would bring all the force of human reason to the study of the mysterious transformation which Paul is content to narrate. He does not give us any answer to such questions as the how of the mysterious change. What he does clarify is the sacrificial aspect of the Eucharist (see article Sacrifice). He recalls that it was "on the night when he was betrayed" that Christ instituted the Eucharist and he makes clear the link with the redemptive death: "For as often as you eat this bread and drink the cup, you proclaim the Lord's death until he comes." The words are immediately after the call of the Lord to *anamnesis*. We need to recall the covenant aspect already mentioned. Nor does Paul state or insinuate the Christ is sacrificed a second time. He has written elsewhere: "For we know that Christ being raised from the dead will never die again; death no longer has dominion over him" (Rom 6:9).

The eschatological aspect of the Eucharistic banquet is emphasized by the Synoptics: "Truly, I say to you, I shall not drink again of the fruit of the vine until that day when I drink it new in the kingdom of God" (Mk 14:25). Paul is not so emphatic, but he was possessed of the idea: "you proclaim the death of the Lord *until he comes*." For him Christ in the Eucharist was essentially the risen Christ, as it was the risen Christ who appeared to him and called him. As recent studies have shown in detail, the Resurrection has a most important place in his soteriology. "If Jesus is to come back one day, it will be with his body transfigured by glory and in order to transform our bodies to resemble his (Phil 3:21; Col 3:1-4) in the power of the Spirit. There does exist, then, an intimate bond between the Eucharist and the return of Christ. The Eucharist is the glorious body of Christ, through which the faithful enter into communion with God and with his life-giving Spirit. When he returns, Christ will perfect the work he began by giving us the the Spirit fully, the principle of the eschatalogical renewal of the world and of our bodies."[3]

Writing possibly under the influence of the Antioch liturgical practice, Paul, nonetheless, gives us testimony of the highest kind on the faith of the early Church in the Eucharist. There is another aspect to his teaching which has been clarified by J. Murphy-O'Connor: "The 'remembrance' for which Paul twice calls must be fully lived. The way in which the Corinthians celebrated the Eucharist showed that they remembered Jesus only as a reality of the past. For Paul, on the contrary, authentic remembrance is concerned with the past only in so far as it is constitutive of the present and a summons to the future. What he desires to evoke is the active remembrance of total commitment to Christ which makes the past real in the present, thus releasing a power capable of shaping the future." To this idea the author relates the phrase "discernment of the body." It has been interpreted in the light of

preoccupation with the real presence as we have seen. "The 'discernment of the body' which he demands in v. 29 is the affirmation in action of the organic unity of the community. Anyone who dares to participate in the Eucharist without adverting to the Body is guilty of perpetuating the divisions which make the Lord's supper impossible (v. 20) and, in consequence, eats and drinks to his own damnation. The Corinthians must sincerely evaluate their relationship to each other in the light of the love shown by Christ (2 Cor 5:15) before celebrating the Eucharist (v. 31). In making this demand Paul is merely restating for a new situation the injunction of Jesus in the Sermon on the Mount. . . . Christ remains incarnationally present in and to the world through the community that is his Body. The organic unity integral to this body is reinforced and intensified by the Eucharist but not by the words and gestures in themselves, because Paul would energetically repudiate any mechanical approach to the Sacrament."[4] The importance of this insight for the social effects (qv) of the Eucharist is overwhelming. But does Fr. Murphy-O'Connor's insight annul the interpretation so many others have given; are they mutually exclusive? Paul is a many-sided spiritual genius (see article Symbolism). Trent (qv) seems to favour the older opinion.

[1]Cf. E.B. Allo, O.P., *La synthèse du dogme eucharistique chez St. Paul, RBib* 30 (1921), 321-343; id., *Première épître aux Corinthiens*, Paris, *Etudes Bibliques*, 1934, 302-309; W. Goossens, *Les origines de l'Eucharistie, sacrement et sacrifice*, Gembloux, Paris, 1931; J. Jeremias, *Das paulinische Abendmahl eine Opfer darbringung, Theol. Studien und Krit.*, 108 (1927), 124-141; F. Amiot, *L'enseignement de Saint Paul*, vol. II, Paris, 1938, 47-49; F. Prat, S.J., *The Theology of St. Paul*, English tr., 1945, I, 123-27; II, 263-68; Teofilo Ab Orbiso, *La Eucaristia in San Pablo, Est. Biblicos*, 5 (1946), 171-213; J.M. Bover, S.J., *Teologia de San Pablo*, Madrid, 1946, *La Eucaristia*, 677-719; V. Jourdan, *Koinonia in I Corinthians, Journal of Bib. Lit.*, 67 (1948), 111-114; O. Cullmann, *Paradosis et Kyrios. Le problème de la tradition dans le paulinisme Rev.d'hist. et de phil. relig.*, 30 (1950), 12-30; H. Schuermann, *Der Einsetzungsbericht*, Muenster Weston, 1955, 73-133; P. Neuenzeit, *Das Herrenmahl*, Munich, 1960; M.E. Boismard, O.P., *The Eucharist according to St. Paul*, in *The Eucharist in the New Testament*, London, 1964, 125-142; L. Cerfaux, *The Christian in the Theology of St. Paul*, London, 1967, 333-335; J. Fitzmyer, S.J. in *Jerome Biblical Commentary*, 824-25; G. Ruffino, *Eucaristia, L'Eucaristia nel Nuovo Testamento*, 48-61; J. Murphy-O'Connor, O.P., *Eucharist and Community in First Corinthians, Worship* 50 (1976) 370-385; 51 (1977), 56-69; id. *First Corinthians*, Wilmington, 1979, 109-115; [2]M.E. Boismard, *op. cit.*, 128, 29; [3]*Ibid.*, 136, 37. [4]J. Murphy-O'Conner, *op. cit.*, 114.

PAUL VI (1897-1978), POPE (from 1963-1978)

The pontificate of Paul VI saw greater changes in the Eucharistic liturgy than had been seen for centuries. It also witnessed an upheaval within the Church, with diverse effects not least on Eucharistic doctrine and practice. To deal with each movement the Pope had to intervene personally or through the Roman congregations responsible to him: restructuring of these bodies, additions to them, were part of his programme. Church government was affected not only by the Council but also by the Episcopal Synod, Paul VI's creation, as by the powers given to National Episcopal Conferences.

A succinct account of so many things is not easy (see New Order of Mass, The; Post-conciliar Documents). Paul VI set up the Consilium for the Implementation of the Constitution on the Liturgy, by *Motu Proprio*, 25 January 1964. The Constitution was promulgated on 4 December 1963, at the end of the second session of the Council (see Vatican II), so that as Pope he lived with the final phase of conciliar discussion on the Constitution, its emergence in the life of the Church and the consequences.

The principal event in post-conciliar Eucharistic history was the publication of the new Order of Mass in 1969. It appeared with a General Instruction which explained various matters deemed to require explanation. A first version of this document had, because of one article, provoked comment and harsh criticism. Article VII read as follows: "The Lord's Supper or Mass is the sacred synaxis or gathering of the people of God as a congregation, with a priest presiding, to celebrate the memorial of the Lord. Wherefore the promise of Christ, 'Where two or three are gathered in my name, there am I in the midst of them' (Mt 18:20) is eminently true of the local congregation of holy Church." This article, an apt description of a Protestant communion service, was significantly altered as follows: "*In the Mass or Lord's* Supper the people of God are called together in one, with the priest presiding over them *and acting in the person of Christ*, so that they may celebrate the memorial of the Lord *or the Eucharistic sacrifice.* Wherefore the promise of Christ, 'Where two or three are gathered in my name, I am there in the midst of them' (Mt 18:20) is eminently true of this *local assembly* of the holy Church. *For in the celebration of Mass, in which the sacrifice of the Cross is perpetuated, Christ is really present in the very community gathered in his name, in the person of the minister, in his word, and also substantially and continuously under the Eucharistic species.*" (Italicised words were added.)

Similar additions were made to other articles: article 48 had read: 'The Last Supper, in which Christ instituted the memorial of his death and resurrection'—it was corrected to: 'At the Last Supper, Christ instituted the paschal sacrifice and banquet'; 'the institution narrative' in article 55d became 'the institution and consecration narrative'; article 60 had

presented the priest as president of the assembly of the faithful—corrected, it reads: 'In virtue of his ordination the priest is the member of the community of the faithful who possesses the power to offer sacrifice in the person of Christ"; there are references added to the Decree on the Ministry and Life of Priests, n. 2, and the Constitution on the Church, n. 28.

Were the Observers, separated brethren, who were present at drafting sessions influential in the composition of the first inadequate text? Fortunately the corrections were made. It is naive to dismiss the uneasiness caused by the first text as groundless. There is no question of impugning the integrity of the Protestant observers—they must speak as they believe.

To reassure entirely those disturbed, Pope Paul had a preface composed which, in fifteen articles, admirably summarized Eucharistic doctrine; direct reference is frequently made to the Council of Trent. To impose the new Order of Mass authoritatively the Pope issued an Apostolic Constitution, 3 April 1969. Therein he explains the alterations.

The Pope devoted, proportionately to other matters, a large section of the Credo of the People of God to the Eucharist. "We believe that the Mass which is celebrated by the priest in the person of Christ in virtue of the power he receives in the Sacrament of Order, and which is offered by him in the name of Christ and of the members of his Mystical Body, is indeed the Sacrifice of Calvary sacramentally realized on our altars. We believe that, as the bread and wine consecrated by the Lord at the Last Supper were changed into his Body and Blood which were to be offered for us on the Cross, so likewise are the bread and wine consecrated by the priest changed into the Body and Blood of Christ now enthroned in glory in heaven. We believe that the mysterious presence of the Lord under the appearance of those things which, as far as our senses are concerned, remain unchanged, is a true, real and substantial presence. Consequently, in this Sacrament there is no other way in which Christ can be present except through the conversion of the entire substance of bread into his Body and through the conversion of the entire substance of wine into his Blood, leaving unchanged only those properties of bread and wine which are open to our senses. This hidden conversion is appropriately and justly called by the Church *transubstantiation.* Any theological explanation intent on arriving at some understanding of this mystery, if it is to be in accordance with Catholic faith, must maintain, without ambiguity, that in the order of reality which exists independently of the human mind, the bread and wine cease to exist after the consecration. From then on, therefore, the Body and Blood of the Lord Jesus, under the sacramental appearances of bread and wine (DS, 1642, 1651-54; Paul VI, *Mysterium Fidei)*, are truly presented before us for our adoration, this being the will of the Lord himself in order that he might be our food and might incorporate us into the unity of his Mystical Body (S. Th. III, 73, 3). The unique and indivisible existence of Christ the Lord, whereby he lives in the glory of heaven, is not multiplied by the Sacrament but rendered present in every place on earth where the Eucharistic Sacrifice is celebrated. Here indeed we have that *Mystery of Faith* and Eucharistic blessings to which we must unequivocally give our assent. And this same existence remains present after the Sacrifice in the Most Blessed Sacrament which is reserved in the tabernacle, the living heart of our churches. It is, then, our bounden and loving duty to honour and adore in the Blessed Bread, which we see with our eyes, the Word Incarnate himself, whom we cannot see, but who, nonetheless, without leaving heaven, is made present before us."[2]

There is a reference in this admirable statement to the Encyclical, *Mysterium Fidei* (qv), issued while the Council was still in session. In 1967 the Sacred Congregation of Rites published a lengthy Instruction, *Eucharisticum Mysterium* (qv and see article Vagaggini, Cipriano). The Pope did his utmost in the difficult situation after the Council to restrain excess on either wing, to correct deviations from true doctrine. In his magisterial *Marialis Cultus* he showed how to unite Marian piety and liturgical excellence.

In the perspective of time Paul VI's contribution to the ecumenical movement takes on special significance. He fostered, encouraged or welcomed dialogue on the Eucharist, and saw the fruits in such agreements as are related in the present work (see articles on ARCIC, Dombes Group, Lutheran-Catholic agreement, Lima agreement). Noting with sadness the difficulties felt by priests the Pope took special initiatives to help them and to fortify their commitment, knowing that thus he served the Eucharistic Lord. For the Church at large the Pope's example was vivid at Eucharistic Congresses, notably in India and Latin America. His was a pontificate centred on the Eucharist, manifold in this service.

[1]Besides, *AAS, Insegnamenti* and *L'Osservatore Romano,* esp. weekly ed., cf. Daniel-Ange, Paul VI, un regard prophétique; 2 vols. I, *Un amour qui se donne,* Paris, 1979; II, *L'éternelle Pentecôte,* Paris, 1981; esp. *Paul VI et la modernité dans l'Eglise,* Colloque 2-4 June, 1983, Rome; ed. G. Vallet, C. Pietri, *Collection de l'Ecole française de Rome,* 1984, 875pp; TSp XII, 522-536.

PECTORIUS, EPITAPH OF

An inscription in Greek found in seven fragments near Autun in 1830, successfully deciphered and published by the great patristic scholar, J.B. Pitra.[1] He and another eminent archaeologist, J.B. de Rossi, dated it to the beginning of the second century; E.L. Blunt and J. Wilker disagreed, opting for the end of the third century. More recent opinion favours between 350 and 400, though the first part may be from an older poem from about the second century. It runs thus: "O divine race of the heavenly Fish, keep your heart pure, for you, among mortal men, have received the immortal spring of divine waters. Friend, refresh your soul in the eternal streams of enriching wisdom. Receive the food sweet as honey, of the Saviour of the saints. Eat your fill, drink your fill when you receive the Fish in the palms of your hands. I pray you, Master and Saviour, give us the Fish for our food. Let my mother rest in peace, I pray you, O Light of the dead. Aschandius, father beloved of my heart, with my sweet mother and my brothers, in the peace of the Fish, remember Pectorius."

The symbolism of the Fish representing Christ is well established. The essence of the epitaph is then Eucharistic.

[1]Tr. L. Deiss, *Springtime,* 261, 62; cf. J. Quasten, *Monumenta,* 24-27; *id., Patrology,* I, 173-75; *id.,* NCE, XI, 49-50; *id., Fish as symbol, ibid.,* V, 943-46; M. Guarducci, *Rendiconti della Pontificia Accademia d'Archaeologia,* 23-24 1947-49.

PETER D'AILLY (1350-1420)

French theologian, one time Chancellor of the then prestigious University of Paris, P. was involved in the ecclesiastical disputes—as to the lawful occupant of the Papacy—took part in the Council of Constance which condemned Wycliffe (qv); he had a considerable literary output, 175 items listed.[1] He deals with the Eucharist in his commentary on the Sentences. Where he surprises is in his readiness to consider impanation (qv). He defines transubstantiation—which he accepts as the official teaching of the Church—thus: "Transubstantiation is the immediate succession of two things not having a common matter or subject, of which the second is the substance which begins to be of itself and principally where the other ceases wholly to be."

P. thinks that though Catholics have agreed that the "body of Christ is truly and principally in the sacrament under the appearances of bread and wine, there have been different opinions on the mode or manner." He considers three theories thereon: "the substance of bread becomes the body of Christ" in the sense that bread as such becomes his body; "the substance of bread does not remain bread, nor does it cease to be *simpliciter,* but it is reduced to matter standing on its own or receiving another form, and this either in the same place or elsewhere, while the body of Christ coexists with the accidents of bread"—he thinks that this theory "could not be rejected on grounds of manifest reason or compelling scriptural authority"; thirdly, "the substance of bread remains."

P. mentions two ways in which this might happen: one, that it would remain where the body of Christ begins to be; the other, that it would move to another place. He deals with the first as he considers the second unreasonable. He thinks that it is possible that the substances of bread and wine could be assumed by the body of Christ—he thinks this is opposed neither to reason nor the authority of the Bible; can see no difficulty if it could "agree with the decision of the Church." He is finally led to opt firmly for the "common opinion of the saints and doctors": "the substance of bread does not remain but ceases to be *simpliciter*." He does not think that this manifestly follows from Scripture and he judges that the Church favours it more than that it has made a clearcut decision. He is also orthodox on the question of the "accidents" existing without their proper subject: he accepts the Scotist idea of annihilation (see Scotus, Duns). Though P's speculation is but theoretical and his orthodoxy certain, he was bound to be misquoted and his doctrine abused later in times of controversy.

---

[1]Commentary on the Sentences, 4th ed., Venice, 1500; cf. *In IV Sent.*, q. 6: quotations here apud E.C. Messenger, *The Reformation*, I, 100-102.

PETER LOMBARD (c. 11-1160)

The master compiler of his age, P. born in Lombardy, educated and a teacher in France, eventually Bishop of Paris, influenced medieval thinking considerably.[1] Besides commentaries on the Psalms and the epistles of St. Paul, he was author of the *Sententiarum libri quattuor*, a text-book not of striking originality but laying out theological material widely collected in an order that suited the growing academic community and invited commentaries from several of the masters then and for some generations. The sources were medieval, patristic—some Greek with the first large borrowing from St. John of Damascus and the Latins, especially Ambrose, Hilary and Augustine (qqv).

P's Eucharistic doctrine is contained in the fourth book of the Sentences, dist. VIII to XIII, and the commentary on 1 Cor, 11:23-24. The theme of the fourth book is the Sacraments and the Last Things and P. finds the place of the Eucharist therein: he first fixed the number of the Sacraments at seven. He is

mostly concerned with the Eucharist as Sacrament. He deals with the institution, matter and form, the twofold eating, sacramental and spiritual, the real Eucharistic presence, the conversion of bread and wine into the Body and Blood of Christ, the accidents, validity of consecration by heretics and those excommunicated.

P. deals briefly with the question of sacrifice (qv). The main preoccupation still in his age was the real presence; the shadow of Berengar (qv) still hung over the schools, and his supporters were not all defunct. "There are some of those mentioned who, beyond lunacy, measuring the power of God by the manner of natural things, contradict the truth boldly and dangerously, stating that the Body or Blood of Christ are not on the altar, that the substance of bread or wine is not converted into the substance of the Flesh and Blood, but that Christ said, *This is my Body*, as the Apostle said, '*But the rock was Christ*'. For they say that the Body of Christ is there only sacramentally, by which they mean only as a sign, and solely as a sign is it eaten."[2]

The idea of transubstantiation was current in P's generation. He does not use the term. But '*substantia*' had been given theological status by the Oath of Berengar and he accepted it. There is some question about his idea of the change. Elsewhere he says: "And thus what was bread before the consecration is already the Body of Christ after the consecration, because the word of Christ changes the creature and thus the bread becomes the Body of Christ and the wine with water put in the chalice becomes Blood by the consecration of the heavenly word. Thus Augustine. As through the Holy Spirit the true flesh of Christ is created without sexual union so through the same Spirit from the substance of bread and wine the same Body and Blood of Christ are consecrated; the Body and Blood of Christ are produced by the power of the Holy Spirit from the substance of bread and wine; what is externally perceived is a figure."[3] Here P. does not use the word substance of the Body and Blood.

P. had given, in the commentary on the Pauline epistle, a summary of what he would give later.[4] Dealing with sacrifice, in the Sentences, he leans particularly on the point of Christ's unique sacrifice: "Christ died once on the Cross and was immolated in himself, but each day he is immolated; in the Sacrament there is a memorial of what was once accomplished.... Yes, we offer every day, but it is in memory of his death; and there is but one victim, not many. How one and not many? Because Christ was immolated only once. But this sacrifice is the copy of that ; it is always and everywhere the same victim who is offered. Are there many Christs? No, the one Christ is everywhere, fully existing here and there.... From which it may be gathered that what takes place on the altar is and is said to be a sacrifice; and Christ was once offered, and is daily offered but in different ways formerly and now."[5]

P. has a strange idea on why communion under both species takes place: the bread represents the body and the wine the blood. He is not consistent in his view on whether heretical or excommunicated priests can consecrate. He thinks in terms of the Church, whose sacrifice it is, whom they cannot represent, and the angels who are called on to bear the sacrifice on high, whose company they cannot share. Elsewhere he is not so sure.[6]

[1]Works PL 191, 192; Sentences ed. Quaracchi, 1871; E. Rodgers, *Peter Lombard and the Sacramental System,* 1917; cf. J. de Ghellinck, S.J., *Le mouvement théologique au XIIe siècle,* 1914, 73-244; id., DTC, V, 1298f; id., DTC XII, 2, 1941-2019; id., *L'essor de la litterature latine au XIIe siècle,* 1946; M. Lepin, *L'idée du sacrifice,* 147-157; EC IX, 1952, 1438-40, A. Piolanti; DSp XII, 1604-12 I. Brady; LTK VIII 367-69, I. Brady, A. Emmen; NCE XI 221-22, I. Brady; [2]*In Sentent.,* lib. IV, dist. X, 1, PL 192, 859; [3]*Ibid.,* 861; [4]PL 191, 1641; [5]Dist. XII, PL 191, 1641; [6]Cf. M. de La Taille, S.J., (qv) 423f.

PETROBUSIANS (12th Century)

Followers of a heretic, Peter de Bruys (d.c. 1140), who seems to have been a priest, who in the course of preaching in the Dauphiné and Provence, attracted a certain following.[1] Among his many errors was denial of the Mass and rejection of church buildings. He was condemned in these terms by Lateran Council II: "Those, moreover, who pretending a kind of piety condemn the sacrament of the body and blood of the Lord, the baptism of children, the sacred ministry and other ecclesiastical orders, and the bonds of legitimate marriages, we drive as heretics from the Church of God, and we both condemn and we command them to be restrained by exterior powers. We bind their defenders also by the chain of this same condemnation." This canon has been taken literally from the Council of Toulouse of the year 1119, which was held in the presence of Pope Callistus II.

[1]Sources: Peter the Venerable, *Tractatus adversus Petrobusianos Haereticos,* CCCM, ed J. Faerns, 10, 1968, and Peter Abelard, *Introductio ad Theologiam,* II, 4, PL 178, 1056; cf. J.J. von Dollinger, *Beiträge zur Sektengeschichte des Mittelalters,* I, 1890, 75-97; E. Vacandard, *Les origines de l'heresie albigeoise, Revue des Questions Historiques,* 55 (1894), 50-83; J. Kamp, *Chronologisches zu Peters* Ehrwurdigen *Epistola adversus Petrobusianos,* in *Miscellanea Francisco Ehrle* (ST 37, 1923, 71-79; J.C. Reagan, *Did the Petrobusians Teach Salvation by Faith Alone? The Journal of Religion* 7 (1927) 81-91; R. Mansell, *Studi sulle eresie del secolo XII, Studi Storici* 5, Rome 1953, 1-23; F. Vernet, DTC VI 2, 2178-81; id., DTC II, 1151-56;

PIOLANTI, MGR. ANTONIO (1911-   )

The present work is much indebted to the published works of this prolific, singularly erudite Italian theologian. His *magnum opus, Il Mistero Eucaristico,* 3rd ed, 1984, 679 pp, has been a constant quarry. He has had a rich, fruitful career in third-level teaching of theology—in the Propaganda and Lateran Universities, in academic administration, directing, as Rector of the Lateran, a programme of expansion to meet modern demands, especially in writing and editorial direction: he is director of the review *Doctor Communis,* organ of the Roman Academy of St. Thomas, of which he is Vice-president. He has founded and continues to edit the review *Divinitas* and two Thomistic collections, *Studi Tomistici* and *Bibliotheca per la storia del tomismo.* He has discharged several functions in the Roman Curia, notably Consultor of the Holy Office and of the Congregation for the Propagation of the Faith. He helped prepare the Roman Synod called by John XXIII, was a member of the Preparatory Theological Commission of Vatican II and an expert to the Council. Apart from articles in theological dictionaries and encyclopedias and 210 articles in EC, of which he was joint editor, Mgr. Piolanti's bibliography runs to 247 items, books and articles for scientific reviews—articles in the Catholic press are not listed.

From his first publications in 1938-39 through the years to the one mentioned for 1984, Mgr. Piolanti has continually chosen Eucharistic themes for his study. He began in 1938-39 with an edition of an unpublished work by Cardinal Francesco Mendoza on *The Eucharist and the Mystical Body,* 1938, and in the following year with a book, 230 pp, on *The Mystical Body and the Eucharist in St. Albert the Great* (qv). Forty-five of the 247 items listed deal directly or indirectly with the Eucharist, as do a much higher proportion of the contributions to EC. Besides *Eucaristia* which he edited and to which he contributed four important articles, he has published substantial works on the Sacraments, many times re-edited, and on the Incarnation, *Christologia* for his students, 1962, *Dio-Uomo,* 1964, 666 pp, for general readership. The breadth of his interests is evident from his profound knowledge of St. Thomas over a wide range of subjects and his attention to the problems raised by Protestantism,[2] as from his presentation of theism in contemporary terms and his frequent essays on divine grace.[3] Paul VI paid tribute in 1969 to the varied, incessant, meritorious services of Mgr. Piolanti to the Church and to higher education.[4]

[1]Much information in the *Festschrift* offered to Mgr. Piolanti on the occasion of his priestly Golden Jubilee, *Cinquant'anni di*

Magistero Teologico in 1984, preface, Card. M.L. Ciappi, O.P., Rome, Pontificia Accademia di S. Tommaso, 1985; bibl. 15-33; [2]'*Il Protestantesimo ieri e oggi*', ed. A. Piolanti, Ferrari, 1958, 1398 pp.; [3]'*Dio nel mondo e nell'uomo*', Rome, 1958, 678 pp; *Aspetti della grazia*, Rome, 1958; *Natura e Grazia*, Rome, 1958; ed. 'Il Soprannaturale' with contributions, e.g. 'La realtà della vita divina,' 281-301; [4]Personal letter to Mgr. Piolanti, *L'Osservatore Romano*, 20 August 1969.

PISTOIA, SYNOD OF (1786)

Bishop Scipio de Ricci, of the diocese of Pistoia-Prato, to support the policy of Leopold I, Grand Duke of Tuscany who had appointed him, called and organised a synod to further Leopold's programme of a reform which would borrow from French Gallicanism and imperial Josephinism.[1] The synod met in Pistoia. The errors contained in the synodal decrees were condemned by Pius VI in the Constitution, *Auctorem Fidei*, 28 August 1794. What concerns the Eucharist is as follows:

The Partaking of the Victim in the Sacrifice of the Mass (The Eucharist, sec. 6): The proposition of the synod in which, after it states that 'a partaking of the victim is an essential part in the sacrifice,' it adds, 'nevertheless, it does not condemn as illicit those Masses in which those present do not communicate sacramentally, for the reason that they do partake of the victim, although less perfectly, by receiving it spiritually,' since it insinuates that there is something lacking to the essence of the sacrifice in that sacrifice which is performed either with no one present, or with those present who partake of the victim neither sacramentally nor spiritually, and as if those Masses should be condemned as illicit, in which, with the priest alone communicating, no one is present who communicates either sacramentally or spiritually, false, erroneous, suspected of heresy and savouring of it.

The Efficacy of the Rite of Consecration (The Eucharist, sec. 2) The doctrine of the synod, in that part in which, undertaking to explain the doctrine of faith in the rite of consecration, and disregarding the scholastic questions about the manner in which Christ is in the Eucharist, from which questions it exhorts priests performing the duty of teaching to refrain, it states the doctrine in these two propositions only: 1) after the consecration Christ is truly, really, substantially under the species; 2) then the whole substance of bread and wine ceases, appearances only remaining; it (the doctrine) absolutely omits to make any mention of transubstantiation, or conversion of the whole substance of the bread into the body, and of the whole substance of the wine into the blood, which the Council of Trent (qv) defined as an article of faith, and which is contained in the solemn profession of faith; since by an indiscreet and suspicious omission of this sort knowledge is taken away both of an article pertaining to faith, and also of the word consecrated by the Church to protect the profession of it, as if it were a discussion of a merely scholastic question—dangerous, derogatory to the exposition of Catholic truth about the dogma of transubstantiation, favourable to heretics.

The Application of the Fruit of the Sacrifice (The Eucharist, sec. 8) The doctrine of the synod, by which, while it professes 'to believe that the oblation of the sacrifice extends itself to all, in such a way, however, that in the liturgy there can be made a special commemoration of certain individuals, both living and dead, by praying God specially for them,' then it immediately adds: 'Not, however, that we should believe that it is in the will of the priest to apply the fruit of the sacrifice to whom he wishes, rather we condemn this error as greatly offending the rights of God, who alone distributes the fruit of the sacrifice to whom he wishes and according to the measure which pleases him'; and consequently, from this it derides 'as false the opinion foisted on the people that they who give alms to the priest on the condition that he celebrate a Mass will receive from it special fruit'; thus understood that besides the special commemoration and prayer a special offering itself, or application of the sacrifice which is made by the priest does not benefit, other things being equal, those for whom it is applied more than any others, as if no special fruit would come from a special application, which the Church recommends and commands should be made for definite persons or classes of persons, especially by pastors for their flock, and which, as if coming down from a divine precept, has been clearly expressed by the sacred synod of Trent (sess. 23, c. 1 *de reform*; Bened. XIV, Const. '*Cum semper oblatas*', sec 2)—false, rash, dangerous, injurious to the Church, leading into the error elsewhere condemned in Wycliffe.

The Suitable Order to be Observed in Worship (The Eucharist, sec 5). The proposition of the synod enunciating that it is fitting, in accordance with the order of divine services and ancient customs, that there be only one altar in each temple, and, therefore, that it is pleased to restore that custom—rash, injurious to the very ancient pious custom flourishing and approved for these many centuries in the Church, especially in the Latin Church.

(Ibid.)

Likewise, the prescription forbidding cases of sacred relics or flowers being placed on the altar—rash, injurious to the pious and approved custom of the Church.

(Ibid., sec. 6)

The proposition of the synod by which it shows

itself eager to remove the cause through which, in part, there has been induced a forgetfulness of the principles relating to the order of the liturgy, 'by recalling it (the liturgy) to a greater simplicity of rites, by expressing it in the vernacular language, by uttering it in a loud voice'; as if the present order of the liturgy, received and approved by the Church, had emanated in some part from forgetfulness of the principles by which it should be regulated—rash, offensive to pious ears, insulting to the Church, favourable to the charges of heretics against it."[2]

It is for historians to evaluate the degree of coercion, moral and even physical, which was used to secure passage in the congregations, of the various decrees which are here stigmatised. This was Jansenism à l'Italienne, deriving from Jansen and Quesnel but adapted for consumption south of the Alps. A wider question is to what extent the synod was deflected from doctrinal pronouncements which would have been beneficial, an anticipation of Vatican II. Whether they would have then found favour is clearly also problematic.

[1]Sources: *Memorie* of Scipio de Ricci, ed. 2 vols, A. Galli, Florence, 1865, and *Atti e decreti del concilio diocesano di Pistoia dell'anno 1786*, Pavia, 1788; decrees widely translated; cf. F. Anfossi, *Difesa della Bolla 'Auctoren Fidei'*, 3 vols, Rome, 1876; G. Baldasseroni, *Leopoldo II, Granduca di Toscano e i suoi tempi*, Florence, 1871; A.G. Jemolo, *Il giansenismo in Italia prima della rivoluzione*, Bari, 1928; B. Matteucci, *Scipione de Ricci: Saggio storicoteologico sul giansenismo italiano*, Brescia, 1941, bibl 228-330; id., *Il giansenismo*, Rome, 1954; E. Passerin, *Il fallimento dell'offensiva riformata di Scipione de Ricci secondo nuovi documenti (1781-1788) Rivista di Storia della Chiesa in Italia*, 9 (1955) 99-131; C.A. Bolton, *Church Reform in 18th Century Italy (The Synod of Pistoia, 1786)*, Archives Internationales d'Histoire des Idées, The Hague, 1969; J. Carreyre, DTC XII, 2, 2176-99; L. Willaert, LTK VIII, 324-25; B. Matteucci, NCE XI, 388-90; [2]DS 2628-2633; Msi 38.

PIUS V, ST. (1504-1572), POPE (From 1566)
In the six years of his pontificate he made a decisive contribution to church life and notably influenced liturgical reform.[1] His predecessor, Pius IV (d. 1565), had set up a commission to implement the decisions of the Council of Trent (qv). We have no minutes of its sessions. It was Pius V who, 14 July 1570, promulgated by a Bull the *Missale Romanum ex decreto ss. Concilii Tridentini restitutum, Pii V Pont. Max jussu editum*. It was accompanied by *Rubricae Generales* and a *Ritus servandus in celebratione Missae*. Reform was thorough. The liturgical cycle was freed of a mass of feasts of saints, accumulated during the Middle Ages and submerging Sundays; only those adopted by Rome before the eleventh century were retained. Thus one hundred and fifty days were free, without counting octaves. The multiplicity of votive Masses was also restrained. The ordinary of the Mass was simplified: most of the Sequences dropped, the private prayers and gestures of the celebrant reduced to order, the hymns which were sung even during the Canon, cut down, drastically. A choice was given between private and conventual Mass, the latter possible because of the many religious still in monasteries. Pius V did not see his ambitious programme fully realised; certain accretions of the Carolingian age remained. But the invention of printing helped to achieve uniformity. The Pope, as we often hear nowadays, laid down that no change was to be made in the Missal he was promulgating. The rule must be seen in context. He wished to bar the frequent rearrangements of medieval times. His successors, Clement VIII, 1604, Urban VIII, 1634, St. Pius X (qv), did not understand it absolutely.

[1]A.G. Martimort, ed. *L'Eglise en Prière*, III, R. Cabie, 191, 2;

PIUS VI (1717-1799), POPE (From 1775)
By the Constitution *"Auctorem fidei"* Pius condemned the errors of the Synod of Pistoia (qv);[1] a number touched Eucharistic doctrine.

[1]Bibl. article Pistoia.

PIUS X, ST. (1835-1914), POPE (From 1903)
The saintly Pope's motto, 'To restore all things in Christ' was applied especially in the domain of Eucharistic worship and piety (see article Communion, Holy).[1] The Decree of 20 December 1905, which ended the "plague of Jansenism" (qv), was issued by the Congregation of the Holy Council and approved by the Pope. It contained the significant words: "But his Holiness, since it is especially dear to him that the Christian people be invited to the sacred banquet very frequently and even daily, and so gain possession of its most ample fruits..." The two essential points in the directives submitted to him were that the one condition necessary was to be "free from mortal sin," and the reduction of the power hitherto used—unfortunately abused—by the confessor: "Let the counsel of the confessor intercede. Yet let confessors beware lest they turn anyone away from frequent or daily communion, who is found in a state of grace, and approaches (it) with a right mind."[2]

The second epoch-making liberating decree was to admit children at an early age to Holy Communion. The "age of discretion," the decree laid down, "is that at which the child begins to reason, that is, about the seventh year, more or less. The obligation of satisfying both precepts of confession and communion begins from that time." "Full and perfect knowledge of Christian doctrine is not necessary ... (the child) in accord with his capacity perceives the mysteries of faith necessary by a necessity of means, and by which he distinguishes Eucharistic bread from the common and corporeal." The duties of those with care for the children are clarified; abuses about refusing confession to them, or, in danger of death, denying them Viaticum, are severely condemned.[3]

The Pope's policy of restoring Plain Chant to its due place in the Liturgy helped promote an atmosphere of piety towards the Eucharist. Indirectly his strictures on the errors of Modernism have an important bearing on the theology of the Eucharist: the error about the origin of the sacraments condemned in the Decree *Lamentabili* (39, 40, 41, 54);[4] the errors about the origin of dogma, and about the authority of the Church set forth in the Encyclical *Pascendi dominici gregis*.[5]

---

[1]Documents in *ASS* and *AAS*; in *Papal Teachings*, St. Paul, Boston, *The Liturgy*, 1962 and *The Catholic Priesthood, Papal Documents*, ed. Mgr. P. Veuillot, Dublin 1957, I, 7-89; *All Things in Christ*, English tr. of the documents of St. Pius X, E. Ysermans, Westminster, Md., 1954; cf. Life by G. Dal-Gal, English tr., ed. G.F. Murray, Westminster, Md, 1954; S. Tramontin, *Profilo di storia della Chiesa italiana dall'Unità ad oggi*, Turin, 1980; id., *Un secolo di storia della Chiesa. Da Leone XIII al Concilio Vaticano II*, Rome, 1980; 51-109, bibl 105-109; A. Zambarbierieri, *Dizionario del Movimento Cattolico*, II, Turin, 1983, 40-53; (see article Teaching Authority); [2]DS 3383; [3]DS 3532; 3536; [4]DS 3440, 1, 2; [5]DS 3475 ff;

PIUS XII (1876-1958), POPE (From 1939)

Before his election as Pope Pius XII—Cardinal Pacelli as he then was—had given evidence of profound Eucharistic idealism and piety: as Legate of Pius XI to the Triduum for Peace at Lourdes in 1935 and as his Legate to two International Eucharistic Congresses (qv), at Buenos Aires in 1934 and Budapest in 1938. At Lourdes he gave a Holy Hour (qv) for priests, in the course of which he spoke with profound insight on the Eucharist in the life of the priest.

As Pope, Pius had many opportunities to expound his views on the Eucharist. Jewels of Eucharistic doctrine, pastorally oriented, are found in the many addresses he gave to Eucharistic Congresses. Thus to the young church of Australia he recalled the memory of the first Mass celebrated one hundred and fifty years previously: "Their Eucharistic Lord was with them again. The Holy Mass had forged a link uniting them with their dear ones far over seas, and surely the hills and dales of their native land were heard to echo the joy that filled their hearts." But this historical memory is to evoke a more solemn one: "The Mass,

your daily Mass, carries the memory back far beyond the brief span of a century-and-a-half. It transports you in spirit to 'a large upper room furnished' of a house in Jerusalem. It is Thursday night, almost two thousand years ago. Jesus had eaten the paschal lamb with his Apostles." There follows the Lucan institution narrative: "On that traitorous, yet never so triumphant Holy Thursday night, the Sacred Heart of Jesus was asking us all, through the Apostles on whom he was to found his Church (cf. Eph 2:20) to remember the sacrifice he so lovingly, so eagerly even, accepted for our salvation: to commemorate it all days, from the rising of the sun to the setting of the same, down through the ages and across the five continents of his kingdom on earth."[2]

Speaking to a congress in Turin, 'City of the Blessed Sacrament,' Pius spoke thus: "In this solemn hour, let us, as Vicar and mouthpiece of Jesus, hidden but truly present, testify once again to you that marvellous, fruitful action exercised by the Blessed Eucharist in the secret depths of souls and among the whole congregation of the faithful. Everything true, everything holy, everything eternal, everything divine accomplished by the Church in her two thousand years of existence has its origin, development and nourishment in the mystery of the Eucharist. History is quick to testify and prove that at every time and in every place where devotion to the Blessed Sacrament flourished, there were recorded those wonderful Christian achievements of which Catholicism is justly proud—from the three centuries of heroic resistance of the first Christian communities, whose indomitable energy was drawn from the hallowed table of the breaking of Bread, to a prodigious expansion of Christian ideas and institutions; and from the prompt recovery of strength after temporary local decline, to the rich harvest of Saints, from charitable, educational and scientific institutions, to the marvellous conquests of missionaries. No holy supernatural action, no good and great deed has ever been performed by Christ's followers on earth, which did not draw inspiration and strength from the Eucharist, that is, from Christ himself become the food of souls."[3]

Again speaking to a congress in Brazil, he extols the Eucharist thus: "Mystery of divine and infinite mercy! Sign and efficacious seal of unity! Bond of charity, symbol of peace and harmony! (August. *in Joann. Ev. tract XXVI, n. 13*; PL 35, 1613; *Conc. Trid., Sess XIII*, c. 8). One and the same Victim to be adored on every altar; one and the same divine food served everywhere at the Holy Table: and all men, without distinction of race or nationality, of social condition or class, all equally called to believe, adore and share, that all might equally partake of his Body and Blood, all be raised to the same noble heights, sharers in the divine nature (Chrysost. *in Joann. hom XLVI*, n. 3, PG 33, 1100; cf. 2 Pet 1:4); that all might feel that, being more than brothers, they are members of the same mystic Body of Christ, loving one another in heart and deed, as though loving Christ himself (cf. Chrysost. in 1 Cor hom *XXIV*, n. 2, PG 61,200)."[4]

In the doctrinal Encyclicals, *Mediator Dei* (qv) and *Mystici Corporis Christi* (qv), the exposition is more theological; in *Haurietis Aquas* the Pope explains the basis of devotion to the Eucharistic Heart (qv) of Jesus. In his exhortation to priests to aim at holiness of life, he speaks of the need for devotion to the Eucharist, and he urges this piety too on seminarists: "Young seminarists will find no great difficulty in acquiring these and all the other priestly virtues, if from boyhood they have imbibed a genuine and tender devotion to Christ Jesus 'truly, really and substantially' present under the species of the most venerable Sacrament and dwelling on earth among us, and if also, all their projects and labours have been inspired by Christ and directed to him."[5] A similar thought is expressed in *Sacra Virginitas*: "The more pure and chaste a soul is, the more it hungers for this bread, from which it derives strength to resist all temptations to sins of impurity, and by which it is more intimately united with the divine Spouse; 'He who eats my flesh and drinks my blood, abides in me and I in him.'"[6]

The Pope knew how to condemn error as he showed in *Humani Generis* in regard to transubstantiation (qv); he also dealt with this subject in his address to the Assisi Liturgical Congress.

[1]For texts besides official collections, *AAS* 1939-1958, *Discorsi e Radiomessagi*, 20 vols, ed. in French, *Documents Pontificaux de Pie XII*, 20 vols., ed. St. Augustin, St. Maurice-Paris, 1950-1962; esp. *Papal Teachings*, St. Paul, Boston, *The Liturgy*, 1962 and *The Catholic Priesthood, Papal Documents*, ed. Mgr. P. Veuillot, 2 vols, Dublin, 1957, 195, vol. I, part 2, 1-309; vol. II, 1-262; cf. esp., D. Bertetto, S.D.B., *Il magistero eucaristico di Pio XII*, Turin, 1957, texts and commentary; A. Piolanti (qv), *De symbolismo et ubiquismo eucharistico a Pio XII proscriptis*, in *Euntes Docete*, 1951, 56-71; M. O'Carroll, C.S.Sp., *Pius XII, Greatness Dishonoured*, Dublin, 1980, 202-209; id., DSp XII, 1438-1442; in *Pius XII. Zum Gedächtnis*, ed. H. Schambeck, Berlin, 1977, Pietro Cardinal Parente, *Philosophie und Theologie in der Lehre von Pius XII*, 29-50; G. Caprile, *Pius XII und das Zweite Vatikanische Konzil*, 649-692; R. Leiber, S.J., NCE, XI, 414-418; (see article Teaching Authority); [2]*AAS* 45 (1953), 296, 97; [3]*AAS* 45 (1953), 552, 53; [4]*AAS* 47 (1955), 612, 13; [5]Apostolic Exhortation *'Menti nostrae,'* *The Catholic Priesthood*, ed. Mgr. Veuillot, I, pt 2, 193; [6]Encyclical *'Sacra Virginitas'* ibid., 305.

PLINY'S LETTER ON THE CHRISTIANS

Eusebius, in his *Historia Ecclesiastica,* gives the background for a much-quoted text from Roman literature on Christianity: "So great a persecution was at that time opened against us in many places that Plinius Secundus, one of the most noted of governors, being disturbed by the great number of martyrs, communicated with the emperor concerning the multitude of those that were put to death for their faith. At the same time he informed him in his communication that he had not heard of their doing anything profane or contrary to the laws—except that they rose at dawn and sang hymns to Christ as God; but that they renounced adultery and murder and like criminal offences, and did all things in accordance with the laws. In reply to this Trajan made the following decree: "that the race of Christians should not be sought after, but when found should be punished."[1]

Pliny the Younger, nephew and adopted son of the elder Pliny, was governor of the Roman province of Bithynia in Asia Minor from 109 or 110 until his death in 113. Of the letter which he wrote to the emperor Trajan, which Eusebius mentions, the passage relevant to our subject is as follows: "They insisted that this was the extent of their crime, or error: It was their practice to meet, on an appointed day, before sunrise, to sing together among themselves a hymn to Christ, as to a god, and to bind themselves by an oath, not for any criminal activity, but not to commit theft, or robbery, or adultery, not to perjure themselves, not to refuse to return property left with them when called upon to do so. Upon the completion of these activities, their practice was to separate, and to assemble again to take food, but of an ordinary and harmless kind."[2]

Is this a reference to a Eucharist, or to an agape? Opinion is affirmed with difficulty. The community life of the Christians was already something noted. It is possible that such a community meeting was the occasion of a Eucharist, or an agape (qv).

[1]Bk III, ch. 33, LNPF, I, 164, 65; cf. D.Sheerin, *The Message*, 31f; A.N. Sherwin-White, *The Letters* of Pliny, Oxford, 1966, 702-708; M. Durry, *Pliny le Jeune: Lettres X et panégyrique de Trajan*, Paris, 1947: J.A. Jungmann, S.J., (qv), *The Mass of the Roman Rite*, I, 18; [2]D. Sheerin, *op.cit*, 32.

POST-CONCILIAR DOCUMENTS

Vatican Council II ed. A. Flannery, O.P., gives a descriptive list of post-conciliar documents down to 1975, two hundred and fifty in number. Of these, one hundred and twenty are liturgical, clearly by far the largest proportion. The editor made a selection, which is followed in the present work; the documents are dealt with briefly, named, according to church custom, from the first Latin words of the original. First there are those texts which relate directly to implementation of the Council teaching and directives: *Sacram litur-*

giam, 25 January 1964; *Inter oecumenici*, 26 September 1964; *Tres abhinc annos*, 4 May 1967; *Missale Romanum*, 3 April 1969; *Liturgiae Instaurationes*, 5 September 1970; *General Instruction on the Roman Missal*, 26 March 1970.

More numerous are the documents dealing with problems arising out of the post-conciliar programme, problems in the area of doctrine or practice: *Ecclesiae semper*, 7 March 1965; *Cum hac nostra aetate*, 14 February 1966; *Musicam sacram*, 5 March 1967; *Eucharisticum mysterium*, 25 May 1967; *Actio pastoralis Ecclesiae,* 15 May 1969; *Memoriale Domini,* 29 May 1969; *Sacramentali Communione*, 29 June 1970; *In celebratione Missae*, 7 August 1972; *Immensae caritatis*, 25 January 1973; *Eucharistiae participationem*, 27 April 1973; *Sanctus Pontifex*, 24 May 1973; *Eucharistiae Sacramentum*, 21 June 1973; *Pueros baptizatos*, 1 November 1973; *Instauratio liturgica*, 25 January 1974; *Firma in traditione*, 15 June 1974; *Conferentiarum episcopalium*, 28 October 1974; *Textus precis eucharisticae*, 1 November 1974; *Opportunum esse*, 1 November 1974; *Accidit in diversis*, 11 June 1976; to which documents of the pontificate of Paul VI must be added these from the pontificate of John Paul II: *Inaestimabile donum*, 3 April 1980; *Officum mihi*, 13 December 1980 (qqv).

PRESENCE, THE REAL

It is Catholic teaching that in the sacrament of the Eucharist the body and blood of Jesus Christ are present truly, really and substantially.[1] This article will show the certainty of the belief from the outset. The content of the biblical revelation is dealt with separately; so are the various heresies which arose during the centuries. A number of these are ultimately traceable to a strange fountain of error, Manicheism; diversity was caused by changing factors and conditions. Two moments when error took a different and more comprehensive form, the eleventh and sixteenth centuries, saw direct action by the Teaching Authority: against Berengar (qv) and the Reformers (qv).

The first non-biblical witness is within the influence of the Apostles: St. Ignatius of Antioch (qv). Here we are concerned only with the texts which are relevant to the Real Presence; other aspects of his Eucharistic doctrine are treated either in the article under his name or in the article 'Transubstantiation.' In the letter to the Smyrnaeans reacting against certain heretics, Docetists, he writes: "They abstain from Eucharist and prayer, because they did not confess that the Eucharist is the flesh of our Saviour Jesus Christ, who suffered for our sins, which the Father raised by his goodness. They then who deny the gift of God are perishing in their disputes; but it were better for them to have love, that they also may attain to the Resurrection."[2] Again we get this realism: "I have no pleasure in the food of corruption or in the delights of this life. I desire the 'bread of God,' which is the flesh of Jesus Christ, who was the 'seed of David,' and for drink I desire his blood, which is incorruptible love."[3]

The historical details added in these passages leaves no doubt about the reality of Christ's presence in the Eucharist. St. Justin Martyr was no less realistic: "For we do not receive these things as if they were ordinary food and drink. But just as Jesus Christ our Saviour was made flesh through the word of God and took on flesh and blood for our salvation, so too we (we have been taught) through the word of prayer that comes from him, the food over which the Eucharist has been spoken becomes the flesh and blood of the incarnate Jesus, in order to nourish and transform our flesh and blood."[4]

The tradition is continued in St. Irenaeus (qv) who refers to the Eucharist as the "blood and body of Christ." Tertullian (qv) many times cites the words of the Lord, "This is my body," with occasional use of symbolism, but many times with strong realism. With Origen there is the problem of his use of allegory. He did write these lines: "But we give thanks to the Creator of the universe and eat the loaves that are presented with thanksgiving and prayer over the gifts, so that by prayer they become a certain holy body which sanctifies those who partake of it with a pure intention."[5]

Four fourth-century Fathers, St. Cyril of Jerusalem (qv), St. John Chrysostom (qv), St. Cyril of Alexandria and St. Ambrose (qv), were singled out for quotation by Paul VI (qv). St. Cyril: "We have been instructed in these matters and filled with an unshakable faith, that that which seems to be bread is not bread, though it tastes like it, but the body of Christ, and that which seems to be wine, is not wine, though it too tastes as such, but the blood of Christ. . . . Draw inner strength by receiving this bread as spiritual food and your soul will rejoice."[6] St. John Chrysostom: "It is not the power of man which makes what is put before us the body and blood of Christ, but the power of Christ himself who was crucified for us. The priest standing there in the place of Christ says these words, but their power and grace are from God. *This is my body*, he says, and these words transform what lies before him."[7] St. Cyril of Alexandria: "Christ said indicating (the bread and wine): *This is my body*, and *This is my blood*, in order that you might not judge what you see to be a mere figure: the offerings, by the hidden power of God Almighty, are changed into Christ's body and blood, and by receiving these we come to share in the life-giving and sanctifying efficacy of Christ."[8] "St. Ambrose: "Let us be assured that this is not what nature formed but what the blessing consecrated; and that greater efficacy resides in the blessing than in nature, for by the blessing nature is changed.". . . "Surely the word of Christ, which could make out of nothing that which did not exist, can change things already in existence into what they were not. For it is no less extraordinary to give things new natures than to change their natures."[9] (For opinion of St. Augustine (qv) see article.)

Let us note, in passing, as more detail is given in the relevant articles, that the Oath of Berengar contains the words "after the consecration it is the true body of Christ . . . and the true blood of Christ."[10] Likewise, the words of Trent are: "First of all the holy Synod teaches and openly and simply professes that in the nourishing sacrament of the Holy Eucharist after the consecration of the bread, our Lord Jesus Christ, true God and man, is truly, really, and substantially contained under the species of those sensible things."[11]

The Church teaching summarized a vast body of continuous preaching, catechesis, liturgical practice, even archaeological (qv) evidence. The Real Presence is implied in the *Didache* (qv), in the Apostolic Tradition (qv) of Hippolytus (qv), in the anaphoras (qv), notably that of Serapion of Thmuis (qv): "O God of truth, may your holy Word come down upon this bread, that it may become the body of the Word, and upon this cup, that it may become the blood of the Truth." The epitaphs of the early centuries also have a message on the belief, as have the images in the Roman catacombs (see Abercius, Pectorius). To the essential truth, the faithful people of God have borne witness in age after age, showing that this is the living, lived faith of the Church. This faith is manifest in times of persecution, when priest and faithful flock assemble in secret; it is boldly professed by multitudes who gather in the great national and international eucharistic congresses, who join with the Pope as he celebrates the Eucharist in one country after another across the globe.

Through the intense controversies of the early centuries, Christological and Trinitarian, the one common bond of belief between heretics and orthodox was in the Eucharist. Different schools of thought interpreted different aspects of the mystery, the Antiochenes and Alexandrians moving along their separate paths to the same reality: the Alexandrians (Clement, Origen, Serapion, Cyril) displaying varying shades of symbolism, as did the Neoalexandrians (Cyril of Jerusalem, Basil, Gregory of Nazianzus, Gregory of Nyssa)—though we have seen examples of realism from them; the Antiochenes (St. John Chrysostom,

Theodore of Mopsuestia, Theodoretus), sticking to concrete realities, an Aristotelian influence, and to the letter of Sacred Scripture, gave prominence to the presence of Christ's real body and blood—they did not delay over the veil which faith must penetrate. In the thoroughness with which he made this approach, St. John Chrysostom was the greatest Eucharistic doctor of the Orient.

The giant intellect of Augustine held together and made a synthesis of the two tendencies, though his symbolism was in an ecclesiological context. In the Eucharist he distinguished: *id quod videtur*, the sensible species; *id quod creditur*, the body and blood of the Lord; *id quod intelligitur*, the whole mystery as a symbol of the Mystical Body. "What you see is the bread and the cup, the reality which meets your eyes. This is what your faith requires: the bread is the body of Christ, the cup is the blood of Christ. This is briefly stated for it suffices for faith. However, faith looks for enlightenment; as the Prophet says: 'Nisi credideritis, non intelligetis.' You can say to me: you have ordered us to believe, now explain so that we may be able to understand. If you wish to understand what is the body of Christ, hear the Apostle: *Vos autem estis corpus Christi et membra.*"[12]

The Middle Ages was to be, in Europe, a time of intense Eucharistic piety and to witness a summit of Eucharistic theology in the works of the scholastic doctors, foremost among them St. Thomas Aquinas (qv). In the ninth century the realists with Paschasius Radbert (qv) as their pioneer, were opposed by the symbolists, Ratramnus (qv), leading. Many names jostle for attention in the years immediately following. All appealed to Augustine as their patron. Symbolism reached a point of danger in the case of Berengar. Another phase opened, a massing of forces against Berengar, with, in succession, the flowering of the twelfth century. A genuine mystical dimension was not wanting.

The scholastic synthesis withstood the shock of sixteenth-century opposition. A whole new wave of Eucharistic theologians, early among them St. John Fisher, Bellarmine and others following, propounded the doctrine of the Real Presence with the intellectual resources and dialectical skills needed in the new situation. The eighteenth century was weak in theology, but the gains of the controversy were not lost. They were ready for full exploitation by Franzelin, Scheeben (qqv) and others in the nineteenth century, by Billot, De la Taille and a diverse company of dogmatic theologians, pastoral figures and spiritual writers in our own time.

Truth is never secure in immobility. So, with the ferment of new ideas and extravagant theories which immediately preceded and followed the Council, without even the most tenuous links with conciliar teaching, some strange perverted growths were to appear in the field of Eucharistic doctrine. They occasioned the Encyclical Letter of Paul VI (qv), *Mysterium Fidei* (qv), which was, among other things, a defence of the truth of the Real Presence—the Pope noted the "opinion according to which in the consecrated hosts which remain after the celebration of the Sacrifice of the Mass, Christ our Lord, is no longer present." These strange ideas and the practices flowing from them also prompted a number of instructions from competent Roman authorities, pointing to abuses and calling for correction, for return to doctrinal and ritual sanity. These Roman documents are treated in separate articles.

[1]Cf. anonymous author: *Le corps de Jesus Christ présent dans l'Eucaristie*, Avignon, 1926; F. de Lanversin, *La présence eucharistique*, RSR 23 (1933), 176-196; A. Verhamme, *De modo praesentiae Christi in Sacramento*, Collationes Brugenses, 1935, 384-86; id., *De desitione praesentiae Christi in Eucharistia*, ibid., 435-39; L. Baudiment, *Notre Seigneur n'est il pas présent qu'une fois dans l'hostie?*, Rev. Apologétique, 65 (1937), 546-61; B. Ayala, *De actuali extensione Christi in Eucharistia in sententia Doctoris Eximii*, Rome, 1939 (Dissertation, Gregorian University); J. Van der Meersch, *De praesentia Christi in Eucharistia*, Collationes Brugenses, 1939, 465-66; R. Masi, *La teoria suareziana della presenza eucaristica*, Rome 1942; F. Orozco, *La explicación de Santo Tomas sobre la presencia del cuerpo de Cristo en la Eucaristía 'per modum substantiae'*, Rome, 1943,(Dissertation, Gregorian University); Y. de Montcheuil, *La raison de la permanence du Christ sous les espèces eucharistiques d'après S. Bonaventure et S. Thomas*, Mélanges théologiques Paris, 1946, 71-82; F. Cardinal Carpino, *De Eucharistia*, Rome, 1946, 322-367; A. Loreti, *La presenza eucaristica in Durando di S. Porziano*, Rome, 1949; L. Nunez Goenaga, *El valor y funciones de la presencia real de Jesu Cristo. El Sacramento segun la doctrina eucaristiologica de Santo Tomas*, Toulosa, 1949; I. Filograssi, S.J., *De Eucharistia*, ed. 5, Rome, 1953, 231-273; U. Bouesse, *Il modo di presenza di Cristo nell'Eucaristia, Eucaristia*, 263-84; A. de Sutter, *La notion de présence et ses différentes applications dans la Somme Théologique de S. Thomas*, EphemCarmeliticae, 17 (1967), 49-69; Ch. Cardinal Journet, *La présence sacramentelle du Christ*, Fribourg, 1966; A. Bertuletti, *La presenza di Cristo nel Sacramento dell'Eucaristia*, Rome, 1969; G. Sohngen, *La presenza di Cristo nella fede e nel Sacramento*, Assisi, 1971; I. Cisar, *Note sulla presenza eucaristica*, Rassegna di Teologia 13 (1972), 225-234; L. Ligier, *Il Sacramento dell'Eucaristia*, P.U.G., Rome, 1977 154-198; Ch. Cardinal Journet, *Le mystère de l'Eucharistie*, Paris, 1981. J. Betz, *Mysterium Salutis*, VIII, pt 2; I. Biffl, *Eucaristia, Teologia e pastorale*, Turin, 1982, 60-63; I. Pintard, *La présence du Christ, Esprit et Vie*, 93, 28 April 1983, 250-55; R. Laurentin, *Jésus Christ, Présent, Paris, 1981;* [2]*VII, 1*, K. Lake, *The Apostolic Fathers*, I, 259; [3]*Romans*, VII, 3, 235; [4]*Apol.* I, 66; [5]*Ad Celsum*, VIII, 33, tr. H. Chadwick, Cambridge, 1953, 476; [6]*Catecheses*, 22, 9, PG 33, 1013; [7]*De prodit. Judae*, Hom I, 6; PG, 49, 380; cp. In Mt Hom 82, 5, PG 58, 744; [8]In Mt 26, 27, PG 72, 451; [9]*De Myster.*, 9, 50-52, SC 25, 124, 25; [10]Msi, XX, 524D, DS; [11]DS; [12]Sermo 272, PL 38, 1246.

PRIESTHOOD

The Eucharist as sacrifice (qv) has a necessary relationship with priesthood.[1] The Eucharist first celebrated at the Last Supper (qv) was an act of the priesthood of Christ. Continued on our altars it is performed by the priests of the New Law. We have, therefore, to consider the priesthood of Christ and that of those who act officially within the Church.

Christ was priest from the moment of his Incarnation. The formal constituent of the Saviour's office was, therefore, the anointing of his sacred humanity by the *gratia unionis*, not the bestowal on his soul of the *gratia capitis*, this latter making him Head of the Mystical Body. Christ was the High-Priest because he was the God-man. He received the priestly office when his human nature was assumed and given personal existence by the Word. "Christus," writes L. Billot, "unctus est sacerdos per ipsam unionis gratiam per quam habet potestatem ad omnia munera sacerdotii."[2] This echoes the word of St. Thomas, "unus tamen et idem fuit sacerdos et Deus."[3]

The idea has ancient lineage. St. Irenaeus (qv) thought that all Christ's activity was priestly. With this general principle assumed he can write thus: "When he was incarnate and became man he recapitulated in himself the long line of men and obtained salvation for us all at once in his flesh, in such wise that what we had lost in Adam, that is, to be made in the image and likeness of God, we could recover in Christ Jesus."[4]

St. Athanasius, doctor of the Incarnate Word, wrote beautifully on this theme: "Now when became he 'Apostle,' but when he put on our flesh? and when became he 'High Priest of our profession' but when, after offering himself for us, he raised his body from the dead, and as now, himself brings near and offers to the Father those who in faith approach him, redeeming all, and for all propitiating God? Not then as wishing to signify the essence of the Word, nor his natural generation from the Father, did the Apostle say, 'Who was faithful to him who made him'—(perish the thought! for the Word is not made but makes)—but as signifying his descent to mankind and High-Priesthood which did 'become'—as one may easily see from the account given of the Law and of Aaron. I mean, Aaron was not born a high-priest, but a man; and in process of time when God willed he became a high-priest; yet became so, not simply, nor as betokened by his ordinary garments, but putting over them the ephod, the breastplate, the robe which the women wrought at God's command, and going in them into the holy place, he offered the sacrifice for the people; and in them, as it were, mediated between the vision of God and the sacrifices of men. Thus then the Lord also, 'In the beginning was the Word, and the Word was with God, and the Word was God,' but when the Father willed that ransoms should be paid for all and to all, grace should be given, then truly the Word, as Aaron his robe, so did he take earthly flesh, having Mary for the Mother of his body, taking the place of the virgin earth, that as High Priest having like others an offering, he might offer himself to the Father, and cleanse us from all sins in his own blood, and might rise from the dead."⁵ "He did not become other than himself on taking the flesh, but, being the same as before, he was robed in it; and the expressions 'he became' and 'he was made,' must not be understood as if the Word, considered as the Word, were made, but that the Word, being Framer of all, afterwards was made High Priest, by putting on a body which was originate and made, and as such he can offer for us."⁶ "And when became he ' a merciful and faithful High Priest' except when 'in all things he was made like unto his brethren?' And then was he 'made like,' when he became man, having put upon him our flesh."⁷

An idea which had occasionally appeared that Christ was a priest before the Incarnation must be abandoned in the light of Heb 5:1: "For every high priest chosen from among men is appointed to act on behalf of men in relation to God, to offer gifts and sacrifices for sins." If the priest must be "among men," then the vital moment in Christ's case was the Incarnation.

It is well known that Jesus does not give himself the title priest; in no book of NT save Heb does he receive it explicitly. The title is applied to the Christian community in 1 Pet 2:5; Rev 1:6; 5:10; the wording is borrowed from Ex 19:6; Is 61:6. Jesus did not belong to the tribe of Levi. His priesthood transcends such relationship of blood and the symbol is fixed in Melchizedek (qv).

Heb points, moreover, to the utter singularity of Christ's priesthood by the use, in his regard, of "great priest" (10:21) and "high priest" (2:17, etc., ten times in all), even "great high priest" (4:14), whereas "priest" is used of Melchizedek (7:1, 3, 11, 15) and of the Levitical priesthood (7:14-23; 8:4; 9:6; 10:11).

Two further moments of importance are to be noted in the priesthood of Christ. With the descent of the Spirit upon him at the moment of his baptism by John, there began the public manifestation of the office. Henceforth the ancient priesthood which Jesus had fully respected is out of date. St. Peter fixed the great initial moment with the words: "You know the word which he sent to Israel, preaching good news of peace by Jesus Christ (he is Lord of all), the word which was proclaimed throughout all Judea, beginning from Galilee after the baptism which John preached: how God anointed Jesus of Nazareth with the Holy Spirit and with power; how he went about doing good and healing all that were oppressed by the devil, for

God was with him" (Acts 10:37-38). Jesus himself announced in his hometown the programme which would give expression to his priesthood: "And Jesus returned in the power of the Spirit into Galilee. And he came to Nazareth, where he had been brought up; and he went to the synagogue, as his custom was, on the sabbath day. And he stood up to read; and there was given to him the book of the prophet Isaiah. He opened the book and found the place where it was written: 'The Spirit of the Lord is upon me, because he has anointed me to preach good news to the poor. He has sent me to proclaim release to the captives, and recovering of sight to the blind, to set at liberty those who are oppressed, to proclaim the acceptable year of the Lord!...', 'Today,' said Jesus, 'this scripture has been fulfilled in your hearing' " (Lk 4:14-21).

Thus anointed by the Spirit, Jesus exercised his priesthood up to and including the paschal mystery (qv). When that was completed and he entered heaven, there came the fulfillment of his priesthood. "By his sacrifice, our high priest entered into possession, in his body immolated and raised, of the heavenly glorification to which he had a right through his dignity as Son of God, but of which he had been deprived in the time of his life on earth, 'for a while made lower than the angels.'" "A second aspect of the fulfillment (consummation) of Jesus consists in the power he henceforth has in his very humanity, of sending as from his origin, the Holy Spirit: royal power, of which his seat at the right hand of the Father is the symbol and which makes of Christ the Head of the new People of God."⁸

Jesus is the priest in glory, active in the Church through his divine power. He acts through his priests, the ministers of the New Law. "Christ," says St. Thomas, "is the source of all priesthood."⁹ Here we meet the problem of the ministerial priesthood and the priesthood of the faithful; the problem of the ministerial priesthood in our time. We must consider some historical background, which is necessary to get the problem in perspective, to understand why Popes have had to issue so many appeals and warnings to priests in recent times (see articles: Abuses in regard to the Eucharist, Post-conciliar documents, *Mysterium Fidei, Inaestimabile donum*).

Vatican II (qv) *seemed*, by certain of its decisions and at certain moments, to devalue the priesthood. The basic text of the Council, the Constitution on the Church, has chapters on Religious and the Laity; none on Priests, who are given a few paragraphs in the chapter on the hierarchical nature of the Church (ch III, n. 28). Even in this short space much of the emphasis is on the *presbyterium*; priests are "prudent cooperators of the episcopal college and its support and mouthpiece."

True, the Council issued a decree on the ministry and life of priests; it did likewise for the laity, religious and bishops. The fortunes of the schema on priests were not such as to display initially very profound concern. The schema was reduced to a set of twelve propositions, a kind of skeleton, in time for the third session of the Council. The propositions had, inevitably, a platitudinous character. This seemed a strange lack of recognition in face of mighty achievement: of heroism to the point of martyrdom—over three thousand priests martyred in Poland alone, of missionary zeal, of labours in every sector of church life, of theological research and reflection which provided the very food of conciliar debates—the "New Theology" was entirely the work of priests, of the immense contribution to education at every level.

Things did not rest there. Between the third and fourth sessions of the Council an effort was made to repair the damage. The propositions were rejected and instructions given to prepare a substantial text. The bishops seemed almost to fear what would, in fact, happen and their eagerness to help prepare a worthy text can be seen in the subsequent history of the Council: the written comments which reached the drafting commission run to over 330 pages of the *Acta Synodalia*;[10] at the final stage over 5,400 amendments, *Modi*, were submitted.[11] The product of these labours, which were coordinated by a great theologian of the priesthood, Fr. J. Lécuyer (qv), is a text which should enlighten and inspire.

It did not seem to do so at once. The years immediately after the Council saw the flight from the ministry, the decline in priestly recruitment and the irregularities which called for the papal interventions mentioned. Was this due to a theology of the priesthood weighted heavily towards the episcopate? The new Code of Canon Law seems to endorse this theology, where it speaks of priests as "helpers and advisers" of bishops (Canon 384). Priests were now seen almost essentially in relation to bishops, not, as we were accustomed to be taught and to believe, in relation to Jesus Christ. The traditional doctrine of *in persona Christi* has not been denied; it is explicitly affirmed: "Partakers of the office of Christ the sole Mediator (1 Tim 2:5) on their level of ministry, they announce the divine word to all. They exercise this sacred office of Christ most of all in the Eucharistic liturgy or synaxis. There, acting in the person of Christ,[12] and proclaiming his mystery, they join the offering of the faithful to the sacrifice of the Head. Until the coming of the Lord (cf. 1 Cor 11:26), they re-present and apply in the Sacrifice of the Mass the one sacrifice of the New Testament, namely the sacrifice of Christ offering himself once and for all to his Father as a spotless victim (cf. Heb 9:11-28)."[13]

With this statement of *Lumen Gentium* (ch III, n. 28) compare the following from the Decree on the Ministry and Life of Priests: "Therefore, while it indeed presupposes the sacraments of Christian initiation, the sacerdotal office of priests is conferred by that special sacrament through which priests, by the anointing of the Holy Spirit, are marked with a special character and are so configured to Christ the Priest that they can act in the person of Christ the Head."[14] But note that this generous statement is immediately preceded by this sentence: "Inasmuch as *it is connected with the episcopal order*, the priestly office shares in the authority by which Christ himself builds up, sanctifies, and rules his body" (italics added).

In the context therefore of purely speculative theory the Council appeared to maintain traditional teaching. In the empirical or existential order the bishops, at least for a while, seemed to take priests for granted. Within a short time it was clear that they could do nothing of the kind. The Catholic priestly body was, in places, disintegrating. At once papal and episcopal initiatives were taken to reassure the priests within the Church. Paul VI, in 1969, sent a special message to them. The priesthood was chosen as the theme of the episcopal synod of 1971. The Pope kept up his words of encouragement, making it clear that he knew what was happening. He spoke of the wave "of doubts, uneasiness and anxiety breaking on the souls of many priests,"[15] of the "identity crisis,"[16] which was now a talking point. He had the requests for laicisation piling up on his desk and news of seminaries closing down. He would probably agree that when he spoke of a campaign of auto-destruction within the Church, he had principally priests in mind.

Serene assessment of the evolution of thought must note some other factors. The entire corpus of spirituality has practically ignored the episcopate: Is there even one pamphlet on the spiritual life of bishops to compare with the thousands of publications on the spirituality of priests? This is a particular glory of the French school from the seventeenth century on. The question turns especially on spiritual works of profound value, substantial in character; these generate still higher theological thinking.

Another fact is noteworthy. Since the beginning of the century Popes have from time to time issued documents, Apostolic Exhortations or Encyclicals on the priesthood: St. Pius X, Pius XI, Pius XII, John XXIII.[17] In not one of these papal documents does one meet the idea of the priest's close association with the bishop, the key idea of Vatican II—nor in the previous code of Canon Law were priests described as "helpers or advisers" of bishops. One Pope, Pius XII, felt authorized to speak for all: "As our predecessors, particularly St. Pius X and Pius XI have taught, and as we ourselves have mentioned in the Encyclicals *Mystici Corporis* and *Mediator Dei*, the priesthood is truly the great gift of the divine Redeemer, who, in order to perpetuate to the end of the ages the work of the salvation of the human race which he consummated on the Cross, has entrusted his power to the Church, and willed that she should participate in his own one and eternal priesthood. The priest is 'another Christ,' because he is marked with an indelible character which makes him a living image, as it were, of the Saviour; the priest represents Christ, who said, *'As the Father hath sent me, I also send you* (Jn 20:21); *he that heareth you, heareth me"* (Lk 10:16).[18]

Pius XI thought that his Encyclical on the priesthood was the most important document of his pontificate. Simultaneously with the publication of it he instituted a Votive Mass in honour of the "supreme and eternal Priest, Jesus Christ." He was the Pope of the Missions, as he launched a vast movement of evangelization. Here is his tribute to missionary priests as written in the Encyclical: "The work of the Missions, which manifests so strikingly the Church's divinely given genius for expansion, is largely in the hands of priests and is successfully carried on by them. They are pioneers of the faith and apostles of charity and, at the cost of many sacrifices, they extend the frontiers of God's kingdom on earth."[19]

The question for the historian of theology is: How did the great Popes of the century miss an idea to which the fathers of Vatican II attached so much attention and importance? How can the discrepancy be explained; should it be eliminated? How will the apparent contradiction with Church history be explained? The history of the Church, especially of the Latin Church, unfolds constant enrichment by priests, not acting as part of a presbyterium, but on their own initiative. With a few exceptions, all the religious orders and congregations since medieval times were founded by priests. Again with few exceptions the great missionary pioneers in every continent were priests. What does theological science through the ages, and in particular in these last two centuries, not owe to personal research, reflection and publication, whether orally or in writing, by priests? Was all this achievement extraneous to their priestly office and duty? In the overwhelming majority of cases the role of a bishop vis-à-vis the priest operative in the domain of his excellence was nil; in some cases, as in that of Don Bosco as a founder or Newman as a theologian, it was almost adverse; Newman was denounced to Rome by a bishop as a heretic: his thinking—on the

sentiment of the faithful—is written into the texts of Vatican II.

This is not to argue for opposition between priests and bishops. It is an affirmation of the might of the Catholic priesthood, which comes directly from Jesus Christ, as the Popes have taught. When Christ acts fully through his priests all the Church benefits. The instinct of the faithful thinks of Christ not as a bishop, but as a priest. Pope John Paul (qv) has followed in the line of Paul VI, using every means available to him to exalt the idea and ideal of the priesthood.

[1]Cf. esp., *Teologia del Sacerdocio*, ed. Facultad Teologica del Norte de España, Instituto 'Juan de Avila,' Ediciones Aldecoe, Burgos, 14 vols, 1969-1982; cf. article bibliography; E. (Cardinal) Suhard, *The Priest in the Modern World*, in *Pastoral Letters*, English tr., London, no date, French original, 1949; H. von Campenhausen, *Kirchliches Amt und geistliche Vollmacht*, 1953; C. Spicq, *L'Epître aux Hébreux*, Paris, II, 1953, 119-31; H. Bouessé, *Le Sauveur du monde*, II, *Le mystère de l'Incarnation*, Paris, 1953; esp. J. Lécuyer, C.S.Sp. (qv), *Le sacerdoce dans le mystère du Christ*, Paris, 1957; id., *What is a Priest?*, London, 1959; id., *Le sacrement de L'Ordination*, Paris, 1982; Cl. Dillenschneider, C.SS.R., *Le Christ, l'unique prêtre et nous ses prêtres*, Paris, 1959; J. Forrestal, *Where are the Priests?*, Vatican City, 1965; K.H. Schelke, *Discipleship and Priesthood*, London, 1966; J. Smith, *A Priest for ever. A Study of Typology and Eschatology in Hebrews*, London, 1969; N. Lash—J. Rhymer, *The Christian Priesthood*, 9th Downside Symposium, 1970; ed. J. Coppens, *Sacerdoce et Célibat*, 20 contributors, Gembloux, Louvain, 1971; ed. G. Concelli, *Il Prete per gli uomini d'oggi*, 33 contributors, 918 pp, Rome, 1975; A. Vanhoye, *Prêtres anciens. Prêtre nouveau selon le Nouveau Testament*, Paris, 1980; J. Galot, S.J., *Teologia del Sacerdozio*, Florence, 1981; G. Martelet, S.J., *Deux mille ans d'Eglise en question. Crise de la foi. Crise du prêtre*, Paris, 1984; K.T. Schafer, M. Schmaus, LTK VIII, 756-58; A. Michel, DTC XII, 1 (1936), 138-161; *Commentary on the Documents of Vatican II*, ed. H. Vorgrimmler, vol IV, London, 1969, J. Lécuyer, F. Wulf, P.J. Cordes, M. Schmaus *on the Decree on Ministry and Life of Priests*; [2]*De Verbo Incarnato*, 7th ed., 347; [3]III, q. 22, art. 3, ad 1; 183-297; [4]*Adv. Haer.*, III, 18, 1, SC 34, M. Sagnard, 312, 313; [5]*Orat. II contra Arianos*, 7, LNPF, IV, 351, 52; [6]*Ibid.*, 8, 352; [7]*Ibid.*, 9, 353; [8]J. Lécuyer, *Le sacerdoce*, 165, 166; [9]III, q. 22, art. 4; [10]Vol IV, Part 5, 209-540; [11]Commentary, j.cit., 206; [12]Notes to Council text: Trent, DS 1743, and Pius XII, *Mediator Dei, AAS* 39 (1947), 553; DS 3850; [13]Notes to Council text: Trent, DS 1739, 40; Vatican II, *Constitution on the Sacred Liturgy*, art. 7, 47; [14]Art. 2; [15]26 February 1968, DCath 481, 5; [16]DCath 1969, 213, 16; ibid., 1966, 482; ibid., 1970, 403; [17]St. Pius X, *Haerent animo, ASS* 41 (1908), 555-577; Pius XI, *Ad catholici sacerdotii fastigium, AAS* 28 (1936), 6-53; Pius XII, *Menti nostrae, AAS* 42 (1950), 657-702; John XXIII, *Sacerdotii nostri primordia, AAS* 51 (1959); [18]Repr. in *The Catholic Priesthood, Papal Documents from Pius X to Pius XII*, ed. Mgr. P. Veuillot, Dublin, vol I, 1957, 157; [19]*Ibid.*, 211.

PROMISE, THE DISCOURSE OF: ST. JOHN, chapter VI

The discourse pronounced in the sixth chapter of St. John's gospel is related to the institution (qv) of the Eucharist as promise to fulfillment.[1] Key phrases in the text are traditionally applied to the Eucharist, "I am the Bread of life"; "I am the living Bread which came down from heaven." The whole chapter may be seen as structured around the Eucharist, the last part, 6:51b-58, it nows seems generally agreed, must be seen in reference to it. This is so evident that exegetes like Bultmann, who do not like the overt Eucharistic doctrine in these verses, seek to challenge their authenticity.

The general paschal character of the gospel is now at times presented, as is the Johannine fondness for sacramental themes. Close examination of the sixth chapter shows that it brings into focus the essential claim of Jesus to his people: he is the fulfillment of their messianic hope. The messianic banquet is honoured, for here unlike the synoptics when the multiplication of the loaves and fishes comes at the end of the day to solve a hunger crisis, here it is given a place on its own. There are echoes of Exodus, the manna, the murmuring: the Hebrews murmured against Moses and God in Mara (Exod 15:24), in the desert of Sin (Exod 16:2, 7-12) and at Massa (Exod 17:3); the Jews of Galilee murmur against Jesus. "And finally,the proximity of the Pasch creates a liturgical link between the two generations. So everything combines to connect the revelation of the Eucharist with the history, cult and hopes of the Jews. The Eucharist will be the manna sent from heaven, the messianic meal, the new Pasch: this will be the food with which God will secretly feed his people now, the food for which the whole of sacred history had aroused their hunger, the food for which the pious Jew was eager, and which he sought in meditation on the Law. To reveal it and he invites men to 'come' to him, offer it, Jesus adopts the tone of Wisdom; like Wisdom he makes them sit down at his table: "I am the Bread of life. He who comes to me will never hunger and he who believes in me will never thirst" (6:35). One can recognize here the appeals of Proverbs (9:5), of Ecclesiasticus (24:26) and of Isaiah (55:1-3). Like Wisdom, Jesus stands at the crossroads, there where the Scriptures—those concerning worship, and those which are historical, prophetic, sapiential—flow together; he is the fulfillment of all the hopes of Israel."[2]

The verses of Jn 6 have a sacrificial import, "my flesh for the life of the world" (6:51); they contain an eschatological element, "He who eats my flesh and drinks my blood has eternal life and I will raise him up on the last day" (6:54). The Eucharist is linked with the mission of Christ, the one "sent" as Jn so often reminds us (3:17; 4:34; 5:30; 6:38; 10:21; 10:36; 1 Jn 4:9-10). "As the living Father has sent me, and as I live because of the Father, so he who eats me he also shall live because of me" (6:57).

It is then the whole Christology of Jn that is crystallised in the sixth chapter. Directly the Eucharist is linked with the Incarnation. Jn has no institution narrative (qv), for in a sense his whole gospel speaks of the Eucharist and reaches in the promise of it the glorious summit of Johannine thought.

[1]Cf. general commentaries, *Jerome Biblical Commentary, New Catholic Commentary*; C.H. Dodd, *The Interpretation of the Fourth Gospel*, Cambridge, 1953, 333-345; C.K. Barrett, *The Gospel According to St. John*, London, 1955, 234-254; R.C.H. Lenski, *The Interpretation of St. John's Gospel*, Minneapolis, 1961, 486-524; R.E. Brown, *The Gospel According to St. John*, Anchor Bible, I, 1966; 268-303, bibl. 303, 4; F.L. Godet, *Commentary on St. John's Gospel*, Grand Rapids, 1980, 574-612; D. Mollat, S.J., *The Sixth Chapter of Saint John*, in *The Eucharist in the New Testament*, London, 1964, 143-156; E. Janot, *Le Pain de vie. A propos des interprétations du ch. 6 de l'Evangile de St. Jean*, Greg., 11 (1930), 161-170; J. Leal, *Spiritus et caro in Jn 6*, 69, Verbum Domini 30 (1952), 357-364; J.L. Lilly, *The Eucharistic Discourse of Jn 6*, CBQ 12 (1950), 48-51; X. Léon-Dufour, S.J., *Le mystère du Pain de Vie (Jean VI)*, RSR, 46 (1958), 481-523; A. Feuillet, P.S.S., *Les thèmes bibliques majeurs du discours sur le pain de vie*, NRT, 82 (1960), 803-822, 918-939, 1040-1062; [2]D. Mollat, *op.cit.*, 150.

PUEROS BAPTIZATOS, 1 November 1973
Directory on Children's Masses, giving directives on how some adults should participate, on the various parts of the Mass as they should be explained to children, on aids, such as singing and music, even visual aids, not overlooking the value of certain moments of silence in these as in adults' Masses.

[1]Text *AAS* 66 (1974), 30-46, English tr. Vatican Press Office, A. Flannery, O.P., 254-270.

Q/R

QUASTEN, JOHANNES (1900-1987)

Q., one of the great patrologists of recent times, was born, educated and ordained priest in Germany, pursuing further studies in Rome; his early special interest was archaeology.[1] Impeded from teaching in the post to which he had been appointed in his native land, he was invited to the Catholic University of Washington, and from 1938 was professor of Ancient Church History, Christian Archaeology and Patrology. With Canon J.N.D. Kelly of Oxford and F.L. Cross of the same University, he helped to secure recognition for Patrology as a most important theological discipline in the English-speaking world. He especially influenced a whole generation of theologians in North America. In the steps of Newman he wished to make the Fathers known in English, launched with W. Burghardt, S.J., ACW, and with F.L. Cross initiated the International Congress of Patristics. As editor, reviewer, contributor to learned reviews and collective works, he kept up a constant flow of scholarly writing. Of special relevance to the Eucharist are *Expositio antiquae liturgiae Gallicanae Germano Parisiensi ascripta*, 1934, the monumental three volumes of *Patrology*, 1950 ... and especially the seven volumes, *Monumenta eucharistica et liturgica vetustissima*, 1935-1937: all marked by impeccable scholarship. Q. was a member of the preparatory liturgical commission for Vatican II, an expert at the Council and a member of the post-conciliar Consilium for the implementation of conciliar directives. Eighty-one scholars from many countries contributed to his *Festschrift*.

[1]Cf. *Kyriakon, Festschrift Johannes Quasten*, 2 vols., ed. P. Granfield, J.A. Jungmann, S.J., Munster, 1970; esp. II, articles by W. Burghardt, 915-916, J. Pelican, 917-920, biographical sketch by P. Granfield, 921-923; *id.*, bibl, 924-935.

QUMRAN

The detailed attention given by scholars to all that concerns the Qumran community, brought to historical knowledge by the epoch-making finds in the Judean desert, must inevitably include interest in what is said in the freshly found documentation about meals with distinctive features: the community meal, the note of messianic expectancy associated with such meals.[1] Inevitably, too, comparison is made with the central dominant meal of the NT and Christian community. The prescription in the *Manual of Discipline*, 1 QS VI, 1-6, is often reproduced: "In these (regulations) they shall walk in all their sojournings. Everyone finding himself with his fellow, the lesser shall hear the greater, with regard to the work and the mammon (wealth). Let them eat communally, bless communally, and take counsel communally. In every place where there are ten men of the Council of the Community, let there be among them a man who is a priest and let each according to his rank sit before him; this is how they shall take counsel with regard to every matter. When the table is laid for the meal or for the must (grape juice, *tirosh*) to drink, the priest shall be the first to stretch out his hand to invoke a blessing upon the first of the bread and the must."[2]

A later find in *Qumran Cave I* OSa ii, 17-22, has a description of the cult meal as follows: "...and when they gather to the table of the community and to the drinking of the wine and when the table of the community is made ready and the wine has been mixed for drinking, then no one is to touch the first portion of the bread and wine before the priest. For it is he who blesses the first portion of the bread and of the wine and who touches as the first the bread. Then may the Messiah of Israel touch the bread and then (only) may (those who belong to) the congregation say the blessing, each according to his rank. And in accordance with this rubric they shall act at each meal, when (at least) ten men are gathered (for it)."

K.G. Kuhn, in his study of this theme compares the first Qumran text here quoted with the description of the Essene meal by Josephus (*Bell.* 2, 8, 5). He speaks of purification, of entry denied to the uninitiated, of the Essenes going to "the refectory as to a sacred shrine." "When they have seated themselves in silence, the baker serves the loaves in order, and the cook sets before each one plate with a single course. Before the meal, the priest gives the blessing, and it is unlawful to partake before the prayer. The meal ended, he offers a further prayer; thus at the beginning and at the close they do homage to God as the bountiful giver of life."[3]

It is not surprising since Qumran is generally taken for an Essene settlement that there is, despite some differences, "general agreement between Josephus and 1 Qs VI."[4]

What of the relationship with the Eucharist? K.G. Kuhn, who also considers an interesting Egyptian-Jewish legend, *Joseph and Aseneth*, is firm: "This is not to say that we encounter in Jesus, and more specifically in the Last Supper, some kind of Essenism. We are confronted with a new and originial phenomenon, but a phenomenon where forms and praxis are often analogous to those of the Essenes."[5] J. Jeremias is still more categorical. After a detailed analysis of all the arguments put forward in support of some dependence he concludes:" Definitely, in my opinion proof of the influence of Essene practices on the narratives of the Last Supper has not been given.... Thus our inquiry ends in a negative result. It has not been proved to the present time that Jesus was influenced by Essene meal customs, and here I am in complete agreement with Kuhn. If new texts do not contain unexpected surprises, Essene meals will be no help to us for an understanding of the Eucharistic words of Jesus."[6] As R.E. Brown says elsewhere in the same collective work: "There remains a tremendous chasm between Qumran thought and Christianity."[7]

---

[1]Cf. K.G. Kuhn, *The Lord's Supper and the Communal Meal at*

Qumran in *The Scrolls and the New Testament*, ed. K. Stendhall, London, 1958; F.M. Cross, *The Ancient Library of Qumran*, New York, 1961, 234ff; G. Vermes, *Discovery in the Judean Desert*, London, New York, 1956; id., *The Dead Sea Scroll in English*, Pelican Books, 1962; cf. index meal; [2]Kuhn, 67; Vermes, *Discovery*, 143; [3]Kuhn, 71; [4]*Ibid.*, 67, 68; [5]*Ibid.*, 84; [6]*La derniere Cène. Les Paroles de Jésus*, Paris, 1972, 34, 36; [7]*Op. cit.*, 205.

RAHNER, KARL (1904-1984)

The great German theologian treats of Eucharistic questions in essays found dispersed in his many works.[1] In one of the volumes on *Mission and Grace* he has papers on *The Sacrifice of the Mass and an Ascesis for Youth, The Mass and Television*, and *On developing Eucharistic Devotion*. His concern here, as so often in his work, is to diagnose honestly the religious situation and to liberate his disciple from constricting views or fashions not theologically justified. He writes thus on Mass and youth: "In this sense every Christian, youth included, should understand his life as lived inwards, towards and outwards from the altar. But this means that he has to be so guided and instructed that in the celebration of Mass, he encounters the deeper content of his own life, and that from the standpoint of his life in the concrete he grasps the ceremony of the Mass in a more living way. And if this is not merely one thing that we might perhaps think about, but a basic condition of the fulfillment of the Mass, if its sacramental meaning and its power are really to be given free rein, then it becomes all the clearer that we must see to it with all our resources that the concrete way in which Mass is celebrated makes this encounter between Mass and life both easy and obvious."[2]

R. defended in this book a view which Church practice has rejected, that the television Mass was an offence against the sacred character of the great religious act. He concludes: "The Church, which thinks in centuries and is not easy to outlive, does not need to use a television camera so as to let an unbelieving world stare dully at the performance of her loftiest mystery until such time as this sensation, too, shall have become just another bore."[3] This conclusion is reached after an argument which goes deep to the root of the question, back to the *disciplina arcani* (qv). In the essay on thanksgiving—part of *On developing Eucharistic Devotion*—he relates the question to the essentials of Eucharistic communion, deals lucidly with the preoccupation some have with the time element. The section of that chapter dealing with Visits is considered separately.[4]

In *Theological Investigations* III, R. writes on the *Eucharist and Suffering*.[5] Three properties, he says, mean that the Eucharist may lead its recipient "into the dark valleys of Christ's suffering." It is a sacrifice; it brings grace, and it brings the communicant more closely to the Mystical Body of Christ which is the Church. "In this respect," he concludes, "it will be a sacred comfort to us if we are able to say to ourselves that what we are suffering is simply a participation in the life of one whom we receive daily as victim and grace and as the bond of love. It is absolutely true to say that if we have died with him (2 Tim 2:11) we share everything with him—both death and life—because we live in him through his Sacrament."

In *Theological Investigations* IV, R. has profound reflections on the *Word and the Eucharist*,[6] dealing first with the *Word and Sacrament* generally. He goes on to deal for a mixed Catholic-Lutheran audience with the question of the real Presence, basing much of what he says on Trent (qv). He makes another significant contribution to a spirituality of the Eucharist in the essay *The Eucharist and our Daily Lives* in *Theological Investigations* VII. Here, in characteristically existentialist fashion, he analyses the concept of the "Everyday." He opens thus: "In this Sacrament saving history as a whole and at the same time our personal saving history attains its highest point."[7] He concludes thus: "Finally these two factors, the experience of the everyday seen through the eyes of faith on the one hand, and the celebration of the Eucharist on the other, must be correlated and made complementary. Each must be interpreted in the light of the other. Only when we do all this do we achieve a real and effective encounter with Jesus Christ, our Lord, our Life, our Judgement, our eternity." Those who may have misunderstood R's treatment of television Mass will be reassured by the profound realism of this passage.

[1]*Festgabe fur Karl Rahner*, 2 vols., Freiburg i. Br., 1964, bibl., II, 900-936; L. Roberts, *The Achievement of Karl Rahner*, London, 1967; [2]*Mission and Grace*, I, London, 1963, 252f; [3]*Ibid.*, 274f; [4]Cf. also *Theol. Invest.*, IV, London, 1966, *On the Duration of Christ after Communion*, 312-320; [5]London, 1967, 161-170; [6]London, 1966, 252-286; [7]London, 1971, 211-226; quotations first and last page.

RATRAMNUS (d. 868)

R., a monk of Corbie, composed a work, *De Corpore et Sanguine Domini*, to oppose the realist views expressed by Paschasius Radbert (qv) in his work with the same title.[1] R's principal objective was to combat the theory of Paschasius that the body of Christ in the Eucharist is identical with his historical body. He thought that Paschasius gravely misrepresented St. Augustine and set about the necessary correction. His phraseology was inexact and though he did wish to

affirm a presence of Christ his mode of expressing it is confusing, practically erroneous: "The body and blood of Christ which are taken in the mouth of the faithful in the Church are figures, according to their visible appearance, but according to their invisible substance, that is the power of the divine Word, they truly exist as the body and blood of Christ."[2] The word 'substance' here has not the Aristotelian meaning it would have with the Scholastics. R's problem was how the Eucharist could be reality and figure at the same time. He was insistent on rejecting the idea of identity between the Eucharistic body and the historic body of Christ: the historic body was visible, palpable; the Eucharistic body is invisible, impalpable, spiritual: "therefore nothing is to be thought of here corporeally, but spiritually"; "it is the body of Christ, but not corporeally, it is the blood of Christ, but not corporeally";[3] "although," says Paschasius, "similarly the mind should strive to grasp things spiritually where nothing bodily can be felt ... all that we eat is spiritual."

There are texts so ambiguous that R. has been accused of holding for the permanence of the substance of bread and wine after the consecration,[5] but the defect is in the formulation not the thinking, for elsewhere we read: "the bread which by the ministry of the priest is made the body of Christ, shows one thing externally to the human senses, while another calls interiorly to the minds of the faithful."[6]

R. uses a text from St. Ambrose which Paschasius had used, but to turn it against him: "the body which was crucified and buried was true; truly sacramental is that which we receive."[7] He was not a symbolist, for he believed in the spiritual, divine presence. With his teaching on the presence of Christ in the Sacraments, especially Baptism, the difference from the Eucharistic presence is unclear. Interestingly though he is desirous to vindicate St. Augustine, it is from St. Ambrose that his arguments are borrowed.

R. has had subsequently mixed fortunes. He was condemned under another name, that of John Scotus Eriugena by Leo IX at the Council of Vercelli. St. John Fisher referred to him in the preface to his *De veritate corporis et sanguinis Christi in Eucharistia*. But the Protestants began to claim him and he was put on the Index (in regard to this book) in 1559; the ban was lifted in 1900.

Dom M. Cappuyns, O.S.B., the expert on John Scotus Eriugena, has shown that he was not the author of R's treatise—he was a mere *"spectateur"* to the debate with, possibly, some sympathy for R.[8]

[1]Text, PL 121: 125-170; ed. J.N. Bakhuizen, van den Brink, Amsterdam, 1954; English tr., C.P. Farrar and A.P. Evans, *Biblio-*

graphy of English translations from Medieval Sources, New York, 1947, Washington, 1960, 3267-3272; also by H.W.-W.C.C., London, 1838 and W.F. Taylor, London, 1880; cf. A. Naegle, *Ratramnus und die heilige Eucharistie*, Theologische Studien der Leo-Gesellschaft, V, 1903; D. Stone 1909, 226-33; J. Geiselmann, *Die Eucharistielehre der Vorscholastik*, Forschungen zur Christlichen Literatur und Dogmengeschichte, XV, Hft 1/3, Paderborn, 1926; C. Gliozzo, *La dottrina della conversione eucaristica in Paschasio Radberto e Ratramno*, Palermo, 1945; J. Fahey, *The Eucharistic Teaching of Ratramn of Corbie*, Mundelein, Ill., 1951; J.N. Bakhuizen van den Brink, *Ratramn's Eucharistic Doctrine and its Influence in Sixteenth Century*, in Studies in Church History, II, (1965), 54-77; F. Vernet, DTC, V, 1213, 1214; H. Peltier, DTC, XIII, 2, 1781-83; K. Vielhaber, LTK, VIII, 1001-2; A. Piolanti, EC, X, 549-50. [2]Ch 49, PL 121, 147; [3]Ch 60, 152; [4]Paschasius, PL 120, 1305, 06; [5]cf. ch 9, 12, 14, 131, 132, 133; [6]*Ibid.*, 131; [7]150. [8]*Jean Scot Erigène, sa vie, son oeuvre, sa pensée*, Louvain, 1933, 86-91.

RESURRECTION, THE

Christ instituted the Eucharist the night before his Passion and death, in the Passover (qv) context, in the context therefore of a meal (qv).[1] When he changed the bread and wine into his body and blood he was still a living being on earth. When we hear of the first celebration of the Eucharist in Acts 2:42-43, Jesus is in a different state: "And they persevered in the apostles' teaching and in the fellowship in the breaking of bread and of prayers. But awe fell on every soul, as many wonders and signs took place in Jerusalem through the apostles," (see article Breaking of Bread). The bread is broken in memory of him, as he commanded. But he is now risen and in glory.

Down to recent times interpretation of the Last Supper (qv), the Mass (qv) and the Real Presence (qv) were in the terms of the Council of Trent (qv) related to the sacrificial death of Christ on the Cross, "so that he might leave to his beloved spouse the Church a visible sacrifice (as the nature of man demands) whereby that bloody sacrifice once to be completed on the Cross might be represented, and the memory of it remain even to the end of the world."[2] This remains true, but by no means excludes another truth, that in the Eucharist from the first celebration of "the breaking of bread" to the present time, it is the risen and ascended Lord who is present. Thus Vatican II, stating that "the Saviour instituted the Eucharistic sacrifice of his Body and Blood" continues thus: "This he did in order to perpetuate the sacrifice of the Cross throughout the ages until he should come again, and so entrust to his beloved Spouse, the Church, a memorial of his death and resurrection."[3]

The reference to the resurrection reflects the recent theology of this event as a mystery of salvation. It is no longer viewed merely as a concluding occurrence in the life of Christ, its relevance principally to apologetics to establish his divinity. Its meaning is not static, but vital, not merely eschatological but immanent, achieving its effect incessantly in souls. When, therefore, we speak of the Eucharist "within the horizon of the mystery of Christ," we are proclaiming the inexhaustible riches the Saviour communicates to us: "When Christ says that this bread and this wine *are* his body and blood, and so already does in a fragmentary way what he will be doing in the parousia in a way that extends to the whole, he is giving himself in person to the Church. The power he exercises of transforming elements into the reality of his body—the body which destroys death—is not a power that lies outside him; that power is Christ himself in person, making the truth of his resurrection valid for us. The whole Lord, therefore, is really present there as the life-giving master of this world.... In giving us this world, clothed in the sovereign identity that he alone will ever be able to confer upon it, it is his own self that Christ gives us." The same author unfolds or suggests the incomparable riches that flow from a synthesis of the two realities, Resurrection and Eucharist of Christ. "This, in truth, is what the Eucharist is: the Sacramental unfolding in history of the world's fundamental identity in the order of the Resurrection."

---

[1]Cf. for the renewed theology of the Resurrection, esp. F.X. Durrwell, C.SS.R., *The Resurrection*, London, 1960; X. Léon-Dufour, *Resurrection of Jesus and the Message of Easter*, London, 1974; D.M. Stanley, S.J., *Christ's Resurrection and Pauline Soteriology (Analecta Biblica 38)*, Rome 1961; on the Resurrection and the Eucharist, cf. esp., G. Martelet, *The Risen Jesus and the Eucharistic World*, London, 1976; J.H. Miller, *Until he comes; The Eucharist and the Resurrection*, Proceedings of the Liturgical Week; 23 (1962), 39-44; [2]G. Martelet, *op. cit.*, 177ff; [3]*op. cit.*, 175.

RITZ, MARIA JULITTA (1882-1966)

This remarkable German mystic, member of the Congregation of the Holy Redeemer, impressed many people who knew her as a person of great sanctity.[1] It was only after her death, with the publication of her *Spiritual Testament* that the singular quality of her mystical experience became known and could be appreciated. The opening of the beatification process in Würzburg, the city of her lengthy religious observance, twenty years after her death, is one sign of the profound posthumous impact of her personality and writing. Her doctrine is centerd on the Holy Trinity (qv), on which in an intensely experiential setting she writes with a doctrinal sureness and depth that are rare in such literature. In that whole background her writing on the Mass deserves consideration: "During Holy Mass the incaranate eternal Wisdom treated me as the confidante of his most Sacred Heart. With kindness that cannot be described and with love, Jesus showed me Holy Mass as a legacy to mankind, his most precious pledge and unique means for achieving his interests in the plan of salvation and sanctification of the whole of humanity redeemed and called to eternal happiness. Yes, he places his interests in my soul and lets me penetrate ever deeper into the sacrificial character of Holy Mass and convinces me ever more clearly of the purifying, atoning and sanctifying power of his blood poured out for us, so that my soul may make ample use of the ransom of souls for eternal life by offering the precious blood of Jesus to the heavenly Father for the whole of needy mankind. I see that souls looking for help receive the first and biggest share, while obdurate unbelievers cause me the keenest, atoning sufferings. For them I must pass through mortal agonies so that they may not fall a prey in the end to their wickedness and to divine anger."[2]

Another characteristic passage is: "Our whole history of salvation and salvific activity on behalf of each individual, I find united and made effective in the sacrifice of the Holy Mass. In the light of faith, I understand the Holy Mass as a true and living sacrifice, a sacrifice of self in holocaust, and sacrificial meal, and therefore an oblation of utter annihilation. At the beginning of Holy Mass, I am allowed to pray with Jesus, 'You have given me a body, O my God; behold I come to do your Holy will.' The divine will is that I should be an atoning sacrifice in, with and through Jesus, with his attitude of perfect surrender to God the Father, and through sharing in Jesus' bitter passion by freely accepted and divinely imposed sufferings for others.... At the Consecration I am allowed to offer myself in sacrifice in union with our gentle Mediator, Priest and Sacrificial Lamb to the heavenly Father for all the redeemed that they may have the grace of redemption in expiation, as well as for the sanctification of the world and for the liberation of the poor souls in Purgatory. Just as Jesus wanted to suffer voluntarily the bitter death of the Cross in our place and still offers himself for us in an unbloody manner in Holy Mass, so am I allowed and commissioned by Jesus to offer expiation in body and soul in others' place, through participation in the holiness of the triune God and in the oblation of myself, body and soul, for love of God and for souls, so that we all may glorify the Father through Jesus whom we have been given for our salvation."[3] Sister Julitta imagines Jesus proclaiming at the moment of the elevation (qv): "Recognize, O world, that I love the Father and do what is pleasing to him." As she says, "The triune God cannot release us from self-sacrifice, from a participation in deep faith and from a surrender in a deep

sacrificial spirit to the divine will." All this is existential Eucharistic theology of the highest quality. Sister Julitta says that at Mass the Father showed himself to her as "the Lord of life, not only of my own life but of that of the whole world, and not only of the world, but also of his much-loved incarnate Son."[4] Those who may have been tempted to cloud the intrinsic reality of the Mass by undue, unenlightened attention to ceremonial will find these words a salutary corrective.

---

[1]Cf. *Schwester Maria Julitta, Ihr Geistliches Vermächtnis*, ed. Andreas M. Back, CMF, 4th ed., Wurzburg, 1970; quotations here from English tr. *Spiritual Testament*, 1987—by numbered sections; [2]103; [3]174, 175.

ROSMINI-SERBATI, ANTONIO (1797-1855)

The prolific and controversial Italian thinker propounded views on the Eucharist which were condemned as were other propositions taken from his works thirty-two years after his death.[1] There is a literature for and against him, that is, in regard to his orthodoxy. His doctrine has been characterised as "vital assimilation" as an explanation of transubstantiation. The condemned propositions are: 29. "We think that the following conjecture is by no means at variance with Catholic doctrine, which alone is truth: In the Eucharistic sacrament the substance of bread and wine becomes the true flesh and true blood of Christ, when Christ makes it the terminus of his sentient principle, and vivifies it with his life; almost in that way by which bread and wine truly are transubstantiated into our flesh and blood, because they become the terminus of our sentient principle. 30. When transubstantiation has been accomplished, it can be understood that to the glorious body of Christ some part is added, incorporated in it, undivided, and equally glorious. 31. In the sacrament of the Eucharist by the power of words the body and blood of Christ are present only in that measure which corresponds *(a quel tanto)* to the substance of the bread and wine, which are transubstantiated; the rest of the body of Christ is there through concomitance. 32. Since he who does not eat the flesh of the Son of man and drink of his blood, does not have life in him (cf. Jn 6:54), and nevertheless those who die with the baptism of water, of blood or of desire, certainly attain eternal life, it must be said that these who have not eaten of the body and blood of Christ, are administered this heavenly food in the future life, at the very moment of death. Hence also to the saints of the Old Testament Christ was able by descending into hell to communicate himself under the appearances of bread and wine, in order to make them ready for the vision of God."[2]

[1]For bibl. cf. standard reference works, e.g., *The Oxford Dictionary of the Christian Church*, 1203, 4, s.v.; A. Piolanti, *Il Mistero*, 239, n. 8, lists the works of R. where the Eucharist is dealt with: *Dell'educazione cristiana*, Rome 1823, 184-218; *Catechismo disposto secondo l'ordine delle idee*, Naples, 1949, pp. 75, 110, 125, 128, 223; *L'introduzione al Vangelo secondo S. Giovanni commentata*, Turin, 1882, lezioni 72, 77, 79, 81-89, 90-93; *Antropologia soprannaturale* III, Casale Monferrato, 1883, 372-502; *Epistolario completo*, XII, Casale Monferrato, 1893, lettera 7679, 354-59; in defence of R., cf. G.B. Pagani, *Le quaranta propozioni rosminiane condemnate*, Rome, 1908, 201-235; L. Lanzoni, *Compendium theologiae dogmaticae*, Turin, 1882, 213-338; G. Morano, *Esame critico delle quaranta propzioni condemnate*, Milan, 1905, 573-678; C. Viglino, *La ragionevolezza dell'Eucaristia*, Domodossola, 1938; against R's orthodoxy, Anonimo, *Rosminiatarum propositionum trutina theologica*, Rome, 1892, 304-329; F. Sala, *Institutiones Theologiae Dogmaticae*, Milan, 1899, treatise on the Eucharist; G. Ballerini, *Gesù Eucaristico e i suoi oppositori*, Pavia, 1922, 144-148, 235-238;
[2]DS 3229, 3230; Decree of the Holy Office, 14 December 1887.

RUPERT OF DEUTZ (c. 1075-1129 or 1130)

R. involved indirectly in the Investiture controversy, for as a monk in Liege he shared the exile of his abbot, dealt with the Eucharist in his first work, *Liber de divinis officiis*, on the ecclesiastical year, but especially in his commentary *In Evangelium Joannis*.[1] His intention in this work, written c. 1116, was to defend the real presence (qv) against Berengar (qv), but his language aroused suspicion. William of St. Thierry rebuked him in his *Epistola ad quemdam monachum*, accusing him of holding the theory known as impanation (qv) There is controversy about R's actual teaching, but such a sentence as this can scarcely be explained away: "The Word already made flesh is made visible bread, not changed into bread, but assuming and bringing the bread into the unity of the person." R. was not felicitous in his phraseology about the Eucharistic species; he did, in his more mature works, seek to attenuate the crudity of some expressions.

[1]*De divinis officiis*, bk. 2, ch. 2 and 9; PL 170, 35, 40; *In Evangelium Joannis*, II, 14, PL 169, 201-826; cf. G. Gerberon, *Apologia pro Ruperto Tuitiensi*, Paris, 1669, PL 167, 23-194; Hurter, I, 25-29; O. Wolf, *Mein Meister R. Ein Monchsleben aus dem 12 Jahrhundert*, Freiburg i.B., 1920; E. Betz, *Rupertus von Deutz. Seine Werke und die bildende Kunst*, Cologne, 1930; J. de Ghellinck, *L'essor de la littérature latine au XIIe siècle*, I, Paris-Brussels, 1946, 118-120; *id.*, *Le mouvement théologique au XIIe siècle*, 2nd ed., Bruges, 1948, *passim*; St. Axters, *La spiritualité des Pays Bas*, Louvain, 1948, 20-22; P. Sejourne, DTC XIV, 201-203; A. Piolanti, EC X, 1446-48; B. Neunheuser, *L'Eucharistie*, II, Paris, 1966, 78-79; A. Piolanti, *Il Mistero*, 237 ff;

S

SACRAMENTALI COMMUNIONE, 29 June 1970
Instruction of the Sacred Congregation for Divine
Worship on the Extension of the Faculty to administer
Holy Communion under both species.[1] The document
takes account of the growing demand for communion
of this kind and states the authorities with competence
and the principles that should guide them. It also
warns against possible abuses.

---

[1]Text *AAS* 62 (1970), 664-667; English tr., issued by the Congregation, A. Flannery, O.P., I, 206-208.

SACRAM LITURGIAM, 25 January 1964
A *Motu proprio* by which Pope Paul VI began the
process of implementation of the Constitution on the
Sacred Liturgy.[1] He notably set up a Concilium or
commission which would be responsible for this work
and he decreed that educational centres undertake the
work of instruction in the liturgy prescribed by the
Council. Diocesan commissions should be set up "to
promote the liturgy and understanding of the liturgy."
The Pope also declared that "territorial" episcopal
conferences, in the areas within their care, should for
the time being mean "national" episcopal conferences.

---

[1]*AAS* 56 (1964), 139-144.

SACRIFICE
The new messianic community established by Jesus
Christ was heir to the OT traditions about sacrifice,
bloody and unbloody, offered in the first case as
holocausts, for atonement or as peace offering.[1] Sacrifice, that is, the offering of a material gift to God to
acknowledge his absolute lordship and man's utter
dependence on him, was an imperative of the religious
mind of the Jews in the time of Jesus and of the first
days of the Church, as it is of all peoples. Whence the
problem: Why did the Gospels and the Pauline epistles
seem to speak so little about it? For the same reason
probably that Jesus never spoke of himself as a priest:
his claim would have been incomprehensible to the
Jews, as he was not a member of the tribe of Levi. He
had a priesthood entirely superior to the Levitical
office based on inheritance, free therefore, and justified
by reference to the priesthood of Melchisedek (Ps
110:4; Heb 5:6; 10; 6:20).

It is Heb which explicitly announces the priesthood
(qv) of Christ and, consequently, establishes fully,
what is implicit in the Gospels and St. Paul, the truth
about his sacrifice: "But when Christ appeared as a
high priest of the good things that have come, then
through the greater and more perfect tent (not made
with hands, that is, not of this creation) he entered
once for all into the Holy Place, taking not the blood
of goats and calves but his own blood, thus securing
an eternal redemption" (9:11, 12). "And every priest
stands daily at his service, offering repeatedly the same
sacrifices, which can never take away sins. But when
Christ had offered for all time a single sacrifice for
sins, he sat down at the right hand of God, then to
wait until his enemies should be made a stool for his
feet" (10:11-13).

Paul in Eph 5:2 leaves little doubt on the sacrifice of Christ: "And walk in love, as Christ loved us and gave himself up for us, a fragrant offering and as sacrifice to God." Examined in the light of this interpretation, the Institution Narratives (qv) of the Eucharist reveal a true sacrificial core. They link up with the sacrifice of Mount Sinai. The texts to compare are Mt 26:26-29 and parallels (Mk 14:22-25; Lk 22:15-20; 1 Cor 11: 23-26) with Ex 24: 4-8. Mt: "Now as they were eating, Jesus took bread and blessed, and broke it, and gave it to the disciples and said, 'Take, eat; this is my body.' And he took a cup, and when he had given thanks he gave it to them, saying, 'Drink of it, all of you; for this is my blood of the covenant, which is poured out for many for the forgiveness of sins. I tell you I shall not drink again of this fruit of the vine until that day when I drink it new with you in my Father's kingdom.'" Ex: "And Moses wrote all the words of the Lord. And he rose early in the morning, and built an altar at the foot of the mountain, and twelve pillars, according to the twelve tribes of Israel. And he sent young men of the people of Israel, who offered burnt offerings and sacrificed peace offerings of oxen to the Lord. And Moses took half of the blood and put it in basins, and half of the blood he threw against the altar. Then he took the book of the covenant, and read it in the hearing of the people; and they said, 'All that the Lord has spoken we will do, and we will be obedient.' And Moses took the blood and threw it upon the people, and said, 'Behold the blood of the covenant which the Lord has made with you in accordance with all these words.'"

It is for biblical experts to look for latent symbolism in the twelve pillars representing the twelve tribes and the twelve apostles gathered around the Lord. But the basic ideas of the covenant and the blood poured out are not latent; they are quite explicit. The idea of the Eucharist as sacrifice is grounded in the New Testament (cp. Eph 2:13; 1 Cor 10:14-18; Rom 12:1).

It can be traced in the early Fathers, who took up and developed the idea which passed from the NT to the early liturgies, the *Didache*, the *Traditio apostolica* probably of St. Hippolytus, the *Euchology of Serapion* (qqv): "For this is the sacrifice of which the Lord says: 'In every place and at every time offer me a pure sacrifice, for I am a great king, says the Lord, and my name is marvellous among the nations'" (Mal 1:11, 14).[2] "And we pray you to send your Holy Spirit on the offering of your holy Church, to bring together in unity all those who receive it."[3] "Lord of the Powers, fill this sacrifice, too, with your power and your participation. For it is you that we have offered, this living sacrifice, this bloodless offering.... For this reason, we, too, celebrating the memorial of his death, have offered this bread and we pray: Through this sacrifice, reconcile us all to yourself, be favourable to us, O God of truth."[4]

Important patristic testimonies include St. Irenaeus: "But giving his disciples advice to offer to God the first-fruits from his creatures, not as if he needed them, but that they themselves should not be unfruitful or ungrateful, he took bread which is a creature, and giving thanks said: 'This is my body.' And likewise he proclaimed that the chalice, which is from our earthly creation, is (i.e., contains) his blood; he taught the new oblation of the New Testament, which the Church receiving from the Apostles, offers to God in the whole world, to him who gives us as food the first-fruits of his gifts in the NT ; of this Malachi, from among the twelve (minor) prophets thus prophesied. (Here he quotes Mal 1:10-11.) He made abundantly clear by this that the ancient people will cease to make offering to God; but in every place a sacrifice will be offered to him and it will be pure; his name is glorified among the nations."[5]

St. Justin (qv) is not less explicit: "Wherefore God says thus concerning the sacrifices that were offered up by you at that time, speaking, as I said before, by Malachi, one of the Twelve (minor prophets): 'I have no pleasure in you, says the Lord of hosts, and I will not accept an offering from your hands. For from the rising of the sun to its setting my name is great among the nations, says the Lord of hosts' (1:10-12). He speaks at that time, so long beforehand, concerning the sacrifices that are being offered to him in every place by us Gentiles, that is to say, the bread of the Eucharist and likewise the cup of the Eucharist saying also that we glorify his name, but you profane it."[6] "God therefore has long since borne witness that all sacrifices offered by his name, which Jesus the Christ enjoined, namely at the thanksgiving of the bread and the cup, which are offered in every place on earth by the Christians, are well pleasing to him."[7]

By the time of St. Cyril of Jerusalem (qv) the idea is firmly established: "After the spiritual sacrifice, the unbloody worship, has been accomplished in this victim that is offered in propitiation, we call on God for peace in all the Churches, for tranquillity in the world, for the emperors, for the armies and the allies, for the ill and afflicted. In brief, for all those in need of help we all pray and offer the sacrifice.... We then remember also those who have fallen asleep: first, the patriarchs, prophets, apostles, and martyrs, that through their prayers and intercession God would accept our petitions; then, for our fathers who have fallen in holiness, for the bishops, and, in short, for all those who have fallen asleep. For we are convinced that our prayers, which rise up for them in the presence of the holy and venerable victim, are most profitable to their souls."[8]

St. Augustine (qv) wrote at length on sacrifice in the *De Civitate Dei*.[9] "Thus a true sacrifice," he says, "is every work which is done that we may be united to God in holy fellowship, and which has a reference to that supreme good and end in which alone we can be truly blessed." In the form of a servant, the great High Priest offered himself to God in his passion for us, that we might be members of this glorious Head, "For it was this form he offered, in this he was offered, because it is according to it he is Mediator, in this he is our Priest, in this the sacrifice." He concludes: "This is the sacrifice of Christians: we, being many, are one body in Christ. And this also is the sacrifice which the Church continually celebrates in the sacrament of the altar, known to the faithful, in which she teaches that she herself is offered in the offering she makes to God."[10] "Thus," he says again, "he is both the Priest who offers and the sacrifice offered. And he designed that there should be a daily sign of this in the sacrifice of the Church, which, being his body, learns to offer herself through him. Of this true sacrifice the ancient sacrifices of the saints were the various and numerous signs; and it was thus variously figured, just as one thing is signified by a variety of words, that there may be less weariness when we speak of it much. To this supreme and true sacrifice all false sacrifices have given place."[11]

St. Thomas Aquinas (qv) deals with sacrifice in the context of the virtue of religion.[12] Don Anscar Vonier has drawn attention to the fact that he "found it possible to state the whole Eucharistic mystery in sacramental concepts.... The Eucharistic sacrifice is entirely subsumed under the concept of the Eucharistic sacrament—nay, more, the Eucharistic sacrament is said by him to have its main expression and celebration in the consecration, which consecration, again, according to him, is the direct and complete sacramental representation of Christ's passion, and as such is sacrifice."[13] "This sacrament," says St. Thomas "is at the same time sacrifice and sacrament; but it has the nature of sacrifice inasmuch as it is offered up, and it has the nature of a sacrament inasmuch as it is partaken."[14] The Angelic Doctor's thinking has the complexity to be expected in such a subject—a fact manifest when he deals with OT types of the Eucharist—the offering of Melchizedek, the sacrifice of expiation and the manna, with the Paschal Lamb as excelling all because it typifies every aspect.[15] Different interpreters have explored and emphasized differing aspects of the saint's thought.

The concept of sacrifice was integral to Catholic teaching and theology and was given the necessary prominence when this teaching and theology had to be clarified by the Council of Trent (qv). Since then, down to Vatican II, much ink has flown on the precise meaning of sacrifice, with two theories apparently in competition, oblation and immolation (qqv).

[1]For bibliography cf. L. Sabourin, S.J., in L. Sabourin *Sin, Redemption and Sacrifice*, Rome Analecta Biblica 48, 1970, 299-333; Bibliographies to other articles: Billot, L. De la Taille, M., Immolation, Oblation, Paschal Mystery; cf. E. Dorsch, *Der Opfercharakter der Eucharistie, einst und jetzt*, Innsbruck, 1909; H. Lamiroy, *De essentia Missae sacrificii*, 1919, Louvain; F. Kramp, *Scripta nuper edita de sacrificio Missae, Greg.*, 2 (1921), 416-442; J. Grimal, *Le sacerdoce et le sacrifice de N.S.J.C.*, 4th ed., Paris, 1926; B. Augier, *L'offrande et le sacrifice, RT*, 29 (1929), 2-34, 117-131, 193-218, 476-488; id., *Le sacrifice ecclésiastique, RT* 32 (1932), 739-57; 1934, 201-222; A. Collart, *Theories sur l'essence de la Messe, Collectiones Namurcenses* 1930, 210-219; 376-391; 1931, 10-25, 207-227; E. Leroux, La controverse sur l'essence du sacrifice de la Messe, Rev. Eccl. de Liege 1930-31, 341-351; G. Petazzi, *La vera natura del sacrificio della Missa; L'essenza del sacrificio eucaristico*, Padua, 1936; W. Goossens, *Les origines de l'Eucharistie, sacrament et sacrifice*, Gembloux, 1931; E.F. Dowd, *Conspectus of Modern Catholic Thought on the Essence of the Eucharistic Sacrifice*, Washington, 1937; *Die Vollendung der Welt im Opfer des Gottmenschen*, Freiburg, i.B., 1938; J. Van Der Meersch, *Annotationes de Sacrificio Missae*, Bruges, 1940; A. Van Hove, *De Eucharistia*, 2nd. ed., Malines, 1941; B. Capelle, O.S.B., *Du sens de la Messe*, in *Les Questions liturgiques et paroissiales*, 1942, 1-25-study of the literature; F.A. Piersanti, *L'essenza della Messa*, Rome, 1942 (Dissert. Angelicum); R. Garrigou Lagrange, O.P., *An Christus non solum virtualiter sed actualiter offert Missas quae quotidie celebrantur, Angelicum* 19 (1942), 105-117; id. *De Eucharistia*, Turin, 1945; G. Anichini, *L'Eucharistia nel dramma della Redenzione*, Lucca, 1947; E. Doronzo, *De Eucharistia*, II *De Sacrificio*, Milwaukee, 1948; E. Masure, *Le Sacrifice du Corps Mystique*, Paris, 1950, 8th ed., 1957; G. Sartori, *Le concezioni sacramentali del Sacrificio della Messa, La Scuola Cattolica* 78 (1950), 3-24; M. Becque, Le Mystère de la Messe, NRT 82 (1950), 27-83; J. Galy, *Le Sacrifice dans l'Ecole francaise de spiritualite*, Paris, 1951; A. Zigrossi, *L'unità fra Cena e Passione alla luce della 'res et signum' del Sacrificio Eucaristico, Divus Thomas* (Piacenza), 55 (1952), 358-374; C. (Cardinal) Journet, *La Messe, Présence du sacrifice de la croix*, Paris, 1957; id., *Le mystère de l'Eucharistie*, Paris, 1981; G. Filograssi, *De SS Eucharistia*, 6th ed., Rome, 1957; R. Tremblay, *Le mystère de la Messe, Angelicum*, 36 (1959), 184-202; R. Masi, *La dottrina sacramentale del sacrificio della Messa, Euntes Docete*, 12 (1959), 141-181; J. Lecuyer, *Le Sacrifice de la Nouvelle Alliance*, Paris, 1962; U. Van Camp, *De habitudine Missae ad sacrificium Crucis apud commentatores latinos Ep. ad Hebr.*, Katanga, 1962, (Dissert. Antonianum); P.M. Matthijs, *De aeternitate Sacerdotii Christi et de unitate Sacrificii Crucis et altaris*, Rome, 1963; F. Quarello, *Il Sacrificio di Cristo e della Chiesa. Rassegna e riflessioni su posizioni recenti*, Brescia, 1970; F. Spadafora, *L'Eucaristia nella Bibbia*, Rovigo, 1971; V. Pagliarani, *Il Sacramento dell'unità di vita e di Sacrificio della Chiesa con Gesu*, Rovigo, 1971; P. Cardeil, *La Cène et la Croix, NRT* 101 (1973), 676-698; Joseph de Sainte-Marie, *L'Eucharistie, salut du monde*, Paris, 1981; P.L. Carle, *Le Sacrifice de la nouvelle alliance*, Paris 1981; E. Galbiati, *L'Eucaristia nella Bibbia*, 2nd ed., Milan, 1982; A. Piolanti, *Il Mistero*, 376-546; A. Gaudel, DTC XIV, 1 (1939), 662-92; E.L. Mascall, *Corpus Christi*, London, 1965; E. Masure, *The Sacrifice of the Mystical Body*, Chicago, London, 1954; C. (Cardinal) Journet, *La Messe, Présence de la croix*, Bruges, 1957; J.A. Jungmann, *The Sacrifice of the Church*, London, 1956; B. Neunheuser, ed., *Opfer Christi und Opfer der Kirche*, Dusseldorf, 1960; R. Daly, S.J., *Christian*

Sacrifice, the Judaeo-Christian Background before Origen, Washington, 1978. [2]*Didache*, 14, L. Deiss, *Springtime*, 77; [3]Epiclesis in the *Traditio apostolica*, *Springtime*, 131; [4]*The Eucharistic Liturgy, Springtime*, 195; [5]*Adv. Haer.*, IV, 17, 5, Harvey, II, 197ff; [6]*Dialogue with Trypho*, 41, 2-3, tr. L. Williams, SPCK, 82; [7]*Ibid.*, 117, 1, *op. cit.*, 240f; [8]*Cat* 23, 8, 9, *Springtime*, 286 (see article Cyril of Jerusalem on Catecheses); [9]Bk X, ch 3-6; [10]*Op. cit.*, ch 6, tr. Marcus Dods for *Great Books*, 302; [11]*Ibid.*, 311; [12]IIa-IIae, qq 85, 86; [13]*A Key to the Doctrine of the Eucharist*, London, 1925, 76; [14]III, q. 79, art v; [15]III, q. 73, art vi.

SANCTI VENITE

The oldest Eucharistic hymn (see article Hymnography) is in the Antiphonary of Bangor, which was compiled in that monastery between 680-691. It was taken from Ireland to Bobbio, is now in Milan, in the Ambrosiana Library, where it was taken in 1609 by Frederigo Borromeo (Cod C 5 inf.). The hymn may well be much earlier than the date of the Antiphonary, though the legend which associates it with St. Patrick is untenable. It runs thus: "Holy ones, come receive the Body of Christ, and drink the holy Blood by which you are redeemed./ Saved by the Body and Blood of Christ fed on them, let us sing praise to God./ By this Sacrament of Body and Blood all are freed from the jaws of Hell./ The Bestower of Salvation, Christ, the Son of God, has saved the world by Cross and Blood./ Sacrificed on behalf of all, the Lord has been himself both priest and victim./ The Law wherein sacrifice of victims was bidden is the foreshadowing of the divine mysteries (Heb 8:4-5)./ The Giver of Light and Saviour of all has granted a glorious grace to his holy ones:/ all approach with pure mind and faith to receive an eternal guarantee of salvation./ The Guardian of the saints, their Ruler as well, is the Lord, the Grantor of everlasting life to the faithful./ He gives the bread of heaven (Ps 77:24) to the hungry, proffers drink to the thirsty from the Living Spring (Jn 6:35)/ Alpha and Omega (Rev 1:8), Christ the Lord himself, has come, will come to judge mankind."[2]

[1]Critical ed. of the Antiphonary, F.E. Warren, Henry Bradshaw Society, IV, X, (1893, 1895); English tr., J.M. Neale, *English Hymnal*, 307; cf. F. Cabrol, O.S.B., DACL II, 1, 183-191; D.J. Sheerin, *The Eucharist*, Wilmington, 1986, 381-82; [2]Apud Sheerin, *op. cit.*

SANCTUS PONTIFEX, 24 May 1973

Declaration of the Sacred Congregation for the Clergy and the Sacred Congregation for the Discipline of the Sacraments on First Confession and First Communion.[1] In certain quarters the custom had been introduced of allowing children to receive their first Communion (qv) without going to confession. This was a tolerated exception to the general practice of the Church. With the approval of the Pope, the Congregation decides that the experiments, which have lasted for two years up to the end of the school year 1972-73, should cease and that everybody everywhere should conform to the decree *Quam singulari* (qv).

[1]A. Flannery, O.P., I, 241.

SCHOLASTIC DOCTORS, THE

Besides the scholastic doctors dealt with separately (see articles, Albert, St.; Thomas Aquinas, St.; Scotus, Duns) their contemporaries, notably St. Bonaventure, Alexander of Hales and Richard of Middleton, discussed, generally in their commentaries on the Sentences, problems of Eucharistic theology.[1] They may vary in the mode of presentation, but are always in agreement on the fundamentals already clarified in the preceding generations, notably the doctrine of transubstantiation (qv).

[1]E. Mangenot, DTC, V, 1309-1315.

SCHEEBEN, MATTHIAS JOSEPH (1835-1880)

Scheeben's Eucharistic doctrine is expressed fully in the dogmatic handbook. In the *Mysteries of Christianity* he related his theory to the dominant Trinitarian theme of that great work. In two chapters he deals in order with the real presence (qv) and the significance of the Eucharist. His thinking, as usual, is nourished by patristic learning, notably a long quotation from an author not frequently quoted in works on the Eucharist, St. Cyril of Alexandria (qv); and he takes account of medieval writers. He is especially good on the Eucharist and the Holy Spirit (qv).[1]

[1]English tr., C. Vollert, S.M., 1946, 469-535.

SCOTUS, JOHN DUNS (c. 1265-1308)

S. held that the Eucharist was the supreme and most excellent of the sacraments; the act of consecration (qv) is most noble. In regard to the sacraments he held that the opinion of the Holy, Roman church must be followed.[1] Some ink has flowed about his theory of transubstantiation (qv), notably on the question of adduction (qv). A student of his doctrine has summarized it thus:

1. "The conversion of the whole substance of bread and wine into the body and blood of our Lord Jesus

Christ, which wonderful and singular conversion the Church calls transubstantiation, is a formal dogma of faith, in the same way as the Real Presence (qv).

2. The principal argument which effectively establishes the dogma of transubstantiation is the supreme and infallible teaching of the Roman Church, which instructed by the Holy Spirit, explained the words of institution, *This is my body*, by an interpretation that was not constitutive but declaratory, as meaning the conversion of the whole substance of the bread into the body of Christ.

3. Eucharistic transubstantiation excludes both impanation (qv) and annihilation (qv), as also the return of the substance of bread into materia prima and it includes the concept or nature of true conversion, that is, the passage of the whole substance of bread into the body of Christ.

4. Eucharistic transubstantiation, though it is true conversion possible to God alone, is not nevertheless a conversion productive of the body of Christ already pre-existing in heaven, but conversion or adductive action of the body of Christ, through which Christ does not acquire a new *esse simpliciter*, but a new *esse hic*, namely, a new and real presence in the most holy Sacrament of the Altar.

5. Therefore the *terminus ad quem* of transubstantiation is not produced, but by the force of conversion it is adduced *(adducitur)*; but the *terminus a quo*, by the force of the same conversion, is by no means annihilated (minime annihilatur), but it ceases totally to be so that the body of Christ should replace it, it does not, therefore, pass into nothingness but into the body of Christ. But if the bread is annihilated, it is so not by force of conversion, but through a mere consequence of conversion. Hence transubstantiation as such could never be called annihilation of the *terminus a quo* but adductive conversion.

6. But this doctrine, which has also always had faithful followers outside the school of Scotus, for example Robert Bellarmine (qv) and among recent writers Ch. Pesch (qv), is entirely safe in faith, in so far as the Church even in the Council of Trent (qv), which maintaining strictly the fact of wonderful conversion, never intended to decide anything about the intimate nature of this wonderful conversion."[2]

More detailed studies deal with subtleties in S's thought; which subtleties have caused controversy.[3] The general summary given of his thought is acceptable.

---

[1]Works, *IV Sent.* dd. 8-13 and aparallel passages; cf. H. Klug, O.F.M. Cap., *Joannis Duns Scoti doctrina de sacrificio praesertim de sacrosancto missae sacrificio*, Barcelona, 1929; V.M. Cachia, O.P., *De natura transubstantiationis juxta S. Thomam et Scotum,* Rome, 1929; A.M. Vellico, O.F.M., *De Transubstantiatione juxta Joannem Duns Scotum, Antonianum* 5 (1930), 301-320; V. Cachia, O.P. *Animadversiones in transubstantiationis doctrinam, Angelicum* (1931), 246-62, reply to the former; [2]A.M. Vellico, *op. cit.,* 331; [3]Cf. V.M. Cachia, *op. cit.*

SERAPION OF THMUIS, ST. (after 360)

The anaphora (qv) of this Euchology of fourth century origin, parts of it earlier, is of interest to Eucharistic history. It runs as follows: *Preface*: "It is right and just to praise you to celebrate you, to glorify you, eternal Father of the only-begotten Son, Jesus Christ. We praise you, eternal God, inscrutable, indescribable, incomprehensible to every created nature. We praise you, who are known to the only-begotten Son, you whom he reveals and interprets, you whom he makes known to created natures. We praise you, you who know the Son and reveal his glory to the saints, you whom the Son whom you have begotten knows, you whom he shows and interprets to the saints." In this opening passage the care to affirm an orthodox belief at the time of Arianism is evident. The text continues:

"We praise you, invisible Father who gives immortality. You are the source of life, the source of light, the source of every grace and every truth. You love men, you love the poor, you reconcile yourself with all, you draw all to you through the coming of your beloved Son." There follows a Trinitarian passage: "We pray you, make living men of us. Give us the Spirit of light 'that we may know you, the True One, and him whom you have sent, Jesus Christ' (Jn 17:3). Give us the Holy Spirit that we may be able to proclaim and tell forth your indescribable mysteries! May the Lord Jesus speak in us and also the Holy Spirit. May he celebrate you with hymns through us! For you are above every Principality, Power, Force and Domination, above every name that is named in this age as in the age to come."

The Sanctus which follows is more elaborate than usual, as is the Institution Narrative: "Lord of the Powers, fill this sacrifice, too, with your power and your participation. For it is to you that we have offered this living sacrifice, this bloodless offering. It is to you that we have offered this bread, figure of the body of your only-begotten Son. This bread is a figure of the holy body. For the Lord Jesus, the night when he was betrayed, took bread, broke it, and gave it to his disciples saying: 'Take and eat, this is my body, which is broken for you for the forgiveness of sins.' For this reason, we, too, celebrating the memorial of his death, have offered this bread, and we pray: Through this sacrifice, reconcile us all to yourself, be favourable to us, O God of truth. For just as this bread, once scattered upon the hills, has been brought together and become one, so, too, deign to gather your Church from every people, from every land, from every town, village and house, and make of her a single Church, living and catholic."

This interruption in the narrative allows the author to insert an anamnesis and a passage borrowed from the *Didache* (qv). He takes up the narrative using here as in regard to the bread the word "figure" which is also found in the anaphora of St. Ambrose (qv):

"We offer, too, the cup, figure of the blood. For the Lord Jesus, after the meal, took the cup and said to his disciples: 'Take and drink, this is the New Testament, that is my blood poured out for you, for the forgiveness of sins.' For this reason we, too, have offered the cup, a figure of the blood."

Then follows an epiclesis, but it is addressed to the Word rather than to the Holy Spirit. The reason is the author's need to affirm orthodoxy in face of Arianism: "O God of truth, may your holy Word come down upon this bread, that it may bcome the body of the Word, and upon this cup, that it may become the blood of the Truth. Grant that all who communicate may receive a life-giving remedy, that will heal every weakness in them and strengthen them for all progress and all virtue; let it not be a cause, O God of truth, of condemnation, confusion, or shame."

There are then mementos of the living and of the dead and the anaphora ends with a prayer of petition and a doxology: "Accept the thanksgiving of your people. Bless those who have presented to you these offerings and thanksgivings. Give all this people health, prosperity, and happiness, all the blessings of soul and body. Through your only-begotten Son, Jesus Christ, in the Holy Spirit, as he was, as he is and will be, from all generations and for ever and ever."

Besides the anaphora, the Eucharistic Liturgy has a prayer for the breaking of the bread, a blessing of the people after the breaking of the bread, a prayer after the communion of the people, a blessing of oil and water and a prayer to accompany the laying on of hands after the blessing of the oil and water.

The distinctive features of the anaphora already noted support the opinion that the author of the Sacramentary, in which it occurs, is Serapion, Bishop of Thmuis, friend of St. Athanasius, who wrote in letters to him the first treatise on the Holy Spirit. He also acted as intermediary for Athanasius to Emperor Constantius. He had been trained as a monk by St. Antony. He may have taken an earlier text and worked on it to give this admirable example of a fourth-century Egyptian anaphora.

---

[1]Text ed. G. Wobbermin, *Altchristliche liturgische Stücke aus der*

Kirche Ägyptens nebst einem dogmatischen Brief des Bischofs Serapion von Thmuis, TU, XVII, 3b, 1898; F.E. Brightman, *JTS* 1, (1899-1900), 88-113; J. Quasten, *Monumenta*, 48-67, bibl. 48; F.X. Funk, *Didascalia et Constitutiones apostolorum*, II *Testimonia et Scripturae propinquae*, Paderborn 1905, repr. Turin, 1964, 172-77; English tr., J. Wordsworth, *Bishop Serapion's Prayer-Book*, Early Church Classics, S.P.C.K., 189; L. Deiss, *Springtime*, (here used), 184-208; *Prex*, 128-133; cf. B. Capelle, O.S.B., *L'Anaphore de Serapion, Essai d'exégèse, Le Muséon*, 59 (1946), 425-443; B. Botte, O.S.B., *L'Euchologe de Serapion, est-il authentique, Oriens Christ.*, 48 (1964), 5056; P.E. Rodopoulos, *The Sacramentary of Serapion*, (Oxford Dissertation) in *Theologia* 28 (1957), 252-275, 420-439, 578-591; *ibid.* 29 (1958), 45-54, 308-217; Bardenhewer, III, 98-102; G. Bardy, DTC, XIV, 2 (1941), 1908-1912; H. Dorrie, PW, Suppl. VIII (1956), 1260-6, 67.

SOCIAL EFFECTS OF THE EUCHARIST

The sign by which, according to Christian tradition, Jesus prefigured the Eucharist, was an act to meet an urgent social need: the feeding of the thousands in the wilderness. He who said, "Man shall not live by bread alone, but by every word that proceeds from the mouth of God" (Mt 4:4; Lk 4:4), worked a miracle to provide bread for those who had none.

In the institution of the Sacrament, Jesus did not create a rite remote from the flow of human existence; he placed it in the setting of a community meal. It is immeasurably more than that, reaching into the very godhead, continuing the mystery of the Incarnation in our midst, for our manifold benefit. But it touches human life in its fullness, has involved from the beginning relationships of diverse kinds, within the family where initiation into its meaning and diffusion can be quite normal, in social structures where the minister of the Eucharist constitutes a centre of multiple social reference, in assemblies and liturgical gatherings where there is an available remedy for evey kind of discrimination, dissension, conflict.

The call to the believing Christian is to make this idealism effective. A weakening in the Church's mission to the world is often caused by the cleavage between prayer and worship on the one hand and, on the other, conduct in the cultural, social, political and economic domains. The divided Christian mind has cost the Church heavily. It is a phenomenon calling for detailed, deep analysis. It is regrettable that in places it has made of the Eucharist a Sacrament of purely private concern—that is, said with full appreciation for the complexities of human behavior. It is true that people are sometimes scandalised at the sight of daily communicants cheating in business, heedless about human rights, indifferent to the many social evils of our time. It is equally true that countless apostles of true social reform throughout the world draw from frequent reception of the Sacrament light and strength to persevere in work that is tiring, dull, at times apparently hopeless.

The remedy is to preach and practise the full truth. Social work is difficult, is often denied any due gratitude, may be foiled of results that could be legitimately expected. In such circumstances inner motivation of a particular kind is called for. It is available to the Eucharistic Christian. Not superficially, but always immediately.

The NT teaching, in particular the directives of St. Paul (qv), insist on the immediate call from the Eucharist to commitment to Christ in his brothers, to endeavour for the elimination of every kind of injustice between man and man, for the relief of the stricken, the creation of a community which will reflect more and more brightly, experience more and more fully, Christ's love, his concern and compassion for his suffering members. The same important truth has been powerfully expressed by the Dombes Group (qv). There must be a concerted effort to establish, strengthen, extend this essential bond between Eucharistic piety and effective love of others.

A challenge to the Christian is the dignity of the potential communicant, the individual who would receive Holy Communion more freely and more frequently if he were relieved of the burden of poverty or social disability. The motive here is realization that others besides the affluent or well-off Christian are called to be beneficiaries of Christ's supreme gift.

There is a call to consecrate the world to God, to free it of destructive, corrosive, pollutant elements, to give it the beauty which, in the design of the Creator, it would have. To make sacred means to draw on that which is the primary source of all the sacred, the Incarnate Word, entering our world to enhance the whole universe, active through his Spirit, he comes to those who receive the Eucharist in an authentic plenary sense.

Who, finally, can estimate the indirect effects of strong Eucharistic faith at certain moments in the Church's history? They compel our attention and evoke our admiration, hopefully our imitation. The desire to create a fitting setting for the Eucharist has influenced the artistic life of peoples, community morale. The most beautiful buildings in the world have been raised as edifices for the celebration of the Eucharist: witness the medieval cathedrals.

Here the Eucharist was a unique source of social inspiration. Community faith, the manifold response of genius and superb craftsmanship, as of sheer human industry, individual and collective, of labour-defying tasks of immense magnitude were all, in the last resort, Eucharistic. All was centred on the Mass, the Lord who is its meaning, the manifold benefaction he distributes to all. One day perhaps in a new, cleaner

and more vibrant universe he will again meet the same generosity, see Christ changing by his divine power the face of the earth .

At the National Eucharistic Congress, December 4-8, 1987, which concluded the National Eucharistic Year in the Philippines, its theme, "One Bread, One Body, One People," the social commitment called for by the Eucharist was a foremost idea, powerfully expressed by some lecturers, notably Bishop Francisco Claver, SJ, and Archbishop Orlando Quevedo, OMI. A book occasioned by the Year, *The Eucharist and the Filipino* by Bishop T.C. Bacani is also highly relevant, as will be the *Proceedings of the Congress.*

---

[1] I. Giordani in *Eucaristia*, 1207-19; bibl. to articles on Spirituality and St. Paul; A. Hamman, *Vie liturgique et vie sociale*, Paris, 1968, Agape, 151-227; X Leon-Dufor, *Le partage du pain eucharistique*, Paris, 1982; *Symposium International du Congrès Eucharistique*, 13-15 juillet, 1981, *Responsabilité, Partage, Eucharistie;* Text of Archbishop Quevedo's lecture, *Doctrine and Life*, 38 (1988), 179-189.

SPIRIT, THE HOLY

Acts 1:14 we read: "All these with one accord devoted themselves to prayer, together with the women and Mary the mother of Jesus, and with his brothers." There is no mention whatever of the Eucharist. Then there occurred the event of Pentecost. It was immediately followed by Peter's striking first sermon. "And Peter said to them, 'Repent, and be baptized every one of you in the name of Jesus Christ for the forgiveness of your sins; and you shall receive the gift of the Holy Spirit'" (Acts 2:38). The sequel was the birth of the new messianic community, the Church: "So those who received his word were baptized, and there were added that day about three thousand souls" (*Ibid.* 41). But now they have a new activity, thus described: "And they devoted themselves to the apostles' teaching and fellowship, to the breaking of bread and the prayers" (*Ibid.* 42). The idea is repeated within a few verses: "And day by day, attending the temple together and breaking bread in their homes, they partook of food with glad and generous hearts, praising God and having favour with the people" (*Ibid.* 46-47).

"Breaking of bread" is a technical term for celebration of the Eucharist. There is no doubt that it took place only after the descent of the Spirit; it is closely linked with this descent. The newcomers who are promised the Spirit by Peter—provided they repent and are baptized in the name of Jesus Christ—at once join in the "breaking of the bread."

Understandably there are two aspects to the question of the Spirit and the Eucharist, distinct but not inseparable. There is the relationship between the

Spirit and Christ present in the Eucharist and the relationship between the Spirit and the grace which comes to the individual through the Eucharist, sacrament and sacrifice.

On the question of the Spirit and Christ, account must be taken of the history of the epiclesis. In the east the epiclesis is considered very differently from western attitudes, at least until recently. This may be due to the more explicitly Trinitarian liturgical outlook of the easterns. In the west the emphasis, in the essential moment of the consecration, that is the change of the bread and wine into the body and blood of Christ, has been on the action of the priest *in persona Christi*, which concept is not dominant in eastern thinking—some think it absent. The subject is dealt with, with ample bibliography, in the present author's *Trinitas*, s.v. In the same work the article on Grace deals with the action of the Spirit in this area, in a Trinitarian context.

---

[1]Add to bibl. P. McGoldrick, *The Holy Spirit and the Eucharist*, *ITQ*, 50 (1883/84), 48-66.

SPIRITUALITY

St. Thomas Aquinas says that the Eucharist is "the consummation of the whole spiritual life."[1] The idea was expanded by Vatican II: "The Sacraments and all the ministries of the Church and apostolic duties are bound to the Eucharist and ordered towards it. For the holy Eucharist contains the whole spiritual treasure of the Church, that is, Christ himself, our Pasch, he who is the living Bread, whose flesh, vivified by the Holy Spirit and vivifying, gives life to men, inviting and leading them to offer, in union with him, their very life, their work, all creation."[2]

Since the spiritual life is the development of the life of grace and through the Sacraments grace reaches the soul, the Eucharist, as the greatest of the Sacraments, must be central in an authentic spiritual life. It brings not only sanctifying grace, but also the Author of grace; it continuously helps the fulfilment of all other sacramental grace; and by the word of the Master it has an infallible eschatological dimension—"he who eats my flesh and drinks my blood has eternal life, and I will raise him up at the last day" (Jn 6:54).

To these immense spiritual advantages of the Sacrament, the Eucharist adds the reality of the true eternal sacrifice. Here it responds to the deepest religious impulse in man, an impulse which must find expression if personal perfection is to be attained. It is in this encounter of person with Person that the mystery of man is established. Religion is a personal exchange, a dialogue at many levels between God and his creature, ultimately a fusion of essential interests through the plenary exercise of the theological virtues.

The Eucharist affords immediate challenge, scope, motivation, for faith becomes increasingly pure and freed of spurious accretion, as the soul adheres unhesitatingly to the truth that here under the appearances of bread and wine, the Eternal Son of the Father is present. Hope which carries the soul unflinchingly into the future, has in the eschatological dimension of this mystery, a support which can carry it forward to the moment of inexpressible bliss, when it is with Christ.

Charity, the supreme commandment, the queen of the virtues, the bond of perfection, meets in the Eucharist the Lord, immediate object of its exercise. The history of spirituality shows that the spirituals may be misled or side-tracked by systems, practices, even a fashionable jargon. Spirituality thus recedes into the subjective domain; the Eucharist gives it an objective world to live in, essentially to love in; it is truly Christocentric, for it is concerned with Christ directly. It is the enemy of illusion for he is the "Way, the Truth and the Life." Desire in the virtue of love is central; how much the history of the Church, especially exemplified in the lives of its saints, teaches us of Eucharistic desire.

For life needs presence, and here presence is most powerful, active, creative, living. Life needs routine, which is a special relationship with time: time, a creature of God which, as with all his creatures, he respects. Routine is called deadly, boring. But acceptance of routine, conformity to it in a spirit of faith is utterly indispensable to true spiritual growth. Only such conformity enables the soul to rid itself totally of illusion. It enters a domain of bare, therefore perfect, faith, and will in due course reap the rewards of its fidelity. As marriage lived faithfully through phases of dullness moves eventually into a period of tranquil fulfillment, of serenity and deep, untroubled joy, so the communicant who, day after day, in a spirit of faith, without any emotional support, clings to the Saviour, will one day savour his delights in peace and joy.

Life needs celebration. It marks great moments, turning-points, commemorates anniversaries, makes the present meaningful in relation to the past, delineates the hope of the future. This vital need is certainly met in the Eucharist, in the great feasts when it is given special solemnity, in the recurring Sunday liturgies, presently given special prominence. There is thus a valid relationship between the interior life and the necessary externals of our religion.

We touch here another factor which has been misunderstood: the link between liturgy and personal spirituality. Not only is there no reason for conflict; there is every reason for harmony and mutual enrichment. The Liturgy without a true interior spirit is mechanical; a true interior spirit may deteriorate without recognition of what ecclesial life, membership of the Mystical Body of Christ, demands.

---

[1]III q. 73, a. 3; cf. *Dictionnaire de la Spiritualité*, ed. S. de Fiores and T. Goffil, Paris, 1983, 336-349, s. v. Eucharistie, E. Ruffini; *Dizionario Enciclopedico di Spiritualita*, ed. A. Ancilli, Rome, 1975, s.v.; *Eucaristia*, 736-753, J. Castellano; K. Rahner, S.J., *The Eucharist and Suffering, Theological Investigations*, III, 161-170; id., *The Eucharist in our Daily Lives, Theol. Investigations*, VII, 211-266; id., *On the Duration of the Presence of Christ after Communion, Theol. Investigations* IV, 312-320; (see articles, Communion, Holy, and Heart of Jesus, the Eucharistic).

STIPENDS, MASS OFFERINGS

Offerings of bread and wine were made from early times to the celebrant of Mass.[1] He was free to use the remnant, after he had duly celebrated with what was required, for the clergy and the poor; the Mass was applied to the donors. Abuses are possible in this area, as in every other department of religious observance. But the practice is not simony. It is not the purchase or attempted purchase of spiritual things with material products. Appeal is made to St. Paul (1 Cor, 9:7-13) for justification. From the eighth century, donations of money were made instead of bread and wine and the practice of offering stipends, as they are called, became widespread. It was regulated by appeal to elementary justice in regard to contracts, and, in important details, by Canon Law. The New Code, 1984, deals with the various questions in canons 945 through 958. Anything in the nature of trafficking or multiple application is forbidden, as is acceptance of more than one stipend for personal retention each day—if another is allowed it is for charity. Amounts are subject to proper control, as are funded Mass intentions and the number of stipends that may be received over a specified period.

The essential justification of the practice of offering stipends is the bond between the ministerial priesthood in its central act and the faithful needing this ministry, willing to share in some way the burden of the priest's life. He is a priest for them, never more so than in offering the sacrifice of the Mass.

---

[1]Cf. T. Ortolan, *Mass Stipends*, Washington, 1925; N.T. Miller, *Funded Masses according to the Code of Canon Law*, Washington, 1926; T. McDonnell, *Sitpends and Simony*, IER 50 (1939), 593-612; 54 (1939), 35-57, 159-175; T. Ortolan DTC VII, 169-91; for church regulations and the competent authority, cf. Paul VI, *Firma in Traditione*, Apostolic Letter concerning Mass Stipends, 15 June 1974, A. Flannery, ed., *Vatican Council II*, 1, 278-280.

SYMBOLISM

As Pope Paul VI says in *Mysterium Fidei*: "It is true that much can be found in the Fathers and in the Scholastics with regard to symbolism in the Eucharist, especially with reference to the unity of the Church. The Council of Trent, restating their doctrine, taught that the Saviour bequeathed the Blessed Eucharist to his Church 'as a symbol . . . of that unity and charity with which he wished all Christians to be most intimately united among themselves' and hence 'as a symbol of that one Body of which he is the Head.'"[1]

The doctrine of symbolism has been thought out anew by modern Catholic theologians. We must admit that it can be proposed, as the Dombes Group note in a report, by Catholic theologians to evacuate the doctrine of realism. In fact this is by no means a consequence of symbolism rightly understood. It is rather, on the contrary, true that a thoroughly grounded realism needs to be viewed in the light of a certain symbolism to save it from deviation.

Karl Rahner says: "All beings are by their nature symbolic, because they necessarily 'express' themselves in order to attain their own nature." Later he asks: "What then is the primordial meaning of symbol and symbolic, and hence (and to this extent) symbolic for another? It is this: as a being realizes itself in its own intrinsic 'otherness' (which is constitutive of its being), retentive of its intrinsic plurality (which is contained in its self-realization) as its derivative and hence congruous expression, it makes itself known. This derivative and congruous expression, constitutive of each being, is the symbol which comes in addition from the object of knowledge to the knower—in addition only, because already initially present in the depths of the grounds of one's being. The being is known in this symbol without which it cannot be known at all; thus it is symbol in the original (transcendental) sense of the word."[2]

Symbolism is thus ontologically and epistemologically grounded. The application to the Eucharist is made possible by the Master's choice of bread and wine as the matter of his great Sacrament. "The symbols in the Eucharist have a dominating tone of food and drink, and it is in that key that they relate to man and, in their own way, throw light on his condition. In the very act by which they communicate Christ to us, they signify and recall that man is compounded of culture, community, body and mortality in a way which we must now define by gradually allowing the Eucharistic symbolism to unfold its immense richness."[3] The author develops his thought to comprise the whole range of life, personal and collective. For the believer the problem is to raise all that to the supernatural level.

Here is where faith illumines symbolism, transforms and elevates it. The bread and wine signify and evoke man's need, his growth, his association with his fellows in a fulfilled relationship; bread and wine consecrated signify the Saviour, who sustains by his nourishing power, heals, beautifies, incorporates in the only truly enduring community, increases and then finally shares his triumph over death. To man, at the natural level, death ensues when food and drink, bread and wine, can no longer be assimilated. Death cannot ensue spiritually for the soul nourished on the Eucharist up to its apparent onset, for it is the Lord who has conquered death who is taken in communion. His conquest is the communicant's.

Understandably then there is a strong thread of thought centred on the Eucharist in its symbolic character. A peak was reached in Augustine's thinking on the subject. He continues his influence through the ages.

[1] *AAS* 57 (1965), Vatican tr.; cf. H. (Cardinal) de Lubac, S.J., *Corpus mysticum, L'Eucharistie et l'Eglise au Moyen Age*, Paris, 1944; L. Zanni, *Il simbolismo eucaristico nella teologia recente*, Rome, 1955 (Dissert. Lateran University); id., *Simbolo e realtà dell'Eucaristia nel pensiero e nella vita della Chiesa*, in *Eucaristia*, 301-327; E. Schillebeeckx, O.P., *The Eucharist*, London, 1968, 130-137; J.-M. Dufort, *Le symbolisme eucharistique aux origines de l'Eglise*, Montreal, 1968; Symposium, *L'Eucharistie le sens des Sacraments*, Lyon, 1971; L. Dussaut, *L'Eucharistie, Pâques de toute la vie, Diachronie symbolique, de l'Eucharistie*, Paris, 1972; J.P. de Jong, *L'Eucharistie comme realité symbolique*, Paris, 1972; A. Vergote-A. Deschamps-A. Houssiau, *L'Eucaristia simbolo e realtâ*, Italian tr., Assisi, 1973; H. Duquaire, *L'Eucharistie symbole et présence réelle du Christ*, Paris, 1974; R. Didier, *Le Sacrament de la foi, La Pâque dans ses signes*, Paris, 1975; G. Martelet, *The Risen Christ and the Resurrection*, London, 1976, esp., ch 2, *Eucharistic symbolism and man's condition*, 30-59; L.M. Chauvet, *Du symbolique au symbole, Essai sur le sacrament*, Paris, 1979; id., Symbole et Sacrament, Paris, 1986; G. Francesconi, *Storia e simbolo "Mysterium in figura"; la simbolica storico-sacramentale nel linguaggio e nella teologia di Ambrogio di Milano*, Brescia, 1982, bibl., A. Piolanti, *Il Mistero*, 345-371; [2] Theological Investigations, IV, 1966, 224; 231; [3] G. Martelet, *op. cit.*, 30; cf. Council of Florence, *Decree for the Armenians*, DS 1320f.

T

TEACHING AUTHORITY, THE

Open exercise of the Teaching Authority is generally linked with error or heresy, which stand in need of correction.[1] Here we are noting the precise character of important interventions by the Church in the field of Eucharistic doctrine.

The first to note is Anathema XI of St. Cyril presented to the Council of Ephesus: "If anyone does not confess that the flesh of the Lord is life-giving and belongs personally to the Word of God, the Father, but that it is of someone else besides him, but joined to him according to worthiness, as having only the divine indwelling, and not rather as we said, is life-giving, since he was made the Word's own, and has power to give life to all things, let him be anathema."[2]

There is no direct reference here to the Eucharist. But apart from the fact that we know that "life-giving" was a key-word with St. Cyril, we read in his commentary on St. John: "The Lord says to us: 'Truly I say to you, "If you do not eat the flesh of the Son of man, and if you do not drink his blood.'" But do not imagine that this flesh of the Son of man is the flesh of a man like us (how could the flesh of a man be life-giving?); it is the very flesh of him who became and called himself Son of man for our sake."[3] The phrasing is identical in the conciliar commentary on the Anathema XI: "In the churches we celebrate the holy, life-giving and unbloody sacrifice, and we hold on faith that the body which is set before us and similarly the precious blood are not of any common man, one like to us, but we receive it as the very body and blood of the Word who gives life to all. For common flesh

cannot give life."[4]

From early medieval, Carolingian times, local councils or synods intervened in Eucharistic matters. Thus Florus of Lyons denounced Amalarius (qv) to the synod of Kiersy, 838, which condemned him;[5] personal animosity was not absent from the incident. Generally Amalarius wrote in terms which can be explained. Two centuries later the synod of Arras, 1025, condemned the Cathari, who rejected the sacraments of Baptism, Penance, Matrimony and the Eucharist. A notable contribution was the speech of Bishop Gerard, an explicit statement of Eucharistic doctrine, in the terms then achieved.[6] Before long the Church had to deal with the problem of Berengar (qv).

Pope Lucius III (1181-1185) sent a letter to the Council of Verona, 1184, which it adopted as a decree: "All who, regarding the sacrament of the Body and Blood of our Lord Jesus Christ, or regarding baptism or the confession of sins, matrimony or the other ecclesiastical sacraments, do not fear to think or to teach otherwise than the most holy Roman Church teaches and observes; and, in general, whomsoever the same Roman Church or individual bishops through their dioceses with the advice of the clergy themselves, if the episcopal see is vacant, with the advice if it is necessary of neighbouring bishops, shall judge as heretics, we bind with a like bond of anathema."[7] The occasion of the papal missive was the spread of the Albigenses.

The thirteenth century would see the flowering of scholasticism and the writings of the great Eucharistic doctor, St. Thomas Aquinas (qv). At the outset we meet the career of Innocent III and the Lateran Council (qv). Wycliffe (qv) occurs in the interval between this council and that held in Florence to promote Christian unity.

We note in the 'Decree for the Greeks' issued by the Council of Florence the following statement on the question of the azymes (qv): "We have likewise defined that the body of Christ is truly effected in unleavened or leavened bread; and that priests ought to effect the body of our Lord in either one of these, and each one, namely, according to the custom of his Church, whether that of the west or the east."[8]

The 'Decree for the Armenians' from the same council treats at length of the Eucharist: "The third (sacrament) is the sacrament of the Eucharist; its matter is wheaten bread and wine, with which before consecration a very slight amount of water should be mixed. Now it is mixed with water because according to the testimonies of the holy Fathers and Doctors of the Church in a disputation made public long ago, it is the opinion that the Lord himself instituted this sacrament in wine mixed with water; and, moreover, this befits the representation of the Lord's passion. For blessed Alexander, the fifth Pope after blessed Peter, says: 'In the offerings of the sacraments, which are offered to the Lord within the solemnities of Masses, let only bread and wine mixed with water be offered as a sacrifice. For either wine alone or water alone must not be offered in the chalice of the Lord, but both mixed, because it is read that both, that is, blood and water, flowed from the side of Christ.' Then also, because it is fitting to signify the effect of this sacrament, which is union of the Christian people with Christ. For water signifies the people, according to the passage in the Apocalypse: 'the many waters . . . are many people' (cf. Apoc. 17:15) And Julius, the second Pope after blessed Sylvester, says: 'The chalice of the Lord according to the precept of the canons, mixed with wine and water, ought to be offered, because we see that in water the people are understood, but in wine the blood of Christ is shown. Therefore, when wine and water are mixed in the chalice the people are made one with Christ, and the multitude of the faithful is joined and connected with him in whom it believes.' Since, therefore, the holy Roman Church taught by the most blessed Apostles Peter and Paul, as well as all the rest of the churches of the Latins and Greeks, in which the lights of all sanctity and doctrine have shown, have so preserved this from the beginning of the nascent church and are now preserving it, it seems very unfitting that any other region differ from this universal and reasonable observance. We order, therefore, that the Armenians themselves also conform with all the Christian world, and that their priests mix

a little water with the wine in the offering of the chalice, as has been said. The words of the Saviour, by which he instituted this sacrament, are the form of this sacrament; for the priest speaking in the person of Christ effects this sacrament. For by the power of the very words the substance of the bread is changed into the body of Christ, and the substance of the wine into the blood; yet in such a way that Christ is contained entire under the species of bread and entire under the species of wine. Under any part also of the consecrated host and consecrated wine, although a separation has taken place, Christ is entire. The effect of this sacrament which he operates in the soul of him who takes it worthily is the union of man with Christ. And since through grace man is incorporated with Christ and is united with his members, it follows that through this sacrament grace is increased among those who receive it worthily; and every effect that material food and drink accomplish as they carry on corporal life, by sustaining, increasing, restoring, and delighting, this sacrament does as it carries on spiritual life, in which, as Pope Urban says, we renew the happy memory of our Saviour, are withdrawn from evil, are greatly strengthened in good, and proceed to an increase of the virtues and the graces."[9]

The teaching of the Council of Trent is dealt with separately. In the summary of its doctrine, the 'Profession of Faith of the Council of Trent,' drawn up by order of Pius IV and promulgated by his Bull, 'Injunctum nobis', 13 November 1565, there is included a section on the Eucharist: "I also profess that in the Mass there is offered to God a true, proper sacrifice of propitiation for the living and the dead, and that in the most holy sacrament of the Eucharist there is truly, really, and substantially present the body and blood together with the soul and the divinity of our Lord Jesus Christ, and that there takes place a conversion of the whole substance of the bread into the body, and of the whole substance of the wine into the blood; and this conversion the Catholic Church calls transubstantiation. I also acknowledge that under one species alone the whole and entire Christ and the true sacrament are taken."[10] Much the same words were used in the Profession of Faith for the Maronites, 16 March 1743, approved by Benedict XIV.

The Catechism of the Council helped to convey its teaching to the faithful and it has a certain status in the ordinary teaching authority. All of chapter IV of Part II, with 81 questions, deals with different aspects of the Eucharist.

The Synod of Pistoia, and the Bull of Pius VI which dealt with it, *Auctorem fidei*, 28 August 1794, are dealt with separately.

The first intervention of the Teaching Authority in

the present century was during the pontificate of St. Pius X (qv). What he did in regard to Holy Communion is told in the article on Communion. In the decree of the Holy Office approved by him, *Lamentabili*, 3 July 1907, two propositions were condemned as follows: "(45) Not all that Paul says about the institution of the Eucharist (1 Cor 11:23-25) is to be taken historically; (49) As the Christian Supper gradually assumed the nature of a liturgical action, those who were accustomed to preside at the Supper acquired the sacerdotal character." The reasons for the condemnation of these and other propositions are set forth in the Encyclical *Pascendi dominici gregis*, 8 September 1907.

Prior to Vatican II (qv), two documents emanating from Pius XII (qv) deserve mention. In *Mediator Dei* (qv) the Pope repeated the doctrine of Trent on the sacrifice of the Mass and the priesthood. Some extracts merit study:

(After recalling the words of Trent, XXII, c. 1) "The august sacrifice of the altar is therefore no mere simple commemoration of the Passion and death of Jesus Christ; it is truly and properly the offering of a sacrifice, wherein by an unbloody immolation the High Priest does what he had already done on the Cross, offering himself to the eternal Father as a most acceptable victim. 'One . . . and the same is the victim, one and the same is he who now offers by the ministry of his priests and who then offered himself on the Cross; the difference is only in the manner of offering.' (*Ibid.*, c. 2). The priest, then, is the same: Christ Jesus, whose sacred body is represented by his minister. The consecration which the minister received when he was ordained to the priesthood assimilates him to the High Priest and enables him to act by the power of Christ himself and in his name. And therefore when he exercises his priestly power, he, as it were, 'lends Christ his tongue and gives him the use of his hand.' (John Chrys. In Joan Hom, 86, 4). The victim, too, is the same: the divine Redeemer according to his humanity and in his true body and blood. But the manner in which Christ is offered is different. On the Cross he offered to God the whole of himself and his sufferings, and the victim was immolated by a bloody death voluntarily accepted. But on the altar, by reason of the glorious condition of his humanity 'death will no longer have dominion over him,' and therefore the shedding of his blood is not possible. Nevertheless the divine wisdom has devised a way in which our Redeemer's sacrifice is marvellously shown forth by external signs symbolic of death. By the 'transubstantiation' of bread into the body of Christ and of wine into his blood, both his body and blood are rendered really present; but the Eucharistic species

under which he is present symbolize the violent separation of his body and blood, and so a commemorative showing forth of the death which took place in reality on Calvary is repeated in each Mass, because by distinct representations Christ Jesus is signified and shown forth in the state of victim."[13]

The Pope then shows how each of the great ends of sacrifice—praise, thanksgiving, propitiation and impetration—is fulfilled in the Mass. Nothing touches the self-sufficiency of Christ's death on Calvary. What is now effected is the application of the fruits of Calvary. "Although Christ, universally speaking, has reconciled the whole human race to the Father by his death, yet he has willed that all men should come and be brought to his Cross, especially by means of the sacraments and the Mass, and so take possession of the fruits which, through the Cross, he has won for them."[14] "Among the instruments for distributing to believers the merits that flow from the Cross of the divine Redeemer, the august sacrifice of the altar is pre-eminent: 'As often as the commemoration of this victim is celebrated, the work of our Redemption is performed.' But this in no way derogates from the dignity of the sacrifice of the Cross; on the contrary it is a clear proof—as the Council of Trent asserts—(XXII, c. 2, can. 4) of its greatness and necessity. The daily immolation is a reminder to us that there is no salvation but in the Cross of our Lord Jesus Christ (cf. Gal 6:14); and that the reason why God wills the continuation of this sacrifice 'from the rising of the sun to its going down' (Mal 1:11) is in order that there may be no pause in that hymn of praise and thanksgiving. This is a debt which men owe to their Creator precisely because they stand in constant need of his help, and in constant need of the divine Redeemer's blood to destroy the sins that call for his just retribution."[15]

Pius XII pointed to some other errors; that which held that prayers could not be addressed to Jesus Christ personally, a view he taught to be "not only opposed to the mind of the Church and to Christian usage, but also false." "For to speak exactly, Christ is Head of the universal Church, as he exists at once in both his natures. Moreover, he himself has solemnly stated: 'If you shall ask me anything in my name, that I will do' (Jn 14:14). Though it is true especially in the Eucharistic sacrifice—in which Christ, at once priest and victim, exercises in an extraordinary way the office of reconciler—that prayers are very often directed to the eternal Father through the only-begotten Son; nevertheless it occurs not seldom even in this sacrifice that prayers to the divine Redeemer also are used. For after all every Christian must know full well that the man Christ Jesus is also the Son of

God and God himself. And so when the Church militant is offering its adoration and prayers to the unspotted Lamb and the sacred victim, her voice comes to us as an echo of the triumphant Church's chorus, singing without end: 'To him that sits on the throne and to the Lamb, benediction and honour and glory and power for ever and ever."[16]

In the Encyclical *Humani Generis*, 12 August 1950, Pius XII censured thus an erroneous opinion on Transubstantiation (qv): "And there are those who contend that the doctrine of transubstantiation inasmuch as it is founded on an outmoded philosophical notion of substance, should be corrected in such wise that the real presence of Christ in the most holy Eucharist, is reduced to a kind of symbolism, so that the consecrated species are no more than efficacious signs of the spiritual presence of Christ, and of his intimate union with the faithful members in the Mystical Body."[17]

Vatican II figures next in the chronology of the Teaching Authority; it is dealt with separately. So are the successive interventions of Paul VI (qv) and John Paul II (qv) in face of the abuses (qv) and intellectual vagaries of the post-conciliar age. (See articles, *Mysterium Fidei, Inaestimabile Donum*, Post-conciliar Documents.)

---

[1]Bibliographies to articles mentioned in the text; cf. DTC V, 989-1430; X, 795-1316; cf. esp. A. Zigrossi, *L'Eucaristia nel Magistero della Chiesa in Eucaristia,* 185-217 with bibl; in the same work, section 3: *Deviazioni sul Dogma Eucaristico*: G. Zannoni, patristic period, 497-501; A. Piolanti, Middle Ages, 503-510; D. Stiernon, A.A., Orthodox differences, 511-531; L. Cristiani, Protestantism, 533-553; S. Zedda, S.J., recent non-Catholics on the origin of the Eucharist, 555-574; A. Michel, recent doctrinal deviations, 575-595; [2]DS 262; [3]*In Jo.*, I, 9, PG 73, 113; [4]Mansi, V, 18; [5]Mansi, XIV, 741-754; [6]Mansi, XIX, 433; [7]DS 761; [8]DS 1303; [9]DS 1320-1322; [10]DS 1866; [11]DS 2534; [12]DS 3445, 3449; [13]CTS tr., 32-33; [14]*Ibid.,* 36; [15]*Ibid.,* 36-37; [16]NCWC tr., 56; [17]DS 3891.

TERTULLIAN (c. 165-c. 225)

The 'Father of Latin theology' presents some problems in his Eucharistic texts. In the *Adversus Marcionem*, he writes thus: "And so having professed that he longed with longing to eat the Passover, as being his own—for it would have been unsuitable that God desire something which belonged to another—he made the bread, which he had taken and distributed to the disciples, his own Body, saying: 'This is my Body,' that is, the figure of my Body. But it could not have been the figure, unless it were the body of something real. Something void, like a phantasm, cannot have a figure.... Similarly, when he established the Covenant sealed with his blood by speaking of the cup, he also proved the reality of his Body, for blood can belong to no other body than one of flesh. For even if some type of body other than one of flesh should be brought forward in argument against us, unless it be of flesh, it surely will not have blood."[2] "That is the figure of my Body" raises a difficulty, explicable, as his great commentator, Fr. D'Alès, explains, by reference to the ancient figure of bread which is now given reality: T. more than once recalls Jer 11:19.

Again T. uses the word *"repraesentare"* in regard to the Eucharist: *Panem, quo ipsum corpus suum repraesentat.*[3] Does this mean merely to represent? Again Fr. D'Ales shows by a detailed examination of T's vocabulary, that the word means "to make present." Finally, there is the claim made by certain Calvinists that T. used the word *"censetur"* to signify that the words of consecration merely meant "it will be taken for." "I," he said, "am the Bread of Life." And a little earlier, the Bread is the Word (*sermo*, T's usage) of the Living God, which came down from heaven. Then as his Body is contained in the Bread *(Tum quod et corpus ejus in pane censetur)*, This is my Body. Therefore begging our daily bread we ask for perpetuity in Christ and not to be separated from his body."[4] The usage by T. is explainable by a study of his vocabulary, as Fr. D'Alès makes clear. His orthodoxy is clear in many other passages through his works.

---

[1]Works PL 1 and 2; CCSL, I, II; CSEL 20, 47, 70, 76; Solano, *Textos*, I, 87-104; cf., A. D'Ales, S.J., *La théologie de Tertullien,* Paris, 1905; J. Quasten, *Patrology*, II, 1953, 246-340; G. Bardy, DTC, XV, 1, 1946, *Tertullien*, 130-171, G. Bareille, *Eucharistie*, DTC V, 1130-1131; B. Stakemeier, *La dottrina di Tertulliano sul sacramento dell'Eucaristia, Rivista storico-critica delle scienze teologiche*, 1909, 199ff; P. Batiffol, *L'Eucharistie*, 204-226; V. Saxer, *Tertullien*, in *L'Eucharistie des premiers chrétiens*, Paris, 1978, 129-150; A. Piolanti, *Il Mistero*, 166-170; [2]*Contra Marcionem*, 4, 40, CSEL 47, 559; PL 2, 460A; cf. D'Ales, *op. cit.*, 356-367; [3]*Ibid.*, 1, 14, CSEL, 3, 308; PL 2,262A; [4]*De Oratione*, PL 1, 1160.

TEXTUS PRECIS EUCHARISTICAE, 1 November 1974.

A justification and explanation of the Eucharistic Prayers for Children—an Instruction from the Sacred Congregation for Divine Worship. Directives are given for translation and for their liturgical use; there is a brief description of each of the three prayers.

---

[1]Text *Notitiae*, (1975), 7-12; tr. A. Flannery, II, 53-57.

THEODORE OF MOPSUESTIA (c. 350-428)

T's name figures in remarkable controversies and in conciliar condemnations over a century after his death; one result of this reversal of accepted views, of the taint of heresy and the dispute about the Three Chapters, was that much of his written work was destroyed or allowed to survive only in fragments wholly inadequate to his thought.[1] Recovery of MSS in the present century has remedied this situation. In particular the discovery of a Syriac version of the *Catechetical Homilies* in 1933 by A. Mingana, who published them with an English translation is a boon to students of T's Eucharistic theology, for Hom XV and XVI are directly relevant to the subject, the first dealing with doctrine, the second with liturgical acts. Patristic scholars like R. Deveresse and E. Amann, and theologians of the priesthood like J. Lécuyer (qv) have fortunately analysed the thought content of the documentary finds.

Antiochene in theological background and method, closely associated with St. John Chrysostom (qv), T. is not quite as realistic in exposition as his friend, nor as St. Cyril of Jerusalem, but there is no doubting his belief in the Real Presence: "It is with justice, therefore, that when he gave the bread he did not say: 'This is the symbol of my body,' but: 'This is my body'; likewise when he gave the cup he did not say: 'This is the symbol of my blood,' but: 'This is my blood,' because he wished us to look upon the (elements) after their reception of grace and the coming of the Spirit, not according to their nature but to receive them as they are the body and blood of Our Lord. We ought not to regard the elements merely as bread and cup, but as the body and blood of Christ."[2] T. repeats this idea, as expressed in the *Catechetical Homilies*, in his commentary on Mt: "He did not say: 'This is the symbol of my body and this of my blood,' but: 'This is my body and my blood,' teaching us not to consider the nature of the laid-out things, but through the accomplished thanksgiving they have been changed into the flesh and blood."[3]

T. is generally thought to provide unusually ample teaching on the role of the Holy Spirit in the Mass, on the *epiclesis* therefore. Quotations are aligned by J. Quasten: "We ought not to regard the elements merely as bread and cup, but as the body and blood of Christ, into which they were transformed by the descent of the Holy Spirit."[4] Fr. Lécuyer thought that T. did not consider precisely the question when the change takes place in the Eucharistic consecration. The great Orientalist, Fr. Martin Jugie, A.A., thought that for T. the *epiclesis* was post-consecratory, showing that the consecration had already taken place.[5]

T. thought of the Eucharist as the food appropriate to those who had been in Baptism born to a new life: "To you also who have been born by grace and the coming of the Holy Spirit, and have received this sanctification, it is fitting that the food should bear its

likeness, as you received by grace and the coming of the Holy Spirit."[6] Here we must note a general principle of T. in regard to sacramental life. The sacraments link us with heavenly reality. The Eucharist is a sacrifice, but it is a sacrifice made in image, which represents the unique sacrifice which Christ introduced to heaven on the day of the Ascension. "To the Eucharist then," says Fr. Lécuyer, "is applicable what we already said of the sacraments in general: it is the image of a heavenly reality, which is the sacrifice of the Saviour; an image and not merely a shadow without substance; in the Eucharist there is already a participation in the heavenly reality which will be given to us in its fulness only later. The reality is the return of Christ, high priest and victim, to the right hand of the Father, as the first-fruits of all mankind, and the communication by him to the elect of the very prerogatives of heavenly glory which he possesses unalterably: not Christ alone, but Christ with his Mystical Body united to him in the participation of the same divine goods."[7]

For T. the Mass is a memorial of the Passion and death of the Saviour. But it is on the Resurrection and Ascension that he will insist in his explanation of the Mass: "The reality to which his eyes instinctively return, to which he wishes to direct all the thoughts of his listeners, is the heavenly reality, of which the Eucharist is the image. The reception 'in images' of the body of Christ is in fact but the prelude, the promise, the pledge of this unchangeable communion 'without sacrament or signs' in the incorruptible life of the risen Lord. Already the Eucharist gives us a share in eternal life; it prepares us, moves us towards this heavenly communion, drawing closer the bonds of unity of the Body of Christ, fruit of Baptism."[8]

Such is the rich theology of the Eucharist revealed in the recovered works of the great Antiochene theologian. An interesting (qv) parallel in texts across the centuries links him with St. Thomas. The latter wrote: *O Sacrum Convivium in quo Christus sumitur, recolitur memoria passionis ejus, mens impletur gratia et futurae gloriae nobis pignus datur.*" T. wrote: "We take the immortal and spiritual food, which is the body and blood of Our Lord,... all of us who believe in Christ and in order commemorate the death of Christ Our Lord, and thereby receive wondrous food, from which we derive hope capable of drawing to us a share in the (good things) to come."[9] T. cannot be invoked, as from passing remarks some Fathers can, to support the theory of mystic immolation by the separate species consecrated (see Billot, Louis).

[1]Works: ed. A. Mingana with English tr. Woodbrooke Studies, V, VI, Cambridge, 1932, 1933; ed. R. Tonneau et R. Deveresse, with

French tr., *Les Homélies Catechétiques de Theodore de Mopsueste*, Vatican City, 1949; J. Solano, *Textos*, II, 77-105; P. Vosté, *Theodori Mopsuesteni Commentarius in Evangelium Johannis Apostoli*, CSCO, Scriptores Syri, 3, Louvain, 1940; cf. E.B. Pusey, *The Doctrine of the Real Presence as contained in the Fathers from the death of St. John the Evangelist to the Fourth General Council*, Oxford, 1855; J. Lebreton, *Le dogme de la transubstantiation et la christologie antiochienne du 5e siècle*, in *Report of the XIX Eucharistic Congress*, London, 1909, 328ff; A. Rücker, *Ritus Baptismi et Missae quem descripsit Theodorus von Mopsuestensis*, Münster 1933; F.J. Dölger, *Teodor von Mopsuest über zwei Zeremonien vor der Genuss des eucharistischen Brotes*, AC 4 (1934), 231; M. Jugie, A.A., *Le liber ad baptizandos de Theodore de Mopsueste*, EO 38 (1935), 263-70; id., *De Forma Eucharistiae, de Epiclesibus eucharisticis*, Rome, 1943, 42-43; W. de Vries, *Der Nestorianismus Theodors von Mopsuestia in seiner Sacramentenlehre*, OCP 7 (1941), 91-148; F.J. Reine, *The Eucharistic Doctrine and Liturgy of the Mystagogical Catecheses of Theodore of Mopsuestia*, SCA 2, Washington, 1942; R. Deveresse, *Essai sur Théodore de Mopsueste*, ST 141, Vatican City, 1948; J. Lécuyer, C.S.Sp., (qv), *Le sacerdoce chrétien et le sacrifice eucharistique selon Théodore de Mopsueste*, RSR 36 (1949), 481-516; id. in *Eucaristia*, 154-59; J. Quasten, *Mysterium tremendum: Vom Christlichen Mysterium*, Düsseldorf, 1951, 66-75;, id., *The Liturgical Mysticism of Theodore of Mopsuestia*, TS 15 (1954), 431-39; id., *Patrology*, III, 401-423; G. Bareille, DTC, V, 1158f.; E. Amann, DTC 15, 268-69; [2]*Cat. Hom.* 15; [3]PG 66, 713; [4]*Cat. Hom.* 15, 76 Mingana; for further quotations, Quasten, *op. cit.*, 421; [5]*Op. cit.*, 42f; [6]*Hom.* 16, 23; [7]*Op. cit.*, 506; [8]*Ibid.*, 512-13; [9]*Hom* 16, 10.

THEODORET OF CYRRHUS (c. 393-c. 460)

T's Eucharistic theology was entangled with his Christology, the latter explicitly oriented against Monophysitism.[1] The problem was to show that the human nature in Christ was not absorbed in the divine. Appeal was then made to the analogy of the Eucharist. But from this arose a misunderstanding—if the divine and human natures could exist together, the temptation was to think that in the Eucharist the bread and wine could coexist with the body and blood of Christ. At its worst this would be impanation (qv), or Luther's consubstantiation (qv). A number of Protestant writers have taken this interpretation, one maintaining that the doctrine held in the fifth century was the same as Luther's. If T. gave any grounds for such an interpretation it was due to his eagerness to resist monophysitism; it must be admitted that he mistook the analogy between the mystery of the Incarnation and the Eucharist. An Antiochene, his relationship to Cyril of Alexandria is a complicated story.

T. had no doubt at all on the Real Presence (qv). This comes out clearly in a dialogue between an orthodox believer and a heretic imagined by T. "After the consecration how do you call them (the gifts offered)? Body and blood of Christ."[2] Unfortunately when it comes to the mode of conversion we have in the same dialogue this passage: "You believe that you participate in the body and blood of Christ? Yes, so I believe. In the same way that the symbols of the body and blood of the Lord are one thing before the priestly *epiclesis* (qv) and after the *epiclesis* are transformed and become something else, likewise the body of the Lord after the ascension was transformed into the divine substance. You are caught in your own trap; for, after the consecration the mystic symbols do not lose their proper nature; these remain in their first substance, in their appearance, in their form, visible and tangible."[3] Evidently these terms and the concepts they express had not yet been fully clarified.

According to T. Christ the high priest according to the order of Melchizedek offered the one perfect sacrifice, which is continued by his ministers as a memorial. T. insists on Christ offering as Head of the Mystical Body.[4]

[1]J. Solano, *Textos*, II, 471-499; cf. M. Richard, *Notes sur l'evolution doctrinale de Theodoret*, RSPT, 25 (1936), 459-481; A.D'Ales, S.J., *De Sanctissima Eucharistia*, Paris, 1929, 98ff; Quasten, Patrology, III, 536-448; G. Bareille, DTC V, 1168; G. Bardy, DTC XV, 1, 299-525, esp. 321; [2]*Eranistes, Dial.* 2, PG 83, 167; [3]*Ibid.;* [4]In Psalm. 109, PG 80, 1772, 73; *In Epist. ad Hebr.*, 7:27 and 8:1-4; PG 82, 733-736.

THÉRÈSE OF LISIEUX, ST. (1873-1897)

The saint is of interest to Eucharistic piety because of her stated aim in entering Carmel, to pray for priests (qv) and for sinners; apart from the immediate relationship between priesthood and the Eucharist, her whole cast of thought was strongly affected by ministry of the kind that recalls the central mystery; she was essentially a missionary, rightly proclaimed Patroness of the Missions after her glorification.[1] Her life was marked by great moments of Eucharistic fervour. Her first Communion was the starting point in this series of events. Her description of it, of the preparation which she was given, and the intensity of the moment itself have marked it in her spiritual legacy; this was evident in the centenary commemorations in 1984. The date was 8 May 1884, when Thérèse was over eleven years of age. The first Communion was a mystical moment: "But I do not wish and I could not say everything.... There are things which lose their perfume as soon as they are exposed to the air; there are intimate thoughts which cannot be expressed in the language of this earth, without losing at once their profound, heavenly meaning.... We (Jesus and Thérèse) were no longer two; Thérèse had disappeared as a drop of water lost in the depth of the ocean; Jesus alone remained; he was Master and King. Had not Thérèse asked him to take away her liberty? This liberty frightened her; she felt so weak, so fragile that she wished to be united forever to divine Strength."[2] Her tears, which caused surprise, were of the purest joy. Again, it was after Communion at Midnight Mass in 1886 that she was healed of undue sensitiveness. Her heroic fortitude was manifest in the course of her last illness, as she dragged herself to the chapel for the Sacrament; her fervour was evident in visits, in the Stations of the Cross prayed in presence of the Blessed Sacrament—once praying thus she received the wound of love—in her loving observance of her duties as Sacristan.

Saint Thérèse's Eucharistic outlook had, soon after her death, an impact wider than the confines of her Carmelite convent. She had written to her cousin, Marie Guerin to dissuade her from her reluctance, caused by scruples, to receive Holy Commmunion: "O my little Marie, do you realise that sweet Jesus is there, in the Tabernacle, expressly for you, for you alone, that he burns with the desire to come into your heart ... don't listen to the demon, laugh at him, and go without fear to receive the Jesus of peace and of love.... Dearest little sister, receive Communion often, very often ... there you have the *sole remedy* if you want to be cured. Jesus has not put this attraction into your heart for nothing. I think he would be glad if you could make up your two lost Communions, for then the demon's victory would be less, since he could not have managed to keep Jesus from your heart" (Marie had missed Communion on Ascension Day and on the last day of May).

When St. Pius X (qv) heard this letter he cried out: "*Oportunissimo! Oportunissimo.* This is a great joy to me; we must proceed with this process (for Beatification) quickly." The saint's ideas on frequent Communion (qv) were much ahead of her time. She believed in daily Communion, disagreeing in this from her Prioress, Mother Gonzaga; she foretold that the latter would change her opinion when Thérèse had died. This happened and a chaplain favourable to frequent Communion was appointed, as she had also predicted.

The saint composed a fresco around the Tabernacle of the inner oratory of the convent; it showed angels surrounding the Host in a monstrance, with the legend: "Did you but know the gift of God." One of her poems was on the Eucharist, *My desires next to the Tabernacle*: it expresses intense love for Jesus in the blessed Sacrament, developed with reference to the physical elements surrounding celebration of the Eucharist and reservation of the Sacrament, the tabernacle, the altar, the corporal, the paten, the chalice, the grapes that give the wine, the wheat that gives the host. The saint returns to the theme of the Eucharist in some of her other poems; this theme was part of her lived spirituality, the very fabric of her astonishing holiness.

[1]Cf. F. Jamart, *The Complete Spiritual Doctrine of St. Teresa of Lisieux*, New York, 1961, 268-69; [2]Tr. from Lisieux ed, *Histoire d'une Ame*, 57; [3]*Collected Letters of Saint Thérèse of Lisieux*, ed. Abbe Combes, tr. Frank Sheed, London, 1949, Letter 30 May 1889, p. 94, 95.

THOMAS AQUINAS, ST., DOCTOR OF THE CHURCH (1225-1274)

The effect of the Angelic Doctor's teaching on Eucharistic theology may be illustrated by the index entry in Mgr Piolanti's (qv) large work, *Il Misterio Eucaristico* (679 pp); "he is quoted on almost every page." This teaching is found in the *Summa Theologiae*, III, qq 73-83, and in many other places in the works, principally in the *Libri Sententiarum*, IV, *Contra Gentes* IV, and in the saint's commentary on 1 Cor XI. As in everything St. Thomas wrote, account is taken of previous development. Among the Fathers, apart from occasional references to others, it is St. Augustine (qv) and St. Ambrose (qv) whom he invokes. But it is especially the far-reaching effects, on all his thinking on the subject, of his synthesis of Aristotelian philosophy and the revealed truth of God that raises his doctrine to unrivalled excellence.

The idea of transubstantiation (qv) had been evolved and the word was accepted. But St. Thomas thought out the theory to a totally satisfactory and compelling conclusion. Though he did not set out to elaborate a doctrine of the sacrifice of the Mass separately from his discussion of the Eucharist as sacrament, the elements of such a doctrine are in his work. He expresses them mostly in dealing with the virtues of religion, *Summa Theologiae,* IIa IIae, esp. q. 85.

The order of topics in the *Summa* is as follows: On the sacrament of the Eucharist in itself; On the matter of the Eucharist as to its species; On the conversion of bread and wine into the body and blood of Christ; Whether the whole Christ is contained under this sacrament; On the accidents remaining in this sacrament; On the form of the sacrament of the Eucharist; On the effects of the sacrament of the Eucharist; On the use or taking of this sacrament in general; On the way in which Christ used this sacrament; On the minister of this sacrament; On the rite of this sacrament: eleven questions, eighty-four articles.

On transubstantiation T. writes: "Every created agent is determined in its act, since it is of a determined genus and species; and therefore the action of every created agent issues in some determined act; each thing in its actual *esse* is determined by its form. Therefore no natural or created agent can act except to effect a change of form; and for this reason every conversion which follows the laws of nature is of the form. But God is infinite act, as has been shown in part one (of the *Summa*, q. VII, art 1, q. XXV, art 2); therefore his action extends to the whole nature of being. He is able therefore not only to effect conversion of form, whereby different forms succeed each other in the same subject, but the conversion of the whole reality, so that the whole substance of this is converted into the whole substance of that. This is what happens by divine power in this sacrament; for the whole substance of bread is converted into the whole substance of the body of Christ, and the whole substance of wine into the whole substance of the blood of Christ. Hence this conversion is not formal, but substantial; nor is it contained within the categories of natural motion, but may be called by its proper name, transubstantiation."[2]

T. in company with all the great founding fathers of scholasticism, Bonaventure, Alexander of Hales, Giles of Rome, Albert the Great, rejected the idea of annihilation as the means of transubstantiation. T. is also insistent on the fact that no change takes place in the body of Christ: "In natural instances of conversion, that which is converted and that into which it is converted are changed. But in the present instance that to which the conversion is made, is already existing and nothing is added to it; therefore that to which the conversion is made, in no way is changed, that is the body of Christ, but only the bread which is subject to conversion."[3]

Dom Anscar Vonier, O.S.B., in a remarkable study of the Eucharistic theology of T., argued very strongly that for the Angelic Doctor sacrament and sacrifice are one: "The sacrament, for St. Thomas, is essentially in the consecration; which, again, is essentially the representation of Christ's passion and therefore sacrifice, as Body and Blood are consecrated separately. Speaking of the celebration of Mass, St. Thomas says that it matters very little whether the sacrament be consecrated by one or many, provided the rite of the Church be observed."[4] Dom Vonier cites another passage wherein, as he says, for T. sacrament and sacrifice are identified: Mass, he says, for St. Thomas is simply the sacrament which is being celebrated: "In Mass there are two things to be considered, namely the sacrament itself, which is the principal thing, and the prayers for the living and the dead which are said at Mass. From the point of view, then, of sacrament, the Mass of a bad priest is not of less value than the Mass of a good priest, because in both cases the same sacrament is being performed."[5] Or again this passage: "The sacrament is accomplished *(perficitur)* in the consecration of the matter; the use of the sacrament by the faithful does not of necessity belong to the sacrament, but is something following upon the sacrament."[6] And finally a lengthy passage wherein the

basic truth, as Dom Vonier sees it, is expressed as is T's theology of the OT and NT: "In this sacrament we may keep in mind three things: what is 'sacrament' only, namely, bread and wine; what is 'thing and sacrament,' namely, the true body of Christ; and what is the 'thing' only, I mean the effect of the sacrament (on man's soul). Considering what is 'sacrament' only, the most perfect figure of this sacrament was the offering by Melchizedek, who offered up bread and wine. But looking at Christ in his passion *(Christum passum)* who is contained in this sacrament, the figures of it are all the sacrifices of the Old Testament, chiefly the sacrifice of expiation, which was the most solemn. Coming now to the effect of the sacrament, its principal type was the manna which had in it 'all that is delicious, and the sweetness of every taste,' as it is said in the sixteenth chapter of Wisdom, just as the grace of this sacrament refreshes the soul in every way. The Paschal Lamb, however, was the figure of the sacrament according to all those three aspects. According to the first aspect, because it was eaten with unleavened bread .... According to the second aspect, because it was offered up by the whole multitude of the children of Israel on the fourteenth day of the month, and this was the figure of Christ's passion who on account of his innocence is called the Lamb. According to the effect, moreover, because through the blood of the Paschal Lamb the children of Israel were protected from the destroying angel, and were brought forth from the slavery of Egypt; for this reason, then, the Paschal Lamb is considered to be the chief figure of the sacrament, because it represents it in every aspect."[7]

On so many other aspects of the Eucharist T. brought completion, precision, wealth of thought, profound insight. Every article in the *Summa* merits study. His doctrine of the Mass is sometimes taken as of the 'immolation' (qv) school.[8] But in the extracts here quoted it is clear that he allowed fully for oblation (qv).

---

[1]Besides the classic commentators, John Capreolus, Thomas Cajetan, John of St. Thomas, among modern writers, Louis Billot (qv) excels; cf. M. Grabmann, *Die Lehre des hl. Thomas von Aquin von der Kirche als Gotteswerk*, Ratisbon, 1903; A. Bassani, *De transubstantiatione ad mentem S. Thomae*, Florence, 1913; A. Von Slpawa-Neyman, *Das Problem der wesenlosen Gestalten im hl. Altarsakrament nach der Lehre des hl. Thomas von Aquin*, Breslau, 1920; A. Zychlinski, *Sincera doctrina de conceptu transubstantiationis juxta principia S. Thomae*, La ciencia tomista, 16 (1924), 28-65, 222-244; J. Puig de la Bellacasa, *De transubstantiatione secundum S. Thomam*, Barcelona, 1926; F. Simonis, *Indagatio critica in opinionem S. Thomae de natura intima transubstantiationis*, Indore, 1939; esp., Anscar Vonier, O.S.B., *A Key to the Doctrine of the Eucharist*, 2nd ed., London, 1931; Henricus a Sancta Theresia, *Notio sacrificii in communi in synthesi S. Thomae*, Rome, 1934; F. Orozco, *La explicación de Santo Tomas sobre la*

presencia del cuerpo de Cristo en la Eucaristia 'per modum substantiae,' Rome, 1943 (Dissert. Gregorian University); Y. de Moncheuil, *La raison de la permanence du Christ sous les espèces eucharistiques d'après St. Thomas*, in *Mélanges théologiques*, Paris, 1946, 71-82; L. Nuñez Goenaga, *El valor y funciones de la presencia real de Jesu Cristo. El Sacramento segun la doctrina eucaristiologica de Santo Tomas*, Tolosa, 1949; in *Eucaristia*, 263-284—on the statement of Pius XII (qv), 22 September 1956, a misrepresentation of St. Thomas; cf. U. Bouesse; A.M. Hoffmann, *De sacrificio Missae secundum S. Thomam, Angelicum,* 15 (1938), 262-85; G. Geenen, O.P., *L'adage 'Eucharistia est sacramentum unitatis ecclesiasticae' dans les oeuvres et la doctrine de St. Thomas d'Aquin*, in *Congreso Eucaristico Internacional de Barcelona*, 1952, Barcelona, 1953, II, 275-81; M. Matthlis, *Mysteriengegenwart secundum S. Thomam, Angelicum* 34 (1957) 393-99; A. de Sutter, *La notion de présence et de ses différentes applications dans la Somme théologique de St. Thomas, EphCarmel* 17 (1967), 49-69; F. Martínez, *La Eucaristia y la unidad de la Iglesia en Santo Tomas de Aquino, Studium* 9 (1969) 377-404; [2]III, q. 75, art 4; cp with decree of Trent (qv), Sess. XIII, ch. 4, almost literal transcription; [3]*IV Sent.*, D. 11, 1, a 3, q. 3, sol. 1; [4]*Op. cit.,* 79; [5]III, 182, art 2; [6]q. 74, art. 7; [7]q. 73, art. 6; [8]Cf. Henricus a S. Theresia, *op. cit.*

TRANSIGNIFICATION

A theory proposed in the late fifties and the sixties of the present century to express in modern phenomenological terms the reality of Christ's presence (qv) in the Eucharist.[1] It emphasizes the reality of the Eucharist as a sign act. It is much linked with the idea of transfinalization, a theory current at the same time. Paul VI (qv) taught in *Mysterium Fidei* (qv) that these ideas were not to be repudiated outright; it is a question of so applying them that the truth held by the Church from the beginning about Christ's presence is not only not endangered but is more vividly shown in its richness. Advocates of transignification speak of the difference between the sensible, scientific and commercial value of things and their significance, which may depend on what they are chosen or fashioned to express, a piece of gold becomes a marriage ring with thereby a new significance—the shortcoming of the example is obvious, for this particular piece of gold has significance as long as it is a ring, owned by someone who invests it with this meaning; even before it is deprived of its design its significance dies with its owner. Fr. E. Schillebeeckx uses the example of the cloth which acquires a new significance when it is chosen to make a national flag. But how many flags lie in museums all over the world, with no significance but that of historical evidence, valuable or negligible, as the curiosity of the public or the need of a historian decides.

Transfinalization views bread and wine used in the Eucharist as changed from what were in the creative intention and finality of God to a new finality: they could not only serve as nutriment, but also as a means of sharing love and friendship. Now they are identified

with a world of inter-personal relationships to be understood in the light of phenomenology. All this needs to be thought out fully, in such wise that the reality of Christ's presence, so far admirably explained by the concept of transubstantiation (qv) is still fully asserted. The claims of valid anthropology can be adequately met without upsetting those of divine revelation and Christian tradition. Inevitably the case for the new concepts was put excessively in places, as the whole air in post-conciliar times was favourable to change and a school of thought, or rather of fashion, welcomed anything that would diminish the prestige of the Council of Trent (qv). Existentialist thinking seemed dominant, "essentialist" theses to be discarded; new ideas, at times confused with mere novelty, were eagerly sought. Time has assured a certain settlement of innovative theory, checked against the truths received from past times. These truths can always be expressed in ways adaptable to a new mentality, for as Pope John said, in his address for the opening of the Council, "The substance of the ancient doctrine of the deposit of faith is one thing, and the way in which it is presented is another ... provided that its essential meaning be preserved."

[1]Cf. E. Schillebeeckx, O.P., *The Eucharist*, London, 1968; H.J. Nicolas, *Présence réelle eucharistique et transignification, RT*, 71 (1971), 448ff; A. Piolanti, *Il Mistero*, 271-278; for a different viewpoint, the Paschal Mystery (qv) entirely consistent with the doctrine of transubstantiation, cf. H.-M. Feret, *Eucharistie, Pâque de l'univers*, Paris, 1966, esp. 98ff.

TRANSUBSTANTIATION

A philosophical term fashioned over the centuries to express a mystery, the change of what was bread into the body of Christ, of what was wine into his blood.[1] Though this mystery is known only by faith, the reality which it expresses is utterly objective (see Presence, Real). So much is involved in this change, so much up to and including God's existence as Creator, his omnipotence, the Incarnation of his divine Son, the relationship between the sacramental order and the human condition, that language was pressed to its limit to serve revealed truth. Such things and so much more must be borne in mind when the word transubstantiation is criticised, as it has been in some recent formal exchanges of opinion in an ecumenical context.[2] It is said to be non-scriptural—as was the *homoousion*—to be tied to one particular system of philosophy, the scholastic, to be outmoded. It is important first to trace the origin and growth of the term.

The truth is fully implied in the institution (qv) narrative, consonant with the discourse of promise (qv). The problem was to clarify its content and express this adequately. The first elements are in the Fathers. Reflecting on the liturgy, which according to the extant *anaphorae* (qv), with the solitary exception of that of Addai and Mari (qv), have the institution narrative in a central place, they began to enunciate the identity of the body and blood of Christ with the bread and wine.

Thus we find St. Ignatius of Antioch (qv) saying: that "the Eucharist is the flesh of our Saviour Jesus Christ"[3] and St. Justin (qv): "For we do not receive these things as if they were ordinary food and drink. But just as Jesus Christ our Saviour was made flesh through the Word of God and took on flesh and blood for our salvation, so too (we have been taught) through the word of prayer that comes from him, the food over which the eucharist has been spoken becomes the flesh and blood of the incarnate Jesus, in order to nourish and transform our flesh and blood."[4] St. Irenaeus (qv) says that the bread and wine "receiving the word of God become the Eucharist, that is, the body and blood of Christ."[5] Tertullian (qv) says: "He took bread, offered it to his disciples, and made it into his body by saying: 'This is my body.'"[6]

The Pre-Nicene Fathers were content to affirm the passage from bread and wine to the body and blood of Christ: one became the other (*ginetai* for St. Irenaeus). In the fourth and fifth centuries the Greek Fathers were seeking to advance the mode of expression towards some kind of adequacy: how to signify the change. Words chosen expressed varied shadings of the idea of profound change, conversion, transference, transformation; the different nuances are considered in the article on each author.

The interesting parallel movement of thought in the west turns on the evolution of the word transubstantiation. It is important to locate the first use of the word *substantia*, from which it came. This first such mention appears to be in a homily, *Magnitudo coelestium beneficiorum*, attributed to Eusebius of Emessa and others, but probably the work of Faustus of Riez (qv).[7] "Therefore the heavenly authority confirms exactly that my flesh is really food and my blood drink. Let every hesitation of unbelief withdraw therefore since the author of the gift is himself also the witness to the truth. For the invisible priest, by a mysterious power of his word changes *(convertit)* visible created things into the substance of his body and blood (*visibiles creaturas in substantia corporis et sanguinis sui*), saying thus: 'Take and eat: this is my body,' and repeating the sanctification, 'Take and drink, this is my blood.'"[8] Faustus, recalling the wonders of creation, urges the Christian regenerated in Christ to ask himself "how it should not be strange or impossible that mortal things should be changed into the substance of Christ *(quod in Christi substantiam et mortalia commutantur)*." Again he says that "the primary created things, at the gesture of divine power through the presence of the majesty, can pass over into the nature of the Lord's body *(in dominici corporis transire posse naturam)*"; the created things placed on the altar are "before being consecrated by the invocation of his name *(antequam invocatione sui nominis consecrantur)*, the substance of bread and wine; after the words of Christ, they are the body and blood of Christ."[9]

Among those influenced by Faustus was St. Paschasius Radbertus (qv) who quotes him and borrows from him. Batiffol's remark about St. Paschasius was first deserved by Faustus. In the oath of Berengarius (qv), as we shall see, the words used were "substantially changed" (*substantialiter converti*). The word 'transubstantiate' occurs first in a twelfth century text: "Let us pray that the food of angels become the food of men, that is, that the offering of bread and wine be transubstantiated *(transubstantietur)* into the body and blood of Jesus Christ."[10] The words are found in the *Tractatus de sacramento altaris*, attributed to Stephen of Beauge (d. 1139/40) but now restored to their true author, Stephen of Autun (d. c. 1189). In the present state of research, the first certain use of the word is by Rolando Bandinelli, later Pope Alexander III (d. 1181) in his *Sententiae*, about 1140/41: "Nevertheless, if, in urgent necessity, under the appearance of another bread consecration takes place, there would certainly be transubstantiation *(profecto fieret transubstantiatio)*, but transubstantiation of the blood never takes place save of wine."[11] The great medieval scholar, J. de Ghellinck, S.J, has shown the word in frequent use from mid-twelfth century on.[12]

From the oath of Berengarius (qv) to John Paul II at the International Eucharistic Congress, Nairobi, 1981, the idea occurs, equivalently in the first instance, explicitly ever since, in the official teaching of the Church. The oath of Berengarius is given in the article on him. The Fourth Lateran Council decreed as follows: "One indeed is the universal Church of the faithful, outside which no one at all is saved, in which the priest himself is the sacrifice, Jesus Christ, whose body and blood are truly contained in the sacrament of the altar under the species of bread and wine; the bread (changed) into his body by the divine power of transubstantiation, and the wine into the blood, so that to accomplish the mystery of unity we ourselves receive from his (nature) what he himself received from ours."[13] The Council of Constance, dealing with the question of communion under one species, notes that "it must be believed most firmly and not at all doubted that the whole body of Christ and the blood are truly contained under the species of bread as well as under the species of wine."[14]

The Council of Florence continues the teaching thus: "The words of the Saviour, by which he instituted this sacrament, are the form of this sacrament; for the priest, speaking in the person of Christ effects the sacrament. For by the power of the very words the substance of the bread is changed into the body of Christ, and the substance of the wine into the blood *(substantia panis in corpus Christi et substantia vini in sanguinem convertuntur)*; yet in such a way that Christ is contained entire under the species of bread, and entire under the species of wine. Under any part also of the consecrated host and consecrated wine, although a separation has taken place, Christ is entire."[15]

It was the Council of Trent which canonised the word transubstantiation: "But since Christ, our Redeemer, has said that this is truly his body which he offered under the species of bread (cf. Mt 26:26ff; Mk 14:22ff; Lk 22:19ff; 1 Cor 11:24ff) it has always been a matter of conviction in the Church of God, and now this holy Synod declares it again, that by the consecration of the bread and wine a conversion takes place *(conversionem fieri)* of the whole substance of the bread into the substance of the body of Christ our Lord, and of the whole substance of the wine into the substance of his blood. This change is appropriately and rightly called transubstantiation by the Catholic Church."[16]

Pius VI, by the Constitution *Auctorem fidei*, 28 August 1794, condemned the errors of the Synod of Pistoia (qv). Recalling that the Synod had discouraged priests from speaking about the manner in which Christ is in the Eucharist—as explained by scholastic theology, and had stated the doctrine in two propositions: (a) after the consecration Christ is truly, really, substantially under the species and (b) then the whole substance of bread and wine ceases, appearances only remaining, the Pope went on to say that the doctrine "absolutely omits to make any mention of transubstantiation, or change of the whole substance of bread into the body, and of the whole substance of wine into the blood, which the Council of Trent defined as an article of faith, and which is contained in the solemn profession of faith; since by an indiscreet and suspicious omission of this sort knowledge is taken away both of an article pertaining to the faith, and also of the word consecrated by the Church to protect the profession of it, as if it were a discussion of a merely scholastic question—dangerous, derogatory to the exposition of Catholic truth about the dogma of transubstantiation, favourable to heretics."[17]

The Profession of Faith of the Council of Trent repeats the formulation of the conciliar decree on the substantial change and the words: "and this change the Catholic Church calls transubstantiation."

Some interventions by the Magisterium in the present century are noteworthy. Pius XII (qv) referred in *Humani Generis* to some erroneous trends: "Some are found who maintain that the doctrine of transubstantiation based, they say, on an outmoded philosophical notion of substance, should be corrected in such wise that the real presence of Christ in the most holy Eucharist should be reduced to a symbolism; in this way that the consecrated species would be only the efficacious signs of the spiritual presence of Christ and his intimate union with his faithful members in his Mystical Body."[18]

The same Pope spoke at length to the international liturgical congress at Assisi, 22 September 1956, on the limits to theological investigation of the mystery: "Certain theologians, while accepting the doctrine of the Council on the real presence and transubstantiation, interpret the words of Christ and those of the Council in such a way that all that remains of Christ's presence is a kind of envelope emptied of its natural content. In their opinion the essential content of the species of bread and wine is 'the Lord in heaven,' with whom the species have a so-called real and essential relation of content and presence. This speculative interpretation raises serious objections when it is put forward as fully sufficient, for the Christian sentiment of the faithful people, the constant catechetical teaching of the Church, the terms of the Council, especially the words of the Lord himself, demand that the Eucharist contain the Lord himself. The sacramental species are not the Lord, even if they have with the substance of Christ in heaven a so-called essential relation of content and presence. The Lord said: 'This is my body! This is my blood!' He did not say: 'This is a sensible appearance which signifies the presence of my body and my blood.' Doubtless he could have arranged that the sensible signs of a real relation of presence would be the sensible, efficacious signs of sacramental grace; but the question here is of the essential content of the *species eucharisticae*, not of their sacramental efficacy. One cannot then admit that the theory, of which we have spoken, takes full account of the words of Christ, that the presence of Christ in the Eucharist means nothing more and that this suffices to warrant saying in full truth of the Eucharist, 'Dominus est.'"

These words caused something like alarm in Thomistic circles in Rome. The Pope, it was felt, had been unduly influenced by some theologians in his immediate entourage, notably Fr. Hurth, who favoured the adduction (qv) theory. An incident in the Roman academic world illustrates the tension created. Fr. I. Filograssi, S.J., of the Gregorian University was suddenly refused the *Nihil Obstat* for a work, *De sanctissima Eucharistia, Quaestiones dogmaticae selectae*, which had been given this approval annually for twenty years. The Pope's theologian disagreed with the reply which Fr. Filograssi gave to an objection: "If there is no change in the body of Christ, then there is no presence under the Eucharistic species." In fact he had borrowed the reply from Cardinal Billot (qv), who had restored the Thomist theology of transubstantiation (see article Thomas Aquinas, St.). Eventually with the support of Roman Thomists, notably Fr. H. Barré, C.S.Sp., who supplied him with the text from *In Distinct*, 10, art. 4, Fr. Filograssi was given the *Nihil Obstat*. The Pope and his theologians were astonished and the Pope did not conceal his displeasure with his theologians: the Assisi discourse is not included in the collection of Pius XII's texts on the Eucharist made by Fr. Bertetto.[19]

Vatican II (qv) did not explicitly formulate a theory of transubstantiation. It taught the presence of Christ in two passages: "He is present in the Sacrifice of the Mass not only in the person of his minister, 'the same now offering, through the ministry of priests, who formerly offered himself on the cross,' but especially in the Eucharistic species."[20] "For in the most blessed Eucharist is contained the whole spiritual good of the Church, namely, Christ himself our Pasch and the living bread which gives life to men through his flesh—that flesh which is given life and gives life through the Holy Spirit."[21]

Paul VI (qv) dealt with the real presence (qv) in the *Credo of the People of God* and continued thus: "Consequently, in this sacrament there is no other way in which Christ can be present except through the conversion of the entire substance of bread into his body and through the conversion of the entire substance of wine into his blood, leaving unchanged only those properties of bread and wine which are open to the senses. This hidden conversion is appropriately and rightly called transubstantiation. Any theological explanation intent on arriving at some understanding of this mystery, if it is to be in accordance with Catholic faith, must maintain, without ambiguity, that in the order of reality which exists independently of the human mind, the bread and wine cease to exist after the consecration.... The unique and indivisible existence of Christ the Lord whereby he lives in the glory of heaven is not multiplied by the sacrament but rendered present in every place on earth where the Eucharistic Sacrifice is celebrated. Here, indeed, we have the *Mystery of Faith* and Eucharistic blessings to

which we must unequivocally give our assent."[22]

Thus Pope Paul in 1968. On 3 September 1965, then still the feast of St. Pius X (qv), he had published the Encyclical Letter, *Mysterium Fidei* (qv). In the section of this document which deals with the present subject he wrote as follows: "To avoid misunderstanding this sacramental presence which surpasses the laws of nature and constitutes the greatest miracle of its kind,[23] we must listen with docility to the voice of the teaching and praying Church. This voice which constantly echoes the voice of Christ, assures us that the way Christ is made present in this sacrament is none other than by the change of the whole substance of the bread into his body and of the whole substance of the wine into his blood, and that this unique and truly wonderful change the Catholic Church rightly calls transubstantiation.[24] As a result of transubstantiation the species of bread and wine undoubtedly take on a new meaning and a new finality; for they no longer remain ordinary bread and ordinary wine, but become the sign of something sacred, the sign of a spiritual food. However, the reason they take on this new significance and this new finality is simply because they contain a new 'reality,' which we may justly term ontological. Not that there lies under those species what was already there before, but something quite different; and that not only because of the faith of the Church, but in objective reality; since after the change of the substance or nature of the bread and wine into the body and blood of Christ, nothing remains of the bread and wine but the appearances, under which Christ, whole and entire, in his physical 'reality' is bodily present, although not in the same way that bodies are present in a given place."[25]

The Pope dealt here in passing with the theories of transignification (qv), and transfinalization, current at the time. In the Encyclical he referred to the address he had given to the Italian National Eucharistic Congress at Pisa in the same year.

In the extensive Eucharistic teaching of John Paul II (qv), there are two explicit references to transubstantiation. Speaking to pilgrims from Milan on 14 November 1981, with the National Eucharistic Congress to be held in that city in mind he said: "The Eucharist is the mystery of mysteries, since its acceptance means welcoming completely the message of Christ and of the Church, from the introduction to faith, to the doctrine of redemption, to the concept of sacrifice and the consecrated priesthood, to the dogma of transubstantiation, to the value of legislation in liturgical matters."[26] At the final Mass of the International Eucharistic Congress in Nairobi, 18 August 1985, the Pope spoke thus: "In fact at the Last Supper, Christ took bread in his own hands, blessed it and said these words over it: 'Take this all of you and eat it: this is my body.' And the broken bread which had become, in a sacramental way, his own body, he distributed to the Apostles. In a similar way, he brought about the transubstantiation of the wine into his blood and distributing it to the Apostles, said: 'This is the cup of my blood; take ye all and drink of it.' And then he added: 'Do this in memory of me.'"[27]

The position of the Orthodox is dealt with separately. Out of the historical survey, including the Teaching Authority arises the question of speculative theology: How is transubstantiation explained? We are here dealing with the precise concept, not with erroneous views, such as impanation (qv), consubstantiation (qv) advocated by Luther, or the recent theories dealt with by Pope Paul VI, transignification, or transfinalization.

As a general principle it must be recalled that in relations between creatures and God, the relationship on the creatures side is real, but on God's, notional only, for God is immutable. So is the glorified body of Jesus Christ. When we seek to explain the passage of a created entity like bread, the *terminus a quo*, to the *terminus ad quem*, his glorified body, we cannot do so by a theory which implies any change in the body of Christ.

One such theory argues that the body of Christ is produced from the bread: the production interpretation. Another, that Christ's body is adduced or brought to the bread: the adduction theory. Each view has to be considered, and in the present case criticised, separately. But first the doctrine preferred because it accords with the Church's teaching and can claim the authority of St. Thomas Aquinas (qv).

To express this doctrine there is no better authority than Cardinal Billot, who succeeded in restoring it in face of the erroneous theories adopted since the seventeenth century: "St. Thomas and the ancient scholastic Doctors, that is, St. Bonaventure, Giles of Rome, Alexander of Hales, Albert the Great, unanimously deny all annihilation of the substance of bread; they deny it, I say, not only as to the word but in reality. 'There is no way,' says St. Thomas (III, q. 73, art 3), 'by which the true body of Christ can begin to be in this sacrament save by conversion of the substance of bread into him *(per conversionem substantiae panis in ipsum)* which conversion is removed, by the annihilation of the substance of bread, or by its return to the underlying matter. . . . From which it is clear that the aforementioned opinion (of annihilation) is false.' And St. Bonaventure (in IV D. 11, pat I q. 2): 'All in common hold that it is not annihilation of the bread, rather a change into a better substance; and, therefore, such conversion is transubstantiation, not

annihilation, and thus it should be called. Further, if the bread were not converted into the body of Christ, one could not understand how the body of Christ could begin to be on the altar without its being changed; on which account it must be called conversion of the bread, not annihilation.[1] Again they unanimously deny any action in any way terminating at the body of Christ, that is, they deny all production or adduction of it, even any change wrought in it by the force of consecration, teaching that transubstantiation is an action by which the *substance of bread is converted into the pre-existing, unchanged, body of Christ*, while the dimensions and other accidents of the converted substance remain.' In the conversion of natural things what is converted and that into which it is converted is changed. But here that to which the conversion is made was pre-existing and there is no addition to it; therefore, that in which the conversion ends is in no way changed, namely, the body of Christ, but only the bread which is converted.' Thus St. Thomas in IV D. 11, Quaest 1, a 3, q 1. St. Bonaventure agrees: 'It must be said,' he says, 'that though nature cannot do this, nor reason understand it, nevertheless, God can convert many things into the body of Christ, and accordingly the body of Christ is in many places, not through any change in Christ, but in the bread which is converted into him.' And later, 'In creation that which was not is made to be; in transubstantiation what was in one place is made to be elsewhere, without any change in itself.' And again, 'By consecration only this is done that what was perfect and glorious in heaven, is, by virtue of transubstantiation, the same on the altar without any change.' And the same is the opinion of Albert the Great in IV D. 11, a. 1, ad 5 et 6; Giles of Rome, on the body of Christ, Theorema 1; Alexander of Hales, Summ. theol., Tome 4, quaest. 10, etc. Therefore, in the doctrine of the ancients, transubstantiation is not the destruction of one thing and its substitution by another by means of production or adduction, but it is one simple action whereby God, who as the author of being has power in all being, changes immediately whatever is of the entity in the substance of bread into what is of the entity in the substance of the body of Christ, in such wise that the subject is in no way Christ, but only the bread, whose substance passes and whose dimensions remain."[28]

As the great dogmatic theologian adds, there were two sacred principles governing the thought of the schoolmen in this matter: the first is that the reality in heaven and in the Eucharist on every altar is "the one individual body born of the Virgin, offered on the cross, raised and taken to glory before the eyes of the Apostles; the second is that any action exercised on the body of Christ so that remaining in heaven it should attain a new and simultaneous presence in the (consecrated) host, is utterly impossible."[29] The action is on the bread and wine; Christ is changeless.

This is the authentic doctrine of transubstantiation, a form of change, conversion, differing totally from all others, respecting the transcendence and power of the glorified Christ. (See articles Presence, Real; Thomas Aquinas, St.; Adduction Theory; Production Theory).

[1]Bibl. A. Piolanti, *Il Mistero*, 216, 17; *Eucharistia*, 261, 62; cf. A. Piolanti, *Il Mistero*, 216-68; id., *Eucharistia*, 221-62; id., *EC*, s.v.; C. van Crombrugghe, *La présence reelle et la transubstantiation*, Gand, 1906; J. Labreton, S.J., *Le dogme de la transubstantiation et la théologie antiochéenne du Ve siècle*, Etudes 117 (1908), 477-87; J. Piccirelli, *Disquisitio de catholico intellectu dogmatis transubstantiationis*, Naples, 1912; A. Bassani, *De transubstantiatione ad mentem S. Thomae*, Florence, 1913; J. de Ghellinck, S.J., *A propos du premier emploi du mot transubstantiation*, RSR 2 (1911), 466-69; 57-72; 3 (1912), 255-59; id., DTC V, 1287-1302; A. von Slpawa-Neyman, *Das Problem der wesenslosen Gestalten im hl. Altarsakrament nach der Lehre des hl. Thomas von Aquin*, Breslau, 1920; J. Bittremieux, *De transubstantiatione quid senserit S. Bonaventura, Collectanea Franciscana*, 1923, 26-39; A. Zychlinski, *Sincera doctrina de conceptu transubstantiationis juxta principia S. Thomae, La ciencia tomista* 16 (1924), 28-65; L. Cardinal Billot, S.J., *De Sacramentis*, I, ed. 7, 1932, 344-360; J. Puig de la Bellacasa, *De transubstantiatione juxta Duns Scotum, Antonianum* 6 (1930); V.M. Cachia, *Animadversiones in transubstantiationis doctrinam*, reply to previous art., *Angelicum* 9 (1931), 246-62; M.T.L. Penido, *Le rôle de l'analogie en théologie dogmatique*, Paris, 1931, 427-41; B. Baur, *Non potest aliter corpus Christi incipere esse de novo in hoc sacramento nisi per conversionem substantiae panis in ipsum, Divus Thomas* (Piacenza), 38 (1934), 120-28; A. Verhamme, *Exponitur notio transubstantiationis, Collationes Brugenses*, 29 (1925), 92-99; id., *Genesis canonis transubstantiationis in Concilio Tridentino*, ibid., 140-49; id., *Refutantur sententiae reproductionis et adductionis*, ibid., 180-89; H.I. Storff, *De natura transubstantiationis juxta J. Duns Scotum*, Quaracchi, 1936; P. Glorieux, *Fieri est factum esse, Divus Thomas* (Piacenza), 42 (1938), 254-78; T. Horan, *Doctrina transubstantiationis secundum F. Suarez*, Rome, 1938 (thesis Greg. University); A. Michel, *Les décrets du Concile de Trente*, Paris, 1938, 259-87; id., *Transubstantiation*, DTC XV, (1946), 1396-1406; H.H. Maltha, *Cosmologia circa transubstantiationem, Angelicum*, 16 (1939), 305-34; F. Simons, *Indagatio critica in opinionem S. Thomae de natura intima transubstantiationis*, Indore, 1939; R. Maglione, *Il concetto di conversione in Egidio Romano*, Benevento, 1941; G. Gliozzo, *La dottrina della conversione eucaristica in Pascasio Radberto e Ratramno*, Palermo, 1945; F. Cardinal Carpino, *De Eucharistia*, 370-75; J. Filograssi, S.J., *De SS Eucharistia*, ed. 6, Rome, 1957, 157-189; 213-231; C. Colombo, *Teologia, filosofia e fisica nella transustanzione La Scuola Cattolica*, 1955, 89-124; id., *Ancora sulla transustanzione*, ibid., 1956, 241-262; M. Ghirardi, *Ai margini di una controversia eucaristica*, ibid., 1956, 263-88; R. Masi, *L'Eucaristia e le scienze*, in *Eucaristia*, 743-777; J. de Baciocchi, *Présence eucharistique et transubstantiation, Irenikon*, 1959, 139-64; id., *La sostanza materiale e i suoi accidenti. La controversia eucaristica*, Studia Patavina, 1957, 125-142; P. Cardinal Parente, *Conversione mirabile*, Symposium, *Eucaristia pane di vita*, Padua, 1962, 21-36; F. Selvaggi, *Realtà fisica e sostanza sensibile nella dottrina eucaristica*, Greg 37 (1956), 16-33; F.J. Leenhardt, *This is my body. Essays on the Lord's Supper*, tr. J.G. Davies, London, 1958; C. Vollert, *The Eucharist: Controversy on Transubstantiation*, ThSt 22 (61), 391-425; id., NCE L. Hodl, *Der Transubstantiationsbegriff in der scholastischen*

Theologie des 12 Jahrhunderts, RTAM 31 (1964), 230-259; H. Jorissen, *Die Entfaltung der Transubstantiationslehre bis zum Beginn der Hochscholastik* (Münsterische Beiträge zur Theologie, 28, Heft i, 1965, bibl.; A. Trape, *Il mistero eucaristico in Egidio Romano, Divinitas* 10 (1966), 440-66; J.F. McCabe, *The Doctrine of Transubstantiation from Berengar through Trent: The Point at Issue, HTR* 61 (1968), 385-430; L. Ligier, *Il Sacramento dell'Eucaristia*, Rome 1977, 199-251; J. de Aldama, S.J., *La doctrina de Lutero sobre la transubstantiación según los teólogos del Concilio de Trento*, Arch. Teol. Granad., 42 (1979); J. Betz, *The Eucharist ... Mysterium Salutis*, VIII, pt. 2, ed. 2; P.-L. Carle, O.P., *Le sacrifice de la Nouvelle Alliance. Consubstantiel et transubstantiation*, ed. 2, Bordeaux, 1981; R. Coggi, *Si può ancora parlare di transustanziazione, Sacra Doctrina*, 1983, 227-232; J. Piccirelli, *De Catholico Intellectu Dogmatis Transubstantiationis*, Naples, 1912; J.H. Nicolas, O.P., *Synthèse Dogmatique*, Fribourg, 1985, 947-981, esp. 953-58; [2]Cf. P.L. Carle, *op. cit.*; [3]*Smyrnaeans*, VII, 1 Lake I, 259; [4]*Apol.*, I, 65-66; [5]*Adv. Haer.* V, 2, 3; [6]*Adv. Marcionem*, IV, 10; PL 2, 491-2; [7]Cf. art. Faustus of Riez; [8]Pl 67, 1052, 53; [9]*Ibid.*, 1056; [10]PL 172, 1291; cf. D. Vanden Eynde, *Le Tractatus de sacramento altaris' faussement attribué à Etienne de Beauge, RTAM* 19 (1952), 225-43; [11]Ed. U. Gietl, Frib in B., 1891, 231; [12]Cf. DTC, l.c.; [13]DS 802; [14]DS 1200; [15]DS 1321; [16]Session XIII, c. 4, DS 1642; [17]cf. Canon 2; DS 2629; [18]*AAS* 42 (1950), 571; [19]Text of Assisi address, *AAS* 48 (1956), 720; for sequel cf. R. Laurentin, *Jesus Christ Présent*, Paris, 1980, 62-65; [20]*Sacrosanctum Concilium*, 7; [21]*Presbyterorum ordinis*, 5; [22]*Vatican Council II*, ed. A. Flannery, O.P., 393; [23]Reference in text to *Mirae Caritatis*, Encyclical of Leo XIII, *Acta Leonis XIII*, vol. 22, 1902-1903, 123; [24]Reference in text to Council of Trent, *Decree on the Eucharist*, ch. 4, and can 2; [25]Tr. CTSI, *AAS* 57 (1965); [26]*AAS* 73 (1981); [27]*AAS* 77 (1985); [28]*Op. cit.*, 346ff; [29]Ibid. 348, 49, n.1.

TRENT, THE COUNCIL OF

The promulgated documents of the Council are reproduced, as to their essentials, at the end of this article.[1] Some background is first sketched. The conciliar decrees on the Eucharist and on the Mass had to deal with subjects in the focus of controversy provoked by the Reformation. At the same time necessary reforms were needed within the Church itself, for many abuses existed. The drafting and discussion of the decree on the Eucharist suffered from the vicissitudes of the Council more than any other document on its agenda; these vicissitudes were political in origin. We are not concerned with the personalities of the Council, the papal theologians, Lainez and Salmeron, the spokesmen for the emperor, Charles V, Melchior Cano and John of Ortega; the emperor took a lively interest in the proceedings, was much concerned with one problem, communion under both species. The Pope's problem at times was to maintain the Council's independence from the emperor. Protestant delegates were expected, which slowed progress.

Inevitably the procedure was dictated by the consciousness of errors to be condemned. Ten articles were, in 1547, ready for rebuttal first by the theologians present, then by the Council Fathers: 1. The body and blood of Our Lord Jesus Christ are not really in the Eucharist, only as a sign, like the notice of an inn; 2.

Christ is given in the Eucharist, but he can only be eaten spiritually by faith; 3. The body and blood of Our Lord Jesus Christ are in the Eucharist, but the substance of bread and wine are there also; thus there is not transubstantiation, but hypostatic union of the humanity of Christ with the substance of the bread and wine; 4. One should not adore Christ in the Eucharist, nor honour him by feasts, nor carry him in procession, nor take him to the sick; those who adore him are really idolators; 5. The Eucharist should not be kept in the sanctuary, it should be consumed at once or given to those present; to act otherwise is to abuse the sacrament; 6. The body of the Lord is not in hosts or particles which remain after communion; he is there only while he is being received, neither before nor after; 7. It is a divine law that the people receive communion under both species; it is a sin, therefore, to force people to take only one; and nevertheless if the Council were to order communion under both species, they would have to communicate under one only; 8. Under one species there is not contained as much as under the two, and he who receives communion under one does not receive as much as he who receives under both; 9. Faith alone is sufficient preparation for the reception of the Eucharist; there is no obligation to receive communion at Easter; 10. No one is allowed to give himself communion.

From 3 to 19 February, Sundays excepted, more than sixty theologians with more than forty prelates present, were engaged in discussing these points. Ten more articles were suggested. The articles distributed to the Council Fathers were accordingly divided into three groups: those which the theologians thought should be condemned outright; those which, in the opinion of theologians, should be amended; new articles to be submitted.

The Council, in general assembly, was to debate these matters on 8 and 9 March. Things went no further, for the Pope, taking many things into account, decided to change the meeting place of the Council to Bologna. There in May the debate was continued. Things were brought to a conclusion and seemed ready for a definition when the Pope suddenly intervened and ordered a delay in procedure. This ultimately led to consideration of the subject when the Council met in Trent in 1551. The eleventh and twelfth sessions took from May to September and in the latter month from 8 to 16, once again theologians were asked to discuss ten articles which seemed to call for condemnation; in content they are broadly similar to those first drafted. Twenty-eight theologians contributed to the debate, including Salmeron and Lainez, and the imperial doctors, Melchior Cano, John d'Ortega and John Arze. The results of their deliberations were submitted to the Council Fathers, who gave their views in general assemblies from 21 to 30 September. A general principle was accepted: the Council had enough to do to condemn heresies; it should not take part in debates conducted in the schools of theology. There was much exchange of opinions on the difference, in grace received, between communion under one or both species, whether it should continue in the German possessions, how should Jn 6:53 be interpreted: "Truly, truly I say to you, unless you eat the flesh of the Son of man and drink his blood, you have no life in you." Was it sufficient to appeal to 6:51: "I am the living bread which came down from heaven; if any one eats of this bread he will live for ever; and the bread which I shall give for the life of the world is my flesh."

A drafting commission was given the task of achieving a final text in the light of so much discussion: ten canons were drawn up on 1 October; next day they were brought to thirteen. They represent a remarkable improvement on the early texts. Before they were finally adopted, a request was made on behalf of the emperor and Ferdinand of Austria to put off a decision until the Protestants could come; the Pope had guaranteed a safe-conduct. A compromise was adopted—the canons to which they might object, those dealing with the obligation to receive under both species, and with the difference in grace between reception under one or both species, would be left in abeyance. A final text of the canons to be defined was reached after further refining. Then it was decided to follow previous procedure and draft a number of chapters to go along with them, a doctrinal summary. Eight chapters were planned: on the real presence, the institution, the excellence and worship of the Eucharist, transubstantiation, preparation for communion, the communion of the laity and communion of children. The question of transubstantiation became polemical between Thomists and Scotists so that a new text was called for. With very little change the Council Fathers accepted it as the commission had drafted it. All was now ready for the definition, which took place on 11 October, before an imposing assembly.

There had been question of reforming canons since 1547, but though draft texts were prepared, the matter was shelved. The vicissitudes of the Council caused further delay in dealing with the question of communion under both species and the communion of children. It was not until June 1562 that discussion could begin on the subject, and 16 July that the canons and corresponding chapters could be approved.

In early June it was announced that the remaining articles on the Eucharist would be discussed. Five questions were proposed to the theologians; they bore on the possibility of a divine precept binding for salvation on communion under both species, the nature of the ecclesiastical precept denying the chalice to all but the priest, the conditions advisable if a concession were made in favour of a particular country—for a motive of Christian charity, the question of difference, for the recipient, in communion under both species, the question whether there was an obligation in divine law to give communion to children before the use of reason.

Four canons were drawn up after the abundant exchange of opinions by the theologians. They were debated with some vigour in six general congregations between 30 June and 3 July and, after amendment, subjected to further close scrutiny—especially in regard to any argument based on Jn 6—further amended and finally approved.

The Mass: The Council's teaching on the Mass was in the context of the doctrines expressed by the Reformers. The formulation of the teaching was at least in its timing affected by the vicissitudes of the Council's history. The first active phase was the drafting and discussion of ten canons, submitted for condemnation, taken from the writings of the Reformers; the references were given. Between 7 and 29 December 1551, these canons were debated by some 70 theologians who mostly agreed with their tenor. The Council secretary summed up the position: "The articles on the Mass should in the judgement of the theologians be condemned, nor were any amendments of consequence made." The Council Fathers debated them from 7 to 14 January 1552. Subsequent commentators like M. Lepin scrutinize these speeches for indications of the thinking on the sacrifice of the Mass, as to what precisely constitutes the reality.

When the debate was ended commissions were named to draft texts. They produced a brief preface, four chapters and thirteen canons: the great truths were affirmed, the reality of the Mass as sacrifice, its intrinsic relation to the sacrifice of the Cross which it did not rival or lessen in uniqueness, its propitiatory character, the importance of the canon—the Reformers contended that this was rife with errors—the validity of private Masses, of Masses in honour of the saints, of Masses said for others, the rule for mingling water with wine, the language used and manner of its use, and the proper ceremonial.

Ready by 20 January, consideration of the document was delayed to await the arrival of a second group of Lutherans—some had come from Würtemberg. Finally the text was a victim of the adjournment of the Council, decreed by Julius III in view of the changing political situation, accepted by the assembly on 28 April, despite the opposition of twelve Council Fathers. Thus what was, with the question of justification, the most important matter on the conciliar agenda, would not be considered for ten years.

When Pius IV recalled the Council to meet in January 1562, reform was a priority on the agenda. It was in session XXI, 16 July that dogma was taken: on the question of communion under both species, as has been seen. Immediately after, attention was given to the Mass. The matters submitted to the Council were broadly the same as had been hitherto discussed, but they were proposed as thirteen questions. Procedure was tightened by limiting the number of theologians, and attempting to limit the time they could take. Commissions from within the Council Fathers were set up to draft a doctrinal statement and canons and to list abuses in the celebration of Mass.

A text was ready by 6 August and engaged the attention of the Fathers. Whereas in the previous session there had been but seventy, there were now one hundred and eighty Fathers. Opinions of interest were expressed, notably on the sacrificial character of the Last Supper (qv), and how this should be defined. Unanimity was reached by 14 September on doctrine and on condemnation of abuses. Some days were taken up with the difficult question of the chalice—offering it to the laity. With the principal texts passed and solemnly promulgated on 17 September in session XXII, there was included a decree reserving this decision to the Pope. The texts finally passed are here given.

Session XIII (October 11, 1551). *Decree on the Most Holy Eucharist.*

The sacred and holy ecumenical and general Synod of Trent, lawfully assembled in the Holy Spirit with the same legates and nuncios of the Apostolic See presiding therein, although it has convened for this purpose not without the special guidance and direction of the Holy Spirit, namely to publish the true and ancient doctrine concerning faith and the sacraments, and to provide a remedy for all the heresies and other very serious troubles by which the Church of God is at present wretchedly agitated and torn into many different factions, yet from the beginning has had this especially among its desires, to uproot the 'cockles' of execrable errors and schisms, which the enemy in these troubled times of ours has 'sown' (Mt 13:25), in the doctrine of the faith, in the use and worship of the sacred Eucharist, which our Saviour, moreover, left in his Church as a symbol of that unity and charity with which he wished all Christians to be mutualy bound and united. Therefore, this same sacred and holy synod, transmitting that sound and genuine doctrine of this venerable and divine sacrament of the Eucharist, which the Catholic Church, instructed by our Lord

Jesus Christ himself and by his Apostles, and taught by the 'Holy Spirit who day by day brings her to all truth' (Jn 14:26), has always held and will preserve even to the end of time, forbids all the faithful of Christ hereafter to venture to believe, teach, or preach concerning the Most Holy Eucharist otherwise than is explained in this present decree.

Chapter I. *The Real Presence of our Lord Jesus Christ in the Most Holy Sacrament of the Eucharist.*

First of all the holy Synod teaches and openly and simply professes that in the nourishing sacrament of the Holy Eucharist, after the consecration of the bread and wine our Lord Jesus Christ, true God and true man, is truly, really and substantially (can. 1) contained under the species of those sensible things. For these things are not mutually contradictory, that our Saviour himself is always seated at the right hand of the Father in heaven according to the natural mode of existing, and yet that in many other places sacramentally he is present to us in his own substance by that manner of existence which, although we can scarcely express it in words, yet we can, however, by our understanding enlightened by faith, conceive to be possible to God, and which we ought most steadfastly to believe. For all our forefathers, as many as were in the true Church of Christ, who have discussed this most holy sacrament, have most openly professed that our Redeemer instituted this so wonderful a sacrament at the Last Supper, when after the blessing of the bread and wine he testified in clear and definite words that he gave them his own body and his own blood; and those words which are recorded (Mt 26:26ff; Mk 14:22; Lk 22:19ff) by the holy Evangelists and afterwards repeated by St. Paul (1 Cor 11:23ff), since they contain within themselves that proper and very clear meaning in which they were understood by the Fathers, it is a most disgraceful thing for some contentious and wicked men to distort into fictitious and imaginary figures of speech, by which the real nature of the flesh and blood of Christ is denied, contrary to the universal sense of the Church, which, recognizing with an ever grateful and recollecting mind this most excellent benefit of Christ, as the pillar and ground of truth (1 Tim 3:15), has detested these falsehoods, devised by impious men, as satanical.

Chapter II. *The Reason for the Institution of this Most Holy Sacrament.*

Our Saviour, therefore, when about to depart from this world to the Father, instituted this sacrament in which he poured forth, as it were, the riches of his divine love for men, 'making a remembrance of his wonderful works' (Ps 110:4) and he commanded us in the consuming of it to cherish his 'memory' (1 Cor 11:24), and 'to show forth his death until he come' to judge the world (1 Cor 11:26). But he wished that this sacrament be received as the spiritual food of souls (Mt 26:26) by which they may be nourished and strengthened (can. 5), living by the life of him who said: 'He who eateth me, the same also shall live by me' (Jn 6:58), and as an antidote, whereby we may be freed from daily faults and be preserved from mortal sins. He wished, furthermore, that this be a pledge of our future glory and of everlasting happiness, and thus be a symbol of that one 'body' of which he himself is the 'head' (1 Cor 11:3; Eph 5:23), and to which he wished us to be united, as members, by the closest bond of faith, hope, and charity, that we might 'all speak the same thing and there be no schisms among us' (cf 1 Cor 1:10).

Chapter III. *The Excellence of the Most Holy Eucharist over the other Sacraments.*

This, indeed, the most Holy Eucharist has in common with the other sacraments, that it is a 'symbol of a sacred thing and a visible form of an invisible grace'; but this excellent and peculiar thing is found in it, that the other sacraments first have the power of sanctifying, when one uses them, but in the Eucharist there is the Author of sanctity himself before it is used (can. 4). For the apostles had not yet received the Eucharist from the hand of the Lord (Mt 26:26; Mk 14:22) when he himself truly said that what he was offering was his body; and this belief has always been in the Church of God, that immediately after the consecration the true body of our Lord and his true blood together with his soul and divinity exist under the species of bread and wine; but the body indeed under the species of bread, and the blood under the species of wine by the force of the words, but the body itself under both by the force of that natural connection and concomitance (qv) by which the parts of Christ the Lord, 'who has now risen from the dead to die no more' (Rom 6:9), are mutually united, the divinity also because of that admirable hypostatic union (can. 1 and 3) with his body and soul. Therefore, it is very true that as much is contained under either species as under both. For Christ whole and entire exists under the species of bread and under any part whatsoever of that species, likewise the whole (Christ) is present under the species of wine and under its parts (can. 3).

Chapter IV. *Transubstantiation.*

But since Christ, our Redeemer, has said that that is truly his own body which he offered under the species of bread (cf. Mt 26:26ff; Mk 14:22ff; Lk 22:19ff; 1 Cor 11:24ff), it has always been a matter of conviction in the Church of God, and now this holy Synod declares it again, that by the consecration of the bread and wine a conversion takes place of the whole substance of bread into the substance of the body of Christ our

Lord, and of the whole substance of the wine into the substance of his blood. This conversion is appropriately and properly called transubstantiation by the Catholic Church. (can. 2).

Chapter V. *The Worship and Veneration to be shown to the Most Blessed Sacrament.*

There is, therefore, no room left for doubt that all the faithful of Christ, in accordance with a custom always received in the Catholic Church, offer in veneration (can. 6) the worship of latria which is due to the true God, to this most Holy Sacrament. For it is not less to be adored because it was instituted by Christ the Lord to be received (cf. Mt 26:26). For we believe that same God to be present therein, of whom the eternal Father when introducing him into the world says: 'And let the Angels of God adore him' (Heb 1:6; Ps 96:7), whom the Magi 'falling down adored' (cf. Mt 2:11), who finally, as the Scripture testifies (cf. Mt 28:17), was adored by the Apostles in Galilee. The holy Synod declares, moreover, that this custom was piously and religiously introduced into the Church of God, so that this sublime and venerable sacrament was celebrated every year on a special feast day with extraordinary veneration and solemnity, and was borne reverently and with honour in procession through the streets and public places. For it is most proper that some holy days be established when all Christians may testify, with an extraordinary and unsusual expression, that their minds are grateful to and mindful of their common Lord and Redeemer for such an ineffable and truly divine a favour, whereby the victory and triumph of his death is represented. And thus, indeed, ought victorious truth to celebrate a triumph over falsehood and heresy, that her adversaries, placed in view of so much splendour and amid such deep joy of the universal Church, may either vanish weakened and broken, or overcome and confounded by shame may some day recover their senses.

Chapter VI. *The Reservation of the Sacrament of the Holy Eucharist and Bearing it to the Sick.*

The custom of receiving the Holy Eucharist in a holy place is so ancient that even the age of the Nicene Council recognized it. Moreover, the injunction that the sacred Eucharist be carried to the sick, and be carefully reserved for this purpose in the churches, besides being in conformity with the greatest equity and reason is also found in many councils, and has been observed according to a very ancient custom of the Catholic Church. Therefore, this holy Synod decrees that this salutary and necessary custom be by all means retained. (can. 7).

Chapter VII. *The Preparation that must be Employed to Receive the Holy Eucharist worthily.*

If it is not becoming for anyone to approach any of the sacred functions except solemnly, certainly, the more the holiness and divinity of this heavenly sacrament is understood by a Christian, the more diligently ought he to take heed lest he approach to receive it without great reverence and holiness (can. 11), especially when we read in the Apostle those words full of terror: 'He who eats and drinks unworthily, eats and drinks judgement to himself not discerning the body of the Lord' (1 Cor 11:29). Therefore, the precept, 'Let a man prove himself' (1 Cor 11:28) must be called to mind by him who wishes to communicate. Now ecclesiastical usage declares that this examination is necessary, that no one conscious of mortal sin, however contrite he may seem to himself, should approach the Holy Eucharist without a previous sacramental confession. This, the holy Synod has decreed, is always to be observed by all Christians, even by those priests on whom by their office it may be incumbent to celebrate, provided recourse to a confessor be not lacking to them. But if in an urgent necessity a priest should celebrate without previous confession, let him confess as soon as possible.

Chapter VIII. *The Use of the Admirable Sacrament.*

As to its use our Fathers have rightly and wisely distinguished three ways of receiving this Holy Sacrament. For they have taught that some receive it sacramentally only, as sinners; others only spiritually, namely those who eating with desire the heavenly bread set before them, by a living faith, 'which works by charity' (Gal 5:6), perceive its fruit and usefulness; while the third receive it both sacramentally and spiritually (can. 8); and these are they who so prove and prepare themselves previously that 'clothed with the wedding garment' (Mt 22:11ff) they approach this divine table. Now as to the reception of the sacrament, it has always been the custom in the Church of God for the laity to receive communion from the priests, but that the priests when celebrating should communicate themselves (can. 10); this custom proceeding from an apostolic tradition should with reason and justice be retained.

And finally this holy Synod with paternal affection admonishes, exhorts, entreats, and beseeches, 'through the bowels of the mercy of our God' (Lk 1:78), that each and all, who are classed under the Christian name, will now finally agree and be of the same opinion in this 'sign of unity,' in this 'bond of charity,' in this symbol of concord, and that mindful of so great a majesty and such boundless love of our Lord Jesus Christ, who gave his own beloved soul as the price of our salvation, and gave us 'his own flesh to eat' (Jn 6:48ff), they may believe and venerate these sacred mysteries of his body and blood with that constancy and firmness of faith, with that devotion of soul, that piety and worship as to be able to receive frequently that 'supersubstantial bread' (Mt 6:11), and that it may be to them truly the life of the soul and the perpetual health of mind, that being invigorated by the strength thereof (III Kings 19:8), after the journey of this miserable pilgrimage, they may be able to arrive in their heavenly country to eat without any veil that same bread of angels (Ps 77:25) which they now eat under the sacred veils.

But whereas it is not enough to declare the truth, unless errors be exposed and repudiated, it has seemed good to the holy Synod to subjoin these canons, so that all, now that Catholic doctrine has been made known, may also understand what heresies are to be avoided and guarded against.

Canons on the Most Holy Sacrament of the Eucharist.

Can. 1. If anyone denies that in the sacrament of the most holy Eucharist there are truly, really, and substantially contained the body and blood together with the soul and divinity of our Lord Jesus Christ, and therefore the whole Christ, but shall say that he is in it as by a sign or figure, or virtually: let him be anathema.

Can. 2. If anyone says that in the sacred and holy sacrament of the Eucharist there remains the substance of bread and wine together with the body and blood of our Lord Jesus Christ, and denies that wonderful and singular conversion of the whole substance of the bread into the body, and of the entire substance of the wine into the blood, the species of the bread and wine only remaining, a change which the Catholic Church most fittingly calls transubstantiation: let him be anathema.

Can. 3. If anyone denies that the whole Christ is contained in the venerable sacrament of the Eucharist under each species and under every part of each species, when the separation has been made: let him be anathema.

Can. 4. If anyone says that after the completion of the consecration that the body and blood of our Lord Jesus Christ is not in the marvellous sacrament of the Eucharist, but only in use, while it is taken, not however before or after, and that in the hosts or consecrated particles, which are reserved or remain after communion, the true body of the Lord does not remain: let him be anathema.

Can. 5. If anyone says that the special fruit of the most holy Eucharist is the remission of sins, or that from it no other fruits are produced: let him be anathema.

Can. 6. If anyone says that in the holy sacrament of the Eucharist the only-begotten Son of God is not to be adored even outwardly with the worship of *latria*

(the act of adoration), and therefore not to be venerated with a special festive celebration, nor to be borne about in procession according to the praiseworthy and universal rite and custom of the holy Church, or is not to be set before the people publicly to be adored, and that the adorers of it are idolaters: let him be anathema.

Can. 7. If anyone says that it is not lawful that the holy Eucharist be reserved in a sacred place, but must necessarily be distributed immediately after the consecration among those present; or that it is not permitted to bring it to the sick with honour: let him be anathema.

Can. 8. If anyone says that Christ received in the Eucharist is received only spiritually, and not also sacramentally and in reality: let him be anathema.

Can. 9. If anyone denies that all and each of the faithful of Christ of both sexes, when they have reached the years of discretion, are bound every year to communicate at least at Easter according to the precept of holy mother Church: let him be anathema.

Can. 10. If anyone says that it is not lawful for a priest celebrating to communicate himself: let him be anathema.

Can. 11. If anyone says that faith alone is sufficient preparation for receiving the sacrament of the most Holy Eucharist: let him be anathema. And that so great a sacrament may not be unworthily received, and therefore unto death and condemnation, this holy Council ordains and declares that sacramental confession must necessarily be made beforehand by those whose conscience is burdened by mortal sin, however contrite they may consider themselves. If anyone moreover teaches the contrary or preaches or obstinately asserts, or even publicly by disputation shall presume to defend the contrary, by that fact itself he is excommunicated.[2]

Session XXI, 16 July 1562.

The Doctrine on Communion under both Species and that of Little Children.

Preface

The holy, ecumenical, and general Synod of Trent, lawfully assembled in the Holy Spirit with the same legates of the Apostolic See presiding, has decreed that those things which relate to communion under both species, and to that of little children are to be explained here, since in different places various monstrous errors concerning the tremendous and most holy sacrament of the Eucharist are being circulated by the wiles of the evil spirit; and for this reason in some provinces many seem to have fallen away from the faith and from obedience to the Catholic Church. Therefore, it warns all the faithful of Christ not to venture to believe, teach, or preach hereafter about those matters, otherwise than is explained or defined in these decrees.

Chapter I. *That Laymen and Clerics who not Offering Mass are not Bound by Divine Law to Communion under Both Species.*

Thus, the holy Synod itself, instructed by the Holy Spirit, who is the Spirit of wisdom and understanding, the Spirit of counsel and piety (Is 11:2), and following the judgement and custom of the Church itself, declares and teaches that laymen and clerics not officiating are bound by no divine law to receive the sacrament of the Eucharist under both species, and that without injury to the faith there can be no doubt at all that communion under either species suffices for them for salvation. For although Christ the Lord at the Last Supper instituted and delivered to the apostles this venerable sacrament under the species of bread and wine (cf. Mt. 26:26f; Mk 14:22; Lk 22:19; 1 Cor 11:24f), yet, that institution and tradition do not contend that all the faithful of Christ by an enactment of the Lord are bound (can. 1, 2) to receive under both species (can. 1, 2). But neither is it rightly inferred from that sixth discourse in John that communion under both forms was commanded by the Lord (can. 3), whatever the understanding may be, according to the various interpretations of the holy Fathers and Doctors. For, he who said: 'Unless you eat the flesh of the Son of Man and drink his blood, you shall not have life in you' (Jn 6:54), also said: 'If anyone eat of this bread, he shall live forever' (Jn 6:52). And he who said: 'He who eats my flesh and drinks my blood has life everlasting" (Jn 6:55), also said: 'The bread which I shall give, is my flesh for the life of the world' (Jn 6:52); and finally he who said: 'He who eats my flesh and drinks my blood, abides in me and I in him' (Jn 6:57), said nevertheless: 'He who eats this bread shall live forever' (Jn 6:58).

Chapter II. *The Power of the Church Concerning the Administration of the Sacrament of the Eucharist.*

It (the Council) declares furthermore that this power has always been in the Church, that in the administration of the sacraments, preserving their substance, she may determine or change whatever she may judge to be more expedient for the benefit of those who receive them or for the veneration of the sacraments, according to the variety of circumstances, times and places. Moreover, the Apostle seems to have intimated this in no obscure manner, when he said: 'This is how one should regard us, as servants of Christ and stewards of the mysteries of God" (1 Cor 4:1); and that he himself used this power is quite manifest in this sacrament as well as in many other things, not only in this sacrament itself but also in some other things set down with regard to its use, he says: 'About the other

things I will give directions when I come (1 Cor 11:34). Therefore holy mother Church, cognisant of her authority in the administration of the sacraments, although from the beginning of the Christian religion the use of both species was not infrequent, nevertheless, since that custom in the progress of time has been already widely changed, induced by weighty and just reasons, has approved this custom of communicating under either species, and has decreed that it be considered as a law, which may not be repudiated or be changed at will without the authority of the Church. (can. 2).

Chapter III. *Christ Whole and Entire and a True Sacrament is Received under Either Species.*

Moreover, it declares that although our Redeemer, as has been said before, at that Last Supper instituted this sacrament and gave it to the apostles under two species, yet it must be confessed that Christ whole and entire and a true sacrament is received even under either species alone, and that on that account, as far as regards its fruit, those who receive only under one species are not to be deprived of any grace which is necessary for salvation (can. 3).

Chapter IV. *Little Children are not Bound to Sacramental Communion.*

Finally, the same holy Synod teaches that little children without the use of reason are not bound by any necessity to the sacramental communion of the Eucharist (can. 4), since having been 'regenerated' through 'the laver' of baptism (Tit 3:5) and having been incorporated with Christ they cannot at that age lose the grace of the children of God which has already been attained. Nor is antiquity, therefore, to be condemned, if at one time it observed this custom in some places. For just as those most holy Fathers had good reason for an observance of that period, so certainly it is to be believed without controversy that they did this under no necessity for salvation.

Canons on Communion under Both Species and that of Little Children.

Can. 1. If anyone says that each and every one of the faithful of Christ ought by a precept of God, or by necessity for salvation to receive both species of the most holy Sacrament: let him be anathema.

Can. 2. If anyone says that the holy Catholic Church has not been influenced by just causes and reasons to give communion under the form of bread only to laymen and even to clerics when not consecrating, or that she has erred in this: let him be anathema.

Can. 3. If anyone denies that Christ whole and entire, who is the fountain and author of all graces, is received under the one species of bread, because, as some falsely assert, he is not received according to the institution of Christ himself under both species: let him be anathema.

Can. 4. If anyone says that for small children, before they have attained the years of discretion, communion of the Eucharist is necessary: let him be anathema.[3]

Session XXII, 17 September 1562.

The Doctrine on the most Holy Sacrifice of the Mass

The holy, ecumenical, and general Synod of Trent lawfully assembled in the Holy Spirit with the same legates of the Apostolic See presiding, has decreed that the faith and doctrine concerning the great mystery of the Eucharist in the holy Catholic Church, complete and perfect in every way, should be retained and, after the errors and heresies have been repudiated, should be preserved as of old in its purity; concerning this doctrine, since it is the true and the only sacrifice, the holy Council, instructed by the light of the Holy Spirit, teaches these matters which follow, and declares that they be preached to the faithful.

Chapter I. *The Institution of the Most Holy Sacrifice of the Mass*

Since under the former Testament (as the Apostle Paul bears witness) there was no consummation because of the weakness of the Levitical priesthood, it was necessary (God the Father of mercies ordaining it thus) that another priest according to the order of Melchizedek (Gen 14:18; Ps 109:4; Heb 7:11) arise, our Lord Jesus Christ, who could perfect (Heb 10:14) all who were to be sanctified, and lead them to perfection. He, therefore, our God and Lord, though he was about to offer himself once to God the Father upon the altar of the Cross by the mediation of death, so that he might accomplish an eternal redemption for them (*illic*, there), nevertheless, that his sacerdotal office might not come to an end with his death (Heb 7:24, 27) at the Last Supper, on the night he was betrayed, so that he might leave to his beloved spouse, the Church, a visible sacrifice (can. 1) (as the nature of man demands), whereby that bloody sacrifice once to be completed on the Cross might be represented, and the memory of it remain even to the end of the world (1 Cor 11:23ff) and its saving grace be applied to the remission of those sins which we daily commit, declaring himself constituted 'a priest for ever according to the order of Melchizekek' (Ps 109:4), offered to God the Father his own body and blood under the species of bread and wine, and under the symbols of those same things, gave to the apostles (whom he then constituted priests of the New Testament), so that they might partake, and he commanded them and their successors in the priesthood in these words to make offering: 'Do this in memory of me, etc.' (Lk 22:19; 1 Cor 11:24), as the Catholic Church has always under-

stood and taught (can. 2). For, after he had celebrated the ancient feast of the Passover, which the multitude of the children of Israel sacrificed (Ex 12:1ff) in memory of their exodus from Egypt, he instituted a new Passover, himself, to be immolated under visible signs by the Church through the priests, in memory of his own passage from this world to the Father, when by the shedding of his blood he redeemed us and 'delivered us from the power of darkness and translated us into his kingdom' (1 Cor 1:13).

And this, indeed, is that 'clean oblation' which cannot be defiled by any unworthiness or malice on the part of those who offer it; which the Lord foretold through Malachi must be offered in every place as a clean oblation (Mal 1:11) to his name, which would be great among the nations, and which the Apostle Paul writing to the Corinthians has clearly indicated, when he says that they who are defiled by participation in the 'table of devils' cannot become partakers of the table of the Lord (1 Cor 10:21), understanding by table in each case, the altar. It is finally that (sacrifice) which was prefigured by various types of sacrifices, in the period of nature and the Law (Gen 4:4; 8:20; 12:8; 22; Ex: passim), inasmuch as it comprises all good things signified by them, as being the consummation and perfection of them all.

Chapter II. *The Sacrifice is a Visible Propitiation for the Living and the Dead.*

And since in this divine sacrifice, which is celebrated in the Mass, that same Christ is contained and immolated in an unbloody manner, who on the altar of the Cross 'once offered himself' in a bloody manner (Heb 9:27), the holy Synod teaches that this is truly propitiatory (can. 3), and has this effect, that if contrite and penitent we approach God with a sincere heart and right faith, with fear and reverence, 'we obtain mercy and find grace in seasonable aid' (Heb 4:16). For, appeased by this oblation, the Lord, granting the grace and gift of penitence, pardons crimes and even great sins. For, it is one and the same Victim, the same one now offering by the ministry of the priests as he who then offered himself on the Cross, the manner of offering alone being different. The fruits of that oblation (bloody, that is) are received most abundantly through this unbloody one; so far is the latter from being derogatory in any way to him (can. 4). Therefore, it is offered rightly according to the tradition of the apostles (can. 3), not only for the sins of the faithful living, for their punishments and other necessities, but also for the dead in Christ not yet fully purified.

Chapter III. *Masses in honour of the Saints.*

And though the Church has been accustomed to celebrate some Masses now and then in honour and in memory of the saints, yet she does not teach that the sacrifice is offered to them, but to God alone, who has crowned them (can. 5). Thence the priest is not accustomed to say: 'I offer sacrifice to you, Peter and Paul' (St. Augustine, *C. Faustum*, 20, 21 PL 42,384), but giving thanks for their victories, he implores their patronage, so that 'they themselves may deign to intercede for us in heaven, whose memory we celebrate on earth' (Missal).

Chapter IV. *The Canon of the Mass.*

And since it is fitting that holy things be administered in a holy manner, and this sacrifice is of all things the most holy, the Catholic Church, that it might be reverently and worthily offered and received, instituted the sacred canon many centuries ago, so free from all error (can. 6), that it contains nothing in it which does not especially diffuse a certain sanctity and piety and raise up to God the minds of those who offer it. For this consists both of the words of God, and of the traditions of the apostles, and also of pious instructions of the holy Pontiffs.

Chapter V. *The Solemn Ceremonies of the Sacrifice of the Mass.*

And since such is the nature of man that he cannot easily without external means be raised to meditation on divine things, on that account holy Mother Church has instituted certain rites, namely, that certain things be pronounced in a subdued tone (can. 9) in the Mass, and others in a louder tone; she has, likewise, (can. 7) made use of ceremonies such as mystical blessings, lights, incense, vestments, and many other things of this kind in accordance with apostolic teaching and tradition, whereby both the majesty of so great a sacrifice might be commended, and the minds of the faithful excited by these visible signs of religion and piety to the contemplation of the most sublime matters which lie hidden in this sacrifice.

Chapter VI. *The Mass in which the Priest Alone Communicates.*

The holy Synod would wish indeed that at every Mass the faithful present receive communion not only by spiritual desire, but also by the sacramental reception of the Eucharist, so that a more abundant fruit of this most holy Sacrifice may be brought forth in them; yet if that is not always done, on that account it does not condemn (can. 8) those Masses in which the priest alone communicates sacramentally, as private and illicit, but rather approves and commends them, since indeed these Masses should also be considered as truly common, partly because at these Masses the people communicate spiritually, and partly, too, because they are celebrated by a public minister of the Church not only for himself, but also for all the faithful who belong to the Body of Christ.

Chapter VII. *The Water to be Mixed with Wine to be Offered in the Chalice.*

The holy Synod then admonishes priests that it has been prescribed by the Church to mix water with the wine to be offered in the chalice (can. 9), not only because the belief is that Christ the Lord did so, but also because there came from his side water together with blood (Jn 19:34), since by this mixture the sacrament is recalled. And since in the Apocalypse of the blessed John the peoples are called waters (Apoc 17:1, 15), the union of the faithful people with Christ, their Head, is represented.

Chapter VIII. *The Mass not to be Celebrated in the Vernacular, and its Mysteries to be Explained to the People.*

Although the Mass contains much instruction for the faithful, it has nevertheless not seemed expedient to the Fathers that it be celebrated everywhere in the vernacular (can. 9). For this reason since the ancient rite of each church has been approved by the holy Roman Church, the mother and teacher of all churches, and has been retained everywhere, lest the sheep of Christ suffer hunger, and 'little ones ask for bread and there is none to break it unto them' (cf. Lam 4:4), the holy Synod commands pastors and everyone who has the care of souls to explain frequently during the celebration of the Masses, either themselves or through others, some of the things which are read in the Mass, and among other things to expound some mystery of this most holy Sacrifice, especially on Sundays and feast days.

Chapter IX. *Preliminary Remarks on the Following Canons.*

Because various errors have been disseminated at this time, and many things are being taught and discussions carried on by many against this ancient faith founded on the holy Gospel, on the traditions of the apostles, and on the doctrine of the holy Fathers, the holy Synod, after long and grave deliberations over these matters, has resolved, by the unanimous consent of all the fathers, to condemn and eliminate from the holy Church by means of the following canons whatever is opposed to this most pure faith and to this sacred doctrine.

Canons on the Most Holy Sacrifice of the Mass.

Can. 1. If anyone says that in the Mass a true and real sacrifice is not offered to God, or that the act of offering is nothing else than Christ being given to us to eat: let him be anathema.

Can. 2. If anyone says that by these words: 'Do this in memory of me' (Lk 22:19; 1 Cor 11:24), Christ did not make the apostles priests, or did not ordain that they and other priests might offer his own body and blood: let him be anathema.

Can. 3. If anyone says that the sacrifice of the Mass is only one of praise and thanksgiving, or that it is a mere commemoration of the sacrifice consummated on the Cross, but not one of propitiation; or that it is of profit to him alone who receives; or that it ought not to be offered for the living and the dead, for sins, punishments, satisfactions, and other necessities: let him be anathema.

Can. 4. If anyone says that blasphemy is cast upon the most holy sacrifice of Christ consummated on the Cross through the sacrifice of the Mass, or that by it he is disparaged: let him be anathema.

Can. 5. If anyone says that it is a deception for Masses to be celebrated in honour of the saints and to obtain their intercession with God, as the Church intends: let him be anathema.

Can. 6. If anyone says that the canon of the Mass contains errors, and should therefore be abrogated: let him be anathema.

Can. 7. If anyone says that ceremonies, vestments, and outward signs, which the Catholic Church uses in the celebration of Masses, are incentives to impiety, rather than the services of piety: let him be anathema.

Can. 8. If anyone says that Masses, in which the priest alone communicates sacramentally, are illicit and are therefore to be abrogated: let him be anathema.

Can. 9. If anyone says that the rite of the Roman Church, according to which a part of the canon and the words of consecration are pronounced in a low tone, is to be condemned, or that the Mass ought to be celebrated in the vernacular only, or that water should not be mixed with the wine that is offered in the chalice because it is contrary to the institution of Christ: let him be anathema.[4]

[1]General literature on Council of Trent, especially H. Jedin, 3 vols, English translation, 1957; for the Eucharist and the Mass, cf. M. de la Taille (qv), *Mysterium Fidei*, 3rd ed., 1931, L. Billot (qv), *De Ecclesiae Sacramentis*, I, 7th ed., Rome, 1932, 356ff, 604ff; M. Lepin, *L'idée du sacrifice*, 293-331; E.C. Messenger, *The Reformation, the Mass and the Priesthood*, I, London, 1936, 202-220; for the Eucharist, J. Godefroy, DTC V, 1326-1355; for the Mass, J. Rivière, DTC X, 1114-1142; A. Michel, DTC, XV, 1459-1461; *id.*, vol X, Hefele-Leclercq, *Histoire des Conciles*, 255-287; 425-466; E. Schillebeeckx, O.P., *The Eucharist*, London, 1967, 29-86; A. Duval, *Le Concile de Trente et le culte eucharistique*, in *Studia eucharistica*, Antwerp, 1946, 379-414; *id., Des Sacrements au Concile de Trente, Rites et Symboles*, 1980, Paris, *Le culte eucharistique*, 22-59; *La Messe*, 61-150; E. Jamouille, *Le sacrifice eucharistique au Concile de Trente*, NRT 67 (1945); *id., L'unité sacrificielle de la Cène, de la Croix et de l'autel au Concile de Trente*, ETL 22 (1946), 34-69; A. Suarez, *La inmolación del sacrificio eucaristico segun el Concilio Tridentino y el Decreto Conciliar*, Quito, 1942; D. Power, *The Sacrifice we Offer: The Tridentine Dogma and its Reinterpretation*, Edinburgh, 1987; [2]DS 1635-1661; [3]DS 1725-1734; [4]DS 1738-1763.

TRES ABHINC ANNOS, 4 May 1967

This is the second Instruction of the Sacred Congregation of Rites on the Proper Implementation of the Constitution on the Liturgy.[1] It explains the stage reached and the attitude towards proposals received from bishops. Increased conscious and more active participation of the faithful in the sacred liturgy, "especially in the holy sacrifice of the Mass" is reported and an admonition of the Council recalled, "regulation of the sacred liturgy depends solely on the authority of the Church.... Therefore no other person, even if he be a priest, may add, remove or change anything in the liturgy on his own authority."[2]

[1]Text *AAS* 59 (1967), 442-448; English tr., A. Flannery, O.P., I, 98-99; [2]Constitution on the Liturgy, 22.

TRIDENTINE MASS, THE

The name given to the Mass as promulgated by St. Pius V (qv), in 1570.[1] But the word is a misnomer, as the *Institutio Generalis* (qv) makes clear: "When issuing decrees that the Order of the Mass should be revised, the Second Vatican Council ruled, among other things, that certain rites were to be restored to the vigour which they had in the days of the Holy Fathers."[2] These are the very words used by St. Pius V in the Apostolic Constitution *Quo primum* whereby he promulgated the Tridentine Missal of 1570. The employment of the very same words indicates that the two Missals, though separated in time by four centuries, are nevertheless inspired by and embody one and the same tradition. In those troubled days St. Pius V was unwilling to make any changes in the rites except minor ones; he was intent on preserving more recent tradition, because at that time attacks were being made on the doctrine that the Mass is a sacrifice, that its ministers are priests, and that Christ is really and abidingly present under the Eucharistic species. "In point of fact the Missal of 1570 differs very little indeed from the first printed Missal which dates from the year 1474, and this in turn follows very closely a Mass book dating back to the time of Pope Innocent III.

[1]Cf. bibl. to article on St. Pius V; [2]Roman Missal, ed. 1970.

TRINITY, MOST HOLY

The real presence (qv) of Christ, eternal Son of God, in the Eucharist, does not alter his personality within the Holy Trinity. The three divine Persons did not become man, so they are not in the Eucharist as he is, for the Eucharist is a prolongation of his Incarnation. His Eucharistic existence is possible because he became man. But as man he was still God the Son, retaining his personal property within the Blessed Three, enjoying the unchangeable circumincession that is his eternal life with the Father and the Spirit, in no way less God, less God the Son, less the Only-begotten, less the One from whom, with the Father, the Spirit proceeds. All this must continue in his Eucharistic life, for the *kenosis* (the self-emptying) which was a condition of his Incarnation did not, could not, diminish the reality of his Godhead and his Trinitarian existence.

Christ in the Eucharist prompts reflection on the Trinitarian role in creation. For the world was created by the Father, through the Son, with the Spirit fully cooperating. It is with part of this creation, interestingly parts of it subjected to the creative power of man, that Jesus Christ chose to identify the Eucharist. For bread and wine are not merely creatures, they are creatures worked on by man. Here we touch the fundamental question of the primacy of Jesus Christ. Was it a primacy of excellence only—that we must believe—or an absolute primacy? On the affirmative answer to the latter question, that given by the present writer with many others of greater importance, we have to think out the divine plan to mould creation around the incarnate Son of God, since creation was intended for him, and God, in his creative act and his Providence, effects the whole and the parts down to their tiniest detail.

V

VAGAGGINI, CIPRIANO, O.S.B. (1909-?)

This Italian Benedictine held important teaching posts in Theology, served as Rector of the Pontifical Liturgical Institute.[1] His attention was especially given to the theology of the Liturgy: *Il senso teologico della liturgia*, ed. Paoline, 1957. Member of the Liturgical Preparatory Commission, he was an expert to the Council and a member of *Consilium*, set up by Paul VI to implement the directives of the Council. He was principally responsible for the instruction on Concelebration (qv) and Communion under both species, and for *Eucharisticum Mysterium* (qv), 25 March 1967, an important practical sequel to Paul VI's *Mysterium Fidei* (qv). His work *Il canone romano e la riforma liturgica*, Turin, 1966, pointed to his most important contribution to liturgical renewal, the preparation of the new Eucharistic Prayers (qv). Author of several books, including *Caro salutis est cardo. Corpo eucaristico e liturgia* and *Liturgia e pensiero teologico recente*, as well as over seventy articles, a number to EC. V. is a member of ITC.

[1]Cf. *Lex orandi, lex credendi*, essays offered to V. on his seventieth birthday, ed. G.J. Bekes, G. Farnedi, esp; Letter to editor by Mgr. A. Bugnini, 11-15: bibl.; *Studia Anselmiana*, 79, Rome, 1980; principal work, English tr. *The Theological Dimension of the Liturgy*, Collegeville, 1958.

VATICAN II

There had been in the decades preceding the Council a shift in emphasis in the theology of the Mass. The generation of De la Taille (qv) and Lepin (qv) and of those who followed them or were contemporary, with less expansive treatises, Vonier, Masure and Journet, gave way to proponents of a new approach, that of the Paschal Mystery (qv). The work of Dom Odo Casel (qv) had contributed to the change, as had the dimensions, worldwide of the Liturgical movement, which Pius XII (qv) welcomed as a sign of the Spirit's action. The preparatory commission for the Liturgy named in 1960 included in its membership scholars of great prestige, such as Mgr. M. Righetti, Fr. John Quasten (qv), Dom B. Capelle, O.S.B., and Fr. J. Jungmann, S.J. (qv); among the Consultors there were some equally distinguished names, Dom Bernard Botte, O.S.B., Fr. Aimé George Martimort (qv), Fr. John Hofinger, S.J., Dom Polycarp Rado, O.S.B. Dom Cipriano Vagaggini, O.S.B. (qv), Fr. Pierre Marie Gy, O.P. The commission elected within the Council was given twenty-five experts to advise on textual drafting. Twelve were members of the preparatory commission.

With such resources to draw on, it is no wonder that the Constitution on the Liturgy was the first to go through drafting stages and was quickly passed by the assembly. No wonder either that in doctrine, in such space as was allowed for doctrine, recent insights would prevail. So much is evident in the first chapter, which sets the liturgy in the whole scheme of redemption by Christ: "Accordingly, just as Christ was sent by the Father so also he sent the apostles, filled with the Holy Spirit. This he did so that they might preach the Gospel to every creature and proclaim that the Son of God by his death and resurrection had freed us from the power of Satan and from death, and brought us into the kingdom of his Father. But he also willed that the work of salvation which they preached should be set in train through the sacrifice and sacraments, around which the entire liturgical life revolves. Thus by Baptism men are grafted into the paschal mystery of Christ; they die with him, are buried with him, and rise with him. They receive the spirit of adoption as sons 'in which we cry, Abba, Father' (Rom 8:15) and thus become true adorers such as the Father seeks. In like manner as often as they eat the Supper of the Lord they proclaim the death of the Lord until he comes. That was why on the very day of Pentecost when the Church appeared before the world those 'who received the word' of Peter 'were baptized.' And 'they continued steadfaastly in the teaching of the apostles and in the communion of the breaking of bread and in prayers ... praising God and being in favour with all the people' (Acts 2:41-47). From that time onward the Church has never failed to come together to celebrate the paschal mystery, reading those things which were in all the Scriptures concerning him,' (Lk 24:27), celebrating the Eucharst in which 'the victory and triumph of his death are again made present' and at the same time 'giving thanks to God for his inexpressible gift' (2 Cor 9:15) in Christ Jesus, 'in praise of his glory' (Eph 1:12), through the power of the Holy Spirit."[1]

The idea of the resurrection as salvific, herein clearly taught, is an idea given prominence in recent times, by writers, such as F.X. Durrwell, C.SS.R. A decline in theology had led to emphasis on the Passion as solely salvific, with the Resurrection considered something relevant to apologetics. The Constitution goes on to explain the varied presence (qv) of Christ in his Church, and the way in which he associates the Church with him in the liturgy as an exercise of his priestly office, so that "full public worship is performed by the Mystical Body of Christ, that is, by the Head and his members; all of this is a "foretaste of the heavenly liturgy which is celebrated in the Holy City of Jerusalem toward which we journey as pilgrims, where Christ is sitting at the right hand of God, Minister of the holies and of the true tabernacle."

It is in this broad setting that we must understand the Council's teaching on the Mass, which is contained in chapter two of the Constitution: "At the Last Supper (qv), on the night he was betrayed, our Saviour instituted the Eucharistic sacrifice of his Body and Blood. This he did in order to perpetuate the sacrifice of the Cross throughout the ages until he should come again, and so to entrust to his beloved Spouse, the Church, a memorial of his death and resurrection, a sacrament of love, a sign of unity, a bond of charity, a paschal banquet in which Christ is consumed, the mind is filled with grace, and a pledge of future glory is given to us."[2]

Thereafter the conciliar document concentrates on practical liturgical matters, participation: "Offering the immaculate victim, not only through the hands of the priest, but also together with him, they should learn to offer themselves." Directives are given on revision of the rite of Mass; on the generous use of the 'treasures of the Bible'; on the homily (qv); on the prayer of the faithful; on the vernacular; on communion under both species; and on concelebration (qv).

One passage on the Eucharist as a source of covenant (qv) grace reflects the biblical approach: "For the goal of apostolic endeavour is that all who are made sons of God by faith and baptism should come together to praise God in the midst of his Church, to take part in the Sacrifice and to eat the Lord's Supper. The liturgy, in its turn, moves the faithful filled with 'the paschal sacraments' to be 'one in holiness.' It prays that 'they hold fast in their lives to what they have grasped by their faith.' The renewal in the Eucharist of the covenant between the Lord and man draws the faithful and sets them aflame with Christ's insistent love. From the liturgy, therefore, and especially from the Eucharist, grace is poured forth upon us as from a fountain, and the sanctification of men in Christ and the glorification of God to which all other activities of the Church are directed, as toward their end, are achieved with maximum effectiveness."[3]

If this is not seen to be a rich theology of the Eucharist, it must be remembered that the passages quoted are from the Constitution on the Sacred Liturgy, which was drawn up and passed early in the Council's history; it was promulgated on 4 December 1963. In the Constitution on the Church, promulgated on 21 November 1964, there are some further elements to note. In the chapter on the Mystery of the Church we read: "As often as the sacrifice of the cross by which 'Christ our Pasch is sacrificed' (1 Cor 5:7) is celebrated on the altar, the work of our redemption is carried out. Likewise, in the sacrament of the Eucharistic bread, the unity of believers who form one body in Christ (cf. 1 Cor 10:17), is both expressed and brought about. All men are called to this union with Christ, who is the light of the world, from whom we go forth, through whom we live, and towards whom our whole life is directed."[4]

In the next chapter on the People of God we are told that the faithful "taking part in the Eucharistic sacrifice, the source and summit of the Christian life, offer the divine victim to God and themselves along with it. And so it is that, both in the offering and in

Holy Communion, each in his own way, though not of course indiscriminately, has his own part to play in the liturgical action. Then strengthened by the body of Christ in the Eucharistic communion, they manifest in a concrete way that unity of the People of God which this holy sacrament aptly signifies and admirably realizes."[5]

The chapter on the Church as hierarchical is, as is well known, heavily weighted towards the episcopate. Priests are in a subsidary role to them. The effects of possible misinterpretation in the immediate aftermath of the Council are dealt with in the article on the Priesthood (qv). The Council's teaching on the essential sacrificing act of the priest is in this passage: "However, it is in the Eucharistic cult or in the Eucharistic assembly of the faithful *(synaxis)* that they exercise in a supreme degree their sacred functions; there, acting in the person of Christ and proclaiming his mystery, they unite the votive offerings of the faithful to the sacrifice of Christ their head, and in the sacrifice of the Mass they make present again and apply, until the coming of the Lord (cf. 1 Cor 11:26), the unique sacrifice of the New Testament, that namely of Christ offering himself once for all a spotless victim to the Father (cf. Heb 9:11-28)."[6]

On the same day as the Constitution on the Church was promulgated, two other documents were issued: the Decree on the Eastern Churches and the Decree on Ecumenism. Two passages in the second document merit attention, though they aim at no exhaustive treatment. On the separated Eastern Churches the Council had this to say: "Everyone also knows with what love the Eastern Christians celebrate the sacred liturgy, especially the Eucharistic mystery, source of the Church's life and pledge of future glory. In this mystery the faithful, united with their bishops, have access to God the Father through the Son, the Word made flesh who suffered and was glorified, in the outpouring of the Holy Spirit. And so, made 'sharers of the divine nature' (2 Pet 1:4) they enter into communion with the most holy Trinity. Hence through the celebration of the Eucharist of the Lord in each of these Churches, the Church of God is built up and grows in stature, and through concelebration, their communion with one another is made manifest."[7]

On the separated churches of the west, the Council had a different comment: "Although the ecclesial communities separated from us lack the fullness of unity with us which flows from baptism, and although we believe they have not preserved the proper reality of the Eucharistic mystery in its fullness, especially because of the absence of the sacrament of Orders, nevertheless, when they commemorate the Lord's death and resurrection in the Holy Supper, they profess that it signifies life in communion with Christ and await his coming in glory. For these reasons, the doctrine about the Lord's Supper, about the other sacraments, worship and ministry in the Church, should form subjects of dialogue."[8]

On 7 December 1965, two decrees were issued, on the Church's missionary activity and on the ministry and life of priests. In the first we read: "Through preaching and the celebration of the sacraments, of which the holy Eucharist is the centre and summit, missionary activity makes Christ present, he who is the author of salvation."[9] In the second there occurs a very strong, rich theological statement: "But the other sacraments and indeed all ecclesiastical ministries and works of the apostolate are bound up with the Eucharist and are directed towards it. For in the most blessed Eucharist is contained the whole spiritual good of the Church, namely, Christ himself our Pasch and the living bread which gives life to men through his flesh—that flesh which is given life and gives life through the Holy Spirit. Thus men are invited and led to offer themselves, their works and all creation with Christ. For this reason the Eucharist appears as the source and the summit of all preaching of the Gospel; catechumens are gradually led up to participation in the Eucharist, while the faithful who have already been consecrated in baptism and confirmation are fully incorporated in the Body of Christ by the reception of the Eucharist. Therefore, the Eucharistic celebration is the centre of the assembly of the faithful over which the priest presides. Hence priests teach the faithful to offer the divine victim to God the Father in the sacrifice of the Mass and with the victim to make an offering of their whole life."[10]

Two other passages in the decree merit attention: "However, no Christian community is built up which does not grow from and hinge on the celebration of the most holy Eucharist. From this all education for community spirit must begin. This Eucharistic celebration, to be full and sincere, ought to lead on the one hand to the various works of charity and mutual help, and on the other hand to missionary activity and the various forms of Christian witness."[11]

That statement is in the context of the priest as ruler of God's people. In regard to the need for holiness in the discharge of priestly duty, the exercise of the threefold priestly function, the Council again speaks of the Eucharist: "Priests as ministers of the sacred mysteries, especially in the sacrifice of the Mass, act in a special way in the person of Christ who gave himself as a victim to sanctify men. And this is why they are invited to imitate what they handle, so that as they celebrate the mystery of the Lord's death they may take care to mortify their members from vices and concupiscences. In the mystery of the Eucharistic sacrifice, in which priests fulfil their principal function, the work of our redemption is continually carried out. For this reason the daily celebration of it is earnestly recommended. This celebration is an act of Christ and the Church even if it is impossible for the faithful to be present. So when priests unite themselves with the act of Christ the Priest they daily offer themselves completely to God, and by being nourished with Christ's Body they share in the charity of him who gives himself as food to the faithful."[12]

There is much to ponder in these passages, due probably to a great theologian of the priesthood who served on the commission, Fr. Joseph Lécuyer, C.S.Sp. (qv). There is a reference to the Spirit's (qv) role in the Eucharist—"that flesh which is given life and gives life through the Holy Spirit"—as there is to the cosmic dimension of Eucharistic life—"men are invited ... to offer all creation with Christ"; as again the faithful are said "to offer the divine victim to God the Father"—as the Eucharist is the very source of community, and should prompt active spirituality. All is brought back to the very centre, "the work of our redemption," and to Christ himself.

---

[1]*Constitution on the Liturgy*, 6, Vatican II, vol 1, A. Flannery, O.P., 4; on conciliar texts, cf. esp. *Acta Synodalia* I, 1 and 2 for the *Constitution on the Liturgy*; IV, 5, 6, 7 for the *Decree on the Ministry and Life of Priests*; IV, 5, 6, 7, esp. 5, for written submissions on the draft schema, 209-541, exceptional as were the 5,671 Modi at a later stage; cf. in collection *Unam Sanctam, 66, La liturgie après Vatican II*, Y. Congar, O.P., P.M. Gy, J.P. Jossua, M.D. Chenu, M. Carrouges, P. Colin, Th. Strothmann, B.D. Marliangeas, J.P. Audet, S. Lyonnet; Paris, 1966; *Unam Sanctam 68, Les Prêtres*, E. Marcus, J. Frisque, H. Denis, Y. Congar, C. Wiener, P. Colin, J. Lécuyer, H. le Sourd, A. Weers, Paris, 1968; *Commentary on the Documents of Vatican II*, ed. H. Vorgrimmler, I, *The Liturgical Constitution*, 1-87; IV, *Priests*, 183-297, esp. J. Lécuyer, History, 183-209; M. Tierney, *The Council and the Mass*, Dublin, 1965; ed. J.D. Crichton, *The Mass of the People of God*, London, 1966; ed. A. Flannery, O.P., *Liturgical Renewal and Adaptation*, Dublin, 1968; J.D. Crichton, *Christian Celebration and the Mass*, London, 1971; [2]art. 47; A. Flannery, 16; on the resurrection (qv) cf. F.X. Durrwell, C.SS.R., *La résurrection de Jésus, mystère de salut*, Paris, 1950, 2nd ed, 1954, English tr., 1960; D.M. Stanley, *Christ's Resurrection and Pauline Soteriology*, Rome (*Analecta Biblica* 38), 1961; [3]art. 10, 11; A. Flannery, p. 6; [4]art. 3, A. Flannery, p. 351; [5]art. 11, p. 362; [6]art. 28, p. 386; [7]art. 15, p. 465; [8]art. 22, p. 469; [9]art. 9, p. 823; [10]art. 5, p. 871; [11]art. 6, p. 874; [12]art. 13, p. 887, 8.

VIRTUALISM

A theory of Eucharistic presence (qv) generally attributed to Calvin (qv): though the elements of bread and wine, the theory maintains, are not altered, they can, within the celebration, give the communicant the power or virtue of Christ.[1]

The opinion was implicit in the teaching of Berengar

(qv) and was countered by Durandus of Troarn (qv).

Calvin's variation on the theme is expressed by the use of the word *exhibited*. "The mystery of the Holy Supper consists of two things, the bodily signs which are set before our eyes and represent to us invisible things in such way as our weakness can grasp, and the spiritual reality which is both denoted and exhibited (exhibetur) by the symbols."[2]

The Council of Trent (qv) in teaching the presence of Christ in the Eucharist "truly, really and substantially" in condemning those who "say that he is in it as by a sign, or figure or force (virtually)" and in declaring Christ in the Eucharist worthy of "latria as to the true God" rejected virtualism absolutely.[3] From Calvin it percolated to Cranmer (qv) whose opinion has been thus summarised: "The faithful communicant receives the virtue and grace of Christ's body and blood, which are themselves absent." "The faithful communicant sacramentally receives those effects of Christ's life and death which would be conveyed if there were a beneficial reception of his actual body and blood, which are themselves absent." "The faithful communicant sacramentally receives those effects of Christ's life and death which would be conveyed if there were a beneficial reception of his actual body and blood."[4]

---

[1]Cf. E.C. Messenger, *The Reformation*, I, 174, 327, 559; [2]Apud E.C. Messenger, *ibid.*, 174; [3]DS 1636; 1643; 1651; [4]D. Stone, *History*, II, 127.

VISITS TO THE BLESSED SACRAMENT

Visits to the Blessed Sacrament are part of the Catholic ethos.[1] The practice is found in regions and countries where the Catholic faith is strong; it has characterized very many saints. About the time of Vatican II the great German theologian, Fr. Karl Rahner (qv) felt obliged to defend this form of devotion, as it was being subjected to criticism. He recalled that though Reservation of the Blessed Sacrament was defended by the Council of Trent explicitly so that the Sacrament should be available to the sick outside the celebration of the Eucharist, the fact of Reservation had implications. One is adoration (qv). Pope Pius XII (qv) in *Mediator Dei* (qv) emphasized the importance of another, "devout and daily visits to the sacred tabernacle." The former code of Canon Law recommended visitation of the most Holy Sacrament as a subject of legitimate instruction for the faithful (Can. 125, no. 2; can. 1273).[2] The present Code is equally explicit: "Unless a grave reason prevents it, the Church in which the most Holy Eucharist is reserved should be open to the faithful for at least some hours each day so that they are able to spend time in prayer before the Blessed Sacrament" (Can. 937).

Pope John Paul II wrote thus: "Adoration of Christ in this Sacrament must also find expression in various forms of Eucharistic devotion; personal prayer before the Blessed Sacrament, hours of adoration, periods of exposition—short, prolonged and annual (Forty Hours)—Eucharistic benediction, Eucharistic processions, Eucharistic Congresses" (qv).

Fr. Karl Rahner (qv) deals at length with the justification of visits to the Blessed Sacrament with the idea in mind, basic certainly, that in the Eucharist Christ is present—it is the Council of Trent which teaches this—that he may be taken. But this taking is a personal relationship, extending to the whole of one's being, with the Lord. The visit in carrying the effect of previous Communions and looking to those in the future leans on the totality of Christ, Lord of the universe, principle of unity in the Church, infinite mystery in his Person, his being, his designs. Was St. Teresa of Avila expressing a profound intuition when she wished to found new monasteries of her order to give him in each case a new roof to live under? Nor should we forget that, as Fr. Rahner says, a custom one thousand years old has rights, even if they are not the first thousand years of Church history.

[1]Cf. K. Rahner, *Mission and Grace,* I, London, 1963, 301-325, with the references in annotation.

W/Z

WOMEN AND MINISTRY

The gains of the feminist revolution in the present century have led to considerable thought and writing on woman's place in church life; eventually this prompted discussion of the ministry which women could exercise, including the priesthood. Such a question would not have been put until quite recently. The collection of papal teaching, *The Woman in the Modern World*, 1957, shows that prior to Pius XII (qv) little was said on the subject at all by Popes, and nothing on the question of possible access to the priesthood.

The official answer to the request for priestly ordination of women so frequently heard in the late sixties and seventies was in the form of a Declaration on the Admission of Women to the Ministerial Priesthood, *Inter Insigniores*, 15 October 1976: "The Catholic Church," it says, "has never felt that priestly or episcopal ordination can be validly conferred on women." This opinion is defended throughout the document, with arguments from Scripture and Church history, with due account of social philosophy and anthropology. There is recognition of and praise for the immense services of women to the Church in so many different areas, mention of the two women Doctors of the Church, whose belated recognition itself tells a story, a delay of 600 years for St. Catherine, 400 for St. Teresa.

John Paul II (qv) repeated the teaching on his first visit to the United States: "The fact that there is a personal individual call to the priesthood given by the Lord to 'the men he himself had decided on' is in accord with the prophetic tradition. It should help us, too, to understand that the Church's traditional decision to call men to the priesthood, and not to call women, is not a statement about human rights, not an exclusion of women from holiness and mission in the Church. Rather this decision expresses the conviction of the Church about this particular dimension of the gift of priesthood by which God has chosen to shepherd his flock."[3]

Women are admitted as ministers of the Eucharist and as lectors, even in the Pope's private oratory. How they should further express the priesthood of the faithful, which they fully possess, through which they share in the unique priesthood of Christ, may be more clearly seen with growing experience in the Church. It is known that the whole question is actively debated in certain regions and milieux, notably in the United States. Not all advocates of the ordination of women are women; not all women are advocates of the ordination of women. It is claimed that biblical scholars, even in the Biblical Commission, support them. It would be utterly unrealistic to ignore the agony of so many who feel that their lot, within the Church, is one of deprivation. How can they be brought to see that the ideal of service inherent in the priesthood is, in so many other ways, open to them? One preliminary to peace in this troubled area, would be whole-hearted acceptance of the ideal of service by priests. As is suggested in the article on priesthood, there has been confusion of thought in places on the meaning, value, dignity, mystery, majesty of the priesthood—the causes of this momentary failure of mind and nerve need careful research. All is summed up in service after the model of Christ: a much misunderstood ideal.

[1]Essential bibliography, *R.I.C., International Bibliography, The Woman in the Church*, Cerdic Publications, Strasbourg, Supplement 70-71 covering years 1975-1982; Supplement 94-95 covering years 1982-1984; some titles from an extensive bibliography: J. Massingberd Ford, *Our Lady and the Ministry of Women, Marian Studies*, 23 (1972), 79-112; H. Rolland, *La condition de la femme dans l'Eglise*, Paris, 1975; K. Rahner, S.J., *Women and the Priesthood, Theological Investigations*, XX, London, 1981, 35-47; *Lumière et Vie*, 151 (1981), several authors, 2-117; *Oser vivre au feminin*, 21 articles, *Communautés Nouvelles*, 58 (1978), 6-94; *Pro Mundi Vita, Ministères et Communautés*, 4 articles, 12 (1977), 4-13; *Ordination for Christian Ministry*, 9 articles, *Review and Expositor*, 78 (1981), 469-590; [2]Tr., A. Flannery, Vatican II, vol 2, 333; [3]*L'Osservatore Romano*, repr., John Paul II, *A Priest Forever*, collected statements to July, 1981, ed. Seamus O'Byrne, St. Paul Publications, Athlone, 73, 74.

WYCLIFFE, JOHN (c. 1330-1384)

With his other many errors which led him into conflict with church authority and were condemned, W., in a work entitled *De Eucharistia* and elsewhere, denied essential doctrines in regard to the Eucharist and the priesthood.[1] As to the priesthood he thought that it could be exercised only by those in the state of grace—this flowed from his curious theory of predestination and "dominion." W. claimed to follow Berengar (qv). He was aware that the Fourth Council of the Lateran had condemned Berengar. But, he asks, were they predested? W., then reviving Berengar's doctrine, contends that the body of Christ is not in the consecrated host either essentially, substantially, corporeally or identically. The effect of the words of institution he interpreted in a figurative sense; the consecrated bread and wine represent Christ sacramentally. "The common people most faithlessly and blasphemously believe that this sacramental sign of the body and blood of Christ is actually Christ himself. And in this heresy clergy and prelates are involved."[2] W. denied transubstantiation and he seems to have denied that the Mass was instituted by Christ. The consecrated host, he thought, should be honoured as an image of God, not adored.

W. was condemned by the Chancellor and Doctors of his own University, Oxford, in 1381: "First, that in the sacrament of the altar the substance of material bread and wine, which were before consecration, really remain after consecration; secondly, which is dreadful to hear, that in this venerable sacrament, the body and blood of Christ are not essentially, or substantially or corporeally *(essentialiter, substantialiter, corporaliter)*, but figuratively or symbolically *(figurative seu tropice)* so that Christ is not really there

in his own bodily presence (*veraciter, in sua propria praesentia corporali*).... We, therefore, have summoned many doctors of sacred theology and professors of canon law ... and it was at length finally decided and declared by their judgement that the assertions are erroneous, and opposed to the decisions of the Church and contrary to truths which are Catholic and plainly result from the words of the saints and the decisions of the Church."[3]

There follows a plenary statement of Catholic doctrine: "By the sacramental words duly pronounced by a priest, the bread and wine on the altar are transubstantiated or substantially converted into the real body and blood of Christ." The statement, which is further amplified, was agreed to by Thomists, Scotists and Nominalists then at Oxford. The condemnation was renewed by a Provincial Council held in London in 1382: present were ten bishops, seventeen doctors in theology, sixteen doctors in civil and canon law, and others. In 1397 another Provincial Council, presided over by Archbishop Arundel of Canterbury, also condemned propositions of W., including three on the Eucharist. Finally, the General Council of Constance, Session VIII, 4 May 1415, condemned the following propositions (the decision being subsequently approved by Martin V, by the Bulls *Inter Cunctas* and *In eminentis*, 22 February 1418): "1. In the sacrament of the altar the material substance of bread and likewise the material substance of wine remain; 2. In the same sacrament the accidents of the bread do not remain without a subject; 3. Christ is not in the same sacrament identically and really with his own bodily presence; 4. If a bishop or priest is living in mortal sin, he does not ordain, nor consecrate, nor perform, nor baptize; 5. It is not established in the Gospel that Christ instituted the Mass."[5]

[1]Wycliffe's works published by the Wyclif Society (35 vols., London, 1883-1914); cf. Darwell Stone, History, I; J.H. Dahmus, *The Prosecution of John Wyclif*, London, 1952; B.L. Manning, *Cambridge Medieval History*, VII (1932), 486-507; bibl. 900-907; Fliche-Martin, XIV, 4th part, 943-988; esp., E.C. Messenger, *The Reformation*, I, 106-112; [2]*De Eucharistia*, apud E.C. Messenger, 107; [3]*Ibid.*, 110; [4]*Ibid.*, 111; [5]DS 1201-1204.

ZWINGLI, ULRICH (1484-1531)

The Swiss Reformer stated his idea of the Mass in article 18 of his 67 articles published in 1523, along with a Defence of them: "Christ, who offered himself once for all on the Cross, is the perpetual and effectual sacrifice and victim for the sins of all believers. Wherefore the Mass is not a sacrifice, but a commemoration of the sacrifice offered on the Cross once for all, and a token of the redemption set forth."[1] Z.

used symbolical language as: "Christ's body and blood are the food of the soul when it firmly believes that the body and blood of Christ are its salvation."

In *The Nature of the Faith* addressed to Charles V, Zwingli was explicit in his denial of the Real Presence (qv): "In the Holy Eucharist, the real body of Christ is present by the contemplation of faith, that is, those who give thanks to the Lord for the benefit conferred on us in his Son recognise that he took real flesh, that in it he really suffered, that he really washed away our sins by his blood, so that everything done by Christ becomes, as it were, present to them by the contemplation of faith. But that the body of Christ, that is, the natural body itself, essentially and actually is either present in the Supper, or committed to our mouth and teeth as the papists and certain others maintain, this we deny." "The opinion which asserts that the body of Christ is eaten in the Supper corporeally, naturally, essentially, is irreligious.... To eat the body of Christ sacramentally is to eat the body of Christ in mind and spirit, with the addition of the sacrament"[2]

Z. thought that to "eat the body of Christ spiritually was nothing else than to lean in spirit and mind on the mercy and goodness of God"; the bread and wine he thought to be the symbolical body of Christ, eaten sacramentally.

Z. rejected the sacrifice of the Mass and the sacrificing priesthood: "Holy Order which they say impresses a certain character on the soul is a human figment. And what they adduce concerning the imposition of hands from Acts and 1 Tim is frivolous. This was an external *consignatio* by which were made known those upon whom the gift of tongues was to come, or who were to be sent forth for the ministry of the word. What has this to do with that figment of character? It is a function, not a dignity; the episcopate is the ministry of the word. Therefore he who administers the word is a bishop, and he who does not is no bishop, any more than a consul or magistrate who does not function is really such."[3]

After Z's death his teaching was set forth in the Confession of Basel, 1534, and in the First Helvetic Confession, 1536. The first was drafted by Oecolampadius, the second by Bullinger, Myconius and Grynaeus. Since this second formula was designed to help approach the Lutherans, it bears a certain mark of Bucer (qv): "The body and blood of the Lord are not naturally united to the bread and wine, but the bread and wine are ordained by the Lord to be symbols by which the real communication of his body and blood may be *exhibited* by the Lord himself."[4] The word exhibited in this passage speaks of Bucer.

---

[1]Works *Corpus Reformatorum,* 98f, 1904 ...; *Zwinglis Hauptschriften*, ed. F. Blanke and others; Zurich, 1940 ...; cf. A. Baur, *Zwinglis Theologie, Ihr Werden und ihr System*, 2 vols, 1885, 1889; W. Köhler, *Zwingli und Luther. Ihr Streit über das Abendmahl nach seinen politischen und religiösen Beziehungen (Quellen und Forschungen zur Reformation geschichte*, VI, VII, 1924, 1953;) J. V. Pollet, O.P., *Huldrich Zwingli et la Réforme en Suisse d'après les recherches récentes*, 1963; H. Sasse, *This is my Body, Luther's Contention for the Real Presence in the Sacrament of the Altar*, Minneapolis, 1959; U. Gabler, *Huldrich Zwingli im 20 Jahrhundert*, bibl. 1897-1972, Zurich, 1975; E. Guder, R. Stahelin, E. Egli, PRE, 3 ed., XXI, 1908, 774-815; L. Cristiani, DTC XV, 2, 1950, 3716-44; J.M.V. Pollet, O.P., *ibid., Zwinglianisme*, 3745-3928; E.C. Messenger, *The Reformation*, I, 170-172; [2]Opera II, 541; [3]De vera et falsa religione, Zurich, 1525, 302; [4]Schaff, *Creeds of Christendom*, III, 225.

Index of Entries

INDEX OF ENTRIES

About the Author

Corpus Christi is the work of Michael O'Carroll, C.S.Sp., Irish
theologian and educator. He has written widely and well, over the
last three decades, on theological and ecumenical topics. He is also
the author of the internationally-acclaimed *Theotokos: A Theological Encyclopedia of the Blessed Virgin Mary* and *Trinitas: A
Theological Encyclopedia of the Holy Trinity.*